International Cuisine & Food Production Management

Chef Parvinder S. Bali

Programme Manager—Culinary Services
Oberoi Centre of Learning and Development
Delhi

OXFORD
UNIVERSITY PRESS

OXFORD
UNIVERSITY PRESS

Oxford University Press is a department of the University of Oxford.
It furthers the University's objective of excellence in research, scholarship,
and education by publishing worldwide. Oxford is a registered trademark of
Oxford University Press in the UK and in certain other countries.

Published in India by
Oxford University Press
YMCA Library Building, 1 Jai Singh Road, New Delhi 110001, India

First published in 2012
Third impression 2013

ISBN-13: 978-0-19-807389-5
ISBN-10: 0-19-807389-5

Typeset in Baskerville Regular
by Innovative Processors, New Delhi 110 002
Printed in India by Radha Press, Delhi 110 031

Dedicated to

my father, late (Major) Ranjit Singh Bali

my mother, Gominder Kaur Bali

my wife, Shalini Bali

and my two lovely children, Ojas and Amora

PREFACE

A chef's role is no different from that of a manager and is more complex than it sounds. A chef has to have three most important qualities: attitude, skills, and knowledge. Everything comes with experience and if budding chefs have the right kind of knowledge and attitude, then acquiring skills will be easy. It is mandatory for chefs to enrich knowledge, be up to date with technology and new products, seek out new ways of doing things, control wastages, and maintain quality. These will go a long way in satisfying the expectations of the guests, the organization, and the stakeholders.

With globalization, the world is increasingly becoming border less. India has carved a niche on the global map and many international companies have set up or are in the process of setting up their business in India. Also, tourism has brought in a steady stream of tourists from all around the world to India. It, therefore, becomes important for chefs to understand the flavour profile of different countries around the world. This would enable production of food by using authentic cooking methods and ingredients to meet the needs of the international traveller/tourist.

Most of the food production books available to Indian students of hotel management and catering are written by international authors. It becomes difficult sometimes for the students to relate to these books, as there are differences in commodities, technology, and even processes used in various parts of the world. Presently, students have to refer to different books for one particular topic and do not even get to see many ingredients, let alone cook with them. Also, there is no textbook that discusses the concepts of cooking keeping in mind the Indian work culture and availability constraints of some commodities in India.

About this Book

Recognizing the need for comprehensive books for students pursuing their career in hotel management, I decided to write books for students and everyone interested in cooking. The first volume, *Food Production Operations,* deals with basic commodities, methods of cooking, and basics of pastry and Indian cuisine. The second volume, *Quantity Food Production Operations and Indian Cuisine,* talks about volume cooking and Indian cuisine. This third volume, *International Cuisine and Food Production Management,* is an extension of the first two volumes. It is expected that the students have read the first two volumes in order to grasp the third one better.

This book has been developed keeping in mind the diversities in cuisines all around the world. It discusses advanced level of kitchen operations that are performed in professional kitchens. This book gives an insight into various aspects of international cuisines such as larder kitchen, sausages, cold cuts, sandwiches, and also modern adaptations of the same; different international cuisines such as Western, European, and Oriental; advanced confectionery skills; and skills for effectively managing production, yield, and cost. Various important concepts have been discussed in tabular form for better understanding.

The book has been specially designed to meet the requirements of students aspiring to become chefs. It would also act as an aid for trained professionals in the industry to brush up their basic knowledge and understand the different cuisines of various countries and the set standards and principles related to their cooking. The accompanying CD contains standard recipes in Excel format which are enabled with formulas. Users can feed the required fields in the Excel sheets and obtain costs of the recipes and apply the same while deciding food costs and selling price of the menus.

This book brings in my 18 years of experience with Oberoi Hotels and Resorts. This professional knowledge percolates down through the chapters in the form of 'chef's tips' that are rarely mentioned in books, but are always followed or practised in the kitchens. These were handed down from our seniors and we have always carried them with us. For example, one should never refreeze a melted ice cream, as it can form large crystals that can hamper the texture of the ice cream; instead such ice creams can be used for milkshakes.

Pedagogical Features

The various student-friendly pedagogical features in the book include the following:

- All chapters begin with learning objectives, introduction, and then discuss in detail the various topics
- The commodities and important information are listed in tabular form and the tables are also numbered for easy reference and accessibility
- The concepts and skills are explained through various figures and chef's tips
- The conclusion and detailed list of key terms at the end of each chapter aid in understanding of the key concepts in the chapter
- The concept review questions at the end of each chapter will test the students' grasp on the chapter and will also prepare them for technical interviews
- The projects given at the end of each chapter will be useful for chef instructors to guide the students for research and initiate the habit of self-learning
- The colour plates aid in a better understanding of the concepts and identification of commodities and ingredients that might not be easily available in India
- The accompanying CD contains recipes which are enabled with formulas to calculate the waste percentage and food cost of the dish

Coverage and Structure

This book is divided into four parts. The first part, *Cold Kitchen*, builds an understanding about various types of jobs that are carried out in the larder kitchen, such as charcuterie, sandwiches, and appetizers.

Chapter 1, *Larder and Cold Kitchen*, covers the layout and equipment used in the larder or *garde manger*, functioning and organizational structure of larder kitchen, and various sections in which different types of jobs are carried out on a day-to-day basis.

Chapter 2, *Charcuterie*, covers different types of cold cuts, sausages, and the methods of preparation of the same. Famous cold cuts from around the world are explained with photographs for better comprehension.

Chapter 3, *Appetizers and Garnishes*, introduces various types of appetizers served from the cold kitchen. In this chapter, the concept of *amuse bouche* in fine dining restaurants and the finer aspects of plating of appetizers in a modern way are discussed in tabular forms.

Chapter 4, *Sandwiches*, introduces various types of sandwiches and the most common types prepared in hotels and restaurants. It enhances knowledge about preparation, storage, and service of sandwiches in hotels.

Chapter 5, *Uses of Herbs and Wines in Cooking*, discusses the selection, identification, and use of various types of herbs and wines in Western cooking.

The second part, *International Cuisines*, introduces the student to the international cuisines such as French, Italian, Spanish, German, Greek, Scandinavian, Mediterranean, Mexican, English, Japanese, Chinese, and Thai. This part also discusses the art of plated food and use of herbs and wine in cooking.

Chapter 6, *Western Cuisines*, discusses cuisines of the Western world such as Italian, Mexican, and the Mediterranean (parts of Italy, Spain, Southern France, Morocco, Lebanon, Turkey, and Greece). These cuisines have been discussed with regard to their geographical location, regions, special equipment used, and a few famous dishes from these countries.

Chapter 7, *European Cuisines*, discusses cuisines of Germany, France, England, and Scandinavian countries (Norway, Denmark, Sweden, and Finland).

Chapter 8, *Western Plated Food*, discusses the art and science behind plating Western food. Various types of crockery and materials used in modern plating are also discussed along with photographs for the students to understand how plating has also been refined over the years.

Chapter 9, *Concept of Health Food*, covers the latest trends of healthy eating and various elements that constitute healthy food. It also discusses various kinds of nutritional software and guidelines to some dietary regulations in the food industry and the increasing demands of organic cooking and the new health menus used in modern hotels.

Chapter 10, *Oriental Cuisines*, primarily discusses the three most popular cuisines of South-East Asia: China, Japan, and Thailand.

The third part, *Advanced Pastry and Confectionery*, discusses various kinds of cakes and pastries, frozen desserts such as ice creams and *parfaits*, chocolates and its usage in confectionery, modern plated and buffet desserts, cookies, and various types of sauces used in pastry and confectionery.

Chapter 11, *Cakes and Pastries*, discusses both classical cakes and modern cakes and pastries, and new ways of presenting them.

Chapter 12, *Chocolates*, discusses the origin and manufacturing processes of chocolates, different types of chocolates, and their applications in confectionery.

Chapter 13, *Desserts*, discusses various types of hot and cold desserts and their presentation.

Chapter 14, *Ice Creams and Frozen Desserts*, discusses methods of making frozen desserts, commodities and equipment used for making these deserts, and their storage and serving.

Chapter 15, *Sauces and Coulis*, covers components and types of sauces, and their uses, storage, and service.

Chapter 16, *Cookies and Biscuits*, discusses various types of cookies and biscuits and the methods of preparing them.

The final part, *Food Production Management,* discusses the various financial and organizational aspects of kitchen management. This part makes the students aware of various types of management functions that are performed in the daily kitchen work and also discusses how to evaluate and conduct trade tests in the kitchen.

Chapter 17, *Production Management,* discusses kitchen organization, various aspects such as production planning and scheduling, production quality and control, forecasting and budgeting, menu costing, and yield management.

Chapter 18, *Research and Product Development,* focuses on the testing of new equipment, food trials, and developing and evaluating new recipes.

The knowledge provided in these chapters can be utilized to prepare various recipes given in the CD. This knowledge, along with right attitude and skills gained through experience, will help aspiring chefs to build a strong foundation for a successful career.

About the Accompanying CD

The book is accompanied by a CD containing PowerPoint presentations on step-by-step preparations of terrine and pâté and over 370 macro-enabled recipes in MS Excel format. The recipes are divided in the following way:

1. Cold kitchen
   - (a) Appetizers
   - (b) Sandwiches
2. International cuisines
   - (a) Western cuisine
     - (i) Italian,
     - (ii) Lebanese
     - (iii) Mediterranean
     - (iv) Mexican
     - (v) Moroccan and Turkish
   - (b) European cuisine
     - (i) English
     - (ii) French and Provencal
     - (iii) German
     - (iv) Scandinavian
   - (c) Health food
   - (d) Oriental cuisine
     - (i) Chinese
     - (ii) Japanese
     - (iii) Thai
3. Advanced pastry and confectionery
   - (a) Cakes and pastries
   - (b) Chocolates
   - (c) Desserts
   - (d) Ice creams and frozen desserts
   - (e) Sauces and coulis
   - (f) Cookies and biscuits

The recipes are designed on Excel sheets with built-in macros. They allow users to calculate waste percentage and food cost of the dish.

System Requirements for the CD

- The CD is compatible with all versions of Windows, starting from Windows 98.
- The computer must have a CD/DVD drive.
- The computer must feature MS Office.

Using the CD

- The step-by-step preparations are given in the folder 'Preparations' and the various recipes are given in three folders: Cold Kitchen, International Cuisines, and Advanced Pastry and Confectionery
- To view the desired file, click on the desired folder
- Click on the preparation (PPT) or recipe (Excel sheet) you wish to view

Acknowledgements

I would like to mention certain people and organizations who have either directly or indirectly contributed towards the completion of this book.

First and foremost I would like to mention our chairman, Mr Prithvi Raj Singh Oberoi, under whose able guidance I have been able to collect all the knowledge pertaining to this book. I would like to thank the Oberoi Centre of Learning and Development (OCLD) for letting me use the resources for research. I gratefully acknowledge the support of my Dean (OCLD), Mr Mark Woodbridge, for allowing me to complete this task. I would specially want to thank all my colleagues and friends who have lent their encouragement and support in this venture of mine. I would also like to mention the kitchen management associates of OCLD 2011–13 batch, who have lent their help and support in the compilation of the recipes in the CD.

My thanks would be incomplete if I did not mention the academicians and the reviewers, who reviewed the book and gave corrective feedback that helped to frame the contents of the book. I would like to thank the editors at Oxford University Press India for their constant follow-ups and all their support that motivated me to accomplish this project.

I would like to thank all the near and dear ones and the professionals in the industry who have in some way or the other influenced the development of this book.

Last but not least, I would like to appreciate the support of my wife, Shalini, and my children, Ojas and Amora, who showed their immense patience while I wrote my third book.

Chef Parvinder S. Bali

BRIEF CONTENTS

DETAILED CONTENTS

PART III: ADVANCED PASTRY AND CONFECTIONERY

PART IV: FOOD PRODUCTION MANAGEMENT

LIST OF COLOUR PLATES

PART I

COLD KITCHEN

- *Larder or Cold Kitchen*
- *Charcuterie*
- *Appetizers and Garnishes*
- *Sandwiches*
- *Uses of Herbs and Wines in Cooking*

CHAPTER 1

LARDER OR COLD KITCHEN

Learning Objectives

After reading this chapter, you should be able to

- trace the background of a larder kitchen
- define the term larder kitchen and its importance in the kitchen division
- analyse the various sections of a larder kitchen and how they support other kitchens
- get an insight into the basic layout of the larder kitchen and how should it be set up to work efficiently and effectively
- identify various kinds of tools and equipment used in the larder kitchen
- understand the hierarchy of a larder kitchen and the specific jobs performed by each section head

INTRODUCTION

The first volume of this book—*Food Production Operations*—focused on the various types of kitchens in the hospitality industry and the range of commodities and cooking methods involved in preparing food. The second volume—*Quantity Food Production Operations and Indian Cuisine*—concentrated on quantity food production, volume forecasting, planning, and Indian cuisine. It also covered cuisines from different regions, *dum* cooking, *tandoor*, Indian sweets, and home style food. This book is an extension to the two previous volumes and is aimed at providing students with an understanding of various international cuisines on a broader perspective. It essentially covers the cold kitchen, international cuisines, advanced pastry, in addition to production management and product development.

Larder essentially means a cool place used for storage. The cold or larder kitchen, in hotel industry parlance, includes appetizers, sandwiches, and salads and cold cuts such as *charcuterie.* The first four chapters of this book cover various aspects of the cold kitchen. In this chapter, we will learn what a larder kitchen means.

In the olden times, when refrigeration was not very common, or rather non-existent, people used to build special places to store products purchased from the market. These places, called larders, were used to store cheese, vegetables, meat products, and even wine. Our ancestors were predominantly farmers and their harvested produce had to be stored for consumption for long periods of time. Human needs for constant supply of food not only led to the practice of farming and domesticating animals but also of preserving food. They mastered the art of preserving fish by salting, curing, and drying it for future use. With the discovery of spices and vinegars, they began to pickle food items and learnt the art of smoking and curing food. In fact, curing of food goes back to 3000 B.C. We will discuss these aspects in the next chapter on *charcuterie* products.

In the hotel industry, larder kitchen refers to a separate department that is associated with the preparation of cold foods. It is also known as *garde manger,* which in French means 'keeping cold for eating later'. This department prepares various items, such as salads and starters, commonly known as *hors d'oeuvres* in French. The larder kitchen also prepares cold meat, such as sausages, forcemeats, pâtés, and terrines, that we will discuss in detail in Chapter 3 on appetizers. The larder kitchen also specializes in preparing decorative items, such as butter sculptures and ice carvings, to decorate the buffet. However, it is now a dying art, as it is highly labour intensive and requires a great deal of skill. Also, with the advent of moulds and specialized tools for carvings, this skill has further diminished. Moreover, modern buffets prefer to focus more on quality food rather than exotic items which drain the time and energy of the staff.

Garde manger or the larder is the support kitchen and is always located in the main kitchen of the hotel. It caters to both à la carte as well as buffet operations. It is thus very important that the larder kitchen be in close vicinity of the hot kitchen to enable close-coordination between the two kitchens and time is not spent in running around between them. For example, a sandwich made in the cold kitchen is generally accompanied by French fries that would come from the hot kitchen.

LARDER WORK

Larder kitchen is a unique kitchen which prepares all types of cold meat, fish, and vegetables for buffets for restaurants, banquets, as well as à la carte. It is a much specialized area of the kitchen as it deals with artistic presentations of food. This department has various sections such as salads, hors d'oeuvres, fish preparation area, butchery, cold sauces, sandwiches, and buffet decorations. Larder also includes several sections that are involved in pre-preparation and fabrication of cold foods, which can either be used for salads, or the processed meat can also be used by the hot kitchen. Certain sections of the larder kitchen can be operational on a 24-hours basis. Larder is one of the most important sections of the kitchen as it is responsible for the first course of meal that a guest encounters and sets the mood for the rest of the meal. A larder chef is therefore, a very skilled chef who has mastery of not only cold food preparation but also has an in-depth knowledge of the culinary skills related to basic cooking, such as blanching, poaching, stewing, and so on. Many of the food items prepared in the cold kitchen are first cooked by hot cooking method and then cooled, glazed, and covered with various toppings and sauces such as *aspic, chaud froid,* and jellies.

SECTIONS AND FUNCTIONS OF A LARDER KITCHEN

In hotels, the larder kitchen has many roles to play. It is a unit which acts as a support kitchen to several other units such as the hot kitchen, bakery, and pastry. The work in the *garde manger* is varied and requires a huge amount of skill as well. The scale of *garde manger* operations depends upon the type and volume of business. In a traditional set-up, a larder kitchen would comprise different sections, which have specific responsibilities and tasks to carry out on a daily basis. The various sections of a larder kitchen along with the tasks undertaken in each of them are discussed in the following sections.

Sauces and Soups Section

This section is responsible for preparing cold soups and sauces for appetizers as well as some hot main courses. The salads are generally made in the *garde manger,* hence different types of dressings are also made and stored in this section. *Garde manger* also prepares the sauces and condiments required for cold buffets. *Vichyssoise,* chilled cucumber, and mint soup are few examples of commonly served cold soups from the cold kitchen. It also supplies sauces, such as tartare sauce and mayonnaise, to the hot kitchen, which serves these as accompaniments with hot food.

Salads Section

This is one of the most important parts of the larder kitchen. It prepares a range of simple and compound salads that are served in à la carte as well as in banquets and buffets. In this section, all cold and hot salads are prepared and readied for service. In the modern fine dining service styles, the meal is usually started with a very small portion of an appetizer known as *amuse bouche,* which is prepared by the larder kitchen. We shall read about appetizers in Chapter 3. Apart from salads, the larder kitchen also prepares cold fruit platters for breakfast and other meal periods. In many hotels, the larder also prepares the fruit baskets that are sent to guest rooms as amenities.

Sandwich Section

This section of the larder kitchen prepares cold sandwiches and cold plates with salads, sauces, and condiments for hot sandwiches that are dished out from the hot kitchen. A range of sandwiches that can be used for high tea, à la carte, or even sold packed in *gourmet shoppe* outlets in the hotel can be prepared in this section. We will discuss the range of different types of sandwiches in Chapter 4. Various accompaniments, such as pickles, salads (such as coleslaw and garden greens), and sauces (such as tartare sauce) are served with sandwiches. These accompaniments are also prepared by the *garde manger.* All these condiments and pickles are also served with salad bars in buffet and the same is prepared by this section.

Charcuterie Section

This is one of the most skilled areas of a cold kitchen. It prepares various kinds of cured and smoked food. Hot and cold smoked food is prepared and served as salads or even as an ingredient to be used in a sandwich. In earlier times, this was one of the areas that a larder kitchen was famous for. Smoked meat items, such as smoked salmon, smoked breast of turkey, brined and cured pork loin, are some of the most popular preparations. This section also makes forcemeats for sausages, galantines, terrines, pâtés, etc. Since this section is the most specialized area of larder, it is often located as a separate unit altogether. Many hotels purchase these products from such places. *Charcuterie* products are discussed in detail in Chapter 2.

Carving Section

This section of larder kitchen is also a highly skilled and specialized area, that makes various kinds of decorative structures from fruits and vegetables or even from softened butter or margarine. Large ice blocks are carved to make logos for events or just used as props in elegant functions. For company-related events, large glass platters with colourful gelatine figurines representing the logos of companies are prepared in this section. This section is the busiest of all in festive occasions such as Christmas or any large banqueting event which requires a display of such artistic show pieces. However, this art is fading away slowly due to the shortage of skilled labour.

Cheese Section

Variety of cheese from all over the world is served in hotels and speciality restaurants. The cheese section of the larder kitchen specializes in preparing cheese platters for buffets as well as à la carte orders. Various kinds of cheese are stored at ambient temperature and in separate areas as cheese can pick up strong odours from other ingredients. This section also prepares cheese platters for any room amenities and also as packaged item to be sold to guests. Some of the dishes prepared by this section are discussed in the section on international cuisines later in the book.

Appetizers and Hors D'oeuvres

This section of the larder kitchen specializes in preparing appetizers for snacks, banquets, as well as restaurant orders. Various kinds of cold appetizers also known as hors d'oeuvres in French are prepared and dished out from here. Several other popular appetizers, such as *antipasti* from Italy, *mezze* from Lebanon, and *tapas* from Spain, are prepared from this section. The hot appetizers are prepared in the hot kitchen, but the cold appetizers are prepared in the larder.

Butchery

This is usually a part of the larder kitchen but it is separated from the main section, as it is advisable to process raw and cooked food separately to avoid contamination. Various types of meat are cut and portioned here and supplied to various kitchens. Fish

CHEF'S TIP
When the cold kitchen prepares mayonnaise, it accumulates lots of egg whites, which can be used by hot kitchen to clarify consommés. If the egg whites do not have a single drop of yolk in them, they can also be used in the bakery kitchen to prepare desserts such as meringues.

are also cut and processed here; but in many hotels, due to health and hygiene reasons, fish is generally processed in an area separate from the butchery section. In some hotels, butchery forms a part of the food stores to have a control over the expensive meat, but in some hotels it is a part of the kitchen and directly under the control of the larder kitchen.

LAYOUT OF A TYPICAL LARDER

The *garde manger* is typically an area used for preparing, processing, and storing cold perishable food, both in raw as well as cooked state. This section is also responsible for processing meat and fish that are eventually used by other sections of the hotel to make dishes. All types of hors d'oeuvres, salads, sauces, etc. are prepared, stored, and served from here. Therefore, for such crucial functions to be carried out smoothly and efficiently, it is important that the larder kitchen is well-planned and laid out.

Larder kitchen is always a part of the main kitchen as it not only serves à la carte and banquets but is also responsible for room amenities, welcome drinks to guests, and many other support roles for other kitchens. Traditionally the larder kitchen also comprised a butchery and fish preparation area, but with the passage of time the concept of larder kitchen got restricted to a section which prepares salads, appetizers, and other support jobs for the hot kitchens. In some hotels, the butchery section comes under food stores. The meat is received and processed and stored back into the stores. The meat is then issued to each separate kitchen on a storeroom requisition. This is done because meat being an expensive commodity it is necessary to control its use.

The *garde manger* is also responsible for decorative props on the buffet such as vegetable and fruit carvings, butter sculptures, and ice carvings. Though there are no separate sections allocated in the larder kitchen for this particular work because of the low frequency of such jobs, in the event of such functions, the ice carving is usually done at a place which is separate from the kitchen area. This is done as it involves a lot of chiselling of ice that can spread over large areas and cause slipping.

It is important to keep the work flow in mind while planning the larder kitchen. Various kinds of jobs would be performed here at the same time so it is important to keep the raw food separate from the processed food to avoid any cross-contamination. Figure 1.1 shows the most traditional layout of the *garde manger* of a five-star hotel, which caters to banquets as well as à la carte operations of a restaurant. Note that each section in the larder kitchen has been separated from others. The following sections are clearly demarcated, starting from the right-hand bottom corner; moving anticlockwise.

Section for Peeling

This is the pre-process section where all the vegetables and fruits are sanitized and peeled for further use. The peeled vegetables are stored in a refrigerated cold room known as 'walk-in' until further use. The peels can be passed on to the hot kitchen for flavouring

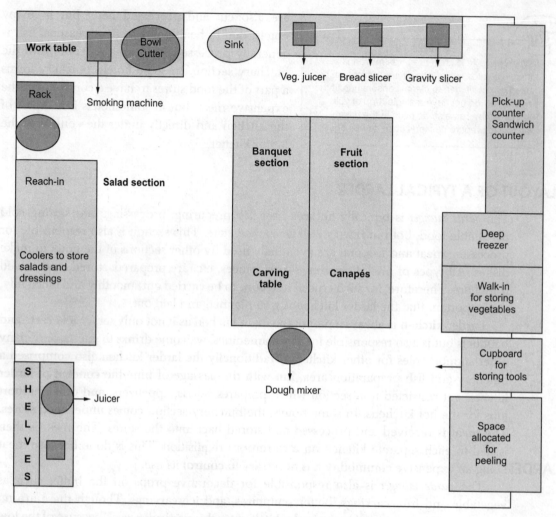

Fig 1.1 Traditional layout of the *garde manger* of a five-star hotel

stocks, provided the peels are clean and safe. This section is usually at the entrance of the kitchen, so that no soil or dirt is carried into the section.

Storage Space for Small Tools and Equipment

It is important to store small tools and equipment in a separate cupboard. Cupboards and other such storage areas should never be fabricated in wood, as they breed germs. Only stainless steel cabinets are to be used.

Pick-up Counter

When the *garde manger* executes food orders on à la carte basis, it is termed as pick-up of food. When the food is dispensed for banquets, it is known as distribution system. It is important that the pick-up area is located in a place that is nearer to the restaurant as well as the banquet premises. This area is used for picking up all the à la carte and banquet orders of salads, appetizers, and also sandwiches. This is a complete refrigerated unit with a refrigerated top as well as cabinets to store *mise en place*. Such a versatile unit allows the chef to dispense all orders from a single place without having to move around too much.

Table for *Mise en Place*

This table can have equipment such as gravity slicers, juice machine, etc. that will enable chefs to do *mise en place*. The sliced meat can be then stored in the pick-up counter or in the walk-in designated for salads and cold cuts. The table on the left top corner can be used for *mise en place* for meat. Buffalo chopper and other related machines can be installed here.

Other Sections

The central table is used for preparing salads for banquets and functions. Canapés and bulk sandwiches for the functions can also be prepared here. The prepared salads and dressings are stored in a separate walk-in until pick up. This table can also be used for various other purposes such as carving and making decorative show pieces.

This is just a basic set-up of a larder kitchen, but in any establishment the set-up of sections in a larder can be different. However, there is one thing that is common, that is, the efficient work flow without any crossing of traffic in the larder.

The cold kitchen can be segregated from the main kitchen and located in a cool place, but it should not be far away from the main kitchen as it directly supports other departments of the kitchen. It is important that this area is well lit, airy, and well planned for the staff to carry out their responsibilities efficiently and effectively.

LARDER EQUIPMENT

Due to the wide variety of tasks performed in the cold kitchen, various kinds of tools and equipment are used in the larder kitchen some of which are unique to it. These could be large equipment as well as small tools. As basic tools in the larder kitchen can be used to perform many intricate tasks, larder chefs become very possessive about the tools and equipment in their kitchen. Although we would discuss the sections of larder in detail and cover all basic tools and equipment in later chapters, Table 1.1 gives an overview of the most commonly used large equipment and small tools in a larder kitchen.

Table 1.1   Equipment and tools used in larder kitchen

Equipment/Tools	Description	Photograph
Buffalo chopper or bowl cutter	This is a versatile equipment used for chopping meat. It consists of a large flat bowl with a cutter blade attached vertically. When the machine is in operation, the bowl moves and the sharp blade rotates simultaneously to cut the meat pieces into desired size. This	

(Contd)

Table 1.1 (Contd)

Equipment/Tools	Description	Photograph
	machine is particularly used for chopping meat, as it cuts the meat including the sinews. The meat can then be ground and used for various preparations such as cold meat and sausages.	
Meat mincer	This equipment is used for mincing meat. It has a spiral metal rod, a cutting blade, dye, and closing rim as shown in Fig. 1.2. The dye is a perforated attachment, which varies depending on the size of the perforations. When mincing meat, it is sensible to begin with using the larger dye and subsequently arriving at the smaller dye. The functioning of the meat mincer is different from that of the bowl cutter—this machine is unable to cut the sinews into smaller pieces.	
Bone saw machine	This machine is generally used in the butcher section of the larder kitchen. It has a sharp saw tooth shaped blade that cuts the bones of the meat without splintering them. This machine should be used with extreme caution and safety guidelines should always be followed when using it. It is common to see chefs use stainless steel netted gloves while working on the bone saw to protect themselves from any injuries.	Bone saw machine Stainless steel glove
Gravity slicer or meat slicer	It is one of the most commonly used machines in the larder kitchen. This equipment is used for slicing meat and other commodities such as vegetables and bread. It is commonly used to slice cold cuts for salads and platters. It is important to clean and disinfect this machine after every use in order to prevent contamination.	

(Contd)

Table 1.1 (*Contd*)

Equipment/Tools	Description	Photograph
Vegetable processor	It is used for various cuts (slicing, shredding, chopping, etc.) so as to obtain desired and uniform shapes and sizes of vegetables. It is generally used in an establishment that operates on volume operations as it helps in saving time and manpower. And the end product is also consistent. This equipment is available in various capacities and one should choose the model according to the kind of operation.	
Dough mixer	Although this equipment is more often associated with the bakery. It comes handy in the cold kitchen too. Here it is used to make emulsified sauces such as vinaigrettes and mayonnaise. Many kinds of dough are also required for certain cold preparations and the same can be prepared in this machine.	
Vacuum packing machine	The main purpose of this equipment is to pack raw or cooked products without any air so as to preserve them for their flavour and freshness. These days it is also used for vacuum packing foods, for sale in the retail market. Some chefs use this equipment to seal the meat and flavours in a plastic bag which is then poached in water to prepare the dishes. This style of cooking is known as *sous vide* and is the latest trend to cook healthy food. Thick plastic bags are used. The commodity to be packed is put inside the bag and kept in the machine in such a way that the opening of the bag protruds out of the machine. When the lid is closed and the machine is put on, it first pumps air into the bag and then extracts all the air with pressure to vacuum seal the bag. The plastic pouch can then be labelled and stored in a freezer or refrigerator.	
Sandwich counter	This is a refrigerating unit that has cabinets and a refrigerated open counter top in which the *mise en place* can be stored in small gastronome pans. This set-up helps to store the *mise en place* at hand and allows the chef to dispense the guest orders of salads, appetizers, and sandwiches efficiently and effectively.	

(*Contd*)

Table 1.1 (Contd)

Equipment/Tools	Description	Photograph
Hanging rail systems	These rails systems are used in larger cold rooms that are used for hanging meat and carcasses. Hanging meat helps to tenderise it and maintaining its quality as hanging helps in air circulation around the carcass. Many different types of hooks are also used along with the railing systems to hang the meat.	
Zesters graters	Various kinds of graters are used in the larder kitchen to extract the zest from citrus fruits. Some of the commonly used ones are: *Micro plane grater* A micro plane grater has a sharp tooth and its sleek shape helps to maintain a grip while grating spices and commodities such as nutmeg, lemon, and oranges, etc. *Zester* This tool is used for removing zest from citrus fruits such as lemon and oranges. It has a slightly curved tip with sharp holes in it, which remove zest without any bitter pith attached to it. *Channeller* A channeller or channel knife is a kind of small peeler that has a curved V shape at the tip or sometimes at its side. It helps to remove a thick strip from the sides of the citrus fruit. The fruit is then sliced to yield decorative slices.	
Utility tools	These are a range of tools used in larder kitchen for various tasks. They not only help to do the job efficiently but also help to get a consistent product. Some of the commonly used tools are: *Can and bottle opener* Larder kitchen uses a lot of canned and bottled products for which this piece of equipment is very handy. These are available in various shapes and sizes.	

(Contd)

Table 1.1 (Contd)

Equipment/Tools	Description	Photograph
Utility tools	*Corer* As the name suggests, this tool is used for coring the central part of fruit without cutting the fruit open. It is used when we need the fruit intact or it needs to be cut into slices. Corers are used mainly for coring apples and pears. Some large corers are also used for coring pineapples. *Pitters* These are the most important small tools used in larder kitchen. They can be used for removing pits from stone fruits such as cherries and olives.	
Slicers and peelers	A wide range of slicers and peelers are used in the larder kitchen to slice/peel various vegetables, fruits and other commodities. A few of the ones used commonly are: *Egg slicer* It is used for slicing boiled eggs. It has a curved base on which the boiled egg is placed. The top cover is made with thin pieces of wires equidistant from each other. When pressed over the base, these wires help to divide the egg into slices of uniform size. *Egg wedger* The concept is same as that of the egg slicer but in this case the placement of the wires is in such a way that it helps to divide the eggs into equal wedges or quarter. *Egg top cutter* This tool can be used to slice off the top of a boiled or even raw egg before being served to a guest. It helps to neatly slice off the top of the egg.	

(Contd)

Table 1.1 (Contd)

Equipment/Tools	Description	Photograph
Slicers and peelers	*Quail egg cutter* This specially designed slicer is used for slicing the top of small quail eggs. The egg fits in the small hole on one of the blades and the other blade with sharp edge slices off the top without damaging the egg.	
	Mango slicer This is a very unique piece of tool that can slice the mango in such a way that it takes the pit out of the mango, giving the maximum yield of the mango without creating any mess.	
	Asparagus peeler The adjustable blade of this peeler helps to peel asparagus without wasting any of its good and edible part.	
	Truffle slicer This tool is used for slicing delicate truffle slices, which are commonly used in larder kitchen. Since truffles are very expensive fungus, it is important to have a good yield and even slices.	
	Cheese slicer This tool is used for slicing hard cheese that would be used for decorating and garnishing salads and appetizers. A very thin flake can be peeled off from the cheese block with the help of this tool.	
	Mandolin slicer This versatile equipment has multiple uses. It can be used for slicing commodities to paper thin thickness. It can also be used for shredding and creating a wafer with holes also known as *gaufrette*.	
	Japanese slicers These are decorative slicers that are used for making spaghetti shapes or ribbons from vegetables, such as carrots, radish, and beetroots, for use in salads and garnishes.	

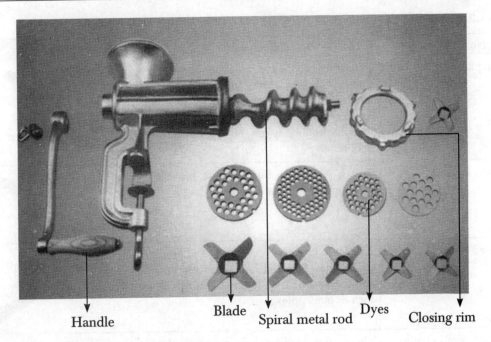

Handle   Blade   Spiral metal rod   Dyes   Closing rim

Fig. 1.2 Parts of the meat mincer

Knives and Shears

Apart from the equipment and tools mentioned in Table 1.1, various kinds of knives, scissors, and shears are used in the larder kitchen for performing small but important jobs. Since it is one of the sections of the kitchen that also carries out lots of vegetable and fruit carvings and decorations, the kinds of tools and small decorating knives used here are varied and unique. Many other kinds of knives apart, from the conventional ones, are used for specific purposes, such as splitting open shells of bivalves (oysters, mussels, etc.) or for giving a decorative edge to vegetables and fruits. Some of the commonly used knives and shears are listed in Table 1.2.

Table 1.2 Types of knives and shears used in larder kitchen

Name of tool	Description	Photograph
Paring knife or vegetable knife	It is used for paring apples and round fruits. The size of the blade varies between 3 and 5 inches.	
Turning knife	This knife is used to give vegetables various ornate shapes such as ovals. Such vegetables are also known as turned vegetables and hence the name of the knife. The knife has a slight curved blade that facilitates turning.	

(Contd)

Table 1.2   *(Contd)*

Name of tool	Description	Photograph
Boning knife	This knife is used for removing bones from the meat. It has a thinner and shorter blade and is used to cut meat away from the bone. The heel of the knife is slightly curved so that the knife can rest on the bone while deboning.	
Filleting knife	This is similar to boning knife but has a flexible blade for the ease of filleting a fish.	
Serrated knife	This knife is used to cut breads and prepare sandwiches. Serrated knives are very sharp and can also be used for cutting tough fruits such as pineapples.	
Smoked salmon knife	This knife is used for slicing smoked salmon into thin slices. It has a long blade measuring up to 30 cm and is very thin, sharp, and flexible.	
Oyster knife	These knives are used for splitting open oysters. These are also known as oyster shuckers, as the process of opening oysters is known as shucking. The oyster knife does not have a sharp edge, but has a sharp tip, so it is important to use stainless steel gloves or a thick duster as a protection while shucking oysters.	
Clam knife	This knife has a unique design with a rounded tip and an edge, which is sharp but not as sharp as the cutting knife. Such unique features of this knife help it to extract clam from its shell in a safe and hygienic manner.	
Buntz knife or wavy knife	It is also commonly known as decorating knife. The unique wavy blade of this sharp knife helps to give vegetables and fruits wavy shapes. It can also be used to make net-shaped or *gaufrette*-shaped vegetables.	

(Contd)

Table 1.2 (Contd)

Name of tool	Description	Photograph
Cheese knife	This knife is used on the cheese board to cut various types of cheese by a guest. The sharp two-pronged tip facilitates in lifting up the cut piece of cheese. The holes in the cheese knife help to cut soft cheese and allow the cheese to stick to the knife.	
Tomato knife	This knife is used for slicing tomatoes. It has a sharp serrated edge and the blade is approximately 6 inches. The serrated edge helps slice the tomatoes with ease without getting mushy. The two-pronged tip helps to remove the eyes of the tomatoes.	
Deveining knife	This knife is used usually for seafood, such as prawns, shrimps, and lobsters, to remove veins from their body parts. The narrow tip of this knife and the broad base facilitate the deveining of prawns and shrimps.	
Grapefruit knife	This is a specially designed knife for removing tender segments from grapefruit, without losing much of the juice. The rounded blade and the curved serrated blade from both the sides help in removing the segments with ease.	
Chestnut knife	Chestnuts need to be scored on the end before roasting or boiling to release steam from inside. This prevents the nuts from popping out and losing their shape. The short and sharp blade of the chestnut knife helps to score the end of chestnuts. The size of the blade is roughly around an inch.	
Mincing knife or *mezzaluna*	It is also known as *mezzaluna* because of its unique half-moon shape with handles at both ends. It can have a single or twin blade. The rocking action of the sharp blades chops herbs to a fine consistency.	

(Contd)

Table 1.2 (Contd)

Name of tool	Description	Photograph
Poultry shears	These are heavy duty shears used for cutting poultry and game birds. The curved shape of the blade allows the shears to cut through the tough bones of chicken. Though these are known as poultry shears, they are in fact heavy duty scissors that can be used for variety of heavy-duty tasks in the kitchen.	
Lobster shears	These are used for cutting and preparing lobsters. The short sharp blades help in splitting the lobster body while the cracker in the middle of the shear helps to crack the lobster claws to extract the meat.	
Kitchen shears	These are heavy-duty pairs of scissors used for various small tasks in the kitchen. Some of the kitchen shears are multipurpose and can be used for various jobs such as cracking nuts and opening cans and bottles.	

HIERARCHY OF LARDER STAFF

Much before the legendary French chef Augustus Escoffier (early part of the twentieth century) invented the brigade system in kitchen and made a reporting structure, kitchens were divided into groups known as guilds. Each guild specialized in a certain skill and art. Thus, there was the guild of bakers, people who made cold cuts and meat, etc. Each of these guilds had a training system in place and after a person had achieved mastery over the skill, which took considerable amount of time, they were conferred the title of master craftsmen. With the onset of modernization in the industry and progression in hotel business, a strong need was felt to classify the craftsmanship of the chefs into some form of hierarchical structure. Chef Escoffier is credited for putting together a brigade system with reporting levels in each section. *Garde manger* too has its own brigade. The larder chef is the master chef who has the technical and managerial skills to perform the tasks of this highly specialized kitchen. Under him/her is a brigade of chefs, cooks, and *commis* who work together as a team to achieve the goals and objectives of the larder section. The second in command of the larder is the position of *sous chef* or even a junior *sous chef,* commonly referred to as kitchen executive who is responsible for carrying out the main operations in the department. He/she heads the brigade of *chef de parties* (CDPs) commonly known as *chef de partie* that are at a supervisory grade. Each CDP is in charge of a particular section and has few *commis* and apprentices working under him/her. An apprentice is entry level staff who is beginning to learn the art and skills of any kitchen. After few years of being an apprentice, he/she would get promoted to *commis* and then up the hierarchical ladder based on performance. Figure 1.2 shows the hierarchical structure of a larder kitchen. In some hotels there are kitchen artists who report directly to the larder chef as theirs is a highly skilled job and the artists are master craftsmen.

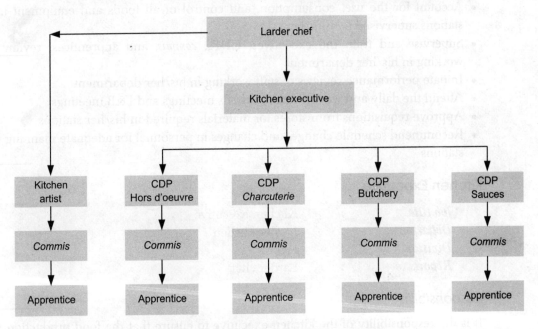

Fig. 1.3 Brigade of a larder kitchen of a five-star hotel

DUTIES AND RESPONSIBILITIES OF LARDER STAFF

With position comes a lot of responsibility and accountability. Each of the levels in the kitchen has a set of duties and responsibilities that makes up the job description of the person at that level. The job responsibilities of each person at various levels in the larder kitchen are discussed below.

Larder Chef

Job title	:	Larder chef
Department	:	Kitchen
Division	:	Food and beverage (F&B)
Reports to	:	Executive *sous chef*

Responsibility

It is the responsibility of the larder chef to organize, develop, and supervise food production in the larder kitchen as per standards and recipes developed by the executive chef. His/Her specific responsibilities are to:

- Train staff on improved work procedures, quality food production, economical use of food materials, and attractive presentation of food items
- Be responsible for all food production in the area assigned to him/her
- Be responsible for overall food cost control without affecting standards and specifications laid out by top management
- Account for the use, consumption, spoilage, and control of foodstuff produced or stored under his/her supervision
- Account for the use, consumption, and control of all foods and equipment in the stations supervised by him/her
- Supervise and train the executives, CDPs, *commis*, and apprentices; review staff working in his/her department
- Initiate performance reviews of staff working in his/her department
- Attend the daily and weekly kitchen chef's meetings and F&B meetings
- Approve requisitions from stores for materials required in his/her stations
- Recommend schedule changes and changes in personnel for adequate manning of all stations

Kitchen Executive

Job title	:	Kitchen executive
Department	:	Larder kitchen
Division	:	F&B
Reports to	:	Larder chef

Responsibility

It is the responsibility of the kitchen executive to ensure that the food production team provides consistent quality of food and beverage in the area/shift under his/her control, as per the corporate preset international standards in order to maximize guest satisfaction and organizational profitability in an atmosphere of high employee morale. His/Her specific responsibilities are to:

- Ensure adherence to organizational standards of food quality, hygiene, preparation, and presentation in his/her kitchen
- Ensure all kitchen equipment and machinery is in good working order at all times, in his/her area of work
- Recommend changes in systems and procedures to increase efficiency and improve service levels
- Ensure prompt, courteous, and accurate service to all guests in order to achieve high levels of guest satisfaction
- Be responsible for maintaining of records/documentation in his/her area as per operational/control requirements
- Ensure quality and availability of raw ingredients at all times for smooth operation
- Ensure that the staff report on duty as per their shift and any sickness of the staff to be conveyed and reported immediately to the human resource (HR) executive and larder chef

- Ensure buffets/food displays are set up and maintained professionally, as per organizational standards
- Ensure hygiene standards of his/her kitchen, storage areas, equipment, and machinery
- Control food wastage, without compromising on food quality
- Ensure cleaning schedules by kitchen stewarding department being followed in a timely manner
- Ensure par level of dry stores and perishables are maintained on daily basis and also ensure correct store requisitioning
- Ensure attendance and punctuality of every team member
- Provide functional assistance to all subordinates and peers of various areas
- Ensure excellent relations and professionalism amongst all staff in his/her kitchen and with related departments and staff
- Coordinate functions and activities with other F&B sections, engineering, housekeeping, etc.
- Work in close coordination with F&B service team
- Ensure appropriate and professional communication with F&B team at all given times and for any special occasions
- Ensure constant on-the-job and classroom training for his/her kitchen employees
- Personally conduct critical training sessions
- Encourage team building through regular informal meetings and keep an open door policy
- Attend behavioural, vocational, and skill-related training, to enhance his/her skills and develop multifunctionality
- Provide cross-training to employees of other departments
- Share his/her skills and knowledge with all employees; drive and follow company standard operating procedures (SOPs) in his/her kitchen
- Counsel subordinates in work-related and personal matters
- Maintain records as required of training in the department

Chef de Partie

Job title	:	*Chef de partie*
Department	:	Larder kitchen
Division	:	F&B
Reports to	:	Kitchen executive

Responsibility

It is the responsibility of the *chef de partie* (CDP) to assist his/her superior in maintaining the highest standard of quality in food preparation by following standard recipes and high level of hygiene standards maintained as per hazard analysis and critical control points (HACCP) standards in his/her area, in order to maximize guest satisfaction and profitability in an atmosphere of high employee morale. The specific responsibilities are to:

- Ensure prompt and accurate service by all kitchen staff under his/her control to all customers in order to achieve a high level of customer satisfaction

- Be responsible for implementing hotel standards on food quality, preparation, and presentation in his/her section/shift
- Recommend changes in systems and procedures to increase efficiency and improve service levels
- Recommend changes in menu at the time of new menu by introducing new dishes and their presentation
- Ensure that the hygiene and cleanliness of the kitchen area is maintained as per predetermined standards
- Be responsible for controlling food wastage, without compromising on food quality
- Ensure proper security and safety of raw and cooked food/equipment by proper storage
- Ensure that all the kitchen equipment are operated, maintained, and stored properly and are safe to use
- Ensure that all the kitchen records are maintained properly at all times
- Ensure that organizational polices and standards are adhered to by all in the department
- Ensure availability of ingredients in the kitchen, at all times, in order to provide prompt service
- Assist kitchen executive and higher authorities to define the organization of work within his/her kitchen department including assignments, time schedules, and vacations
- Ensure that inter-kitchen food transfers are accurate and conform to hotel policy
- Ensure proper *mise en place* in his/her production sections for speedy preparation and service
- Ensure production planning is being discussed with his/her *commis* and the concerned higher kitchen authorities
- Ensure all company SOPs are followed by all the team members
- Ensure cleaning schedules by kitchen stewarding department being followed in timely manner
- Ensure par level of dry stores and perishables are maintained on daily basis and also ensure correct store requisitioning
- Requisite daily requirement from storeroom and get it checked and duly signed by the kitchen executive
- Recommend quality status on all the products in the kitchen to senior authority and rectify it as soon as possible
- Register complaints regarding improper machinery functioning or employee misbehaviour to the kitchen executive
- Brief the team members on menu changes or introduction of new ingredients/new dishes on the menu
- Provide functional assistance to all subordinates and peers of various kitchens
- Ensure excellent relations and professionalism amongst all staff in the kitchen and with related departments
- Ensure appropriate and professional communication with all team members at all given times.

Commis

Job title	:	*Commis*
Department	:	Larder kitchen
Division	:	F&B
Reports to	:	*Chef de partie*

Responsibility

It is the responsibility of the *commis* to prepare and provide the highest quality food in his/her area by following standard recipes and high level of hygiene standards maintained as per HACCP standards in order to maximize guest satisfaction and optimum profitability in an atmosphere of high individual morale. His/Her specific responsibilities are to:

- Prepare food and provide prompt, courteous, and accurate service to all customers as per organizational standard of quality, as directed
- Control food wastage without compromising on food quality
- Prepare all *mise en place* in production sections for smooth kitchen operation, as directed
- Ensure hygiene and cleanliness of his/her area at all the times
- Assist CDP and above in implementing and following organizational standards on food quality, preparation, and presentation
- Be responsible for maintaining all kitchen equipment in his/her area in good working condition
- Be responsible for adherence to all organizational policies and procedures
- Ensure complete hygiene in his/her work area and adhere to HACCP standards
- Ensure exact collection of perishables, grocery, and meat/fish items as per the store-room requisition
- Ensure timely cleaning and sanitisation of all equipment and tools in appropriate hygienic manner
- Recommend daily requirement from storeroom to CDP
- Maintain a daily logbook and registering equipment issues, and any critical information to be passed on to higher authority or next shift
- Recommend quality status on all the products in his/her kitchen to CDP
- Provide assistance to all subordinates and peers of various kitchens
- Ensure excellent relations and professionalism amongst all staff in his/her kitchen and with related departments
- Coordinate with other F&B sections, engineering, housekeeping, etc. whenever required
- Ensure appropriate and professional communication with all team members at all given times
- Attend behavioural, vocational, and skill-related training, to enhance his/her skills and develop multifunctionality

Apprentices

These are trainees who help out in day-to-day operations and are learning the art and skills of the larder kitchen. Their main role is to practise and hone their knife skills. For a few months they practise cutting and chopping of vegetables and other items so that they become proficient at using various kinds of knives.

The positions defined here are in a classical sense. In the real world, they are combined, altered, and adapted to fit the specific goals of individual operations.

SUMMARY

In the hotel industry, larder kitchen refers to a separate department that is associated with the preparation of cold foods. It is also known as *garde manger,* which in French means keeping cold for eating later. The larder kitchen specializes in making cold salads, appetizers, soups, and other specific tasks such as making decorative cold foods and platters for receptions and big banquets.

Today, one cannot even think of a modern food establishment that does not have a larder kitchen. In this chapter, we discussed at length the significance of larder kitchen in catering to à la carte orders, as well as for banquets, functions, and guest rooms in addition to providing support to other kitchens. We also discussed various sections of larder kitchen and the specific jobs that are performed in each section. We learnt about the various kinds of large equipment and small tools used in the larder kitchen to perform the specialized tasks. Due to the shortage of skills

in the carving section, much of the specialized work is getting outsourced, as it is not required on daily basis. Ice carvings, butter sculptures, and vegetable carvings are a few examples of such skills. We also discussed the layout of a larder kitchen and understood the importance of planning the area with regard to placement of various tools and equipment to perform the job effectively and efficiently. The work flow is kept in mind while designing the layout of any section, so that the staff does not have to move around too much in order to complete a job.

The discussion on the hierarchical structure of the larder kitchen explained the sections and levels of the staff in this section. We also discussed the jobs and responsibilities of staff at various levels. This would help students understand the jobs carried out by various people in the same section to meet organizational goals and objectives.

KEY TERMS

Amenities These are complimentary gratuities sent to the guest rooms.

Antipasti It is the Italian term for appetizers.

Aspic Aspic is a clear reduced stock that becomes so gelatinous, that it can be used to cover cold meat and vegetables, to give them a shiny appearance.

Brined This is meat that is dipped in salted flavoured solution before smoking or cooking.

Canapé These are small pieces of bread that are topped with meat and vegetables and served as snacks.

Cellar It is a cool and airy room that is used for storing food and wine.

Charcuterie It is a section of the larder kitchen that is responsible for preparing cold meat, sausages, and cured meat.

Compound salad It is a salad made by combining two or more ingredients.

Consommé It is clarified meat broth that is served as hot or chilled soup.

Curing It is the process of treating the meat with salt and sugar in order to preserve them.

Deveining It is the process of removing veins from the body of prawns and lobsters.

Forcemeats   These are chopped or pureed meat that are used for stuffing or put into moulds and cooked.

Galantine   It is deboned whole chicken stuffed with minced chicken meat and poached. It is usually served cold.

Garde manger   It is the French term for larder kitchen, which translates to keeping cold to eat.

Gaufrette   It refers to netted shape, usually of potatoes, achieved by using mandolin slicer or buntz knife.

Gourmet shoppe   It is an outlet in the hotel that sells snacks and sweets such as chocolates, sandwiches, cold cuts, cakes, etc.

Guild   Before the advent of kitchen brigade, guilds were group of professionals who were responsible for a particular craft.

HACCP   It is the acronym for hazard analysis and critical control points, which is a food management system that ensures that hygiene standards are up to date.

Hors d'oeuvres   It is the French term for appetizers that are served at the beginning or the first course of the meal.

Mayonnaise   It is a cold emulsified sauce of egg yolks and oil flavoured with mustard.

Meringue   It is a type of dessert made from whipped egg whites along with sugar.

Mezze   It is the Lebanese term for appetizers.

Pâtés   It is the French term for meat pastes.

Relish   These are vegetable condiments flavoured with spices and flavourings served as an accompaniment with sandwiches, etc.

Salting   It is a process of preservation, where the food is preserved by adding large quantities of salt.

Sausages   These are chopped or pureed meat filled in intestines of various animals and eaten grilled or smoked.

Scoring   It means making an incision with a sharp knife.

Shucking   It is the term used for opening of oysters.

Simple salads   These are salads made by only one major ingredient.

Sinews   These are fibrous strands that attach meat muscles together.

Smoked salmon   It is cured and cold smoked salmon that is served as an appetizer.

Sous vide   It is a style of cooking, where the food commodity is sealed in a plastic pouch and cooked to retain all flavours and juices.

Tapas   These are small tidbits from Spain usually served as snacks and appetizers.

Tartare sauce   It is a cold sauce made by combining mayonnaise sauce with acidic vegetables such as gherkins and chopped pickled onions.

Terrines   These are chopped or pureed meat or vegetables either cooked or set with gelatine and served cold.

Truffle   It is a kind of fungus that has a delicate flavour.

Vichyssoise   It is a chilled creamy soup of pureed potatoes and leeks that is usually served chilled.

Walk-in   It is a large cold refrigerated room, where a person can walk inside.

Zest   It is the rind of any citrus fruit, usually obtained by grating.

CONCEPT REVIEW QUESTIONS

1. What do you understand by larder kitchen and how did it get this name?
2. What are the various ways of preservation of food that are ancient but still followed today?
3. What do you understand by the term *garde manger*?
4. Why is larder kitchen so important in modern hotels?
5. Briefly describe the sauce and soup section of larder kitchen.
6. What work is carried out at the salad section of larder kitchen?
7. What are the various sections of larder kitchen and how do these support the hot kitchen?
8. What do you understand by cured and smoked foods?
9. What are hors d'oeuvres?
10. Briefly describe five types of large equipment that are used in larder kitchen.
11. How should one choose the kind of dye for mincing the meat?
12. What care should be taken while operating a bone saw machine?

13. What is *sous vide* and how is a vacuum machine helpful to the process?
14. Explain the uses of hanging rail systems.
15. What is the difference between a paring knife and a turning knife?
16. Apart from the usage, how is a boning knife different from filleting knife?
17. Describe three kinds of shears commonly used in larder kitchen.
18. How is a clam knife different from an oyster knife?
19. Why does the cheese knife have holes in it?
20. What is so unique about the tomato knife?
21. What is the use of chestnut knife?
22. Describe a *mezzaluna* and its uses.
23. Describe the mandolin.
24. List the parts of a meat mincer.
25. What parameters should be kept in mind while planning a larder kitchen?
26. Explain the brigade of larder kitchen.
27. What are the broad responsibilities of a larder chef?

PROJECT WORK

1. In groups of five, conduct a market survey of hotels and speciality restaurants. Make a note of the set-up of the cold buffet and list the various kinds of salads, meat, and vegetable platters that are served. Also observe the way the buffet is spread out and if any decorative props are used.
2. Visit a factory nearby that specializes in making cold cuts and meat. Observe how the meat is received, treated, and processed for various kinds of cold cuts and cured meat. Make a report and submit it to your faculty for evaluation.
3. Conduct a market survey of a place that sells imported vegetables and meat. Make a note of various kinds of ingredients that can be used in larder kitchen.
4. Collect the various kinds of knives as explained in Table 1.2. Now use each knife for the purpose explained and write down your comments with regards to the use, yield it gives, etc. Observe if any other knife can give similar results and record your observations.

CHAPTER 2

CHARCUTERIE

Learning Objectives

After reading this chapter, you should be able to

- understand the basic concept of *charcuterie*
- comprehend the purpose of smoking, curing, and other processes involved in the preparation of *charcuterie* products
- identify various kinds of tools and equipment used for making sausages
- explain the purpose of components of any *charcuterie* product such as main meat, binders, sweeteners, and other seasoning agents
- examine the effects of dry curing and wet curing on a product and its uses in *charcuterie*
- evaluate cold smoking and hot smoking and their effects
- identify the ingredients used in sausage making
- comprehend the use of different types of forcemeats and their effect on the texture of the final product
- differentiate the various types of sausages, their production, shapes, and origin
- identify *galantine*, *ballotine*, and *dodines* and their importance in larder kitchen
- understand the differences between a pâté and a terrine
- analyse the techniques used in preparation of foie gras
- identify various types of truffles and their uses in *charcuterie*
- comprehend the uses of aspic and *gelée* in *charcuterie* and larder kitchen

INTRODUCTION

In Chapter 1, we read about the cold or larder kitchen, which is also commonly known as *garde manger*. In this chapter, we will learn about the various products that form a section of *garde manger*. On a smaller scale of operation, these products can be made in the larder kitchen, but sometimes the same operations can constitute a full-fledged mechanized and centralized kitchen producing products that are sold around the world.

Charcuterie is derived from a French word meaning 'cooked flesh'. Over the years, as trade and business developed across regions, countries and across the globe, food habits and tastes also changed as a result of influences, new ingredients, etc. For instance, certain special items, such as cheese and smoked cold meats, became such cherished delicacies that they began being traded for goods. It thus, became necessary to evolve certain standards on preparation of these dishes and codification of rules on the sale and purchase of such food items to control the money and price abuses. This led to formation of groups known as *guilds*. Each guild was responsible for a certain type of product and it was the responsibility of the guild to train people and make them master craftspersons. Each guild had a specified charter which listed its specific rights. By the end of the sixteenth century, there were approximately 24–30 guilds that were specific to only food items. One such guild that was responsible for preparing dishes from pig's meat was referred to as *charcuterie*. This guild maintained the tradition of preparing a range of products from pig's meat. Items such as hams, bacon, sausages, and pâtés further led the chefs to become more creative—such that specialization in this field has reached its zenith. Certain units around the world specialize in making smoked and cold meat. Germany and Italy are the largest producers and consumers of cold meat and sausages. In the modern world, *charcuterie* products are not only limited to a few slices on the plate, but also used in breakfast such as sausages and bacon. They are commonly used as fillings in sandwiches and burgers and as cold displays in the event of festive buffets such as Christmas and royal/state banquets.

In this chapter, we will focus on a range of *charcuterie* products that are made in the larder kitchen. We will discuss various kinds of meat, stuffing, techniques, etc. that are employed for the preparation of many types of cold meat. We begin with the most commonly used cold meat in the kitchen called sausages.

SAUSAGE

A sausage is a generic term for the wide range of preserved meat products made out of mincemeat, combined with fat and spices and stuffed or enclosed in some form of casing. A sausage could be preserved by cooking, smoking, or drying or, at times, be stored fresh chilled and cooked at the time of serving.

The word 'sausage' is said to be derived from the Latin word *salsus,* which means salted. Meat was earlier dry salted for preservation and it was heavily spiced with ginger and pepper to mask the flavour of high salt content. The prime reason was to preserve the meat. Nevertheless, families perfected recipes and handed them down for generations to create signature products. This elevated sausage making into an art form. From early times, people realized the fact that many parts of animals, such as intestines, stomach, and bladder, were perfect pouches for the meat to be placed inside and then cooked or cured to create sausages. All these casings formed the base of preparing sausages. Till date the process of basic sausage making remains the same. The meat is first ground and then mixed with spices, seasonings, and curing agents. It is then stuffed into various casings and then cured, brined, smoked, or cooked. In Italy, sausages are known as *insaccati,* which means 'in the sac'. There are few important elements of sausage making. We discuss each of these elements in the following sections.

Elements of Sausages

The various elements used to make sausages include meat, fats, seasoning and cure mixes, binding agents, and sweeteners.

Meat

The main ingredient of any sausage is meat. Usually pork is the most preferred meat due to its neutral flavour and colour, but meat such as lamb, beef, chicken, and game such as rabbit, squirrel, wild boar, venison, and pheasant can all be used for preparing different kinds of *charcuterie* products. Many people think that sausages are prepared from cheaper cuts of meat or leftover meat. This, however, is not true, as the quality of the meat will determine the final quality of the product. It is important to choose prime quality of meat. One of the most important things to keep in mind is that the meat should be from tougher cuts, such as legs, shoulder, or butt, as these are more exercised muscles in animal and tougher cuts of meat yield better flavours compared to the lean ones. The toughness of the meat can be overcome by grinding it to various degrees which varies from one product to another. This type of meat is known as forcemeat. Apart from meat, various other ingredients, such as offal, are used in the preparation of many *charcuterie* products. Offal is defined as the inside parts of an animal, such as the heart and liver, cooked and eaten as food. It is important to follow safety and hygiene while handling offal as it is highly perishable in nature. Some of the commonly used offal in *charcuterie* are described in Table 2.1

Fats

As a ratio, 25 per cent of fat is used in forcemeat to prepare stuffing for sausages and other *charcuterie* products. Fat is one of the most important ingredients in sausage making. However, the ratio of fats used has to be maintained for less amounts will make the final product dry and crumbly while excessive amounts will lead to shrinking of the final product. In modern times, people have become very conscious about health. The old recipes mentioned close to 50 per cent of fat being used in sausages. The fat commonly used in sausage making is taken from the jowl of the pig or from the back of the pig, which is commonly known as *fatback.* Some forcemeat recipes that utilize meat from chicken and fish also use double cream as fat.

Fat provides the richness and smoothness to the sausages and also helps in adding flavour and moisture to the final product. When using meat, it is important to use well-marbled meat. In case of using lean meat, extra fat has to be added. One should avoid using fat from lamb as it is too strong in flavour and also avoid chicken fat as it is too soft and can spoil the final texture of the product.

Table 2.1 Types of offal used in charcuterie

Offal	Description
Brain	The brain used in *charcuterie* often comes from lamb, sheep, hogs, and cow. The brain should be used within one day of receiving. When received it should be plump, firm, and light pink in colour. Upon receiving, it should be soaked in water and lime juice for at least two hours. The water should be constantly changed to remove the off flavours and traces of blood. To cook brain, it should be simmered in water flavoured with lime juice for not more than 20 minutes, after which it can be cooled in ice water and used accordingly.
Tongue	The tongue used should be from a large animal and should weigh less than 1.2 kg. After receiving, the tongue should be washed and scrubbed under running water and it should be simmered in water flavoured with lime juice for at least 20 minutes. It should then be chilled in ice water and only when it has cooled enough, should the skin be removed. Tongues can be smoked, boiled, or pressed and used in various *charcuterie* products.
Liver	Liver is the most popular and widely used offal in *charcuterie*. Liver from many animal sources, such as beef, lamb, veal, and pork, are commonly used in *charcuterie* products. The blood from liver is used for preparing blood sausages, which are very popular in Germany. After the liver is received, it should be drained to get rid of the blood. The liver should be blanched or sautéed and cooled quickly. This procedure helps the liver to firm up and it become easy to process the same. Ensure that the liver is never overcooked, as it makes the meat tough.
Sweetbreads	Highly appreciated by gourmets, these are basically thymus glands of lamb, pork, young beef, and veal. The sweetbreads should be washed and soaked in several changes of water flavoured with lime juice. Blanch in hot water for a short time and remove the membrane before serving. Sweetbreads should be used immediately. Sweetbreads are commonly used for making *pâtés* and *terrines*.
Pig's feet	Pig's feet are often available split lengthwise. These are a good source of gelatine and are commonly used for preparing aspic and *gelée*. It is commonly used to prepare rich stocks, which are sometimes used for binding sausages.
Blood	Highly perishable in nature, this ingredient should be used straight away after straining it to get rid of certain impurities. Blood is a very common ingredient used for preparing black pudding, tongue and blood sausages, and other blood sausages such as *boudin blanc* and *boudin noir*.
Caul fat	*Caul* fat is a remarkable item used in *charcuterie* in many different ways. *Caul* is a lacy membrane of fats that usually lines the abdominal cavity of animals. Fat from hogs, pigs, and sheep are much preferred because of their white colour and neutral flavour. The *caul* fat can be used for wrapping ground meat, securing pieces of rolled meat, adding moistness to the ground meat, etc. to retain the shape while cooking. When the meat cooks, the *caul* fat melts away naturally basting the meat.

Seasoning and cure mixes

If there is no seasoning and flavour in the sausage, the food will taste bland and will not be favoured and relished by people. Seasoning in the olden times was done for various other reasons and not necessarily for flavour. Before the advent of sophisticated refrigeration, butchers would tend to heavily season and spice *charcuterie* products to mask the flavours of ageing meat. Today, access to fresh and aromatic seasonings has added a whole new dimension to cold cuts and meat. Many seasonings are native to certain countries and provinces. For example, Italian sausages are known for their fresh aromas of thyme, oregano, and black pepper in their sausage, and English sausages boast of fresh herbs such as tarragon and parsley.

Seasonings in a sausage can depend upon the creativity of the chef. From spices, to fresh herbs everything can be used to flavour and season a sausage. A mixture of four spices, also known as *quatre épices,* is usually a mix of ground cinnamon, cloves, pepper, and nutmeg. Care should be taken to add dried herbs and spices unless specified fresh. Dries herbs have a stronger aroma as compared to fresh ones, which is often more desirable in *charcuterie.*

Apart from salt, various other seasonings, such as dried onion, garlic, celery, are mixed to give subtle flavours to the meat. It is also common to add sautéed onion and shallots that have been *deglazed* with white wine and mixed with diced meat and marinated overnight before being ground and mixed. This method gives an excellent seasoning to the final product.

It is important to cure the sausages, especially the ones that would be dried or cold smoked. The term curing refers to treating the sausage meat with chemical salts. The three main curing agents used in *charcuterie* are sodium chloride (common salt), sodium nitrite, and sodium nitrate. Though sodium chloride is used for preservation and flavour only, nitrite and nitrate are used to impart a rosy colour to the sausage, apart from acting as preservatives. Some of the commonly used curing agents are described in Table 2.2.

> **CHEF'S TIP**
> The two Prague powders mentioned in Table 2.2 should only be used as specified and should not be used in place of the other.

Table 2.2 Commonly used curing agents

Curing agent	Description
Nitrites	Nitrites are used to preserve meat. Also, sodium nitrite (NaNO3) is added, apart from salt and sugar (in small quantities), to prevent the growth of a very harmful bacteria—*Clostridium botulinum.* It is also added for colour retention or colour enhancement, e.g., bacon, ham, smoked sausages, and other cured products. Sodium nitrite combines with *myoglobin* to form *nitrosomyoglobin* a bright red stable compound. This colour remains even on cooking above 75°C.
Phosphates	Phosphate compounds are added to stabilize the texture of the emulsion in sausages. These help to retain juices and water in the meat. These also aid in the water binding capacity, due to which even after cooking, the sausages do not get dried and retain their natural juices.
Ascorbic acid	The addition of ascorbic acid preserves the flavour of the meat and prevents it against fungi and yeast. It is also a good antioxidant, as it prevents oxidation and aids colour retention.
Prague powder 1	It is a preserving compound that is sold premixed in the ratio of 94 per cent common salt and 6 per cent sodium nitrite. It is usually used in wet cures and for products that are to be smoked or canned.

(Contd)

Table 2.2 (Contd)

Curing agent	Description
Prague powder 2	It is a preserving compound that is sold premixed in the ratio of 94 per cent common salt and 5.8 per cent sodium nitrite and 0.2 per cent sodium nitrate. It is usually used in dry cures and is most suitable for salamis which need long drying and smoking times. However, it should not be used on any product that is to be fried at high temperature, such as bacon.
Tinted curing mix (TCM)	It is a mixture of 94 per cent common salt and 6 per cent sodium nitrite. This mixture has to be used very carefully and measured accurately, as only 113g of TCM suffices for 45 kg of meat. Tinted curing mix is usually available tinted with pink colour, so that it can be identified easily and not confused with common salt.

Binding agents

While preparing the mix for sausages, it is important to bind the meat together. Most of the times a procedure called 'mixing the meat' is followed. In this, the meat is kneaded manually or mechanically with the help of a machine. A protein in the meat called myosin helps to naturally bind the meat together. In many cases, products such as soy proteins, milk powder, and corn syrup solids also help to bind the meat together and improve the flavour as well. Soy protein and milk powder help to retain the natural meat juices while smoking. However, care should be taken to limit soy proteins concentrate to 5 per cent of the total mix and the milk solids to 12 per cent of the total mix. Other traditional binding agents commonly used are eggs and cream, or mixture of starches also known as *panada*. These can be a mixture of *choux* pastry, cooked rice, and soaked bread slices. The *panada* is particularly useful when using forcemeat that contains wet ingredients such as liver.

Though the amount of *panada* in each recipe will depend upon the type of forcemeat, on an average, *panada* constitutes 10 per cent of the total weight of the forcemeat.

Sweeteners

Sweeteners, such as honey, corn syrup, etc., play a major role in sausage making than just flavouring the mix. They serve as food to the necessary bacteria to thrive in the meat, which in turn develops the mellow flavours. Sweeteners also help to promote browning in *charcuterie* products. Dextrose, rather than normal granulated sugar, is the most preferred sugar in making sausages, as it has the ability to penetrate more quickly and effectively.

Forcemeat

Forcemeat is the base for all *charcuterie* products. It can be described as an emulsion of meat and fat that is created by mixing meat and fat either by chopping, grinding, or puréeing them together to create a smooth paste. The texture of the sausage is determined depending upon the method used. If the meat is chopped, then the resulting sausage will be coarse in texture. This style is popular in many countries. Smooth textured sausages, such as frankfurters and *bratwurst*, are prepared by puréeing the meat and fat together. In *charcuterie*, forcemeats are not only limited to sausage making, but are used in various types of products such as pâtés, terrines, *roulades*, and *galantines*. The texture and type of a *charcuterie* product depend on the type of forcemeat used to fill in the casing. Also, the size of the grind of the forcemeat will determine the finished texture of the sausage. Coarser grind will yield a product that will have a chunky and crumbly texture, whereas a smoother grind will have a smooth textured sausage.

Types of forcemeat

There are four basic styles of forcemeat, each of which is discussed in Table 2.3.

Casings

Sausage starts with a ground meat mixed with spices and seasonings and some curing salts, such as nitrates, and are forced or packed into casings or sacs. The casing not only holds the meat together, but compactly packed meat in casing undergoes complex chemical reactions in controlled environment, which results in a flavourful sausage. Just like wine is matured, sausages and cold meat are left to mature and ripen to develop the flavour. Some of these processes can last from a few hours to few months depending upon the type of sausage. A sausage is often smoked to add pleasant flavour and also acts as a preservative

Table 2.3 Types of forcemeat

Forcemeat	Description
Basic forcemeat	This style of forcemeat is also known as straight mix as the meat and fat (usually pork meat and fat) are ground together from a coarser mixture to a smoother emulsified mix through progressive grinding. The mix is then allowed to rest for few hours and used accordingly. Preferably, the fat used should be *fatback* as it holds well even when the meat is ground progressively. This kind of forcemeat is usually used for stuffing in pâtés, terrines, *galantines*, and sausages.
Country style	This type of forcemeat is of much coarser texture and is made of one or several types of offal. Such forcemeat can be hand-chopped or ground through a large perforated plate of meat mincer until emulsified. Sometimes chopped meat is also added to the emulsified mixture to give a country style look and appearance. Many a time a mixture of starch (*panada*) is used for holding the meat together. This type of forcemeat is used for preparing pâtés, terrines, and few large sausages.
Gratin	This kind of forcemeat is usually used in terrines and pâtés as an inlay or stuffing. The piece of meat may be cured or marinated and browned or sautéed to give a characteristic brown colour to the meat. The browning is also done to shrink the meat and it can easily be used as an inlay. During the process of cooking, the forcemeat and meat will congeal together and thus, no air pocket would be created. This type of forcemeat is used as an inlay for pâtés, terrines, and *galantines*.
Mousseline	This is one of the lightest and smoothest of all forcemeats and is usually made with soft white meat such as veal, chicken, and fish. The meat is emulsified with ice and fat and these result in a paste, which can also be enriched with eggs and cream. This type of forcemeat is used as a filling for appetizers or as stuffing for fish and chicken supreme. Sometimes various types of mousseline are layered to create pâtés and terrines.

and colour enhancer. Here casings again play an important part, as the semi-permeability of the casing allows the smoke to penetrate right through keeping the meat intact. Casings give the sausage its desired size, shape, and also characteristic colour.

There are two types of casings: natural and man-made or synthetic casings. With the increase in demand of sausages and cold meat, it was important to create man-made casings as the demand could not be met just through natural casings.

Natural casings

As the name suggests, these casings are obtained naturally from animals. Usually, the small and large intestines of animals are used for casings. The intestines are preserved at the time of slaughter and are cleaned and segregated on the basis of their size and shape. Sometimes they are also cut into uniform lengths. The size of the casings varies between 16 mm and 127 mm in diameter, however, some casings are custom made for some sausage making firms. These are made by sewing small and big intestines together to create large sizes. These are often known as sewed beef middles or sewed hog bungs. The natural casings are preserved in two ways: the first style is to dry salt the casings. These are quite popular as they need no refrigeration and can be stored up to few years. Another style is to wet pack the casings in brine solution and these can be used straight away without any pre-preparation such as soaking in warm tepid water or dipping in saline solution. Such casings are perishable and cannot be stored for a very long time.

Man-made casings

These casings are artificially made and are preferred over natural casings, as they offer better quality control because of the standard sizes and shapes. There is a wide range of man-made casings that use products such as animal collagen, synthetic food grade plastic and polymers. Let us discuss few of the commonly used man-made casings in *charcuterie*.

Plastic casing Made of plastic, this type of casing is suitable for scalded or cooked sausages and is non-edible. Products can be stored in it and the casing needs to be peeled off before eating. It is available both in transparent and coloured form.

Collagen casing This type of casing is made of animal collagen extruded into shape of casing, which is edible. It is more expensive than natural casing and is comparatively easier to use. It is usually used for smoked and cooked sausages and is available both in straight and curved forms. Since this is a man-made casing using animal product, it requires refrigeration below 10°C.

Fibrous or cellulose casing This is good for air-dried sausages such as salamis, and as it is permeable, it should not be used for cooked or scalded sausages. It is made using non-edible plant protein.

Polymer casing This type of casing is made up of high-strength polymer, which can withstand high temperature of cooking. The products can be cooked and stored in this itself with no secondary packing/vacuum required.

Sausage Making

A sausage is a mix of the main ingredient with other agents and then stuffed in a casing as discussed above. It can then be grilled, cured, brined, or smoked, depending upon the type and variety. Although the process is fairly simple, yet making sausages is an art. One would realize this when he/she starts to stuff the mixture in the casings. Often, the casings break and the sausages get distorted in shape and size. Every step of sausage making is crucial and chefs need to understand each step carefully before attempting to make a sausage. As one practises, one develops a fairly good speed and becomes skilful in sausage making. However, before we go into the various steps of making sausages, let us first discuss some basics of *charcuterie* such as various kinds of tools and equipment used in the process, the types of forcemeat used, the methods of curing, brining, and smoking.

Tools and equipment used in sausage making

The types of tools and equipment used in sausage making are described in Table 2.4.

Table 2.4 Tools and equipment used in sausage making

Tools/Equipment	Description	Photograph
Brine pump or spray pump	This tool is like an injection with a large needle. It is used for injecting brine solution in the meat, so that curing can be achieved evenly.	
Hanging sticks	These metal sticks are usually made of steel and are used for hanging meat and sausages in the smoking machine. Although most of the machines come with this accessory, yet it is a good idea to order an extra set.	
Hog rings	These are special metal crimps that are used to seal both the ends of large sausages. Smaller sausages can be tied with the casing itself, but larger sausages require hog rings.	
Hog ring clipper	It is a small tool that has nose clips which help to seal the hog rings onto the ends of a large sausage.	

(Contd)

Table 2.4 (Contd)

Tools/Equipment	Description	Photograph
Hydrometer	This is a small equipment with a delicate glass that measures the percentage of salt in a solution and even measures the specific gravity. This equipment is used for obtaining accuracy and consistency of the product every time. Since salt plays an important role in sausage making, it is important to measure the salinity.	
Meat tumblers	This equipment is available in various shapes and sizes. The common one is a barrel-shaped container with an attachment like a flat paddle inside. It tumbles the meat and helps to massage leading to the development of myosin.	
Sausage stuffer	This equipment works on hydraulic principle and forces the stuffing mixture into small tubes of various diameters to fill the casings. The tubes, often known as sausage tubes, can be detached and changed depending upon the type of sausage. There are models available in the market that range from domestic types to commercial ones which can stuff up to 200 kg of mix.	
Smoking machines	This machine is used for both hot and cold smoking at desired pressure and temperature control. It is available in a wide range of domestic style to large *smokehouse* chambers for commercial production.	
Spray head	Many sausages require a shower of cool water or even warm water during the production stage. The shower helps bring sheen to the product and washes off the smoke particles sticking to the surface.	

Note: The equipment mentioned above does not exclude other tools and equipment, such as meat mincers, bone cutters and weighing scales, which are used in the larder kitchen as discussed in Chapter 1.

Curing

Curing is one of the most important things to do when preparing meat for *charcuterie* as it is meant to prevent bacterial contamination. If it was not for this process, many *charcuterie* products would not be seen on market shelves. Curing of food means preserving food and this particularly becomes necessary in *charcuterie* production, which is very vulnerable to bacterial contamination called botulism. It is caused by a bacterium called *Clostridium botulinum*, which can thrive at temperatures as low as 4°C. Since ages, raw or unrefined salt has been the most commonly used curing agent in food, be it pickles or cold meat. The first curing agent discovered was potassium nitrate commonly known as saltpetre or saltpeter. However, this did not produce consistent results so it has been banned in commercial units since 1975. The nitrates take long to breakdown in cured meat and hence it is important to follow the measurements accurately. High amount of nitrates and nitrites can cause chemical food poisoning, which could prove fatal for the consumer. Curing is always done prior to cooking or smoking the cold meat. There are two kinds of cures: dry cure and wet cure (or brining).

Dry cure As the name suggests, the appearance of this cure is dry in nature. It is usually used for products such as salami, smoked salmon, etc., where a dry texture is required and also for products that require a long time to cure. Dry cure is a combination of salt, sweetener, and curing agents, and herbs and seasonings required by the recipe. Usually 300g of dry cure is used for every 5 kg of meat. This is a basic rule and can be applied to cures of various meat with little variations. Table 2.5 provides the formula for preparing dry cures for the meat.

Table 2.5 Formula for preparing dry cure for meat

Ingredient	Quantity
Salt	4.5 kg
Sweetener	2.25 kg
TCM	450 g
Seasoning	As desired

Dry cure is usually rubbed on to the surface of the fabricated product making sure that all of it is completely covered with the dry cure mix. The contact time would vary from one product to another and generally depends upon the thickness of the prepared meat. For instance, meat with 1/4th inch of thickness can be cured in two to three hours, whereas a 2-inch thick pork belly can easily take eight to ten days to be cured. Some products such as ham on bone take almost 45 to 50 days to cure. Also, temperature and humidity play a crucial role, especially when curing things for more than two days.

Once dry cured, the product is rinsed and left to dry in cold storage for over 12 hours. This helps to form a dry skin on surface also known as *pellicle*, which is essential prior to smoking and ensures that the smoke adheres to the surface.

Brining or wet cure As the name suggests, the appearance of this cure is liquid in nature. It contains the same ingredients as a dry cure with water added to it make it a salty solution also known as brine. It is generally used for products which are going to be cooked and the final product may have more moisture than the original weight. It is also fairly a quicker process as brine injectors are commonly used to inject wet cures that

Table 2.6 Formula for wet cure or brining

Ingredient	Quantity
Salt	1 kg
Sweetener	600 g
TCM	110 g
Seasoning	As desired
Water	12 litres

reach almost every part of the meat. Although taste wise dry cured products are considered superior, yet wet curing is preferred over dry curing because if environment control is not cautiously exercised, then the area around the bone can start getting contaminated. This is, however, avoided when brine is injected right near the bones and other vulnerable parts.

Wet cure is a combination of salt, sweetener, curing agents, and seasoning with an addition of water. The amount of wet cure should be enough to submerge the meat product and care should be taken to wet cure products in non-corrosive materials such as tubs made of food-grade plastic or stainless steel. When preparing wet cures for meat, such as beef and pork, refer the formula in Table 2.6. The ratios might change in case of fish and poultry.

Wet cure is usually used for submerging the fabricated product ensuring that all of it is completely covered with brine solution. For larger joints, one can use the brine injector to inject the wet cure inside the meats joints. The contact time would however vary from one product to another. Usually it depends upon thickness of the prepared meat and also if it has been injected or not. Table 2.7 shows the time taken for wet curing of various meat commodities.

Table 2.7 Time required for wet curing or brining

Products	Not injected	Injected
Breast of poultry and game birds	18–20 hours	Not advisable
Whole poultry or duck	22–24 hours	12–14 hours
Pork loin	24–30 hours	20–22 hours
Boneless ham	5–6 days	3–4 days
Ham with bone	20–23 days	6–7 days

Once wet cured, the product is rinsed and then left to dry in cold storage for over 12 hours, which helps form *pellicle*. As discussed, *pellicle* is essential prior to smoking to ensure that smoke adheres to the surface. Brining also deepens the colour of the meat and is ideal in case of garnish forcemeat.

Smoking

Smoking of meat and meat products has been very popular since thousands of years. Early on itself, while preserving meat, it was understood that drying of meat took place faster when stored close to fire. It not only dried and cured the meat faster, but also prevented animals from savaging on the food. The smoke from the fire gives a subtle flavour to the food, which has now been associated with *charcuterie*. Most of the *charcuterie* products are smoked. Smoking not only imparts flavour and colour, but the chemicals present in the smoke also inhibit bacterial growth thereby preserving food. Smoke is quite a complex composition of compounds that are formed when the wood burns.

Various types of smoking equipment are available in the market these days, but the main function of smoking remains the same. There is a compartment in which the meat is hung or placed and a source where the smoke is produced, with ample ventilation and circulation space for the smoke to spread in and around the food item. Some of the most commonly used wood for smoking are oak, cider, hickory, cherry, etc. The wood should be hard as soft wood burns out too easily thereby spoiling the taste and colour of the end product. Since smoking is always done after the meat has been cured, it helps in further intensifying the flavours and preserving the food. There are two kinds of smoking, namely hot and cold.

Cold smoking This is a kind of smoking that does not cook the product, as the temperature maintained in the smoke chamber is less than 30°C. The product though gets slightly dehydrated during the cold smoking; hence it is advisable to keep a bowl of ice in the smoking chamber. Cold smoke is applied to products that need not be cooked, e.g., smoked salmon. It can be applied to products that only require smoking at this point and will undergo the cooking process later. Also, cold smoke is usually used for items that have been through the process of dry curing. Sausages, such as chorizos and salamis, are cold smoked.

Hot smoking This kind of smoking also helps in cooking the product, while it is being smoked. Hot smoking is particularly useful for certain *charcuterie* products as the heat in the smoke chamber coagulates the proteins on the surface of the meat, thereby creating a barrier for the moulds to grow. It is important to control the temperatures of the hot smoking chamber as too high temperatures would render the meat dry and chewy and lower temperatures would leave the meat undercooked, thereby aiding microbial growth. When applying hot smoking, the internal temperature of the meat should be around 65 to 70°C.

It is, however, important to apply smoking to the product only after it has been rested in a cold place after curing, as it leads to the development of *pellicle*. This in turn is very important as it will enable the smoke to stick to the surface of the product.

Preparation of Sausages

We have thus far learnt the basic principles involved in the preparation of *charcuterie* products. Now, it will be easier for us to understand the production of sausage. The step-wise preparation of sausage is discussed next.

Step 1: Select the ingredients

This first step is very crucial to all kinds of food preparations more so in the case of making sausages, where it is mandatory to use fresh and prime quality ingredients to prepare quality products. The main ingredient is any kind of meat, but the meat to fat ratio should be 75 per cent meat to 25 per cent of fat and the meat should be free from any contamination. Since sausages will be either cooked or dry cured, it is important that they are cured before they are prepared.

It is also important to trim the meat of excessive gristle, sinews, and connective tissues, as they will not give consistent forcemeat. This is particularly significant for dried and cured sausages as the connective tissue will not get cooked because there is no heat applied to the mixture. Ensure that all the ingredients are chilled as chilled meat and fat form a stable emulsion, which results in good texture of the sausage.

To start any sausage, chopped shallots and chopped garlic are sautéed in small amounts of oil until very lightly coloured. *Deglaze* with white wine and take the mix off the fire. Chill the mixture and add to the meat cut into small dices. Marinate and let it rest in refrigerator for a couple of hours.

Step 2: Grind the ingredients

Set up the meat mincer. All the parts of the mincer should be chilled in ice water for around 30 minutes. If the mince required is fine, then it is also mandatory to start with a mesh that has large holes and then move towards the mesh with smaller holes. Mince the mixture, along with fat until the desired texture is achieved. Transfer the mixture into a mixing bowl and mix the forcemeat with the help of a dough hook for around one to two minutes. It is important that the parts of the dough mixer are also chilled in ice water. Mixing at this stage will make the mixture sticky as *myosin* is developed, which helps bind the meat. Any other seasonings, curing mixes, binding, and sweetening agents are added at this stage. The mixture should be used immediately and cannot be stored for long once the emulsion has been formed. In case of making emulsified sausages, the meat at this stage is blended with ice until a smooth paste is obtained.

Before we start to fill the sausages, it is important to test a small batch to ensure that the mixture is seasoned and well blended. To do this, a small amount of prepared meat is poached in water and then tasted for any adjustments.

We have discussed different types of stuffing, also known as forcemeat, earlier in the chapter. The forcemeat will be finally stuffed into the casing. Forcemeat is prepared in many different ways, depending upon the type of product that it is intended for. There are various types of sausages that are made using various types of forcemeat in the preparation. Few types of sausages commonly prepared are as follows.

Fresh sausages   These are made out of a coarse mixture of meat, fat, and spices, ground together. These sausages are made from the basic forcemeat and they can be shaped into patties and shallow-fried or deep-fried. These are supposed to be stored chilled or frozen.

Fresh smoked sausages   These sausages are prepared with strong spices and smoked such as chorizo, *kielbasa*.

Emulsified sausages   Forcemeat based mixture of meat, fat, and ice is made into an emulsion and cooked, then chilled and stored for later use. This includes sausages such as *boudin blanc* and *bratwurst* and frankfurters. Such sausages are also known as 5-4-3 sausages as they contain 5 parts of meat (usually pork), 4 parts of fat, and 3 parts of water in the form of ice. Many of the emulsified sausages are poached before they are allowed to smoke.

Smoked cooked sausages   These sausages are made up of either emulsion or a coarse mixture of meat and spices. Smoked sausages could be coarse such as Spanish chorizo or fine emulsion based such as frankfurters or franks. These are made with the addition of curing salt to acquire the colour of smoke.

Dried sausages Also known as fermented sausages, these have been around for hundreds of years and are still the most favoured of all because of the robust flavours and texture. These are basically dry (smoked in some cases) sausages, which are fermented and dried. The procedure is to age them for around two weeks or more. During this process, lactic acid develops, which in turn makes the meat acidic thus inhibiting the growth of harmful bacteria. These are slightly acidic in nature, due to low pH value, which inhibits bacterial growth and have usually longer shelf life. Salamis and pepperoni are examples of dried sausages.

Step 3: Prepare the casing

We have read in this chapter about various types of casings both natural and manmade. The casings are received either dry or wet. Before stuffing the sausage, it is important to prepare the casings, so that they can be stuffed easily. Casings need to be uncoiled and soaked in warm water for at least 30 minutes. This allows them to become soft. They should then be washed in several changes of water. Flush the openings with fresh water to ensure that the salt from inside also is drained out. This method also helps to identify if there are any holes in the casings (Fig. 2.1). The cleaned sausages should be cut into the

(a) Cleaning casings with water

(b) Putting casing on the feeder tube

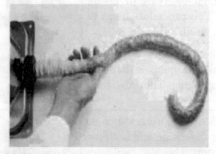
(c) Stuffing the sausage into the casing

(d) Making link shapes of sausage

Fig. 2.1   Steps for stuffing sausages (see also Plate 1)

required length and soaked in acidulated warm water for at least 30 minutes. This makes the casings stretchable and they usually do not break easily when stuffed.

Step 4: Stuff the casings

To stuff the casings, tie one end of the casing with butcher's twine to lock the end and slide on the other part of the casing onto the sausage stuffing tube. It is important to lubricate the sausage stuffing nozzle and the work table with water to prevent the casings from sticking and drying out. The casing is now ready to be stuffed with the forcemeat that will be forced out from the sausage filling machine into the casing (Fig. 2.1). There are many ways in which sausages are stuffed and prepared. Some of the styles and resulting shapes are discussed in Table 2.8.

Step 5: Cook, cure, smoke sausages

This step is one of the most crucial steps and can affect the final texture of the product. When the sausage is stuffed, it should be checked for any air pockets. If there are any, they should be pricked by a sharp needle. Sausages can be cooked straight away or can be hung at controlled temperatures to mature the flavours. In such cases, it is important that the sausages are either wet cured or dry cured. Not all sausages are smoked, however smoking can be done immediately. Some sausages, such as breakfast sausages, are served cured and raw and they have to be cooked by the methods of poaching, sautéing, or grilling close to service. Some sausages are chilled overnight and then poached or grilled and finally refrigerated for two to three days and used as desired.

Table 2.8 Shapes of sausages

Style of sausage	Description	Photograph
Rope sausage	While filling sausages into the casings, the latter are slowly drawn off the feeder tube, when the forcemeat is being extruded out of the sausage filler tube. Rope sausages are prepared by coiling around the filled casings to form spirals. These sausages are often sold coiled and can be raw, cooked, or smoked. They look very attractive in butchers' shops and on displays.	
Linking sausage	In this type of the sausage, while being filled, the casing is pinched and twisted around at equal intervals to create linking sausages of the same length. This procedure helps to prepare sausages that are of uniform weight and size.	
Chaining sausage	In this type, the ends of a few linked sausages are joined together to form a chain. This procedure helps in hanging the sausages in the smokehouse for smoking. They also look good on displays.	
Looping sausage	This type of shape is particularly used for sausages such as *kielbasa*. The forcemeat is stuffed into the casing and both the ends are joined together to form a loop. This also facilitates the sausages to be hung in the smokehouse.	

Popular Sausages Across the World

Some of the popular sausages served in hotels across the world are described in Table 2.9.

Table 2.9 Popular sausages across the world (see also Plate 1)

Sausage	Description	Photograph
Kielbasa or Polish sausage	This large loop-shaped sausage from Poland is made by stuffing emulsified forcemeat consisting of pork butt and *fatback* with crushed ice. It is dry cured by adding TCM and seasonings such as black pepper and garlic. The sausage is hung in controlled temperatures for few days and then cold smoked.	
Bratwurst	This is a German delicacy made from emulsified forcemeat of pork, veal, and sometimes beef. The word is derived from the German words *brat* which means 'chopped meat' and *wurst* which means 'sausage'. *Bratwurst* is generally the most preferred choice for grilling and barbequing.	
Frankfurters	This is a very popular German sausage that has become famous the world over because of its use in the popular sandwich 'hot dog'. It is made with emulsified forcemeat prepared from veal/beef and fat from jowl of pig. The sausage is prepared into link shapes and then cured for a day to develop the traditional orange colour. They are then hot smoked.	
Salami	Salami has been the most popular of all sausages because of its keeping qualities. It is a cured and fermented sausage most popular in Italy, France, Hungary, Germany, and other European countries. It is prepared from the forcemeat of country style and the traditional specked appearance comes from the fat of neck of the pork. Spices, such as crushed black pepper, and herbs are popularly used in salamis.	
Mortadella	*Mortadella* is a large Italian sausage that is made from emulsified forcemeat, in which fat from the neck of the pork and chopped pistachios are added to give it a traditional specked look. The meat from the pork butt is cured with the dry cure mix and then proceeds as for emulsified forcemeat. Spices and seasonings, such as white pepper, ground mace, Spanish paprika, ground nutmeg, coriander, cloves, bay leaves, and garlic powder, are added, along with bindings such as dry milk.	

(Contd)

Table 2.9 (Contd)

Sausage	Description	Photograph
Breakfast sausage	As the name suggests, this sausage is commonly eaten for breakfast. In the USA, this sausage is made from the basic forcemeat mix and is shaped into patties and shallow-fried. English breakfast sausages are usually stuffed into the casings and made into link shapes. The size of the breakfast sausage is roughly around 3 inches long.	
Cumberland sausage	As the name suggests, this sausage comes from Cumbria, which is in the north-west of England. These are traditionally made into long rope shapes, but these days it is common to see link shapes as well. It is prepared from the country style forcemeat of pork and fat and seasoned with spices, such as pepper, and herbs. The meat is chopped to give it a characteristic chunky texture.	
Chorizos	Chorizos come from Spain and Portugal. These sausages are fermented and air-dried. They get their distinctive red colour from the smoked red peppers. The Mexican chorizos are flavoured with Chile peppers. Chorizos can be eaten sliced or they can be barbequed or even deep-fried.	
Loukanika	This popular sausage from Greece is made from pork and is flavoured with aromatic herbs, fruits, and vegetables such as orange peel, fennel, allspice, ground bay leaves, cayenne pepper, oregano, thyme, onion, and garlic. This sausage mix is made by basic forcemeat method and stuffed into casings or simply, the mixture is packed into *caul* fat. The sausage is then grilled, broiled, or pan-fried and then chilled in refrigerator for at least three to four days.	
Merguez	*Merguez* is a spicy sausage from North Africa. It is made from strong flavoured meat such as mutton or beef. It is made by basic forcemeat, which is marinated in red wine before being ground. It is flavoured with *quatre épices*, *harissa*, and red peppers. It is shaped into small ropes or can be looped as well.	
Boudin blanc	*Boudin* is a common word used for many sausages in and around France. The *boudin blanc* is a white-coloured sausage that is prepared from emulsified forcemeat. Traditionally, it is made from pale-coloured pork meat and is enriched with cream, eggs, etc. *Boudins* are stuffed into casings and are refrigerated for at least 12 hours. These are then poached in a mixture of milk and stock and are refrigerated for up to three days.	

(Contd)

Table 2.9 (Contd)

Sausage	Description	Photograph
Boudin noir	Also known as blood sausage, they are so called because of their black to deep purple colour owing to the principle ingredient—blood. The forcemeat of this sausage is an emulsified pork blood and suet and is flavoured with seasonings. This sausage is particularly famous during Christmas. The *boudin noir* is chilled for at least 12 hours before they are poached.	

GALANTINES, BALLOTINES, AND DODINES

Galantines were popularized during the French revolution between 1789 and 1799. It was a cold savoury dish made from boned poultry which was stuffed back into the skin and poached in a gelatinized stock and left in there to mature. *Galantines* are essentially prepared from poultry, but chefs since the eighteenth century have been using various kinds of meat, such as lamb, beef, and even pork, to prepare *galantines*. In European cookery, we often come across two more dishes, namely *ballotine* and *dodine,* which seem to be similar to *galantine* as the basic style of preparation and ingredients are similar. The difference, however, is in shape and the temperatures at which these dishes are served. A *ballotine* refers to the *ballot* shape, which means a bundle, and can be served hot or cold. It is meat, fish, or fowl that is boned, stuffed, and rolled into the shape of a bundle. It is then braised or roasted and can be served hot or even cold. But *galantine* always pertains to the cold savoury dish made from boned chicken. A *dodine* is similar to *ballotine* and is usually prepared with the legs of duck or goose and is roasted instead of being poached. Moreover, *dodines* are always served hot. Though it is claimed that *ballotine* is made from leg meat of game birds only, but any piece of meat can be used for preparing *ballotine*, as long as it is rolled into a bundle or a pouch and then poached.

Galantine Making

The important steps to be followed to prepare galantines are as follows.

Step 1: Prepare the bird

It is important to select a fresh and plump poultry to make galantine. The first important step to make galantine is to carefully bone the chicken, without damaging or puncturing the skin. It is fairly easy to start from the back of the chicken. Make an incision on the backbone of the chicken with a sharp knife and carefully remove the skin in one piece and keep it aside. Now remove the meat from the bone and keep it separate. Certain parts of the boned meat may be cured to add as a garnish to the *galantine*. The breast and the supreme are the commonly used cuts for curing for *galantines*.

Step 2: Fill and roll the galantine

To fill the galantine, spread the skin on a plastic wrap or preferably a cheesecloth, which is damp. Trim the chicken skin to a neat rectangle and place it on a cheese cloth. Place the filling which has been made as basic forcemeat and lay the cured cuts as a garnish in the centre. It is also common to see the chicken breast being flattened and used on top of the skin and then stuffing the *galantine* with the forcemeat. Roll the *galantine* carefully around the forcemeat in such a manner, that the skin just overlaps creating a neat seam. The *galantine* is now twisted from both the ends to give it a smooth and a firm *roulade* shape. The ends are tied with a butcher's twine to form a tight *roulade*.

Step 3: Cook the galantine

Galantine is usually cooked by poaching. The *galantine* is lowered in a pot of simmering stock flavoured with aromatic herbs. It is a good idea to keep some weight on the *galantine* to keep it submerged in the stock throughout the poaching. Usually, *galantine* is poached until the internal temperature is around 65°C. The *galantine* should be allowed to cool in the same poaching liquor and it is removed when the internal temperature is at 65°C and not 75°C as there will be a carry over cooking in the hot liquid. *Ballotines*, on the other hand, can be removed after poaching and can be seared in a pan to acquire a golden brown colour if serving hot. *Dodine* will be prepared the same way as a *ballotine*, but will be roasted instead.

> **CHEF'S TIP**
> Allow the *galantine* to cool in the same liquid that it is poached in or it will shrink if taken out and chilled.

HAM, BACON, AND GAMMON

The differentiation between a ham, bacon, and gammon can get very confusing for a beginner. Understanding these terms would become very simple if we understand the anatomy of a pig in the context of making *charcuterie*. Once a pig is salted and cured, it is referred to as ham, bacon, or gammon. The hind leg is composed of middle gammon, hock gammon, and knuckle. When the entire hind leg is salt cured and smoked, it is known as ham. When pieces are portioned out and salt cured and smoked, then they are referred to as gammon. The gammon can also be termed so when a salt cured ham is portioned out to smaller pieces. Figure 2.2 shows the parts of a pig that are used for *charcuterie*.

Bacon can be prepared from any other parts of the pork, apart from the hind legs. If the meat is taken from the collar and salt cured, it will be known as collared bacon and so on. To prepare the pig for *charcuterie*, it is split into two halves along the backbone and then divided into three parts: fore end, middle, and hind leg. The middle is commonly used for various kinds of bacons.

Types of Ham and Bacon

The various kinds of ham and bacon as obtained from pig meat are described in Table 2.10.

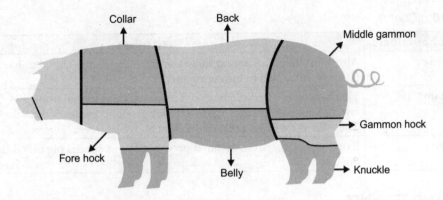

Fig 2.2 Parts of a pig used for *charcuterie*

Table 2.10 Types of ham and bacon

Type of bacon/ham	Description
Collared bacon and picnic ham	The collar is cut from the shoulder area of the pig. The meat from the collar is salted and cured and then smoked. It is called collared bacon. If the entire shoulder is boned, rolled, cured, and smoked, then it is referred to as picnic ham or shoulder ham.
Guancialle	*Guancialle* is the cheek of the pig's meat when salt cured, air-dried, and smoked. It is commonly used in Italian cuisine.
Canadian bacon	It is bacon obtained from the loin or back of the pig. The process remains the same. The meat is boned and then salt cured and smoked.
Streaky bacon	This is the most commonly used bacon and is obtained from the belly of the pig. It is boned and then salt cured and smoked. If the bacon is only cured and not smoked, then it is referred to as green bacon.
Prime bacon	This is obtained from the belly part, but does not have as much fat as streaky bacon. The streaks in the bacon are formed due to the layering of the fat and the meat in the pig's belly. This bacon contains some part of the fatty belly and a larger part of loin.
Pancetta	*Pancetta* is a type of Italian bacon that is prepared from a cured belly of pork. It is traditionally rolled and is available in the market as a roll or in dices.
Bayonne ham	It is air-dried salted ham prepared from pigs reared in Bayonne, a city in France.
Black Forest ham	This speciality from Germany is also known as *Schwarzwälder Schinken*, owing their name to the black forests of Swabia. This ham is seasoned, dry cured, and then smoked over sawdust and wood shavings from fir tree.
Westphalia ham	This popular ham from Germany is also reared from special pigs that are always fed on corn. The meat is then dry cured and smoked with beech wood and branches of juniper berry tree.
Prosciutto	This famous ham comes from the Parma region of Italy and can be cured or cooked. The cured variety is called *prosciutto crudo* and the cooked variety is known as *prosciutto cotto*. Parma ham has a unique flavour as the pigs reared for it are fed with whey leftover from the production of parmesan cheese from that region. This ham can be cured and air-dried for almost 12 months.

(Contd)

Table 2.10 (Contd)

Type of bacon/ham	Description
San Daniele	Also from Italy, this ham is quite similar to the Parma ham, but has fairly lower levels of salt added to the curing mix.
Serrano ham	This ham comes from Spain and is prepared from special white pigs. These hams are slightly sweet in taste due to very less amount of salt added in the curing mix. This ham is air-dried at almost 1200 m above sea level.
Jamón Ibérico	Iberian ham, also from Spain, is prepared from a special pig called Iberian black pig.

PÂTÉS AND TERRINES

In the olden times, when each guild was responsible for a particular dish and other guilds could not prepare and sell the same item, some innovative and creative *charcuterie* guilds prepared savoury pies and tarts, which were not prepared by the guild of bakers. The *charcuterie* guild began to prepare forcemeats and vegetables enclosed in various kinds of dough pastries, or even earthen moulds and served them attractively garnished.

In general, the word pâté comes from paste or dough, which was used for lining the savoury pies. Pâtés can be served hot or cold while terrines are always served cold. The word terrine comes from a French word *terre* which means earth. In the olden times, terracotta moulds were used to make terrines, which were served in the same pot that they were cooked in. Over the years, earthen moulds have been replaced with moulds of ceramic, stainless steel, and other metals. There is a very thin line of difference between a pâté and a terrine. Many chefs can debate over the differences between pâtés and terrines. Terrines are not lined with any pastry and can be lined with slices of meat such as ham, bacon, or even slices of *fatback*. The main differences between a pâté and a terrine are highlighted in Table 2.11.

Terrine Making

Both terrines and pâtés use forcemeat as the main ingredient. The basic steps of preparing forcemeat for terrines as well as pâtés remain the same as discussed for sausages and other *charcuterie*. Terrines are prepared in special earthen or metallic moulds. Let us now discuss the step-by-step method of preparing terrines (see Fig. 2.3).

Table 2.11 Differences between a pâté and a terrine

Pâté	Terrine
For making a pâté, forcemeat is encased in a paste or dough like a pie.	For making a terrine, forcemeat is cooked in an earthenware mould.
It is cooked in an oven and the pastry is sometimes decorated with designs made out of dough.	It is usually poached in water bath or bain-marie.
A pâté is always taken out from the mould before being served.	A terrine is served in the dish that it is prepared in. With the advent of metallic moulds, terrines are taken out of the moulds and served sliced on platters.
It can be served hot or cold depending upon the preparation.	It is always served cold.

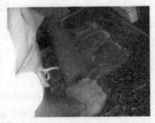

(a) Prepare the lining by layering the sliced ham on plastic and rolling them

(b) Measure the length of a terrine mould

(c) Line the terrine with the ham

(d) Ensure that an overhang is left

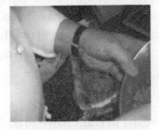

(e) Fill the forcemeat

(f) Lay the garnish inside

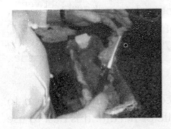

(g) Cover with more forcemeat

(h) Tap and close the overhang

(i) Sliced terrine platter

Fig. 2.3 Step-by-step preparation of a terrine (see also Plate 1)

Step 1: Choose the mould

The first step is to choose the right kind of mould. There are many types of moulds available for making terrines; select the one which is clean and not chipped.

Step 2: Line the mould

The mould is first lined with a plastic wrap to facilitate the removal of the terrine after it is cooked. Now line the base and the sides of the mould with sliced fat from the *fatback* of pork. This is traditional; however, it is very common to see other kinds of products such as cold smoked hams, such as Parma ham and slices of bacon, being used for lining the moulds. This gives a good and appetizing appearance to the terrine if served without the mould. The items used are known as liners and one can use many other products, such as blanched spinach leaves and seaweed, as liners. The fat liner also helps to baste the meat while cooking and keeps the terrine moist and flavourful. When lining the mould, ensure that extra fat hangs from the end which will finally be used for covering the filling.

Step 3: Fill forcemeat

Terrines are prepared by artistically layering or assembling the forcemeat with patterns and inlays to create a good visual impact. The garnish style of forcemeat is used in combination with other kinds of forcemeat. Ensure that the forcemeat is not filled up to the brim but a space of at least quarter of an inch is left for expansion of the meat. Ensure that the forcemeat is spread to every corner of the mould using a spatula to avoid any air pockets. Smoothen the forcemeat and cover the top with the hanging *fatback* and plastic to completely encase the forcemeat in the *fatback*. Tap the mould a couple of times on the table to release any air pockets which might have been created while layering the terrine. Some moulds come with tight-fitting lids; however in the absence of one, cover the terrine mould with a double layer of aluminium foil, crimping it on edges to seal the top of the mould.

Step 4: Cook the terrine

The next step is to cook the terrine. It is advisable to cook the terrine in a water bath. Invert a cake cooling rack in a pot and place the terrine on it. Avoid the terrine touching the base of the pot. Now fill hot water up to two-third or three-fourth of the mould and bake in an oven where the temperature of the water does not exceed 77–78°C. The temperature of the water bath is very essential to monitor and should not go beyond 78°C or else it will affect the texture of the final product. An oven temperature set between 150–155°C should be able to maintain the temperature of the water at 77°C.

Step 5: Remove and cool the terrine

It is important to know when the terrine is cooked. The cooked terrine feels firm to touch and the juices run clear when inserted with a sharp knife or needle. It is best to use a thermometer which can give more accurate results. The internal temperature of the terrine should be around 70–75°C. Some terrines have to be pressed for the firm texture and to eradicate the air gaps which will result as breeding spaces for microorganisms. The terrine should be taken out of the water bath and allowed to rest at room temperature until the internal temperature comes to around 30–35°C. The terrine can now be pressed by putting some weights on top and refrigerated for at least 2–3 days for the flavours to intermingle and mellow down. If desired, the terrine can be completely covered in aspic, which we will discuss later in this chapter.

The terrine can now be served in the mould itself or be removed from the mould and sliced and served. Some terrines, such as pastes of chicken liver, can be covered with a layer of fat and served as they are on the dining table.

Components of Pâté

Pâtés can be handcrafted to make shapes or these days, collapsible hinged metal moulds are commonly used for special pâtés such as *pâté en croûte*. Dough crusts can be baked

Table 2.12 Components of a pâté

Components of pâté	Description
Pastry	This is one of the most essential components of a pâté that separates it from a terrine. Various types of pie crusts can be used for preparing pâtés. The pie crust can be made with shortcrust pastry, brioche, or even pastry and yeast-leavened dough. The dough for the pastry should be made at least 24 hours before and chilled, so that it can be handled easily. It is important to gauge the thickness of the pastry while lining the moulds. If the forcemeat contains lot of fat, then the pastry has to be rolled slightly thicker, as it would absorb the fat that melts during the cooking process much better.
Stock	It is a reduced flavoured concentrate of meat that is to be used as forcemeat for pâté. The leftover trimmings of the meat can be combined and made into a reduced stock. Stock can be incorporated into the forcemeat while mixing or it can be used as aspic and poured into the pâté when baked.
Forcemeat	The various kinds of forcemeat have been discussed in Table 2.3. The principles of preparing the forcemeat also remain the same as discussed earlier.
Aspic jellies	The pie is baked by drilling a hole on top of the pastry to allow the steam to escape during cooking. This process also creates an air gap in the pâté, when the pâté is cooked and cooled. The air gaps in the pâté are then filled by pouring the aspic through the vent until all the spaces are filled with the aspic jelly. The pâté is then refrigerated for at least 24 hours and then served sliced.

more evenly in metal moulds. Pâtés can be made into cylindrical shapes, pie shapes, or cut out in designs to make any shape. A pâté therefore has few components, which are described in Table 2.12.

Pâté Making

Most of the pâtés made in the dough or pastry lining are known as *pâté en croûte*, which means 'pâté in a crust'. To prepare a classical *pâté en croûte*, one has to select a clean rectangular pâté mould, which is collapsible and made out of metal. The step-by-step procedure for making a pâté is explained below. Refer Fig. 2.4 for the overall procedure.

Step 1: Choose the mould

The first step is to choose the right kind of mould. There are many types of moulds available for making pâté; select the one that is collapsible (Fig. 2.5) and is made of metal as the metal mould helps to develop a better crust.

Step 2: Line the mould

The mould is first lined with rolled-out pie dough. To line a mould, roll out the pie dough to a large square and place the mould in the centre. Now cut out in a manner so that it easily fit inside the mould with few inches hanging outside the mould as this would be used as a covering for the final pâté. Refer Fig. 2.6 to see how the dough is to be cut and placed inside the mould.

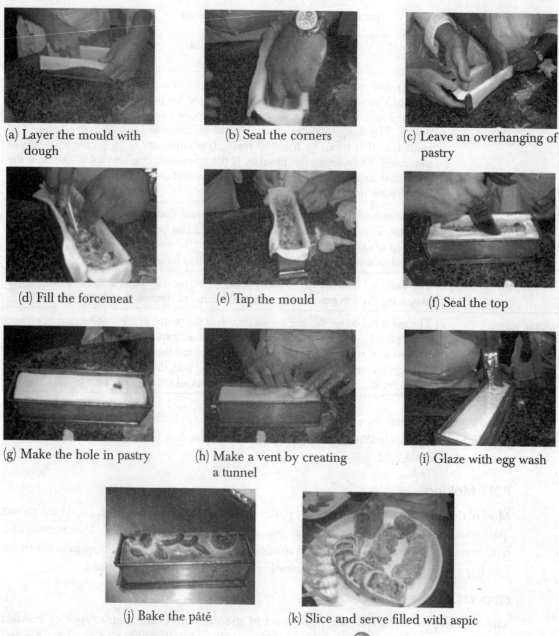

(a) Layer the mould with dough

(b) Seal the corners

(c) Leave an overhanging of pastry

(d) Fill the forcemeat

(e) Tap the mould

(f) Seal the top

(g) Make the hole in pastry

(h) Make a vent by creating a tunnel

(i) Glaze with egg wash

(j) Bake the pâté

(k) Slice and serve filled with aspic

Fig. 2.4 Step-by-step preparation of a pâté (see also Plate 2)

Fig. 2.5 Collapsible pâté mould

Fig. 2.6 Cutting the dough for lining the pâté mould

Step 3: Fill forcemeat

Pâtés, like terrines, are also prepared by artistically layering or assembling the forcemeat with patterns and inlays to create a good visual impact. The garnish style of forcemeat is used in combination with other kinds of forcemeat. Ensure that the forcemeat is not filled up to the brim but a space of at least quarter of an inch is left for the expansion of the meat. Ensure that the forcemeat is spread to every corner of the mould using a spatula to avoid any air pockets. Smoothen the forcemeat and cover the top with the hanging pie dough to completely encase the forcemeat in the mould. Tap the mould a couple of times on the table to release any air pockets which might have been created while layering the pâté.

The mould can then be turned upside down to face the seamed edge at the base and the neatly finished top will be exposed, which is much desirable. It is now important to cut out a small hole or vent on the side to allow steam to escape during the cooking process. If this is not done, then the steam will rupture the pastry during the cooking process. A small pipe or one created by using aluminium foil is inserted in the vent to prevent the vent from closing up during the baking process. The leftover dough can be used to make small cut-outs and decorations that can be used to decorate the pâté. The top should then be brushed with egg yolks to darken the colour of the crust during the baking process.

Step 4: Bake the pate

The next step is to cook the pâté. The pâté should be baked around 175°C until the pâté is golden brown in colour and the internal temperature is around 75°C.

Step 5: Remove and cool the pate

It is important to know when the pâté is cooked and it is best to use a thermometer, which gives more accurate results. The internal temperature of the pâté should be around 70–75°C. The pâté should be allowed to rest at room temperature until the internal temperature comes to around 30–35°C. During the baking process, the pastry and the meat would have expanded and this would have led to a big air gap between the dough and the forcemeat. Since these are not pressed like terrines, it is important that the gaps are filled. For this purpose, melted aspic is used and the same is ladled through a funnel kept on the vent that was created earlier. The pâté should be allowed to rest for at least 24 hours, before it can be sliced and served.

Types of Pâté

Though many types of pâtés are made in the pie crust, there is a range of pâté that closely resembles the making of terrine and the prime ingredient for such pâtés is liver. Such pâtés get their name from the kinds of liver used in their production. This name is probably given due to the paste-like consistency of the forcemeat. The cooking principles of such pâtés are also similar to that of terrine. Let us discuss various kinds of pâtés.

Pâté de foie gras

Pâté de foie gras is made from both geese and ducks. From time immemorial, humans have used the art of overfeeding animals to obtain higher yields of meat and internal organs. A special variety of ducks called *Moulard* is used for rearing foie gras (liver). Foie gras from geese are far superior to those obtained from ducks. Geese are force-fed and this results in an enlarged liver, which is then used. Foie gras is commonly available in three grades—A, B, and C—depending upon its size and appearance. A grade could weigh between 650–700 g, B weighs between 500–550 g, and grade C roughly weighs around 450g. It is one of the most expensive ingredients and thus it should be received, stored, and handled with care or else it could burn a hole in the pockets of the owner. Upon receiving, the foie gras must be inspected for any foul smells and blemishes or cuts, which would have damaged the delicate meat. If it is not being used immediately, the foie gras must be stored on a bed of crushed ice in a perforated pan and covered with more crushed ice and stored in a refrigerator.

Cleaning foie gras Before one attempts to clean the foie gras, it is important to understand the anatomy of the liver, which will help him/her to clean it without any damage to it. It is important that the foie gras is stored in milk flavoured with salt for at least 2 hours before processing. This process is also known as *tempering* and it helps to handle the liver while cleaning. The network of veins in foie gras is shown in Fig. 2.7.

The foie gras comes wrapped and resembles an oval ball. The two lobes of foie gras are folded over one another. Hold the liver carefully in your hands and gently pull the two lobes apart. These

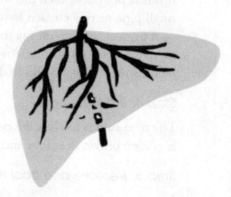

Fig. 2.7 Vein network of foie gras

would open up naturally at their own seam. Slice with a very sharp knife in the two lobes to expose the vein structure as shown in Fig. 2.7. Be careful not to cut through. A combination of pulling and small incisions with the tip of the knife should be enough to perform this act. Once exposed, pull out the veins from the top of the lobe where the veins are thickest. Try using tweezers, fingers, or tip of knife to pull out the veins preferably all in one piece. This has to be done quickly as foie gras is very soft and cannot be handled for too long for the warmth of the hand will start to destroy the texture of this product. The foie gras is now ready to be used as listed in the recipe. If it is not to be used immediately, then wrap in plastic and store refrigerated at 1°C. This temperature will enable the foie gras to firm up and thus can be easily sliced or cut according to the desired shapes.

Commercial pâté and pâté maison Varieties of pâtés are prepared by using foie gras and liver from other poultry as well. Few are also prepared bottled or packed, but it is fairly easy to make them in hotels as well. Some common types of liver pâtés are described in Table 2.13.

Table 2.13 Types of pâtés

Pâté	Description
Pâté grand-mère	This pâté is commonly made at homes by grandmothers and hence the name. The forcemeat of this pâté is made in an emulsion style, where the chicken livers are cleaned of sinews and sautéed in hot oil, along with chopped shallots. This mix is then flambéed with cognac or any other brandy and is mixed with diced pork meat and chilled for few hours. The mixture is then progressively ground and then emulsified by adding eggs, cream, spices, and binding agents such as bread soaked in milk (*panada*). Terrine mould is lined with *fatback* lined with plastic and the forcemeat is layered inside the mould and covered with *fatback*. The pâté is allowed to cure in a refrigerator for 24 hours and then poached in the water bath like a terrine, until the internal temperature is 74°C. Remove from the water bath, cool, then press with a weight, and refrigerate overnight. Cover with aspic and serve sliced with toasted bread.
Pâté de Campagne	This country-style pâté is prepared by using pork butt and chicken liver or foie gras. This pâté is prepared by using a mixture of basic forcemeat style combined with diced meat to give it an appearance of country-style forcemeat. In this pâté, pork butt, chicken liver, and *fatback* are progressively ground and then combined with diced pork meat and *panada*. The forcemeat is garnished with sliced truffles, spices, seasonings, pistachios, and diced *fatback* and put in a terrine mould lined with sliced ham. The pâté is poached in a water bath like *pâté grand-mère*. If using pâté de foie gras, then ensure that the internal temperature is 63°C. Refrigerate for up to 24 hours and then slice accordingly and serve.
Chicken liver pâté	This pâté is commonly served as terrine and it is known as potted liver mousse. It is quite a popular appetizer on buffet and à la carte menus. To prepare this pâté, the chicken liver is soaked in milk, salt, and TCM for at least 24 hours to cure. The livers are drained and patted dry and emulsified forcemeat is prepared by adding cream, *fatback*, spices, and dry sherry, binding such as bread flour and breadcrumbs and small amount of gelatine. The mixture is then sieved through a wire mesh to remove any particles. It is now layered in a terrine mould lined with plastic and poached in a water bath until the internal temperature is 74°C. Remove from the water bath, cool to 30°C, press weight, and refrigerate overnight. Slice and serve with toasted brioche.

TRUFFLE

Truffle is a fruiting body of a fungus, which is a multicellular microorganism. There are two types of fruiting bodies of fungi: the one that grow above the ground called 'mushroom' and the ones that grow deep into the ground known as 'truffle'. Truffles grow in wild habitats and special sows (female pigs) are reared to sniff them out of the ground. The pungent odour that the truffle emits is quite similar to that of the boar (male pig) and that is the reason why sows are used for this purpose. Truffle is one of the most expensive commodities that was first used in cooking by a famous French gastronome Jean Anthelme Brillat-Savarin who described truffles as the 'diamonds of the kitchen'.

Just like mushrooms, not all truffles are edible and that is one reason why these are expensive. Truffles grow in many parts of the world. The famous edible ones come from France, Italy, Croatia, and Greece. These also grow in few parts of the USA and North

Africa. Each variety of truffle differs in shape, colour, size, as well as flavour. Truffles have irregular shapes and may at times be smooth or wrinkled. They can be used in a variety of ways. They are commonly paired with foie gras to prepare highly priced pâtés and terrines. It can also be shaved onto pastas and salads. Truffle is usually served uncooked and is packed in oil for preservation. Truffle oil is obtained by flavouring high-grade olive oil with synthetic flavours. It is usually a cheaper option than expensive truffles.

Types of Truffle

There is a variety of edible truffles available around the world. Some popular ones are described in Table 2.14.

Table 2.14 Types of truffle

Truffle	Description	Photograph
Italian white truffle	Italian white truffles grow commonly in Umbria, Alba, or Piedmont regions of Italy. It is one of the highly prized truffles at the gastronomic table as it is the rarest form of truffle. It is commonly known as white diamond. These truffles get their name from the place where they come from and are not usually white as the name suggests. The truffle is more yellowish in colour and the skin is smoother than black truffles. The white truffles are also harvested during winter and summer months and the flavour of both these truffles is very different from each other.	
Winter black truffle	Also known as *périgord*, black truffle is harvested during the months November to March in the Périgord region in France and hence the name. It grows in Italy, Spain, and France, where it is usually found under oak, hazelnut, and chestnut trees. The truffle gets its name from the region that it is harvested from, such as Burgundy truffle and Alsace truffle.	
Summer black truffle	The summer black truffles are harvested around summer months and the colour of these is usually deep brown as compared to the winter truffles.	

ASPIC OR GELÉE

Aspic or gelée is one of the most important items of the larder kitchen and finds many uses in *charcuterie*. Aspic can be defined as any liquid or stock that is fortified with gelatine. Gelatine is an extraction of the collagen, a protein found in skin and bones of animals. It is a sticky and clear substance obtained from the gelatinous parts of animal such as bones, cartilages, horns, and hoofs. Thus, aspic can be made from animal stock, vegetable, or fruit juices as well. When an animal stock is left to simmer, then a stage comes, when it transforms into a jelly-like substance commonly known as natural aspic or *gelée*, which is the French term for jelly. As there are different applications of aspic, the strength of the jelly also differs depending on the purpose for which it is required. The concept will be understood better by discussing the various practical uses that aspic is subjected to in the larder kitchen, particulary *charcuterie*.

Uses of Aspic or Gelatine

The various applications of aspic or gelatine in *charcuterie* are described in Table 2.15.

Table 2.15 Uses of aspic and gelatine

Uses of aspic/ gelatine	Description
Coating	As the products made in the larder kitchen are ready-to-eat foods, it is important to form a covering on top to seal it, thereby protecting it from drying out which will spoil its appearance. Many sliced pâtés and terrines are coated with melted aspic to give a presentable mirror-type appearance and clean look and also help to seal the product.
Chaud froid	*Chaud froid* in French literally translates to hot and cold. This is a type of sauce that is prepared hot but used with cold meat. There are many kinds of *chaud froid* made from base sauces such as béchamel, *demi-glaze*, or even *velouté*. The sauce is cooked and mixed with aspic or gelatine and allowed to cool. Then it is used for covering cold meat such as *galantines*, *ballotines*, terrines, and pâtés. It was customary in old times to decorate the festive buffet with a range of cold meat platters and elegantly decorated galantines with *chaud froid* and garnished with truffles and vegetables that were cut into fancy shapes and patterns.
Sealing a garnish	Aspic is also used for sealing garnishes on a plate. A fresh herb or any cut shape of vegetable is placed on a white plate and aspic is poured over it to seal the garnishes on a plate, on which other items, such as sliced forcemeat, will be presented. These are, however, old styles of presentation and are rarely used nowadays.
Filling	Melted aspic is also filled in the *pâté en croûte* to seal air gaps and make the pâté more presentable when sliced.
Binding agent	Aspic or gelatine is also used as a binding agent while preparing forcemeats for pâtés and terrines.
Decorations	Gelatine and aspic are also commonly used for making jelly displays, especially for logos or presentations used for food competitions. The strength of gelatine has to be more to prepare a hard jelly that can be cut into required shapes. These shapes are also known as aspic *croûtes*.

The consistency of set aspic is very important. It should be firm enough to hold and should melt away when put in the mouth. The strength of aspic may be altered according to the weather as well. In warm weather, it should be made stiffer; otherwise it will melt on the buffet.

Aspic and glazes are very rich in proteins and hence very susceptible to bacteria. It is therefore, important not to touch the product with bare hands when coated in aspic.

The aspic must be cooled in an ice bath before applying on the product. A product coated with aspic should never be frozen as it will spoil the appearance of the aspic.

Commercially, gelatine is available in two forms: powdered and sheets. Powdered gelatine is most commonly used in larder and confectionary works. Sheet gelatine, as the name suggest, is available in sheet form and has stronger setting qualities compared to powdered gelatine. The vegetarian version of gelatine comes from a seaweed known as agar-agar. Agar-agar is a white-coloured ruffled seaweed that contains natural setting properties like gelatine.

Proportions of Gelatine

Using gelatine is an art and one must follow the proportions that vary according to the intended use. Table 2.16 provides an idea of the varying proportions of gelatine that are used in different applications.

CHEF'S TIP

When adding melted gelatine to cold mixes, add a small amount of cold mix to the warm gelatine to stabilize the temperatures and then mix together. Otherwise, the gelatine may form strands in the mixture.

There are specific ways in which the powdered and sheet gelatine are used for application in the larder and other areas of kitchen such as bakery and confectionery. The powdered gelatine must be carefully weighed and then soaked in water at room temperature to swell. This process is normally known as *bloom* and it usually takes 3–4 minutes. When the gelatine has *bloomed* well, the bowl should be placed in a hot water bath to melt the gelatine. Upon melting, the gelatine becomes a thick and clear liquid, which can be used according to requirements.

Sheet gelatine seems more convenient to use and that is why it is also the preferred choice of most chefs. It is used by soaking the gelatine leaves in cold water to allow softening or blooming. The soaked gelatine can straightaway be added to warm liquid and does not have to be melted separately.

Aspic and gelatines are also used in various other products, such as mousses and *timbales*, that are commonly served as appetizers. We will discuss appetizers in the next chapter.

Table 2.16 Proportions of gelatine to water in different applications

Delicate	Coating	Slices	Firm
12–14 g of gelatine in one litre of liquid: It is most delicate of all and usually used for brushing on top of products.	28 g of gelatine in one litre of liquid: All *chaud froid* sauces contain this proportion.	50–52 g of gelatine in one litre of liquid: This proportion is used in *pâté en croûte*, when the gel has to be sliced.	65–70 g of gelatine in one litre of liquid: This is used for coating platters with garnishes for displays.

SUMMARY

In this chapter, we discussed one of the most important products of the larder kitchen—*charcuterie*. The term *charcuterie* is derived from a French word that means 'cooked flesh'. The main soul of any *charcuterie* is the meat that is formed into an emulsion, which is cured and then cooked or poached to form various products such as sausages, pâtés, and terrines. Though it is a fairly easy process, it involves great skills, and an in-depth knowledge about the techniques regarding selecting and grinding the meat and the art of curing and smoking.

One such product which we discussed in detail was sausage. A sausage is a generic term used for a wide range of preserved foods that are prepared from minced meat, seasoned, and stuffed in a casing. Sausages were created to preserve meat and in olden times, it was common to see minced meat stored in sacs of animal organs such as stomach and intestines. Till date, natural intestines are used as casings to prepare sausages, but the increasing demands have created a demand for man-made and synthetic casings. Some of these are prepared from natural products such as cellulose, but there is a huge range of synthetic casings also that are commonly used for stuffing sausages. In this chapter, we discussed various kinds of casings that are used for stuffing.

We also discussed various kinds of offal commonly used in *charcuterie*. These can be used in preparation of sausages, terrines, or pâtés, are nutritious and provide variety on the dining table. Even animal blood is used for preparing a type of sausage that is known as black pudding or *boudin noir*, which gets its name form the customary deep purple to black colour of the sausage. It is obtained when blood is cured and smoked in the casing. Various kinds of special equipment that are used for preparing sausages were also explained along with photographs for easy identification. The step-by-step procedure for making a sausage is given. Some popular sausages around the world and their shapes have also been discussed.

We discussed the main ingredient used in preparing *charcuterie* products—forcemeat. This is a mixture of main meat along with fats, binding, seasoning, and flavours. We discussed various kinds of forcemeat of varied textures that are used for producing a range of *charcuterie*.

We also discussed the range of chemicals that are used as curing agents and the cautions that that must be exercised while using them. Most of these chemicals are nitrates and nitrites of sodium and potassium that can be very poisonous if they are not used in recommended doses. Various types of curing and brining methods are explained with the time periods for which the meat should be in contact with the curing agents.

Smoking, which is also an important aspect of *charcuterie* products, is explained in detail explaining the reasons why a product is smoked. Both cold smoking and hot smoking impart a different flavour to the product and the method of smoking is carefully selected depending upon the end product.

In this chapter, we also discussed another application of forcemeat, that is, the preparation of pâtés and terrines. Though there is a little difference in the product, a pâté is prepared and served hot or cold and can be made in a mould or without mould. A terrine is prepared in a special earthenware mould and served in it. The differences between a pâté and terrine are listed in a Table along with step-by-step procedures of preparing a pâté and a terrine. We have also discussed some special pâtés such as *pâté en croûte* and pâté de foie gras.

The way the foie gras should be received, processed, and stored is explained in detail. The pictorial representation of the vein structure of the foie gras would enable the students to figure out how to clean the foie gras before serving.

We also discussed another important aspect of larder kitchen known as *galantine* and *ballotine*. The step-by-step instructions for the production of *galantine* highlight the critical points that should be kept in mind while preparing them. We discussed other *charcuterie* products made from pig such as ham, gammon, and bacon. We also discussed various types of famous ham and bacon from all over the world and their countries of origin.

Certain special commodities, such as truffle, its production, and types, are also discussed along with pictures. It is one of the most expensive commodities used in the larder kitchen as well as hot kitchen and is commonly used with delicate products such as pâté de foie gras.

In the last part of the chapter, we discussed aspic and *gelée* that are important commodities used in larder kitchen. These have many uses apart from being used as coatings and bindings for forcemeat and decorations. Types of gelatine and their uses are explained in detail.

KEY TERMS

Agar-agar It is a white seaweed that is used as a gelling or setting agent.

Aromats These are a mixture of flavousome herbs and salts used for flavouring food.

Aspic croûtes These are small cut-outs of a set aspic jelly that are usually used for decoration.

Aspic It is flavoured liquid or stock that is fortified with gelatine.

Ballotine It is bundle-shaped preparation of forcemeat stuffed into the leg of chicken or any other part. It can be served hot or cold.

Blooming It is a process in which gelatine is soaked in water at room temperature and allowed to soften and swell up.

Boudin blanc It is a popular white-coloured sausage prepared in France.

Boudin noir Also known as black pudding or blood sausage, it is prepared by adding blood in the forcemeat. It is deep purple to black in colour.

Bratwurst It is a sausage from Germany that is usually made from emulsified forcemeat.

Breakfast sausage It is a sausage from England that is stuffed in cases or shaped into patties. It is shallow-fried before serving.

Brine A salt solution of high concentration is called brine.

Canadian bacon This is bacon obtained from the back or loin of pig.

Caul fat This is the inner lining of the stomach of an animal.

Cellulose It is a fibrous protein found in the cell wall of plant cells.

Charcuterie These are cold products made from meat which are cured, air-dried, or smoked. These comprise an important output of the cold kitchen.

Chaud froid *Chaud froid* is a sauce which is prepared hot and served with cold meat. It is fortified with gelatine and aspic, and meat is covered with this sauce.

Chorizo It is a fermented and air-dried spicy sausage from Spain and Portugal.

Collagen It is a type of protein obtained from bones and skin of animals.

Corn syrup It is a sweet thick syrup obtained from corn.

Cumberland sausage It is a large rope-shaped sausage from Cumbria in north-west England.

Dodine It is a savoury dish like *ballotine*, but is always served roasted and hot.

Fatback This is a layer of fat, which is obtained from the back of a pig.

Frankfurters Also called franks, frankfurters are emulsified sausages usually deep orange in colour.

Galantine This is a cold preparation of chicken where the forcemeat is stuffed back into a boned chicken skin and then poached.

Gammon This is portioned out hind leg of pig which can be cured and/or smoked before or after portioning out.

Guancialle It is bacon obtained from the cheeks of pig.

Guilds These were groups formed in France that were responsible for production and selling of a particular product.

Ham Cured and/or smoked hind leg of pig is called ham.

Hog bungs Large intestine obtained from the lower abdomen of pig is called hog bungs.

Hog rings Special crimps that are used for securing the ends of large sausages are called hog rings.

Hot dog It is one of the most popular sandwiches in the world prepared with frankfurters.

Hydrometer This is a device used for measuring the specific gravity or concentration of salt in a liquid.

Jowl of pig The lower jaw of pig is called jowl of pig.

Kielbasa A loop-shaped sausage from Poland, it is also known as Polish sausage.

Linking sausage It is a type of a sausage wherein it is tied at desired intervals to give it a linked shape.

Looping sausage It is a type of a sausage wherein it is tied in the middle to make it appear like a loop.

Loukanika This is an aromatic sausage from Greece.

Merguez It is a sausage from North Africa which is richly flavoured with spices.

Mortadella It is a large Italian sausage made from emulsified forcemeat.

Myoglobin It is an enzyme present in the muscle of meat that is produced when the meat is massaged or rubbed. It helps in binding of the forcemeat.

Offal It is a generic term used for edible organs of an animal.

Panada This is a starchy mixture of mashed potatoes or bread soaked in milk, usually used as a binding agent.

Pancetta It is bacon obtained from the rolled belly of pork.

Parma ham It is cured ham from Parma region of Italy, also known as *prosciutto* Parma.

Pâté It is a preparation in which forcemeat is encased in a paste or dough like a pie.

Pâté de Campagne It is country-style pâté prepared form pork meat and foie gras.

Pâté de foie gras It is a pâté preparation from fattened liver of geese or duck.

Pâté de grand mere It is emulsified pâté prepared form chicken livers and pork meat.

Pellicle It is dry skin formation on a cured meat which is left in cold place to mature for at least 12 hours.

Pheasant It is a type of game bird commonly found in the USA.

Picnic ham Cured and smoked part of the shoulder of pig is referred to as picnic ham.

Pork butt Meat from the rump of pig is called pork butt.

Potted pâté It is prepared in a mould and served pressed in a ceramic pot.

Prague powder 1 This is a mix of preserving chemical agents usually used in wet curing of forcemeat.

Prague powder 2 This is a chemical agent used in dry curing of forcemeat.

Prime bacon Bacon obtained from the middle part of the belly of pig is called prime bacon.

Progressive grinding It is a procedure involving the grinding of meat from a larger plate to a smaller plate to get a fine mince.

Quatre épices It is a mixture of four ground spices such as nutmeg, cinnamon, cloves, and pepper.

Rope sausage It is a long rope-shaped sausages that is packaged as coils for sale.

Salami It is a very popular dry cured and fermented sausage that traces its origin to Italy.

Saltpeter It is the common name for sodium nitrate.

Sausage This is a generic term for minced and seasoned forcemeat stuffed in a casing and cured or smoked.

Streaky bacon Bacon obtained from the lower belly of pig is called streaky bacon.

Supreme of chicken It is the thin tenderloin of chicken attached to the breast piece.

TCM It is the acronym for tinted curing mix. Tinted curing mix is a mixture of common salt and sodium nitrite.

Tempering of foie gras The process of dipping foie gras in salted water for at least two hours to enable the handling of liver while cleaning it is called tempering.

Terrine It is a type of forcemeat usually cooked and served in special earthenware pots or moulds in which it is cooked.

Venison Meat from deer is called venison.

CONCEPT REVIEW QUESTIONS

1. What do you understand by the term *charcuterie*?
2. Define a sausage and its components.
3. Write short notes on the main ingredients used in sausage preparation.
4. Define offal and give at least five examples that can be used in *charcuterie*.
5. Define a sweetbread and explain how it is used.
6. What is *caul* fat and what are its uses?
7. What natural casings and man-made casings are used for forcemeat stuffing in sausages?
8. What are middle or bungs and where are they used?
9. How should the casings be stored and used?
10. What kinds of fats are used in *charcuterie* and what is the importance of the same?
11. What are the different types of spices and seasonings added in the sausage mixes?
12. Why are nitrates and nitrites used in *charcuterie*?
13. Explain the uses and difference between Prague powder 1 and 2.

14. Why is it important to bind the forcemeats? Name any three binding agents commonly used for forcemeats.
15. What role do sweeteners play in fabrication of meat for *charcuterie*?
16. Explain *myosin* and its uses.
17. What is a brine pump and what is its use?
18. How does one clip the hog rings onto sausage casings?
19. What is a hydrometer and what is its use?
20. Describe forcemeat. What are the different types of forcemeat?
21. What is the difference between country-style and *gratin* forcemeat?
22. Describe the process of curing and the types of curing.
23. What is the procedure for dry and wet curing?
24. Differentiate between hot smoking and cold smoking.
25. List the steps in the preparation of sausages.
26. Explain four types of sausages.
27. What care should be exercised while handling the casings for the filling?
28. Write short notes on rope, linked, loop, and chain sausages.
29. What is *kielbasa*?
30. What is the difference between a *bratwurst* and a frankfurter?
31. Differentiate between a *mortadella* and a salami.
32. What is the difference between an English breakfast sausage and a Cumberland sausage?
33. Write about the famous sausage from Greece.
34. What is the difference between a *boudin blanc* and *boudin noir*?
35. Differentiate between a pâté and a terrine.
36. Write down the step-wise preparation of a terrine.
37. What cautions should be followed while cooking terrines?
38. How is a terrine cooled? Explain the significance of the steps followed.
39. What are the components of a pâté?
40. Describe the step-by-step preparation of *pâté en croûte*.
41. Write a short note on pâté de foie gras.
42. How should the foie gras be stored, cleaned, and processed?
43. Differentiate between *pâté de Campagne* and chicken liver pâté.
44. Differentiate between *galantine, ballotine,* and *dodine*.
45. Write down the step-by-step preparation of *galantine*.
46. Differentiate between ham, bacon, and gammon by drawing the body of a pig.
47. Name at least three types of bacon and the body parts that these come from.
48. What is the difference between Black Forest ham and Westphalia ham?
49. Name three famous hams from Spain.
50. What is *prosciutto* and how many types of *prosciutto* are available in market?
51. How are truffles different from mushrooms?
52. Name two white truffles and give reasons why they are so expensive.
53. What is the difference between summer and winter black truffles?
54. What is the difference between an aspic and a *gelée*?
55. What are the uses of gelatine or aspic in larder kitchen?
56. Define a *chaud froid* and its uses.
57. Name two types of gelatine used in kitchen and what is the difference between the usages of these.
58. What do you understand by the word blooming of gelatine? Why is it important?
59. What care should be taken while adding gelatine to the cold mixtures?
60. How does the amount of gelatine impact upon the texture of the final product?

PROJECT WORK

1. In groups of five do a market survey of any shop or establishments that sell cold cuts and *charcuterie* items. List these and find out more about these products and add your findings in the following table:
   Share the information with the rest of the groups.

Product	Country of origin	Type of forcemeat	Method of curing	Method of smoking	Uses

2. In groups of five, research about at least 10 unique sausages from around the world. Give short description of the same and mention what is unique about these. Share the information with the other groups.

3. With the guidance of an expert, prepare some sausages, using various kinds of forcemeat. Create your own smoking chambers and smoke the products and compare the same with original products. Note the observations and taste the products.

4. Within a group of 20 students, prepare a jelly by varying the amounts of gelatine by 5 g. The first student should use 5 g in one litre and the second should use 10 g, the third 15, and so on. The twentieth student should be using 100 g in one litre. Allow the jelly to set for at least three hours. Now compare the results and make observations on the same. This will enable the students to understand about the various strengths of gelatine and its uses.

CHAPTER 3

APPETIZERS AND GARNISHES

Learning Objectives

After reading this chapter, you should be able to

- understand the basic concept of hors d'oeuvre
- comprehend the purpose of classifying hors d'oeuvre
- identify various kinds of appetizers served around the world
- explain the key features in the preparation of hors d'oeuvre
- evaluate cold and hot hors d'oeuvre
- identify the principles behind preparing mousse, *timbales*, *rillettes*, and confits
- comprehend the use of different types of garnishes
- recognize the differences between different types of caviar
- differentiate between *antipasti*, tapas, *mezze*, smorgasbord, and *antojitos*
- analyse the techniques used in preparation of *amuse bouche*
- identify various types of tools and techniques used for preparing modern hors d'oeuvre

INTRODUCTION

An appetizer, as the name suggests, is a food item that is served to whet the appetite or prepare the customer for the meal to follow. It is an age old custom to serve titbits of food and beverages to guests, while they are waiting for the food to be served. Typically, appetizers or starters are small bite size portions of food that are neatly decorated and served well garnished. It is widely believed that food is first eaten through the eyes. This holds true for an appetizer, as it creates the first impression of the meal to follow. Thus, appetizers are not just flavoursome but are carefully planned for they are a prelude to the meal. There should be a connect between the appetizer and the subsequent meal.

In this chapter, we will discuss various kinds of appetizers and their classification. We shall also discuss some of the classical hors d'oeuvres and understand how these are prepared. We shall also discuss the significance of different appetizers and the approach to be adopted while planning them. Appetizers for pre-plated food are very different in approach to the ones served for volume. We will discuss the range of elaborate set ups and the modern approach to appetizers. In the previous chapter, we read about various kinds of *charcuterie* products such as pâtés, terrines, and sausages that are commonly served as appetizers. Now, we cover a range of cold appetizers such as mousses and *timbales*.

Appetizers are served around the world and are known by different names. In France, these are commonly known as hors d'oeuvres. Just as aperitifs are drinks served before meals, hors d'oeuvres are served as starters to meals. In olden times, these were served outside the main dining hall in a lounge, along with the drinks. The purpose was to prepare the guests for the main meal to follow and also to control their hunger pangs, while the dinner was being readied. The custom is still prevalent in this day and age and there are some events, called cocktails events, in which only a range of small tit bits, both hot and cold, are served and passed around.

As per the classical French menu, hors d'oeuvres are served as the first course on the menu and such hors d'oeuvre is called tabled hors d'oeuvre while some are passed around like cocktail snacks, called butler or butlered hors d'oeuvre. The butler hors d'oeuvre are usually standing meals, wherein people mingle with each other and alcoholic beverages and infused drinks called cocktails are served apart from other soft drinks. Such lavish events are mostly hosted at dinner functions, where people have enough time to enjoy the wining and dining till late in the night. However, nowadays it is not unusual to see cocktails and butlered hors d'oeuvres being served at even public gatherings, which may not culminate in a dinner. Whatever be the hors d'oeuvre, it is important to keep the following salient features in mind while preparing and serving these.

- Hors d'oeuvre should be carefully selected and should complement the event and the main meal to follow.
- The hors d'oeuvre should be bite-sized or at the most two mouthfuls. Larger appetizers tend to fill up the stomach and render futile the efforts put in the preparation of main meal.
- While preparing and handling hors d'oeuvres, hygienic and sanitary precautions should be followed scrupulously For instance, raw items such as caviars, sashimi and oysters should be served on a platter of crushed ice to avoid any kind of contamination and spoilage.
- Appetizers presented on the plate should be very decorative and appealing to the eye. This being the first course and an introduction to the meal needs to be exciting and fresh. Even the appetizers presented in the butlered service, should be arranged in such a way, that the last person served is not left with a mess of garnishes on the serving platter.

CLASSIFICATION OF APPETIZERS

Appetizers are generally classified on the basis of the temperatures that they are served at—hot hors d'oeuvre and cold hors d'oeuvre. There is also another category of appetizers known as canapés. Variety in the menu can be created by choosing and selecting hors d'oeuvre of these types. Let us discuss these hors d'oeuvres.

Canapés

Miniature varieties of open-faced sandwiches are known as canapés. These are popularly served as cocktail snacks and as tabled hors d'oeuvre in French classical menu. Any canapé has four major parts such as base, spread, main commodity, and garnish. The range of bases, spreads, main commodities, and garnishes are discussed in detail in the next chapter on sandwiches. Canapés are usually open faced so that the garnish looks attractive and appetising to the patron or customer. The word canapé comes from the French word that means sofa or couch. The spread and food commodity are placed on a base of bread that acts like a couch and thus, the name. The bread for canapés is cut into attractive geometrical shapes and presented. Many other forms of canapés such as Italian *crostini*, which literally means 'little toasts', are Italian equivalents of the French canapé.

Canapés can use fillings such as roasted meat, various kinds of seafood, chicken, and other meat. It can be also topped with cold sliced *charcuterie* products, cheese, pâté de foie gras, etc. Figure 3.1 illustrates some canapés that are a foodie's delight.

The following are some important points that must be kept in mind while working on canapés.

- Canapés should be made as close to service as possible. Since these are small pieces of toasted or grilled breads that are covered with spread and toppings, there is a possibility that they can become soggy.
- They should be fairly easy to assemble and the flavours should complement the following meal. This has to be especially kept in mind when they are being prepared for a large gathering, when it would take more time to garnish and prepare canapés at the last minute.
- Prime quality ingredients should be used for making canapés, as they will make first impression on the minds of the guests.
- The assembly and lay of the canapés should be well-organized and planned, as many individual components have to be placed at the last minute. It is good to follow the assembly line workflow, wherein each person has a specific responsibility. One person lays out the prepared bread, another person places the spread, and so on.

Fig. 3.1 Various types of canapés

- Keep safe and hygienic practices in mind at all times, as these are ready-to-eat foods and thus classified as high-risk items. Handle the finished product with gloves or tongs which have been sanitized.
- The spreads, toppings, should be flavoured well as the main purpose of serving canapés is to induce thirst so that the customers can order more drinks.
- Each canapé should look the same, as they would be presented together. If they all look different, they will not appear presentable.

Cold Hors d'oeuvres

Cold hors d'oeuvres are appetizers that are served cold or at room temperature. Initially all the starters that were served in old times used to be cold, as they were combinations of certain foods that were left over from the production of main meals. However, to provide variety to appetizers some extraordinarily creative chefs came up with some brilliantly successful hors d'oeuvres that were served hot. As time progressed, these became a category in itself. There are many varieties of classical appetizers some of which are popularly served till date with few minor changes in presentation and appeal. Some popular cold hors d'oeuvres are as follows.

Crudités

Various kinds of crunchy and fresh vegetables are cut into finger shapes and served with flavoursome dips (Fig. 3.2). They are still popular and are commonly served on various events. Vegetables such as carrots, cucumbers, celery sticks, bell peppers are few of the vegetables commonly served as crudités. The vegetables, after processing, are neatly cut into long sticks and are chilled in ice water to get a crunch. They are commonly served with dips such as curried mayonnaise, cream cheese, yoghurt dips, or even sour cream.

Fig. 3.2 Various types of crudités

Shell shapes

Shell shapes (Fig. 3.3) are short paste savoury *tartlets* and *barquettes* commonly served as hors d'oeuvres. These are filled with various kinds of fillings. The round shells of tartlets or boat-shaped *barquettes* can be filled with sautéed vegetables, cold smoked meat, or even miniature salads. The range of fillings can be unlimited as it depends upon the creativity of the chef. Shells can also be elegantly piped with various kinds of vegetable and meat mousses, which has been discussed later in the chapter. One has to be careful while deciding on the fillings for the shells, as moist fillings can make the shells soggy and such an assembly should be done only at the last minute.

Fig. 3.3 Various types of shell shapes

Bouchees

The word *bouchees* come from the French word *bouche* which means mouth. These are small bite-sized vol-au-vent shells made from puff pastry. The shells in this case are packed with hot or cold fillings as depicted in Fig. 3.4. So, these can also be classified as hot appetizers if served hot.

Fig. 3.4 Various types of *bouchees*

Profiteroles

These are small, round hollow shapes prepared from choux pastry. They can be filled in a variety of ways; the top can be sliced to obtain a shell which can be filled with creamy or dry fillings as showed in Fig. 3.5. Creamed cheese mousse, smoked meat, and many other fillings can be put inside and served. Another way to serve the shells is to keep them intact and stuff the mousse with a piping nozzle from the base in which a small hole is cut off. These types of appetizers are easy to prepare for large functions as the shells can be made in advance and frozen for further use.

Fig 3.5 Various types of profiteroles

Mousses

The word mousse comes from the French word *moussoir* which means frothing or foam. A mousse by definition is always served cold and the ingredients can be cooked and cooled but never heated after preparation. Mousse is a very popular dessert made in confectionary, but in *garde manger*, a cold mousse is always a savoury dish that has three major components: base, binder, and aerator.

Mousses are used in variety of ways. They can be piped onto various bases such as shells, profiteroles, or even *bouchees*. The mousse can also be neatly piped in small vegetables shaped into small cups or hollowed out cases. The mousse can be layered in a clear glass mould and topped with aspic mixed with decorative vegetables and herbs. The mousse can also be layered into moulds and then demoulded, sliced, and served like terrines or pâtés. The three components of mousse are discussed below.

Base A variety of ingredients can be used for preparing the mousse. The base is the main ingredient of the mousse. It can range from various kinds of fruits and vegetables to cheese, meat, and seafood, and *charcuterie* products. The first step is to puree the main ingredient and pass it through a fine sieve to obtain a smooth puree. Cooking might be involved to cook many vegetables, meats, and seafood to facilitate pureeing. In many cases, where the puree is too dry, the consistency can be adjusted by adding items such as béchamel sauce, *velouté*, cream, or even mayonnaise. It is always a good idea to sieve the mixture to remove any unwanted particles, which will hamper the final consistency of the smooth mousse.

Binder As the name suggests, this part is used for binding the ingredients together to create a well formed gel or stable structure. Ingredients such as aspic, powdered or leaf gelatine are most commonly used binders for the mousses. The gelatine must be bloomed and then melted, before it is added to the base (refer Chapter 2 for the uses of gelatines). The amount of gelatine to be added to the mixture will depend upon many factors such as viscosity of the main ingredient, the kind of ingredient itself, and even the acid or the alkaline content of the ingredient. For example, when making cheese mousses, cheese itself can play the role of a binder effectively and an extra binding agent might not be required at all.

The whole reason of adding a binder to the mousse is to create a stable mousse, which can be shaped or piped and would hold its shape when chilled and not collapse when presented on the buffet. On the other hand, too much of a binder can make the mousse too firm and rubbery, thereby, spoiling the texture of the final product. Twenty-five grams of bloomed gelatine is a good bet for 1 kg of the total mixture. This quantity can be adjusted depending upon the intended use of the mousse. If the mousse is to be piped into *tartlets*, then the consistency will be different than what will be prepared in a mould and then sliced and served.

Aerator These add volume to the mixture. Aeration can be achieved by adding traditional aerators such as whipped creams and egg whites. Care should be taken not to over-whip the aerators as that can give a curdled appearance to the final product. Care should also be taken while stirring or folding the aerators into the mixture. Do not add all at once; start with a small amount of aerator to be folded in the mixture and then allow the rest to fold in, as it will help the aerator to get evenly dispersed, thereby resulting in a desired texture of the final product. The aerator should be folded in chilled mixture and on a bed of ice to maintain consistent temperature at all times. The difference in temperatures will result in curdling of the mousse. The mousse once formed should be immediately shaped as required or if they set with gelatine, then it will be difficult to shape and pipe. The mousse can also be rolled like a *roulade* or it can be made into galantine-like style, by using the outer covering of sliced vegetable or cheese, etc. The mousse can also be layered in a *terrine* mould, demoulded, sliced, and served glazed with aspic.

Savoury water and jellies

In the previous chapter we learnt that flavoured water, such as reduced stocks and fruit juices, have been popularly used in larder kitchen for various reasons. These highly flavoured and seasoned water form very good appetizers when served as they are or by allowing them to set into a jelly. Other ingredients, such as meat and ornately cut vegetables, could be added to enhance their visual appeal. The amount of gelatine required for this purpose would depend upon the service style of the jelly. It should be firm, if it has to be demoulded and sliced. The amount of gelatine is also affected by the kind of liquid that is used for preparing the jelly. Acidic items, such as pineapple juice, lemon and wine, weaken the strength of gelatine. Also, enzymes present in pineapple and papaya weaken the action of gelatine. Nonetheless, jellied appetizers are added on the appetizer selection as they provide an interesting experience when eaten. The appetizer maintains its shape on the platter or plate and is firm to lift, but when eaten, it subtly melts away from the heat in the mouth, leaving the diced commodities to chew upon.

Caviar

Caviar, once the most classically served hors d'oeuvre, is rarely served in hotels nowadays. This is because of its rare availability and also because of animal rights activists, who are seeking ban on animal products from endangered species. Caviar is obtained from the roe (eggs) of the sturgeon fish—a highly labour-intensive job. Its low shelf life or highly perishable property makes it an extremely expensive commodity.

Caviar is manually harvested from the roe sac of the fish while it is still alive. If the fish is dead, then the membranes that surround the individual eggs or roe get damaged and begin deteriorating. The roe sac, once obtained, is carefully rubbed over a sieve and the roe or small eggs are collected, washed in fresh water, and then graded by connoisseurs on the basis of the size of the eggs, their colour, firmness, gloss, and other features. The caviar is then salted carefully to preserve it and to infuse the desired flavour. Salting is an art and the amount of salt in caviar determines its quality and price. The most regarded process for salting caviar is called *malossol*, which in Russian means 'little salt'. The salt added in this process is not more than 5 per cent of the total weight of the caviar.

There are many types of caviar available in the market. In France, caviar is a term for the roe of sturgeon fish only, but in other parts of the world roe of other fish are sold as caviars as long as the name of the fish is mentioned on the packaged container. The name of the caviar is derived from the species of sturgeon fish it comes from. Some of the common types of caviar are described in Table 3.1.

Table 3.1 Types of caviar

Caviar	Description	Photograph
Beluga	Apart from the size of caviar, it is also graded on its colour. The colours on caviar are represented by 000 on the packaged jars. 000 would indicate lightest coloured caviar and 0 would indicate the darkest. The beluga caviar is the most expensive of all caviars because of its quality and grading. Another reason is that beluga sturgeon takes a minimum of 20 years to attain maturity. An adult on maturity could weigh up to 1,200 kg. The colour of the beluga is light to dark grey. Beluga caviar is sold in blue jars or tins. The colour grading is 000.	
Ossetra	The roe of *ossetra* species of sturgeon is graded as the second best caviar after beluga. The size of the grain is medium. This sturgeon takes between 14 and 15 years to attain maturity and weighs around 220 kg. The colour of the *ossetra* caviar is brownish with a golden tinge and has a strong nutty flavour that makes it unique and different from other caviars. It is commonly available in yellow jars or tins. The colour grading is 00.	
Sevruga	It is fairly less expensive than beluga or *ossetra* and has a smaller grain graded as 0. It is the smallest of all caviars and has a stronger flavour with a dark brown colour. *Sevruga* sturgeon is ready to be harvested at 8 years and it weighs around 70–80 kg. It is normally sold in red jars or tins.	
Sterlet	It is one of the rarest forms of caviar as this sturgeon species is nearly extinct. This prized caviar is light golden in colour and graded 000. It was once named the golden caviar of the Czars in Russia.	
Pajusnay	*Pajusnay* means 'pressed' in Russian. This Russian caviar is a mix of mature, small, broken, or overripe eggs which are put in linen sacks and pressed to release all the fatty acids. The resulting caviar is more like a paste and it is common in Russia to apply it on dark bread like a spread and consumed along with vodka. The flavours of this caviar are very intense and are also used for preparing cold sauces.	
Salmon roe	Roe obtained from fish other than sturgeon such as salmon, trout, and cod, are also harvested for human consumption. However, the caviar thus obtained must mention the fish on the packing jar. It cannot be sold as true caviar, which is obtained only from sturgeon. The roe from salmon are light golden to pink in colour and are of large size. This caviar is not graded as 000, which is only used for true caviars.	

(Contd)

Table 3.1 (Contd)

Caviar	Description	Photograph
Tarama	Cod and carp are usually used for harvesting this caviar and is quite popular in Mediterranean countries, especially Greece, where it is harvested from grey mullet. In the USA, *tarama* is also referred to the roe obtained from tuna fish.	
Botarga	Special grey mullet fish are used to harvest this caviar in Italy. The grey mullet is common in the Mediterranean region. In Italian cuisine, this fish is also dried and salted and commonly eaten as an appetizer	
Tobiko	This is roe of flying fish and is popular in sushi bars In Japan. These are available in bright yellow, red, and green colours and flavoured with various flavours such as wasabi, pale orange called *yuzu,* and even squid ink.	
Tarako	This is same as *tobiko*, but is obtained from the cod fish. The use of *tarako* is similar to that of *tobiko*.	

Caviars are highly perishable in nature which is why these are generally served straight from the jars and tins. The size of the packaging is also the serving size of one portion, which is one ounce (28 g). It has to be served elegantly to do justice to the expensive commodity. Caviar is generally served in glass bowls placed in a container containing crushed ice. The other accompaniments served along with caviar are sieved hard boiled eggs, boiled and grated egg whites, chopped chives, freshly whipped cream, chopped shallots, and toasted brioche or blinis.

Stuffed vegetables

A variety of vegetables can be stuffed with a range of products and even mousses to make cold appetizers. Preparing any vegetable depends upon the creativity of the chefs. Vegetables can be used raw or blanched depending upon the type selected. For example, mushrooms can be scooped out, blanched, and stuffed with cheese mousse to make wonderful cold appetizers. Blanched and scooped cherry tomatoes can also be used as casings for stuffing various kinds of mousses. Vegetables can also be sliced, marinated, and grilled, and then arranged on a plastic sheet and filled with varieties of fillings and rolled like a *roulade*. The *roulades* can be sliced individually and decorated with garnish or glazed with aspic. Thus, sky is the limit to the kind of product that can be prepared using vegetables for stuffing.

Timbales

In olden times, *timbales* referred to small and round drinking cups made of metal. It is believed that the word *timbale* comes from an Arabic word, *thabal* meaning drum. A *timbale* is a pasty mould in which food is baked. *Timbales* were popularized by King Edward VII of England, whose royal banquets were incomplete without this appetizer. *Timbales* can be prepared in various ways and filled in a variety of ways. Those can be lined with pastry, meat, sliced vegetables, or even aspic. But the dish is always served without the mould. *Timbales* can be served hot or cold depending upon the filling. Hot *timbales* are also known as custard *timbales*, where a mixture of meat, cream, seasoning, and eggs put in greased moulds and poached in water until the custard is cooked. *Timbales* can also be coated with aspic and served cold. Some aspic-lined timbale moulds are packed with flavoured aspic and the moulds are put in a container of ice cold water, until the water comes up to the rim of the *timbale*. Leave the moulds in the water for 10 minutes or until the aspic has set around the mould. Remove the moulds and pour out excess aspic. This would leave a cavity inside, which can be packed with any kind of fillings such as mousses, cheese mixtures, or even meat. The *timbales* can then be chilled and served with attractive garnishes after taking them out of the moulds.

Confits

These appetizers originated from the Southern west region of France, where they were a favourite amongst farmers. Just like vegetables were preserved for the winter months, it was always an ongoing phenomena to preserve meat and offal such as tongue, shoulder, hocks, wings, and neck, which were cooked and stored in their own fat. The word confit is derived from the French word *confire* which means to preserve. Even today, the confits are popularly served in the main meal or as appetizers. Poultry such as duck and goose and game such as rabbit, quails, and pheasants, are very popular in making confit. Traditionally, confit were prepared by putting meat, herbs, and flavourings, along with fat of the same animal or lard and cooked in earthenware crock pots which were placed near smouldering charcoal. This ensured slow cooking that gave the meat its delicate flavours and texture. The principle of cooking meat, that is cooking at very low temperatures for a long duration of time, remains the same today except that the traditional hearths and smouldering charcoals have been replaced by electric ovens and hotplates. The meat is first marinated with salt and seasoning. The salt helps to extract the perishable meat juices. The meat is then covered with rendered fat and allowed to slow cook for 6–8 hours depending upon the type and cut of meat. Slow cooking helps in maintaining the smooth and soft texture of the meat as the fat under the meat slowly melts away and provides moistness to the meat. Once the meat is cooked, it is allowed to cool in the same fat, so that it can maintain its firmness. A confit can be eaten immediately or it can be stored in the same fat for almost 3 months.

The confits can be served on any base or in a small pot. To present a confit, remove the meat from the fat and remove the excess fat from the meat. Sear the meat on a skillet and warm in a steamer to soften the meat for 5–10 minutes. The confit can be served warm or just shredded and served topped on bread.

Rillettes and Rillons

Rillettes can be described as the by-products of confits. The English call them potted meat and these can be made from confits. Also, traditionally in Europe, these were prepared by leftover cooked meat, which were pounded or shredded into thin fibres and mixed with rendered fat or butter and then packed into stone wares or small porcelain pots, where it could stay up to a few months. The other method is to pulverize the leftover meat with few cubes of ice in a food processor and grind the meat until a very coarse texture is obtained. Care should be taken not to puree the meat to the textures of *mousseline* as the texture is not suitable for a *rillette*. When the meat are cut into small cubes, browned well, and mixed with butter and seasonings, it is known as *rillons*. A *rillon* is never shredded like a *rillette*. Both *rillettes* and *rillons* form a good variety of appetizers when served with crackers or crusty bread slices. These can also be stuffed in various mousses and cups of vegetables or profiteroles to prepare interesting hors d'oeuvre.

Hot Hors d'oeuvres

As the name suggests, this range of appetizers is served hot. Generally, a mix of canapés, cold and hot appetizers are creatively planned by chefs to make an event successful. Hot appetizers are common around the world and known by different names in different regions. They can be baked, deep-fried, grilled, or even steamed such as Chinese dim sums.

The following are some of the most popular hot hors d'oeuvres served in hotels across the world.

Beignets or Batter-fried Hot Hors d'oeuvres

These hors d'oeuvres are prepared by coating meat or vegetables in a batter and deep-frying until crisp. Any fried food coated in batter and deep-fried is known as *beignets* in France. These can be sweet or savoury. Commonly known as fritters in English, these appetizers are prepared with various kinds of batters across the world and are served as hot snacks. Table 3.2 describes some famous beignets popular in various countries.

Brochettes or skewered appetizers

Brochette, meaning skewer in French, have been popular since centuries. Small chunks or marinated food such as meat, fruits, and vegetables are skewered onto skewers and cooked on smouldering charcoal. The brochettes can be served along with appropriate dips and sauces and can also be a mini meal, if served in large portions. One can use metal skewers or small wooden or bamboo sticks as used in oriental cuisines. There are many types of skewered brochettes served around the world. Some of the common brochettes are described in Table 3.3.

Table 3.2 Various kinds of beignets or batter-fried hot hors d'oeuvres

Beignets	Description	Photograph
Tempura	This Japanese snack is prepared by making a batter with help of flour, eggs, seasoning, and ice cold water to prepare a lumpy kind of batter in which a variety of meats, seafood or even vegetables can be coated and crisp-fried. The tempura is fried in such a manner that the colour remains creamy yellow.	
Orly	*Orly* is a batter prepared by mixing flour, beer, eggs, and seasonings and is also known as beer batter. Variety of foods but most commonly fish can be coated in this batter and deep-fried until crisp.	
Pakora	This is an Indian snack made from a batter of gram flour, Indian spices, and water. Items such as chicken, fish, cottage cheese, and a variety of vegetables are coated with the batter and fried until crisp. These are however, not served as prelude to the main course, but they are popular snacks during tea time.	
À l'anglaise	This is a method of preparing food items, where these are first coated with flour and egg batter and then with fresh or dried breadcrumbs and are fried until crisp. Fish fingers, chicken nuggets, etc. are most commonly served hot appetizers in cocktail events. One can also use commodities such as Mozzarella sticks, Camembert cheese wedges, and stuffed mushrooms for this preparation.	

Table 3.3 Types of skewered hot appetizers

Brochettes	Description	Photograph
Brochettes	These are small chunks of meat, vegetables, fruits, cheese, or a combination of all the four, marinated and grilled.	
Kebobs	These are vegetables or meat skewered on metal skewers and cooked over smouldering charcoal. *Kebobs* are a speciality of Middle Eastern countries such as Tunisia, Morocco, and Iran.	

(Contd)

Table 3.3 (Contd)

Brochettes	Description	Photograph
Shashliks	These are same as brochettes but are commonly prepared in Russia.	
Satays	These are marinated slices of meat skewered onto bamboo sticks. These can then be grilled or pan-fried. These are popularly prepared in South-East Asian countries such as Malaysia, Indonesia, Thailand, and Vietnam.	

Kebabs

These are very common starters used in Indian cuisine and can be made from a range of meat, seafood, vegetables, fruits, cottage cheese, and many other commodities. The commodities are marinated in hung curd, cream, and spices depending upon the products and then cooked in *tandoor*, deep-fried, or shallow-fried as per the desired product. Please refer the chapter on *tandoor* cooking in the book *Quantity Food Production Operations* to know about different types of kebabs.

Bruschetta

Bruschetta is a popular Italian appetizer, very similar to the canapé. While the process of assembling in both the appetizers is same, in bruschetta, the bread is sliced thicker and is pan-fried on both the sides. The toppings on the bread could be hot, warm, or cold depending upon the type of bruschetta. Various kinds of Italian breads are used for preparing bruschettas.

Croquette

This is a classical hot hors d'oeuvre served in France and other European countries. It is a mixture of meat, seafood, vegetables, or a combination of these, which are combined with *panada* such as thick white sauce and bread soaked in milk. The mixture is then shaped into various shapes such as ovals or cylinders, which are then coated with batter of eggs and flour and finally coated in fresh or dried breadcrumbs and deep-fried until crisp. Chefs are being more creative these days and the coatings of breadcrumbs are being replaced with commodities such as vermicelli, crushed nuts, and semolina to give a different appearance and to create a variety in the croquettes. To understand the *mise en place* and work flow for breading procedure or crumbing the food items, which is also known as *pane a l'anglaise* method.

The work flow is as follows.

(a) The food item is first cut into equal shapes and size. This is important as different sizes will not cook evenly.

(b) The prepared items are first coated into seasoned flour to fill up any dentures and create a surface which will allow the eggs and other coatings to stick onto the food commodity.

(c) The food is then dipped into an egg or sometimes into a batter prepared from eggs, flour, salt, and liquid.

(d) The food item is then coated in breadcrumbs and extra crumbs are removed by shaking the product.

(e) The crumbed-product is ready to be deep-fried.

This *mise en place* can be prepared in advance and kept up to two days depending upon the food product.

Another hot appetizer that resembles a croquette is called rissole. In this, the mixture is wrapped in dough or any covering and then dipped in batter, crumbed, and deep-fried.

Dough-wrapped hors d'oeuvres

Many creative hors d'oeuvres are prepared by covering or encasing a range of food products in various kinds of dough and then baked, grilled, or deep-fried according to the recipe. Dough that are commonly used wraps are *phyllo* pastry, puff pastry, tortillas, noodles, etc. Table 3.4 describes some very popular dough-wrapped hot hors d'oeuvres.

Table 3.4 Types of dough-wrapped hot hors d'oeuvres (see also Plate 2)

Hors d'oeuvres	Description	Photograph
Sausage puffs or pigs in blankets	These are very popular hot hors d'oeuvres prepared by marinating frankfurters with grain mustard sauce, salt, and sometimes Tabasco. Puff pastry is sheeted out to a large rectangle, and the franks are arranged in one single line. The rectangle is now brushed with beaten eggs and rolled over to form a cylinder in which the franks are encased. It is then cut into equal sizes and baked until the puff is crisp. Other food products, such as minced meat, vegetables, can also be used to give variations. They are also commonly known as pigs in blankets.	
Strudel	Though a strudel is commonly used for making a popular dessert in Austria, small individual savoury strudels are commonly served as hot hors d'oeuvres. Refer the chapter on laminated pastry in the book *Food Production Operations*, to understand the making of a strudel.	
Börek	This is a popular hors d'oeuvre from Mediterranean cuisine, particularly Greece and Lebanon. It is made from *phyllo* pastry and any kind of filling can be used. The most popular is *spanakopita*, wherein the filling is of spinach and feta cheese. To prepare *böreks*, *phyllo* pastry is cut into 2-inch wide strips and brushed with melted butter. The desired filling is placed on one of the corners and the long strip is folded at right angles to prepare a triangular pocket, which is baked or deep-fried.	

(Contd)

Table 3.4 (Contd)

Hors d'oeuvres	Description	Photograph
Spring roll	This is very popular hot hors d'oeuvre from South-East Asian countries and China. Various kinds of cooked fillings are rolled in readily available spring roll sheets or flat dough sheets commonly known as *wonton* skins. This hot hors d'oeuvres is rolled into a cylinder with both ends closed. Springs are deep-fried until crisp and served hot.	
Wonton	A very popular hot hors d'oeuvre from China, it is similar to the spring roll, but the only difference is in the shape. In case of *wonton*, the square piece of sheet is stuffed with a filling and folded into a triangle and then both the ends are pinched together to form a unique shape.	
Turnovers	These are made from puff pastry and variety of fillings such as meat, vegetables, and seafood, are encased in puff pastry and baked until crisp. Traditionally, the shape of the turnover is determined by the filling inside. Chicken turnovers are shaped into half moon, vegetables into triangular, and lamb turnovers into square or rectangular. The shapes are consistent so that they can be easily identified.	

Flat Breads

Various types of flat breads are served as hot hors d'oeuvres, some are plain, while some with toppings. Varieties of flat or yeast leavened breads such as mini pizzas are also commonly served as snacks. Some of the common flat breads served as hot hors d'oeuvres are described in Table 3.5.

Table 3.5 Flat breads served as hors d'oeuvres

Flat bread	Description	Photograph
Pizza	Yeast leavened bread from Italy, it is topped with tomato sauce, main ingredients, seasonings, and Mozzarella cheese and baked in hot oven until the crust is formed and cheese has evenly melted. Pizza can be served as a main meal or when served in miniature versions, it is a popular hot hors d'oeuvre. Some flat breads are also served with slices of *haloumi* cheese as starters.	
Crostini	It is an Italian version of a canapé. The sliced bread can be spread with various kinds of spreads, such as garlic butter, pesto, olive, and anchovy paste, and grilled or pan-fried before serving.	
Calzone	It is a folded pizza. The pizza is topped with sauce, filling, and cheese and is folded to form a half-moon shape. If made in miniature size, it can be served as a hot hors d'oeuvre.	

Pies and Tarts

Small savoury shells can be made using puff pastry, *phyllo*, or shortcrust and baked with filling or can be filled after they are baked. Depending upon the kind of pie, these can be served hot or cold. Just like we discussed shell shapes in the section on cold appetizers, hot pies are popularly made by using different types of fillings. Some classical pies served as hot hors d'oeuvres are listed in Table 3.6.

Miscellaneous hot hors d'oeuvres

We have discussed a range of hot hors d'oeuvres in the previous sections; however there is yet another range of hot appetizers that are unique and prepared classically since centuries. Some classical hot hors d'oeuvres are listed in Table 3.7.

Table 3.6 Classical pies served as hot hors d'oeuvres

Pie	Description	Photograph
Quiche	This is a small tart shell lined with salt paste and filled with different types of meat, *charcuterie*, seafood, or vegetables and savoury custard made from eggs, cream, and milk, and poured in and baked until cooked. There are different types of classical quiches that have classical fillings such as quiche *lorraine* that has a filling of leeks and bacon. Quiche for hors d'oeuvres can be made in small individual shells, but for large banquets, they can be prepared in sheet pans and then cut into squares or rectangles.	
Australian leek pie	This is prepared by lining small tartlet moulds with puff pastry. The filling is of sautéed leeks with herbs and the top is also covered with puff pastry. It is then baked until crisp and served hot. It is also commonly known as pot pie as it is made in a tart shell to hold the shape.	
Scotch pie	Originally from Scotland, this is a slightly raised pie made in a cylindrical mould with a filling of meat—usually mutton seasoned with herbs. It is also known as mince pie as it is made from minced meat.	

Table 3.7 Miscellaneous classical appetizers (see also Plate 3)

Appetizers	Description	Photograph
Angels on horseback	A very popular hot hors d'oeuvre, it is prepared by wrapping marinated oyster meat with sliced bacon and grilling the same. In the event of non availability, oysters are also substituted with scallop meat.	

(Contd)

Table 3.7   (Contd)

Appetizers	Description	Photograph
Devils on horseback	The concept is quite similar to the *angels on horseback*, the only difference is that the oyster is replaced with prune or dates that are stuffed with mango chutney and then wrapped in bacon. Unlike *angels on horseback*, these are popularly baked and served hot.	
Dolmas	This word comes from the Turkish word *dolmak*, which means stuffed. Various kinds of vegetable leaves such as cabbage leaves and spinach, but most commonly grapevine leaves, are stuffed with an assortment of fillings such as meat, rice, and vegetables, and steamed until cooked. They are commonly served as hot hors d'oeuvres with a curd-based dip.	

GARNISHING HORS D'OEUVRES

Although the use of garnish is mostly governed by tradition, yet in modern times, chefs are switching over to more trendy garnishes to adorn the dishes. Here we focus on the changing trends in garnishes and some modern and contemporary ways of garnishing food. The role of garnish and few types of garnishes are dealt with at length in Chapter 4 on sandwiches.

Types of Garnish

Some of the common types of garnishes used in hors d'oeuvres are described in Table 3.8.

Table 3.8   Types of garnishes used in hors d'oeuvres

Garnish	Description
Vegetables	Vegetable carvings is a specialized section of larder kitchen, where special people are hired to create large displays of showpieces made from carved vegetables such as watermelon, papaya, and pumpkin. This, however, is a fading art. Various types of vegetable garnishes are described in Table 4.4 in Chapter 4 on sandwiches.
Bread	Breads are commonly used as garnish in appetizers. They are used in many forms. Thinly sliced rye bread is toasted to make attractive garnish or it is commonly served as an accompaniment to many hors d'oeuvres such as caviar. *Pita* bread, tortilla chips, baked or fried *phyllo* pastry are all common types of breads used as garnish.
Salads	Few salads, apart from micro greens and lettuce, are used as accompanying garnish with appetizers. Depending upon the dish, the vegetables are sliced thinly and refreshed in ice cold water to get crisp. These are then used as garnish in various appetizers.
Sauces	Accompanying sauces are used as attractive garnishes in cold appetizers. The sauces can be thickened with gelatine and then pureed to obtain a thick and viscous liquid, which can be squeezed onto the canapé or any appetizer.
Compotes, chutneys, etc.	Various types of pickles, compotes, chutneys, and relishes are also commonly used as garnish, as they add flavour and contrasting taste to the hors d'oeuvres.

Importance of Culinary Garnishes

Hors d'oeuvres are the first course of the meal and hence it is very important to present the same in the most artistic and decorated form. Garnishing the appetizers plays a very important role in service of hors d'oeuvres. Sometimes the accompaniments served along with the main appetizer are also known as garnishes, as the dish would look bare and incomplete without the same. Imagine a small portion of caviar; if it is served as it is, it would look incomplete. The guest would feel no value for the money that they would be paying for such an expensive dish. Thus, accompaniments served along with the caviar would be considered as garnish.

The main purpose of the garnish is to add colour, texture, taste, nutritional value, and an element of surprise to the dish. However, it is important to focus carefully on the garnishing of a dish. Whenever a garnish is chosen, its use should be kept in mind; if it is only adding colour, then it should be treated as non functional garnish. However, one should avoid using a non-functional garnish, as it does not serve any purpose.

Garnishing a food should be fairly easy and not complicated. Complicated garnishing can result in delayed food orders, and sometimes a hot dish would get cold by the time the work on the garnish is completed. Also, over-garnishing a dish should be avoided as it would take away the real flavour of the food.

POPULAR TRADITIONAL APPETIZERS FROM THE WORLD

Appetizers, snacks, hors d'oeuvres are all synonymous to each other. Today, with more creative ideas and availability of products, it is not uncommon to find a range of appetizers from around the world being served on buffets and à la carte menus of many hotels and restaurants. Unlike France, where the starters are formally passed around or served pre-plated, the starters or hors d'oeuvres are arranged as a spread for the guests. This spread of hors d'oeuvres can at times culminate into main meals also. In different countries, it is known by different names. For example, in France it is termed as *hors d'oeuvre varie*, in Italy is called *antipasti*, and in Russia, it is known as *zakuski* wherein the spread consists of smoked fish with salads, toasted *blinis* with caviar, sauces, etc. The appetizer spread in India is called by different names. For instance, in Gujarat, such a spread is called *farsaan* and in many banquets, it is common to see chaat counters that serve an array of savouries. Please refer the section on Indian sweets in the book *Quantity Food Production Operations* to understand more about the different types of street food that are served as appetizers in India. Some of the most commonly served traditional appetizers from various countries that have become popular internationally are discussed next.

Antipasto

The plural for *antipasto* is *antipasti*, which means before pasta or the main meal in Italian cuisine. Exhibit 3.1 gives us a fair idea of the selection in *antipasti* menus often served in speciality Italian restaurants. Various items such as cold sliced meat, pâtés, terrines, pickled vegetables such as peppers, olives, artichokes, cheeses, and even assortment of crusty breads, *crostini*, bruschettas, etc. are presented in large platters and liberally dressed with olive oil and parmesan cheese in *antipasti* buffets. In fact, Italians take great pride in showcasing their gastronomic fare on this buffet. Fresh, simple, high qualities are few adjectives that define *antipasti*. Seasonal and variety are other important aspects of an *antipasti* buffet. The four main courses of Italians are *antipasti*, *Primi piati*, which means the first plate, followed by pasta or the main course, and finally the dessert known as *dolce*. While *Primi piatti* courses involve starch, pasta, and risottos, are some commonly served items in the main course. We will discuss about these in more detail while discussing Italian cuisine in Chapter 6.

Exhibit 3.1   Selection in *Antipasti* Menus

Vegetarian Selection
- Asparagus with goat cheese, cherry tomatoes, pine nuts in shallot vinaigrette
- Grilled Mediterranean vegetables with shaved parmesan cheese and hazelnut tapenade
- Salad of butternut pumpkin and porcini mushrooms with truffle oil and garlic chips
- Roast baby potato with zucchini in basil balsamic dressing
- Ricotta stuffed bell peppers on potato shingles
- Potato bean and *borolotti* bean with shallot vinaigrette
- Salad of couscous with artichoke, peppers zucchini, and basil
- Balsamic marinated tomato petals with basil, goat cheese, and Kalamata olives
- Salad of zucchini, eggplant with pesto pine nuts and *reggiano* shavings
- *Ricotta* stuffed green peppers with garlic parsley dressing
- *Porcini* stuffed *capelletti* with artichokes, basil, and white wine dressing
- *Fagioli* bean with sun dried tomato, braised radicchio, and shallots
- *Panzanella* with *pesto croutons* and avocadoes
- Truffled broccoli and asparagus with gorgonzola cheese
- Balsamic marinated tomato and Mozzarella stack with rocket lettuce and *tapenade* vinaigrette.

Condiments
- Sun-dried tomato in oil
- 4 green olives
- Black olives

- Artichoke in oil
- Zucchini in oil
- Peppers in oil
- Mushrooms in oil
- Eggplants in oil
- *Grissini* sticks: black olive, rosemary, oregano, sun-dried tomato
- Water crackers
- Lavash triangles: with black pepper, white sesame, with black sesame, with poppy seeds

Assorted Lettuce in Bowl with Condiments
- Chopped truffles
- Truffle vinaigrette
- Truffle oil
- Truffle essence

Cheese
- *Caprino fresco*
- *Prato fiorito*
- *Castelmango*
- *Gorgonzola piccante*
- *Pecorino di pienza*
- *Robiole d alba*

Meat Selection
- Tuna with potato, beans, capers, and garlic dressing
- Roast chicken with asparagus in mustard garlic dressing
- Sweet bay scallops with prawns and broccoli in *gremolata* vinaigrette
- Cold cut salad with pineapple and *cilantro* dressing
- Tenderloin and *peperonata* rolls on grilled zucchini with rocket leaves
- Cold cut and bean salad with almonds and gherkins

(Contd)

Exhibit 3.1 *(Contd)*

- Balsamic chicken with wild mushrooms and artichokes
- Tenderloin and roast vegetable medley with sun dried tomatoes
- Scallop, shrimp, and lobster trio with asparagus and lemon zest
- Stacks of boiled eggs with tuna mousse, beans, and black olives
- Potato, bean, and bacon salad with shallot parsley dressing
- Roast tenderloin with asparagus and *porcini* in mustard vinaigrette
- Braised octopus with peppers and cherry tomato in garlic dressing

- Sauté chicken livers with goat cheese and zucchini in balsamic dressing
- Lobster medallions with *frisee* lettuce in truffle vinaigrette
- Parma ham and melon platter
- Cold cuts: *mortadella*, Farmers *salami*
- Potted goose liver *terrine*: Served along with potato bread *croutes*

Gravalax: Condiments of salmon Gravadlax

- Lemon muslin
- Sour cream
- Capers
- Melba toast
- Chopped onions
- Parsley

Mezze

Mezze or *meze* is a selection of small dishes or large platters served in the Middle East or in the Mediterranean countries as a prelude to the main meal or as a meal by itself. The word *mezze* is derived from Turkish word *meze* which means taste or snacks. In Arab countries, it is known as *muqabillat*, in Morocco it is called *mezedakia*, and in Greece, they are called *mezzethes*. The range of products served in *mezze* would depend upon the availability and the geographical location of that particular place. We will discuss a range of *mezze* in the section on international cuisines especially in Mediterranean cuisine in Chapter 6. The most common items served on *mezze* in many hotels around the world are described in Table 3.9.

Table 3.9 Types of *mezze*

Mezze	Description
Dips	Many dips such as *salsa* are prepared with diced vegetables in tomato puree. *Baba ghanoush* is made by pureeing roasted aubergines and seasoned with olive oil and herbs. *Moutabel* is also made with roasted aubergines and seasoned with a sesame paste called *tahini*. *Tzatziki* is made by combining hung curd with grated cucumber and olive oil. *Rouille* is a sauce prepared by pureeing red chillies, garlic, and breadcrumbs. *Begendi* is similar to *moutabel* but is smoked. *Taratoor* a kind of paste made with blanched and skinned almonds, lemon, garlic, and bread. *Mast-o-khiar* is a hung curd with pomegranate seeds, sultanas, olives, olive oil, and rose petals. *Hummus* is made by pureeing boiled chick peas, olive oil, and lemon juice etc. The above dips are commonly served and eaten with flat breads such as *pita*, *lavash*, *khubz*, etc.
Salads	Various types of salads are served on *mezze*. Some of the these are *fattoush*, which is a tossed salad of cucumbers, onions, lettuce, and tomatoes; *melitzanosalata*, which are grilled baby eggplants marinated in olive oil, chopped parsley, and grilled zucchini; Greek salad or *horikita* which is mixed salad of diced cucumbers, onions, peppers, lettuce, and feta cheese, and *tabouleh*, which is prepared by mixing one part of *burghul* with three parts of chopped parsley and seasoned with olive oil and lemon juice, grilled pepper, salads, etc.

(Contd)

Table 3.9 (Contd)

Mezze	Description
Pickles	Marinated dates, figs, olives are commonly marinated in olive oil and lemon salt and served as pickles. Hung curd cheese is rolled into chopped parsley and pepper and also pickled in olive oil. It is called *laban* or *labneh* and is common *mezze*.
Meat	Some hot *mezze* comprise *seekh kebabs* known as *shish taouk,* minced meat dumplings called *kibbeh,* grilled fish, *jawaneh* or chicken wings marinated and broiled in *tandoor. Shawarma* or *doner kebabs* are skewered on to large rods and broiled in a special rotating griller. The meat is sliced thin and served encased in *pita* bread with salads and dips.
Vegetables	Hot vegetarian *mezze* include falafel, which is prepared by mincing soaked chickpeas with onion, garlic, and parsley and shaped into flat cakes and deep-fried. Falafels are served encased in *pita* pockets and served along with salads and dips.
Cheeses	Some grilled cheese such as *haloumi,* and *sanganaki,* from Greece are very popular part of *mezze*.

Tapas

Tapas is the *hors d'oeuvre varie* selection from Spain. The concept of tapas is unique and interesting. In olden times, a slice of bread was used to cover drinks to avoid any foreign particle from falling into it. This was known as *tapar,* which means to cover in Spanish. Later the bread was served with a topping to make the bread also edible to form a part of the snack. Thus, tapas is always associated with drinks and that is the reason why places where drinks are served are called tapas bars. With chefs being creative, more and more varieties of snacks, cold meat, hot snacks, pickles, and dips got added to tapas bars which have gained popularity as places where people can drink as well as dine. The whole concept of tapas is to encourage people to interact with each other informally. It is a place where family and friends can get together and celebrate an occasion or just unwind. Tapas are gaining popularity across the world because of its concept and lively atmosphere and culture. Since Spain was ruled by several races, its food too has been influenced by various cuisines. Romans introduced olives, the Moors enriched Spanish cuisines with nuts such as almonds, walnuts, citrus fruits, and spices; while the discovery of the new world gave Spain its tomatoes, sweet and chilli peppers, corn, and potatoes. Some of the commonly served tapas in hotels across the world are described in Table 3.10.

Table 3.10 Types of tapas

Tapas	Description	Photograph
Olives	Range of olives, especially the ones stuffed with red peppers, anchovies, almonds, and even gherkins are popularly served marinated in olive oil and herbs as tapas.	
Albondigas	These are deep-fried meat balls made from minced meat, onion, garlic, and herbs. These are commonly served hot with spiced tomato sauce.	

(Contd)

Table 3.10 (Contd)

Tapas	Description	Photograph
Banderillas	These are skewered olives, pickled onions, and anchovies skewered on to a stick.	
Fried meat	These are batter-fried meat and seafood, such as squid rings, chicken supreme, fish fingers, octopus, served on hot tapas with garlic dip called aioli.	
Boquerones	These are white anchovies and can be pickled and served in vinegar or can be deep-fried and served hot.	
Charcuterie	Grilled and sautéed sausages such as *merguez*, chorizos commonly adorn the tapas table. The sausages can be cooked in different ways. They can be stewed in wine or served fried.	
Empanadas	These can be called turnovers. Any kind of filling can be enclosed in a pastry and then deep-fried or baked. They are usually served hot with a dip.	
Gambas	Prawns are quite popular in tapas bar and they can be served grilled, sautéed, or even batter-fried to make interesting tapas.	

Antojitos

These are famous appetizers from Mexico, but are hardly used as such. In most cases, *antojitos* are considered to be street food that is often eaten as snacks. The word comes from a Spanish word *antojo,* which means craving. Like tapas and *mezzes, antojitos* are always eaten as snacks, as they are considered to be less expensive food. The concept of an *antojito* is very similar to the chaats and street food of India. We will discuss a few of these in Chapter 6 when talking about Mexican cuisine.

Smorgasbord

Smorgasbord or *smörgåsbord* is a type of cold and hot buffet which is very popular in Scandinavian countries. The word comes from two words, *smörgås* that means an open-faced sandwich and *bord* which means a table on which the buffet is laid out. The most common items found on smorgasbord are cold fish dishes such as various forms of herring, smoked eel, and salmon. Varieties of pickles, cheese, and bread are also served on this buffet table. We will also discuss this in detail in Chapter 7.

MODERN PLATED APPETIZERS

The world is changing constantly and new developments are taking place in each and every field, including cooking. Many years ago, cooking was only restricted to homes and the main focus was always nutrition and fresh food. As trends changed gradually, food began to be sold and served in special dining places. It thus became important to prepare and present food in an attractive manner, so that it could not only be marketed but also have an edge over competition or rivals in the field.

In olden times, the buffets used to be elaborate with large spreads of meat, cheese, vegetables, sauces, and master-crafted showpieces of huge vegetable carvings, ice sculptures, and a whole plethora of *charcuterie* products. Such lavish buffets were limited to the rich and famous. In the modern age, however, hotels began to take into account factors such as wastage in terms of energy, food, manpower, and also high inventories of platters and plates. Gradually, there was a shift to less elaborate buffets and the focus was on à la carte dishes being made in moderation and prepared and served to guests on order.

The modern age thus, has seen a new range of serve wares, tools and equipment, and commodities that have taken food and its presentation to the next level. Today, the very high-end restaurants process and cook the food item in its most traditional form, but what makes the restaurant different is the presentation of the food served, the overall ambience, and the style of service.

The appetizers in the hotels are particularly given importance as they are the first course of the meal that is expected to leave a long-lasting impression on the guest's mind.

A range of crockery is used for serving appetizers in an attractive fashion. The illustrations in Table 3.11 provide a fair idea of crockery used nowadays for serving appetizers. Some chefs also create bowls of ice in which they can serve chilled appetizers.

A tasting platter or combination of appetizers have created concepts such as tasting menus that are gaining popularity day by day. Chefs have recently switched to starting with a tiny portion of appetizers known as *amuse bouche*.

Modern Concepts

The traditional French courses of menu have become a thing of the past in hotels of today. People want their meals to be fairly quicker than what they used to be in olden times because of paucity of time. We have discussed a range of appetizers earlier in the chapter. These can be served in different ways. They can be arranged on a serving platter and passed around as in case of standing cocktail functions, or can be served to the guest's

Table 3.11 Types of *amuse bouche* or *amuse guele* (see also Plate 3)

Type	Description	Photograph
Israeli couscous	Israeli couscous are prepared from semolina but the grain is larger than the normal couscous. In this *amuse bouche*, they are boiled and tossed with a sauce of sundried tomatoes and herbs and presented on a leaf of rocket lettuce.	
Chilled lettuce soup	This *amuse bouche* is a tasting platter of three different types of appetizers served on a plate. The picture shows a chilled lettuce soup being served with a *crostini* of blanched tomatoes and a salad of micro greens.	
Mushroom *gallete*	Mushroom is sautéed and deglazed with white wine. It is then flavoured with herbs and bound with a *panada*. The mixture is then shaped into *galettes* and pan-fried. In the photograph, it is garnished with a curl of parmesan shaving and micro green.	
White asparagus mousse on jellied beet consommé	In this *amuse bouche*, a white asparagus mousse is presented on lightly jellied beetroot consommé and garnished with a beetroot chip and chopped chives. A very classical appetizer, it is combined together and served in a modern style.	
Grilled fish on wok-seared vegetables	This appetizer is presented in a Chinese soup spoon. The advantage of such an *amuse bouche* is that it can be presented with sauce and such presentations can replace tart shells, which otherwise can get soggy with such fillings. The wok-seared vegetables flavoured with light soy sauce are presented with pan-seared chunk of fish and garnished with chives.	
Prawn cocktail	This is the modern adaption of classical prawn cocktail as served in cold hors d'oeuvre. Here the poached prawns are arranged on *mesclun* mix dressed in cocktail sauce and poached prawns are placed garnished with micro greens.	
Chilled celeriac puree served with *quenelle* of *mascarpone* cheese	A chilled soup of celeriac is served with *mascarpone* cheese that is flavoured with dry vermouth and herbs. The unique way of serving this as an *amuse bouche* is in a deep bowl.	

(Contd)

Table 3.11 (Contd)

Type	Description	Photograph
Lemon and cod liver pâté on bed of pea mash and ginger emulsion	This is an *amuse bouche* which is prepared in the most modern style. A classical cod liver pate is prepared by adding a lemony flavour and is presented on mashed peas and the emulsion is foam that is prepared by using nitrous oxide canisters.	
Carrot jelly with *beluga* caviar on bed of toasted pumpernickel	In this *amuse bouche,* a chilled carrot jelly is presented on a toasted dark rye bread from Germany called pumpernickel and garnished with caviar. Such expensive *amuse bouche* should be served in a very high-end and special function.	
Grilled eggplant on soft polenta	The eggplant is sliced and grilled. It is then stuffed with grated cheese and seasonings. It is then rolled and heated under a salamander. It is served on a creamy polenta in a spoon.	

plate from a large platter, or even featured on the à la carte menu, where the guest would get a plate of well-presented and decorated hors d'oeuvre. Many a time it is seen that guests skip this course and order a salad or a soup as an appetizer and the appetizer course or a hors d'oeuvre that was very popular once upon a time was getting relegated to the background. This lead to another innovation in the culinary world—the chefs came up with a unique idea of presenting a very small miniature food item in the form of hors d'oeuvre to the guest no sooner than they were seated at the table. This small dish commonly came to be called *amuse bouche* or *amuse guele*. The word literally means a bite-sized piece of a dish that creates an amusement in the mouth (which is the literal translation of the French word). In other words, it lets the saliva start its action and prepares the palate to go through the various courses of menu.

Any cold or hot, vegetarian or non-vegetarian hors d'oeuvre can be served as an *amuse bouche*. It is common to see this course being served with compliments of the chef, who proudly presents these as an introduction to his/her style. Many hotels have also started the concept of grazing menu, which is also known as degustation menu. In this type of menu, smaller tasting portions of many dishes are served. It is not uncommon to see appetizer degustation menus featuring a range of hot and cold appetizers that can eventually form a whole meal by itself.

A fancy range of platters and serve ware is used for presenting *amuse bouche*. Table 3.11 describes some popular *amuse bouche* served in the hotels.

We have thus seen the uses of various kinds of crockery and modern ways of presenting appetizers. Even though the classical ingredients, such as jellies and aspic, are used, they can be presented in more stylish and fashionable ways. For example, in Table 3.11, we saw how a mousse made from white asparagus is presented over consommé aspic. One can also create bite-sized appetizers by making cut-outs of aspic and arranging them on a different base such as puff base and then topping it with a *quenelle* of mousse. Thus, we should not restrict ourselves but should try and use flavours from all around the world to prepare an appetizer. Caution should however be taken while combining the flavours as too much clash of flavours takes away the main purpose of an appetizer. Also, the appetizer should be planned keeping the theme of the food in mind.

The use of foams

One of the most commonly used styles in food service is to make foams. Though foams, such as whipped cream and mousses, have always been a favourite in culinary applications, recently a new style of making cold and hot foams has emboldened chefs to frequently use it creatively and effectively. Both cold and hot foams use a basic principle of agitation through special equipment that works with nitrogen oxide canisters. Eighty per cent of our atmosphere is made up of nitrogen gas, which helps create an emulsion or foams in the presence of stabilizers or gelling agents such as milk fats and gelatine. The liquid that is to be foamed is mixed with gelatine and then chilled. It is then pureed and added to the machine plugged with a nitrogen canister. Upon shaking the equipment and pressing the lever, a foamy liquid comes out which can stay as it is for a considerable amount of time. Sometimes ingredients such as soya lecithin are added to provide more stability. Figure 3.6 depicts a foaming equipment.

Encapsulation

Another recent development in the larder kitchen is the use of certain chemicals to produce a gelled liquid substance that resembles a fish roe or caviar. These are also known as false caviar or *faux caviar* and the process is known as encapsulation. The concept behind preparing these is very old, but the application has been quite prominent in the recent years.

A carbohydrate-based gelling agent obtained from a brown seaweed called *alginate* is commonly used in the preparation of this caviar. This product only gels in the presence of calcium. Any liquid fruit or vegetable juice, or any liquid is mixed with *alginate* and then the same is dropped like droplets into a calcium solution. The more the concentration of the calcium, the thicker becomes the film. Once formed, the spheres are taken out and washed. They can also be served cold or warm as desired.

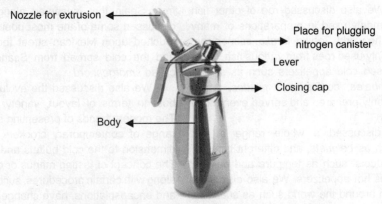

Nozzle for extrusion ◄

Place for plugging
nitrogen canister

Lever

Closing cap

Body ◄

Fig. 3.6 Foaming equipment or foamer

SUMMARY

In this chapter we discussed the products used to create sumptuous cold buffets as well as à la carte preparations for the first course known as hors d'oeuvres. Hors d'oeuvres are the first meal served as small titbits to guests to prepare them for the main meal to follow. Therefore, these products have to be flavoursome and appetizing. In this chapter, we have discussed various kinds of hors d'oeuvres such as cold, hot, and canapés. Some hors d'oeuvres are served as pass-around snacks, called butlered hors d'oeuvres whereas many are served at the table and are known as tabled hors d'oeuvres. Canapés can be served both hot and cold and the same has also been discussed in detail in Chapter 4 on sandwiches. We also discussed the important features that must be kept in mind while preparing canapés to ensure that the product is of high quality and standard.

We discussed various types of cold hors d'oeuvres, such as crudités, bouchees, shells prepared from shortcrust pastry, and choux pastry, which can be used as base for creating assortment and variety of cold appetizers. We also discussed the principles behind preparing cold savoury mousses and the role played by the various ingredients such as the base, aerator, and the jellying agent. We also discussed the role of gelatine and aspic in preparing savoury jellies and how they are used as cold hors d'oeuvres.

In this chapter, we also discussed one of the most important dishes of cold hors d'oeuvres called caviar. Caviar is a roe of the sturgeon fish and various kinds of caviars are obtained from the different types of sturgeon fish and graded accordingly. The service of caviar has always been very royal and special. We discussed various kinds of caviar and what makes them special. We also discussed roe of other fish which are commonly used in preparations of many dishes around the world. Tobiko, tarako, salmon roe, etc. are commonly used roes from various fish.

We discussed cold appetizers such as stuffed vegetables, timbales, confits, and rillettes, which are very commonly prepared and served even these days.

We also discussed a whole range of hot appetizers, such as beignets, and different types of batter-fried products, such as tempura and pakora, that are used as hot appetizers. We also discussed brochettes from around the world such as shashliks from Russia, satays from South-East Asia. Other hot hors d'oeuvres such as kebobs from Persia, Iran, and other Middle Eastern countries were described. We also read about preparing croquettes and the mise en place and work flow that needs to be followed while making the same. Among the hot appetizers, we discussed those wrapped in dough such as pigs in blanket, böreks, and spring rolls. We also discussed various types of tarts and pies that can be used as hot hors d'oeuvres. Apart from these, we also discussed some of the classical hors d'oeuvres such as devils on horseback and angels on horseback.

It is important for all the food items to be garnished, particularly the hors d'oeuvres, as they are the first course and create the first impression on the guest. Thus, we discussed various types of garnishes such as vegetables, breads, sauces that are commonly served as garnishes and also as accompaniments. It is important to serve garnish for a purpose other than just adding colour to the dish.

Appetizer is an age-old concept and it is known by different names in different parts of the world. In France, they are known as hors d'oeuvres, while in Italy they are called antipasti, which means before pasta or the main meal. We discussed various components of antipasti and also the selection of vegetarian and meat items listed in menu so that the students can understand the diverse variety that can be served in an antipasti buffet. We also discussed mezze and its components. Mezze is very popular in Arab and Mediterranean countries. Various types of dips, breads, cheese, vegetables, and meats are served in a mezze table.

Another very popular appetizer that is catching on with hotels and restaurants of modern times are tapas bars. Tapas are the elaborate spread of food from Spain that is served along with drinks. We discussed some of the most popular tapas and also touched upon Mexican street food called antojitos and the cold spread from Scandinavian countries called smorgasbord.

We also discussed the evolution of appetizers, both in terms of layout, variety, and presentation. The modern trends of presenting amuse bouche and range of contemporary crockery has given a new dimension to the cold buffets and à la carte menus. The concept of tasting menus or degustation menus along with certain procedures, such as creating foams and encapsulations, have changed the look and feel of modern appetizers.

KEY TERMS

Amuse bouche These are small plated appetizers served to the guest in a fine dining restaurant.

Amuse guele Same as *amuse bouche*

Aperitifs These are drinks served before meals to increase the appetite.

Appetizer An appetizer is a mini food item that is served as a prelude to the meal.

Barquettes These are boat-shaped savoury pastry shells.

Blinis These are thick pancakes made from rye flour or buckwheat flour.

Brioche It is yeast-leavened bread enriched with sugar, butter, and eggs.

Butlered hors d'oeuvres These are starters served passed around by stewards or butlers.

Canapés These are bite size hors d'oeuvre of vegetables, meats, etc. topped on a fancy-shaped bread.

Capeletti It is a cap-shaped paste from Italy.

Caviar It is the roe of sturgeon fish.

Celeriac This is a type of starchy tuber.

Cocktail event An standing event where hard and soft beverages are served along with hot and cold appetizers.

Cocktail sauce It is cold sauce prepared by combining mayonnaise with tomato ketchup.

Couscous It is a by-product of semolina; popular in Mediterranean cuisine.

Crostini It is the Italian version of canapé.

Crudités These are raw crisp vegetables served as hors d'oeuvre along with dips.

Degustation menus Also known as tasting menus, these are a selection of few dishes of the menu and served as miniature portions.

Dim sums These are tiny steamed appetizers from China.

Fattoush It is Mediterranean salad of diced cucumbers, peppers, and lettuce.

Fritters This is the English term for fried products.

Galette It is small and flat-shaped patty of meat or vegetable.

Gravad lax It is cured salmon with dill and black pepper.

Gremolata It is a sauce prepared from chopped ingredients in olive oil.

Haloumi It is a type of cheese from Cyprus. It is like Mozzarella, but can withstand higher temperatures and is ideal for grilling and frying.

Horikita It is a Greek salad prepared by combining cucumbers, onions, olives, tomatoes, and feta cheese.

Israeli couscous It is large-grain couscous (semolina) from the Mediterranean.

Kalamata olives It is a type of black olive from Greece.

Lavash This is a thin flat bread often served along with appetizers.

Malossol It refers to low salt content in caviar.

Melitzanosalata It is small brinjal salad served in *mezze*.

Melba toast It is thinly sliced rye bread served toasted as an accompaniment.

Mesclun It is assortment of baby lettuce.

Nuggets These are small pieces of meat that are crumbed and fried.

Orly It is kind of batter made by using flour, eggs, and beer.

Oysters These are a kind of bivalve shellfish.

Panzanella It is an Italian salad made by combining vegetables and crusty bread.

Peperonata These are roasted, skinned, and sliced bell peppers marinated in herbs and olive oil.

Porcini It is a type of Italian mushroom.

Quiche lorraine It is bacon and leek quiche.

Reggiano It is another name for parmesan cheese.

Ricotta It is Italian soft cheese.

Sanganaki It is a type of cheese from Greece usually grilled and served as hot appetizer.

Sashimi A Japanese dish consisting of raw slices of fish is called sashimi.

Tabled hors d'oeuvres These are starters served at the guest's table.

Tabouleh It is salad prepared by combining broken wheat and chopped parsley.

Tapenade It is a paste of ingredients, generally olives and nuts.

Tempura These are fried appetizers from Japan.

Tabasco It is a type of chilli sauce from the USA.

Tortillas It is a flat flour bread from Mexico.

Wonton skins These are readily available sheets made from flour.

Water crackers These are thin crisp savoury biscuits served along with cheese.

Zakuski These are appetizers from Russia.

CONCEPT REVIEW QUESTIONS

1. Describe an appetizer or an hors d'oeuvre.
2. What are different types of hors d'oeuvres and how are these classified?
3. What criteria would you keep in mind while preparing and serving hors d'oeuvres?
4. Describe a canapé. How is it different from a *crostini* and open-faced sandwich?
5. List at least five points that you would keep in mind while preparing canapés.
6. What are *crudités* and how are they served?
7. Explain how choux pastry can be used to prepare hors d'oeuvre.
8. List two ways in which puff pastry can be used for preparing bases for hors d'oeuvre.
9. Describe a mousse and its components.
10. What is caviar and how is it harvested?
11. Name three types of true caviars and describe their difference.
12. What is the grading of caviar and what do you understand by the word *malossol*?
13. What is the pressed Russian caviar called and how is it used?
14. Name at least three other fish used for making caviar and name the roe obtained from these fish.
15. What is a *timbale* and how are they prepared?
16. Differentiate between confits, *rillettes*, and *rillons*.
17. Describe a *beignet* and list at least two types.
18. What are brochettes? Name at least two types of brochettes.
19. Define a bruschetta and how is it different from a *crostini*.
20. What are *croquettes*? What would be the procedure of crumbing the same?
21. Describe at least three types of dough wrapped hors d'oeuvres.
22. What are *böreks* and *spanakopita*?
23. Differentiate between a mini pizza and a *calzone*.
24. Describe a *quiche lorraine*.
25. What is the difference between a scotch pie and pot pie?
26. What is the difference between *angels on horseback* and *devils on horseback*?
27. What is the importance of a garnish in hors d'oeuvre?
28. What are *antipasti* and what does it comprise of?
29. List at least 5 types of vegetarian and meat *antipasti*.
30. What is a *mezze*? How is it known in other parts of Middle Eastern countries?
31. Name at least five dips that one could serve on *mezze*.
32. Name at least three salads that can be served on *mezze*.
33. Name three hot *mezze*.
34. What are tapas and how are they different from *antipasti* and *mezze*?
35. List at least five types of tapas.
36. Write short notes on *antojitos*, *smorgasbord*, and *zakuski*.
37. Describe the evolution of hors d'oeuvre and mention how they have changed over the years.
38. What do you understand by the term *amuse bouche* or *amuse guele*?
39. Describe the points to be kept in mind while plating *amuse bouche*.
40. Describe a tasting or a degustation menu.
41. Explain the use of foaming machine in the modern presentations.
42. What is encapsulation and how is it useful?

PROJECT WORK

1. In groups of five, conduct a market survey of hotels and speciality restaurants that specialize in serving *antipasti*, *mezze*, tapas, and other specialities. Record your observations with regard to the choice of the menu, ingredients, and equipment used in cooking and serving and share your findings with the other groups.
2. In groups of five plan a menu for 100 people. Each group should research about one particular style of appetizer layouts such as *antipasti*,

zakuski, *mezze*, *mezzethes*, *mezedakia*, tapas, smorgasbord, and *antojitos*. The menu should comprise at least five vegetarian and five meat items along with condiments and accompaniments such as breads and pickles. Share the menu with each other and see what is common to most of these. Now prepare these items in the lab kitchen and present to the other teams.

3. In groups of five each, research at least two *amuse bouche* for a fine dining menu of various cuisines such as Chinese, Indian, Italian, Greek, and Japanese. Prepare the same in lab kitchen and present for evaluation.

4. In groups of five, research about various kinds of crockery that you would use for presenting hors d'oeuvre.

CHAPTER 4

SANDWICHES

Learning Objectives

After reading this chapter, you should be able to
- understand the basic concept of sandwiches and their types
- comprehend the various parts of a sandwich and their importance
- appreciate the range and types of sandwiches, such as hot and cold, and their sub-classifications
- prepare various kinds of sandwiches that are served in hotels and restaurants
- analyse the salient features and techniques used in making quality sandwiches
- claim an insight into the basic features of storage and service of sandwiches

INTRODUCTION

The most basic definition of a sandwich is two slices of bread enclosed with a filling that could be meat, vegetables, or cheese. Sandwiches are named after John Montagu, the fourth Earl of Sandwich, in the UK. It is believed that he was a chronic gambler who acquired the habit of eating his meal of sliced cold meat pressed between two slices of bread, at the gambling table. He did it so that he would not have to leave the gambling table to have his meals. Although the term sandwich is of recent origin, the concept of eating fillings between bread slices dates back to many centuries. It was a customary practice in France to feed the labourers working in farms with sliced cold meat sandwiched between crusty slices of brown bread. This would give the necessary nutrition and it would be fairly easy to eat such food. Even people setting out on journeys would pack sliced and cooked meat pressed between slices of bread. It was not until the nineteenth century that sandwiches started to feature on the menus of hotels and restaurants.

In modern hotels, sandwiches are classified into a category of foods known as 'convenience food'. England and the USA are the largest consumers of sandwiches. Even today, packed food for guests contains sandwiches as part of the meal. Sandwiches are skilfully and creatively made by using various kinds of breads and fillings. Nowadays, the sandwiches are not just limited to a simple filling, but can consist of composite fillings in several layers of bread which can be served hot or cold. Some sandwiches are served without a covering of another slice of bread and are known as open-faced sandwiches. Some sandwiches have exotic fillings and can be served as snacks in very high-end cocktail functions.

In this chapter, we will discuss various components of a sandwich and types of sandwiches that have always been popular on the menus of hotels worldwide. We will also discuss the contemporary approach to sandwich making in hotels.

PARTS OF SANDWICHES

There are four major components or parts of any sandwich:
- Bread
- Spread
- Filling
- Garnish

Let us discuss each of these in detail as understanding of these components will go a long way in helping you prepare various kinds of sandwiches.

Bread

Various kinds of breads are used for preparing sandwiches. In olden times, any available bread could be used for preparing sandwiches, but with the passage of time as sandwiches became popular, it became important to use the range of breads available around the world. White plain bread made in large rectangle moulds is the most commonly used bread for making sandwiches because of its neutral flavour and shape that facilitates the preparing and portioning of a sandwich. This large bread is also commonly known as sandwich bread in hotels. Contrasting breads are used these days to provide variety to the sandwiches on the menu. Due to healthier eating trends, wholewheat and multigrain breads are also getting popular with chefs. Sandwiches are best prepared to order. However, this might not always be possible, especially in volume cooking, where the bread needs to be stored under damp cloth, so that it does not dry out. Over a period of time and research, some bread has gotten associated with typical kinds of fillings that are followed till date. For example, fillings made with fish are generally sandwiched in brown bread, whereas roasted chicken is filled in white bread. Some special breads, such as German sour dough bread, are much stronger in flavour and complements the dried and salted meat such as *salami, bresoala,* and ham. Breads for sandwiches can be toasted, grilled, or served plain. Some of the commonly used breads are discussed in Table 4.1.

Table 4.1 Various types of breads used for sandwiches

Bread	Description	Photograph
Sandwich loaf	Also known as pullman loaf, it is a white bread made in a large mould that yields a bread of size 6 × 6 inches. It is the most preferred bread because of its neutral flavour. The bread is baked in loaves and then sliced to prepare sandwiches. A range of sandwiches can be prepared using this type of bread because of its unique square shape that allows the sandwich to be cut into various shapes such as triangles and finger shapes.	
French baguette	This crusty bread from France is a long bread ranging between 12 and 24 inches with a diameter of 2–3 inches. The unique shape of this bread allows the chefs to make sandwiches known as foot longs. The bread can be split open and various types of fillings can be put inside to make sandwiches.	
Rye bread	Rye flour is used for preparing breads that have more intense flavour. This brown coloured bread is commonly used for making seafood sandwiches such as smoked salmon and creamy tuna. It is common to see brown breads being used for seafood fillings.	
Wholewheat bread	As people are becoming more health conscious worldwide, wholewheat breads are gaining popularity in the preparations of various kinds of sandwiches. These breads can be made into various shapes depending upon the type of sandwich required. These can be baked into logs like baguettes or like a loaf.	
Pumpernickel	This dark bread from Germany is normally made with rye flour but small amounts of wheat flour are added to the dough to lighten the texture. The bread has a dark colour, dense texture, and a sour and earthy flavour. It is generally consumed with smoked sausages and meat, marinated fish and cheese.	
Pita bread	*Pita* is a Lebanese bread that is baked on hot stones or on the hearth of an oven. The bread puffs up when baked and it is normally split open into half to create pockets that can be stuffed with various kinds of fillings to create a range of sandwiches. The famous *gyro* sandwich from Greece is made using *pita* bread.	
Soft rolls	A range of shapes is made using the soft roll dough that can be used for preparing sandwiches. The round flat shape is commonly used for preparing burgers, whereas 6 inches long rod-shaped soft roll bread is used for making chicken frank sandwiches also known as hot dogs.	

(Contd)

Table 4.1 (Contd)

Bread	Description	Photograph
Bagel	The bread is made with both refined flour, wholemeal flour, and multigrain flour. It can include vegetable oil, or margarine or butter, along with eggs and yeast. After shaping and proving, the bread dough is poached or steamed for a minute or two and then given an egg wash and baked, which helps in the formation of a glossy crust and dense interior. They are served commonly in breakfast. Bagels are Jewish bread, which resemble a doughnut with a hole in the centre but it can also be served as sandwiches. Smoked salmon in mini bagels are very popular canapés.	
Multigrain bread	This bread is made with different cereals which include wheat, corn, rye, millet, oats, malted wheat, sunflower and sesame seeds. More of a health fad, this type of bread goes into the preparation of sandwiches for health-conscious clients.	
Sour dough bread	This German bread is made from a mixture of flours such as rye, oats, and multigrain, that are left to ferment to develop flavours and dark colour. Being intense in flavour, it pairs up well with cream cheese and smoked meat.	
Ciabatta	This bread from Italy is a crusty and has a soft interior. The flat slipper shape of this bread makes it ideal for preparing both close and open-faced sandwiches.	
Focaccia	This bread has a lot of olive oil, thus it needs to be kneaded for a longer time, which enhances its taste as well as texture. The texture is a hard and sharp crumb contrasting with a soft interior. There are many different flavours, such as tomatoes, olives, cheese, and nuts, which can be added in this bread. Prior to baking, a lot of olive oil is spread on the surface and fingers are dug into the dough to make indentations. This helps the oil seep in and give more flavour to the bread. It is used for making open-faced sandwiches.	

Spread

Spread is a creamy paste applied on the surface of the bread. This is done for the following reasons.

- It provides moistness to the slices so that the resulting sandwich is not dry to eat.
- It provides contrasting flavours such as mustard with dried salted meat or creamy mayonnaise with roasted chicken.
- It helps in preservation as the layer of butter on a slice of bread will seal the pores of the bread and prevent microbial growth.

Table 4.2 Various kinds of spread used in sandwiches

Spread	Description
Plain butter	This is the most commonly used spread. Both unsalted and salted butter can be creamed until light and fluffy and then spread on the surface of the bread. Americans also use peanut butter for some sandwiches, which is very popular in USA.
Compound butter	This butter can be a combination of other ingredients combined with butter. Paprika butter, herb butter, anchovy butter, parsley butter, garlic butter, etc., are all examples of compound butter that can be used as spread on bread.
Mayonnaise	Mayonnaise can be used plain or flavoured like compound butter and applied on bread as a spread. It can also be used as a filling by mixing it with various other ingredients. Many chefs mix mayonnaise and butter as a spread for sandwiches.
Cheese spreads	Various types of cream cheese are used as bread spreads. Smoked salmon on rye bread smeared with Philadelphia cream cheese is a very traditional sandwich commonly found on the menus of hotels. Other cheeses can be grated and creamed with ingredients such as cream, butter, or mayonnaise and used as a spread.
Mustard	Mustard is a very commonly used ingredient in spreads. Various kinds of mustard such as creamy *Dijon* mustard paste from France or grainy *pommery* mustard from France and Germany is commonly used alone or paired with mayonnaise before being applied on the bread.
Herb and spice paste	Various kinds of herb and spice pastes such as pesto from Italy, mint chutney from India, *chermoula* from South America, olive paste from France, and *harissa* from Morocco are used as spreads. Refer the chapter on sauces in the book *Food Production Operations* to know more about contemporary sauces that can be used as spreads.
Tomato ketchup	This sauce is often used as a spread for certain sandwiches. The tangy and sweet taste of sandwiches using this sauce is, however, not very popular in high-end hotels and restaurants.

- It helps the filling to stick to the surface of the breads.
- It is used to create variety on the menu.

Chefs can be very creative with the spreads as a range of ingredients are available to create various kinds of spreads. The only point that one needs to keep in mind is that the spread should be creamy enough to ease out the application of the same on the bread. Some of the commonly used spreads are described in Table 4.2.

Fillings

This is the most important part of the sandwich as it gives taste, texture, flavour, and name to the sandwich. A filling can be called the heart of the sandwich. Traditionally, sandwiches were combinations of roasted and sliced meat paired with greens such as lettuce, but with creative chefs and the demand for variety, innumerable kinds of fillings are now available for the discerning customer. Vegetarian options are also unlimited as the guest can choose from a simple cucumber and cheese sandwich to more complex sandwiches such as creamy corn with grilled peppers and so on. A few of the most commonly used fillings in sandwiches are described in Table 4.3.

Table 4.3 Various kinds of fillings used in sandwiches

Fillings	Description
Meat	Various kinds of meat such as chicken, turkey, lamb, beef, pork, and pork products (discussed in Chapter 2) can be used as a filling in sandwiches. The meat can be cooked and processed in various ways depending upon the type of sandwich. Some meat are roasted and sliced, whereas some are grilled and used. Meat could be air-dried or smoked as well to add variety and flavour to sandwiches. Though chicken and roast beef are the most popular choice when it comes to meat, one can use almost any kind of meat as filling. Meat can also be prepared into *pâtés* and *terrines* as discussed in Chapter 3 and used as filling in the sandwiches. Game birds, such as turkey and duck, are also a popular choice with customers.
Vegetables	Various kinds of vegetables are used as fillings in sandwiches. Lettuce is a classical example and is found in almost every sandwich. Vegetables can be grilled, sliced, or diced and mixed with various kinds of spreads listed above or used on their own. Many vegetables are combined, along with meat. Smoked salmon and cucumber with cream cheese is one such classical filling of a sandwich.
Seafood	Seafood is used in a variety of ways in preparing sandwiches. It can be cooked, canned, cured, and smoked. Seafood sandwich is traditionally made using brown bread and can be combined with other ingredients to make nutritious and tasty fillings. Canned tuna and boiled egg paired with mayonnaise is a popular filling. Many chefs have started using tempura fried soft shell crabs and prawns to prepare sandwiches that result in a crunchy filling. Other popular seafood fillings are smoked fish such as salmon, trout and herring, sardines, shrimps, prawns, deep-fried *calamari*, etc.
Salads	A range of salads can be used as fillings for sandwiches, but mayonnaise-based salads are far more popular because of their moist textures. Russian salad, coleslaw are some such examples. Refer the chapter on salads in the book *Food Production Operations* to know more about salads.
Cheese	Cheese is another popular filling used in a sandwich. It can be used sliced or prepared as a spread. Usually, cheese is paired up with meat or vegetables but one can use it all by itself too.
Eggs	Eggs have always been a popular ingredient because of its nutritious characteristics and easy availability. Eggs are a natural source of protein and on combining with starch like bread and fat like spreads, it forms a complete and balanced meal. Eggs can be poached, boiled, scrambled, or prepared into omelettes before being used as a filling. Boiled and diced eggs combined with mayonnaise are very popular. Single fried eggs are classically used as a filling in club sandwiches.

Garnish

Though every sandwich does not need to be garnished, there are some that are garnished before service. Garnishing is mostly done in case of open-faced sandwiches which have been discussed later in this chapter. Closed sandwiches do not require any garnish but sometimes ingredients such as olives and gherkins are secured, along with a small stick and inserted into the sandwich. The prime reason for the same is to secure both the slices together and facilitate in eating. Some of the commonly used garnishes in sandwiches are highlighted in Table 4.4.

Table 4.4 Various kinds of garnishes used in sandwiches

Garnish	Description
Olives	Various kinds of olives such as *Kalamata*, queen's olives, olives stuffed with almonds can be used along with a cocktail stick to secure the filling in the sandwich.
Gherkins	These are small cucumbers that are pickled in brine. These can be used whole or sliced to garnish a sandwich.
Capers	These small round salted or brined berries are classical garnish for smoked salmon sandwiches. These can be sprinkled over the filling. It should be used sparingly as they are very sour.
Sun-dried tomatoes	These are usually used in Italian sandwiches. Tomatoes are marinated with olive oil and sliced garlic and left to sun dry in the open or in a low heat oven. After the tomatoes are dried, they are preserved in olive oil and used as required.
Herbs	Fresh sprigs of herbs are a wonderful garnish in open-faced sandwiches. Refer Chapter 5 for various kinds of herbs that can be used as garnishes.
Lettuce	Usually small lettuce such as watercress, lamb's lettuce, and micro greens are used as garnishes for open-faced sandwiches.

TYPES OF SANDWICHES

A wide variety of sandwiches are available for guests to choose from. Classification of sandwiches into subgroups is necessary to facilitate easy remembrance and to maintain a level of consistency around the globe.

Sandwiches are basically classified into two types—hot and cold—and are further divided into subtypes depending upon the methods of preparation and the occasion for which they are being made. Let us discuss these in detail.

Cold Sandwiches

As the name suggests these sandwiches are served cold or at room temperature. Many such sandwiches are made using pullman loaf, but a variety of other breads can also be used for this purpose. Table 4.5 describes some cold sandwiches that are popular in hotels and restaurants around the world.

Table 4.5 Types of cold sandwiches (see also Plate 3)

Type of sandwich	Description	Photograph
Conventional sandwiches	Also known as closed sandwiches or lunch-box sandwiches, these are traditional sandwiches in which the filling is enclosed between two slices of white or brown bread, along with spreads and garnish. These sandwiches are usually served sliced into half diagonally to make two equal triangle shapes. The sides can be trimmed or left on depending upon the standards set by the establishment.	
Buffet sandwiches	These sandwiches are prepared like conventional sandwiches, but the sides are trimmed and the sandwich is cut into small fancy shapes such as squares, triangles, and fingers. These are also known as afternoon tea sandwiches.	

(Contd)

Table 4.5 (Contd)

Type of sandwich	Description	Photograph
Continental sandwiches	These sandwiches are traditionally prepared using French bread sticks, also known as baguettes. Whole bread stick is buttered and packed with various kinds of fillings. They can be served whole or cut into smaller pieces and served. When served whole, this sandwich is known as foot long because of the size of the baguette.	
Open-faced sandwiches	As the name suggests, these sandwiches are served with the filling neatly arranged on a slice of bread. Since these sandwiches are served open, it is important that they are decorated and garnished with prime quality ingredients and that they look attractive. A combination of fillings, such as rolled ham and shaving of cheese with fresh sprigs of herbs, can be used to prepare open-faced sandwiches. These are also known as Scandinavian sandwiches, as they are commonly prepared in Scandinavian countries (Finland, Norway, and Denmark.) These are always served with the crust on. Miniature varieties of these sandwiches are known as canapés and are popularly served as cocktail snacks and hors d'oeuvres in French classical menu. Open-faced sandwiches are also known as bruschettas in Italy and can be served as snacks or as an appetizer.	
Rolled sandwiches	These sandwiches are prepared by buttering a large slice of bread with the required filling. It is then rolled tightly and secured in a plastic film. The sandwiches are allowed to chill at least for an hour and then served with the sides trimmed. Few of the items such as *kathi* roll* from India, and *shawarma** from Lebanon can be classified as rolled sandwiches.	
Pinwheel sandwiches	These sandwiches are prepared in the same manner as rolled sandwiches. The only difference is that it is prepared on a long slice of bread and rolled until the sandwich is at least 5–6 cm in diameter. The roll is then sliced into 1 cm thick slices and served with accompaniments such as tartare sauce and French fries.	
Ribbon sandwiches	These sandwiches are prepared by layering white and brown slices of bread with colourful fillings until a square block is obtained. The block is then chilled until firm and then it is sliced into 1 cm thick slices and served.	

* Both *kathi* roll and *shawarma* are served hot.

Hot Sandwiches

These sandwiches are prepared and served hot. It is not necessary that they are served piping hot, but the sandwiches are served from warm to hot temperatures. The three main methods of preparing hot sandwiches are grilling, toasting, and bevelling. To understand these terms, let us discuss them as follows.

Grilled Sandwiches

These are the most popular of all hot sandwiches. In the olden times, the concept of hot sandwiches was limited to a slice of roasted hot meat between two slices of bread. The availability and range of equipment, such as sandwich grillers, have changed the way hot sandwiches are prepared and served. Sandwich grillers are also known as contact grills as they have two surfaces that can be closed like a box, trapping the sandwich between two metal sheets that are available in different designs such as ridged or squares. Sandwiches can also be grilled on a hot plate or simply on a pan. The advantage of using a contact grill is that it helps to seal the sandwich together and also gives a uniform colouring on all the sides. Some classical grilled sandwiches are discussed in Table 4.6.

Table 4.6 Types of grilled sandwiches (see also Plate 4)

Sandwich	Description	Photograph
Grilled ham and cheese	An old time favourite of all, this sandwich is prepared using pullman loaf. The two slices of bread are buttered on both the sides. A slice of cheese such as *emmental* or *gruyere* is placed in such a way that it covers the entire slice. A slice of sandwich ham is placed on top of the cheese and sprinkled with salt and pepper. The sandwich is covered with another slice of buttered bread and grilled until the cheese has melted. The sandwich can be served cut into half or in triangles and served with French fries, tartare sauce, and pickled vegetables.	
Croque monsieur	This famous sandwich from France is prepared by enclosing a slice of ham between two slices of cheese, which are then enclosed between two slices of buttered bread and grilled or pan-fried until the cheese has melted and the sandwich is golden brown. The sandwich is cut diagonally into two triangles and served with tartare sauce, French fries, and green salad.	
Croque madame	It is similar to *croque monsieur*; the only difference is that a shallow-fried egg is served on top of the sandwich.	
Stammer max	This sandwich is like an open-faced sandwich in which a slice of bread is grilled or pan-fried in clarified butter and arranged on a serving plate. Sautéed *lardons* of bacon are placed on top of the warm bread and topped with single fried egg. This sandwich can be garnished with fresh watercress leaves.	

(Contd)

Table 4.6 *(Contd)*

Sandwich	Description	Photograph
Hot dog	This popular sandwich is prepared by grilling chicken franks and hot dog bun. The hot dog bun is split open, buttered, and grilled. Grilled chicken franks are placed inside along with mustard spread and sometimes lettuce.	
Gyro	This sandwich is from Greece and is pronounced as *yee roh*. Various kinds of meat, such as grilled pork, roasted beef, along with lettuce, mustard, mayonnaise, and tomatoes, are stuffed in grilled *pita* bread and served with pickles and accompaniments. *Gyro* can be served rolled up or served in an open *pita*.	
Burgers	These are prepared in various ways. One can slice the burger into two or three parts depending upon the type of burger and the fillings. Usually, the burger bun is grilled and sandwiched with a grilled patty of minced chicken, lamb, or beef. The burger is garnished with sliced tomatoes, caramelized onions, cheese, and mustard spreads. It is often eaten as a meal and thus, served with a small portion of salad, French fries, and sauces such as mustard and tartare sauce.	
Panini	Panini is an Italian sandwich that is prepared by slicing focaccia bread into two or more layers. It is packed with different kinds of fillings and grilled in a contact grill, which is pressed so that it flattens the sandwich.	

Toasted Sandwiches

These are popular hot sandwiches on the menu as they use less butter as compared to grilled sandwiches. A wide range of sandwiches is prepared in hotels using this method. The toasted sandwiches can be served hot as well as cold and are usually served with the sides trimmed off, as they become too crisp and cumbersome to eat. Though the choice of trimming the sandwiches varies from one establishment to another, the general rule is that grilled sandwiches are served untrimmed whereas toasted and plain sandwiches are served with sides trimmed off. Some popular toasted sandwiches are described in Table 4.7.

Table 4.7 Popular toasted sandwiches

Sandwich	Description	Photograph
Club sandwich	This is the most popular sandwich and is commonly served in almost every hotel in the world. It is prepared by using white pullman loaf. Three slices of bread are toasted and spread with mayonnaise or butter. The first slice is topped with lettuce, sliced tomato, and single fried egg. The second slice is buttered on both sides and placed on top of the first slice. The second slice is topped with grilled or roasted chicken and grilled bacon rashers. The third slice is placed buttered side down and the sandwich is firmly pressed to secure the filling. The crusts are trimmed off and the sandwich is cut into two triangles or into four small triangles and served with coleslaw salad and French fries. Because of the thickness of the sandwich, it is a good idea to secure each triangle with a cocktail stick embedded with olives.	
Bookmaker	This sandwich is made by toasting two slices of white bread and buttering them well. Grilled minute steak is placed on the toasted bread and mustard paste is smeared on top. Another buttered toast is placed on top and the sandwich is pressed between two thick metal plates so that the juices from the steak moisten the bread. The sandwich is then sliced into three rectangles and served.	
Denver	This sandwich is prepared by toasting and buttering two slices of bread. The first slice is topped with chicken liver pâté and slice of smoked gammon or ham. It is topped with sautéed onions, salt, and pepper and covered with another slice. Reheat the sandwich and serve cut into two without the crusts.	
Western sandwich	This sandwich is prepared by toasting and buttering two slices of pullman loaf. The first slice is topped with shredded lettuce, pimento stuffed sliced olives, sliced roasted beef, and roasted walnuts. More roasted beef and shredded lettuce are topped and seasoned with salt and pepper. The second buttered toast is closed and sandwich is pressed firmly and served with crust removed along with an avocado dip called *guacamole*.	
Danish hot tartare	This unique sandwich is made by using one slice of bread that is toasted on one side and minced steak is spread on the other side. The sandwich is pan-fried in clarified butter until golden brown on both sides. The top is garnished with sautéed onion rings, sliced gherkins, and quartered tomatoes.	

Bevelled Sandwiches

These sandwiches are prepared in a special equipment known as *bevelled* toaster. It helps to seal the edges of the bread, thereby enclosing the filling inside them. Certain models of this equipment can also cut the sandwich into two triangles or four triangles while sealing all the edges.

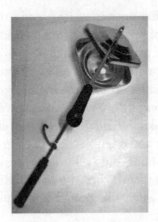

Fig. 4.1 Types of *bevelled* toasters

This kind of sandwich is very popular in north India where the filling of curried potatoes, curried vegetables such as cauliflower, beans, and green peas, is put between two slices of bread and grilled in a bevelled toaster. There are two kinds of models available: one that can be used for cooking on a flame directly and an electrical model as shown in Fig. 4.1.

One can use any kind of filling for *bevelled* toasts. The toast is served hot with a small portion of salad and French fries.

MAKING SANDWICHES

Making sandwich is an art that has evolved over the years. Chefs and connoisseurs have perfected many recipes and documented many salient features of the ingredients to produce the finest sandwiches on the menus of five-star establishments and even fast food outlets. Some of the food joints specialize only in sandwiches and are known as sandwich bars. In hotels, sandwiches are usually prepared by the larder kitchen and hot accompaniments, such as French fries, are provided by the hot kitchen.

We have read in this chapter that the four basic components of sandwiches are bread, spread, filling, and garnish. Whatever may be the type and kind of sandwich, these components will be common except the garnish, which might not be used in every sandwich. Some of the tips and features regarding the use of each of the components of sandwiches are discussed in the succeeding subsections.

Guidelines for the Use of Bread

Bread is the main component of a sandwich. It can be used as a base for open-faced sandwiches, or two or more than two slices can be used to hold the fillings. The following are some significant points or guidelines that must be observed while using breads for sandwiches.

- A wide variety of breads, as discussed in Table 4.1, can be used in preparation of sandwiches. However, the general rule is that fish fillings are used with brown breads and other meat in white bread. Also, due to consciousness about healthy eating, many types of bread, such as multigrain loaves, cereal breads, wholegrain breads. are being used to prepare sandwiches.

- If the bread is supposed to be toasted, then it should be done in a toaster that evenly browns the bread. One must adjust the settings on the equipment, so that each time a consistent brown colour is achieved.
- For making toasted sandwiches, always use one-day-old bread. Fresh bread is difficult to slice and crumbles easily. Plain sandwiches can be made with fresh bread, that is, at least 6-hours old as this helps the bread to slice easily.
- Ensure that the bread is firm and not too moist when sliced, otherwise it will become soggy when the spread and filling are arranged and it will break when lifted for eating.
- The thickness of the slice of the bread varies for different types of sandwiches, but the most commonly used thickness is around 8–9 mm.

Guidelines for the Use of Spread

The spread has many uses apart from just flavouring the sandwich. It is usually used to prevent the bread from getting soggy. It also lends its unique taste and texture to the sandwiches. The following are the guidelines for using spreads in sandwiches.

- Various kinds of spreads are used, as discussed in Table 4.2, and the most commonly used spread is butter.
- Butter should be creamed well to soften as that would allow it to evenly spread on the slice of the bread. It is important to cover the entire slice, including the corners of the slice with butter as butter forms a seal over the slice and prevents it from soaking moisture that would result in a soggy and wet sandwich.
- When preparing sandwiches that require three slices of bread, it is important to butter both sides of the middle slice.
- The spread should be fresh and the flavour should complement the filling and overall taste of the sandwich.

Guidelines for the Use of Filling

As we read earlier in the chapter, filling is the most important part of a sandwich as it gives taste, texture, flavour, and also name to the sandwich. Varieties of fillings, as discussed in Table 4.3, can be used. Following are the guidelines on using fillings for the sandwiches.

- The fillings should be fresh and handled with gloves, as the sandwiches will not be cooked further. Hygiene is of utmost importance while preparing sandwiches as these could be an easy source of food poisoning.
- Fillings should be evenly spread around on the sandwich and should be seasoned well, as it is not possible to open up a sandwich and season it if it is underseasoned.
- When preparing salads for sandwiches, ensure that the ingredients used in the salads, such as lettuce, are drained well or else they will make the sandwiches soggy.
- Avoid using very strong flavours in case of fillings.

Guidelines for the Use of Garnish

Garnishes are mainly used for adding visual appeal to the sandwiches besides making the fillings secure in certain cases. There are many types of garnishes, as discussed in Table 4.4, which are commonly used as garnish. Few guidelines to adding garnish to sandwiches are as follows.

- Not all sandwiches are garnished but whenever garnish is used, it needs to be fresh and crisp.
- Micro greens and baby lettuces often need to be refreshed in chilled water and then dried before being used as a garnish.
- Use garnish that adds colour and texture to the sandwich.

STORING SANDWICHES

Sandwiches must always be prepared fresh and to order. This might not be possible when preparing for large functions or buffets, but in that case the sandwiches should be stored in a cold room covered with a wet cotton duster, so that the bread does not dry out. Plain and toasted sandwiches are often served with the crust of the bread removed; but while storing sandwiches for later use, one must keep the crust on and cut it only at the time of service. Cutting the crust off in advance might wilt the sides, which would give it an old and wilted look.

Sandwiches are often sold in gourmet shops and are one of the most favoured packed foods, due to ease of service and eating. If the sandwiches are to be displayed or packed, these should be packed in a plastic wrap. This helps the sandwich to retain its shape and also helps in keeping it moist and fresh. Nowadays, special boxes are available for packing and displaying sandwiches which make them look attractive.

MODERN APPROACH TO SANDWICHES IN HOTELS

We all know that presentation of food is constantly evolving and chefs are striving to create dishes that can make their establishment unique. With the world coming closer and a whole lot of information available on the Internet, people are creating sandwiches by using various kinds of breads and fillings that were almost unheard of a few decades ago. A humble sandwich of two slices of bread filled with sliced or minced meat has undergone a lot of transformation. A few contemporary trends in sandwich making are enlisted as follows.

1. Range of breads from around the world, such as Jewish bagels, *challah*, kaiser rolls from Germany, and ciabatta from Italy, are being used to prepare a variety of sandwiches.
2. Traditional sandwiches, such as club sandwich that is prepared by using white sandwich bread, is often made with other varieties of bread such as ciabatta. The concept of the fillings however remains the same.
3. Various creative fillings, such as tempura fried seafood, meat, and vegetables with Japanese mayonnaise, are commonly seen on menus these days.

4. With people becoming more and more health conscious, it is common to see many types of healthy and nutritious sandwiches made by using wholewheat bread and sprouted salad fillings.

5. Presentation platters have also improved the overall look of the sandwiches. Choice of stoneware, glass, and geometrical-shaped crockery has enhanced the visual appeal of presentations. Figure 4.2 shows various sandwich presentations seen on platters of five-star establishments and speciality restaurants.

6. Sandwiches are cut into attractive shapes using cutters and moulds to enhance their appearance.

In short, we can say that the modern trends of sandwich making have focused more on presentation of the product and combining flavours from all around the world. It is now common to see a chicken tikka sandwich, which was probably unheard of few years ago, but people are being experimental with food and they need variety and change in flavours.

Fig. 4.2 Modern presentations of sandwiches (see also Plate 4)

SUMMARY

Sandwiches have always been a balanced meal. It was customary in France to serve sandwiches to the labourers working in the fields, as these would provide the required carbohydrates (from the bread), protein (from the meat used as a filling), and fats (from the butter or mayonnaise that was used as spread). Several centuries down the line, components such as breads, fillings, spreads remain constant and the tradition carries on.

This chapter presented the evolution of the sandwich from a simple dish that served as a convenient meal to exotic presentations seen in plush hotels and gourmet shops today. Earlier sandwiches never featured on the menu of high-end restaurants, as they were considered to be quick meals or snacks that were the need of the hour and any leftover meat

were stuffed or rolled between few pieces of bread and eaten. The chefs of today have gone a step ahead. Creativity and the demands of the modern customer have literally forced the food industry to design and create gourmet sandwiches that can be featured on the menus today. Many food and beverage (F&B) outlets specialize only in sandwiches and they have a huge variety to offer.

In this chapter, we discussed each of the sandwich components under a separate heading. A range of commonly used breads in sandwich preparation was discussed, although the ones listed in the chapter are only selected and not a complete list. To read more about breads, refer the chapter on breads in the book *Food Production Operations*. We also discussed a range of spreads that can be used in making sandwiches. The role of spread and its importance in making sandwiches were discussed, so that one can appreciate the use of ingredients while preparing sandwiches. Though the fillings used in sandwiches can be endless and would depend upon the creativity of the chef, yet we have tried to broadly classify the fillings into groups for the reader to understand what range of fillings can be used for preparing sandwiches. There are some classical sandwiches that use a particular kind of filling only, but chefs can create their own unique sandwiches as well.

In this chapter, we also discussed two major types of sandwiches: hot and cold. Each of these was discussed in detail along with illustrations. The recipes of these sandwiches are included in the CD. Apart from hot sandwiches, such as grilled and toasted varieties, we have also listed a fairly new kind of hot sandwich, called *bevelled* sandwich that is prepared in a special *bevelled* toaster.

We also discussed the guidelines for preparing good quality sandwiches under various headings such as breads, fillings, and spreads. The aim is that the student understands the importance of each step and understands the significance of detailing and the principle underlying each and every step of sandwich making. We concluded this chapter by discussing the storage of sandwiches and modern trends in sandwich making.

KEY TERMS

Anchovy   It is a small salted fish often sold canned.

Calamari   It is a term used for seafood comprising squids and cuttlefish. These aquatic animals are also referred to as shellfish.

Chermoula   It is a South American paste of herbs such as parsley, coriander roots, and chillies.

Convenience foods   It is a term used for food items that are ready-to-eat and do not require elaborate crockery and set-up for service.

Gammon   The whole smoked and brined leg of pork is called gammon.

Gherkins   These are small pickled cucumbers.

Harissa   It is a spicy paste of red chillies, black pepper, parley, cilantro, and mint from Morocco.

Hearth   The stone floor of an oven is referred to as hearth.

Hors d'oeuvre   It is a term for the first course of French classical menu which refers to starters.

Kalamata olive   These are popular black olives from Greece.

Kathi roll   It is an Indian sandwich prepared by rolling flat bread with a filling.

Micro greens   This is a term used for small sprouts of vegetables.

Open-faced sandwich   It is a type of sandwich wherein the filling is arranged on one slice of bread only and is left open and not covered with another slice of bread.

Paprika   Chilli powder from Hungary is called paprika.

Philadelphia cream cheese   It is a type of cream cheese popular in the USA. It is mainly used in desserts.

Pimento   These are some kind of sweet peppers.

Queen's olive   Large sized olives are also called queen's olives.

Sandwich bread   This is large white bread used for making sandwiches. It is also known as pullman loaf.

Shawarma   This is Lebanese sandwich prepared by rolling *pita* bread with roasted meat.

Soft-shell crabs   These are crabs with soft shell that can be eaten along with the shells.

Tartare sauce   It is a sauce which is prepared by mixing mayonnaise sauce with pickled onions, chopped parsley, gherkins, etc. It is served with snacks as a dip.

Tempura   This is the Japanese style of batter-fried products.

CONCEPT REVIEW QUESTIONS

1. How did the word sandwich originate?
2. Describe the major components of a sandwich.
3. Name at least five breads that can be used for preparing sandwiches. List the speciality of each bread.
4. What is a pullman loaf? Why is it the most popular sandwich bread?
5. What criteria would you keep in mind while choosing the breads for sandwiches?

6. Name at least three health breads that can be used for making sandwiches.
7. In which ways can *pita* bread be used as sandwiches?
8. Write down any three uses of spreads on sandwiches.
9. Name at least three types of spreads that one can use for sandwiches.
10. What are the kinds of fillings that one can use in sandwiches?
11. What is the difference between continental and buffet sandwiches?
12. How are continental sandwiches different from open-faced sandwiches?
13. Name and describe at least three types of rolled sandwiches.
14. What is the difference between pinwheel sandwich and ribbon sandwich?
15. How is *croque monsieur* different from *croque madame*?
16. Describe a *gyro* sandwich.
17. Describe the procedure of making a club sandwich.
18. Differentiate between a *bookmaker* and *Denver* sandwich.
19. Analyse any three salient features of using breads for sandwich.
20. What care should be taken while using butter as a spread and why?
21. Describe how sandwiches should be stored.
22. Write short notes on the modern trends of sandwich making.

PROJECT WORK

---

1. In groups of five, undertake a market survey of hotels and speciality restaurants that serve sandwiches on their menus. Record your observations with regard to the choice of the bread, spread, filling, garnish and service in the following chart.
   Share this information with the rest of the groups and debate on similarities and differences.

Name of sandwich	Bread	Spread	Filling	Garnish	Accompaniments	Photograph

2. In groups of three each, prepare at least two creative sandwiches by using various kinds of ingredients. Display your creations for tasting and critique the product and evaluate the same.

CHAPTER 5

USES OF HERBS AND WINES IN COOKING

Learning Objectives

After reading this chapter, you should be able to
- select various kinds of herbs used in cooking
- understand the basic concepts of storage and use of herbs
- appreciate the use of the right kinds of herbs for the right commodity to enhance flavours
- differentiate between various kinds of herbs on the basis of flavour and aroma
- analyse the ways in which wines can be used in cooking
- get an insight into the basic uses of wines in cooking

INTRODUCTION

Herbs and wines have been used in cooking since ages for various reasons. The prime reason for using herbs was to mask the flavours of certain strong smelling foods. Over a period of time, people began to realize their nutritional benefits and medicinal values; hence herbs have carved a niche for themselves and are on top of the food list of health-conscious people. Herbs are most sought after as they are a symbol of natural and healthy way of living.

The art of making alcohol was discovered in the very ancient times. Epics and literature across the world are rife with examples about alcohol being consumed by kings and noblemen. In cooking, wine found its place in the Western culture, especially in the French and Italian cuisines, wherein it was used to impart flavour to the food.

Every country and region in the world uses herbs in one form or the other. Recorded historical evidences suggest that cultivation and use of herbs was predominant in the cuisine of countries such as China, India, Egypt, Persia, and Greece. Over time, so many herbs were discovered that it gave rise to an independent subject of study and the people who studied the properties of herbs are known as herbalists. Not all herbs, however, are edible and some of them can be poisonous if consumed in large quantities. These are available in both fresh and dried forms. However, it is best to use herbs when they are fresh as dried herbs are stronger in flavour. Apart from being used in the kitchen, these also add to the environment and are used in medicines and in making cosmetics. The subtle smell of herbs planted in the kitchen garden adds a freshness and natural perfume to the air. Herbs are extensively finding their way into medicines, teas, organic and healthy products, and even into cosmetics. Ancient texts, such as the *Vedas,* talk extensively about various kinds of herbs that were used as medicine in the olden days.

Herbs are versatile and they can grow in gardens and even in small pots or hanging baskets. They can be placed on the window sill of the kitchen where some amount of sunlight is available. Herbs planted this way not only add freshness to the environment but it is also easy to have them at hand while cooking. Leaves are the most edible part of such plants, but sometimes small flowers and stems also find their use in flavouring food. In some herbs, such as celery and leeks, the leaves are discarded and only the stem is used. In this chapter, we shall read about various kinds of herbs, their selection and storage, and their uses in food and drinks.

HERBS

Various kinds of herbs are used in different cuisines across the world. In this chapter, we will discuss common herbs that are most frequently used in kitchens. Although herbs should be used fresh, yet many a time drying of some herbs, such as bay leaves, improves their flavours. The drying of herbs is an art in itself. The aroma of the herbs indicates

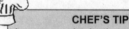

CHEF'S TIP

A common mistake that most chefs make is that they dry their herbs on the top of an oven or a hot place. Herbs should be hanged to dry at a temperature of not more than 30°C. In this way, herbs retain their aroma and colour.

the freshness of the product. A herb that emits a weak or a stale aroma indicates that it is old or not preserved properly. Another way to select herbs is to choose those that have an even and bright colour and do not have discoloured leaves. The stems should be tender and moist and they should have a bright light green appearance. The colour of the stems also determines the quality and age of the herb.

The Use of Herbs in Cooking

Herbs have many uses in the kitchen. Herbs are the most frequently used ingredient for flavouring food. The selection of a herb for a particular dish depends upon its ready availability and its affinity towards the commodity to which it is added. Apart from flavouring and adding aroma and nutritional value to food, herbs are put to several other uses, such as potpourris, that are used as aromatic placements in houses. Some herbs are also used in making herbal pillows that are believed to induce sleep. Table 5.1 highlights various uses of herbs in cooking and related applications.

Table 5.1   Uses of herbs in cooking

Uses of herbs	Description
Flavouring	Herbs can be chopped, minced, torn, or bruised and added to soups and stocks, or they can be added in the form of bouquet garni which means a bouquet of flavours. A traditional bouquet garni consists of a few sprigs of parsley, thyme, leeks, and bay leaves tied together in a bundle so that these can be removed after the flavour has been infused into the cooking liquid. Chopped herbs are used in sausages and stuffing for various kinds of cold cuts. Sage and onion stuffing for turkey is the most classical combination. Various kinds of herbs pair well with creamy sauces while some go well with meat and game. Herbs can also be used for flavouring cheese, cakes, breads, and cookies.
Garnishing	Herbs are commonly used for garnishes. They can be minced finely as in case of parsley or used whole in food and also desserts. Sweet flavouring herbs, such as mint, *lemon verbena*, and bergamot, are used in desserts as garnish. Some of the classical ways of using herbs for garnish are: *Fines herbes* This is a popular herb mixture used for garnish in French cuisine. It generally comprises fine minced herbs such as parsley, tarragon, chervil, and chives. *Deep-fried* Herbs such as curly parsley, basil, curry leaves, and rosemary are deep-fried in oil at a temperature of 80°C. This helps the herbs to retain their colour and yet become crisp. Sometimes rock salt crystals can be sprinkled over the fried herbs and they become wonderful garnishes. *Sprigs* The fresh sprigs of herbs are kept in iced cold water until they become crisp. These are used as garnish on various food items.
Seasoning	*Saltless seasoning* A mixture of dried herbs, such as dill, thyme, and oregano, are combined with dried onion, sesame seeds, black pepper, dried lemon peel, paprika, and garlic powder to make saltless seasoning. Because of rising health problems, salt-free seasonings are becoming common in health food. *Herbal salts* Powdered or rock salt is mixed with dried herbs to make herbal salts. Celery salt is the most commonly used herbal salt in cooking. To make herbal salt, store the fresh herb in salt in an airtight container for few months or until the herb inside has dried. The salt can then be churned in a mixer or ground in a mortar and pestle so that the dried herbs blend well. One can similarly make rosemary salt and other herbal salts.
Herbal oils	Oils can be flavoured with one or more herbs. These oils are used for making vinaigrettes or dressings for salads and also used for glazing meat or used as a sauce such as basil oil in Italian cuisine. Herbal oils are also used as marinating agents for various meat. Virgin olive oils are best suited for making herbal oils, which are made in two ways: 1. Heat oil up to 80°C and put whole herbs in the oil and let it infuse for one week. 2. The second and the most popular is to poach the herb leaves in warm olive oil and then blend it into a puree. The oil is then strained through a cheese cloth and stored in plastic squeeze bottles. Basil oil, parsley oil, chive oil, thyme oil are all made in a similar way. These flavoured oils are also used for garnishing soups, or mixed with fresh green salads.
Herbal vinegars	In olden days, herbs were infused in vinegar or wine for their preservation. This led to flavoured vinegars and wine. Tarragon vinegar is one of the most commonly used vinegar in cooking. To make herbal vinegars, combine fresh herbs with good quality white wine vinegars and keep the jar in sunlight for at least two weeks so that the flavours infuse in the vinegar.

(Contd)

Table 5.1   *(Contd)*

Uses of herbs	Description
Herb butter	Herb butter is made by combining softened butter with chopped herbs. This kind of flavoured butter is also known as compound butter, which can be used for serving along with fish and grilled steaks. A mixture of herb butter is also stuffed inside a chicken breast, which is then rolled and crumb-fried. This is a classical preparation known as *chicken à la Kiev*. Many other kinds of herbal butters are made and used for various dishes. Some of the most commonly made herbal butter are: *Café de Paris butter* This butter was created by the chef of *Café de Paris* restaurant in Geneva, hence the name. The butter is creamed and mixed with ingredients such as herbs, spices, and other condiments such as oregano, marjoram, dill, rosemary, mustard, tarragon, garlic, shallots, parsley, chives, and capers, Worcestershire sauce, and anchovies. This butter is prepared and chilled in the refrigerator. A slice of this is placed on top of a grilled steak and gratinated under a salamander before serving. *Maitre d'Hôtel butter* This butter is made by creaming butter, along with lemon juice and chopped parsley. It is also known as *buerre à la bourguignon* in French. The butter can be used for making sauce or as a stuffing in *poulet à la Kiev*. The butter is usually rolled like a log and refrigerated. It is sliced and served on top of grilled fish as well. *Chive butter* This is made by creaming butter and adding finely sliced chives. The butter is rolled into logs and refrigerated. It can be sliced and served with meat or spread on breads for making *crostini*.
Herbal drinks	Since centuries, herbs have been drunk as herbal decoctions that are believed to be a cure for many ailments including cancer. Before the advent of medicines, it was herbs and spices that were used as medicines. In hotels, herbs find their use in various beverages such as the following. *Herbal teas* Chilled iced tea is a commonly served beverage in all hotels. Mint sprigs are used as the main flavouring agent with lightly brewed tea. Other common herbal teas served in hotels could range from chamomile, bergamot, to oswega tea. *Herbal water* Many eateries that specialize in spa and health restaurants serve water with sprigs of fresh herbs. This acts not only as flavouring for the water but also provides a soothing effect to the eyes. *Cocktails and Mocktails* Herbs, such as mint and *lemon verbena,* are commonly used in flavouring and garnishing various cocktails and mocktails. Cocktails are a mix of two or more spirits or liqueurs flavoured with herbs and other agents, whereas mocktails are non alcoholic. Freshly crushed mint with ice and topped up with fresh orange jus is the most sought-after summer drink in hotels and bars.
Sauces and spreads	Apart from flavouring, herbs can also be combined and cooked to make sauces, soups, and spreads that can be served in variety of ways. Some common sauces and dips made with herbs in the kitchen are as follows. *Herb sauce* Fresh herbs can be made into a sauce in many ways. One way is to flavour any sauce with lots of chopped herbs while the other is to blanch the herb and puree it to a smooth texture. The puree can be mixed with flavoursome stock to make herb sauce. Commonly prepared sauces made in this way are parsley sauces, tarragon sauce, chervil sauce, dill sauce, etc.

(Contd)

Table 5.1 (*Contd*)

Uses of herbs	Description
	Mint sauce Mint sauce is a very common accompaniment to roasted lamb. Freshly chopped mint is added to the reduced lamb jus to make an accompanying sauce. Mint is also used for making mint jelly that is served with cold roasted lamb.
	Spreads and marinades Various herbs are combined together with other condiments, such as shallots, garlic, and spices, to make thick coarse pastes that can be used in various ways. These can be served as sauces or even used for marinating meat for grilling and other cooking principles to create a range of products. Few of the popular herb pastes are pesto from Italy, *chermoula* from Morocco, *chimichurri* from South America, and mint chutney from India.
Pastes and crusts	Herbs can be used to make the crusts or covering for various food commodities to give them a unique flavour and texture. Meat, chicken, and fish can be rolled in an herb mixture to form a crust around and then the item can be grilled, pan-fried, or even roasted. Herb crusts can also be used for curing salmon. Fillet of salmon is cured with salt and sugar and then spread with an herb mixture of dill and black pepper. This preparation is known as *Gravad lax*. Sometimes a variety of cream cheese can be rolled into an herb mixture which helps in preservation and flavouring of cheese. Many types of bread, before baking, are rolled into herb mixtures to improve the appearance and add flavour to the bread.

POPULAR HERBS USED IN COOKING

Some herbs that are are very popular in modern cooking are discussed in this section.

Basil

Other Name: *Tulsi*

Basil is the most commonly used herb in Mediterranean cuisine (refer Chapter 6). The origins of basil (Fig. 5.1) can be traced to India where it is a highly venerated plant, that is an integral part of offerings to gods such as Lord Vishnu and Krishna. Even today, most Indian households would have a basil plant.

Fig. 5.1 Basil leaves

Varieties of basil

There are various varieties of basil such as the following.

Sweet basil This is the most commonly available basil and is used in Italian cuisines. It has large leaves with a dark green, smooth, and shiny skin.

Bush basil This is similar in flavour to sweet basil, but does not grow in height. These grow in bushes and the leaves are smaller.

Hot basil It has a different flavour from sweet basil and is used for religious purposes in India, which is why it is also called holy basil. This basil is also known *krapao* in Thailand where it is commonly used for cooking.

Purple basil   Also known as purple ruffles, these plants have dark purple coloured leaves that have a stronger flavour compared to sweet basil.

Selection, storage, and use

How to select   Basil should be purchased in bunches, which helps to keep them fresh for few days. While selecting, smell the aroma, which should be sweet and strong but pleasing as well. The leaves should be bright green and crisp.

How to store   Basil is highly perishable in nature, so care has to be taken while storing it. Fresh basil can be kept refrigerated for three to four days. Before storing, pick out the dark and black leaves that are bruised and keep them aside for making a sauce called pesto, which is made by crushing basil, garlic, olive oil, parmesan cheese, black pepper, pine nuts, and parsley. Wrap loosely in wet kitchen tissues and store them in a basket, so that they can breathe. If you want to store for a longer period, then dry the basil in bunches by hanging or by packing with salt.

Culinary use   Basil is popularly used in Italian cuisine as it pairs up very well with tomatoes, olive oil, and garlic. The leaves are always torn with hands and added to the dish or the sauce in the last stage of cooking. It is also made into pesto. Basil leaves can also be used in salad mixes. In Thailand, it is chopped and stir-fried with meat such as chicken and fish. Hot basil is one of the most important ingredients in a Thai curry.

Fig. 5.2   Bay leaves

Bay Leaf

Other Names: Laurel leaf, *tej patta*

Bay leaf is also known as laurel leaf because the Greeks used to wear it on their headgears. It symbolized courage and was indicative of the laurels they had achieved (Fig. 5.2).

Varieties of bay leaf

There are many varieties of this leafy spice that can range from small musty olive green colour to large beige-coloured dry leaves. It is an aromatic leaf of an evergreen shrub that belongs to the Mediterranean belt. The leaves are bright green which turn to beige colour on drying.

Selection, storage, and use

How to select   These are available in the market in both fresh and dried forms. For selecting a fresh bay leaf, make sure that its tip is crisp and the stem is green and shiny. There should be no holes, as that indicates that it is been infected with insects. The leaves should break into half when folded and creased. For selecting a dried bay leaf, ensure there are no holes as it would mean that it was infested with insects. The leaves should have a lustre.

How to store   Bay leaves can keep very well after they are dried. Storing these in an airtight jar will keep them good until two years. Fresh bay leaves can keep well in plastic bags for a couple of days and should not be refrigerated.

Culinary use It is always included in bouquet garni to flavour soups and stocks. Bay leaf is available as whole dried leaf or in crushed form. In Indian cuisines, it is used for flavouring rice dishes and also curries. The bay leaf is only used for flavouring and never eaten. So, it is advisable to remove it from the dish before serving.

Fig. 5.3 A chervil shrub

Chervil

Other Names: *Cerfeuil,* garden chervil, French Parsley

Chervil is the most commonly used herb in European countries, especially France. It is believed to have been brought into France by Romans. Chervil (Fig. 5.3) is one of the prime ingredients in the mixture of fines herbes, wherein it is chopped along with chives, tarragon, and parsley. This herbal mixture is used popularly in French cooking. The leaves resemble flat leaf parsley and hence are also known as French parsley. Chervil is believed to have blood-cleansing properties and is also used as a skin cleanser.

Selection, storage, and use

How to select The leaves should be bright green and crisp. If the tips of the leaves have a pinkish hue, it means that the plant has been subjected to heavy sunlight. It, however, does not impact the flavour and quality of the herb.

How to store These leaves should always be used fresh, as they are highly perishable and lose their flavour very quickly. The only way to store chervil is to dry it for winter months, but in summers, it should be used fresh.

Culinary use Chervil is a versatile herb and its unique flavour makes it ideal for salads. It is used in the preparation of fines herbes. Hot chervil soup in winters and chilled chervil soup in summers is an all time favourite of the French. Chervil pairs very well with omelettes and egg dishes. Chervil is also added to vinegars to flavour them.

Fig. 5.4 Bunch of chives

Chives

Other Names: Rush leek, *hara pyaaz*

Chives are long and slender green shoots of the onion bulb. These are hollow and tubular and because of their mild onion flavour, they are used in the flavouring of eggs, salads, and soups. Chives (Fig. 5.4) were believed to have originated in China and then spread to the rest of the world. In cooking, when referring to chives, we generally refer to onion bulbs, but sometimes the green part of garlic shoot, called garlic chive, is used. Those, however, are flat in shape.

Selection, storage, and use

How to select It is important to be able to select chives as they are rarely cooked and often used chopped or snipped on top of salads. While selecting, ensure that the chives are small and tiny. The large ones are strong flavoured and will overpower delicate dishes.

The shoot should be straight and firm with an even bright green colour. The appearance should be smooth and the tip of the chives should be firm.

How to store The chives should be stored refrigerated and covered with a wet tissue. They can also be stored in a bowl of water in an upright position.

Culinary use Chives are one of the components of *fines herbes*. They can be chopped finely and used on salads and egg dishes such as creamy scrambled eggs, salads, and omelettes. Chopped chives are also put on jacket potatoes and they pair up very well with sour cream.

Cilantro

Other Names: Coriander leaves, *dhaniya*, Chinese parsley

Coriander or cilantro (Fig. 5.5) is a commonly used herb in Asian cuisines. In China, it is known as Chinese parsley. All the three parts of this plant—roots, leaves, and seeds—are commonly used in cuisines. The roots are used for flavouring stocks, soups, and sauces, whereas the seeds can be crushed and used as a spice. The leaves can be used whole or chopped as a garnish or ground to a paste and used with various culinary applications. Medicinally, this herb is used for curing stomach pains and ailments.

Fig. 5.5 Bunch of cilantro

Selection, storage, and use

How to select The cilantro should be fresh and vivid green and it should be crisp. The leaves should be flat, without any distorted edges. The bunch of leaves should be stiff when held together and they should emit a pleasing aroma.

How to store Cilantro is best consumed fresh and it is rarely dried. In case we wish to keep it for a longer time, it is advisable to mince it and put in ice cube trays, along with water. The frozen ice cubes can be put in sauces at the time of finishing.

Culinary use Cilantro is used in many ways in various cuisines around the world. The leaves are chopped and mixed with food at the last minute, as it has a very delicate flavour. The seeds can be used whole or can be broiled and powdered and used in curries and pickles.

Dill

Other Names: *Sowa*, dill weed

The dill plant is believed to have originated in southern Europe and western Asia. Both leaves as well as seeds of this herb have various culinary applications. The leaves of dill are feather like (Fig. 5.6), which is why they are often referred to as dill weed. The leaves can, at times, be confused with fennel plant, but the flavour of dill and fennel are very distinctive. The seeds of this plant are sedative in nature and comprise one of the most important ingredients of gripe water that is given to babies for colic pain.

Fig. 5.6 Dill leaves

Selection, storage, and use

How to select While selecting dill, ensure that the leaves are dark green and crisp. The tips of the leaves should be bright and not discoloured. It should be smooth with no blemishes.

How to store Dill is used fresh. In case it has to be stored for a couple of days, wrap the stems in wet tissue paper and keep them in an upright position in a perforated tray or basket. For storage for long time, this herb can be dried by hanging them in a dry place with temperature not exceeding 30°C.

Culinary use The fresh leaves are used in various ways. They combine very well with fish such as salmon, prawns, sea bass, and even with cheese. *Gravad lax* is a cold preparation of salmon, which is cured with salt and sugar and coated with a mixture of chopped dill and black pepper. Dill also pairs up well with sour cream and cucumbers. This herb is very popular during summers and hence its use in salads, egg preparations, steamed fish, etc. is very common. It is also used as a pickling agent with small cucumbers known as gherkins.

Marjoram

Fig. 5.7 A bunch of marjoram

Other Names: *Maruva,* sweet marjoram, knotted marjoram, oregano

There are many kinds of marjoram (Fig. 5.7) available in a herbal garden, but the sweet or knotted marjoram is the best variety that should be used in cooking. Wild variety of marjoram is also known as oregano in Italy and is commonly used with pastas and pizzas. Some of the varieties of marjoram are sedative in nature and hence only small quantities of the same should be used.

Selection, storage, and use

How to select Marjoram should be selected with leaves attached to the stem. The woody stem should be flexible and the leaves should be thin, bright green, and crisp. Ensure that the herb is free from soil and debris.

How to store Fresh marjoram can be stored up to three or four days by wrapping the stems in wet tissue paper and leaving them upright in a perforated basket. It can also keep well in plastic bags that have holes for the herb to breathe.

Culinary use Marjoram pairs very well with meat and potatoes. The strong flavour complements game animals such as rabbit, venison, and quails. Marjoram is often chopped and rubbed on the flesh of the animal before roasting. The herb also helps as a tenderizer. They are also used sparingly in salads and vegetable dishes such as stews and casseroles.

Fig. 5.8 Mint leaves

Mint

Other Names: *Pudina, garden mint, spearmint*

Mint is used in many ways and forms around the world. In countries like Africa, it is brewed and drunk as tea; while in India, it is also made into a paste and served along with kebabs. Mint (Fig. 5.8) is used both in fresh and dried forms, but the taste of fresh mint is more pleasant and refreshing.

Many varieties of mint are available in the market. Each variety of mint has a specific taste and flavour. Spearmint is a variety of mint that has a cooling aroma and flavour to it.

Selection, storage, and use

How to select   Mint leaves should be crisp and should be received in bunches. The tips and edges of the leaves should be bright and without any black or dark spots. The stems when broken should be moist.

How to store   Fresh mint can be wrapped in wet kitchen tissues and stored in a perforated basket. For longer storage of mint, it can be dried or blanched and frozen until further use. It can also be stored in a plastic bag with holes to allow the herb to breathe.

Culinary use   Mint is used in both fresh and dried forms. The leaves turn black when it comes in contact with oxygen as the juices oxidize. That is the reason mint is chopped along with sugar, so that the sugar can absorb any liquid that oozes out from the leaves, thereby preventing it from discolouration. Mint is also made into mint jelly or mint sauce and is a classical accompaniment to roasted lamb. As it has a pleasing flavour, it is also used to flavour liqueurs and is used as a garnish for desserts and pastries.

Fig. 5.9 Parsley leaves

Parsley

Other Name: *Ajmud*

Flat leaf parsley from Italy and curly leaf parsley from France are the two most popular varieties of parsley used in kitchens. Curly leaf parsley (Fig. 5.9) is used mainly as garnish, whereas the flat leaf parsley is used in cooking.

Selection, storage, and use

How to select   Parsley should be selected in bunches. The curly leaf parsley should be dark green and crisp. The leaves should rustle when shaken. The stems of parsley should be bright green and firm and they should snap when bent.

How to store   Parsley should be stored in plastic bags that have holes, so that the herb can breathe. It can also be stored by wrapping up in wet kitchen tissues and storing in a perforated tray in a refrigerator.

Culinary use   Curly parsley is mainly used for garnishes either as whole leaves or in chopped form. Flat leaf parsley is used in cooking in many different ways. The stems of parsley are used as one of the prime ingredients in bouquet garni, to flavour stocks, soups, and sauces. The leaves are finely minced and used as a garnish on stews and braised dishes. It is also one of the ingredients of *fines herbes*.

CHEF'S TIP

Mince parsley until fine. Put in a muslin cloth and wash it under running water and squeeze dry. The resulting parsley will be free flowing and will be easy to sprinkle on top of dishes.

Fig. 5.10 A rosemary quill

Rosemary

Other Name: *Romarin*

Rosemary (Fig. 5.10) grows wild around the coasts of the Mediterranean sea. It is a very aromatic herb with needle shaped leaves that resemble those of pine. The herb has a hard woody stem and the leaves are also tough. The strong aroma of this herb pairs up very well with root vegetables and meats. There is a mythological belief associated with Virgin Mary. It is believed that the blue flowers of this herb got their colour from the blue cloak that she spread on this bushy herb to dry. Greeks and Romans strew it in their hair as it said to be good for sharpening one's memory.

Selection, storage, and use

How to select Rosemary is usually available in small quills, where the needle-shaped herb is attached to the woody stem. The leaves should be firm and light green in colour. The stem should be greyish in colour and the tips of the leaves should be pointed and not discoloured. When the herb is getting old, the leaves tend to acquire a grey to black tinge.

How to store This herb will keep for quite some time in a refrigerator, if stored in plastic bags. The other way to store them is to hang them dry or to pack with salt.

Culinary use Roast leg of lamb with rosemary jus is the most classical of combinations. When chefs hold and smell rosemary, they think of lamb and potatoes, as this herb is used generously with these two food iems. Being hard, this herb is used in methods such as roasting, stewing, braising, and even deep frying. In modern times, rosemary is also used for flavouring tea cakes and cookies. Addition of a few sprigs to a fruit salad gives a pleasant unusual flavour.

Fig. 5.11 Sage leaves

Sage

Other Names: *Salvia, sefakus*

Sage or *salvia* comes from the Latin word *salvere*, which means to save. This herb was used for curing many ailments. Its culinary applications are believed to have started in England in the Medieval period.

It is a strong-flavoured and a popular herb in Mediterranean cooking, as it grows on the coasts of the Mediterranean Sea. Sage leaves (Fig. 5.11) are greyish green in colour. There is also a variety of sage that has purple shaded leaves, which is known as purple sage. This is stronger in flavour than the regular sage. The leaves of sage are rough and matte in texture and the plant often bears purple flowers, which are rarely used in cooking.

Selection, storage, and use

How to select The leaves should be crisp and the edges of the leaves should not be discoloured. The stem of the herb should be firm and tough. When held upright, the herbs should stand up and not wilt.

How to store Sage can be stored up to a week in plastic bags with perforations. It should be stored separately, as its odour can intermingle with other ingredients. For longer storage, sage is dried or stored in olive oil

Culinary use Sage is very popular during Christmas. It is the prime flavouring in onion stuffing, which is used for accompanying roasted turkey. Apart from this, it is commonly used as flavouring in sausages and meats. In Italy, it is often served deep-fried in olive oil or butter and served with pan-fried escalope of veal also known as *saltimbocca*. Chopped sage leaves are also added to salads and tomatoes and they are a perfect flavouring for cream cheese dips. In Belgium and Germany, this herb is used for flavouring oily fish such as eels and mackerels.

Savory

Other Names: Summer savory, winter savory

Fig. 5.12 A small branch of savory

This herb from the Mediterranean region has two varieties: summer and winter savory. The flavour of winter savory is stronger than summer savory. The flavour of the savory herb reminds one of thyme and has always been a great favourite of Italians and English. It has a slightly hot flavour with a bitter after taste. It is believed that Romans introduced it to England. The leaves of savory (Fig. 5.12) are dark green and needle shaped, like in the case of rosemary. However, the resemblance seems only from a distance. When observed closely, the leaves are flat and needle shaped much unlike those of rosemary.

Selection, storage, and use

How to select The leaves should be crisp and bright green. The stems of savory should have a light pinkish hue to them and they should be firm yet tender when broken.

How to store Savory can be stored wrapped in a moist kitchen tissue paper or kept for few days in a plastic bag. For longer storage, this herb can be dried like other herbs or stored in vinegar, which can then be used for making dressings.

Culinary use Savory is the most popular herb used in sauces and meat (such as pork and game). It is also a popular flavouring in soups and used in the stuffings for sausages and pâtés. Fresh summer savory pairs up very well with green peas and fresh green beans. It can also be chopped and sprinkled over green salads.

Fig. 5.13   The leaves of tarragon

Tarragon

Other Name: Estragon

The word tarragon reminds one of the chefs from France and cuisines of the region such as *Béarnaise* sauce and *fines herbes*. The name of this herb is said to have originated from the word *little dragon,* as in the olden times, it was used to cure snake bites. The long slender leaves are used in variety of ways in cooking, particularly around France. It is a tall plant that can grow up to a height of one meter. The leaves are shiny and narrow as seen in Fig. 5.13.

Selection, storage, and use

How to select   Care should be taken while selecting French tarragon as its Russian counterpart (also known as false tarragon) is also available but does not have the same flavour. The leaves of Russian tarragon are coarser and pale green in colour with a slight bitter taste. The leaves of tarragon should be bright green and crisp. The stems should be hard and pale green in colour.

How to store   Tarragon is a highly perishable herb because of its thin leaves that discolour very fast. They can be wrapped up in moist kitchen tissues and kept upto two days. For longer storage, the herb is dried, or traditionally, it is stored in vinegar, which is then used for making various salad dressings.

Culinary use   Tarragon is an excellent flavouring for meat, eggs, creamy sauces, and raw vegetable salads. It is used for flavouring the classical French sauce *béarnaise*, which is a derivative of hollandaise sauce. The light and pleasing aroma of this herb makes it ideal for light flavoured meats such as fish and chicken.

Fig. 5.14   A small branch of thyme

Thyme

Other Name: *Zaatar*

Thyme (Fig. 5.14) is one of the oldest herbs that are referred to in texts as a medicinal herb that was very successful in removing headaches. There are around 50 varieties of thyme that grow abundantly but only three are commonly used in culinary applications—lemon thyme that has a slight citrus flavour, caraway/garden thyme, and English wild thyme. Each of these has a slightly different flavour but the culinary applications of these herbs remain the same.

Selection, storage, and use

How to select   Thyme should have a distinctive aroma and the leaves should be bright green and crisp. The woody stems should be light green in colour and as the thyme gets older, the colour of the stems tends to get darker.

How to store   Thyme can be stored wrapped in moist kitchen tissues and kept standing in upright position in a perforated tray. It can also be stored in plastic bags. For longer storage, it can be dried or infused with oil, which is then used in cooking.

Culinary use Thyme is paired with chopped parsley and used in stuffing for meat such as chicken and pork. It is one of the prime herbs used in bouquet garni to flavour stocks, soups, and sauces. Chopped thyme is commonly used as a garnish for soups such as cream of mushroom and pumpkin. Thyme is also infused with oil, which is then used as a dressing for various salads. It is also paired up with Mediterranean vegetable such as tomatoes, aubergines, courgettes, and sweet bell peppers.

Lemon grass

Fig. 5.15   Lemon grass

Other Names: Citronella grass, fever grass

Lemon grass is one of the perennial varieties of a grass that is commonly used as a flavouring agent in South-East Asian cuisines, especially Thailand, Indonesia, and Malaysia. This herb (Fig. 5.15) is native to India, though it is not commonly used in Indian food. It is used in villages to make a bitter concoction known as *kadha*. It has a lemony flavour because of its oil that is also present in lemon peel.

Selection, storage, and use

How to select Lemon grass should be bright green in colour, as it tends to take on a woody colour when it gets old. The hanging grass should be bright green and the root should have a slight greenish tinge.

How to store Lemon grass can be wrapped in wet kitchen tissues or kept in paper bags. This way they can be stored from two to three weeks. To store it for a longer time, it can be frozen or dried in dry climates.

Culinary use When used in cooking, only the lower bulbous part is used in curries and stir-fries. It can be smashed and added to soups or even sliced or chopped and added to fillings and stir fries.

Pandan Leaves

Fig. 5.16   Pandan leaves

Other Names: Palmyra, *daun pandan, pandanus*

Pandan leaves (Fig. 5.16) or *pandanus* as they are commonly known are used in Thai and Malaysian cuisines for flavouring. Its subtle flavour is preferred by chefs in cooking. This plant has many uses apart from cooking. In many South-East Asian countries, it is used for weaving mats and boxes that are also used for keeping jewellery and other items. A variety of this plant grows in south India and the famous *kewda* water or *vetiver* is extracted from the leaves.

Selection, storage, and use

How to select The *pandan* leaves selected should be dark green in colour and have shiny and smooth skin. When held between the hands, the long leaf should stand firm. The rib (centre line) should be firm yet supple and delicate. The tip of the leaf should be pointed and there should be no black marks on the leaves.

How to store *Pandan* is a perishable herb and should be used fresh. It can be stored in plastic bags for up to a week. For longer storage, they can be frozen. The only issue in freezing is that this herb will become soft and loose its crispness.

Culinary use *Pandan* leaves are tied into a knot and brewed along with soups and stock. This facilitates the removal of these leaves prior to serving the dish. It is also used for wrapping up meat, such as prawn or chicken, and steamed, so that the flavour seeps in the meat. The *pandan* leaf is usually not eaten and is discarded after it has imparted its flavour to the dishes. It is also used as flavouring in preparing rice dishes in Thailand and Indonesia.

Curry Leaves

Other Names: *Kari patta,* sweet neem leaves

This herb is so commonly used in curries that it gets the name curry leaves (Fig. 5.17). It is very commonly used in western, eastern, and southern India. In north India, the usage of curry leaves is limited to a few dishes only. Though it is commonly used in cooking, this plant also has various medicinal properties.

Fig. 5.17 Curry leaves

Selection, storage, and use

How to select Curry leaves that are selected should always be dark green and attached to the stems. The light colour stem would indicate young curry leaves and these have a better flavour. The surface of the leaves should be smooth and shiny.

How to store Curry leaves can be stored up to one week in a plastic bag. It can also be wrapped in wet kitchen tissues and stored in a perforated container.

Culinary use Curry leaves are used in many ways in Indian cuisine. It can be ground to a paste with other ingredients and used as an accompaniment or as a base for curries. It can also be deep-fried and used as garnish. The most common way of using curry leaf is to temper it in oil and use it for flavouring curries.

Borage

Other Name: *Borag*

Borage (Fig. 5.18) is a medicinal herb that has been in use since medieval times. Its botanical name is *Euphorisinum,* derived from the word euphoria as it was said to bring joy wherever it grew. This tall plant with ruffled leaves has an untidy appearance which is compensated with

Fig. 5.18 Borage plant

small star-shaped blue flowers that find its way into culinary applications. The leaves have a cucumber-like flavour and are often used instead of spinach. The flowers however are used in many ways. They are used in salads or even candied and used in desserts.

Selection, storage, and use

How to select Borage has pale green rough leaves that should be selected along with the bright blue star-shaped flowers. The leaves should be crisp and the stems should be tender and green. The flowers should be fresh and bright.

How to store   This herb can be stored up to a couple of days with its stems immersed in cold water in an upright position in a refrigerator. To store for a longer period of time, the flowers should be candied and the leaves should be dried in bunches.

Culinary use   Borage with its leaves and flowers are commonly used in flavouring salads. The leaves and flowers are also used traditionally for gin-based summer cocktails. Sometimes the flowers are set in ice cubes and used for garnishing other drinks as well. Chopped flowers and leaves have an excellent flavour when mixed with fresh salads. These can also be used in pickling as they impart a pleasant cucumber flavour to the pickles.

Chamomile

Fig. 5.19   Flowers of chamomile

Other Names: Apple weed, camomile

The very mention of chamomile brings to our mind freshly brewed chamomile tea. This annual herb is a low-growing plant which bears white daisy-like flowers (Fig. 5.19) that have a distinct scent and aroma. It is a medicinal plant and a substance called *azulen,* which is used as a healing agent, is extracted from its fresh flowers. Usually two varieties of chamomile are available: Roman chamomile and apple-scented chamomile.

Selection, storage, and use

How to select   Chamomile should be purchased with flowers attached, as it is the flowers that are mostly used.

How to store   Chamomile should be stored refrigerated in plastic bags or it can be dried for longer storage.

Culinary use   Though this herb is not very commonly used in culinary applications, the flower is brewed to make chamomile tea that aids in digestion and stomach disorders.

Bergamot

Fig. 5.20   Flowers of bergamot plant

Other Name: Bee balm

Bergamot (Fig. 5.20) is also known as bee balm as bees are attracted to its scented flowers. This is a fragrant plant that has a pleasant smell somewhat reminiscent of mint and orange. The herb is native to North America and was used by American Indians in their food and drinks.

Selection, storage, and use

How to select   The leaves should be crisp and should not have blemished edges. The flowers should be bright red and supple. The stems should be green and pliable.

How to store   Bergamot can be stored in a refrigerator in a plastic bag up to few days. To store it for long, they should be dried in shade, where it is not humid.

Culinary use   Chopped flowers and leaves are added to salads and also wine to flavour it. Bergamot herb and leaves are also brewed to create a delicious herbal tea. The leaves and fruits are often added to fruits salads and jellies.

Fig. 5.21 Leaves of lemon balm

Lemon Balm

Other Names: Sweet balm, citronella

Native to Southern Europe, this herb has been cultivated for almost 200 years now. The citrus flavour from the leaves makes it the most preferred herb for flavouring dessert sauces and wines. Bees love this herb and the famous Melissa honey is obtained from bees which suck nectar from the flowers of lemon balm. The oval-shaped leaves (Fig. 5.21) have serrated edges.

Selection, storage, and use

How to select The leaves should be bright green and the edges should be firm and spiny without any black edges. The stems should be green and tender. When held in a bunch, the leaves should not wilt down and should emit a pleasing citrus aroma when rubbed.

How to store This herb is stored wrapped in wet kitchen tissues and refrigerated. This keeps it good for few days. For longer storage, it can be stored along with castor sugar or can be dried.

Culinary use This herb is commonly used in desserts but it is also brewed as a tea and drunk in Middle East. Melissa tea is another name for the tea obtained by drying the leaves. Because of its unique citrus flavour, it is also commonly used for flavouring ice creams and iced teas. In Italy, it is also used for making a lemon balm pesto.

Fig. 5.22 A small branch of purslane

Purslane

Other Name: *Kulfa*

Purslane is a herb that finds its usage even in Indian cuisine. An annual plant, it has smooth shiny green thick leaves that bear orange flowers. They have a sharp and sour flavour and are mixed with other herbs before being used. *Purslane* (Fig. 5.22) also has medicinal properties; its leaves and seeds were brewed in olden days to make tea that was considered a tonic.

Selection, storage, and use

How to select While selecting purslane for salads, ensure that the leaves are tender and small. The leaves should have a shine and the stems should be reddish to pink in colour. The edges of the leaves should be vivid green.

How to store Purslane can be stored in a plastic bag for up to three days in a refrigerator. It is never dried and is always used fresh.

Culinary use Purslane leaves are used in salads. It can be chopped and used in mixed green salads. Whole purslane leaves can be sautéed and mixed with cream and served as an accompaniment. In Indian cuisine, curry prepared from purslane and lentils is very common in Hyderabadi cuisine.

Fig. 5.23   Lemon verbena

Lemon verbena

Other Name: Louisa

A native of Argentina, this herb (Fig. 5.23) has leaves that have a strong lemon flavour. The characteristic citrus aroma makes it a favourite for flavouring many dishes, specially desserts.It thrives in hot climates and the aroma is quite powerful in the evening hours. The narrow leaves with a hard woody stem resemble laurel leaves.

Selection, storage, and use

How to select   This herb should be selected with fresh and light green leaves that have a smooth and shiny surface. The tips of the leaves should be crisp and the edges should not be black or shrivelled.

How to store   *Lemon verbena* should be stored in plastic bags with perforations. This way it will keep fresh for a couple of days. This herb can also be dried and stored for long time in sealed jars.

Culinary use   This strong lemon-flavoured herb can be sparingly used in desserts such as fruit salads, jellies, and beverages such as fresh summer drinks. It is also paired with ice cream for the wonderful citrus flavour and aroma. *Lemon verbena* is also used as a herbal tea that has medicinal properties. In South America, the brew of this herb is used as mouth cleaner as it is considered to be a mouth freshener and also strengthens the gums.

Lovage

Fig. 5.24   Lovage plant

Other Names: Maggiplant, Love parsley

Lovage (Fig. 5.24) is quite similar in usage to Angelica plant. The stems of this herb are candied and eaten as dessert and the large leaves can also be cooked as vegetables. It was commonly used in Great Britain during the medieval times, but slowly faded out of fashion. The leaves are very similar to celery leaves and the flavour is somewhat like celery.

Selection, storage, and use

How to select   The fresh and bright green leaves with thick texture and celery-like aroma should be selected. The edges of the leaves should be crisp and not damaged. The stem should be firm and fibrous and when bent, it should snap into two.

How to store   *Lovage* can be stored wrapped in wet kitchen tissues for a couple of days. This herb is rarely dried and seeds of this plant are used to flavour the food.

Culinary use   Lovage has many culinary applications. The stem is candied and used in desserts, whereas the leaves are used for making vegetable preparations. The seeds can be used to flavour breads such as oats bread. The leaves of this herb are also used for flavouring vegetable soups, meat broths, and casseroles. Chopped *lovage* leaves also add flavour to eggs and green salads.

WINES USED IN COOKING

Wines have been used in cooking since ages. Historical evidence tells us that even in India, the distillation process for making wines for consumption and medicine was used almost 3500 years ago. Wines were probably accidentally discovered when a bunch of grapes got fermented and someone happened to taste them. With the passage of time, the art of wine making got refined and people also started to drink them along with food. Today, there is arguably no better beverage to accompany a meal other than wine. With its infinite variety of tastes, textures, and aromas, there is no dish in the world that would not find its perfect match in a glass of wine. The total experience of the entire meal doubles up—the wine tastes better and so does the food, it culminates in a perfect sensory harmony.

Though admittedly this 'holy grail' of delight is not always easy to achieve, as it requires from the diner an elevated and educated palate and from the *sommelier*, an in-depth familiarity with both the food and the wine, it not all that difficult to raise one's dining experience to new levels. Wines exist for the pleasure of pairing them with food, and if they are paired wisely, the resulting harmony of smells and flavours will enhance their characteristics.

Wine Pairing

It is impossible to establish strict rules on wine pairing because both food and wine are complex substances that can be easily altered. As the taste of a dish depends on its ingredients and its cooking process, the same holds true for wines. The taste of the wine will differ on the types of grape used, the different soils, climatic conditions, as also the techniques of cultivation and manufacture. The general rule is that the flavour of the wine should not prevail over food and vice versa. A thumb rule is that a delicate dish requires a light wine, while a rich dish calls for a well-structured wine.

Here are some of the commonly accepted rules that are by no means hard and fast.

Rule 1

Always drink white wine with white meat and seafood. However, this concept is changing today and it is very common to see white wine being paired with red meat as well. The justification of this is that wine should complement the flavours of the food. With a spicy seafood dish, a herbaceous New World *Sauvignon Blanc* would do well, but so would a Chianti or new season Beaujolais. Red fish, such as salmon and tuna, particularly go well with wines of its own colour. Again a light *Pinot Noir* or perhaps a *Dry Rose* or *Blush Zinfandel* would be the best wines.

Rule 2

Always drink red wines with red meat. This rule probably works well. But choose the right red wine with the right meat. Duck goes well with *Pinot Noir* as lamb does with *Cabernet Sauvignon* and most game dishes match perfectly with a peppery, full bodied *Shiraz*.

Rule 3

Drink sweet wines only with dessert. One of the greatest matches is foie gras and *Sauternes*. The sticky sweetness helps to assimilate the fatty richness of the liver on the palate. *Sauternes* also goes well with pork.

Rule 4

With Champagne, there is no rule. If you enjoy it, have it as an aperitif, to finish the meal, or drink it throughout the meal.

Uses of Wine in Cooking

Apart from drinking, wines are used in various other applications in culinary world. Some of these applications are discussed in Table 5.2.

Table 5.2 Uses of wine in cooking

Uses of wine	Description
Marinades	Both red and white wines are used as marinades for meat. One of the primary uses is for the flavour, but wine also helps to tenderize the meat and remove offensive flavours, if there are any. Most of the braised meat preparations require the meat to be marinated in wine for at least 24 hours. The resulting marinade is then used for making sauces that are served along with the meat.
Sauces	Wines are used for making sauces, both for savoury items as well as desserts. Most of the stock-based sauces are a mixture of stock and wine reduced to a glaze and then thickened with soft butter or various thickening agents to create sauces. Red wine also gives a dark red colour to the reduced lamb stock to make lamb jus. For making sauces for desserts, the wine can be reduced along with fruit purees or on its own to create light and flavoursome sauces. Wines in desserts are also used for making *sabayon* by combining egg yolks, sugar, and wine and cooking over a *bain-marie* until the mixture is thick and foamy. *Zabaglione* is one such Italian dessert made from Marsala wine.
Deglazing	This is one of the most versatile methods employed to retain the flavour of the sauce. Deglazing is a process where the liquid, such as wine and stock, are used for dissolving the remains of the cooked food in a pan. When meat or vegetables are roasted or pan-fried, it leaves some fat and the remaining sediments, such as carbohydrates and proteins, stick to the bottom of the pan. These remains are also known as sediments and contain most of the concentrated flavours. Wine is a best medium to deglaze the same and this liquid can then be added to the sauce.
Flaming	Wines and spirits are alcohol. Thus, upon igniting, these wines flare up and burn until the alcohol has burned off. This principle is often used for flaming desserts that give a good visual appeal. Desserts such as baked Alaska and plum puddings are often served flambéed with wine and spirits.
Stocks	Wine is commonly used for flavouring stocks. Apart from adding flavour, wines are also added for various other reasons, one of them being to make an acidic stock called *court bouillon*. The acid in *court bouillon* is, required especially for poaching oily fish. The acid in the *court bouillon* helps to extract the oil from the fish and keeps it firm.
Flavouring	Wines are commonly added for flavouring in Western food. These can be used to flavour cakes, pastries, sauces, and stocks. Wine is whipped with egg yolks and sugar to make a *sabayon* and whipped cream and other flavourings are folded in to make wine-flavoured mousses and creams for filling various cakes and pastries.

Earlier, wines were mainly made in regions of France, Italy, and Germany, but slowly and steadily the cultivation of grapes led to wine production in various countries around the world. Wines from countries such as Chile, South Africa, and India, are also getting very popular with customers and these wines are classified as New World wines. Nashik in Maharashtra, is home to famous vineyards and wines from this region are carving a niche for themselves in the international market.

SUMMARY

The herbs and wines used in cooking were discussed in this chapter in detail. Before we dwell into the use of herb in kitchens, it is important to understand the characteristics of an herb and wine. Each herb can have many varieties and this diversity results in each herb having its own unique and peculiar flavour. Before we start using herbs in the kitchen it is important for us to know various kinds of herbs, their selection, storage, and uses.

In olden times, herbs were used mainly as a medicine. Today herbs find their uses not only in food, but also in beauty treatments and naturopathy. Herbs are used fresh, but drying of some herbs improves their shelf life and one can use herbs even when it is not in season. Care must be exercised when drying herbs, as they have to be hung dry in a shade where the temperature does not exceed 30°C. Dried herbs are stronger in flavour as the oils present in the herbs get concentrated after drying.

Herbs add freshness to the environment. These add a pleasing scent to the areas where they are grown and hence it is very common to see herbal gardens in kitchen areas. In this chapter, we discussed various kinds of herbs with a photograph for easy identification. Many herbs are also known by other local and scientific names. These have also been mentioned along with a brief description and varieties of herbs. The ways of selecting, storing, and their use in culinary world are also discussed in detail.

This chapter also discussed the uses of wine in cooking. It is interesting to read about various ways in which wines are used by chefs to enhance the taste of a dish as also its visual appeal.

This knowledge on herbs and wine in cooking will come handy in the following chapters on International cuisines.

KEY TERMS

À la Kiev It is a preparation of chicken where it is stuffed with herb butter, crumbed and deep-fried.

Anchovies These are small salted fish sold canned.

Azulen It is a substance extracted from chamomile flowers that is used as a medicine.

Baked Alaska It is a dessert made by layering sponge and ice cream and covered with whipped meringues and baked until the meringue gets colour.

Béarnaise sauce It is a derivative of hollandaise sauce.

Beaujolais This is high quality red wine from Beaujolais region of France.

Bouquet garni It is a bundle of herbs used for flavouring soups, stocks and sauces.

Casserole It is a style of cooking in closed containers known as casseroles.

Chianti It is an Italian white wine.

Chinese parsley Fresh coriander leaves are known as Chinese parsley in China.

Compound butter It is softened butter flavoured with herbs and other ingredients.

Court bouillon It is flavoursome stock made with acidic medium, such as wine, and is used for poaching oily fish.

Crostini It is a thin and long slice of bread spread with herbs and butter and toasted.

Escalope It is a thin slice of meat often used for grilling.

Fines herbes   It is a mixture of herbs used in French cuisine.

Flat leaf parsley   It is a variety of parsley used in Italian cuisine.

Garlic chives   These are green shoots of garlic pod.

Gratinating   This is a method of cooking, where the food is cooked or given a colour under a hot grill.

Gravad lax   This is salt and sugar cured salmon covered with a mixture of dill herbs.

Gripe water   It is a herbal decoction used for stomach ailments in babies and children.

Herbalist   A person who studies herbs as a profession is a herbalist.

Hollandaise   It is an emulsified sauce made by combining egg yolks and clarified butter over a *Bain* bain-marie.

Jus   This is reduced stocks of meat along with wine and flavourings served as sauces.

Kadha   This is a bitter decoction of herbs and spices made in India and used as a medicine to cure diseases.

Kewda   Essence extracted from a *pandan* plant also known as vetiver.

Krapao   It is another name for hot basil commonly used in Thai cuisine.

Mediterraneancuisine   These are the cuisines of countries bordering the Mediterranean sea.

Oswego tea   It is a herbal tea from South Africa having bergamot as a principal ingredient.

Paprika   It is a spice from Hungary that is made from red peppers with smoky flavour.

Pesto   It is a paste of basil, garlic, pine nuts, parmesan cheese, and parsley commonly used in Italian cuisine.

Pinot Noir   It is red wine from France made from *pinot noir* grapes.

Pot pourris   Herbal arrangement of dried herbs that are used as perfumes for environment are potpourris.

Sabayon   It is whipping of egg yolks and sugar with white wine over mild heat source such as bain-marie.

Saltimbocca   It is an Italian preparation of veal *escalopes* served pan-fried.

Sauternes   It is a type of white wine from France with a slight sweet taste.

Sauvignon blanc   This is a type of white wine from France.

Shiraz   It is a kind of red wine.

Vedas   These are ancient religious texts.

Virgin olive oil   It is oil obtained by the first crush of olives.

Zinfandel   It is a white wine from Italy.

CONCEPT REVIEW QUESTIONS

1. Why were herbs used in cooking in old times?
2. What are the various forms in which herbs are available?
3. What are the other uses of herbs apart from cooking?
4. What parts of the herbs can be used in cooking?
5. How should a herb be dried and what key points should be kept in mind while drying them?
6. List various types of basils used in kitchen. How is Thai basil different from the Italian variety?
7. How should herbs be stored?
8. Why are bay leaves also known as laurel leaves?
9. How are bay leaves used in the culinary world?
10. What are the components of *fines herbes*?
11. What are the culinary uses of chervil?
12. Define Chinese parsley and its use in kitchens.
13. What is a dill herb and what are its uses?
14. What care should be taken while using marjoram herb?
15. Why should mint be chopped along with sugar?
16. Name at least three herbs that can be paired up with desserts.
17. How should parsley be chopped and used in garnishes?
18. Name three herbs that pair up best with lamb dishes.
19. Name at least two herbs popularly used in Christmas dishes.
20. What is savoury herb? How is it useful in kitchen?
21. Which herb is also known as *little dragon* and why?
22. What should be kept in mind while selecting tarragon?

23. What is *zaatar* and what are the various varieties?
24. What are the other names of *pandan* leaves?
25. Name three herbs whose flowers are used as herbs.
26. Name five herbs that are commonly used as tea.
27. Which herb produces Melissa honey?
28. Describe a bouquet garni.
29. What are the various ways in which herbs can be used as garnishes?
30. What are saltless seasonings and how are they made?
31. What are herbal oils and how are they made?
32. Describe compound butters and name at least three of these and their uses.
33. What are the various ways in which herbs are used in herbal drinks?
34. How are wines used as marinades?
35. What are the different ways of making sauces with wines?
36. What is deglazing and how does wine help in that process?
37. Why is wine added to make *court bouillon*?
38. How can wines be used for making desserts?
39. Name a dessert from Italy that uses white wine.
40. What is flambé and how is it done?

PROJECT WORK

1. In groups of five, undertake a survey of a vegetable market and list various kinds of herbs available. Take photographs and write short notes on its culinary uses, country of origin, and the seasonal availability of the product. Make a presentation and share it with other groups.
2. Take a bunch of fresh herbs and dry half of them for a couple of days and store the rest for few days as described in the chapter. After few days, compare the two with regard to colour, flavour, texture, and aroma.
3. Organize a wine tasting exercise wherein assortments of white and red wines are tasted. Make notes of which wine can go with a particular food and share your findings with the entire group.
4. Take a sample of seven to eight kinds of herbs and store in the refrigerator as described in the chapter. Make a note of changes that happen in the herb on a daily basis. Record your observations and collate the results to find out as to how long the herbs can be stored refrigerated.

PART II

INTERNATIONAL CUISINES

CHAPTER 6

WESTERN CUISINES

Learning Objectives

After reading this chapter, you should be able to

- understand the basic concept of European and Western cuisine
- comprehend the difference between various Western cuisines such as Italian, Mediterranean, and Mexican
- identify various kinds of tools and equipment used for making food in various countries in the West
- explain the different types of pastas, olive oils, cheeses, and *charcuterie* products used in Italian cooking
- comprehend the use of common ingredients in Mediterranean cooking
- examine the effects of demography on the cuisines of various countries in the West
- identify the ingredients of various countries and what makes them unique
- comprehend the use of different types tools and equipment and their effect on the final product
- recognize the various regions of Italy and intra-regional differences with respect to cuisine
- analyse the techniques used in the preparation of Mediterranean food
- identify various types of Mexican dishes and what makes them unique
- identify various kinds of chillies used in Mexican cooking

INTRODUCTION

In India people classify all food from the Western world as Continental food; however, this is not true. Continental food mainly comprises food from France and England. It was very popular once upon a time when these countries had colonized a larger part of the globe. With the onset of industrialization and advancement in technology the world became smaller, and we came across the cuisines, and cultures of more and more countries. Therefore, there arose a need to classify food afresh. In this section on international cuisines, we have broadly classified food from the world into three major subheadings such as Western food, European food, and food from the Orient. In this chapter, we will discuss the most popular cuisines such as Italian, Mexican, and Mediterranean. Though there are many cuisines in the West, such as North American and South American cuisine, we will restrict ourselves to the most popular ones that are served in hotels worldwide. Mexican food has a strong influence on some parts of North America which serves a cuisine called Tex-Mex; 'Tex' referring to Texas region in the USA and 'Mex' to Mexico.

The cuisines of the countries that touch or surround the Mediterranean Sea are referred to as Mediterranean cuisine. Although the region is part of Europe, food here is somewhat different from European cuisine and is distinct in more ways than one, perhaps due to the unique climate and the different agricultural produce of the region. Similarly, although Italy too is part of Europe, its cuisine is so different from the rest of the continent that it merits a separate classification and study. We will also discuss how the geographical location and the climate of a country play an important part on the flavours of the cuisine. We have already discussed about various food products that come from a particular cuisine or a country in the earlier chapters. Now, we will study some international cuisines in greater detail.

ITALIAN CUISINE

Italian cuisine is considered the mother of all Western and European cuisines. It is believed that the art of fine dining actually originated in Italy and spread to France with Queen Catherine de' Medici, when she got married to King Henry II of France. Italy has been the cradle of ancient civilizations and home to many ancient dynasties and clans. Thus, its culture and lifestyle as also cuisine has evolved over the years as a result influence of the different communities and regions.

Italian cuisine is one of the best known outside the country of its origin. Pasta, risotto, *fritto misto,* and pizza are enjoyed worldwide, together with excellent *charcuterie* including *mortadella, salumi,* Parma ham, etc. which we briefly discussed in the chapter on *charcuterie.* Italy is also home to many varieties of cheese that are commonly used in kitchens worldwide.

Most of the Western food is influenced by Italian cuisine, which was the first fully developed cuisine in Europe. Its pioneers, the ancient Romans, found some of their culinary inspiration in Asia Minor* and Greece and they also drew on many resources and ingredients that were homegrown. Italian cuisine took almost 1,500 years to get refined as the earlier history suggests that Italian food was all about grilled meat. It were the Romans who are credited with having influenced the Italian cuisine and what we see today is a far more refined version of that food. Since Romans were essentially shepherds and farmers, the basic essence of Italian food to strive for fresh quality produce is still followed in kitchens worldwide. Earlier, Romans used to consume a starchy porridge

---

* Asia Minor is a region of Western Asia, comprising a large part of the modern Republic of Turkey.

called *puls* that was made from millets, wholewheat, or chickpeas. Over time, millets were replaced by corn and the modern version of polenta is still a popular form of starch. Romans also learnt the art of making cheese and bread. It is believed that around 170 BC, it were the Roman cooks who commercialized the production of bread. Romans were far more advanced than other European countries and used pots and cauldrons made from bronze and iron to cook meat, while their French counterparts cooked meat by spit-roasting method, which often made the meat dry and les nutritious.

Historically, Italy has been the seat of political and intellectual power in Europe since ancient times. Not only did the Roman civilization emerge here, it is also the birthplace of Renaissance, the intellectual and cultural movement in medieval era, which shaped modern thought in Europe. This was an era of art, literature, paintings, and gastronomy. The art of preparing breads, cheese, wine, and *charcuterie* began to flourish in many parts of the country. Italy thus, became a trendsetter for many European countries. The Italians started trade with many other regions, such as the Middle East and South-East Asia, to bring in food products, such as melons, that were not found in Italy. Melons were imported from Persia and were first grown in Italy in the Cantalupo region, where the famous melon called cantaloupe comes from.

Geographical Location of Italy

Italy is located in Southern Europe and comprises the boot-shaped Italian Peninsula and a number of islands including the two largest, Sicily and Sardinia. The country is supposed to take its name for the southern part of peninsula called *Italia* which meant land of oxen or the grazing land. Another popular belief is that it is named after *Italus*, an ancient King who ruled the region.

The typical boot shape of the Italian peninsula makes it geographically very unique. The heel and the toe of this boot-shaped peninsula extend into the Mediterranean Sea and provinces such as Sicily, Calabria, and Puglia form a part of the Mediterranean region. It is a land of mountains, seas, lush green meadows. It is known for its cultural heritage, food, fashion, and natural beauty. The countryside has warm sunny beaches, ice-covered mountain peaks, and hills giving in to lush meadows that are home to many famous vineyards. Being a peninsula, it is bound by the sea on three sides and the Alps to the north. It extends into the Mediterranean Sea from southern Europe. Its neighbours to the north are France, Switzerland, Austria, and Yugoslavia. The country also includes two large islands: Sicily and Sardinia. Two independent states lie within the country: the tiny Republic of San Marino in north central Italy and Vatican City, the seat of the Roman Catholic Church. The geographical location has played a significant role in the evolution of Italian cuisine due to the availability of a wide variety of ingredients grown locally at different times of the year. Consequently, ingredients and dishes vary by region. In the following section, we will discuss the various regions of the country, from the gastronomic point of view.

Italian Regions

The various regions of Italy famous for their gastronomic fares are Abruzzo, Basilicata, Campania, Emilia-Romagna, Liguria, Lombardy, Piedmont, Puglia, Sardinia, Sicily, Tuscany, and Veneto. Each of them is discussed separately as follows.

Abruzzo

Abruzzo is situated in the central part of the Italian peninsula facing the Adriatic sea in the east. It is the most mountainous part of Italy surrounded by the Apennine mountains on the west and the coastline on the other. This region boasts a robust cuisine and variety of seafood. The Abruzzi flavour their dishes with hot chilli peppers, aromatic saffron, and olive oil. As the life is predominantly pastoral, rustic broths and meat of sheep, lamb, and mountain goat are quite prominent. Herbs, such as rosemary and garlic, are favourite ingredients of this cuisine. A pasta dish called *aglio olio pepperoncino* is a a popular Abruzzi dish.

Basilicata

This region, also known as Lucania, in Southern Italy has a rough and hard terrain and sunny weather. It is also referred to as a land of mysteries as even today life here is governed by ancient rules and philosophies. The cuisine of Basilicata is not very popular outside Italy, as food here is mainly made from meat of sheep and pigs. Fish is hard to find because it has a very small coastline. Pork is an integral part of this region and the famous sausage called *loukanika* comes from this region. The pigs in this region are quite lean and thin as they graze on land, along with sheep.

Campania

It is one of the most talked about regions of Italy with regard to food, as it has lent its most popular dish, pizza, to the world. Campania is also known as the culinary capital of southern Italy, while Bologna is regarded as the country's northern culinary capital. The region is famous for its fresh vegetables such as tomatoes, peppers, potatoes, artichokes, fennel, lemon, and oranges. The vegetables and fruits have a unique taste as they grow in fertile soil. This region is located near the active volcano of Mount Vesuvius on one side and the coast line of Naples on the other. Hence, the cuisine form this place is also known as Neapolitan. Campania is also known for its fresh Mozzarella cheese. That, perhaps, is a reason why the popular pizza originated in Campania. A variety of hard wheat known as *durum* grows here abundantly, and is a reason for pastas for originating from this place. It is one of the largest producers of pasta in Italy, and spaghetti is popularly consumed here.

Emilia-Romagna

Emilia-Romagna in northern Italy are believed to be the creators of fresh and flat pastas. Popular pastas such as lasagne, *tortellini*, and *tagliatelle*, are all from this part of the country, which is also regarded as the northern culinary capital of Italy. The region has lent the most unique and integral ingredients to Italian cuisine such as balsamic vinegar, without which

Italian cuisine would have been incomplete. The much talked about cheese *Parmigiana*, cold cuts such as *prosciutto Parma*, and Bologna sausage are from the contribution of this region. We shall discuss these unique ingredients later in this chapter.

Liguria

Liguria is a coastal region in north-western Italy. It touches the sea in the south, the Alps in the north and Apennine mountain range in the east. Thus, this region has a wonderful melange of gastronomic fares that include ingredients from the sea, the kitchen gardens, and the forests. The temperate climate of this region, thanks to presence of the sea and the cold from the Alps lends a unique flavour to the ingredients grown here. The produce is a delightful combination of fresh fruits, vegetables, and seafood. The famous basil herb (refer Chapter 5) grows in Liguria and Genoa. Thus, a famous paste made by combining basil leaves with garlic, parmesan cheese, pine nuts, and olive oil called *pesto genovese or ligurian pesto* is commonly used as flavouring agent and as a cooking ingredient. As it is located on the sea coast the cuisine of this region reflects influence from many countries including Southern France, which has an evident impact on its cuisine. The cuisine of this region also has had an influence of its Muslim past. *Minestrone* and pesto are supposed to have been invented in Liguria.

Flat breads such as *focaccia* comes from this region. Since this region is not very prone to growth of hard wheat, this region chickpeas and polenta are used in most of dishes. Gnocchi made from potatoes is also a popular dish here.

Liguria is also famous for its unique olives and olive oil. It is the producer of one of the finest 'extra virgin' olive oils of the world. Ligurians are not just seafood lovers but *porcini* and *ovoli* mushrooms are favourites here too.

Lombardy

The Lombardy region is situated in the north. The northern half of the region is mostly covered by Alpine mountains while the southern parts border with Piedmont and Emilia-Romagna. It is an agricultural province with Milan as the centre of all industrial activities. Parts of Lombardy are watered by rivers originating as streams from the melting ice of the Alps and Apennine ranges and hence the soil is very conducive to growing rice. Risottos and various other rice preparations come from this part of the land. The cattle are reared here both for milk and meat and hence butter and cream are more liberally used in this region compared to olive oil. The region is also a major producer of a wide variety of cheeses and is fondly referred to as the cheese lovers paradise of Italy. Some famous cheeses such as Gorgonzola, *Provolone*, and *Taleggio*, hail from this region. *Osso buco*, a traditional preparation of veal shanks, also comes from this region. Being very close to France and Switzerland, the cooking styles seem to be influenced more by these regions rather than Italian. A famous Christmas sweet bread preparation called *panettone* also comes from Lombardy. The cooking style of Lombardy is also called Milanese style and is usually flavoured with saffron. This style emphasizes on slow cooking in a covered dish for a long time. Only fried dishes, such as *scaloppini*, and soups are cooked on high flame. Boiled dishes should be simmered; roasts should not be cooked rapidly, but cooked slowly until the meat acquires a golden-brown colour. Historically, this region has been under Austrian dominance which has resulted in a lot of French and German influence on its cuisine and culture.

Piedmont

The cuisine of Piedmont region in north-western Italy is amongst the most varied and refined in both taste and presentation. The people of Piedmont are believed to be lovers of food and like to eat a wide spread of quality produce but in moderation. As this region borders France to its north, the influence of French cooking and eating habits is widespread. The style of service is quite reminiscent of France with the food eaten course wise. The distinctive use of lard and butter in their cuisine is however, seeing a downward trend because of high cholesterol levels. The frequent use of garlic, fresh raw vegetables, as well as truffles have led to the creation of a famous sauce called *Bagna càuda,* which is served along with boiled or roasted vegetables. Piedmont also produces the biggest number of cheeses, out of which eight are protected under a geographical status called DOP (or Denominazione di Origine Protetta) which is a classification given to a food item which denotes the origin of a product from a particular region. The chief agricultural products of the plains in Piedmont are grains. It is the greatest rice-producing area of Italy. The streams that run off the mountains are diverted to flood the fields in which rice is cultivated. Since rice cultivation involves the flooding of fields, carp are bred in the still water. The most famous wheat products of the region are breadsticks called *grissini.* These breadsticks are from Turin (capital of Piedmont). French Emperor Napoleon was very fond of these and he called them 'those little Turinese sticks'.

Fresh homemade pastas such as the famous *agnolotti* (pasta folded over like a shape of a rectangle) is quite popular here. Piedmont is also famous for its pastry and chocolate confections. The hazelnut flavoured chocolate called *gianduja* is from Piedmont. The most prized truffle is the white truffle, now also called the Piedmont truffle, which comes from the Lange region south of Alba. The white truffle has a stronger flavour than the black variety.

Puglia

Situated at the south-eastern tip of the Italian peninsula, Puglia is also known as Apulia in Italy. Puglia is one of the largest food producing regions of the country. Located on the heel of the boot-shaped map, this region produces wheat, tomatoes, zucchini, fennel, endives, and a variety of lentils such as chickpeas, cannellini beans, and fava beans. It is also the largest producer of olive oil in Italy and its cuisine predominantly serves a range of seafood and shell fish such as oysters and mussels. It, thus, contributes to the Mediterranean cuisine also. This region is also famous for its durum wheat pastas; a traditional pasta from this region is *orechiette* which is ear-shaped pasta. One of the unique things about this cuisine is that nothing is wasted here. Stale bread is pan-fried in olive oil and used as garnish in pastas or broths. Extra vegetables are sun-dried and stored for winters.

Sardinia

Situated in the Mediterranean sea, Sardinia is the second largest island in Italy after Sicily. The moment we hear the word Sardinia, sardines come to our mind. This region of Italy uses a bountiful amount of seafood in its regional cuisine. Sardinia has been influenced by explorers of various countries such as Greece, France, and Spain and that is quite evident in its food. Stews, roasts, and broths are the most common type of food style of this region. The botarga caviar discussed in Chapter 3 also comes from this region. Mint and myrtle are popular herbs used in regional cuisine. Apart from seafood and shellfish, pork and suckling pigs are also very popular here. One such preparation is *porceddu* that is a suckling pig cooked on a spit. The breads here made are dry rather than moist in order to improve their keeping qualities.

Sicily

Sicily is the largest island in the Mediterranean Sea. The cuisine of Sicily has been influenced by the Greeks, Spainish, and Arabs, though the base is predominantly Italian. The cuisine of Sicily and Puglia form a part of Mediterranean cuisine also. The use of vegetables such as tomatoes, peppers, and eggplant is in abundance, and fish such as tuna, sea bass, and swordfish are commonly eaten, along with shellfish. Lots of couscous (an influence from Morocco in Africa) is also found in Sicily. Influence from the Mediterranean cuisines has led to a range of appetizers or *antipasti* being served in this cuisine. Hot *antipasti* such as *arancine* which are deep-fried rice croquettes and cold *antipasti,* such as *Sicilian caponata,* are very popular. The famous and popular desserts of Sicily, such as *cannoli, Cassata, and granita* are the influence of the Arabs. Sicily uses lots of citrus fruits in its cuisine. Varieties of blood orange are commonly found in Sicily. The famous *ricotta* cheese comes from Sicily. The olive oil used in this part is very robust.

Tuscany

Tuscany is the heartland of Italy. It takes up a large part of the coastline on the Tyrrhenian Sea and so seafood plays an important part in the Tuscan cuisine. It is a land of olives, wheat, and wine. The major food of the land are bread, pasta, fruits, vegetables, high-quality cheese, and cured meat. The style of cooking in Tuscany is simple and the flavours are preserved while cooking. While many people associate Italian food being rich in garlic, tomatoes, olive oil, and herbs, the cuisine of Tuscany uses seasonings sparingly to merely enhance the flavours of the natural ingredients. The famous minestrone soup is from this region.

Umbria

Umbrian cuisine is not very refined in nature. It is derived from the *cucina povera,* which mean food of the poor or peasant cooking. Though it has such a name, it does not mean that this cuisine uses low-quality ingredients. On the contrary, this region relies heavily on fresh produce and seasonal cooking. A land of valleys and mountains, Umbria has a very rich cuisine. Olives and fresh herbs are used in abundance. The food includes beef, pork, veal, baby lamb, game birds, and seafood such as trout and crabs. *Prosciutto* and fresh sausages from this region are very famous. This region is also famous for Umbrian truffles and mushrooms and vegetables, such as wild asparagus, *chayotes*, and *courgettes*, form a large part of the vegetarian meal. Another remarkable product of this region is its dark green and robust olive oil. The pastas and risottos are adorned with sliced fresh truffles and olive oil. This is the only region in Italy without a coastline and thus fish from the natural lakes adorn the tables. Fish such as trout, mullet, and carp are often grilled and served with fresh sautéed mushrooms and vegetables.

Veneto

It is a region of simple but charming towns including its crowning jewel, Venice. Venice once was a powerful city supplying Europe with spices, salt, and goods from the Orient. The most important food here is rice, polenta, beans, and *baccalà*, which is a salted cod. Pasta is not used much here except for gnocchi which is a part of festivals. Though *arborio* is commonly used for risotto in most of the parts of Italy, but special rice called *carnaroli* and *vialone nano* are particularly grown in Veneto to make delectable risottos. This region is particularly famous for its mushrooms, asparagus, and pumpkin. Though this region does not boast of a great variety of cheese, however, a famous cheese called *Asiago* comes from here. Squid and cuttle fish are commonly used seafood and squid ink is often used to colour and flavour risottos and pastas. The famous Italian dessert *tiramisu* comes from this region as well.

Special Ingredients in Italian Cuisine

Italian cuisine is as diverse as Indian food. Each region has a typical flavour profile associated with it and the reasons too are similar to Indian cuisine; such as influences, availability of ingredients, and location of the place. Ingredients form a backbone of any cuisine, but Italians are very particular about seasonal and fresh produce and this is reflected in their cooking. Though pasta is the commonly eaten staple food across Italy, yet it is made in many different shapes and dough. Let us examine the unique ingredients of Italian cuisine.

Cheese

Cheese has always been the basic ingredient on every table in the European continent. The various cheese varieties in the continent are distinctive to the region or places of their origin. In fact, the Italians boast of a larger variety of cheese than the French. Most of the Italian cheeses are DOP. There are many types of cheeses available in Italy, but we would discuss some of the most commonly used ones in hotels around the world in Table 6.1.

Salumi

Salumi is an Italian word for *charcuterie* that we discussed in Chapter 2. Italy has always been famous for its *salumi*. Italians mostly preserve their *salumis* by air-drying and like to eat a lot of ham and bacon in different styles. Some of the common *salumis* used in Italian cuisine in are discussed Table 6.2.

Table 6.1 Common types of Italian cheeses (see also Plate 4)

Cheese	Description	Photograph
Parmesan or *Parmigiano-Reggiano*	It is a grainy and hard cheese which is and is particularly used for cooking. It is usually grated over pastas or split open with a special wedge-shaped knife. It is also popularly referred to as the 'king' of cheeses and is aged for 12 months to 2 years. The older the cheese, the more expensive it is. The cheese takes its name from Parma and nearby places in Emilia-Romagna region of Italy, where it is produced and is a DOP certified variety. The cheese would be called *Grana Padano* if it is made in Lombardy region. Parmesan, which is the French adjective of *parma*, cheese is commonly known as *Parmigiano-Reggiano*. It is one of the oldest varieties of cheeses of Italy and is cooked from cow's milk but is not pressed. It is packed as large wheel-shaped cakes, each weighing around 30 kg. Traditionally, the whey obtained from making this cheese is fed to the pigs that are reared for *prosciutto* Parma ham.	
Pecorino	It is a pungent cheese made from sheep's milk. This cheese is produced in almost every province of central and southern Italy. It matures faster than Parmesan cheese and becomes hard within 7–8 months only. It is used in making sauces and pastas. The *Pecorino* that is made in Emilia Romagna, called *Pecorino Romano*, is pepper flavoured while the one from Sardinia, called *Pecorino Sardo*, is slightly more acidic and sharp.	
Ricotta	It is a soft creamy cheese made from ewe's milk. The unique thing about this cheese is that it is made from whey which is low in fat content. *Ricotta* cheese is drained in special baskets and the marks of the basket can be easily seen on the surface of the cheese. *Ricotta* cheese is often used as stuffing for pastas and also commonly used for making desserts.	
Mascarpone	This creamy cheese comes from Lombardy region and is made from cow's milk. It is prepared by adding tartaric acid to warm milk and allowed to curdle. It is then drained in cheesecloth and allowed to ripen for a few days. *Mascarpone* is commonly used for preparing a famous Italian dessert called *tiramisu* but it can also be used as stuffing for pasta.	
Gorgonzola	Gorgonzola is a famous blue-veined cheese from the regions of Piedmont and Lombardy. Since these regions border France, it is quite possible that the French blue cheese called Roquefort was also inspired by this cheese. Made from cow's milk, this cheese is curdled with starter bacteria and *Penicillium glaucum*, which are responsible for creating the traditional greenish blue streaks in the cheese. Gorgonzola melts easily and it is thus commonly used in cooking as well.	

(Contd)

Table 6.1 (Contd)

Cheese	Description	Photograph
Asiágo	Also made from cow's milk, this cheese is from Veneto region and is a DOP cheese. *Asiago* can be aged for short or for long durations. When aged for a long time, this cheese can become hard and resemble the texture of Parmesan cheese. *Asiago* is a good table cheese, but it can also be used in salads, soups, and sauces. When fresh, it can be used for sandwiches such as panini.	
Caciocavallo	This cheese, predominantly produced in Sicily, is prepared from cow or sheep's milk. It takes its name from *cavallo*, which in Italian means horseback and this is so because the cheese is shaped like saddlebags. This is done by kneading the cheese in lukewarm water. It is manually given the pouch shape.	
Taleggio	This cheese is unique to the Lombardy region. It is a soft cheese that is made from full cream cow's milk. The cheese is mild with a citrus fruit aroma. The crust is very thin and studded with small salt crystals. It is commonly served with fruits and can be paired with salad greens such as radicchio, Belgian endive, rocket, or added onto risottos and polenta.	
Castelmagno	*Castelmagno* is among the oldest cheeses from Piedmont region and carries a DOP certification. The whole milk of cows of Piedmontese breed is typically used for producing this semi-hard cheese. Apart from being served as an elegant table cheese, it is also used in many Italian dishes, especially sauces as it melts easily.	
Caprino	*Caprino* is made from goat's milk. The name comes from Capra for goat in Italy. The cheese can be aged for 25–30 days depending upon the desired product. *Caprino fresco* or fresh cheese is aged for only 3–4 days, while 25–30 days aged *Caprino* is called *Caprino stagionato* which means seasoned. Fresco is more like a creamy cheese and can be used in cooking and served on table as well.	
Robiola	It is a soft-ripened cheese from Piedmont and Lombardy regions. It is made from combinations of milk from cow, sheep, and goat. The *robiola* from Piedmont is eaten with honey as it is a fresh cheese, whereas the one from Lombardy is a DOP cheese that is seasoned. It develops a sour acidic taste which is quite mild and special. It is usually served as table cheese but can be paired with risottos.	

(Contd)

Table 6.1 (Contd)

Cheese	Description	Photograph
Mozzarella	Mozzarella is a native of Campania and is made from the milk of water buffalo. It is a fresh cheese and low in fat content. Mozzarella is always associated with pizza and the unique property of this stringy melting cheese makes it an ideal medium for topping on pizzas and other dishes.	
Scarmorza	This cheese is quite similar to Mozzarella cheese. However, its unique pear shape due to the fact that this cheese is tied in plastic bags and hung to dry. It is also commonly served smoked and can be used instead of Mozzarella.	
Provolone	*Provolone* is made in Veneto and Lombardy regions of Southern Italy. It is a semi-hard cheese that is seasoned for at least 3–4 months. *Provolone* comes in fancy shapes as it is sometimes tied up with strings to give it its traditional oval shape. Three different types of *provolone* are quite popular such as mild called *dolce* which means sweet, *picante* which means sharp, and *affumicata* which means smoked.	
Bocconcini	It is a small bundled cheese prepared from milk of water buffaloes. It is a *pasta filata* cheese, which means that it is prepared by dipping curd cheese in warm salted water and then stretching and folding it to give smooth shapes. They are small dumplings of fresh cheese packed in its own whey and finds its use in salads to prepare tomato and mozzarella salad or used in bruschettas and sandwiches. It can also be coated in *anglaise* style and deep-fried and served as popular snack.	

Table 6.2 Types of *salumi* in Italian cuisine

Salumi	Description	Photograph
Salami	Refer Chapter 2, Table 2.9.	
Prosciutto	Refer Chapter 2, Table 2.10.	
Bacon	Refer Chapter 2, Table 2.10.	
Salami Milano	This is probably the most common salami that is popularly eaten and served around the world. It is made in Lombardy, especially Milan, by grinding pork and beef, along with some bacon. The salami becomes more and more seasoned as one travels southwards in Italy. These are air-dried and some can be matured up to 10 years as well.	

(Contd)

Table 6.2   (Contd)

Salumi	Description	Photograph
Cotechino	*Cotechino* is an Italian *salumi* that resembles salami when purchased. It is prepared from lean meat from head and neck of pig and is highly seasoned. One of the most important ingredients of this product is the chopped and salted rind of pork that provides it its characteristic flavour as well as name. The name comes from the Italian word *cotica* which means rind. *Cotechino* is slowly cooked for at least 4 hours which give the fat around jelly-like consistency that oozes out when it is sliced. It is therefore, customarily served with lentils and boiled potatoes or polenta, so that they can soak up the fat. It is quite popularly served on new year eve dinners.	
Bologna	Bologna is the capital of Emilia-Romagna and it is also the name of a large sausage that resembles *mortadella*. Surprisingly, this sausage is not Italian except its name. It was popularly made by the Americans after being inspired by the *mortadella* from Bologna. The meat is ground finely and the texture of the cooked sausage resembles frankfurters.	
Mortadella	Refer Chapter 2, Table 2.9.	
Bresaola	It is air-dried salted beef from Lombardy region, which is aged for almost 2–3 months until it becomes hard and turns deep red to purple in colour and acquires a sweet musty smell. Thin slices of *bresaola* combine very well with bitter greens, such as *rucola*, and pair up well with olive oil.	
Baccalà	A very popular Mediterranean dish, *baccalà* is salted cod fish. The tradition is to preserve the fish by salting and drying, so that it lasts up to a few months. Before cooking, the cod must be soaked and washed several times to remove the salty flavours.	

Olive oil

Olive oil is the most popular cooking medium in the Mediterranean countries. Apart from Italy, Greece, Spain, Turkey, and Tunisia, nowadays, olive oil is also produced in many other countries of the world. It is extracted from the olive fruit, the procedure of which is the same as it was thousands of years ago. The only difference is that new equipment and machinery have replaced stone grinders. The cultivation of olive tree requires a climate which is typical of Mediterranean countries. Olive oil is graded and classified on various parameters such as its level of acidity, taste, and aroma. Some of the common olive oils used in Italian cuisine are described in Table 6.3.

Table 6.3 Types of olive oils used in Italian cooking

Olive oil	Description	Photograph
Extra virgin olive oil	When the olive is graded, it is checked for acidity levels, which is measured as percentage per 100 g. If the acidity is around 1 per cent or less than 1 per cent, then the oil is classified as extra virgin olive oil. The word 'virgin' in olive oils implies that it is made by physical means and no chemicals or refining has been done. An extra virgin olive oil is dark green in colour and is commonly used to sprinkle on salads and pastas. It is quite sensitive to sunlight and hence packed in dark coloured bottles.	
Virgin olive oil	Olive oil that has between 1 and 2 per cent acidity is classified as virgin olive oil. It is also drizzled on pastas and salads.	
Pomace oil	To make olive oil, the olives are crushed to a paste and allowed to percolate through straw mats. Pressure is applied to extract as much oil as possible. The remaining paste after pressing still contains around 10 per cent olive oil that cannot be pressed or extracted further. Thereafter, a chemical solvent is used which enables further extraction. Oil thus obtained is called pomace oil. Pomace can be used in deep-frying as it has a high smoke point.	
Pure olive oil	This term can cause a lot of confusion among people who do not know about olive oil and its production. Pure olive oil is regarded as low quality oil compared to virgin and extra virgin olive oils, as they are made by refining. Refined or pure olive oils are prepared by chemical treatments that neutralize the acid content and it could be a blend of various olive oils. It is also sold as 100 per cent olive oil.	

Starches

Various kinds of starches are used in Italian cooking. These can be prepared and served as accompaniments or they can be used as a main meal as well. Some starch such as *durum* wheat semolina is used for making products such as pasta and couscous, whereas some ground corn is used for making creamy and soft polenta that are served as accompaniment or as a dish itself. Some of the commonly used starches in Italian cooking are discussed in Table 6.4.

Table 6.4 Various types of starches used in Italian cooking

Starches	Description	Photograph
Risotto/rice	What pasta is to southern Italy, rice is to the north. Short grain plump rice that grows in the regions of Lombardy, Piedmont, and Veneto are typically used for making risotto. Italian rice is graded into four types: *ordinario*, *semi fino*, *fino*, and *super fino*, according to the grain size. Risotto is prepared from the *fino* and *semi fino* varieties, as they can hold their shape on slow cooking, while *ordinario* is commonly used in desserts. The following are some of the common varieties of rice used for making risotto. *Arborio* It is one of the most popular known risotto rice varieties that is native to north-west Italy. It has a large plump grain compared to finer varieties of risotto rice *Vialone nano* It has a plump grain and a firm inner starch which gives risotto a slightly more bite. *Carnaroli* This premium variety of risotto rice is the hybrid of an Italian and a Japanese variety. It has a soft starch outside which dissolves during cooking leaving behind the inner grain which gives it a firm bite. Risotto rice absorbs more liquid than other rice and thus more liquid is added at frequent intervals.	
Couscous	Couscous is a product obtained from semolina and is usually steamed and tossed with olive oil, lentils, and seafood. It is commonly eaten in and around Sicily and it is influenced from Morocco which also forms part of Mediterranean cuisine. Nowadays, instant couscous is available in the market which needs to be rehydrated in boiled water.	
Polenta	Polenta is cornmeal flour obtained by grinding maize or corn. It can be ground coarsely or into fine powder depending upon how it is used and the region it comes from. It may be yellow or white in colour depending upon the variety of the corn used. Polenta is one of the oldest eaten dishes in Italy since the times of the Romans. Earlier it was eaten like a porridge, but nowadays polenta can be ground into various textures such as soft, grainy, and firm and served as accompaniment or made like cakes, set, cut, and then grilled or pan-fried and served as a dish in itself.	
Chickpeas	Also called garbanzo beans or *cecci* in Italy, it is commonly used in all Mediterranean countries. These are commonly used in Southern Italy for making stews or broths and served with couscous.	

(Contd)

Table 6.4 (Contd)

Starches	Description	Photograph
Farro	Also known as *emmer* or *spelt, farro* wheat is commonly used in Italian cuisine to make breads and various types of pastas. It may also commonly be used to thicken or add body to soups and broths or simply boiled and added to salads.	
Durum wheat	*Durum* in Latin means hard. This wheat produces hard flour that is most apt for pastas because of its high gluten content. *Durum* wheat is milled to obtain fine semolina that is traditionally used for making pastas. More milling would result in finer *durum* flour, which is used for making breads.	

Pasta

The word pasta comes from Latin word *pastos* which means dough. Pasta is a firm dough made from *durum* wheat semolina and eggs, and can be flavoured with vegetable purees, squid ink, herbs, etc. to make different varieties. There are two major types of pasta: dried and fresh. Dried pastas can be prepared at home or procured packaged. Fresh pastas are highly perishable and should be used within two days. However, it can be stored for long if it is frozen. Pasta is believed to be introduced by the legendary traveller Marco Polo, who saw it in China in the form of noodles. Though this is traditionally made with *durum* wheat, it is not uncommon to see pastas being made with variety of other flour such as wholewheat buckwheat, rye flour, spelt flour, etc.

The making of pasta dough is simple; It is basically a dough made of flour, egg yolks, olive oil, and some salt. No water added to the dough, which is quite firm as compared to the soft dough. Pasta dough would comprise 25 per cent of liquid to the weight of the flour. The eggs are mainly used to add flavour, colour, nutrition, and moisture to the dough. The following steps are involved in making a pasta dough.

Step 1 Weigh out all the ingredients such as flour, egg yolks, eggs, salt, and olive oil. Though only egg yolks can be used but a combination of few yolks and few whole eggs give good results.

Step 2 Sieve the flour on the table and make a well in the centre. Add salt all around the well and pour olive oil, yolks, and whole eggs in the centre as shown in Fig. 6.1 (a) and work the fingers in a circular motion to collect all the flour to form a dough as shown in Fig. 6.1 (b). Do not knead too much as more gluten will be formed during the sheeting and rolling of pasta dough.

CHEF'S TIP

While sheeting and rolling keep the rest of the dough always covered, so that it does not form any scales and dry surfaces.

Step 3 Wrap the dough in a plastic film or wet duster and chill in refrigerator for at least 2–3 hours to relax. This will help to roll out the dough easily and effectively. Now the dough is ready to be rolled out. This can be

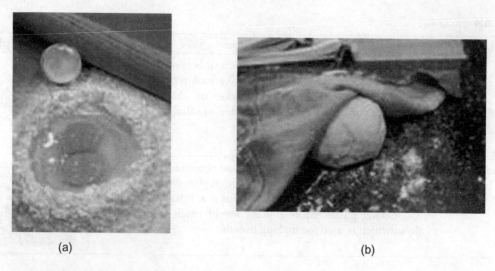

(a)   (b)

Fig. 6.1 Steps involved in making a pasta dough

achieved by rolling by hand or using a machine called pasta machine. The pastas in hotels would be rolled using such machines to cut down on labour and time.

Step 4 Sheet the dough and cut according to desired shape and size. To sheet out the dough, divide the large dough into smaller portions.

Hand roll the dough to form a thin rectangle and then start to sheet on a pasta machine through the widest setting to the small setting but gradually and progressively. It is important to fold the pasta a couple of times and then sheet again. This not only gives a smooth finish to the pasta but also develops gluten. If the dough does not roll smoothly, rest it for a while as sometimes overstretching of gluten can cause this to happen.

The pasta is sheeted out to the desired thickness which can depend upon type of pasta and the purpose. When making pasta sheets, they must be floured well and stacked well, sprinkled with flour to avoid sticking of the pasta. If being used fresh, they can be boiled in salted water and cooked till *al dente* which is an Italian term that denotes 'a bite' or a crunch. The pasta can then be drained and tossed up with prepared sauce and served hot. If the pasta is to be frozen, then the pasta should be arranged on a tray far from each other and then frozen. After it is frozen, they can be put together in a box and kept frozen until further use. While cooking frozen pastas, boil them in salted water in the frozen state or else thawing will make the pasta sticky and soft.

Many variously shaped pastas are commercially made from special machines, whereas hand-made pastas can also be rolled out into various shapes, albeit lesser in number as shown in Fig. 6.2.

Common types of pastas Some common types of pastas used in hotels and restaurants are described in Table 6.5.

 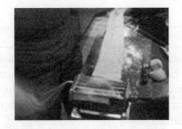 

Fig. 6.2 Rolling out pastas of various shapes

Table 6.5 Commonly used pastas in Italian cuisine (see also Plate 4)

Pasta	Description	Photograph
Penne	It is a tubular pasta, which has pointed ends. In Italy, it can be of two types: smooth and ridged. *Penne* pasta goes well with chunky sauces as due to its tubular design, it can hold the sauce very well.	
Farfalle	This is a bow-shaped pasta prepared by cutting a small sheet with combed edges and pinched in the centre to form a bow. *Farfalle* is best paired with creamy sauces.	
Fusilli	*Fusilli* is a long, narrow pasta that resembles a corkscrew. It pairs best with tomato sauce.	
Maccheroni	Commonly called macaroni in English, it is a short curved hollow tubular pasta that is commonly used for saucy and baked dishes.	
Rigatoni	*Rigatoni* is tubular pasta that is slightly larger than a penne. It can be pointed like a *penne* or even be straight-edged. Since it has a larger area inside, it pairs up well with chunky sauces.	

(Contd)

Table 6.5 (Contd)

Pasta	Description	Photograph
Cannelloni	*Cannelloni* is a tubular pasta that is at least 3 inches long and 1–1.5 inch in diameter. It is used for stuffing and then baked. It can also be made by rolling out the pasta sheet and then rolling it again to form a cylinder after stuffing with a savoury filling.	
Conchiglie	*Conchiglie* is a sea shell- or conch-shaped pasta which is very popular as it can hold a good amount of sauces because of its shape.	
Orecchiette	It is an ear-shaped pasta from Puglia region. Its unique shape of a small disc with a bulge in the centre resembles a small ear and thus the name.	
Lasagna/Lasagne	This is one of the most popular pasta dishes eaten across the world. It is a large sheet of pasta sometimes with wavy edges. It is blanched and then is layered with cheese, tomatoes, béchamel sauce, and baked in large pans.	
Pappardelle	This word comes from an Italian word *papare* which means to gobble up. This pasta is a 5-inch long strip of 2–3 cm width. It is usually paired with creamy mushroom sauces.	
Fettucine	This is a thin long strip of pasta less than 1 cm wide. This pasta pairs well with creamy sauces. *Fettuccine carbonara* is one such classical preparation.	
Capellini	This pasta is also known as angel hair because of its very thin noodle-like shape. One has to be careful while cooking it, as overcooking can spoil its taste and texture.	
Malfatti	*Malfati* is prepared in the same manner as *pappardelle,* but instead of 5-inch long strips, this ribbon pasta is cut at an angle and at a distance of 1–1.5 inch intervals to obtain a rhomboid design.	

(Contd)

Table 6.5 (Contd)

Pasta	Description	Photograph
Garganelli	*Garganelli* is made by rolling the *malfatti* pasta over a bamboo stick. The shape thus becomes tubular like *penne*, but what makes it different from a penne is the overlap of the edges.	
Tagliatelle	This pasta is made in a unique manner. The dough is sheeted out and then rolled up lengthwise to form a cylinder. It is then sliced at an interval of half inch and unrolled to obtain this pasta.	
Tagliolini	It is same as *tagliatelle* but the only difference is that it is sliced at intervals of one-fourths of an inch.	
Paccheri	*Paccheri* pasta is a tubular pasta that resembles *cannelloni* but this pasta is only 1.5–2 inches long. It is not stuffed like *cannelloni*, instead it is boiled and tossed with garlic-flavoured sauces.	
Spaghetti	This is one of the most commonly eaten pastas. It is thin and rod shaped, and usually 30 cm in length. It is paired with tomato or meat sauce called *bolognese*.	
Linguine	*Linguine* is like spaghetti but the shape is slightly concave (imagine a flattened spaghetti). When one looks at the cross-section of this pasta, one can see the oval or boat shape.	
Bucatini	*Bucatini* is a very thin tubular and long pasta. It is different from spaghetti as the former is thin, long but tube shaped, whereas spaghetti is thin and long and solid.	

Stuffed pastas   There is yet another range of pastas that are very popular on the gourmet table. These are hand rolled, stuffed, and covered with another sheet of pasta and cut into various shapes. The fillings can range from cheese and vegetables to roasted meats. A few stuffed pastas are discussed in Table 6.6.

Table 6.6 Special types of hand-made stuffed pastas

Pasta	Decription	Photograph
Ravioli	It is made by rolling out a sheet of pasta and placing the filling on it at equal intervals. The dough is then brushed with egg mixture while another sheet is placed on top to encase the fillings. Thereafter, it is cut into a round or square shape and the edges are pinched with fork to seal the fillings. This is the underlying principle behind the making of stuffed pastas.	
Cappelletti	It is a cap-shaped pasta which is made by cutting out round disc shapes from a pasta sheet. After placing the fillings, it is folded and then the edges are joined together to resemble a hat.	
Agnolotti	*Agnolotti* is small rectangular ravioli which is prepared by sheeting out the pasta dough and cutting it into 3-inch-wide strips. Filling is placed at equal intervals and the sheet is folded into half in such a way that a ribbon is obtained with a filling inside. Now the pasta is cut into rectangular shapes and the three cut sides are pinched to secure the filling inside.	
Pansotti	*Pansotti* in Italian means 'pot-bellied'. This triangular-shaped pasta is made by rolling the pasta into a sheet and then cutting it into desired squares. The filling is placed in the centre and folded along the diagonal to form a triangle with the filling inside. The free edges are pinched to secure the filling.	
Tortellini	There are many legends about this pasta. One of them is that *tortellini* is shaped like the navel of goddess Venus. It is one of the most popular pastas of Emilia-Romagna and is prepared by rolling the pasta and cutting into round discs. These are then folded into half after filling and the edges pulled together and joined to resemble the shape of a navel.	
Gnocchi	This is an altogether different type of pasta but we will discuss it here along with hand-made pastas. Gnocchi is prepared with potatoes. The potatoes are roasted and then mashed. The mash is then mixed with egg yolks, parmesan cheese, and a small amount of flour. Care should be taken not to over-knead the dough. The knead is then rolled into small ropes and pinched to make small balls. These are then thumb pressed onto special ridged wooden gnocchi boards and poached in salted water. Once cooked, these are tossed in sauce and served as a pasta dish.	

Preparing pastas Preparing or tossing pasta is an art. Boiling the pasta to the right degree, allowing for the carry over cooking time in the pan to ensure the all important *al* *dente* texture are significant aspects of pasta preparation. Numerous kinds of sauces and stew, such as ragout, napolitaine and pesto, are prepared and served along with pasta. At imes the pasta is tossed along with the sauce or the tossed pasta is placed in a serving plate and topped with sauces. In many establishments, sauce is served separately and the guest is given the privilege to add it according to their choice. There are many shapes and styles of pastas in Italy and there is no hard and fast rule of serving pasta with any sauce in particular. However, the following two points must be kept in mind while deciding upon the sauce.

- Serve flat pastas with creamy sauces. Because of their shape, they allow the sauce to coat the pastas without giving a feeling of being too creamy.
- Lighter pastas must be accompanied with light sauces and more robust pastas must be paired with robust sauces.

The pasta, whether dried or fresh, needs to be boiled in heavily salted water before it can be tossed in sauces in the pan. The cooking time for each pasta would depend upon its shape and the flour it is made from. It is important to read the cooking time which is given on the package. For fresh pasta, one should rely on the touch and feel of the pasta and in many cases, fresh pasta only takes about 2–3 minutes to get cooked. Though pastas should be blanched or boiled to order, but where it is not possible, it is a good idea to boil the pasta and drain out the water and then coat with olive oil and keep refrigerated until further use. Even when using pre-boiled pasta, it is important that it is refreshed in hot water for at least a minute, before it is plunged into sauce and tossed. The end product must have a crunch and a bite which is referred to as al dente. Pastas can be tossed in a variety of sauces, some of which are listed in Table 6.7.

Balsamic vinegar

Yet another unique ingredient used in Italian cooking is the famous balsamic vinegar. The most popular and famous one comes from the Modena and Emilia-Romagna regions of Italy. Though classified as vinegar, it is not vinegar in the true sense. It is prepared traditionally by cooking the juice from white *Trebbiano* grapes, which is the second most popular grape grown in the world. This condiment is protected by the DOP. Balsamic vinegar is sold under two names, namely

- *Aceto Balsamico Tradizionale di Modena*
- *Aceto Balsamico di Modena*

The former is more expensive while the second one is a less expensive vinegar that is commonly used around the world. Traditionally, the reduced grape juice is aged for a period of 12 years during which it acquires a deep red colour and a sweet taste.

Balsamic vinegar is often used in dressings or can be paired with red wine and cooked until it reduces to a thick syrupy called balsamic reduction. Gnerally, it is liberally sprinkled over salads, main courses, or on a plate to add colour and flavour to the dish.

Table 6.7   Common pasta sauces

Pasta sauce	Description
Napolitana	It is also known as *sauce de pomodoro* because it is made from tomatoes which are called *pomodoro* in Italian. The tomatoes are blanched and the skin is removed. They are then deseeded and chopped to obtain a tomato *concassé*. In a pan, heat olive oil and sauté chopped onions, garlic, carrot, and celery and deglaze with white wine. Now add *concassé* and stew for around 45 minutes until a thick sauce is obtained. It is flavoured with chopped flat Italian parsley and can be used as it is or pureed to obtain a smooth sauce.
Arrabbiata	Same as *napolitana* sauce but it has more garlic and chilli flakes. It is quite a popular pasta in India because of the spicy taste.
Puttanesca	It is an extension of the *arrabbiata* pasta sauce, wherein ingredients such as capers, sliced olives, and parmesan cheese, and anchovy fillets are tossed along with the pasta and *arrabbiata* sauce.
Amatriciana	This sauce is prepared by rendering some bacon such as *guanciale* or *pancetta* and then adding *napolitana* sauce. The smoky flavour added by the bacon is peculiar to this sauce.
Carbonara	This is an emulsified sauce prepared by heating a liaison of cream, egg yolks, and parmesan cheese to produce a smooth and a creamy sauce that pairs up well with flat pasta such as *fettuccine* or *pappardelle*. The cooking procedure is very simple yet requires a lot of skill, as the sauce can easily get curdled if the heat is not regulated well.
Alfredo	This is one of the most basic sauces made by combining cream and butter and bringing them to a boil. Thereafter, Parmesan cheese is added and the pasta is tossed in it. Usually, diced ham and mushrooms are also added to *alfredo*.
Cream sauces	Many types of creamy sauces are used as pasta sauces. Some of these, such as *carbonara* and *alfredo,* have been discussed above. Another way of making creamy sauces is to boil the cream with *mirepoix* (combination of carrots, onion, and celery) and then thicken with small amounts of *béchamel* sauce. To this, various types of ingredients can be added to make cream sauces. The most popular ones are Gorgonzola cheese sauce, *pesto* cream sauce, creamy tomato sauce, etc.
Butter and herb sauces	These sauces are very popular in Piedmont and Lombardy regions where butter is commonly used for cooking. Butter is combined with sage herb and then cooked until nut brown. This sauce goes very well with raviolis and other stuffed pastas.
Pesto	*Pesto* is a green paste of basil, parsley, Parmesan cheese, pine nuts, salt, and black pepper. It is tossed with boiled pasta.
Aglio olio pepperoncino	This sauce is a combination of chopped garlic (*aglio*) and olive oil (*olio*) flavoured with chilli (*pepperoncino*) and hence the name. First, the oil is heated and chopped garlic is sautéed in it. Chopped chilli flakes are added and then freshly boiled pasta is added to the pan and tossed until the sauce coats the pasta. Freshly chopped parsley and Parmesan cheese are sprinkled liberally and tossed well.

Special Equipment Used in Italian Cuisine

Every region in the world utilizes some special equipment for the production of its unique cuisine. In the book *Quantity Food Production Operations and Indian Cuisine,* we read about the regional cuisines of India and saw the diversity in the equipment used in our cuisine. Similarly, Italians use some special equipment and tools for the production of their dishes and *mise en place.* Some of the commonly used equipment in Italian cuisine are described in Table 6.8.

Table 6.8 Equipment used in Italian cooking

Equipment	Description	Photograph
Paiolo	This is a traditional cast iron kettle or pot used for making polenta. It could also be made of copper and aluminium. The pot is slightly rounded at the base to prevent polenta from sticking to the dish while cooking.	
Chitarra	*Chitarra*, also known as pasta harp, is traditionally used in the Abruzzo region of Italy. It is called so because it looks like a harp with 36 strings on one side and 72 on the other side. The side with 72 chords yields pasta called spaghetti *chitarra*. It was common in Italy during the Renaissance Era. Pasta sheets are placed over the wires and then pressed to obtain the string-shaped pasta.	
Pizza oven	This is an oven made of fire bricks. Wooden logs are burnt inside until they turn to amber colour. Then burning coal is pushed to one side of the oven while the hearth of the oven is used for baking pizzas.	
Scolapasta	A must for any Italian kitchen, *scolapasta* is basically a strainer used to drain pasta. This equipment has now been replaced with electric pasta cookers, which are like bain-marie, in which perforated baskets containing pasta are lowered into boiling water and cooked.	*Scolapasta* Electric pasta cooker
Mozzarella slicer	It is an equipment used to cut slices of Mozzarella cheese in even circular shapes. It efficiently reduces wastage of the same.	
Mezzaluna	It is a half-moon cutter used for fine chopping. It is specially used for chopping herbs such as parsley, thyme, and oregano. *Mezzaluna* means half moon and the name is unique to the shape of this chopper.	
Gnocchi board	This is a small wooden bat with ridged lines. It is used for shaping and giving the *gnocchi* its traditional shape and look.	

(Contd)

Table 6.8 (Contd)

Equipment	Description	Photograph
Mortar and pestle	This equipment is used all over the world. In Italy, it is particularly used for making *pesto.* It consists of two parts— a bowl and a crusher. The items required to be crushed are placed in the bowl and manually crushed with the crusher that is pounded on the ingredients to make a paste. In India, it is commonly used to grind wet masalas and make chutneys.	
Pasta machine	This machine is used for rolling the pasta dough to form sheets. The machine also has few attachments that allow the sheets to be cut into small noodles to *fettuccine.* The modern pasta machines also have an attachment that can make stuffed pastas such as raviolis and *pansotis.*	

Special Italian Dishes

Italy is a country of good food and wine and people enjoy eating a spread of food ranging from *antipasti* to *dolce,* which is a dessert course. Italian food has also been gaining popularity across the world compared to French cuisine, which was once a hot favourite among gourmet diners. Earlier in this chapter, we read about different regions of Italy and some foods that were unique to those regions. Let us now discuss some Italian dishes that are very popular on the world. These are described in Table 6.9. However, we will not discuss pasta and sauces, as we have already discussed these earlier.

Table 6.9 Popular dishes of Italy (see also Plate 5)

Dish	Description	Photograph
Minestrone	It is one of the most popular soups on the menus of many hotels. Minestrone is a vegetable broth with a variety of vegetables such as cabbage, carrots, zucchini, peppers, and tomatoes. It is thickened with starch such as potatoes, pasta, or barlotti beans. It is a very flavoursome soup and the method adopted to prepare this is stewing. Minestrone in South Italy is made with lots of tomatoes, whereas in Northern Italy, tomatoes are optional. Though very popular as a vegetarian soup, many recipes suggest rendering of bacon and sautéing vegetables before stewing them.	
Pollo alla cacciatore or hunter's chicken stew	*Cacciatore* means hunter in Italian. This dish reflects the hunter style of cooking, in which the chicken is braised in fresh tomatoes, mushrooms, onions, and few fresh herbs. In south Italy, red wine is also used in this dish, whereas in the north, people use white wine.	

(Contd)

Table 6.9 (Contd)

Dish	Description	Photograph
Saltimbocca	It is a very popular dish from the northern part of Italy and also in Mediterranean cuisine. In this dish, veal escalopes are wrapped or lined with sliced *Prosciutto* (ham) *di parma* and then pan-fried. It is then simmered in veal stock and lemon juice. Sometimes capers are also added. Nowdays, people also using meat, such as chicken, lamb, and pork, for preparing this dish.	
Osso buco	*Osso buco* is a Milanese speciality of sliced veal shanks, which are braised with vegetables, tomatoes, and red wine. It is traditionally served with risotto Milanese and *gremolata*, which is a mixture of freshly chopped flat parsley, lemon zest, and garlic. *Osso buco* in Italian means a bone with a hole, a reference to the marrow hole at the centre of the cross-cut veal shank.	
Melanzane alla parmigiano	This dish is commonly made in southern Italy by layering grilled or pan-fried brinjal with Mozzarella cheese and tomato sauce. It is popularly flavoured with basil and served as a vegetarian meal.	
Fritto misto	This assorted dish of fish and shellfish is a very popular dish served on New Year's eve. It can be eaten as a meal or as a snack. Assortment of fresh seafood is tossed with flour and then deep-fried until crisp. It is served sprinkled with salt, chopped parsley, and lemon wedges.	
Risotto alla Milanese	Risotto is a popular Italian dish made from rice and hot broth (vegetable, fish, or meat based) and cooked until creamy. Butter and Parmesan cheese are added to add more flavour and creamy texture. *Risotto alla Milanese* is typically flavoured with saffron and green peas and is a popular accompaniment with *osso buco*.	
Gnocchi alla Romana	This is a unique kind of gnocchi prepared like polenta. Semolina is cooked with milk and herbs and spread on a tray until set. It is then cut into desired shapes and pan-fried and served with tomato sauce and shavings of Parmesan cheese.	
Vitello tonnato	This is a very popular cold Mediterranean dish served as *antipasti*. It is made by slicing a braised piece of veal into thin slices and topped with tuna-flavoured mayonnaise.	
Insalata caprese	This fresh salad is made by combining fresh tomatoes with buffalo Mozzarella and dressed with *pesto* and extra virgin olive oil. The presentation of this salad can vary according to the creativity of the chef.	

(Contd)

Table 6.9 (Contd)

Dish	Description	Photograph
Insalata de Cesare	Though very popular in Italy, this salad originated in Mexico. It is made by tossing cos or romaine lettuce with a dressing made from coddled eggs, garlic, lemon juice, black pepper and Worcestershire sauce. The salad is then tossed with grated Parmesan cheese and croutons. In olden days, it had become a tradition to serve this salad from a *guéridon* trolley. As it was difficult to separate the egg yolks from the whites in front of the guests, eggs were briefly washed under boiling water. This also gave an impact that the egg was being cleaned but actually when cracked open the egg white would coagulate and the yolk get separated. This preparation is known as coddled egg.	
Acqua pazza	Literally meaning crazy water, it is a classical Italian dish which is prepared by poaching fish in a flavoured broth of vegetables, tomatoes, olives, capers, and olive oil.	
Bistecca alla Fiorentina or beefsteak Florentine style	A Tuscan delicacy, *Bistecca alla Fiorentina* is steak made from chianina breed of cattle, which are prized for their tenderness and flavour. It consists of T-bone grilled over charcoal or wood, and seasoned with olive oil, rosemary, and salt. Seasonings are needed to highlight the rich flavour of the grilled meat.	
Panettone	It is a type of sweet fruit bread, usually prepared and enjoyed for Christmas and New Year in Italy. It is baked in a special tubular mould to give it height of about 12–15 cm. The dough is leavened with yeast and mainly consists of candied orange, nuts, raisins, lemon zest, etc. In many parts of Italy, it is served with *amaretto* and *mascarpone* cheese.	
Tiramisu	*Tiramisu* literally means 'pick me up' in Italian. This popular dessert, made by layering a sweetened *mascarpone* with coffee-soaked *savoiardi* biscuits, comes from Veneto region. *Mascarpone* is mixed with sugar, egg yolks, and sometimes meringue and layered with a sponge biscuit called *savoiardi*. It is flavoured with coffee decoction, although sometimes coffee liquor, such as *kahlua* or *Tia Maria*, could also be used.	
Zabaglione	This is another popular dessert from Italy made by whisking egg yolks, sugar, and Marsala (a sweet Italian wine). It is a very light custard like dessert that is traditionally served warm with fresh figs. In French it is called *sabayon*.	
Sicilian Cassata	As the name suggests, this dessert comes from Sicily. It is prepared by layering sponge slices with *ricotta* cheese, candied fruit, and whipped cream. The top is covered with coloured marzipan stripes and garnished with candied fruits. In many other parts of the world, cheese is often substituted with ice creams.	

MEDITERRANEAN CUISINE

Mediterranean cuisine can be aptly described as a melting pot of cultures—European, Asian, and African. Literally meaning 'the middle of the Earth', the almost landlocked sea is the only one in the world to have on its rim countries of three continents. Not surprisingly, the region served as an important route for ancient merchants and travellers, which facilitated trade and cultural exchange among various societies (Greek, Egyptian, Turkish, Byzantine, Roman, etc.) that emerged there. The history of the Mediterranean region, thus, is crucial to understanding the origins and development of many modern societies and the lifestyles associated with them.

This is also reflected in the cuisine of the region. The Mediterranean food of modern times is very different to what was eaten in the medieval era. It is believed that the Mediterranean cuisine has evolved not because of the lavish eating habits of the people living there, but because they were forced to create food with the limited ingredients as the land is not very conducive to growth of vegetables and fruits. Most of the vegetables and fruits that we see there today are not native to the region. As the countries are situated along the coastline, trade has played a significant role shuffling and exchange of food items and ingredients with distant lands. For instance, rice was introduced by the Arabs, peppers from South America, potatoes from Africa, and maize from North America. The scarcity of ingredients also led to their exchange between different countries across the shores and that is the reason why there is so much of similarity between the ingredients used in Mediterranean cuisine. Today, it is impossible to think about Mediterranean cuisine without these items. Also, people living in the region have over the years perfected various ways of growing fruits and vegetables which is why the food around the Mediterranean is largely dependent on fresh and seasonal items. The harsh and arid climate, however, is very conducive to the growth of some herbs and plants, such as olives, and wheat, which form the basis of Mediterranean cuisine. Olive, from which olive oil is extracted, is the most popular cooking medium throughout the region.

Mediterranean cuisine, is considered to be very healthy. Interestingly, countries like Italy and Turkey despite being situated far from each other, are bound by a common cuisine, albeit with unique local flavours and style of cooking. Experts attribute it to the climatic conditions, which infuse a unique flavour and taste to the common ingredients. For instance, the olive oil in Spain is very different in flavour from the one in Italy or in Greece. As the Mediterranean region is composed of many different cultures, there is also a large variety in its cuisine for it is difficult to find a uniting element in the cooking styles.

Geographical Location of Mediterranean Region

The cuisines of the Mediterranean region were predominantly influenced by Greeks, Romans, Egyptians, Persian, Turks, and Moors in particular. Since these people were efficient in trade and wanted to extend their empire, they travelled to distant places to conquer alien lands and spread their culture as well as cuisine. As many as 20 countries including a few islands are situated along the Mediterranean Sea, which is almost landlocked at the converging point of the continents of Africa, Asia, and Europe. One thing that is common to the countries in this region is their climate—hot and humid

Table 6.10 Regions that comprise Mediterranean belt and contribute to its cuisine

S. No.	Country	Regions
1.	Italy	Sardinia and Sicily
2.	Tunisia	Tunis (Northern Tunisia) and Eastern Tunisia
3.	Algeria	Algiers (Northern Algeria)
4.	Morocco	Morocco (Northern Morocco)
5.	Spain	Almeria, Valencia, Barcelona (Eastern Spain)
6.	France	Marseille, Nice, Corsica (Southern France)
7.	Turkey	Southern and Western Turkey
8.	Greece	Southern coast of Greece
9.	Israel	South-western coast of Israel
10.	Syria	Western coast of Syria
11.	Lebanon	Western coast of Lebanon
12.	Libya	Northern coast of Libya
13.	Cyprus	All areas as it is an island
14.	Bosnia	South and western coast of Bosnia
15.	Slovenia	Western coast of Slovenia
16.	Albania	Western coast of Albania
17.	Monaco	Monaco
18.	Malta	Valletta

summers, and wet and warm winter months. Since these countries are located around the Mediterranean Sea, it is difficult to ascribe geographical particular location to the entire cuisine. In some countries, it is the east that faces the sea, while in some others it is west or north and even south that have Mediterranean weather. The countries and regions that form the Mediterranean belt are listed in Table 6.10.

If we were to summarize the entire Mediterranean cuisine in a tabular form, we would be able to relate everything and understand the commonalities in the diverse Mediterranean cuisine that merit their classification under one heading. Table 6.11 presents the commonalities in the cuisines of various Mediterranean nations.

Seasonal Availability

In the Mediterranean region, food is in tune with the seasons and natural products play a significant part in its cuisine. Being near the sea, seafood dominates this cuisine. Whether it is Italy or the tip of Africa, fish and seafood is found aplenty. Since the land is very dry and arid, lack of greener pastures does not favour the breeding of many cattle so it is not common to find beef on the Mediterranean menu. Lamb has always been popularly used for special occasions. The three major ingredients that dominate the Mediterranean cuisine can be condensed into an acronym WOW: wheat, olive oil, and wine.

Table 6.11 Commonalities in Mediterranean cuisines

Ingredient	Italy	Spain	Greece	Lebanon	Morocco	Turkey	France
Starch	Polenta, pasta, couscous, beans, and lentils	Pasta, rice, beans, lentils	Beans, lentils, rice	Bulgur, couscous, beans, lentils	Couscous, beans, lentils, rice	Couscous, rice, beans, lentils, bulgur	Polenta, couscous, rice, beans, lentils
Fats	Olive oil	Olive oil	Olive oil	Olive oil	Olive oil	Olive oil	Olive oil
Vegetables	*Courgettes,* tomatoes, olives, artichokes, onions, garlic	*Courgettes,* tomatoes, olives, artichokes, onions, garlic	*Courgettes,* tomatoes, olives, artichokes, onions, garlic	*Courgettes,* tomatoes, olives, artichokes, onions, garlic	*Courgettes,* tomatoes, olives, artichokes, onions, garlic	*Courgettes,* tomatoes, olives, artichokes, onions, garlic	*Courgettes,* tomatoes, olives, artichokes, onions, garlic
Fruits	Figs, melons, dates, almonds, walnuts, raisins	Figs, melons, dates, almonds, walnuts, hazelnuts	Figs, melons, dates, almonds, walnuts	Figs, melons, dates, almonds, walnuts	Figs, melons, dates, almonds, walnuts	Figs, melons, dates, almonds, walnuts, raisins	Figs, melons, dates, almonds, walnuts, hazelnuts
Liquor	*Sambuca*	Absinthe	*Ouzo*	*Arak*	*Mahia*	Raki	Pastis
Sauce with garlic olive oil salt	Pesto with addition of basil and pine nuts and parmesan	*Alioli*	*Skordalia* with addition of potatoes, soaked bread and nuts	Hummus with addition of chickpea paste and lemon juice	*Chermoula* with addition of fresh coriander and parsley	*Tarator* with addition of nuts	*Aioli*
Cheese	Parmesan	*Manchego*	Feta	*Akkawi*	Feta	*Beyaz Peynir*	*Banon*

The food in the Mediterranean region is 'family style', implying that it is informal and there is no fuss or much ado about presentation and garnishing. Taste and freshness are the two most important factors that define the principles of this cuisine. Plant food is given preference over lamb and other meat products. Even seafood is considered vegetarian and commonly referred to as *Fruits de Mer* (fruits of the sea). The temperate climate naturally produces olives, wheat, pepper, and garlic and one can easily identify food from the Mediterranean region as it uses these ingredients generously.

It is very difficult to describe the tastes of Mediterranean cuisines because of its diversity with regard to different cultures and countries. The term Mediterranean cuisine conjures up images of warmth, home style and earthy colours, fresh vegetables, salted meat and preserves, robust taste of olives, tomatoes, peppers, artichokes, eggplants (brinjals), onion, and garlic. Figs, nuts, perfumed oranges, dates, etc. are commonly used in their desserts and main courses as well. Whole grains, pastas, wheat products such as semolina in Italy, couscous in Morocco, and bulgur in Lebanon and Greece are by-products of wheat, used in different forms. The Moroccan couscous is commonly used in Italian cuisine as well. Cheese is another commodity that is popularly eaten across the Mediterranean and each country has its own types and varieties of cheeses.

The countries listed in Table 6.10 form a part of the Mediterranean cuisine, but only few popularly feature on the menus of hotels and restaurants catering to international clientele. Therefore, in this section, we will only discuss foods from Lebanon, Greece, Turkey, Morocco, Spain, Italy, and southern France, which are commonly served in hotels. Let us now discuss the broad flavour profile of these countries as it will give us a better understanding of the Mediterranean cuisine.

Lebanese Cuisine

The cuisine of Lebanon is commonly referred to as Lebanese cuisine. It is a part of Middle Eastern cuisine, but since this part of Middle East was influenced by many foreign powers, Lebanese food is very different from the other Middle Eastern foods. Turks ruled this country for over 400 years, after which it was colonized by France for almost 25 years.

Special ingredients in Lebanese cuisine

Olive oils, lemon, and garlic are few of the typical flavours that determine Lebanese food. *Mezze* (that we discussed briefly in Chapter 3 on appetizers) is among the most internationally popular Lebanese dishes that are served in hotels across the world. The Lebanese like to include fresh vegetables and fruits into their diet. Thus, fresh fruits such as melons, apples, oranges, grapes, and figs are served along with desserts such as baklava (refer Table 6.14) that is made by layering filo pastry with an assortment of nuts. Wine is another common ingredient in the Mediterranean cuisine. Interestingly, each country has its own version of native wine, which turns milky white on addition of ice. *Arak* made from fennel is the traditional alcoholic beverage of Lebanon. Herbs, such as mint and parsley, dominate the flavours of the food as is quite evident from its salad *tabouleh*, which is prepared by mixing three parts of chopped parsley with one part of mint and Bulgur and served as *mezze*. The cooking style is mostly grilled, sautéed, or baked and like other Mediterranean countries, Lebanese cuisine also relies on fresh and seasonal vegetables and fruits. Red meat is rare on the menu and lamb often features on special occasions. Christianity and Islam are the predominant religions in Lebanon; thus, Christmas and Easter are celebrated with same fervour as Eid and other Islamic festivals. Whatever the occasion, food and drinks form a major part of the celebrations with family and friends.

Special Lebanese dishes

Some of the most popular dishes in Lebanese cuisine are discussed in Table 6.12.

Table 6.12 Popular dishes from Lebanon

Dish	Description	Photograph
Mezze	*Mezze* is a selection of small dishes served in the Mediterranean and Middle East as dinner or lunch, with or without drinks. There could be around 30–40 dishes, usually small tidbits and snacks, that are served as *mezze*. *Mezze* is the quintessence of lavish hospitality that the Arabs are known for. Various kinds of *mezze* are popularly served around the world. These could include other dishes that are listed below.	
Babaganouj	Eggplants are roasted, peeled, and then mashed and mixed with various seasonings such as tahini (which is a sesame seed) paste, olive oil, and garlic. This *mezze*, with a smoky taste, is often eaten as a dip with pita bread, and is sometimes added to other dishes. It is usually of an earthy light-brown colour.	
Hummus	It is made from boiled chickpeas, which are then pureed with olive oil and seasoned with lemon juice, garlic, chopped parsley, and *tahini* paste. Hummus is popularly eaten with *pita* bread and also served along with meat preparations.	
Kibbeh	A popular hot *mezze*, it is prepared in almost all Middle Eastern countries and served with other *mezzes*. It is called *Köfte* in Turkey. It is prepared by coarsely grinding meat with bulgur, spices, and herbs such as *sumac* and flat parsley.	
Jawaneh	These are popularly served as *mezze* and are prepared by marinating chicken wings with olive oil, lemon juice, crushed garlic, and chopped parsley. These can be broiled in a tandoor or cooked under a salamander.	
Moutabel	*Moutabel* is prepared in the same way as *babaganouj* , the only difference is that it is spiced with crushed black pepper and green chili peppers.	
Muhammara	*Muhammara* is a dip that is popularly served on the *mezze*. It is typically made in Syrian cuisine but common in other Middle Eastern countries too. It is made by pureeing fresh red pepper, walnuts, breadcrumbs, garlic, lemon juice, and olive oil. *Sumac* berry or molasses from pomegranate are also added for extra colour and appearance. It is usually flavoured with chopped mint leaves and eaten as dip with kebabs. It is also known as *acuka* in Turkish cuisine.	

(Contd)

Table 6.12 (Contd)

Dish	Description	Photograph
Labneh	*Labneh* is a strained or hung yoghurt cheese that is very popular in Greek cuisine also. The hung curd cheese is popularly known as *laban*. It is used in variety of ways such as a base for marinating meats for kebabs or eaten as a spread on pita bread or *lavash*. Another popular way to preserve and serve this is to form oval dumplings of *laban* and dip them in olive oil. The *laban* can also be rolled in fresh herbs such as chopped parsley, crushed black pepper, etc. to give it more flavour. This type of preparation is also called *shanklish* in Turkish cuisine. *Labneh* is also commonly used as a stuffing for *kibbeh*.	
Tabouleh	It is a very popular salad served on *mezze* bar. It is prepared by combining finely chopped parsley with *bulgur*, mint, and chopped deseeded tomatoes and seasoned with lemon juice and olive oil.	
Fattoush	It is a fresh salad of seasonal vegetable, such as cucumbers, tomatoes, and onions, that are mixed with leftover flat breads such as *pita* or *lavash*, which are deep fried and tossed, along with lemon juice and olive oil. *Fattoush* is commonly served in the pita pockets and in such a case, it is not mixed with the bread.	
Akkawi	It is a popular cheese made from cow, goat, or sheep's milk. It is a soft white cheese with a smooth texture and a mild salty taste. It is popularly served on *mezze* as a table cheese and is accompanied very well with fruits such as apricots and figs.	
Falafel	Falafel is prepared by coarsely grinding soaked chickpeas, or fava beans, or sometimes both and mixing it with chopped parsley. It is deep fried and served wrapped in pita pockets and eaten as a snack or popular *mezze*. It can also be rolled in flat bread called *khubz*, along with dips such as tahini and hummus.	
Shawarma	*Shawarma* is popularly eaten in Turkey, Greece, Lebanon, and other parts of the Middle East. The meat, usually chicken, is marinated and skewered onto a thick rod which rotates on its axis with the heating element to one side. So the meat gets uniformly cooked on all sides. To serve *shawarma*, the meat is sliced off thinly and is arranged on a large flat bread topped with *fattoush*, hummus, tahini, pickled vegetables and folded like a roll. *Shawarma* in Greece is called *gyro*, and in Turkish cuisine, it is called *doner*, both the words mean 'turning of a kebab'.	

(Contd)

Table 6.12 (Contd)

Dish	Description	Photograph
Tahini	Tahini is a paste of sesame seeds and olive oil. It is commonly served as a dip or can be combined with other ingredients to make items such as hummus and *babaganouj*. It can be prepared in hotels but it is also available as a ready-made condiment.	
Tarator	*Tarator* or *taratour* is commonly prepared in almost all Middle Eastern countries but is most popular in Turkish and Lebanese cuisines. It is a kind of cold soup made with yoghurt, shredded cucumber, chopped garlic, walnuts, olive oil, and dill. *Taratoor* can also be made with thick *labneh* and served as a dip on *mezze*. In Turkish cuisine, it is eaten as a dip with fried squids.	
Warak inab	This is a preparation made from stuffed wine leaves. The boiled and pickled wine leaves are available in bottles and these are stuffed with various kinds of mixtures such as rice, ground meat, and spices and also nuts such as raisins, pine nuts, almonds, and steamed on a bed of potatoes and tomatoes. It is then served hot or cold on *mezze* table.	

Greek Cuisine

Greek food has influenced most cuisines of the Western world as it has a culinary tradition of more than 4,000 years. It spread its culture and cuisine through Rome to Europe and other parts of the world. In 350 BC, Alexander the Great extended his Greek empire to India and introduced spices, such as coriander and fenugreek, to the Indians and in turn took some native culinary practices back to his country. Greece was under the rule of Turks for almost 400 years. This also left an impact on its cuisine. The rocky mountainous regions of Greece are surrounded by the Mediterranean Sea on three sides. Since very less land was available for agriculture, it opened up vistas in trade. The Greeks also led conquests to distant lands to bring in more food into the country. They traded with their olive oils, wheat, and wine, which are common to Mediterranean cuisine. Fish and seafood too is integral to the Greek cuisine. Seafoods, such as tuna, sea bream, octopus, and squids, are still very popular among the Greeks, who have perfected the art of pickling fish. Cattle were hardly present due to scarcity of green pastures hence, goat and sheep were reared not so much for consumption, but for milk and cheese. Greeks also have a 4,000-year-old tradition of making cheeses such as feta and *kasseri*, which are the most popular varieties in the country even today.

Special ingredients used in Greek cuisine

Some of the ingredients native to Greece that are popularly used around the world are described in Table 6.13.

Table 6.13 Famous ingredients used in Greek cuisine

Ingredient	Description	Photograph
Kalamata olives	These are dark, purple, and slightly elongated olives that are hard to grow in other regions. This is why the olive oil from Greece is very much different in flavour from that in Italy or Spain.	
Rigani	This is Greek oregano. When in full bloom, it can reach up to a height of two feet. Its leaves are large, oval, and dark green in colour when fresh.	
Grape/vine leaves	Grape leaves or vine leaves are commonly used for making the *mezze* called *warak inab*, which are known as *dolmades* or *dolmathes*. In Greece, these are stuffed with ground lamb and rice and steamed. They are highly perishable and hence are difficult to find fresh. They are pickled and packed in bottles and sold around the world. They are preserved in brine, so it is always important to wash them to remove extra salt before using.	
Phyllo pastry	Also called filo, these are paper-thin layers or sheets of rolled dough that are readily available in frozen state. Various dishes, both sweet and savoury, are prepared from this pastry. This pastry is also used in Turkey, Lebanon, and Syria. The popular dessert baklava and savoury snack *spanakopita* are prepared using filo pastry. Each sheet is spread with melted butter and then made into a product. This style of applying butter yields a flaky pastry of layers.	
Knafeh	Also known as *kunafa* or *kadaif* in other parts of Middle East, it is basically a shredded form of filo pastry commonly used for making desserts.	
Feta cheese	Feta is an aged cheese that is prepared from goat or sheep milk. It has a granular texture and is used as a table cheese or in salads. This cheese is also crumbled and used as stuffing for many baked pastries like *spanakopita*. The feta cheese is salty in taste and should be used accordingly.	
Kasseri cheese	This cheese is prepared in Greece and also in Turkey. It is a hard pale yellow coloured cheese prepared from sheep milk. The texture is soft but stringy like a Mozzarella. It is aged for at least three to four months to get the full flavours and texture. This cheese is served in sandwiches and also can be pan-fried in olive oil and served drizzled with lemon juice.	

(Contd)

Table 6.13 (Contd)

Ingredient	Description	Photograph
Mastic	Also called Arabic gum, mastic is resin obtained from mastic tree. The sap of the tree oozes out and dries up like teardrops. These are then sun-dried to obtain hard and brittle resin. This is used in the preparation of desserts.	
Greek honey	Greek honey is among the most sought after because of its flavours due to the presence of almost 7,500 flora in the region. Special honey flavours, such as thyme honey, and other herbal honeys are not found anywhere else in the world.	
Mahlab	Also known as *Mahlepi*, this is the crushed powder of seeds of a special variety of cherries called St Lucien. The cherry stones are crushed open to extract these seeds and ground to a powder. The aroma is very strong and reminiscent of bitter almond and cherry. It is commonly used for flavouring Christmas cakes called *Tsoureki*.	
Ouzo	*Ouzo* like *arrack* in Lebanon is an anise-flavoured aperitif that is widely consumed in Greece as well as Spain.	

Famous Greek dishes

The food and flavours of the Greek cuisine can easily be reflected in Turkish as well as Syrian cuisines. Other than simple foods such as grilled dishes, Greek cuisine is also famous for its casseroles and desserts. Some of the popular dishes from Greece are described in Table 6.14.

Table 6.14 Popular dishes of Greece

Dish	Description	Photograph
Horta vratsa	This is a dish of boiled leafy vegetables. Greens such as wild spinach, Swiss chard, and dandelions are boiled until tender and then strained. These are then arranged on platter and served drizzled with olive oil and fresh lemon juice.	
Spanakopita	These are savoury triangles made with *phyllo* pastry. *Phyllo* pastry is cut into a long strip and brushed with melted butter or olive oil. The filling of sautéed spinach and feta cheese is put in a corner and then the strip of *phyllo* is folded over alternately to form a triangle. *Spanakopitas* can be baked or deep-fried. The full name is *spanakotyropita* in which *spanaki* is for spinach, *tyro* for cheese, and *pita* for bread or pie. When only cheese is used in the filling, it is called *tyropitakia*.	

(Contd)

Table 6.14 (Contd)

Dish	Description	Photograph
Avgolemono	This dish is considered to be the national soup of Greece. There are various variations to this soup, which is commonly made with eggs (*avgo*) and lemon (*lemono*) and hence the name. The chicken broth is cooked with chicken, vegetables, and flavourings, and then seasoned with a mixture of egg and lemon. This soup can also be thickened and is commonly used as an accompanying sauce for *dolmas*.	
Skorthalia	*Skorthalia* is a popular dip in Greek cuisine that is made by flavouring any thick puree of starch or nuts with crushed garlic and olive oil. The base could be almonds, walnuts, or even potato puree. Vinegar is added to give the tangy flavour and sometimes bread is added to give it the body. *Skorthalia* is often served with batter-fried fish and batter-fried vegetables.	
Melitzanosalata	This dip is inspired from the *babaganouj* in Lebanese cuisine and is made in a similar fashion. The only difference is that in Greece, it is served with salty cheese and anchovies.	
Horiatiki	Meaning warmth or summer in Greek, it is a fresh salad in Greek cuisine. Commonly featuring on the menus of most hotels and restaurants by the name Greek salad, it is made by combining fresh tomatoes, sliced cucumbers, peppers, red onions and dressed with a dressing of olive oil, vinegar, salt, pepper, and dried oregano. The dish is garnished with diced feta cheese, *kalamata* olives, and chopped fresh parsley.	
Taramosalata	This popular *mezze* from Greece is made from the roe of cod fish. It is salted and then pureed along with bread, mashed potato, vinegar, and olive oil. It is usually served as a dip, along with bread or raw vegetables.	
Tzatziki	This is another popular dip served on a Greek *mezze*. It is made from drained yoghurt like *labneh* and mixed with grated cucumber, salt, olive oil, chopped mint, parsley, and dill. *Tzatziki* is always served as an accompaniment but in Lebanese cuisine, it can be served along with *pita* crisps.	

(Contd)

Table 6.14 (Contd)

Dish	Description	Photograph
Moussaka	*Moussaka* is prepared commonly in all Middle-Eastern countries, but the preparation from Greece is by far the most popular. It is prepared in an oval baking dish and in layers. The layers comprise grilled eggplant slices, tomato sauce, ground and cooked meat and topped with béchamel sauce and cheese and baked until the top layer turns brown.	
Souvlaki	This is a popular fast food of Greece consisting of meat and vegetables on skewers that are served grilled and accompanied with dips and bread. These are commonly eaten wrapped in *pita* breads.	
Dolmathes	Also known as *dolmas,* they are made from grape/vine leaves (refer Table 6.13).	
Gyro	Same as *shawarma* in Lebanese and *doner* in Turkish cuisine (refer Table 6.12).	
Tsoureki	*Tsoureki* is sweet egg bread similar to a brioche. It is traditionally made in braided style and sprinkled with poppy seeds. The presentation of *tsoureki* depends upon the occasion. During Easter, this bread is served garnished with sliced almonds and deep-dyed red eggs to represent the blood of Christ.	
Kourabiethes	These are popular shortbread cookies made with butter, eggs, almonds, and flour. After baking, these are rolled into icing sugar and decorated with whole clove.	
Baklava	This hot dessert can be served cold as well. It is a made phyllo pastry with lavishly added nuts. Its preparation seems simple. In a pan, layer a sheet of filo and brush with melted butter, place another sheet on top and repeat the process until at least six sheets are used. Sprinkle with crushed nuts and sugar and repeat the process until baklava is 2 inches thick. Brush the top with melted butter. Traditionally, it are cut into diamond shape, prior to baking, as the crisp pastry will be difficult to cut after baking. Bake till golden brown and while it is still hot, pour in rose-flavoured sugar syrup. The cuts help to let the syrup seep into the layers. Serve the pastry warm or cold.	

Spanish Cuisine

Looking at the map of Spain, one would realize that in spite of being a part of Europe, it is very near to the African continent. Thus, it is not uncommon to find a distinct Moorish influence on Spanish cuisine. Mediterranean Spain extends from Barcelona to Cartagena and Andalusia in southern Spain, which is famous for its cold soup called *gazpacho*.

Since prehistoric times Spain was ruled by Iberians, Greeks, Celts, before it became a part of the Roman empire in the Middle Ages. It was later conquered by the Moors, who ruled the country till it emerged as a unified country in the fifteenth century. As a result, it came under the influence of various external cultures and also became a source of influence for other regions. For instance, the Moors lent their Muslim culture and ingredients such as dates, raisins, and fruits such as figs and pomegranate that are very popular in Spanish cuisine. Also, medieval explorer Christopher Columbus brought back a lot of ingredients to Spain. It is also known in the world for the best quality saffron; the second best being produced in Kashmir, India.

When talking about Spainish food, the first thing that comes to our minds is the most popular tapas (that we discussed in Chapter 3 on appetizers). There is an interesting fact justifying the existence of tapas in the Spanish culture. The Spanish siesta or the long afternoon break is a must for every Spaniard. Life literally comes to a halt between 2 to 5 pm. Most shops close down, except eating joints and restaurants. The mid-day Spanish meal extends for many hours, wherein people get together and spend time over food and drink. The restaurants usually shut down at 5 p.m. and then reopen at 9 p.m. People meet again in the evening for a drink to the accompaniment of tapas till midnight. The sessions could at times culminate in a dinner.

The flavour profile of Spain is similar to that of other Mediterranean countries. Food is cooked with lots of olives, olive oil, parsley, almonds, garlic, saffron, etc. The land around the Spanish coast is quite fertile and is conducive to the growth of fresh fruits and vegetables that form the essence of Spanish cuisine as in other countries of the region. As Spain has one of the largest coastlines in the European continent, seafood also plays an important role in the country's food basket.

Special ingredients used in Spanish cuisine

Let us discuss some of the most commonly found ingredients in the Spanish cuisine in Table 6.15.

Table 6.15 Popular Spanish ingredients

Ingredient	Description	Photograph
Saffron	Saffron is obtained from the stigma of a flower called *Crocus sativus*. It is one of the most prized herbs in the world as there are only 3 stigmas in one flower and it takes 14,000 stigmas to make up to 30 g of saffron. Each of them is handpicked and graded accordingly. Thus, it is one of the most expensive herbs in the world. The Spanish garnish their dishes with saffron.	

(Contd)

Table 6.15 (Contd)

Ingredient	Description	Photograph
Sherry	One of the most popular wines, Sherry comes from the town of Jerez in Andalusian region and hence the name. Most experts attribute the existence of tapas to Sherry. Sweet sherry attracted lots of flies and to avoid them, the wine was covered with a piece of bread when being served. Thus, tapas was born. Sherry is consumed as aperitif or had along with the meal.	
Aguardiente	It literally translates to tooth water. Commonly used in Spanish cooking, it is an anise-flavoured liquor quite similar to *arrack* and *ouzo* in Greece. It is also popularly made from grapes as a brandy and from skins and pips as well.	
Baccalào	It is same as *baccalà* as discussed in Table 6.2. The art of salting fish was popularized by Romans, which is why this is also found in Italian cuisine.	
Alubias	This is a generic term for various varieties of dried beans that grow abundantly in different parts of Spain. Each area has its own favourite depending on the local produce. All dried beans are soaked, cooked, and then served with salted meat, as they pair up very well with them.	
Butifarra	These are like *boudin blanc* and *noir* (refer Chapter 2 on *charcuterie*). It is very popular in Catalonia and is made from pork, tripe, and pine nuts. It is usually spiced with cinnamon and cumin and can be served grilled or pan fried. The other popular sausage from Spain is chorizo (also discussed in Chapter 2).	
Manchego	*Manchego* cheese is a popular aged cheese. The aging determines its flavour and texture. Spanish cheeses are quite popular in the world. Like in other Mediterranean countries, Spaniards also prepare their cheese from ewe or goat milk.	
Jamón serrano	The Spanish ham called *serrano* is a much sweeter ham as compared to the *Parma* ham of Italy. The best *serrano* ham comes from black Iberian pigs that are fed on acorns, which help in good marbling in this ham.	

(Contd)

Table 6.15 (Contd)

Ingredient	Description	Photograph
Rice	Rice was introduced in Spain by Arabs around the same time that it was introduced in Italy. The Spanish rice is also medium grain and starchy like risotto rice, but prepared very differently. Unlike risotto, this rice is washed several times to remove extra starch and cooked without stirring, allowing the grains to swell along with meat and vegetables. The famous dish called *paella* is made with Spanish rice.	
Piquillos	This is a variety of chilli peppers that grow in Northern Spain. *Piquillos* in Spanish means little beaks and this pepper resembles the pointed beak of a bird. These peppers are roasted, then peeled and deseeded. They are usually available canned. These are popularly eaten stuffed with meat, seafood, or cheese and served as tapas in Spain.	

Popular Spanish dishes

Apart from tapas there are many other dishes from Spain that have acquired global popularity and are a regular feature on the menus of hotels and restaurants across the world. *Gazpacho* and *paella* are two such dishes. Spanish food is redolent of spices, such as cinnamon and saffron, while the food is essentially based on availability of seasonal and fresh vegetables and fruits. Chickpeas and other beans are very popular and olive oil and garlic are the principal flavourings. Spanish olive oils are very aromatic and popularly exported around the world. Some of the dishes that have become popular internationally are discussed in Table 6.16.

Table 6.16 Popular Spanish dishes

Dish	Description	Photograph
Paella	This is one of the most popular dishes that are made by combining rice, vegetables, and different types of meat or seafood and are flavoured with saffron. It is made in a large and shallow cast iron pan and is a sticky kind of pilaf or pilau.	
Gazapacho	This dish from Andalusia was prepared to quench the thirst of labourers working in hot fields. It is a pureed cold soup of fresh vegetables such as tomatoes, cucumbers, red bell peppers, red wine vinegar, one-day-old stale bread, and olive oil. In hotels, the ingredients are combined together and kept marinated in the refrigerator overnight, so that they chill properly. The next day, it is churned until pureed and served chilled. This soup is also served in small shot glasses on cold buffets.	

(Contd)

Table 6.16 (Contd)

Dish	Description	Photograph
Tortilla	This is also known as Spanish omelette and is made by combining eggs, potatoes, olives, vegetables, and herbs. The word comes from the Spanish word *torta* which means a cake. The tortilla, when cooked, looks like a small cake as it is at least an inch thick when prepared. It is normally eaten hot or cold and served on tapas bar.	
Albondigas	These are small dumplings made from ground meat and served in a sauce. The ground meat is mixed with chopped onions, garlic, and herbs and sometimes bound with eggs and bread. These can be deep-fried or steamed and then braised in a sauce.	
Rabo de Toro	One of the traditional dishes, it originated in Cordoba in Spain. It is an oxtail dish that is braised in red wine, tomatoes, and flavoured with herbs such as rosemary, oregano, and thyme. It also has vegetables such peppers, carrots, and onions and is flavoured with paprika and saffron.	
Ensaladas arroz	This is a rice salad, often prepared from leftover rice. One could combine a range of ingredients such as diced peppers, tomatoes, artichokes, olives, and even cold and cured meat. It is dressed with olive oil vinaigrette that is sweetened with some honey.	
Calamares en su tinta	As the name suggests, it is a dish of squids in its own ink. In this north Spanish dish, the squid is braised until tender in a sauce made from onion, tomatoes, peppers, and squid ink.	
Gambas al Ajillo	Usually served as snack or in tapas, these are prawns sautéed in olive oil, garlic, and mushrooms. The dish has a fairly large amount of garlic and hence the name *ajillo;* the dish can sometimes be spiked with red pepper and paprika.	
Pollo al Chilindron	This is a popular braised preparation of chicken with *serrano* ham, onion, garlic, peppers, and tomatoes. This dish comes from Aragona region and the red peppers from this region are the traditional ingredient of this dish.	
Piquillos rellenos	The *piquillios* chillies are available canned, but if using fresh, these can be grilled, peeled, deseeded, and stuffed with various kinds of mixtures, ranging from meat, cheese, vegetables, or a combination of all of these. It is served as tapas as well as eaten in main meals.	

Turkish Cuisine

The people of Turkey are believed to be descendants of the nomadic tribes who moved towards the West from Asia and Mongolia. These people were mainly herdsmen and would rely on their flock of sheep and thrive on natural vegetation and farming. Of the many states in Turkey, two major states (Anatolia and Istanbul) became regions of interests for foreign invaders, who influenced the cuisine of Turkey in a big way. Greeks ruled Anatolia while Istanbul was ruled by the Ottoman Empire. The Turks embraced Islam following their encounters with Persia. It is still the predominant faith in the country.

Turkey, like the Arabian region, is known for its hospitality. Offering food to strangers (believed to be sent by God), is a largely followed custom.

Special ingredients in Turkish cuisine

The cuisine of Turkey is based on fresh and seasonal fruits and vegetables; the flavour being similar to other Mediterranean cuisines. Typical Turkish breakfast comprises fresh cheese made from sheep milk, cucumbers, bread, olives, and tomatoes. The major meal of the day is eaten at noon while dinner is usually had between 7 and 9 pm. Turkish cuisine is not at all spicy except in certain parts of the south, which uses pepper as a result of Arab influence. The foods are seasoned with fresh herbs such as parsley, mint, dill, paprika, cumin, and a special sour berry called *sumac*. Use of olive oil, garlic, and onions is predominant. Greek influence of sauces thickened with lemon and egg is also very common to Turkish preparations.

Like the Spanish tapas, Turkish *mezze* is also very popular and serves many kinds of dishes that are common to Lebanese, Greek, and Arabic cusines. *Raki,* a popular anise-flavoured drink made from grapes, is the national drink of turkey. Turkish cuisine, however, uses a lot of lamb in its dishes, which is not as common in other Mediterranean countries. Turkish kebabs marinated in hung yoghurt and creams are very popular in and outside the country. Seafood is another favourite and mostly served grilled or deep-fried. Fried mussels are popularly eaten as snack along with a nut sauce called skordalia or with almond *taratoor.* Vegetables, such as courgettes, brinjal, pepper, and tomatoes, are predominant in Turkish cuisine. Fresh fruits, such as strawberries, figs, melons, apricots, and quinces, are influences from Arab countries. Fresh fruits are usually eaten after dinner, while desserts are generally eaten with tea and not after main meals. Pilafs redolent with spices and nuts are another speciality of Turkish cuisine, Nuts, such as almonds, walnuts, raisins, and currants, are used liberally for making flavoursome pilafs on special occasions. Instead of rice, even bulgur is used for making pilafs.

Popular Turkish dishes

Traditional Turkish dishes include soups, kebabs, seafood, rice pilafs, delectable desserts, as well as pickles. Pickling of food was invented in Syria and then spread to other parts of the world through various travellers. Though the Mediterranean countries strictly rely upon fresh fruits and vegetables of the season, yet due to long sea voyages, it became important to preserve foods so that they could last during the journeys. Hence, it is quite common to see pickled dishes on Mediterranean menus. Turkey, like other Middle Eastern countries, is quite popular for its *mezze*, but as discussed, it is more popular for its kebabs that feature in menus of hotels and restaurants worldwide. Some of the internationally popular dishes of Turkey are described in Table 6.17.

Table 6.17 Popular preparations of Turkish cuisine

Dish	Description	Photograph
Shish taouk	*Shish* means skewer in Turkish and *taouk* or *tawook* refers to chicken. These are cubes of chicken that are marinated in yoghurt; cream, and *zaatar* spice and are skewered and roasted on charcoal grills. There could be many variations of the marinade depending upon the region. *Shish taouk* or *touk* is commonly served with a garlic paste called *toum*. *Shish taouk* is commonly eaten in other cuisines such as Syrian and Lebanese as well. It can be eaten as a sandwich rolled in a flat bread or eaten as snack too.	
Doner kebab	It is also called *shawarma* in Lebanese cooking (refer Table 6.12).	
Dolmasi	Same as *warak inab* (refer Table 6.12).	
Acuka	Also known as *muhammara* in Lebanese cuisine (refer Table 6.12).	
Manti	These are prepared by grinding meat, such as lamb or beef, and flavoured with spices and wrapped in a dough. These are often served baked.	
Icli kofte	These are commonly known as *kibbeh* in Lebanese cuisine (refer Table 6.12).	
Ali Nazik Kebabi	These are home style Turkish kebabs—a speciality of the Gaziantep province. These are prepared by combining sautéed cubes of baby lamb marinated with spices, along with smoked and grilled eggplant puree.	

(Contd)

Table 6.17 *(Contd)*

Dish	Description	Photograph
Caciki	It is also known as *tzatziki* in Greek cuisine (refer Table 6.14).	
Gozleme	It is a traditional hand rolled pastry that is stuffed and cooked over griddle. The fillings can range from spinach and feta cheese to even ground meat and spices.	
Turkish baklava	This dessert is similar to the Lebanese baklava, but instead of being made in layers, it is made into a roulade and shaped as rings. The *phyllo* sheet is brushed with melted butter and the filling of nuts is placed on one end of the pastry. The *phyllo* is now rolled to form a cigar and then the ends are joined together to form a circle. It is then baked and dipped in sugar syrup before serving.	

Moroccan Cuisine

Morocco is one of the oldest monarchies of the world and the country on the northern tip of African continent is influenced by its immediate neighbours—Spain and France. Thousands of years ago, merchants from North Africa, commonly known as Phoenicians, established a series of ports along the coast of Morocco to trade with other countries. Along with their traded goods, they brought in skills such as arts, metal crafting, and architecture. Today, Moorish architecture is one of the most renowned in the world. It is reflective of strong Arab influence. The Romans made use of the fertile lands of Morocco and Tunisia like they used Sicily and Spain to grow wheat for their consumption. These regions acted as a granary for the Roman Empire. The influence of ingredients such as couscous, corn, and maize is still very prominent in the diets of Mediterranean Italy such as Sicily and Sardinia.

Morocco was once under the control of Roman Empire. In the seventh century, Arabs took control over the land, as a result of which Islam grew roots in the region. Even today, Islam is followed by majority Moroccans. The traditional dining style of Moroccans is very much similar to the Kashmiris. The Moroccan meal, which begins with washing of hands in a basin, is laid on a comfortable carpeted floor.

Special ingredients in Moroccan cuisine

Moroccan cuisine is very unique as it is a subtle combination of Arabic food with a Mediterranean touch, especially the Spanish and French flavours. The food is done with unique ingredients, some of which are described in Table 6.18.

Table 6.18 Unique ingredients of Moroccan cuisine

Ingredient	Description	Photograph
Zaatar	Also known as *zahtar*, it is a blend of few spices such as *sumac*, roasted sesame seeds, and green herbs (such as mint and parsley) that are ground and used to flavour meat and vegetables. It can also be mixed with olive oil and used as a marinade for olives, or as a spread for *pita* or flat bread. The taste of a *zaatar* mixture can be tangy, herbal, or nutty.	
Sumac	*Sumac* is a berry obtained from a shrub. It is dried and used as powdered spice. It is also a common ingredient in the Lebanese cuisine. It is dark red to purple in colour in dried form.	
Ras el hanout	It is a popular blend of various spices used across Africa. The word literally means the 'head of the shop' and thus each shopkeeper blends up their top spices. It is ground and then used in almost every kind of dish.	
Tabil	*Tabil* in Arabic means seasoning. It is a common mixture of ground coriander and caraway seeds, garlic powder, and chilly powder. It is used as a seasoning for various Moroccan dishes.	
Baharat	This spice mixture consisting of black pepper, cinnamon, and rose petals is used for flavouring meat dishes in Tunisia. It is also used in Turkish cuisine.	
Orange flower water	This is clear distilled water obtained from the blossoms of orange. The essence is used for flavouring many desserts in Morocco as well as in Spain and France.	
Couscous	Refer Table 6.4.	
Preserved lemons	It is a condiment made of pickled limes. Diced, quartered, halved, or whole lemons are pickled in a brine of water, lemon juice, and salt; occasionally spices are included as well. The pickle is allowed to ferment at room temperature for weeks or months before it is used. The pulp of the preserved lemon can be used in stews and sauces, but it is the peel (zest and pith together) that is most valued. The flavour is mildly tart but intensely lemony.	

Special Moroccan dishes

Moroccan food is served in courses and is flavoured with spices such as ginger, peppers, cumin, as also fresh herbs such as mint, oregano, parsley and other flavours such as musk and rosewater. Tagine and *mashwee* are the most internationally popular dishes, featuring on hotel menus along with the popular Moroccan preparations listed in Table 6.19.

Table 6.19 Popular Moroccan dishes

Dish	Description	Photograph
Tagines	In Moroccan cuisine, tagine is a stew of slowly cooked less expensive cuts of meat with aromatic vegetables, thus resulting in very tender meat and a sauce. It is traditionally cooked in a special utensil known as tagine, which helps to retain the flavours of herbs and spices. Traditional spices that are used to flavour tagines include ground cinnamon, saffron, ginger, turmeric, cumin, paprika, pepper, as also the conventional spice blend *ras el hanout.* Though tagines are usually meat based, yet it is common to see vegetarian tagines with chickpeas as the main ingredient.	
Mechoui/ Mashwee	Pronounced as *mashwee*, it literally means to roast on a fire. It can be called a Moroccan barbecue dish, where the whole lamb is first marinated with spices, such as paprika, cumin, salt, and butter, and then spit roasted until tender. The whole lamb is roasted along with offal that lends their distinct flavour to the meat and prized organs such as the kidney and liver, which are offered to the guest of honour. This dish is served during the festival of *Eid el Kabir* (*Bakri Id*), 70 days after the end of the month of Ramzan marked by *Eid-ul Fitr.*	
Fatah	It is ground meat mixed with browned almonds and parsley, served over a bed of hummus and drizzled with olive oil. *Fatah* is normally consumed as *mezze*.	
Fuul	It is almost like a hummus and is made by grinding a mix of *fava* beans and chickpeas and is flavoured with olive oil and lemon juice. Unlike *mezze, fuul* is eaten for breakfast.	
Harira	This is the traditional and most famous soup of Morocco, which is commonly eaten in the month of Ramzan when the fast is broken. The recipe could differ from one region to another, however the base ingredients for it are lentils (such as chickpeas), onions, and thickeners such as rice, flour, or even egg. Herbs such as celery, parsley, mint, or coriander are commonly used, along with spices such as cumin, saffron, ginger, and pepper. Diced meat can also be added and the soup is finished with a small amount of olive oil. Lemon juice is always added at the time of serving and it is garnished with hard boiled eggs, dates, and other dry fruits. Although this is a soup, it is considered a meal in itself and is popular during Ramzan.	

(Contd)

Table 6.19 (Contd)

Dish	Description	Photograph
Bisteeya	Also known as *b'stilla*, it is a famous flaky pie that is made traditionally with squab or sometimes with chicken. It is a typical Moroccan dish and is often considered the national dish of Morocco. It has a combination of sweet and savoury flavours and is made with meat which is cooked and then mixed with raisins and roasted almonds, stuffed in layers of *phyllo* sheets, and then baked.	
Kefta	*Kefta* or *koftas* consist of balls of minced or ground meat (usually beef or lamb) that are flavoured with different kinds of spices and other ingredients such as chopped onions and herbs. They can be grilled, fried, steamed, poached, baked, or marinated, and may be served with a rich spicy sauce.	
Baghrir	These are Moroccan pancakes that resemble *appams* from Kerala. It is a popular breakfast item during Ramzan and is made by combining flour, semolina, eggs, sugar, olive oil, and leaveners such as yeast and baking powder. It is left to ferment and baked on a griddle like thick pancakes.	
Maamoul	These are small shortbread balls shaped as domes and filled with dates, walnuts, pistachios, or other fillings and commonly eaten with tea.	
Sfenj	These are Moroccan doughnuts, which are fried in oil and dusted with sugar or soaked in honey.	
Chermoula	It is a typical marinade in Moroccan cuisine comprising coriander, garlic, parsley, cumin, paprika, herbs, oil, lemon juice or pickled lemons, cumin, and salt. It may also include onion, fresh coriander, ground chilli peppers, black pepper, or saffron. It can be used as a marinade for grilled meat and fish or served as a dip.	

Provencal Cuisine

The southern eastern part of France on the Mediterranean adjacent to Italy is referred to Provence. Marseilles, Nice, and Antibes are important cities of this region, which has a rich heritage and history dating prehistoric times. Some earliest human settlements have been found in this region, which was colonized by the Greeks some time around 540 BC. The Romans also established their first province outside the Alps in this region, giving it the name, Provence. The cuisine of this part of France, known as Provencal cuisine, bears strong similarities with Mediterranean region rather than the country of which it is a part. In the world of cooking, Provencal cuisine thus, is classified as Mediterranean cuisine.

Special ingredients in provencal cuisine

Olive oil is the main cooking medium in Provencal cuisine unlike other parts of France where butter is used in cooking. Bouillabaisse is a famous Mediterranean preparation of the region made with seafood, tomatoes, olive, olive oil and flavoured with fennel and saffron, that are typical to Provence. Fresh stew of vegetables, such as eggplants, artichokes, peppers, and tomatoes, flavoured with basil is another popular Provencal dish that is served as vegetable accompaniment to many seafood and meat items. Provencal food is all about garlic, olive oil, fresh cheese, flavours of basil and wild saffron.

Today, Provencal food is an amazing amalgamation of items and eating habits of the various settlers and invaders during its course of history. For example, olives and olive oil are a contribution of the Greeks, pastas, and raviolis of the Romans, couscous of the Moroccans, vegetables and fruits such as raisins and sultanas from Arabs. The style of cooking, by and large, lean, uncomplicated, and healthy as it relies on fresh and seasonal ingredients. Herbs such as basil, chervil, tarragon, fennel, marjoram, mint, thyme, rosemary, and sage combined with olive oil, and sometimes saffron are predominant flavours of Provence. The cuisine, thus, is very aromatic and flavoursome. People usually use a dried herb mixture, which is generally added to impart flavour and aroma to the dishes. This classical Provencal mixture of herbs comprises dried herbs such as thyme, savoury, rosemary, lavender, rosemary, bay leaves, cloves, nutmeg and dried orange peel. The herbs are dried carefully in shade and then ground together to form an aromatic powder.

Special Provencal dishes

Provencal cuisine is very popular all over the world. Some of the common Provencal dishes are described in Table 6.20.

Table 6.20   Common dishes of Provencal cuisine

Dish	Description	Photograph
Cassoulet	One of the most famous dishes of Southern France, *cassoulet* is a slow-cooked bean stew. It contains pork skin, meat such as game birds and sausages, and haricots beans. It is made in a deep round earthenware pot with slanting sides also known as *cassole*.	
Piperade	This dish is served as an accompaniment to many dishes or sometimes served as a dish by itself. It is prepared by sautéing onions, green peppers, and tomatoes that are flavoured with red peppers from southern France called *espelette* peppers. The colours of this dish represent the colours of France and Spain from where it originates.	
Bouillabaisse	Bouillabaisse is a traditional fish stew that is prepared with different kinds of cooked fish. A variety of herbs and spices are used to add flavour to it.	

(Contd)

Table 6.20 (Contd)

Dish	Description	Photograph
Rouille	The word *rouille* comes from the French word for rust, as the colour of this sauce. It is prepared by puréeing breadcrumbs, olive oil, garlic, saffron, and chilli peppers. It is traditionally served as an accompaniment to bouillabaisse.	
Ratatouille	This is a traditional vegetable dish. The complete name is ratatouille *niçoise* and it consists of stewed vegetables. It is generally served as a side dish but it can be served as a complete dish on its own also. This dish is generally prepared in summer with fresh vegetables.	
Tapenade	It is a Provencal dish of finely chopped olives, capers, anchovies, and olive oil. The most desired component on this dish is the capers, as in southern France capers are known as *tapenas* that lend its name to this dish. *Tapenade* is like paste and is commonly applied on crusty breads and eaten as hors d'oeuvres.	
Pissaladière	This Provencal dish is inspired from Italian pizzas, which is prepared by topping a thin sheet of dough with very finely chopped onions, garlic, and anchovies. The anchovies are also arranged in a peculiar fashion or can be pasted and applied on the dough before it is baked. It does not use tomatoes and cheese as in Italian pizzas.	
Civet de Lapin	A traditional winter dish of Provencal region is a rabbit or hare stew that is cooked in red wine and the sauce is traditionally thickened with rabbit blood. This dish is also very popular in English countries, where it is also called jugged hare.	
Aioli	Aioli can be called garlic mayonnaise. It traditionally uses olive oil, garlic paste, egg yolk, and mustard. It is usually served as a dip along with olives and fried items.	

MEXICAN CUISINE

As we read more and more about various cuisines of the world, we learn about the diversity in each cuisine and the various factors that have inspired or completely changed the cuisine and food habits of different regions. Mexican food is no exception. It is widely believed that contemporary Mexican cuisine is completely different from what it used to be thousands of years ago.

Mexico is the birthplace of the highly advanced Mayan or Aztec Civilization in ancient times. However, the Mayans were mainly nomadic hunters and food gatherers and not growers. Traces of this influence can still be seen in Mexican cuisine. Mayan food included wild and game animals, such as armadillos, monkeys, and iguana, and over 200 species of insects, which were considered to be a rich source of proteins. In the modern world too, it is quite common to see certain insects being consumed by rural Mexicans, though not very popular outside the country.

Ancient Aztec food was roasted in fire or cooked in pots called *cazuela*, which was hung over the fire. Cooking methods such as deep frying and pan searing, were literally unknown to the natives. It was much after the Spanish invasion in the sixteenth century that the method of making lard and suet transformed the cooking habits of Mexicans. The art of making cheese, sour cream, and breads constitute a sizeable portion of modern Mexican cuisine. There would not have been popular *quesadillas* or nachos with cheese dips if the Mexicans had not perfected the art of cheese making. The cuisines of Mexico further influenced the cuisines of South America as well as North America, especially Texas in the USA, which borders Mexico. The cuisine of that region, which has an overwhelming influence of Mexican style is popularly known as Tex-Mex cuisine. Invaders from all over the world lent special ingredients, such as squashes, eggplants, onions, garlic, and tomatoes, while the Portuguese helped grow peppers and chillies in and around Mexico. Some of the Mexican chillies such as *habanero* are ranked among the hottest chillies in the world. Thus, the food in Mexico today is largely reflective of the Spanish influence and it is common to some Spanish dishes on Mexican menu. However, the cuisine of the country also has traits form the Portuguese, French, Caribbean, and South American cuisines.

Geography

The geographical location of Mexico is by itself an indicator of its biodiversity and also cultural diversity, which has had a profound impact on its cuisine. Located in North America, it is bordered by the USA on its north; by the Pacific Ocean on its south and west; by Guatemala, Belize, and the Caribbean Sea on its south-east; and on its east is the Gulf of Mexico. The Tropic of Cancer divides Mexico in two halves, with its northern region experiencing temperate climate and the other half having tropical climate. Thus, some parts of Mexico experience cold temperatures in the winter months while some have a constant temperature throughout the year. The climate of Mexico is quite dry and wet. Rainfall, especially in the Eastern region near Gulf of Mexico, lasts from July to September. The climatic conditions are very conducive to growth of tropical fruits and vegetables that dominate the cuisine of Mexico, and South as well as North America. Food items such as nachos with cheese and enchiladas, are American dishes that have been inspired by Mexican ingredients and rarely eaten in Mexico but are very popular in North America.

Special Ingredients in Mexican Cuisine

Since Mexico was a passing route for Medieval Portuguese explorers, ports built on the city of Veracruz attracted lots of traders and travellers who majorly influenced its cuisine.

They added a few ingredients to the Mexican cuisine and also took a lot from them into their own country. The land of Rocky Mountains, green pastures, and coastal areas produces a unique set of flora and fauna including some cacti that are commonly used in cooking. Some are also used for making the popular drink, tequila. Chocolate, as we will learn in Chapter 12, originated from Mexico (and was popularly drunk as a beverage or used to prepare a chicken dish called *mole poblano*). Chocolate and tomatoes are the most popular ingredients in Mexican cuisine. Apart from these, the Mexicans use a wide range of ingredients some which are highlighted in Table 6.21.

Table 6.21 Common ingredients in Mexican cuisine (see also Plate 5)

Ingredient	Description	Photograph
Avocado	Also known as alligator pear, butter fruit, or *makhan phal* in Hindi, this fruit is commonly used in salads and to make one of the most popular Mexican sauces called *guacamole*. Avocadoes were known as fertility fruits by Aztecs. It is always eaten ripe. The outer skin turns dark brown on ripening, which can also be achieved by wrapping in newspapers and left at room temperature for a few days.	
Chillies	There are around 250 varieties of chillies that grow in Mexico and each one has a different culinary use. It is commonly used as an ingredient in sauces and dishes. Some of the most common ones varieties are as follows: *Habanero* Counted among the hottest chillies, it is green when unripe but takes on various colours, such as orange, yellow, and even white, as it ripens. It is the second hottest chilli in the world after the Indian variety called *Naga jolokia*. *Poblano* It is a mild chilli pepper from the Puebla region of Mexico. It can be harvested green and at this stage is mild. When ripened and dried, it is called *anchos* which is significantly hotter than the green variety. It is commonly used in the dish *mole poblano*. *Serano* This chilli from the mountainous region of Mexico gets its name from Sierras which means mountains. Unripe chillies are green which turn red, yellow, or orange as they ripen. They resemble jalapeño chillies but are hotter than them. These chillies are commonly used for making *Pico de Gallo* and is one of the most commonly used chillies in Mexican cooking. *Jalapeño* Pronounced as *halyapeeno,* it is a chilli of Spanish origin. It is a thick chilli between 4 and 9 cm long, with a smooth and shiny texture. It is harvested green. Jalapeños are also commonly sold sliced in a brine. *Anaheim* It is a mild variety of chilli pepper used in many Mexican preparations. It is also called Californian pepper.	 *Habanero* *Poblano* *Serano* Jalapeño *Anaheim*

(Contd)

Table 6.21 (Contd)

Ingredient	Description	Photograph
Chillies	*Pasilla* This chilli is also known as *pasiua negro* because of the black colour that it attains upon drying. When fresh and green, it is also called *chilaca* and is a medium hot and very flavoursome chilli. It pairs up well with duck, lamb, and mushrooms. *Tabasco* This pepper comes from the Tabasco region of Mexico and is one of the most popular chillies in Tabasco sauce. The chilli grows in a unique manner, by growing upwards from the plant. It is available in many colours on the same plants. These chillies are small but quite hot and pungent. *Chipotle* It is a smoked variety of dried jalapeño chillies. It attains a shrivelled look upon smoking and is used for flavouring tomato-based sauces.	 *Pasilla* *Tabasco* *Chipotle*
Jicama (Mexican potato)	It is a sweet root vegetable that looks like a turnip but has an earthy colour like potato, which is why it is also called Mexican potato. It can be eaten raw but is commonly eaten in salads.	
Epazote	Also known as wormseed, is a herb native to Latin America and Southern Mexico. This plant or herb has many uses in Mexican cuisine. The leaves are used to flavour many dishes such as black bean dishes, *ranchero* sauce, and *chipotle* sauce. It pairs up well with tomato and cheese.	
Platanos	It is a banana like fruit that is used in cooking. It is not as sweet as a banana and does not break in cooking. It is also called plantains.	
Frijoles	*Frijoles* or beans are popularly used in Mexican cuisines. Depending on their colour like black or red, they are known as *frijoles negro* or *frijoles roco* respectively. They are cooked like stews or combined with meat or even boiled and served as salads.	
Tortilla	The Mexican tortilla is very different from the one discussed in Spanish cuisine in Table 6.16. Tortilla in Mexico is a flat bread made from flour, similar to a chapatti in India. It has various uses and can be served along with the meal or used for making sandwiches.	
Corn	Corn is one of the most commonly eaten foods in Mexico since the time of the Aztecs. There are two types of corn popularly grown in Mexico—yellow corn is usually for feeding livestock, whereas the white variety is used for human consumption. The leaves of corn are also used for preparing a dish called *tamale*. Corn is also used as a grain, and it can be crushed to make flour that is commonly used for making enchiladas and tacos.	

(Contd)

Table 6.21 (Contd)

Ingredient	Description	Photograph
Nopales	This is the green cactus which is also known as prickly pear. The cladodes or pads of this plant are sold fresh, canned, or dried around the world. It can be cut and prepared like a vegetable, salad, or combined with meat.	
Monterey Jack cheese	It is an American semi-hard cheese quite popular in Mexico. It can be combined with peppers and also made into a spicy cheese. It is cooked to make a jack cheese sauce that is served as condiment along with nachos or can be grated and added in *quesadillas*.	
Achiote	This is the plant which yields the annatto beans. The Spanish were so intrigued by the colour of these beans that they took it to Spain and substituted it in place of saffron. It is commonly used as a colourant for various foodstuffs such as cheeses and butter.	
Tomatillo	It belongs to the family of tomatoes and is related to cape gooseberries. Also known as *tomate verde*, it is a green coloured tomato which is used in preparation of many dishes such as salads, accompaniment with grilled meats, and also for making salsas.	

Special Equipment used in Mexican Cooking

There are many traditional and some unusual equipment used in Mexican cooking such as special mortar and pestles made from lava stones and griddles to cook tortillas. Each equipment is for a particular purpose. Most of the mechanical equipment used for functions such as grinding or blending have been replaced with electric machines and blenders. Nonetheless, the use of traditional kitchen tools is still popular in rural areas. Some popular equipment used in Mexican cuisine are described in Table 6.22.

Table 6.22 Equipment used in Mexican cooking

Equipment	Description	Photograph
Cazuela	It is a traditional earthenware casserole used for making traditional soup of the same name using both meat and vegetables. *Cazuelas* were traditionally hung over wood fires and were very popular in preparing stews. The modern version of *cazuela* is a glazed ceramic pot in attractive colours, which can be placed directly on flame while cooking the soup.	
Olla	It is a ceramic jar used for cooking stews and soups and also for storing dry products and water. *Ollas* have a short wide neck and resemble bean pots or *handis*.	

(Contd)

Table 6.22 (Contd)

Ingredient	Description	Photograph
Molcajete	It is a mortar and pestle that is used for grinding spices, chillies, and other ingredients to make salsas, *guacamole*, etc. A similar larger equipment called *metate* is often made from lava stones and is used for grinding large quantities.	
Tortilero	Originally made from wood, these are two flat wooden or metallic surfaces that are used for pressing a ball of dough to make tortillas or enchiladas.	
Comal	It is a large round griddle usually made of cast iron and is used for cooking tortillas. It is quite similar to the *tawa* in India.	

Special Mexican Dishes

The eating habits of Mexicans have been greatly influenced by the Spanish. Though there is no concept of tapas, Mexico street food (known as *antojitos*) is popular all over the country. Traditionally, Mexicans have four meals—those who get up early, start their day with some sweet pastries, juice, or coffee. That is followed by a mid-morning breakfast called *merinda* consisting of eggs and even small portion of steaks. At 2 p.m., the main meal or *comida* is eaten. As discussed earlier, corn is the basis of Mexican diet and is used in many forms. Vegetables such as tomatoes, tomatillos, squashes, *jicama*, *napoles*, and *frijoles* form a large part of the diet. Meat, such as lamb, beef, and pork and chicken, is commonly eaten. The food is made with a variety of chillies. At times a particular dish is only made with a particular chilli. Seafood is commonly eaten in the coastal areas because of its abundant availability. Though many types of dishes are prepared in Mexico, the more common ones are discussed in Table 6.23.

Table 6.23 Popular dishes in Mexican cuisine (see also Plate 6)

Dish	Description	Photograph
Refried beans	Refried beans are a very popular Mexican dish. These can be made using red beans or black beans and can be seasoned and spiced with chillies. These are cooked until they get a mushy texture. These are usually eaten as an accompaniment, and also used as a stuffing in enchiladas, burritos, etc.	

(Contd)

Table 6.23 (Contd)

Dish	Description	Photograph
Guacamole	It is a kind of dip or a sauce made by crushing the pulp of ripened avocadoes in a *molcajete*. Chopped tomatoes and onions are added for flavour and colour and lime juice is added to prevent the *guacamole* from turning black on exposure to air. It is the most popular dish of Mexico and is quite popular in Spain as well.	
Fajita	*Fajita* commonly refers to any grilled meat served on a bed of corn or flour tortilla. Sometimes in hotels and restaurants, it is often a kind of stir fried meat with onions and bell peppers. It is generally served along with salsa, sour cream, and *guacamole*.	
Salsa	Salsa is a generic word for Mexican sauces. The term is derived from the Latin word *sal* which means salty. A salsa is popularly made with freshly pureed or chopped tomatoes, combined with herbs and seasonings.	
Pico de Gallo	Also known as salsa *cruda*, it is a mixture of chopped onions, tomatoes, and cilantro. It is actually a form of salad but is served in small portions to accompanying dishes. At times, it is sprinkled over dishes to add texture and flavour.	
Enchilada	This is actually a more popular dish in the USA and is made by stuffing a corn or flour tortilla with refried beans, cheese, meats, etc. and covered with chilli pepper sauce and baked. *Enchiladas* can be eaten as snacks or served as a main meal with rice and refried beans.	
Taco	A taco is a half moon corn tortilla shell, that is popularly filled with a salad, refried beans, grilled meats, or sour cream and served along with salsa, *Pico di Gallo*, or *guacamole*. A variety of fillings can be used to fill these crunchy shells that are often sold ready made.	
Tostadas	These are same as tacos; the only difference is that the shape is like that of a shell or a tart. The word comes from toasted as these are toasted and crunchy shells that do not go soggy easily.	

(Contd)

Table 6.23 (Contd)

Dish	Description	Photograph
Burrito	This is a flour tortilla that is stuffed with any kind of filling and rolled up like a roll. Different types of ingredients such as rice, meat, lettuce, *guacamole*, and sour cream, are commonly used but the choice is unlimited.	
Chimichangas	These are deep-fried burritos that are commonly stuffed with ingredients which will not ooze out while frying. It is also accompanied with salsa, sour cream, and *guacamole*.	
Quesadilla	It is probably one of the most popular of all Mexican dishes and can be made in variety of ways. Two tortillas can be sandwiched with caramelized onions, sliced grilled meats, and large quantity of grated cheese. It is then pan fried on both sides until crisp and served with sour cream, salsa, guacamole, and *Pico di Gallo*. Traditionally, it is filled with a special stringy cheese called *Oaxaca* but Mozzarella substitutes well.	
Tamale	*Tamales* are popularly made by filling a flour or corn tortillas with assorted fillings. These are then wrapped in corn husks and secured with string. These are then steamed until firm and then served. The corn husks are discarded before eating. Almost every region in Mexico has its own *tamale* speciality.	
Mole poblano	In Mexico, *mole* is a popular word for all kinds of sauces. This dish is made using the *poblano* chillies and the sauce is flavoured with bitter chocolate. It is popularly combined with chicken or turkey and is an ancient Aztec dish.	
Helado frito	*Helado frito* or fried ice cream is commonly served on menus to add an element of surprise for the guests. An ice cream is scooped and frozen. It is then dipped into a sweet batter of flour and eggs and then coated in corn grits or flakes. Close to service, the ice cream is briefly lowered into hot oil to quickly colour the corn flakes and is served immediately. The coating is hot, while the ice cream still stays in a frozen state.	

SUMMARY

This chapter primarily discussed the food of the Western world. Earlier, the term Western cuisine was used interchangeably with Continental or European Cuisine. However, in this age of globalization and frequent travel, many more delectable dishes from other countries have gained popularity and made it to the international gourmet list. In this Chapter, we discussed non-European or continental Western cuisines such as Italian, Mediterranean, and Mexican. These cuisines that have become equally, if not more, popular than European cuisines.

Although Italy is a part of the European continent, we discussed it in this chapter because it also forms a part of the Mediterranean cuisine along with other countries that surround the Mediterranean Sea. Italian food is gaining more popularity than European cuisine. French cuisine is losing in popularity as it is laced in butter. Comparatively, Italian food is fresher and seasonal. Italian food is cooked in olive oil, which is considered to be healthier than the saturated fat in butter.

It is believed that the fine dining concepts originated in Italy and were taken to France with the marriage of Queen Catherine de' Medici to King Henry II of France. Italian cuisine is as distinct and diverse as the kind of people who emerged and settled in the country at various points of time in history. Besides the result of historic interactions among various races on the food, Italian cuisine also owes its diversity to diverse topography of various regions, as also the climate and *terroir*, which imparts a unique flavour to the vegetation. Therefore, in this chapter, we discussed the cooking styles of as many as 13 regions in Italy including Abruzzo, Basilicata, Campania, Emilia-Romagna, Liguria, Lombardy, Piedmont, Puglia, Sardinia, Sicily, Tuscany, Umbria, and Veneto. The mountainous region of Abruzzo is very famous for its *Aglio Olio* pasta and Basilicata, which was once called Lucania, is famous for its *charcuterie* such as *loukanika* sausage. Campania is famous for its cheesy pizzas and pasta *napolitaine*. Emilia-Romagna is famous for *prosciutto Parma* and Parmesan cheese which is among the most popular ingredients of Italian cooking. Emilia-Romagna is also home to many home-made pastas such as *tortellini* and lasagne. Liguria lies on the foot of Alps. Its cool climate and fertile land produces fresh fruits and vegetables such as olives and basil. The cuisine of Lombardy region, which is famous for its risotto rice, is called Milanese. Dishes such as *osso buco* and *panettone* come from this region. Piedmont borders southern France and the influence of Provencal cuisine can be seen on the region's cuisine. Puglia, on the heel of the boot-shaped country map, is famous for its *durum* wheat pastas such as *orechiette* pasta.

Sardinia and Sicily form a part of Mediterranean cuisine and are famous for their sea food, wheat, wine, and olive oil. The food is robust and seasonal. Dishes such as Sicilian *Cassata*, *Arancine* come from Sicily. Tuscany is part of a large coastline that faces the Tyrrhenian Sea and thus seafood from this region is very popular. Umbria is famous for its white truffles, olive oil, and fresh herbs while Veneto is the place where the famous *tiramisu* comes from. Cheese such as *Asiago* also popularly come from Veneto.

In this chapter, we also discussed a range of ingredients used in Italian cooking such as famous cheeses—Parmesan, *Pecorino*, Gorgonzola, and *mascarpone*. *Charcuterie* products commonly known as *salumi* were also explained with illustra-tions. We also discussed other ingredients of Italian cuisine such as olive oil and its varieties and balsamic vinegar from Italy. Various kinds of ingredients, such as polenta, couscous, and *durum* wheat, were also discussed along with their use in Italian cooking. We also discussed the soul of Italian cooking—the pasta. Various shapes of fresh and dried pasta are discussed in tabular form along with illustrations for easy understanding. Few commonly prepared Italian sauces which are popularly used around the world were discussed in great detail. A range of special tools and equipment that are required in preparing Italian dishes were also discussed along with some popular Italian dishes such as *osso buco* and *saltimbocca*. The recipes of these dishes are included in the CD.

We also discussed the cuisines of Mediterranean region. Though there are nearly 19 countries that form a part of Mediterranean cuisine, we discussed some famous cuisines that are commonly prepared in the hotels and restaurants worldwide. We discussed the cuisines of countries such as Lebanon, Greece, Spain, Turkey, Morocco, and Southern France with regard to their speciality, ingredients, equipment used, and famous dishes from the region that make this cuisine popular and unique.

We talked about the cuisines of Mexico with regard to its history and how the food and habits of its people have evolved over the years. We also discussed the unique ingredients used in Mexican cuisine and some of its most internationally popular dishes. Since Mexican chilli is one of its unique ingredients, we also discussed few types of famous chillies that are popular in Mexican cuisine.

KEY TERMS

Absinthe   It is an anise-flavoured drink from Spain.

Aceto Balsamico   It is Italian for balsamic vinegar.

Acorns   Also known as oak nuts, acorns are obtained from oak trees.

Affumicato   It is Italian for smoked.

Aglio   It is Italian for garlic.

Al dente   It is a term used to denote the cooking of the any ingredient, especially pasta, to a stage where it has a bite to it and is not overcooked.

Artichoke   Also called globe, artichoke is a flower vegetable with scales.

Bagna càuda   It is a dip of anchovies made in the Piedmont region of Italy.

Banon   It is sheep-milk cheese from southern France.

Barlotti beans   These are a type of beans that resemble kidney beans.

Beyaz penir   It is cheese obtained from sheep milk in Turkey.

Bulgur   It is cracked wheat which is par boiled and dried.

Cantaloupe melon   This is a variety of melon from the Cantaloupe region of Italy.

Caponata   These are stewed vegetables such as olives, capers, tomatoes, and aubergines often served as an accompaniment.

Castelmagno   It is a popular Italian cheese commonly used in cooking.

Cecci   It is Italian for chickpeas or garbanzo beans.

Coddled eggs   These are eggs on which boiling water has been poured for a minute or two.

Concassé   It is a term used for de-skinned, deseeded, and chopped tomatoes.

Continental food   It is a term used for food from European countries particularly France and England.

Dandelions   These are bitter arrow-shaped small leaves used in salads as well as stir fries.

Dolce   It is Italian for sweet.

DOP   It is the acronym of *Denomininazione di Orgini Protetta*—a classification of a product in Italy that comes from a certain region only.

Durum   It is a variety of hard wheat grown in Italy popularly used for makings breads and pasta.

Endive   It is a type of lettuce.

Escalopes   These are thin slices of meat.

Espelette peppers   It is a variety of very mildly hot red peppers from southern France.

Ewe   A female sheep. A milch animal.

Extra virgin olive oil   It is olive oil with less than 1 per cent acidity.

Fava beans   These are flat and broad beans found in Mediterranean countries.

Fennel   It is a green vegetable with a bulbous part. The fennel bulb is used in cooking, whereas the leaves are used as garnish.

Focaccia   It is a soft bread from Italy flavoured with vegetables and olive oil.

Fresco   This is Italian for fresh.

Fritto misto   An assortment of fried seafood served in Italy.

Gianduja   It is a paste of hazelnuts mixed with chocolate.

Grana Padano   It is Parmesan cheese from Lombardy region in Italy.

Granita   It is shaved flavoured ice commonly served as dessert in Italy.

Guéridon trolley   It is a trolley in restaurants, where the food is prepared in front of the guest and served by the steward.

Lavash   It is a flat and crisp bread made in Mediterranean countries.

Mahia   It is anise-flavoured drink from Morocco.

Marzipan   It is preparatory almond paste used in confectionary.

Milanese style   It is a style of cooking followed in the Lombardy region of Italy.

Moors   They were ancient inhabitants of Africa.

Mozzarella cheese   It is a soft to semi-hard cheese in Italy that melts to form a stringy texture.

Myrtle   It is a kind of Mediterranean herb that comes from an evergreen shrub.

Nachos These are toasted corn tortilla chips, usually served with cheese dip and salsa.

Olio It is Italian for oil.

Ovoli mushroom It is a kind of Italian mushroom that resembles an egg.

Panini It is a layered grilled sandwich that is served hot.

Parmigiano-Reggiano This is Parmesan cheese from Emilia-Romagna.

Pasta filata It is the process of pulling cheese to give it stringy appearance after it has been softened in warm water.

Pastis This is anise flavoured drink from Southern France.

Pecorino Sardo It is a firm cheese from the Italian island of Sardinia obtained from sheep's milk. It is acidic and sharp.

Pecorino It is pungent cheese made from sheep's milk.

Pepperoncini These are sweet chillies from Italy used in pasta sauces.

Pesto It is paste obtained by crushing basil with garlic, pine nuts, parmesan, and olive oil in a mortar and pestle.

Pita bread It is puffed bread made from flour and yeast.

Polenta It is coarse flour obtained from maize.

Pomace oil It is olive oil extracted by adding solvents to the olive mush.

Pomodoro It is Italian for tomatoes.

Porcini It is a kind of Italian mushroom with earthy colours and flavour.

Puls It is a starchy porridge consumed by the early Romans which was made from wheat.

Pure olive oil It is refined olive oil.

Sabayon This is an Italian sauce obtained by cooking egg yolks with sugar to form a stable emulsion on a double boiler.

Salumi It is Italian for charcuterie products.

Sambuca It is anise flavoured drink from Sicily and Sardinia.

Savoiardi It is Italian sponge biscuit usually used for making *tiramisu*.

Spelt It is a kind of wheat grain commonly used for making pasta.

Stagionato It is Italian for seasoned.

Suet It is a term used for fat obtained from beef or mutton.

Sumac It is a kind of berry that is used as spice in Lebanese cuisine.

Swiss chard It is a kind of leafy vegetable with broad leaves.

Terroir A French term in wine, coffee and tea used to denote the special characteristics that the geography, geology and climate of a certain place bestow on particular plant varieties.

Tex-Mex cuisine This is Mexican cuisine which is popular in the Texas region of North America.

Virgin olive oil It is olive oil with acidity between 1 and 2 per cent.

CONCEPT REVIEW QUESTIONS

1. What do you understand by the word Western and Continental cuisines?
2. What do you understand by the term Mediterranean cuisine?
3. Name the various regions of Italy with regard to cuisines.
4. Critique the food of Abruzzo.
5. What famous dish comes from Basilicata region of Italy?
6. Which region in Italy is famous for its pizzas?
7. Parmesan cheese, Parma ham, and Balsamic come from which region of Italy?
8. What role does geographical location of Liguria play in its cuisine?
9. Describe a *gnocchi* pasta.
10. What is *osso bucco* and which region of Italy it belongs to?
11. How is the cuisine of Piedmont different from Italian cuisine and why?
12. Describe three regions of Italy that form a part of the Mediterranean cuisine.
13. Which region of Italy is near the Tyrrhenian Sea?
14. Which is the most famous dessert from Veneto?
15. Which regions in Italy are famous for its truffles?
16. Name at least three cheeses that are DOP.
17. What is the difference between a *Parmegiano-Reggiano* and *Grana Padano*?

18. Name the cheese obtained from whey.
19. Name one cream cheese from Italy that is used for making a famous dessert called *tiramisu.*
20. What is the difference between Mozzarella cheese and *bocconcini?*
21. What is a *baccalà.*
22. Differentiate between extra virgin, virgin, pure, and Pomace olive oil.
23. Name at least three varieties of rice that are used for making risotto.
24. What is the difference between a bulgur, polenta and couscous?
25. What is the difference between *farro* and *durum* wheat?
26. Describe the ingredients and the method of making fresh pasta.
27. What do you mean by the word *al dente*?
28. Name at least three tubular pastas.
29. Name at least three ribbon-shaped pastas.
30. What is the difference between a *tagliatelle* and *tagliolini?*
31. Name the famous cap-shaped pasta from Abruzzo.
32. What does the term *pappardelle* mean?
33. What is the difference between a spaghetti and *bucatini* pasta?
34. Name at least five stuffed fresh pasta.
35. Differentiate between *napolitana, arrabbiata,* and a *puttanesca* sauce.
36. Name at least three cream-based sauces used in pasta.
37. Evaluate the use of the equipment called *chitarra* in Italian cuisine.
38. Name at least five special dishes of Italy and describe them.
39. Name and describe at least two Italian desserts.
40. Name the countries that contribute to the Mediterranean cuisine.
41. What does the acronym WOW mean in Mediterranean cuisine?
42. What is so unique about the cuisines of the Mediterranean region?
43. Describe the flavours of Lebanese cuisine.
44. Name at least five dips served in Lebanese cuisine.
45. Name at least three hot *mezzes* from Lebanon.
46. Describe a *shawarma* and what is it called in Turkish and Greek cuisines.
47. The dish *warak inab* is prepared in many Mediterranean countries. What is it called in different countries?
48. Describe the flavour profile of Greek cuisine.
49. Name at least three cheeses from Greece.
50. What is the difference between a *phyllo* pastry and *knafeh*?
51. Name three ingredients unique to the Greek cuisine.
52. Describe a *horiatiki.*
53. What is the difference between a *spanakopita* and *tyropitakia?*
54. Name at least three desserts from Greece.
55. How is a Turkish baklava different from the Greek baklava?
56. Describe the food of Spain.
57. Name the famous cheese from Spain.
58. Name two famous cold cuts from Spain.
59. Describe a paella.
60. What is the difference between a Spanish and Mexican tortilla?
61. Describe at least five famous dishes from Spain.
62. Differentiate between a *shish taouk* and *doner kebab.*
63. Name at least five famous dishes of Turkey.
64. Name at least three famous spice mixes from Morocco.
65. Describe a tagine and its importance.
66. Describe the famous dish called *mechoui* from Morocco.
67. Describe *harira*? How is it prepared.
68. What is a Provencal cuisine and how is it different from other Mediterranean cuisines?
69. Name at least five Provencal dishes.
70. What do you understand by the word Tex-Mex cuisine?
71. Describe at least five chillies of Mexico.
72. Describe at least five ingredients used in Mexican cooking.
73. What is *molcajete*?What are its uses in Mexican cuisine?
74. Describe any five famous dishes of Mexico.
75. What is the difference between an enchilada, burrito and a *chimichanga*?
76. What is *Pico de Gallo* and how is it served?
77. Describe *tamales.*
78. What are *quesadillas* and how are they made?
79. What is *helado frito* and how is it made?
80. What are refried beans and their importance in Mexican cuisine?

PROJECT WORK

1. In groups of five, conduct a market survey of hotels and speciality restaurants that specialize in Italian cooking. Make a list of their menu and a few unique ingredients used in the cuisine. Try to find out which part of Italy does the dish comes from.

2. In groups of three each, prepare a range of fresh home-made pastas and combine with a few sauces mentioned in the recipies in the CD. Make your observations on the shapes that go well with various sauces. Justify your observations.

3. In groups of five each, prepare a *mezze* buffet from Greece, Turkey, Lebanon, and Morocco and then compare the similarities and differences.

4. Carry out a research on ancient and traditional Mexican dishes and compare how various influences have led to a change in the food of today.

5. Research at least three special ingredients used in Mediterranean cooking that come from the wild or forests. For example, the cactus used in Mexican cuisine. Share your observations with colleagues and discuss how food has changed and evolved over times.

CHAPTER 7

EUROPEAN CUISINES

Learning Objectives

After reading this chapter, you should be able to

- understand the basics of European cuisine
- differentiate between various European cuisines such as French, German, English, and Scandinavian
- identify various kinds of tools and equipment used for making food in France
- explain the different types of cheeses, vegetables, and *charcuterie* products used in French, German, and English cooking
- comprehend the use of uncommon ingredients in Scandinavian cooking
- examine the effects of topography on the cuisines of various countries in Europe
- identify the cooking ingredients in various countries and what makes them unique
- recognize the various regions of France, England, Germany, and Scandinavian countries and their regional differences with regard to cuisine
- analyse the techniques applied in preparation of Scandinavian food
- identify various types of Scandinavian dishes and what makes them unique

INTRODUCTION

Europe, the world's second-smallest continent, is a large cluster of countries surrounded by the Arctic Ocean in the north, Atlantic Ocean in the west, Mediterranean Sea towards the south and the Black Sea and Caspian Sea towards its south-east. European cuisine is thus understandably wide and varied because of the culture and geographic location that determines the availability of ingredients used for cooking. For this reason, the cuisine from the continent is broadly studied under various sections such as south, west, north, and eastern European cuisine. The southern European cuisine reflects the cooking styles of several countries such as Italy, Greece, Portugal, Spain, and Turkey. Western European cuisine, however, is the most popular among them and is widely available in hotels internationally. This region boasts of cuisines from Austria, Germany, Switzerland, and from France, popularly referred to as French cuisine. Northern European cuisine includes British cuisines and those from the Scandinavian countries of Denmark, Finland, and Norway. The cuisines of Eastern Europe are unique in their own ways. The most popular cuisines from this region are from Russia, Hungary, Poland, and Romania. Though there are many countries in Europe with their own special cuisines, we have restricted ourselves here to the most popular ones that feature on the menu lists of hotels worldwide.

There is a very thin line of difference between the Western and Continental cuisine. The latter is a term generally used for food that particularly came from the UK, France, and Russia, as these were the most popular cuisines in the medieval times. Chef Augustus Escoffier, who first set up the hierarchy and the classical brigade of professional kitchen, was French and the French cuisine of that time was considered to be food for the rich and famous. In this chapter, we will discuss cuisines of France, Germany, Great Britain, Greece, and Scandinavian countries. Italian and Greek cooking are a part of European cuisine, but we discussed it in Chapter 6 on Western cuisines.

In this chapter, we will understand the diversity of each cuisine and its unique approach to cooking and serving food. We will also try to understand the role of ingredients and the unique equipment used for preparing food in different regions. Some dishes from each of these cuisines are very popular worldwide and it is common to see them featuring on the menus of good quality establishments. Thus, we would study these dishes as well.

FRENCH CUISINE

The cuisine of France is one of the most ancient and well-known cuisines in the world. In Chapter 6, we discussed the cuisine of southern France, also known as Provencal cuisine, which is a part of Mediterranean cuisine. The cooking style in the rest of the country is, however, very different from Provence. The modern style of French cuisine, which is popularly served in hotels and restaurants, is understood to have started in Paris and then spread to other parts of the world. Like all other cuisines, French cuisine too has undergone a lot of change over the years. For instance, in the olden medieval times French cuisine flaunted elaborate buffets with elegant presentations and decorations. It was in a way a statement on the social and financial status of the host. The food was richly flavoured with spices, such as cinnamon, nutmeg, and cloves, and use of cold meat and *charcuterie* was prominent. The seventeenth century saw the emergence of the *haute* or high cuisine. This style was popularized by famous chef La Varenne who modified the heavy dishes of medieval times and made dishes that were light and easy to prepare. He also popularized various kinds of pastries and desserts and wrote a book on *haute* cuisine.

The eighteenth century saw further refinement of French cuisine under the guidance of Chef Marie-Antoine Carême, who is credited for creating and classifying mother sauces and basics of culinary preparations. Speciality dishes such as soufflé were created during this time. It was around nineteenth century that the French cuisine was modernized and popularized in hotels. The father of modern French cuisine—Chef Escoffier—was responsible for creating the kitchen brigade system and organizing the French cuisine. The twentieth century saw many innovations in the classical French cuisine. This beginning of this period is around 1960, when Portuguese travellers immigrated to France during colonial wars that were being fought between Portugal and African colonies. The salient features of this style, popularly called the *nouvelle cuisine* or new cuisine, were the presence of light sauces, small portions, and multiple courses. The cooking principles were made simpler and the ingredients were cooked just until done to retain the flavours and textures. Heavy sauces laced with butter were replaced with reduced stocks to form *fumets* which were then thickened with cold butter. This style of cooking is still popular in France as there is increasing preference for healthy cooking styles and fresh ingredients cooked with minimum flavours and sauces. *Nouvelle* cuisine was popularized by chefs such as Paul Bocuse and Michel Guérard.

Geographical Regions

France is located in western Europe. It is famous for its lush green meadows, serene rivers, and picturesque mountains. It is bordered by the English Channel and Atlantic Ocean on its north and west respectively. To the north-east of the country lie Belgium and Luxembourg while Germany, Switzerland, and Italy lie to the east. The Mediterranean Sea lies to the south of France while Spain and Andorra border it in the south-west region. The country has a long coastline along its northern, southern and western regions. The eastern region is mountainous and has a cold climate whereas western France has plains. Such a terrain renders a very unique climate to the country that favours a wide variety of home-grown ingredients.

Like Italy, France also has regions that have particular kinds of food with many French specialities originating from these regions. The southern part that touches Spain and Italy on the south-east is famous for its Provencal cuisine, which we discussed in Chapter 6. The diversity in cuisine is attributed to its demography and close proximity to other countries. For example, the food of France is thought to be laced with butter and heavy sauces, but the cuisine of Provence which borders Italy uses olive oil, saffron, and tomatoes in the food, which is not seen in other regions of France. The food of Alsace has German influence and the famous German dish *Sauerkraut is* very popular in Alsace. Another example of strong German influence is preference for *charcuterie* and cold smoked meat in eastern France even as the north-west uses butter and sour cream. In the following section we shall focus on the features of eight regions in France and their effect on local cuisines.

South-western France

This region comprises provinces such as Aquitaine, Bordeaux, Périgord, Gascony, and the Basque country that influences the cuisine of this part of France. Since Bordeaux borders with Spain through the Pyrenees mountain range, it is common to see the influence of saffron, mushrooms, and rice on its cuisine. Sheep and goat cheese from this region are very popular as people rear lamb and sheep for a living and mountain lambs such as *Agneau de Pauillac* is considered to be the gourmand's choice. Popular cheeses such as *petit Basque* and *Rocamadour* come from this region as does the famous Bayonne ham.

Bordeaux is also popular for its high quality wines. The main specialities of this region are duck; foie gras, prunes, oysters, and *Bayonne* ham. *Périgord* truffles are considered to be one of the finest in the world. The cuisine of this region is full of flavours and is based on products obtained directly from farms.

North-western France

This region includes provinces such as Brittany and Normandy. Normandy is famous for its apples, which are aplenty and found in a large number of preparations from this region. Cider brandy and Calvados are prepared from apples and come from Normandy. Since this region lies on the coast off the English Channel, seafood, such as oysters, clams, and mussels, are very popular here. Cattle are also popularly reared here. Thus, Normandy is home to many Appellation d'Origine Contrôlée (AOC) cheeses such as famous *camembert, Brillat-Savarin* and *Neufchâtel*. Appellation d'Origine Contrôlée, which literally translates to controlled designation of origin, means that an AOC product has to originate from one type of region only. *Crêpe* from Brittany is most famous and commonly eaten with sugar and lemon butter sauce. Butter from Brittany is considered to be among the best in the world.

Eastern and North-eastern France

This region includes provinces such as Lorraine, Alsace, Franche-Comté, and Champagne, which is known for its famed sparkling wine. The food from this region, however, is considered less exciting than other French cuisines due to a limited variety of vegetables comprising potatoes, cabbage, and beetroot as other vegetables are difficult to grow. *Charcuterie* is quite popular in this part of France as also many AOC cheeses such as *Brie, Chaource,* and *Langres* and *Munster* from Alsace. *Sauerkraut*, a German delicacy, served with air dried *charcuterie* and boiled meat, is very popular in Alsace. This region also produces one of the finest white wines. *Quiche Lorraine* from Lorraine is yet another example of German influence where bacon and leeks are cooked in a pie and baked with cheese and savoury custard. Alsace is also famous for its dessert called *baba au rhum*.

Northern France

This region includes provinces such as Picardy and Nord-Pas-de-Calais. The coastline to the Nord-Pas-de-Calais is very popular for its crustaceans, monk fish, and herrings. This region grows plants such as wheat, sugar beets, and chicory. The produce of northern France is considered to be of very high quality and the food is generally composed of rich stews such as *carbonade, Marmite Dieppoise,* and *Coq à la Bière* (which is made by using beer and beef stock). Some good quality *pâtés* and terrines are also very popular from Northern France.

South-eastern France

This region includes provinces such as Côte d'Azur and Rhône-Alpes. Many celebrated chefs such as Paul Bocuse and Fernand Point were native to this region. The food of South-eastern France uses young vegetables and fruits in its cuisine. This region is also popular for its high-quality *charcuterie* and a popular liqueur called chartreuse, which comes from the Chartreuse Mountains. The Côte d'Azur region borders the Alps and Italian coast and the cuisine is very similar to Provencal cuisine. Herbs, such as lavender, savoury, basil, fennel, and marjoram, are commonly used as flavours. The famous *camargue* rice also comes from this region.

Southern France

This region includes provinces such as Midi-Pyrénées and Languedoc. The cuisine of southern France is known as Provencal cuisine and forms a part of the Mediterranean cuisine. This region has already been discussed in detail in Chapter 6. The famous blue cheese Roquefort comes from Toulouse in southern France.

Western France

This region includes provinces such as Pays dela Loire and Poitou-Charentais. The cuisine of this region is robust yet refined. The quality ingredients produced in this region are considered to be a gourmand's choice. Some of France's best dairy produce, such as butter and cream, come from this region. The coastal area of Charentais and Nantes are home to mussels and oysters. Lamb and poultry, such as duck, are reared in abundance as the land is fertile and green. The famous brandy called cognac also comes from this region. Charentais is also famous for its mushrooms and goat cheese.

Central France

This region includes provinces such as Auvergne, Burgundy, Paris, and Loire Valley. The cuisine of Auvergne is very rustic—the main meals consist of heavy vegetable soups flavoured with bacon and cheese. The region is a famous hub for cheese production, which includes many AOC cheese varieties such as *Salers Haute Montagne, Saint-Nectaire,* and *Bleu d'Auvergne* among others. Burgundy, on the other hand, is famous for its red wines and beef. Famous dishes such as *coq au vin, boeuf bourguignon, pot-au-feu* are stews that use liberal amounts of red wine for cooking. *Dijon* mustard from France also comes from Burgundy (see Table 7.1). Paris and *Île-de-France* is a region of multicultural diversity and most of the Michelin star restaurants are located in and around this region.

Popular Ingredients used in French Cooking

France is one of the largest producers of quality wines in the world. The food is considered incomplete if it is not paired with a matching wine. Every region in the country specializes in a particular type of wine that is also controlled by AOC. If produced elsewhere it would be known by different name. For example, the wine champagne can only come from Champagne region and when produced elsewhere in France, it will be known as sparkling wine, but not champagne, even though the method and procedure for making the product is similar. Similarly, we learnt in the previous section that every region in the country has a typical cuisine that is impacted by the availability of a particular ingredient at a particular place. For instance, apples are very common in dishes from Normandy, while butter and cream are very common in dishes from the Loire Valley.

Some of the popular ingredients used in French cuisine are highlighted in Table 7.1.

Table 7.1 Popular ingredients in French cuisine (see also Plate 6)

Ingredient	Description	Photograph
Pig trotters	These are the feet of the pig and were introduced in the menus by King Charles VII around 1435. This famous preparation using pig trotters originated in Champagne. Popularly the pig trotters or feet are braised with aromatic herbs and vegetables such as thyme, marjoram, bay leaves and carrots, leeks and celery for nearly three to four hours. The meat is then separated from the bone, chopped and mixed with *Dijon* mustard, seasonings, and sautéed shallots. After that it is packed into a round mould and allowed to set for easy slicing. It is then sliced and pan-fried until crisp. It can be served with pickled vegetables and mustard.	
Herring	This is an oily fish which grows up to 10 inches and is found abundantly in Atlantic Ocean on the coasts of Normandy. The two traditional methods for conserving herring are salting and smoking.	
Belon oysters	These are flat oysters with a unique nutty taste from coastal waters of Breton (earlier known as Armorica) and are labelled as *Huitres de la riviére du Belon*. These oysters are found in Picardy, Normandy, and Brittany regions of France which are very popular for their seafood.	
Charolais	It is the most famous beef cattle in France specially reared for meat since the 1920s. The bull tends to be large and well muscled with an adult weighing up to 1,200 kg and cows weighing up to 1,000 kg. This breed of cow is reared in Charolles which lies to the south of Burgundy.	
Tripe	Tripe is edible offal of various farm animals. In France, it is prepared in the Normandy region in the form of a stew known as *Tripes à la mode de Caen*. Tripe must be cleaned well before it can be eaten.	
Agneau de Pauillac	*Pauillac* lamb comes from Bordeaux. A unique thing about this breed is that they are allowed to graze on the marshes of Medoc region and on the vines after grapes are harvested for making wines.	
Escargots	Escargots or snails are usually cooked in garlic-flavoured herb butter and served as hot hors d'oeuvres. These are also known as *Escargots à la bourguignon* locally. Not all types of snails, however, are edible. Some of the commonly eaten varieties in France are *helix pomatia, helix aspersa*, and *helix lucorum*. This dish is usually eaten in Burgundy.	

(Contd)

Table 7.1 (Contd)

Ingredient	Description	Photograph
Poultry of Bresse	Poultry of Bresse near Burgundy is renowned for its meat and flavour. It has been granted AOC certification. It is unique white coloured chicken with red crest and blue feet chicken that is allowed to grow in controlled outdoors and is fed on cereals and dairy products.	
Moutarde de Dijon	It is the most valued and popular mustard from Dijon, in Burgundy. It was accidentally invented in 1856, when a person trying to make normal mustard paste added the juice of acidic grapes instead of vinegar. Mustards from Dijon today contain both white and red wines instead of vinegar.	
Camargue rice	Often known as red rice due to its red colour, it is a short-grained rice commonly eaten and grown in southern France. When cooked it has a sticky texture. It is cooked almost like a risotto in Italy.	
Globe artichokes	These are shoots of a plant called *Cynara cardunculus*. Earlier, it used to be imported from the Mediterranean region. Now it is grown in Brittany, which has a similar Mediterranean climate. Brittany accounts for 95 per cent of the total production of artichokes in France.	
Chicory	Chicory or *cornet d'anjou* remains one of the most popular specialities of central France used in winter salads. It has deep green elongated leaves that curl in the mid-vein region which acquires a white colour on maturity.	
Périgord truffle	It is a highly favoured variety of mushroom which grows underground. Truffle grows in the wild habitat and is never reared. Dogs and pigs are used to hunt these mushrooms. To know more about truffles, refer Chapter 3 on appetizers.	
Brie cheese	*Brie* is like camembert; the only difference is that *Brie* comes from Champagne region, whereas *camembert* comes from Normandy. *Brie* is a soft pale white cheese made from cow's milk. The whitish mouldy rind with slight ammonia flavour is edible. *Brie* is also available in large wheels.	
Roquefort	Roquefort is a blue-veined cheese made from sheep's milk. It is one of the best-known cheeses in the world. It is also an AOC cheese. The cheese is white in colour with green moulds. It is a slightly tangy cheese and commonly served on cheese platters.	
Saint-Nectaire	This cheese is made from cow's milk and is from the Auvergne. The texture of the cheese is semi-soft and is aged for around 8 weeks. This cheese is also an AOC cheese.	

(Contd)

Table 7.1 (Contd)

Ingredient	Description	Photograph
Petit Basque	*Petit Basque* is buttery yellow cheese made from sheep's milk. It is aged for at least 70 days. This cheese is produced in the Pyrenees mountain region.	
Rocamadour	This cheese comes from the Périgord and is an AOC cheese. *Rocamadour* is made from goat's milk and is aged only for 12–15 days. The soft texture of this cheese makes it a popular ingredient for salads and sandwiches.	
Brillat-Savarin	It is a soft white cheese made from cow's milk, mainly produced in the Normandy region and comes in 12–13 cm wheels. It is aged only for few weeks and is also available as fresh cheese, just like cream cheese.	
Neufchâtel	This cheese is also produced in Normandy and has a soft to crumbly texture. The outer look of the cheese resembles camembert but the taste is much saltier and sharp as compared to *camembert*. *Neufchâtel* has a typical mushroom flavour and this cheese is usually moulded in the shape of a heart.	
Chaource	This cheese is largely produced in Champagne. It is made from cow's milk and is aged for around 2–4 weeks. The texture of this cheese is soft and crumbly and is usually available in a cylindrical shape.	
Langres	It is an AOC cheese from the plateau of Langres in Champagne. It is prepared from cow's milk and is aged for at least 5 weeks. The texture of the cheese is slightly crumbly and is creamy in colour.	
Munster cheese/ Munster Gerome	It is a strong flavoured soft cheese made of cow's milk. The name comes from the little town of Munster in Alsace and traditionally this is aged in the monks' cellars. It is an AOC cheese and should not be confused with the American cheese called *Muenster*.	
Camembert	It is a soft white mould cheese made from unpasteurized cow's milk in Camembert village of Normandy. It is one of the famous cheeses of France and is an AOC cheese. *Camembert* can be presented on cheese display or can be commonly eaten pan-fried as a hot hors d'oeuvre.	

(Contd)

Table 7.1 (Contd)

Ingredient	Description	Photograph
Saint-Marcellin	This is a small soft cheese made from cow's and goat's milk made in Rhone-Alpes. This cheese gets its name from the small town of Saint-Marcellin, which is also called Isere.	
Beurre Echire	The finest variety of butter produced in France comes from a village called Echire in western France. It is a butter that has been granted an AOC.	

Speciality Cuisines

France is famous for its cuisine and until a few decades ago, it was one of the most popular cuisines served in most hotels in India. Continental food, by default, refers to food from France and Great Britain. France has a varied kind of cuisine. We read about some classical French hors d'oeuvres in Chapter 4 on appetizers and dishes such as *cassoulet* and *bouillabaisse* from Provence in the section on Mediterranean cuisines in Chapter 6. Some of the popular dishes of France are described in Table 7.2.

Table 7.2 Popular dishes of French cuisine (see also Plate 7)

Dish	Description	Photograph
Baguette	A baguette is a long thin loaf of bread that is commonly made from basic lean dough. It is characterized by its length, crisp crust, and slits that enable the proper expansion of gases.	
Purée Saint-Germain	It is a puree soup made up of green peas and bacon. It is one of the most classical soups of medieval French cuisine.	
Sauerkraut	The *sauerkraut* is very popular in Eastern France as it borders with Germany. It is prepared with cabbage and allowed to ferment. The typical taste of a *sauerkraut* is sour and hence the name.	
Quenelle de brochette	Any kind of pureed meat or vegetable with firm texture can be shaped into an oval shape which is known as *quenelle. Quenelles* are usually poached and served masked with a creamy sauce.	

(Contd)

Table 7.2 (Contd)

Dish	Description	Photograph
Bouillabaisse	Bouillabaisse is a traditional fish stew that is prepared with different kinds of cooked fish. A variety of herbs and spices are used to add flavour to the same. It is a popular Provencal dish.	
Foie gras	Refer Chapter 2 on *charcuterie* and Chapter 3 on appetizers and garnishes.	
Ratatouille	This is a traditional vegetable dish. The complete name is *ratatouille niçoise* and is made of stewed vegetables. It is generally served as a side dish but can be served as a complete dish as well. It is generally prepared in the summer season when lots of fresh vegetables are available.	
Blanquette de veau	This is a famous French veal dish made by stewing veal meat with root vegetables and herbs.	
Poulet Sauté Chasseur	Chasseur refers to cooking food in hunter style. This is a chicken stew combined with tomatoes and mushrooms and cooked on a low heat for a long duration.	
Coq au vin	This is a braised preparation from Burgundy. The chicken is marinated in red wine along with aromatic vegetables overnight. It is then braised until the chicken is tender. The sauce is strained and thickened and combined with root vegetables.	
Pot-au-feu	The literal translation is 'pot on fire'. In this preparation, the tougher cuts of meat are stewed on a slow fire along with root vegetables and herbs until the meat is very soft and gelatinous.	
Boeuf bourguignon	This is a stewed preparation of chunks of beef with root vegetables in a red wine-based sauce. It is one of the classical dishes from Burgundy.	
Gateau Opera	*Gateau Opera* is a traditional cake made with almond sponge that is alternately layered with chocolate truffle and coffee butter cream.	

(Contd)

Table 7.2 (Contd)

Dish	Description	Photograph
Tarte tatin	This traditional dessert from Normandy is made by sautéing apples in sugar and butter and then covering the pan with puff pastry and baking in the oven. The dessert is then served inverted, where the baked puff forms the base and the caramelized apples form the top.	
Crêpe Suzette	*Crêpe Suzette* is a flat French pancake that is stewed in orange-flavoured caramel sugar. It is flamed with cognac brandy and requires showmanship. It is often prepared in front of guests on a *guéridon* trolley.	
Madeleine	Madeleine is a traditional cake of France. It is a very small-shaped cake which has a shell-like appearance.	

Special Equipment in French Cuisine

Professional cooking as prevalent in modern hotels today is the gift of French cuisine. That is the reason why many equipment used in hotels across the world are still known by the French terms such as *chinoise* for a conical strainer and *sauteuse* for a small sauté pan. For hundreds of years, French cuisine has relied upon small and traditional equipment such as whisks, spatulas, pots, and pans. Certain parts of France such as Provencal region use an equipment called *cassoulet*, that has been discussed in Chapter 6. Some of the commonly used equipment and tools in French cooking are discussed in Table 7.3.

Table 7.3 Special equipment used in French cuisine

Equipment	Description	Photograph
Cocotte en fonte	A *cocotte* dish or a casserole is a tight fitting lid on heavy bottom pan. It is ideal for braising and poeling. It is used most popularly in Provencal cuisine.	
Passoire chinoise	It is a conical strainer used for straining liquids or soups. The conical shape allows the contents to be pressed down with the back of ladle and letting the liquid spill out. It is one of the most popular equipment used in kitchens worldwide.	
Terrine mould	It is a ceramic mould used for making terrine. The uses of terrine moulds have been discussed in detail in Chapter 2 on *charcuterie*.	
Essoreuse	This is a salad spinner in which washed lettuce is spun to remove the extra moisture and make it crisp. The extra moisture in the greens dilutes the dressings and makes the salad go limp.	

(Contd)

Table 7.3 (Contd)

Equipment	Description	Photograph
Mandolin slicer	It is a universal grater used for slicing and grating vegetables and even truffles. It has two types of blades: plain and serrated. The thickness of the slices can be adjusted depending upon the requirement.	
Hachoir	A half-moon-shaped chopper, also known as *mezzaluna* in Italian, is used for mincing herbs. It can have a single blade or double blade as shown in the picture.	
Lame	*Lame* is a sharp blade that is mounted on a stand and is used for marking slits on baguette bread.	
Moule àsavarin	A ring mould with a hole in the centre is commonly used for cakes and fish terrines and many other pastry applications such as making the classical *baba au rhum* dessert, and caramel custard.	
French fry cutter	This equipment is used for making sticks of potatoes that are used for preparing French fries. It comes with different attachments that can be used for making French fries of various thickness.	
Escargot dish	It is used for serving classical snails in herb and garlic butter sauce. The snails are served as hot appetizers with a snail fork.	
Crêpe Suzette pan	*Crêpe Suzette* is prepared in this pan. *Crêpe Suzettes* pancakes cooked in orange sauce and flambéed with cognac in front of guests by stewards on a *guéridon* trolley.	
Sauté pan	This is a shallow pan with raised slanting sides that is used for tossing food. It comes handy for many preparations such as pan frying, sautéing, and even cooking sauces.	
Fondue pots	Fondue is classically a mixture of melted cheese with wine and vegetables or one day old bread is dipped in the mixture and eaten. This pot is placed over a stand in which fuel is kept burning all the time to keep the cheese in a molten state.	
Baguette tray	This is a baking tray with a wavy finish. Baguettes are rolled out and placed in grooves. The typical shape of a baguette tray helps to retain the round shape of the bread.	

CUISINE OF THE UK

The food of the United Kingdom (UK) is termed as English cuisine or British cuisine. Though this food is quite popular in the UK, it has not been able to establish its repertoire in many other countries due to various reasons. The main focus of British cuisine is more on the use of high quality local ingredients and not as much on the presentation of food. The sauces used in English dishes are used to bring out the flavour of food and complement the dish rather than disguise or mask the original flavour of the food. For example, the juices obtained by roasting a meat are used for preparing sauce also called as roast gravy that is served along with the meat.

Geographical Regions

The UK comprises Scotland, Northern Ireland, Wales, and England. It lies between the North Atlantic Ocean and the North Sea. It borders France and Germany on its south and is separated by the famous English Channel.

The UK is surrounded by four water bodies—the English Channel on the south, the Irish Sea and the Atlantic Ocean on the west, and the North Sea on the east. Therefore, consumption of seafood is prominent in many parts of the UK. The countryside, with its lush green meadows, is rendered fertile by several deltas and tributaries formed by the rivers flowing into the seas. This fertile land has been a boon to the agriculture, where a large variety of fresh fruits and vegetables thrive. Raising cattle, sheep, and livestock was always popular with farmers and that is the reason why beef is so commonly found in English cuisine. Let us now discuss the cuisines of the UK.

Scottish cuisine

Scotland is a close neighbour to the Scandinavian countries, the influence of which is quite evident in Scottish cuisine. Scottish cooking relies heavily on local produce and has few famous dishes such as Scotch broth which is made by cooking vegetables and meat together. Haggis, made by stuffing the stomach of sheep and then boiling it for hours, is another popular Scottish food (refer Table 7.5). Scotland is also famous in the world for its Scottish salmon that is often smoked and cured and served on buffets and salads, and also for its Scotch whisky.

Irish cuisine

This cuisine developed in Ireland. The country has a temperate climate that is suited for growing crops and farming animals. Potatoes form a large part of Irish diet. Ireland is also famous for its beef that is exported all over the world. Several famous dishes, such as Irish stew and fish and chips, are representations of Irish cuisine. Black pudding sausage is an influence of *boudin noir* in France. Ireland is also famous for its whisky and seafood.

Welsh cuisine

Welsh cuisine is popular for its seafood and lamb dishes. Roast leg of lamb served with mint sauce is a traditional Welsh dish. Leek is considered to be the national vegetable of Wales. Welsh cuisine is also mostly dominated by potatoes which are a common ingredient in most preparations. The world-famous shepherd's pie originated in Wales. Cockles are also very popular and can be commonly seen in Welsh cooking.

English cuisine

The dishes in England are unique in their own self, even though the basis of the cuisine is strongly influenced by neighbouring British cuisines such as Welsh, Scottish, and Irish. Traditionally, however, English cuisine has not been as popular as its other European counterparts across the world mainly because of the use of lard and suet that are considered heavy and unhealthy. Another reason attributed to its low popularity is the World War II years, when the concept of rationing and dishes from leftover foods such as 'toad in the hole, and 'bubble and squeak'; were introduced as an austerity measure. These are understood to have projected the English cuisine in poor light. Although the typical or classical English food is not very famous, yet various ingredients, such as Cumberland sausage, English cucumber, and Stilton cheese, have made their mark in the world. Also, the English breakfast is the most popular form of breakfast on the planet.

A typical English breakfast is a hearty meal consisting of breads served with butter and marmalade, eggs served with sausages, bacon, and grilled vegetables such as tomatoes and mushrooms, and accompanied with tea or coffee. The meal often starts with a bowl of cereal and cold or hot milk. This is invariably a large affair and the preparations are now limited to weekends when family and friends get together. The English Christmas dinners are fanfare events where a lavish meal consisting of roast beef, plum puddings, and Christmas cakes have again influenced the Christmas buffets of many countries in the world. Popular dishes, such as fish and chips and bread and butter pudding, that can be seen on the menu of every big hotel in the world is another gift from England.

The English are fond of eating and this culture has been an influence of India, which was a British colony for nearly 200 years. Their meals usually start with a breakfast of eggs, toasts, and cereals. During the day, elevenses is a regular practice. An elevenses is cup of tea or coffee accompanied with biscuits and is popularly had at 11 a.m. and hence the name. The lunch is usually a sandwich and around 4 p.m., afternoon tea is drunk with open-faced sandwiches, scones, jam, clotted cream, and few dry cakes. The dinners are usually an elaborate fare eaten between 6 and 8 p.m. Sometimes supper (last meal of the day) is usually a sandwich with a cup of tea. Many Britons have a practice of drinking a glass of milk before going to bed. This practice is also very common in India, though our afternoon tea is replaced with local snacks. Tea at 11 a.m. and 4 p.m. is also a common practice in India.

Over the years, British food has absorbed the cultures and food ethos from different communities staying in the UK for the past many years. The location of England attracted lots of travellers who brought in ingredients and cooking styles to English cuisine. Various forms of curries from India and Bangladesh are quite popular there. English cuisine also adapted the fast food culture of the USA and it continues to absorb culinary ideas and delights from all over the world. London, for example, is a melting pot of cultures and one can see the most popular restaurants of almost every cuisine in the world there. The British got influenced from Indian cultures and traditions during their long rule in the subcontinent. It is very common to see many Indian influences such as the style of eating, use of spices, and so much so that chicken tikka masala is considered the national dish of England.

Original British food is considered to be unimaginative and heavy by many experts and to some extent, it is true. The use of lard and suet in the old English dishes is avoided by the modern generation because of health reasons. Modern British cuisine has evolved through the adaptation of many cuisines, such as Italian, French, and Mediterranean, and also by preserving the traditional British food of the old era.

Popular Ingredients

The British prefer beef over any meat, though other meat such as lamb, pig, and game birds such as geese, duck, and pigeons called *squabs* are also popularly eaten. Meat are roasted, boiled, and stewed. They can also be made into sausages, which are popularly known as bangers in England. The famous Cumberland sausage from England is quite popular in the world. England is also known for its cheeses that get their names from the regions they come from. Few examples of such famous cheeses are Stilton, Cheddar, and *Derby*. Many of these cheeses are controlled by Protected Designation of Origin (PDO). Table 7.4 highlights some popular ingredients of British cuisine.

Table 7.4 Popular ingredients of British cuisine

Ingredient	Description	Photograph
Stilton cheese	Stilton is one of the famous blue cheeses from England. It is known for its characteristic strong smell and taste. This cheese is guarded by the PDO status and can be called Stilton only if it is made in Derby, Leicester, or Nottingham following a particular recipe. Made from cows milk, the cheese has a soft and crumbly texture. It is usually aged for at least 2–3 months.	
Red Leicester	This hard cheese produced in Leicestershire takes its name from the reddish-to-orange tinge acquired during its aging process between 5 and 9 months. It has a nutty taste. It is mild in taste at 5 months and develops a tangy taste as the ageing progresses.	
Cheddar cheese	Cheddar is a hard cheese with creamy-to-off-white colour. It is the most popular cheese of England and is made in Cheddar town of Somerset and hence the name. It is one of the largest exported cheeses out of the UK. The ageing time of this cheese could vary between 3 months and 5 years depending upon the texture and flavour required. It is commonly used in cooking as it melts away easily.	
Gloucester	This cheese is prepared from cow's milk in Gloucestershire region. It is a semi-hard cheese that is aged for at least 9 months. It has two types: single Gloucester and double Gloucester. Double Gloucester is allowed to ripen for a longer time and this yields in a sharper and more savoury flavour.	

(Contd)

Table 7.4 (Contd)

Ingredient	Description	Photograph
Derby	It is a medium hard cheese made from cow's milk and is known for its buttery flavour. The distinctive pale golden orange colour of this cheese differentiates it from Cheddar, as this cheese is very similar in texture and taste to that of Cheddar. It is aged between 1 and 6 months.	
Lancashire	This cheese is made from cow's milk and the texture is creamy to hard to crumbly, depending upon its ageing. It is aged between 1 month and 2 years. It is a popular cheese used in cooking and is granted PDO accreditation.	
Swede	Also known as *rutabaga* or yellow turnip, it is a root vegetable commonly eaten in England. This vegetable is also popular in Scandinavian cuisine. In England, it is commonly mashed or roasted and served with meats. The leaves are also cooked as vegetables.	
Parsnip	This vegetable is related to the carrot family but is dirty white in colour. When cooked, it emits a buttery taste with a tinge of spiciness. Though it can be eaten raw, it is popularly roasted or boiled and served in soups or as an accompaniment to meat.	
Skirret	*Skirret* is a root vegetable that resembles sweet potatoes. It grows in bunches on a root and are small and long like baby carrots. The inner woody core, which is inedible, needs to be removed before they are cooked. This starchy vegetable is often boiled or roasted and served with meat.	
English cucumber	Traditionally sold wrapped in plastic to reduce water loss, this juicy and long cucumber has a dark green skin which is smooth and the seeds are very small. It is often known as seedless cucumber and is very popular in salads and sandwiches.	
White horseradish	White horseradish grows wildly in certain parts of England. This pungent root is eaten with cold cuts and pickled fish.	
HP sauce	One of the most commonly found ingredient in every household, HP sauce is also known as brown sauce or steak sauce. It is used as a table condiment and is a proprietary sauce made by using tomatoes, dates, tamarind extract, sweeteners, and spices. The recipe of this traditional sauce is a guarded secret. The name HP refers to 'House of Parliament', where this sauce was popularly served.	

(Contd)

Table 7.4 (Contd)

Ingredient	Description	Photograph
Worcester-shire sauce	There is a story that two pharmacists, J.W. Lea and W.H. Perrins, formulated this sauce at an order given by one retired Army officer, who had savoured this recipe in India. Not impressed with the result, he returned the sauce and it was kept away in a store and forgotten. When discovered some time later, the sauce had matured and was pronounced excellent. The manufacturers then perfected the recipe and developed it on commercial scale. It soon became popular as a table condiment. Traditional Worcestershire sauce is thin, dark brown, and pungent, with visible sediment. It is soy and vinegar based but also contains an assortment of exotic ingredients, the proportions and precise details of which remains the manufacturer's secret.	
English mustard	English mustard is prepared from brown and white mustard seeds. It has a tangy flavour and is often served with pickled vegetables and cold meat. English mustard is also used extensively in sandwiches. Colman is one of the oldest companies that has been preparing this mustard in the UK.	
Clotted cream	Clotted cream is a smooth cream that contains at least 55 per cent of butter fat. It is made from high quality and high fat content milk from Jersey cows. The milk is allowed to sit for at least 12 hours and then warmed over a low heat. The cream rises to the top. It is left in a cool place to chill. It is then skimmed off and traditionally served with scones or a hot cup of tea.	
Haddock	This popular fish is found in the waters of North Atlantic Sea. It is mostly pickled and smoked and is served as a breakfast preparation in England. It is also commonly in fish and chips.	
Dover sole	Commonly found in the European waters, it is a very expensive fish and is usually eaten grilled or pan-fried. This fish is a flat fish and can yield four fillets. The flesh is very soft and has a sweet taste.	

Speciality Cuisines

England has been known as the country of beef-eaters and thus, it is very common to see beef in many forms on the English menus. Roast beef served with Yorkshire puddings and leftover meat being used in sandwiches is a common practice there. Beef also finds its place in famous dishes such as steak and kidney pie. Lamb is also a preferred meat that is popularly seen in dishes such as shepherd's pie and Lancashire hotpot. Sandwiches are also supposed to have originated in a place called Sandwich as we had read in Chapter 4 on Sandwiches. British cuisine has also been influenced by Indian culture and food as it is very common to see very high-end Indian restaurants with Michelin star ratings in London today. Among the popular Indian influences are the chicken tikka masala, and *kedgeree*, a popular breakfast item, that is similar to the Indian *khichdi*. Table 7.5 showcases some popular dishes of British cuisine.

Table 7.5 Popular dishes of British cuisine (see also Plates 7 and 8)

Dish	Description	Photograph
Fish and chips	This is one of the most popular dishes of Great Britain. The fish is usually batter-fried or can be crumbed and deep-fried and hence the name *à l'anglaise*, which means English style. It is served with French fries or potato chips and with accompaniments such as tartar sauce and tomato ketchup and in some cases, mushy peas (peas that are sautéed and cooked until they become slightly mushy).	
Steak and kidney pie	This dish is considered to be the representative dish of Great Britain. It is made with a mixture of diced beef and kidneys, which are braised and then thickened with flour. The prepared meat is then encased in a shortcrust pie and baked until the pie crust is cooked and is golden brown.	
Shepherd's pie	It is a very popular dish made with meat of lamb or mutton. The minced meat is cooked with herbs and seasonings and is put in an ovenproof casserole. Mashed potatoes are piped over the same and baked in an oven for a short period of time. It is popularly eaten as a meal.	
Bangers and mash	Sausages are called bangers in England. Usually, Cumberland sausage is used in this dish. It is grilled and served on a bed of mashed potatoes and served with rich onion gravy or sometimes garnished with fried onion rings.	
Bubble and squeak	This dish is named so because of the noise that is produced when it is pan seared on a hot pan. The dish is usually made from left over vegetables that are finely minced or mashed and Seasoned with salt, mixed herbs and cream. It is then shaped into small patties and pan fried on a hot pan until golden and crisp. It is often served garnished with crisp bacon chips.	
Haggis	Haggis is a popular dish from Scotland. It is made by stuffing the stomach of sheep with minced lamb, offal such as liver and heart, chopped onions, egg, spices such as nutmeg and cayenne pepper, and oats. The haggis is boiled in simmering water for at least 3 hours. It is then sliced and served with fried potatoes, vegetables, and Scotch whisky. It is typically eaten on Burns' night, which is the birthday of the famous poet Robert Burns.	
Cornish pasty	This dish is made by placing uncooked and marinated meat on a rolled out shortcrust pastry circle, which is then folded into half to enclose the filling inside. The sides are crimped to seal the filling. The pasty is baked until golden brown and served hot. The fillings of the Cornish pasties can vary from one region to another, but the traditional Cornish pasty is made with beef, potatoes, and swede which is also known as yellow turnip, and onions.	
Yorkshire pudding	Though the name is pudding, yet it has nothing to do with sweets or desserts. It is a savoury dish made from a batter of flour, which is allowed to ferment and then poured into moulds that contain hot beef suet. The pudding is baked until it rises and becomes crisp. Yorkshire puddings are traditionally served as an accompaniment with roasted beef.	

(Contd)

Table 7.5 (Contd)

Dish	Description	Photograph
Welsh rarebit	This is a dish from Wales. It is made by spreading a mixture of mashed cheese, seasoned with mustard and some Worcestershire sauce on bread and gratinated under a hot grill. It is usually eaten as a hot hors d'oeuvre.	
Toad in the hole	Toad in the hole is made by cooking sausages in the Yorkshire pudding batter. It is eaten as a main meal, along with roasted onion gravy. The Yorkshire pudding upon cooking gets a dent like structure which often has a hole. The sausages often pop out of the hole resembling the head of a toad and hence the name.	
Roast beef	Roast beef is the most commonly eaten dish around the world. The portioned out beef cut is marinated and roasted to medium doneness and served sliced with roast gravy, Yorkshire pudding, and roasted potatoes. It is one of the most popular dishes eaten on get-togethers and festivals.	
Chicken tikka masala	Though this might be very surprising, but chicken *tikka masala*, popularized by the British in India, is considered to be the national dish of England. Morsels of chicken are marinated in yoghurt and chilli paste and broiled in oven. It is then tossed in tomato-based gravy.	
Lancashire hotpot	This dish is traditionally made from lamb or mutton, sliced onions, and sliced potatoes. It is usually prepared in a cast iron casserole, wherein the marinated lamb is placed and covered with slices of onions and potatoes. It is then covered with lamb stock and allowed to cook slowly in the oven for at least 10–12 hours. The resulting broth-like dish has gelatinous meat and caramelized flavour of onions. Different types of vegetables, such as mushrooms and leeks, can also be added.	
Cumberland sausage	As the name suggests, this sausage comes from Cumbria, which is in the north-west of England. These are traditionally made into long rope shapes, but it is common to see link shapes as well these days. It is prepared from country-style forcemeat of pork and fat and seasoned with pepper and herbs. The meat is chopped to give it a characteristic chunky texture. It is the most commonly used sausage for making bangers and mash and is also eaten in breakfast as an accompaniment with fried eggs.	
Bacon roly poly	This dish is made by filling a shortcrust pastry with a mixture of onions, leeks, and bacon, seasoned liberally with pepper and herbs such as sage. The dough is rolled out and the filling is placed in the centre. The pastry is now rolled to form a *roulade* and the edges are sealed. The prepared roulade is now packed in an aluminium foil and allowed to steam for at least 2 hours. The foil is carefully removed and the pastry is then baked in a hot oven until the dough on the outside turns to golden brown.	

(Contd)

Table 7.5 (*Contd*)

Dish	Description	Photograph
Scones	These are leavened with baking powder. Scones are also known as quick bread from Scotland. They are popularly eaten during afternoon teas with clotted cream and jam or marmalade.	
Kedgeree	This dish was taken to England by the British colonials who stayed in India for a long time. The Indian dish is also known as *khichdi* and is made with rice and lentils. The British commonly eat it for breakfast and in addition to rice and lentils, they also add flaked haddock fish, boiled eggs, and chopped parsley.	
Flapjack	This is a crisp cookies-like dessert made by cooking butter, sugar, and golden syrup until these boil. Oats are added and the mixture is poured into a baking tin and baked. When it cools, the cake become crisp with a brittle texture.	
Bread and butter pudding	This dessert is prepared from leftover bread and in hotels; it is often prepared from leftover breakfast rolls such as croissants, muffins, and even doughnuts. Traditionally, jam or marmalade is spread over one side of the sliced bread and butter is applied on the other side. The bread is arranged in such a way that the buttered side is always up. Custard prepared with eggs, sugar, and milk is poured over the top and allowed to soak up. The dish is now baked until golden brown and served hot.	
Simnel cake	This cake is popularly eaten during Easter. It is similar to Christmas cake and is usually covered with rolled marzipan and then grilled under a griller, so that the marzipan gets a toasted texture. Some people also put a piece of marzipan in the middle of the cake whilst baking it.	
Fruit trifle	It is a classical English dessert which is made by sandwiching vanilla sponge cake with mixed fruit jam and cutting it into small dices. Chopped fruits, sandwiched sponge cubes, freshly whipped cream, and custard cream are layered together in a serving dish and the top is decorated with a feathered icing.	
Dundee cake	This is a rich fruit cake from Scotland and is made by creaming butter, sugar, eggs, and flour. Candied fruits, almonds, and other nuts are added to the mixture and the batter is poured into a round cake tin. The top is decorated with blanched and peeled almonds and are arranged on top in a circular fashion covering the cake.	

SCANDINAVIAN CUISINE

Scandinavia comprising countries such as Finland, Norway, Sweden, and Denmark is located in the Northern Europe. Its cuisine is less famous in the world as compared to other Western and European cuisines perhaps because of the climate, lifestyle of people, etc. Long and harsh winters in these countries, where the sun can be seen only for few hours in winters, force people to rely on meat and seafood for a large part of their diet. Due to the climatic conditions, vegetables are grown scarcely and are poorly reflected in the diet of many Scandinavian countries. The light summers on the other hand are most favourable for producing berries and other kinds of vegetables such as beet, cabbage, and swede. The cold and long winters have also created the need for preserving food and hence *charcuterie* and pickles are particularly popular in Scandinavian countries.

This cuisine has not been very famous outside in the world due to many reasons such as the isolation from other countries, their climate, limited modes of travel, and also because the industrial revolution happened late in these nations and their food did not get influenced from other lands. Separately, each of the Scandinavian countries has lent something interesting to the world of cuisine. The most famous of all is the cold buffet known as smorgasbord or *smörgåsbord*, which is a Scandinavian buffet that consists of cold cuts, pickled fish, breads, and pickled vegetables, and even roasted meat that are eaten with gusto.

Norway, Denmark, and Sweden share the same culinary history as Denmark ruled Norway from the eleventh until the twelfth century, and the Queen of Denmark and Norway also became the Queen of Sweden. Though during the nineteenth century, the influence of Denmark and Norway faded away from Sweden, yet the traditions in cuisine have stayed on till date. Scandinavians are great craftspersons. They specialize in porcelain, silver, and crystal ware. They love decorating the table as much as they love decorating their food. Largely, a Scandinavian diet would consist of fish, pork, poultry, as well as vegetables such as beet, potato, cucumber, and parsley. Most of the Scandinavian ingredients are sea based because of the large coastlines. In some parts of Sweden, sliced horseflesh is marinated and smoked, whereas in Norway broiled whale steaks are popular. Scandinavian food is simple and mild. To an outsider, it might taste bland as the food is very simple and relies on high quality ingredients. Dinner is the major meal of the day. Breakfast and lunch are comparatively simple fares. Breakfast could be only tea with some cookies and often bread with butter and preserves. Lunch is eaten around 12.30 pm with mostly sandwiches and snacks. Dinner is fairly a large meal and starts as early as 6 p.m. It is the time when people come back from work and this meal is considered an occasion, where members of the family meet and enjoy each other's company.

Regions

Scandinavian countries form a large part of a peninsula that is situated in North Europe. While Norway and Sweden are on the Scandinavian peninsula, Denmark is situated on the Danish islands and Jutland. Finland is joined to Sweden in the north and north-west, but is separated in the south with the Gulf of Bothnia and the Gulf of Finland. Denmark, on the other hand, borders Germany. Iceland is located as an island in the Atlantic Ocean.

All these countries are referred to as Nordic countries, while Scandinavia is a term used for Norway, Sweden and Denmark. The key points of cuisines of each of the Scandinavian countries are discussed in the following paragraphs.

Norway

The cuisine of Norway is known as Nordic cuisine. Most of the Nordic cuisine is based on seafood and farm-raised fish due to the large coastline facing the Norwegian Sea. It is famous for fish, such as salmon, cod, and herring, which forms a large part of their meal. The Norwegian salmon is highly praised across the world and is prepared in many ways. The most popular preparation is smoked salmon which is served as an appetizer, as a topping for open-faced sandwiches, and also as filling for sandwiches. Another popular way of preparing salmon is by curing it with salt and sugar for 3–4 days. This is commonly known as *gravalax* and is very popular in the world. Norway is also known as the land of the midnight sun as for almost 3–4 months the sun is visible throughout the night. The sunlight favours the growth of some fantastic berries, fruits, and vegetables that are a favourite among the Nordes. Another famous produce of Norway is its *tørrfisk,* or dried cod fish. This famous Atlantic cod is traditionally dried in the winds without any salt. The Nordes used it for trading with other European countries to bring rare commodities back home. Norway is also famous for its paper-thin crisp bread, which is popularly eaten with fish and vegetables. Milk from cow and goat is used for making some fantastic cheeses. The famous brown goat cheese called *geitost* is the most popular topping on an open-faced sandwich in Norway.

Denmark

The Danish cuisine is influenced by its neighbouring countries, such as Holland and Germany, thus the food is heavy and rich in fat. The reason for this is the cold climate of Denmark. Long winters have created the need for pickling (fish and vegetables) and preserving food, and reliance on smoked and cured meat, which is common to Danish cuisine. During the short summer season, emphasis is laid on fresh agricultural produce.

The cuisine of Denmark is quite diverse. People living on the coast largely eat fish, whereas people living in the plains prefer pork, cabbage, and other vegetables such as swede, potato, and artichoke. Denmark too is famous for its cheese. It has also given its famous breakfast pastry, the 'Danish pastry' to the world. Today, no breakfast buffet in any good hotel is complete without a Danish pastry. The most famous part of Denmark is its Jutland peninsula that touches the north of Germany. The south of Jutland is famous for its smoked meat and *charcuterie* products.

Finland

The Finnish cuisine like its Scandinavian counterparts is largely non-vegetarian. While the western part mainly relies on meat and fish, the eastern part has inclusions of vegetables such as mushrooms, potatoes, and beetroot. In traditional Finnish dishes, the use of vegetables is very limited, as the harsh winters last for almost nine months, which is not conducive to growth of fruits and vegetables. Therefore, the cuisine relies on use of tubers such as swede, potato, and various kinds of turnip. Like other Scandinavian countries, the climate is just right for berries. The use of wholemeal products, such as rye, barley, and oats, is commonly reflected in Finnish cuisine. Due to the geographical location of Finland, its travel and trade with its neighbouring countries have influenced Finnish cuisine in a big way. Today, Finnish food is quite popular, as chefs try and combine the traditional food with contemporary food presentations and flavours. Chefs happily blend the traditional Finnish cuisine with imported ingredients, such as pastas, herbs, and exotic vegetables, which have replaced the mundane cabbage, swede, and herring that were associated with the so-called 'inferiors'. Finnish cuisine bears more resemblance to Russian and German cuisines and very little resemblance to Swedish cuisine. The Finnish have a penchant for robust flavours, though their taste can be termed as mild or bland. The people like sour taste and pickles in their diet. They do not have a particularly sweet tooth as is evident from negligible emphasis on desserts or sweets. Very few desserts are prepared on special occasions.

Sweden

Like other Scandinavian countries, the Swedish cuisine is largely traditional and non-vegetarian with mild flavours and a sprinkling of fresh produce. However, being the fourth largest country in Europe straddling the entire length of the Scandinavian peninsula, its cuisine shows marked variation between the northern part and the southern part. In the far north, where the climate is extremely cold, meat such as reindeer venison, and geese are eaten whereas in the south, the use of fish and vegetables is not uncommon. Apart from being traditional in their approach, the Swedes have always been open to foreign influences, particularly France. Tea from England, honey cakes from Germany, and French sauces and soups are particular influences on Swedish cuisines. The Swedes like their food slightly sweet. They coat their breads with small amounts of sugar and the traditional meat balls are served with sweet lingonberry jam. Fruit soups, such as the one made with rose hips and blueberries, are also very popular. Let us now discuss the unique ingredients used in Scandinavian cooking.

Popular Ingredients in Scandinavian Cuisine

As discussed, Scandinavian countries have varied kinds of climate. Most of Norway and Sweden have cold harsh winters that last for almost seven to nine months and only some parts of Denmark have summers that are moderately cool. Such extreme climatic conditions leave the Scandinavians with little choice than to rely on seafood and meat, which are pickled, preserved and smoked for consumption. Dependence on fruits and vegetables is limited to the short summer season when production is limited as we have studied earlier. Since industrialization started quite late in these countries due to their isolated location, the influence of European ingredients is also limited. Pork is the largest consumed meat in all Scandinavian countries followed by beef. Milk and milk products, such as cheese and yoghurt, are quite popular and relished throughout the year. Some of the popular ingredients used in Scandinavian countries are discussed in Table 7.6.

Table 7.6 Popular ingredients in Scandinavian cuisine (see also Plate 8)

Ingredient	Description	Photograph
Lingonberry	Also known as cowberry, it is a sour berry that often grows in the wild. It is popularly eaten as preserves, and jams. Its juices are extracted and used in cooking. Since it is a sour berry, it is often cooked with sugar before consumption.	
Bilberry	It resembles blueberries, but should not be confused with them. The bilberry fruit is smaller than blueberry and commonly grows wild in Scandinavian countries as they grow in acidic soils. Bilberries are eaten fresh or can be made into jams and preserves and also used in desserts.	
Cloudberry	This amber-coloured fruit resembles raspberries. It is eaten ripe but often have a sour taste. It is often used for making jams, juices, and liquors. The jam of cloudberries is commonly used as toppings on ice cream in Sweden.	
Sea buckthorn	It is also known as sea berry as it commonly grows on the coast of Atlantic Ocean. It is nutritious but has an acidic taste. It is one of the berries that contain polyunsaturated fats. Though this berry is used for making medicines and cosmetics, in Sweden, it is combined with sugar to make jams and served with breads, cheese, and meat.	
Rose hip	Also known as rose haw, it is the fruit of the rose plant. It is commonly used for making preserves and marmalades in many European countries. But in Sweden it is popularly used for making a dessert known as rose hip soup (refer Table 7.7).	
Salmon	Almost every chef will agree that the best salmon comes from Norway. This fish is prepared and served in a variety of ways. It can be eaten grilled, smoked, and served as an appetizer, or it can be cured to make *gravalax*.	
Atlantic cod	Atlantic cod is the most popular fish eaten by the Nordes. Though they prefer to eat it fresh whenever possible, their love for it has led to its traditional preservation by air-drying. Even the salted cod, called *bacalao*, is popular among the people. It is also exported to countries such as Italy and Spain.	
Sprat	It is a herring-like fish found in the Atlantic Ocean and grows up to a maximum of 16 cm. It is often pickled and canned, and also dried and used as spice in Swedish cuisine. This fish is popularly eaten in all Scandinavian countries.	
Herring	It is one of the oily fishes, which is very popular in all Scandinavian countries because of its habitat in North Pacific and Atlantic Oceans. It can be eaten smoked, salted, or marinated. Pickled herrings have been popular in Scandinavian countries since thousands of years and are eaten with boiled potatoes, boiled eggs, and sour cream.	

(Contd)

Table 7.6 (Contd)

Ingredient	Description	Photograph
Geitost	It is one of the most popular Scandinavian cheeses. In Sweden, it is known as *mesost* and in Norway as *brunost* or *geitost*. It is made from goat's milk by boiling the milk with cream and whey and reducing it to a caramelized texture. It is eaten fresh without ageing.	
Reindeer meat	Low fat meat of reindeer has always been popular with the Nordes. It has a natural flavour and is a delicate and tender meat. It is often cooked as steaks, roasts, or made into stews.	
Ridder cheese	This popular cheese of Norway is comparable with the *Saint-Nectaire* or *Port Salut* of France. It is semi-soft with little or no holes. It is considered to be one of the elite cheeses of Norway.	
Blue *Brie*	Made from cow's milk, the texture of this cheese is very soft. It is often used in cooking or eaten as a snack. It is also known as *cambozola* and made in France and Germany.	
Danish Blue	This blue cheese from Denmark is made from cow's milk and is often known as *Danablu*. Like other blue cheeses, it has a sharp and sour taste with a salty flavour. The texture is creamy. It is aged for 2–3 months, when it develops the typical blue to black mould. This cheese has also been awarded PDO accreditation. It is one of the two cheeses to get a PDO in Denmark. The other is *esrom*.	
Esrom	*Esrom* comes from the Esrom town in Denmark, hence the name. It is a semi-soft cheese made from cow's milk and has a traditional sticky texture with yellow colour and holes scattered all around the cheese. It is aged for 10–12 weeks, but the longer it matures, the better it becomes.	
Havarti	This semi-soft creamy cheese from Denmark is probably the most popular cheese there. It has distinctive small holes scattered throughout the cheese. It is served as a table cheese and often served in desserts with wine.	

(Contd)

Table 7.6 (Contd)

Ingredient	Description	Photograph
Kreivi	*Krievi* is a light yellow-coloured cheese with a semi-hard texture produced in Finland. This cheese has distinctive small and large holes spread throughout. It pairs up very well with dark rye bread and is often used as a topping for open faced sandwiches.	
Kohlrabi	Also known as German turnip, this vegetable is a root vegetable from the brassica family of vegetables that includes cabbage and broccoli. It is also eaten commonly in India as *ganth gobhi or knol khol* in Hindi.	
Kale	It is a form of cabbage with curly and shrivelled leaves that do not close up to form a head like cabbage. It is also known as curly kale due to its appearance. It is used in salads or braised to make vegetable accompaniments. Since this vegetable grows in the winter and tastes better when exposed to frost, it is the most preferred vegetable in Scandinavian countries.	
Swede	Refer Table 7.4.	

Speciality Cuisines

One of the most popular foods of Scandinavian countries is the *smörgåsbord*. It is known as *smörgåsbord* in Sweden, *koldtbord* in Norway, *koldebord* in Denmark, and *seisova poyta* in Finland. *Smörgåsbord* is usually a buffet style table laid out with many cold and hot dishes. The word *smörgås* means open-faced sandwiches while *bord* means table. *Smörgås* in turn consists of two words, *smör* that means butter and *gås* that stands for goose in local language. The earlier *smörgåsbord* were pieces of rye breadspread with goose liver pâté, and this gave rise to different types of open-faced sandwiches that are referred to as *smörgåsbord*. The traditional Swedish *smörgåsbord* consists of hot as well as cold dishes. Varieties of bread, spreads, salads, and cheese are the most popular choice on this buffet and cold fish, such as herring, salmon, cod, and eel, are often the main dishes. Roast meat and desserts are also included in *smörgåsbord*. The *smörgåsbord* laid out during Christmas in Sweden is commonly known as *julbord*, which includes the normal *smörgåsbord* with addition of *charcuterie* products such as Christmas ham, liver pastes, pickled vegetables, and a variety of cheeses. Hot dishes such as meat balls called *köttbullar*, roasted pork ribs, sausages, and few hot vegetable preparations are often added for this fare. Some of the commonly consumed dishes in various Scandinavian countries are described in Table 7.7.

Table 7.7 Popular dishes in Scandinavian cuisine

Dish	Description	Photograph
Skyr	This preparation is like a strained yoghurt and is often eaten salted or with addition of sugar. The whey obtained from the curd is used for pickling and marinating meat. It is believed that this dish was brought from Iceland to Norway many years ago. It is also commonly known as *villi piima* in Finland.	

(Contd)

Table 7.7 (Contd)

Dish	Description	Photograph
Hákarl	It is a preparation of fermented shark popularly eaten in Norway. Since sharks contain poison, the Nordes invented a complex process to remove it. The fish is packed in sand and gravel and stones are put on top and left for 6–12 weeks. The weight presses down the flesh and squeezes out the poisonous liquid. The fish is then taken out, cut into strips, and hung to dry. The fish acquires a distinct taste and smells strongly of ammonia.	
Gravalax	This is preparation of salmon packed with salt and sugar and left to cure for at least 2–3 days. It is then covered with chopped dill and eaten as an appetizer or used as topping for open-faced sandwiches.	
Rommegrot	It is a porridge made with sour cream, flour, and milk. This popular Norwegian dish is eaten on special occasions, along with cured meat.	
Fàrikål	It is a dish like Irish stew that is prepared by stewing lamb with cabbage, black pepper, and flour and is cooked for long hours in a casserole and served with potatoes boiled in their skin. It is a traditional dish served on many festive occasions.	
Eel roll	This is one of the oldest dishes made in Denmark. The eel is skinned and deboned and then stuffed with chopped onions, salt, and pepper and rolled up. It is then rolled inside a cheese cloth and poached. The roll is served sliced and cold with potatoes that have been cooked in white wine.	
Frikadeller	This Danish and Swedish speciality of ground meat patties are made by mincing pork meat with herbs and onions and are shallow-fried in lard or hot oil. It is commonly served with *remoulade* sauce, which is an influence of France. This sauce is similar to Tartar sauce.	
Stegt flæsk	It is one of the most popular home-made dishes of Danish cuisine. Fried slices of pork that are served with boiled potatoes and creamy parsley sauce. This dish is not be confused with *Flæskesteg*, which is roasted pork served with pork cracklings.	
Leverpostej	This is a paste made from liver and is often used as a spread on rye bread and eaten as a snack or a meal. It has become so popular that there are now packaged and ready-to-use liver pastes available in the market.	

(Contd)

Table 7.7 (Contd)

Dish	Description	Photograph
Mustamakkara	Literally meaning black pudding, it is a typical Finnish sausage eaten with sweet lingonberry jam. It is made by mixing pork mince, pork blood, and rye flour and stuffed into casing and cooked like other sausages.	
Köttbullar	This is a very popular Swedish preparation made by mincing meat along with minced onions, herbs, eggs, and breadcrumbs. The ingredients are rolled into dumplings and are usually deep-fried, baked, braised, or even steamed. They are popularly served with mashed potatoes, pickled vegetables, brown sauce, and lingonberry jam. Various kinds of meat, such as pork, beef, or even reindeer, can be used for making this dish.	
Smörgåstårta	This dish originated in Sweden and is now very popular in Scandinavian countries. The appearance of this dish is like a well-decorated cake, but it is a type of sandwich made by layering rye bread or white bread with creamy fillings in the centre. The top of the cake can be decorated with hard boiled eggs, shrimps, and even pickled sardines. It is often served sliced on the *smörgåsbord*.	
Pitepalt	This is a traditional Swedish dish made from potatoes. The potatoes are boiled and mashed along with flour and salt to form dough. The dumpling is formed by filling it up with shredded and sautéed bacon and rolled to enclose the filling. The dumplings are poached in boiling water for at least 35–40 minutes and then removed from the liquid and served along with butter and lingonberry jam.	
Pyttipanna	It is one of the most popular Scandinavian dishes made at home from leftover vegetables. Usually vegetables consisting of potatoes, onions, and various kinds of diced meat and sausage are sautéed with salt and pepper and served with fried egg and pickled beets. Though this dish was usually made from leftover vegetables, it is common to see stores selling readymade packets of *pyttipanna* vegetables pre-cut and ready to be cooked.	
Rødgrød	This Danish dessert has strong German influence. It is made from potato starch and red currants. The red currants are stewed with sugar and water until soft. These are then strained to obtain a juice which is again cooked and thickened with potato starch. It is poured into bowls and allowed to set. It is often served along with custard sauce or whipped cream.	
Kiisseli	It is a fruit soup from Finland made from red currants and blueberries. It is similar to *rødgrød* and can be served hot or cold.	

(Contd)

Table 7.7 (Contd)

Dish	Description	Photograph
Mämmi	This is a traditional Finnish dessert eaten commonly during Easter. It is made from rye flour, dark molasses, salt, and candied orange peel. The mixture is allowed to mature and sweeten naturally before it is baked. The baked product is allowed to mature in cold storage for at least 3–4 days before it can be eaten with cream and sugar or even vanilla ice cream.	
Rose hip soup	This is a very popular fruit soup relished in Sweden. The rose hips are put in a pot and crushed with a wooden spoon. Water is added and the soup is allowed to simmer until the rose hips are tender. The rose hips are pureed and cooked with sugar and thickened with cornstarch. It is usually chilled before serving and served with whipped cream or ice cream.	
Blåbärssoppa	This is a Swedish fruit soup made from bilberries (refer Table 7.6). The procedure is same as that of *rødgrød* or *kiisseli*. Bilberry juice is sweetened with sugar and thickened with potato starch. In Sweden, this soup is drunk to cure stomach ailments.	

GERMAN CUISINE

The cuisine of Germany is very popular in hotels across the world. Like British cuisine, German cuisine is not widely spread, but few of the special dishes have always been very popular on the menus of hotels. Germans have always been traditional in their approach to cooking and ingredients. However post World War II, the influence of foreign food has also impacted German cuisine. Germans love beer. Germany also produces some of the finest wines which are very popular in the world. The cuisine and beverages of Germany have also influenced its immediate neighbour France and vice versa.

Germans are hale and hearty eaters. They start their day with a sumptuous breakfast which consists of bread and toasts with butter and marmalade, eggs, and a strong cup of coffee. *Charcuterie* products, such as ham, sausage, and salami, are also a common feature on the breakfast menus. Traditionally, the main meal of the Germans is lunch which is usually eaten around noon. Dinner, on the other hand, is a small affair with sandwiches and soup. Food has always been a major part of the German culture and they eat ample portions of meat with bread. German breads are more flavoursome and chewy with whole grains. Potatoes form a large part of their diet and many other ingredients such as cabbage, beetroot, kohlrabi (refer Table 7.6), and turnips also feature commonly in German cuisine. Fruits, such as apples, raisins, and prunes, are often added to meat to impart sweetness to the dish. Most of the German meal comprises pork, beef, and chicken, though game animals, such as wild boar, duck, and geese, are also eaten. Lamb is rarely seen on German tables. The methods of cooking usually are braising, stewing, and roasting, combined with some frying. German *charcuterie* is famous all over the world. Their sausages called *wurst* are eaten worldwide. The most common one is *bratwurst* made from ground pork and spices. There are more than a thousand types of cold cuts prepared in Germany. Most of the *charcuterie* products are served with dark rye bread, pickled vegetables, and mustard. German mustards, also known as *senf* (refer Table 7.8), are very popular in the world because of their low acid content compared to American and English mustards.

Seafood in German cuisine is restricted to coastal areas such as north and along the Rhine River; the most sought after fish is the trout. Pickled herrings along the northern coasts are used for rolling up into cylindrical shapes and covered with sliced pickled gherkin and eaten as snacks with pumpernickel bread.

Germany has a fine produce of vegetables and fruits. Asparagus, especially white asparagus, known as *spargel,* carrots, turnips, green peas, beans, beetroot, and fruits such as cherries, apples, peaches, and pears are of high quality and paired with roasted meats and eaten in desserts.

Geographical Regions

Germany is located in Western Europe. Its topography is diverse. It includes the black forests of Swabia and the green meadows and valleys of Rhine (home to world's famous vineyards), apart from the high mountains and deep forests. The north of Germany has a wide coast that faces the North Sea and Baltic Sea. The Jutland peninsula jutting out in the extreme north borders with Denmark. On the west, Germany borders countries such as The Netherlands, Belgium, and France and on the southern side, lie Switzerland and Austria. The East of Germany borders Czech Republic and Poland. The neighbouring countries have impacted the cuisine of Germany to quite an extent. Germany is composed of 16 states and the regional cultural heritage with regard to food is quite evident in this country. After the World War II, Germany was split into East and West Germany. East Germans imbibed certain cooking styles of Russia, whereas the West Germans continued with their style of traditional cooking.

Despite the reunification of Germany in 1990, most of the states have retained their specific cooking styles and regional diversity that are guided by the geographical location, culture and traditions, and regional agricultural practices. The major regions of Germany with respect to their typical culinary traditions are discussed in the following paragraphs.

Bavaria and Franconia

Bavaria and Franconia lie in the south of Germany. One can clearly see the influence of Swiss food in terms of their dairy products. Pork is commonly eaten here in barbeque style; *spanferkel* is the most popular dish wherein baby pigs are roasted over spitfire. The Swiss influence can also be seen on some of the famous German desserts especially made for Christmas. One such dessert is *dresden stollen* that is shaped to depict baby Jesus wrapped in cloth. Other famous dishes of this region are *leberkäs* (a chilled mould of minced pork, beef, and liver), *knödel* (dumplings or soaked bread), *haxen* (pork or veal trotters, most often consumed with *sauerkraut*), *rostbratwürste* (small finger sausages), and *Leberknödel* (large liver dumplings in a clear broth).

Lower Saxony and Schleswig-Holstein

These states lie in north-west Germany facing the North Sea. Thus, the cuisine of this part uses lots of seafood such as eel and herrings. The typical local dish is *aalsuppe* which is a sweet and sour eel soup flavoured with bacon. At times, it is also combined with vegetables or with pears and prunes. Some cured and salted meats such as *buntes huhn* (salt beef on a bed of diced vegetables) and *rollmop,* which are prepared by rolling pickled herring fish, are other popular dishes. This part of Germany is influenced by the cuisine of Scandinavian countries. The famous Danish dessert *rødgrød* is prepared in Germany as well and is called *rote grütz.*

Berlin, Hesse, and Westphalia

Being a cold region, this part of Germany produces some of the finest *charcuteries* of the world. The famous Westphalia ham, *bratwurst,* and rabbit pâté come from this region.

As this region is comparatively cold, Berliners have incorporated in their menu hot soups such as cabbage and pea soup, which are popularly relished with dark pumpernickel bread.

Baden-Württemberg

This is the southern region around Stuttgart and the cuisine shows perceptible Italian influence of *gnocchi* and pasta dishes through Switzerland. German pastas are slightly different from those of Italy. The most popular Italian style pasta is *spätzle* which is made with flour, eggs, and water and is sieved through a *spätzle* strainer into a pot of boiling water. A famous dish that resembles Italian ravioli is *maultaschen,* which is stuffed with ground meat, spinach, and calves' brains. Another dish inspired from Italian *vitello tonnato* is *Geschnetzeltes* which are slices of veal served with cream sauce.

Saxony and Thuringia

The eastern part of Germany is famed for preparations such as *Linsensuppe mit Thüringer Rotwurst* (lentil soup with Thuringian sausages), *Rinderzunge* in *Rosinen-Sauce* (calves' tongues in grape sauce). *Kartoffelsuppe* (potato soup) remains a favourite of the district, as does a baked appetizer, *Quarkkeulchen,* made from curd, boiled potatoes, flour, sugar, and raisins, topped with cinnamon and served with apple sauce. Each city in the district also has its own popular local dishes. Leipzig, for example, has its *Leipziger Allerlei,* a blend of carrots, peas, asparagus, cauliflower, mushrooms, crayfish, ox tails, bits of veal, and dumplings.

Rhineland

Rhineland features some of the most popular dishes that are influenced from France and Belgium. For example, there is *saumagen,* stuffed pork belly with pickled cabbage which is also served in French cuisines as *sauerkraut.* Other dishes include *schweinepfeffer* which is a highly seasoned and spicy pork ragout that's thickened with pig blood, *hähnchen* are pork trotters served with pickled cabbage and potatoes, or *sauerbraten,* which is beef marinated in wine vinegar and spices. *Reibekuchen,* small potato pancakes served with blueberry or apple sauce, are also favourite dishes in this region.

Popular Ingredients

When one thinks of German food, the first thought that comes to the mind are cold meat and *charcuterie* such as frankfurters and *bratwurst*, German mustard, potatoes, roasted beets, pickled cabbage, and the most popular Black Forest cake. Apart from food, Germany is the one of the largest producers of beer and white wine. Most of the land is quite fertile, but less than 5 per cent of the population is into farming and agriculture. Therefore these days, Germany has to rely a lot on imports of foodstuff. Like India, Germany is a land of varied cultures and the unique demography of states is reflected in their ingredients as well as its cuisine. Some ingredients unique to the German cuisine are listed in Table 7.8.

Table 7.8 Special ingredients of German cuisine

Ingredients	Description	Photograph
Spargel	*Spargel* is white asparagus that is highly perishable and seasonal. It is usually available in May and June and because of its perishability, it is often sold canned.	
Kohlrabi	Refer Table 7.6.	
Morello cherries	These are a special variety of sour cherries that grow around the Black Forest regions of Swabia. They are used for making *kirsch* liqueur, the prime ingredient Black Forest cake. Morello cherries are often sold cooked with sugar and cornstarch and are readily available canned.	
Westphalia ham	The speciality of this ham from Westphalia is that the pigs are fed with acorn and the meat is cured and smoked over the branches of Juniper berries.	
Senf	This German mustard is made from different types of mustard seeds, mostly dark and white varieties. The mustard seeds are crushed to a paste or left grainy and mixed with vinegar and oil. The uniqueness of this mustard is that it is made from a mild variety of mustard.	
Quark cheese	It is a type of fresh cheese that is quite similar to curd cheese. It is prepared by warming sour milk until the cheese curdles and then it is strained away. Quark cheese is an un-aged cheese made from low-fat milk.	

(Contd)

Table 7.8 (Contd)

Ingredients	Description	Photograph
Caraway seeds	This spice is very similar to black cumin and is also known as Persian cumin. It is commonly used in desserts, breads, and vegetable dishes. The flavour of caraway seed is like anise seed. It pairs up well with rye flour. It is also the most popular spice added in *spätzle* and *sauerkraut*.	
Juniper berries	Though the name is a berry, but it does not belong to the berry family. It is the fruit of the juniper pine. It is commonly used as a spice and is often used in dried form.	

Speciality Cuisines

German food is quite diverse. Unlike other countries, breakfast and lunch are the main meals, where family members and friends get together for a meal. Germany is influenced by its neighbouring countries most of which are famous for their desserts. Thus, desserts for Germans are very special and extensive. The most famous Black Forest cake known as *Shwarzwalderkirsch torte* is prepared by using *kirsch* liqueur that is obtained from the Black Forest region, and hence the name. Pork meat, beef, and fish are the commonly eaten meat. The overproduction of meat has resulted in a wide selection of *charcuterie* products. Germany also has a repertoire of nearly 6,000 different types of breads. One of the most famous bread is pumpernickel. Germans educated the rest of the world on making sour dough starters to enrich and leaven the bread. Some popular German dishes are described in Table 7.9.

Table 7.9 Popular German dishes (see also Plates 8 and 9)

Dish	Description	Photograph
Aalsuppe	This is one of the most popular dishes from Hamburg. It is a broth of fresh eel made by adding wine and beer and flavoured with herbs such as thyme and parsley. The soup is thickened with broken pieces of pumpernickel bread and is served with boiled potatoes.	
Leberknödel	Commonly called *leberknoedelsuppe,* it is a Bavarian specialty. *leber* stands for liver and *knödel* for dumpling. The base of this soup is a strong beef broth in which the dumplings (made of liver, ground beef, chopped onions, herbs such as parsley, chives, tarragon, thyme, and eggs) is slowly allowed to poach and served with rye bread.	

(Contd)

Table 7.9 (Contd)

Dish	Description	Photograph
Kartoffelsalat	Also known as German potato salad, it is prepared and served hot or cold, or several other ways. Although it is called a salad, it is commonly used as a vegetable accompaniment. To make this salad, thick slices of potatoes are braised with chicken stock and pieces of bacon, until the potatoes are tender and have absorbed most of the stock. It is then mixed with vinegar and grain mustard. In northern Germany, the potatoes are mixed with mustard and mayonnaise.	
Rollmops	These are pickled fillets of herring rolled onto a gherkin of pickled onion to form a cylindrical shape. They are also sold canned and can be eaten as they are or as a topping on breads.	
Sauerkraut	In German, this literally translates to sour cabbage. Red or white cabbage is allowed to ferment naturally with lactic acid bacteria naturally present in air. The shredded cabbage is slated and then packed into a crock pot and pressed down with weight. It is then allowed to ferment for at least two to three weeks. It can be flavoured with caraway seeds and eaten with braised meat.	
Spätzle	These are a type of egg noodles made from flour, eggs, and seasoning. This dish is a speciality of the Swabia region. The thick batter of flour and egg is forced through a special sieve with large holes directly into a pot of salted boiling water. The *spätzle* is tossed in butter and caraway seeds and served with meat.	
Pumpernickel	This dark bread is normally made with rye flour and a small amount of wheat flour is added to the dough to lighten the texture. The bread has a dark colour, dense texture, and a sour and earthy flavour. It is generally consumed with smoked sausages and meat, marinated fish, and cheese.	
Pretzel	This knot-shaped bread is popularly eaten during the Oktoberfest in Germany. The uniqueness about this bread is that it is dipped in a lye solution (sodium hydroxide). This procedure of dipping bread gives it a characteristic flavour and colour. It also induces thirst and thus increases the sales of beer.	

(Contd)

Table 7.9   (Contd)

Dish	Description	Photograph
Wiener schnitzel	This popular dish is also made in Austria. Veal escalope is marinated with salt, pepper, and mustard and is dipped in egg batter and crumbed with fresh breadcrumbs and pan-fried until crisp. It is usually served with fried potatoes, lemon wedges, and cranberry sauce.	
Badener Schneck-ensuepple	This is a broth made from snails and is topped with fresh parsley. Many of us would think of France when it comes to snails, but this popular dish is from the Black Forest region of Germany, which is close to both French and Swiss borders. It is influenced by French cooking style and is served with herbs and garlic butter.	
Rheinischer Sauerbraten	This is a traditional German pot roast, usually made of beef. The meat is allowed to marinate in a marinade of vinegar, spices, and seasonings for a minimum of 3 to 10 days. The acidic action helps to soften the tough meat. The meat is first allowed to dry; when it is taken out of the marinade it is browned in hot oil, before it is braised or pot roasted with the remaining marinade. The dish is usually served with potatoes and *sauerkraut.*	
Spanferkel	This is a special barbecue dish of baby pigs. It is made for special occasions and gatherings such as Oktoberfest. It is traditionally cooked whole over a spitfire.	
Hasenpfeffer	It is a traditional stew made of rabbit. The rabbit meat is stewed with onions, wine, and pepper and the liquid is often thickened with rabbit's blood.	
Schwarzwalder kirsch torte	This is also known as Black Forest cake in English (refer Chapter 10 on cakes and pastries). This traditional cake is prepared by layering three slices of chocolate *Genoese* sponge with whipped cream and morello cherries. The sugar syrup must be flavoured with *kirsch* liqueur or else it cannot be called Black Forest cake. The top of the cake is decorated with lots of chocolate flakes to denote the black forests of Swabia.	
Berliner	Berliners are deep-fried dumplings of yeast leavened dough. The dough is same as that of doughnuts (refer Chapter 10). The dumplings are usually filled with raspberry jam and served rolled in castor sugar.	

(Contd)

Table 7.9 (Contd)

Dish	Description	Photograph
Baumkuchen	This cake is made in various countries under different names. Since the typical rings of this cake resemble lines of a tree trunk, it is often called *tree trunk cake* in Indonesia. Even in Germany, *baume* means log or tree and *kuchen* is a cake. A dessert similar to this in India is called *bebinca*. Traditionally, baumkuchen is made on spit fire by brushing even layers of the cake batter over metal rollers. When the layer browns, more is poured and it continues until the cake is thick enough. It is then taken off the roller and sliced to even thickness.	
Lebkuchen	This is a traditional sweet made during Christmas. The most famous *lebkuchen* comes from *Nürnberg* and hence it is often known as *Nürnberger lebkuchen*. It looks like gingerbread and is made from rye flour, molasses, and honey. It is usually used for making cookies, decorative motifs such as Christmas stars and boots. Many a time *lebkuchen* is cut into pieces and dipped in chocolate.	
Stollen	It is a loaf-shaped cake that is leavened with yeast and made with candied fruits, flour, and butter. Traditionally, this cake is made for Christmas and the special shape denotes baby Jesus wrapped up in a cloth. Sometimes marzipan is put inside and such a *stollen* is called *dresden stollen*. The cake after being baked is dipped in clarified butter and sprinkled with icing sugar.	
Gugelhupf	This is a tea cake made in special deep ring-shaped mould, which gives the cake a bulgy appearance on demoulding. The cake is generally sliced and eaten with tea. It is made with a sweet and leavened dough that often consists of raisins, almonds, and candied fruits soaked in *kirsch* liqueur.	

After having read this chapter, we can now appreciate the diversity in European cuisine with respect to adaptations, ingredients, and cuisines of various nations. Even though European countries are small and often belong to the same region, they have a unique cuisine of their own, with few influences from the neighbouring nations. Europe is famous for its dining culture and some of the most successful chefs hail from this continent and own their restaurants that are internationally acclaimed and world famous.

Now that we are familiar with the Western and European cuisines, in the next chapter we will discuss contemporary presentations and the adaption of such dishes in modern hotels and restaurants.

SUMMARY

In this chapter, we broadly discussed European food, mainly cuisines of France, England, Germany, and Scandinavian countries such as Denmark, Norway, Sweden, and Finland.

European food is also popularly known as Continental food. The concept of professional kitchen set-ups and brigade system was set up by a French chef called Augustus Escoffier and is followed till date in hotels worldwide. In the section on French cuisine, we discussed the various regions of France and how their location influences the food and cooking styles. We also read about how the food in France evolved over the years. The cuisines of medieval times, *haute* cuisine, and also *nouvelle* cuisine were all invented in France and then spread to other parts of the world. In this section, we also discussed the various popular ingredients used in French cuisine. We also discussed few of the famous cheeses such as *Roquefort, camembert,* and *brie*. Some of the popular meat such as *charollais* cattle, *bresse* poultry, and *Pauillac* lamb are highlights of French food.

Some of the French classical equipment used for cooking are also described here with pictures for easy identification. In most of the European cuisines, the food is mainly cooked in pots, pans, and casseroles; however, France has few unique tools and equipment that are used for preparing some unique dishes. We also discussed some popular French food that is regarded as classical and is still features on the menus of modern hotels. It is a popular belief among French chefs that if the basic dishes cannot be perfected, then there is no point in creating contemporary dishes. Some of the classical dishes such as *poulet sauté chasseur*, *pot au feu*, and *coq au vin*, are be known to almost all the chefs in the world.

We discussed British cuisines. British food is considered to be quite unimaginative and there is a lot of emphasis on fresh ingredients with good flavours. Though the cuisine of Great Britain has not been very popular outside the area because of various reasons, this food remains the favourite of British people. Over the years, the British have absorbed food and cooking style from the communities that they colonized earlier in history. It is not uncommon to see Indian influence on many of their dishes.

We also discussed the various kinds of British cuisines such as Irish, Welsh, and Scottish cuisine. English cuisine, even though not popular outside England, has given many dishes to the world. Few such dishes are the English breakfast, fish and chips, and shepherd's pie. England is also famous for its cheeses, such as Cheddar, Stilton, and *Derby*, which are popular all around the world. In this section, we also discussed about the popular dishes of British cuisine.

Later in the chapter we discussed the German and Scandinavian cuisines with respect to the flavour profile and type of cuisine. Scandinavian cuisine includes the cuisines of Finland, Denmark, Sweden, and Norway. *Smörgåsbord* is one of the most popular features of Scandinavian countries, which was discussed in detail. Scandinavia is famous for its different types of berries and unique processes involved in processing fish. The famous *hakarl*, which is a preparation of dried and fermented shark can be a put off for beginners, but is relished all over the Scandinavian countries. Scandinavian countries are also famous for their salmon, which is processed in several ways. It can be smoked, cured like *gravid lax*, or eaten grilled or pan-fried.

Germany is popular for its cold meat and *charcuterie*. Germany's most popular dessert the *Schwarzwalder Kirsch torte* or the Black Forest cake, has been discussed with regards to its uniqueness. We have also discussed the different states of Germany and the flavour profiles of these regions. Many of these regions exhibit influences of the countries they border. The regions have varied temperatures that have an impact on both food as well as the ingredients. We also discussed the most popular ingredients and preparations from the country.

In the next chapter, we will discuss the styles of presenting the European and Western food in form of an à la carte or in buffet by using techniques of food presentation.

KEY TERMS

À l'anglaise This is deep-fried style of preparation, where the food item is first coated in batter and then in breadcrumbs.

AOC It is the acronym for Appellation d'Origine Controlee. It is a recognition given by the government of a (European) country to any food product, that must come from the specified area of origin.

Bacalao It is salted and dried Atlantic cod fish eaten in Mediterranean countries.

Bangers It is the English term for sausages.

Brassica It is the Botanical name of the mustard family comprising leafy vegetables such as cabbage, broccoli, kohlrabi, and cauliflower.

Candied fruits These are dried fruits soaked in high density sugar syrup.

Champagne It is sparkling wine from the Champagne region of France.

Chartreuse It is anise-flavoured liqueur from France.

Continental cuisine The Cuisines of European countries are also termed as Continental cuisine.

Cornet d'anjou It is a variety of Chicory found in Central France.

Crepes These are French pancakes usually served as a dessert.

Crock pot These are ceramic pots usually used for pickling.

Danish pastry It is a breakfast pastry from Denmark, which is made from laminated yeast leavened dough.

Elevenses It is the popular British practice of having tea at 11 a.m.

Feather icing It is a style of decorating where the lines made by syrup or chocolate sauce are dragged with help of toothpick or sharp pointed object to resemble small feathers.

Fumets It is a term for reduced meat or vegetable stocks often used as sauces.

Gherkin These are small pickled cucumbers in brine.

Gravalax A preparation of salmon that is cured in salt and sugar and flavoured with dill.

Guéridon trolley It is a trolley used in restaurant, where the food can be cooked or prepared in front of the guests. It is a classical style of service in French cuisines.

Haute cuisine It is a term for French cuisine around the seventeenth century when the concept of plated presentations was introduced.

Julbord It is a reference for Christmas buffet in Sweden.

Juniper berries These are dried black berries often used for pickling and in marinades in Scandinavian cuisine.

Khichdi It is an Indian preparation of rice and lentils usually tempered with cumin seeds and ghee.

Kirsch This is cherry liqueur obtained from Morello cherries in Swabia region of Germany.

Lavender These are purple coloured scented flowers often used in cooking.

Leavening It is the airy texture produced in a baked item due to the addition of leavening agents such as yeast, baking powder, and baking soda.

Lye It is a mixture of water and sodium hydroxide solution.

Marzipan This is paste made from almond meal and sugar and cooked together until a dough is formed.

Medium doneness It is a stage of cooking meat which is more than rare and less than well done.

Michelin star It is an esteemed industry recognition given to restaurants for high quality food and service.

Mother sauces It is a term used for the four basic sauces that are the base for French cuisine. These sauces are Béchamel, Espagnole, Tomato and *veloute*.

Nouvelle cuisine It is a term for French cuisine around 1960 that promoted contemporary presentations.

PDO It is the acronym for Protected Designation of Origin. It is a recognition given by the English government for the products that come only from the designated region.

Prunes It is a dried variety of black plums.

Quick bread It is a term for baked products that use baking powder for leavening.

Reindeer It is a species of deer family with large antlers on their heads native to the Scandinavian region.

Remoulade sauce (See tartare sauce)

Scandinavia Countries on the Scandinavian peninsula are together referred to as Scandinavia. These comprise Denmark, Sweden and Norway. Finland is also included in the list and referred to as Nordic nations.

Senf This is German for mustard.

Shallots These are small slender onions with a flavour of onion and garlic.

Smörgåsbord It is a term for buffet laid out in Scandinavian countries.

Soufflé A savoury dish from France, which has starch as a base and the mixture is whipped with egg yolks and whipped egg whites. It is baked in special ceramic dishes called soufflé pots and served hot.

Spargel It is German for white asparagus.

Squab It is a special breed of pigeons that are eaten for their meat.

Tartare sauce This is a derivative of mayonnaise sauce with addition of pickled onions, capers, chopped parsley and seasoning.

Vitello tonnato This is an Italian speciality of sliced poached veal served with tuna flavoured mayonnaise.

Western cuisine It is a term used to denote cuisines from the Mediterranean region and Western countries other than Europe such as Mexico.

CONCEPT REVIEW QUESTIONS

1. Which are the countries that contribute to European cuisine?
2. What is the difference between French cuisine, *haute* cuisine and *nouvelle* cuisine?
3. Describe the impact of the geographical location of France on its cuisine.
4. Describe the cuisine of south-western France.
5. What are the popular food commodities that come from North-western France?
6. What regions are included in the eastern and north-eastern France and what famous commodities come from this region?
7. How is the food of northern France different from southern France?
8. What do you understand by AOC?
9. Name at least 5 French cheeses that have acquired an AOC.
10. What is the difference between *brie* and *Camembert*?
11. What are *belon* oysters?
12. Name one famous brand of cattle, lamb, and chicken in France.
13. What kinds of snails are used for making *escargots a la bourguignon*?
14. What is so unique about *Dijon* mustard?
15. Name the famous blue cheese from France.
16. What is *lame* and what is its use?
17. Name three desserts from France.
18. Describe three classical chicken preparations from France.
19. Describe the salient features of the cuisine of Great Britain.
20. What is the difference between Irish, Scottish, and Welsh cuisine?
21. Name the popular blue cheese from England.
22. Describe at least three unique vegetables used in English cuisine.
23. What does HP in HP sauce stand for?
24. What is a clotted cream and how is it used?
25. Name at least two fish used in English cuisine.
26. What is the difference between a steak and kidney pie, and shepherd's pie?
27. What do you mean by bangers and mash?
28. What is bubble and squeak and why is it called so?
29. Describe *haggis* and why is it special?
30. Name three popular desserts from English cuisine.
31. What countries contribute to the Scandinavian cuisine?
32. Describe the food of Norway.
33. What is Finnish cuisine and how is it different from Danish cuisine?
34. Describe at least three unique berries used in Scandinavian cuisine.
35. Name three popular fish used in Scandinavian cuisine.
36. Describe a *geitost*.
37. Describe at least 3 cheeses from Scandinavian countries.
38. Name two PDO cheeses from Denmark.
39. Differentiate between a *kale* and a *kohl rabi*.
40. Describe *smörgåsbord* and its composition.
41. What is *hakarl* and what is so unique about it?
42. Describe *gravalax*.
43. Name at least 5 dishes from Scandinavian countries.
44. What is *mustamakarra* and how is it served?
45. Describe the features of German cuisine.
46. What role does geographical location play on the cuisine of Germany?
47. Describe *spargel*.
48. Describe *Schwarzwalder kirsch torte* and name the cherry used for making it.
49. Name the most popular cream cheese from Germany.
50. Describe a *leberknödel*.
51. What is a *spatzle*? How is it made?
52. Describe rollmops.
53. Describe *sauerkraut* and its use.
54. What is the difference between a *baumkuchen* and a *lebkuchen*?
55. Name the popular bread made on Christmas which is similar to cake.

PROJECT WORK

1. French cuisine is dying its natural death. In groups of four, research the statement and find out the reasons for the same. Devise a French menu that you would serve at a fining dining restaurant and prepare the same for panel tasting.

2. In groups of five, prepare at least two popular dishes each from France, Scandinavian countries, England, and Germany and ready for tasting and evaluation. Record your observations and share with the group.

3. Conduct a market survey of hotels and markets and list down the various kinds of cheeses available. Now classify these cheeses according to their country of origin and find out what kind of cheeses are more popular in India and why?

4. During Christmas time, visit various pastry shops in your city and list the items being sold. Research the products and see how many of these come from European cuisines, especially Germany. List all such products and see what makes them unique.

CHAPTER 8

WESTERN PLATED FOOD

Learning Objectives

After reading this chapter, you should be able to
- understand the basic concept of plating food
- appreciate the use of the right kinds of plates for food presentation
- analyse the components of presenting food
- understand the importance of balance in plated presentations
- claim an insight into the emerging trends of new plate presentations and modern techniques used in the same

INTRODUCTION

In the previous two chapters, we discussed the various cuisines of Western and European countries. No matter which country or province a dish belongs to, chefs over the years have strived to present it on a plate to enhance its visual appeal. This is also commonly known as plated presentation. Such presentations are not only limited to hot or cold food, but are also used in large platters that are served in buffets and large set-ups. The food is presented attractively to stimulate all the sense organs of a person; it is a known fact that a tastefully presented food enhances the appetite and motivates the desire to taste the food. With the concepts of fine dining, restaurants that are opening in the world are increasingly focussing on modern styles of food presentations to make their food unique and an experience to remember.

The art of plate presentations has been mastered by chefs in such a way that on being shown a photograph of a dish on a plate, people can correctly associate with the chef responsible for the presentation. Food presentation is not only about different colours on the plate and how a dish is arranged, but the most important thing or the soul of food presentation is the 'balance'. It is actually the balance of various aspects such as colours, flavours, textures of the dish, and even the balance in choice of platters used for presenting the food.

In this chapter, we intend to discuss the various aspects and concepts behind plated presentations. We will largely talk about balance in flavours, texture, and colour of the food and how to harmoniously present them on a plate. We will also discuss the emerging trends in food presentations and how chefs across the world are using modern technologies to make the food more appealing and decorative. We will discuss the presentations of various foods and see the new concepts underlying modern world cuisine and also discuss the new trends and ideas in food art and critique the same from a professional chef's point of view.

THE CONCEPT OF PLATE PRESENTATIONS

The art of presenting food on a plate is called plate presentation. Presenting the food on the plate is like an artist painting a canvas. The plate is the canvas for the chef and the ingredients are the colours. Like each artist has his/her own style of painting, so does a chef. But, plate presentation is not an easy task. At times, one could land up in a mess while trying to create things with weird combinations that do not justify the use of those components on a plate. Therefore, in order to master the art of plated presentations, it is important to understand the science and art behind the procedure as also the balance between the elements that impact food presentations. The following are the elements that have a significant impact on plate presentation.

- Colour
- Cooking method
- Arranging food
- Garnish
- Plate selection

Colour

Colour is one of the most important components in a food preparation and more so in presentations where creativity can make big difference to the overall feel and appearance of the dish. Colour reinforces quality in terms of freshness and even right cooking method. For example, chlorophyll turns grey when cooked in an acidic medium; grey or discoloured spinach would not be appealing as chefs have to use colour on the plate imaginatively to produce effective results. However, this must never be at the expense of flavour, texture, or balance. For example, a tomato slice may look more appealing when plated next to a slice of fresh Mozzarella, instead of sliced carrots as there would be very little contrast in colour or even texture to a certain extent. The following are some useful tips that should be borne in mind when choosing the colours on plate.

- Earthy tones of colours will blend or harmonize with vibrant colours. It is often observed that foods that taste good together naturally blend with regard to colours as well. The classical example is the tomato and Mozzarella salad from Italy. This classical combination is a favourite of chefs and one can easily find it on menus of various hotels around the world.

Imagine presenting a poached chicken breast with mashed potatoes and volute sauce. The entire combination of the dish is white in colour—white chicken, white sauce, and white sauce. This combination, however tasty, will not invigorate the taste buds. On the other hand, a poached chicken served with caramelized jus and steamed broccoli will make the plate look appetizing. Many of the meat used in western cooking have shades of brown, golden, or caramelized colour and thus it becomes all the more important to choose a contrasting colour. This is the reason that green vegetables, such as asparagus, beans, and spinach, are commonly used as accompaniments for plating non-vegetarian dishes in Western cuisines.

- The use of two or three colours on a plate gives an interesting touch to the plate, however, more than three colours would add too much of colour and will make the plate look crowded and messy.
- When using foods of brown tones, enhance with accompaniments that are bright in colours such as green, yellow, and red.

Garnish

It is important to garnish the food to make it look attractive. We have read briefly about garnishing food in Chapter 3. Garnishes have a much broader role to play apart from adding colour to the food. They add texture, contrasting flavours, and even nutritional aspect to the dish. One has to be careful while choosing a garnish. It is quite a possibility that some dishes might not need any garnish. This is where the art of plating comes into play. Any garnish which is just added to provide an extra colour and does nothing to enhance the texture or flavour of the dish, is not required to be on the plate, and such garnishes are known as non-functional garnishes. Let us discuss some of the points that need to be kept in mind, while garnishing the food on a plate.

Use a garnish that complements the dish Referring again to the tomato Mozzarella salad, just the red tomatoes and white cheese may look boring. So elements such as fresh basil sprigs neatly placed along with sliced tomatoes and cheese, makes it look fresh on the plate. Basil pairs up well with both tomato as well as Mozzarella cheese and apart from adding colour, it also adds to the flavour and taste.

Always focus on the look of the garnish As the garnish is used for adorning the plate, the ingredients must be of high quality. The herbs should be bright and fresh, the crackers should be crisp, and the salads should be well moistened with dressings.

Use for best judgement of an eye appeal when adding an herb as a garnish For example, a piece of steak served with mashed potatoes and green vegetables might not require a garnish of green herb. However, a classical steak served with jacket potato will require some herb as a garnish to make it look attractive.

Cooking Method

Each different method of cooking produces different results in food (taste, appearance, and texture). Most cooking processes use some form of heat transfer which includes the following.

PLATE 1

(a) Cleaning casings with water

(b) Putting casing on the feeder tube

(c) Stuffing the sausage into the casing

(d) Making link shapes of sausage

Steps for stuffing sausages (Chapter 2, Fig. 2.1)

Kielbasa or the Polish sausage

Frankfurters

Salami

Breakfast sausage

Loukanika

Merguez

Boudin blanc

Boudin noir

Popular sausages across the world (Chapter 2, Table. 2.9)

(a) Prepare the lining by layering the sliced ham on plastic and rolling them

(b) Measure the length of a terrine mould

(c) Line the terrine with the ham

(d) Ensure that an overhang is left

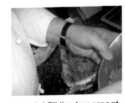

(e) Fill the forcemeat

(f) Lay the garnish inside

(g) Cover with more forcemeat

(h) Tap and close the overhang

(i) Sliced terrine platter

Step-by-step preparation of a terrine (Chapter 2, Fig. 2.3)

PLATE 2

(a) Layer the mould with dough

(b) Seal the corners

(c) Leave an overhanging of pastry

(d) Fill the forcemeat

(e) Tap the mould

(f) Seal the top

(g) Make the hole in pastry

(h) Make a vent by creating a tunnel

(i) Glaze with egg wash

(j) Bake the pâté

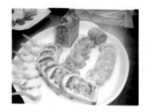

(k) Slice and serve filled with aspic

Step-by-step preparation of a pâté (Chapter 2, Fig. 2.4)

Sausage puffs or pigs in blankets

Strudel

Böreks

Spring rolls

Wonton

Turnover

Types of dough-wrapped hot hors d'oeuvres (Chapter 3, Table 3.4)

PLATE 3

Angels on horseback

Devils on horseback

Dolmas

Miscellaneous classical appetizers (Chapter 3, Table 3.7)

Israeli couscous

Chilled lettuce soup

Mushroom *gallete*

White asparagus mousse on jellied beet consommé

Grilled fish on wok-seared vegetables

Prawn cocktail

Chilled celeriac puree served with *quenelle* of *mascarpone* cheese

Lemon and cod liver pate on bed of pea mash and ginger emulsion

Carrot jelly with *beluga* caviar on bed of toasted pumpernickel

Grilled eggplant on soft polenta

Types of *amuse bouche* or *amuse guele* (Chapter 3, Table 3.11)

Conventional sandwich

Buffet sandwich

Continental sandwich

Open-faced sandwich

Rolled sandwiches

Pinwheel sandwiches

Ribbon sandwich

Types of cold sandwiches (Chapter 4, Table 4.5)

PLATE 4

Grilled ham and cheese

Croque monsieur

Croque madame

Stammer max

Hot dog

Gyro

Panini

Types of grilled sandwiches (Chapter 4, Table 4.6)

Modern presentations of sandwiches (Chapter 4, Fig. 4.2)

Parmesan or *Parmigiano-Reggiano*

Pecorino

Gorgonzola

Asiago

Taleggio

Castelmagno

Mozzarella

Provolone

Common types of Italian cheeses (Chapter 6, Table 6.1)

Penne

Farfalle

Fusilli

Bucatini

Commonly used pastas in Italian cuisine (Chapter 6, Table 6.5)

PLATE 5

Minestrone

Pollo alla cacciatore or
Hunter's chicken stew

Osso buco

Fritto misto

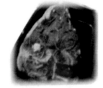

Gnocchi alla Romana

Insalata caprese

Insalata de Cesare

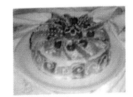

Aqua pazza

Bistecca alla Fiorentina or
Beefsteak Florentine style

Panettone

Tiramisu

Sicialian Casatta

Popular dishes of Italy (Chapter 6, Table 6.9)

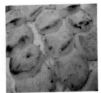

Avocado

Habanero

Pablano

Serano

Jalapeño

Anaheim

Pasilla

Chipotle

Plantanos

Frijoles

Nopales

Achiote

Common Ingredients in Mexican Cuisine (Chapter 6, Table 6.21)

PLATE 6

Refried beans

Guacamole

Fajita

Salsa

Pico de Gallo

Enchilada

Taco

Tostada

Burrito

Chimichangas

Quesadilla

Tamales

Mole Pablano

Helado Frito

Popular dishes in Mexican cuisine (Chapter 6, Table 6.23)

Moutarde de Dijon

Camargue rice

Globe artichokes

Chicory

Périgord truffle

Roquefort

Neufchâtel

Chaource

Brillat Savarin

Saint-Marcellin

Langres

Camembert

Popular ingredients in French cuisine (Chapter 7, Table 7.1)

PLATE 7

Baguette

Puree Saint-Germain

Sauerkraut

Quenelle de brochette

Bouillabaisse

Foie gras

Ratatouille

Blanquette de veau

Poulet Sauté Chasseur

Coq au vin

Pot-au-feu

Boeuf bourguignon

Gateau Opera

Tarte tatin

Crêpe Suzette

Madeleine

Popular dishes of French cuisine (Chapter 7, Table 7.2)

Fish and chips

Steak and kidney pie

Shepherd's pie

Bangers and mash

Bubble and squeak

Cornish pasty

Yorkshire pudding

Welsh rarebit

Popular dishes of British cuisine (Chapter 7, Table 7.5) contd

PLATE 8

contd

Toad in the hole

Roast beef

Chicken tikka masala

Scones

Flapjack

Bread and butter pudding

Simnel cake

Fruit trifle

Dundee cake

Popular dishes of British cuisine (Chapter 7, Table 7.5)

Bilberry

Cloudberry

Sea buckthorn

Rose hip

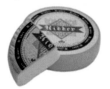
Ridder cheese

Blue *Brie*

Danish Blue

Kohlrabi

Popular ingredients in Scandinavian cuisine (Chapter 7, Table 7.6)

Aalsuppe

Leberknöedel

Kartoffelsalat

Rollmops

Sauerkraut

Spätzle

Pumpernickel

Pretzel

Popular German dishes (Chapter 7, Table 7.9) contd

PLATE 9

contd

Wiener schnitzel

Badener Schneckensuepple

Rheinischer Sauerbraten

Hasenpfeffer

Schwarzwalder kirsch torte

Lebkuchen

Stollen

Gugelhupf

Popular German dishes (Chapter 7, Table 7.9)

Modern ways of plate presentation (Chapter 8, Table 8.1)

Hargao

Shaomai

Char siu bao

Hot and sour soup

Wonton soup

Kung pao

Peking duck

Drunken chicken

Specialities from the Chinese kitchen (Chapter 10, Table 10.2) contd

PLATE 10

contd

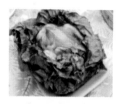
Beggar's chicken

Sweet and sour pork

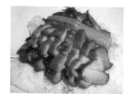
Char siu

Mapo doufu

Dan dan noodles

Hai nan kai fann

Hakka noodles

Moon cake

Mongolian hotpot

Shantung chicken

Shaobing

Date pancakes

Specialities from the Chinese kitchen (Chapter 10, Table 10.2)

Maki

Temaki

Uramaki

Inari sushi

Nigiri sushi

Hosomaki

Kinds of sushi (Chapter 10, Table 10.5)

Mochi

Dango

Tamagoyaki

Tempura

Speciality dishes in Japanese cuisine (Chapter 10, Table 10.6) contd

PLATE 11

contd

Black miso cod

Donburi

Chazuke

Tonkatsu

Gyoza

Okayu

Yakitori

Age bitashi

Hiyayako

Udon

Tsukemono

Chawanmushi

Speciality dishes in Japanese cuisine (Chapter 10, Table 10.6)

Lemon grass/*Takrai*

Thai ginger/*Galangal*

Kaffir lime/*Makrut* leaves

Mango ginger/*Krachai*

Bird's eye chillies/*Prik kee noo*

Tofu/*Tou hu*

Pandan leaves/*Bai toey hom*

Thai cardamom/*Loog gra waan*

Ingredients used in Thai cuisine (Chapter 10, Table 10.9)

Satay

Thod man pla

Larb gai

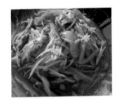
Som tam

Popular dishes of Thai cuisine (Chapter 10, Table 10.10) contd

PLATE 12

contd

Yam woon sen chae

Tom yam

Tom kha

Krathong thong

Kai takrai

Krapao

Patani

Kaeng kiew wan

Paneng

Phad Thai

Kai hor bai toey

Popular dishes of Thai cuisine (Chapter 10, Table 10.10)

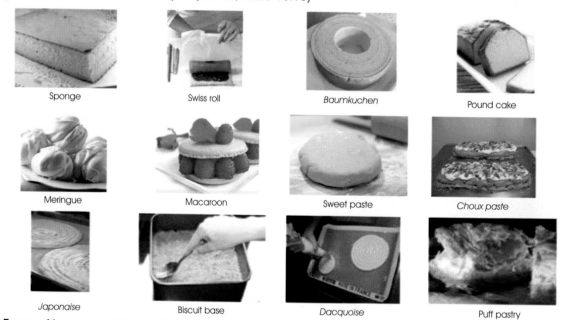

Sponge

Swiss roll

Baumkuchen

Pound cake

Meringue

Macaroon

Sweet paste

Choux paste

Japonaise

Biscuit base

Dacquoise

Puff pastry

Types of bases used for making cakes and pastries (Chapter 11, Table 11.1)

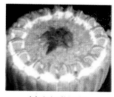

Sacher torte

Dobos torte

Malakoff torte

Linzer torte

Classical cakes and pastries (Chapter 11, Table 11.2) contd

PLATE 13

contd

Battenberg

Black Forest gateau

Napoleon gateau

Gateau St Honore

Praline gateaux

Charlotte russe

Devil's food cake

Croquembouche

Mud cake

Walnut brownies

Baked cheese cake

Chilled cheese cake

Alhambra gateau

Yule log

Gateau Pithivier

Pavlova

Classical cakes and pastries (Chapter 11, Table 11.2)

Pastries prepared in flexipan moulds (Chapter 11, Fig. 11.3)

PLATE 14

Victorian sponge

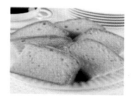

Madeira cake

Banana bread

Carrot cake

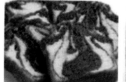

Marble cake

Various kinds of high-tea cakes (Chapter 11, Table 11.5)

Sugar work

Spun sugar

Spun sugar dome

Spun sugar tool

Sugared flowers

Touille

Chocolate

Sponge

Icings and creams

Various types of garnishes used on cakes and pastries (Chapter 11, Table 11.8)

PLATE 15

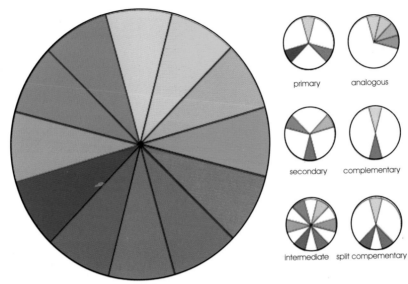

primary   analogous   hue

secondary   complementary   tint

intermediate   split complementary   shade

Colour wheel (Chapter 11, Fig. 11.5)

Feuillant

Chocolate leaves

Chocolate flowers

Flame

Chocolate cut-outs

Nets

Chocolate basket

Sides and collars

Twists and curls

Bows

Chocolate box

Chocolate cone

Three-tier cake with black
and white chocolate cigars

Chocolate garnishes (Chapter 12, Table 12.4)

PLATE 16

Dark chocolate mousse with caramel sauce

Gratinated summer berries with fresh strawberry ice cream

Mille feuille of blueberry mousse with poached pears

Banana chocolate *marquise*

Modern pre-plated desserts (Chapter 13, Table 13.12)

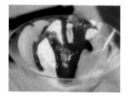

Arlesienne

Black Forest

Jacques

Banana split

Classical *coupes* and sundaes (Chapter 14, Table 14.5)

Oatmeal raisin cookies

Chocolate chip cookie

Macaroon

Crunchy drops

Florentines

Amaretti

Rock cakes

Anzac biscuits

Bull's eye

Derby cookies

Pinwheel

Chequered

Cressini

English tea cookie

Pizelle

Ginger bread

Some examples of cookies (Chapter 16, Tables 16.2, 16.5, 16.8, and 16.11)

Convection   This type of heat is normally found in a heated closed environment, like an oven. The air and oven surfaces are heated which, in turn, heat items inside.

Conduction   This method of heat transfer involves the food coming in contact with the heat source such as boiling, poaching, frying, and deep frying.

Radiation   Radiated heat usually involves a dry heat process wherein the food does not come into contact with the heat source. This type of dry heat is produced by grills, charcoal grills, salamanders, etc.

Let us discuss some of the salient features that need to be kept in mind with regard to the cooking methods vis-à-vis plate presentation.

- One must avoid using foods cooked with a single method of cooking on the same plate. Using dishes cooked by different methods not only adds texture, but also adds a different colour and balance to the entire dish.
- A dish ingredient must reflect the way it has been cooked. For example, a roast chicken must have a caramelized exterior and the boiled vegetables should not have a wilted or deep-fried appearance
- Combine hard and soft textures, smooth and rough type of food together to add an element of interest in the plate.
- Involve the cooking methods that will help retain or intensify the natural colours of the food rather than discolouring them. Discoloured spinach would mean that the right kind of cooking technique has not been employed.

Plate Selection

Plates come in many shapes, sizes, patterns, and colours. The primary role of the plate is to serve food to the guest. It is very important to choose the right type of plate for the right type of food. White is the most preferred colour among chefs as it does not mask the colours of the food.

When it comes to choosing the plate, modern chefs are definitely more creative than their yesteryear counterparts. Apart from porcelain or bone china crockery, they now use wooden boards, textured glass, granite slabs, and even stoneware. In India, it has been a common practice to present food in earthenware dishes to add the rustic touch to traditional presentations. Whatever may be the type of plate, certain factors such as the following should always be kept in mind while presenting the food.

- The most appropriately sized and designed plates should be used to enhance food presentation and provide a balance of plated ingredients. The amount of food placed on a plate also affects the overall look. If the plate is too small, the amount of food placed on it will look messy. On the other hand, an oversized plate will make even substantial portions appear small. However, in many fine dining restaurants, the concept is slightly different, which we will discuss later in the chapter.
- The right plate should be chosen for right kind of food. For example, pasta cannot be served in a flat plate; rather a deep plate called pasta bowl or plate would be advisable because one wants the sauce to stay along with pasta and not fall off the plate. Similarly, serving a steak in a pasta plate would be uncomfortable for the guest to eat as one has to

use knife and fork to eat and due to the raised edges of pasta plate, it becomes difficult to use knife and fork.

- Coloured plates should be carefully chosen. Dark coloured plates should be used for light coloured foods and vice versa.
- Plates of different shapes, such as rectangles, squares, and other geometrical designs, should be chosen to present food on the plate. The arrangement of the food will however differ when the shape of the plate is used. Also, the guest's convenience should be given prime importance when presenting food in rectangular plates. Remember that food is plated to be eaten and not always for taking photographs.

Arranging Food

Arrangement of food is one of the most important aspects of plate presentation. Gone are the days when the food was presented in the classical fashion of the main ingredient at 2 o'clock position, vegetables at 6 o'clock, and sauces and starch at 11 o'clock position of the plate. These days the stress is on heights and arranging the food together as a unity. This not only helps in retaining the temperature of the food, but gives an added dimension, thereby making the food look attractive.

The ingredients placed on the plate should complement each other as a unified dish, rather than each component being placed on the plate apart from each other. The arrangement should be simple and should not take too much time, as the food will become cold before it reaches guests. It is important for the food to taste as good as the presentation itself. The following points should be kept in mind while arranging food.

- *Food items should be kept close to each other in the centre of the plate.* These should be arranged in such a manner that it givers a heightened appearance. For instance, refer the two presentations in Fig. 8.1 and decide which looks more appetizing and why.

  Indeed, the plate in Fig. 8.1(a) looks more sumptuous because of the unity of ingredients, balance of colours, and the heightened or heaped appearance of the food. The plate in Fig. 8.1(b) looks as if someone has already started eating the food.

- *Do not overcrowd the plate.* The basic essence of good food presentation is to keep it simple with a maximum of three to four components on a plate. Too much of food on

(a)   (b)

Fig. 8.1 Plate presentation

plate gives a cluttered appearance and makes it looks overworked and messy. Put only what is required on the plate. If salad has to be presented and a plate is already full, serve it separately in a bowl or use a bigger plate instead.

- *Use coloured spice powders and dried vegetable powders, also known as dusts, to break monotony.* Sometimes spice powders or vegetable powders, such as olive dust, tomato dust, and dried herbs dust, can be sprinkled around on the plate to break the monotony of the empty white plate areas. For dessert plates, you can sprinkle cocoa or powdered sugar. Care has to be taken while doing this as adding too much of powder can be considered as over garnishing and can give the plate an untidy look.
- *It is important to establish a focal point on the plate.* A focal point would be the area, where the eye is immediately drawn and this is where the main ingredient is placed on the plate. For instance, if the guest has ordered grilled chicken, then that should be the focal point and other entire accompaniments, such as vegetables and sauces, should flow out from it. The focal point is the centre of attraction and should be larger than the accompaniments. Do not let the main item get eclipsed by excessive garnish and huge portions of vegetable and starch items. Where there is no main item, as in some vegetable plates, strive for a logical balance of portions.
- *Before the food is placed, add an extra shine by sprinkling finely chopped herbs, nuts, or spices on the plate.*
- *Do not leave too much space between the items while arranging the food.* You need not arrange all the items in the centre which would make it look overcrowded or messy. Place the main dish at the front of the plate. If you have different sizes of food items, place the tallest item at the back and follow it in a descending way.

> **CHEF'S TIP**
> Avoid serving salads on the meat or any hot item. A salad is meant to be cold; if placed on a hot dish, it will not only mask the colour of the main ingredient but will also wilt and become soggy.

MERGING OF FLAVOURS, SHAPES, AND TEXTURES ON THE PLATE

Food presentation is not only about making the food look attractive on the plate. The food presented well should also taste well. When the food comes well presented, it increases the expectations of the guest, therefore, it is important to look into finer details such as balance of textures, temperatures of the food, colours, and the other fine aspects such as the types and consistency of accompanying sauce, deciding whether the rice would be served on the plate or separately, the number of accompaniments, etc.

It is important that the flavours be presented and combined in such a way that they complement each other. Let us talk about these aspects in detail.

Flavours

A right balance of flavours is very essential for the plate. A complete plate must comprise a main item which can be a meat, vegetable preparation, or starch, accompanied with a sauce and a suitable garnish. With the world coming closer, various types of ingredients are available in most of the markets. Today, chefs have a wider range of ingredients to choose from compared to a decade ago, when one had to make do with limited items that were available locally. It is important to choose the flavours in such a manner that they do not clash with each other. Avoid creating a contrast of too many flavours on the same plate. It is a good idea to work with a maximum of three to four flavours in a dish at one time.

There is a favourite saying 'what grows together, goes together'. It is important to use ingredients that grow in the same season. They complement each other's flavours and provide the required nutrition that is needed by the body in that climate and season.

Shapes

Another food presentation tip is to plan for a variety of shapes and forms as well as of colours. One should aim at serving food of different shapes on the plate. For example, you probably do not want to serve Brussels sprouts with meatballs and new potatoes. Green beans and whipped potatoes might be better choices for accompaniments. Cutting vegetables into different shapes gives you great flexibility to present on a plate. For example, carrots, which can be cut into dice, rounds, or sticks, can be adapted to nearly any plate.

Textures

Though not usually included in food presentation tip lists because they are not strictly visual considerations, textures are as important in plating as in menu planning. Good balance requires a variety of textures on the plate. Perhaps the most common error is serving too many soft or pureed foods, such as salmon pâté with whipped potatoes and pureed squash. Instead serve pâté with a crunchy salad or serve a grilled salmon steak with mashed potatoes.

EMERGING TRENDS IN FOOD PRESENTATIONS

Today people have many dining options. Also, food plays an important part on any occasion. In order to make dining a memorable experience for the guests, chefs have started presenting their food in unique ways so as to attract guests and position themselves on top of business. In the last two decades, a new profession called 'food stylist' has come into fashion. These are people who specialize in the art of presenting food in the most attractive manner that can be used in advertisements or even culinary books and covers of magazines. Many a time these presentations do not always use real ingredients and the food is barely cooked to retain the colours and shape. In this chapter, however, we will not discuss this aspect of food presentation and our focus will be on emerging trends in plating food for the guests. Nowadays, chefs have adopted a different approach towards classical cuisine. The methods of cooking, however, remain the same, but the way the food is combined on a plate makes it unique and different. The concept of serving meat with vegetables and starch is still a common practice but the way it is done these days is quite spectacular.

In Chapter 3, we discussed modern presentations of various appetizers. The same holds true for all the other courses also. You can refer Table 3.11 for other kinds of plates and platters used for presenting food.

There was a time when plates were classified on the basis of their size and each plate was meant to be used for a particular course of the meal. For example, a 6-inch plate was used as a side plate, an 8-inch plate for a salad, 10-inch plate was for dessert, 12-inch plate for used for the main course. The concept is quite different now. Chefs have started using large plates of various shapes and sizes to present their food. Table 8.1 describes various types of modern presentation, which increases your understanding on the modern concepts of plated food.

Table 8.1 Modern ways of plate presentation (see also Plate 9)

Description	Photograph
The food in the first picture is presented on a long rectangular plate. When the food is presented on such plates, it is important to present it in a linear fashion to flow with the symmetry of the plate. If the food is presented in the centre, it would not be pleasing to the eye. The rectangular plates also have an extra advantage of presenting various types of components on the same plate. This is usually known as *trio*. In this presentation technique, food can be presented in three different forms. For example, a small portion of tomato soup in a square bowl, a salad of yellow tomatoes, and pickled cherry tomatoes would be known as *trio* of tomatoes or simply tomatoes served in three ways. This is quite a unique concept and many chefs present small portions of many dishes on the same plate to give a more varied choice to the guest.	 
In this presentation, the chef has used an unusual shape of a plate that has a round deep bowl and large shoulders. This plate can be used for presenting soups, pastas, and also small portions of meat, vegetables, or seafood decorated like a masterpiece. The empty white spaces on the large plate makes the dish look neat and less cluttered.	
In this presentation, the chef has used a rectangular plate with wavy borders to present a dish. Geometrical shapes are very common these days and the focus is on the arrangement of food in linear fashion on the plate. Although the shape of the food is in spheres, which is to break the monotony of square shape, it is still presented in straight lines to bring about the linear effect.	

(Contd)

Table 8.1 (Contd)

Description	Photograph
Another presentation is done in a deep bowl that is tilted towards one side. This dish can be used for serving any kind of course. In the first picture, a dessert is presented and in the second picture, a small portion of salad is presented to enhance the overall appeal of the food. In the first dish, the prawns are layered with avocadoes and made to stand like a tower. When the guest starts eating, this tower will collapse but it will stay in the bowl and will still be easy for the guest to eat.	
In these pictures, there are more unusual shapes of plates in two different colours as well. Due to the constant development in the field of food presentation, companies have also started making plates and platters with unique designs that can be used both for à la carte presentations as well as buffets. Apart from ceramics, chefs use slabs of granite, wood, and even glass tiles and slabs to present food. Individual dishes presented on Chinese soup spoons or in small glasses look very pretty on a plate.	
Chefs extensively use glass plates and platters to present food, especially cold salads and sushi and sashimi. These plates can be clear glass or even frosted in appearance. Hot food is seldom presented on glass plates.	
New techniques for presenting food are also becoming common. One such equipment called foamer (refer Fig. 3.2, Chapter 3) is used for transforming liquids into hot or cold mousse that be accompanied with a dish to break the texture and also to add an aspect of modernity to the dish.	

(Contd)

Table 8.1 (Contd)

Description	Photograph
A unique way of presenting food that is required to be smoked is to serve it infused with smoke. Modern equipment as shown are available that can induce smoke into the dish. In the first photograph, a steak is being smoked under glass cover and is served to the guest. The steward removes the glass cover in front of the guest and allows him/her to smell the flavour of the smoke. Various kinds of dry herbs, spice and wood like cherry, hickory, and apple wood is commonly used for smoking.	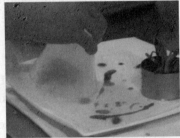
Another interesting way of presenting food is to serve the dish in a deconstructed manner. In this presentation, the ingredients are placed differently and individually garnished on the plate. When the guest mixes the items, it turns into a classical dish. For example, imagine a classical green salad with goat cheese. In the photograph, this salad has being served as individual components but cooked and processed, so that when they are combined, they form the classical salad, but even if not combined, they can still be eaten as individual component. The salad leaves are rolled in an edible rice paper and dressed with vinaigrette. The goat cheese is baked separately to get the baked effect and the dressing is served in a small glass, along with a garnish of olive paste. The plate has been divided with help of reduce balsamic glaze. This kind of presentation is also gaining popularity these days.	

Every chef wants to showcase his/her local or mother cuisine in the most fashionable way so as to enhance its global appeal and acceptability. Indian food in many restaurants in London and various European countries is presented in a modern plated form ensuring that the authentic tastes and flavours are not compromised with. The Japanese have always excelled in the art of presenting their food. Japanese food presentations are most intricate in the world as also their skilful carved garnishes and accompaniments.

There is no end to creativity, but as professional chefs, it is important to keep the following key points in mind, while presenting food on a plate.

Keep it clean and simple   Clean plates look more attractive. Decide your presentations in advance, draw or sketch them if you have to. Moving the food around, once it has been placed on plate, will make the plate look messy and unclean.

Keep it short   The presentations should not be too elaborate or else one would spend too much time plating the food and this can compromise on the temperature of the food. Also too much of handling of food loses its freshness.

BUFF Always remember BUFF (balance, unity, focus, and flow) when presenting food on a plate. We have already discussed these elements. The flow really depends upon the shape of the plate. The food would look more appealing in a linear flow on rectangular plates and on round plates, present the food in a round or circular fashion. Start presenting the food from the centre and let it flow out in a symmetrical fashion.

Everything edible Everything that is put on plate should be edible. Do not garnish food with large sprigs of herbs that cannot be eaten raw. Sometimes rosemary herb is deep-fried and salted to make it edible.

Add height Food presented in heights is very attractive. Use starch and vegetables as a base to provide height. One can also use metal rings of different shapes to arrange food on a plate. Putting a salad in a metal ring and lifting it off the plate gives an unusual height to the dish. Heights can also be given by placing the meat in an upright fashion leaning against some starch or vegetables. Build the food up in height starting from the front. The height of the dish should increase from front to back.

Use odd numbers Use odd numbers of vegetables, meat, or any ingredient on a plate. Even numbers do not look as good and appealing to the eye as the odd numbers do.

Do not clutter the plate Leave empty spaces on the plate when presenting the food. It not only makes the food look clean but also adds an appeal to the plate. Present food in the centre and put nothing on the rim as the steward would be holding the plate and serving to the guest.

SUMMARY

It is an age-old saying that we always eat with our eyes first. It is for this reason that the food is presented beautifully and artistically in hotels, restaurants, and even in take away eateries. Even when we organize parties at home we like to adorn our dining tables with the best of linens, candles, and make an extra effort to decorate and garnish the food we intend to serve—what we do not do on a daily basis. Since in hotels, we get guests everyday and most of them go there to celebrate an occasion or a special day, it is important that the food is presented with flair and creativity.

In this chapter, we discussed the art of presenting food on a plate. There are, however, no rules behind presenting food, but it is our gut feeling which indicates that the food is appealing. Over the years, food presentations have undergone a lot of changes. The concept of plate presentations is understood to have been introduced with the French classical cuisine in the olden days. According to it, the plate was viewed like a clock with the meat placed at 2 o'clock position, the starch at 11 o'clock, and vegetables at 6 o'clock position. This holds true till date for many plates. Chefs have, however, over the years, been experimenting with new forms of presentations. The latest is combining more than one food item on a plate and creating a focal point on which the main dish is placed, and everything else is arranged symmetrically around it or flows from it in a bid to complement the dish.

One has to strike a balance between various elements on a plate and the plate itself. It is the balance with regard to colours, textures, flavours on a plate, and how each element should complement each other in a plate presentation that counts more than simply making the best tasting food look appealing on the plate. In this chapter, we discussed each aspect of plate presentation such as colour, flavour, and texture. We discussed plated presentations in two other chapters of this book: Chapter 3 on appetizers and garnishes and Chapter 13 on desserts. In all these chapters, you must have noticed that various types of plates and equipment are used nowadays to enhance the presentation of the food on plate.

We also discussed emerging trends in food presentation and understood the philosophy and logic behind each presentation along with the salient features that need to be kept in mind when presenting food on a plate.

KEY TERMS

Avocado It is a fruit used as a vegetable in South American countries.

Balsamic It is brown-coloured vinegar from Italy.

Brussels sprouts These are small round vegetables that look like mini cabbage.

Chlorophyll It is the green-coloured pigment found in plants. When green leafy vegetables are cooked in acidic medium, it turns grey.

Crackers These are crisp biscuits or bread used as a garnish.

Fine dining It is a term used for restaurants that serve pre-plated food with exotic ingredients paired with wine.

Foamer It is a small equipment used for incorporating air into liquids.

Food stylist It is a term used for professionals who decorate plates for food photography.

Jacket potato A potato roasted in its skin and served with a slit on top garnished with melted butter and sour cream is called jacket potato.

Jus It is a term for meat juices reduced to form a sauce.

Mashed potato These are boiled and pureed potatoes cooked with cream and butter.

Mozzarella It is a fresh Italian stringy cheese.

Olive dust It is a term for powdered dried olive.

Salmon pate It is a dish made from paste of salmon that can be poached or smoked.

Sashimi This is sliced raw fish in Japanese cuisine.

Sushi It is a Japanese dish of rice and fish presented in different shapes.

Trio It is a style of presenting three different types of food on a plate with individual garnishes and sauces.

Velouté sauce It is a classical French sauce prepared with chicken stock.

Vinaigrette It is a salad dressing made with oil and vinegar.

CONCEPT REVIEW QUESTIONS

1. What do you understand by plated food and why is it done?
2. What role does colour play in plating the food?
3. How would you enhance the brown tones of a food on a plate?
4. What factors would you keep in mind while garnishing the food?
5. What do you mean by non-functional garnish?
6. How does the cooking method influence the presentation of a dish?
7. What factors would you keep in mind while selecting a plate for presentation?
8. Mention at least three materials that can be used for presenting food.
9. Why is the size of plate important with relation to food?
10. What should you consider before choosing the colour of a plate?
11. What key points would you keep in mind while arranging food on a plate?
12. Describe the focal point in a plate presentation and how it is beneficial.
13. How do shapes and texture of the food impact on food presentation?
14. Describe the emerging trends of food presentation.
15. Name various kinds of equipment used in food presentations.
16. What do you understand by deconstructed approach to plate presentation?
17. What is a *trio*? How is it used?
18. What would you keep in mind while presenting food on round and rectangular plates?
19. What does BUFF stand for?
20. Describe at least five crucial points that you would keep in mind while plating the food.

PROJECT WORK

1. In groups of five, undertake a market survey of hotels and speciality restaurants that specialize in serving plated food? Record your observations with regard to the choice of plates, colour combinations, components on plate and accompaniments and share with other groups.

2. In groups of five, plan a three-course menu and present it on various kinds of plates. Let the other groups critique the presentations. Record the suggestions and share in the class.

3. In groups of five each, research the different types of plates and platters and other materials that can be used for enhancing food presentations and make a PowerPoint presentation of the same and share with other groups in the class.

CHAPTER 9

CONCEPT OF HEALTH FOOD

Learning Objectives

After reading this chapter, you should be able to
- understand the basic concept of healthy cooking
- appreciate the types of nutrients available in diet and their applications
- analyse the techniques used in creating healthy preparations
- claim an insight into basic nutrients such as carbohydrates, protein, fats, vitamins and minerals, and their sources and uses in food
- understand the different types of phytochemicals and antioxidants in food sources
- appreciate the use of nutritional software in preparing nutritional analysis of menus
- claim an insight into food pyramid and dietary requirements of an healthy individual

INTRODUCTION

The term SPA is very common these days, especially in the hospitality industry. It is an acronym for *salus par aquam*, a Latin word meaning health from water. Spa is a section in a hotel that deals with health and aims at rejuvenating the body. The increasing demands for healthy lifestyle and eating habits have inspired hotels across the world to focus on health and fitness of the guests. Some finest resorts in the world specialize in this field and have done good business by focusing on health as their unique selling proposition (USP). This has encouraged chefs to prepare food to meet the needs of such guests. Exercise alone cannot help keep an individual healthy. It has to be complemented with healthy eating and a balanced nutritional diet. The basic necessity of food is to provide health and nutrition but with the kind of modern sedentary lifestyles coupled with poor eating habits, food has become a major source of diseases and malnutrition. There is thus, a great need to educate people about the importance of a balanced diet and the role played by various nutrients in the basic metabolism of our body. In the past, Indians were very focused on healthy eating. There are ancient texts, such as *Charaka Samhita* written by sage Atreya Purnarvasu several thousand years ago, which stress on the effect of healthy eating and good lifestyle that eventually leads to a healthy life.

Eating healthy is a broader term used for intake of balanced food. The word diet, which is often used in the context of eating has various meanings. Simply speaking, it refers to intake of food and water for a normal living. The term diet is also used for describing the food items that are prescribed to a person for a specific purpose or for a certain period of time. It is also used to describe the food being taken by a person who is trying to shed some extra weight or gain some weight. Such a person is said to be on a diet or is 'dieting'. A diet is prescribed by nutritionists or dieticians, who determine the foods that need to be consumed in the correct proportions. A poor diet refers to food that lacks nutritional value and which is not in balance with regard to the nutritional elements.

In this chapter, we will discuss the various kinds of nutrients and elements of food that are required in a healthy diet. We will also discuss the importance of balanced nutrition and obtain an insight into various kinds of nutritional software that can help chefs determine the nutritional value of specific food items. We will also discuss various methods of cooking that can be effectively used for preparing dishes for a healthy menu.

A healthy menu should not be confused with hospital food. In this chapter, we are referring to healthy food and not lean cuisine. Food in hospitals is prepared on certain dietary guidelines. For example, a patient suffering from glycaemia will be on a no-sugar diet and a patient suffering from heart disease would be on a low- or no-oil diet. A healthy menu stresses on the balance of fats, carbohydrates, and proteins, as all of these are essential for a healthy body. Before we get into the intricacies of healthy cooking, let us understand the nutrients that make up food from the flow chart depicted in Fig. 9.1.

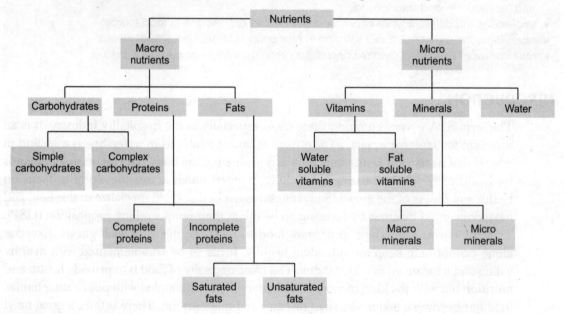

Fig. 9.1 Types of nutrients

TYPES OF NUTRIENTS

Nutrients are compounds essential for the growth and basic metabolism of our body. They are present in the food we eat. Nutritionists classify nutrients into two major types: essential and non-essential. These terms do not mean that one is less important than the other. It only means that essential nutrients are ones that cannot be manufactured or produced by the body itself. For example, cholesterol performs several important functions in the body that regulate our nervous system and other metabolic activities, but since the body has the ability to produce cholesterol, it is considered to be a non-essential nutrient.

The essential nutrients are further classified into macro and micro nutrients. Let us discuss these nutrients and their significance to enhance our understanding as future chefs and help in the creation of balanced and healthy menus for the discerning customer.

Macro Nutrients

Macro nutrients, as their name suggests, are required in large quantities by our body. These provide energy or calories for the body to function efficiently in order to perform daily activities. These are of three types namely carbohydrates, proteins, and fats. This category of nutrients is also known as *nutritive nutrients*.

Carbohydrates

Carbohydrates provide fuel to the body. This category of nutrients are also called short term fuels as they are used directly by cells for providing energy, specially the nervous system and regulation of red blood cells. Carbohydrates are not necessarily building blocks of other molecules, and the body can mobilize its own energy from fats and proteins. If we take less amounts of carbohydrates, then our body will start using proteins as fuel which is less efficient than carbohydrates. On digestion, carbohydrates break down into sugars that can be easily absorbed by the body and thus provide energy for doing work (such as movement of muscles) and also helps to burn the fat efficiently. Carbohydrates are composed of sugar molecules. When only one or two molecules of sugar are present in a compound, then they are known as *simple carbohydrates* or *monosaccharides* (one molecule) and *disaccharides* (two molecules). Simple carbohydrates are easy to digest and are commonly found in fruits, juices, refined sugars, refined flour, and dairy products. These carbohydrates are often low in fibre.

Complex carbohydrates, on the other hand, contain chains of sugar molecules and are known as *polysaccharides*. Complex carbohydrates take more time to digest as first they have to be broken down into simple sugars, which can be then absorbed by the body to release energy. Since they take longer to digest, hence they provide a feeling of satiety and fullness. Complex carbohydrates are found in natural plants such as whole grain cereals, nuts, and vegetables. Upon food digestion, carbohydrates are broken down into glucose, which is reflected as sugar levels in blood. When the levels of glucose increase in the blood, a hormone called *insulin* is secreted by the pancreas that enables the glucose to be absorbed by the cells either for producing energy directly or for being stored in the form of glycogen in liver and muscle cells.

Fibre Another term commonly associated with carbohydrates is fibre. *Fibre* is a form of carbohydrate that is not digestible and therefore, is non-nutritive. It is a combination of many compounds. Different types of food contain different levels of fibre. Since fibre is not digested, it forms the bulk of the diet, thereby giving us the feeling of fullness and zero calories. There are two types of fibres: soluble and non-soluble.

Soluble fibres These dissolve in water and help to regulate many functions in the body. They help to reduce cholesterol levels in the blood, by binding with them in the intestinal tract. Foods such as beans, oats, barley, and fruits are good sources of soluble fibre.

Non-soluble fibres These do not dissolve in water. They absorb water and provide bulk in the diet. Insoluble fibres help clear our intestinal tract and prevent our body from many types of diseases, especially colon cancer. Wheat bran, wholegrain flours, etc. are good sources of non-soluble fibres.

Each gram of carbohydrate gives 4 kcal of energy. It is recommended that 40–55 per cent of energy or calories requirement of an adult human being should be sourced from carbohydrates.

Proteins

Proteins are also called the building blocks of the body. They help in overall growth of the living organisms. It repairs damaged cells and tissues. Proteins are also responsible for carrying oxygen to other parts of the body. In the absence of carbohydrates, proteins also can be used up as the fuel to provide energy.

Proteins are made up of complex compounds known as *amino acids*. A human cell contains 20 types of amino acids. Out of these, eight are essential, which means that they cannot be produced by the body. But when these are supplied to the body, then it has the capability to produce the remaining 12. Many foods contain all eight amino acids that are required by the body and such proteins are known as *complete proteins*. Meat, poultry, eggs, fish, and other animal sources contain all eight types of amino acids and are therefore, known as complete proteins. Plant-based proteins often need to be combined with other foods to result in complete proteins. Rice, lentils, hummus, *pita*, etc. are all examples of complete proteins diet. Some plant sources such as *amaranth*, quinoa seeds, and soy are said to contain all essential amino acids and hence considered complete proteins (refer Fig. 9.2).

It is recommended that 25–30 per cent of the energy requirement should come from proteins. Each gram of proteins gives 4 kcal energy. Excess of proteins in diet can cause disorders such as gout. It is a condition wherein uric acid increases in the body and its crystals get deposited on the joints of the bone causing discomfort and pain.

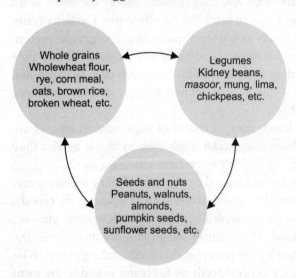

Fig. 9.2 Combinations of complete proteins

Fats

Fats are one of the most essential nutrients required by the body, but when talking about healthy cooking, these are one of the most ignored nutrients. Many people think that healthy cooking means using less fat in the diet. However, this is not at all true and nutritional experts advise that at least 20–30 per cent of energy requirement should be sourced from fats. Each gram of fat provides the highest amount of calories as compared to carbohydrates and proteins. One gram of fat gives 9 kcal of energy and that is why it is important to use the right types of fats in the diet. Apart from protecting the vital organs by surrounding them, fat plays another pivotal role in providing nourishment to the body. It is because of the fat that body is enable to assimilate and absorb the fat-soluble vitamins A and D. Too much of fat or wrong type of fat can, however, lead to coronary heart ailments and other disorders such as obesity.

Fatty acids Just like amino acids are the building blocks of a protein molecule, fatty acids are the building blocks of a fat molecule. Each molecule of a fatty acid consists of atoms of carbon, hydrogen, and oxygen bonded together. It is the bonded structure of the fatty acid that determines whether a fat is saturated, monounsaturated, or polyunsaturated. The number of bonds available for a hydrogen atom to bond with a carbon atom determines its saturation levels. If there are no bonds available, then the fat molecule is said to be saturated and if there are at least two slots available for the bonding, then the molecule is called monounsaturated fatty acid (MUFA) and if more that two slots are available, then the fat molecule is referred to as polyunsaturated fatty acid (PUFA).

The MUFA and PUFA fats are considered healthy to eat, as they increase the good cholesterol in our body. Saturated fats, on the other hand, increase the levels of bad cholesterol, thereby causing risk of coronary heart ailments. Cooking oils made from olives, mustard, canola, pumpkin seed oil, and some nuts such as Brazil nut oil, cashew nut oil, and avocado oil are rich sources of MUFA. Cooking oils made from safflower, corn, sunflower seeds, soyabean and from Omega 3 and Omega 6 fatty acids are polyunsaturated in nature. Unsaturated fats are liquid at room temperature while saturated fats are solid. Fats such as ghee, butter including oils such as coconut and palm oil are saturated fatty acids. At this point, it is also important to understand *trans fats*.

Trans fats These fats are formed when a vegetable oil or unsaturated oil is artificially bonded with other hydrogen atoms in a process known as hydrogenation. Hydrogenated vegetable oils, such as margarine and shortening, are known as trans fats. Such fats have a high smoke point and shelf life and are ideal for baking and deep frying for commercial purpose and hence are popular. While planning health menus, it is important not to choose trans fats in the diet as they not only increase the bad cholesterol in the body but also decrease the good cholesterol, thereby making it even worse for the heart. Table 9.1 categorizes the various kinds of fats along with their sources and effects.

Table 9.1 Types of fat, their sources and effects

Type of fat	Main source	State at room temperature	Effects
Monounsaturated	Mustard oil, canola oil, groundnut oil, almond oil, walnut oil, avocado oil	Liquid	Lowers bad cholesterol and increases good cholesterol
Polyunsaturated	Corn oil, soybean oil, safflower, cottonseed oil, fish oils, flax oil	Liquid	Lowers bad cholesterol and increases good cholesterol
Saturated	Whole milk, butter, cheese, *desi ghee*, coconut oil, cocoa fat	Solid	Raises both good and bad cholesterol
Trans fat	Margarine, vegetable shortening	Solid or semi-solid	Raises bad cholesterol and lowers good cholesterol

Micro Nutrients

Micro nutrients are also known as *non-nutritive nutrients*. This, however, does not mean that they are less important to the body. The name only reflects that unlike macro nutrients, these nutrients do not give or provide calories or energy to the body. On the contrary, these are essential nutrients and are required for many metabolic functions such as fighting diseases and increasing our ability to repair the body. Nutrients such as vitamins, minerals, and water fall this category.

Vitamins

Vitamins are organic compounds present in food that are needed in minute quantities for normal growth and activity. These are of two types:

Water soluble These are vitamins that are soluble in water and are transported through the bloodstream in the body. These include vitamin B complex (thiamine, riboflavin, niacin, folacin, biotin, pantothenic acid, and B6), vitamin B12, and vitamin C or ascorbic acid. Vitamin B complex compounds are found in grains, legumes, various vegetables and meat of various animals. Vitamin B12 is found only in animal foods. Water-soluble vitamins help in building up the nervous system and blood formation. Vitamin C is commonly found in fruits and vegetables. Citrus fruits, such as oranges, are considered to be rich in Vitamin C. Other rich sources of Vitamin C include broccoli, bell pepper, strawberries, and guava. Vitamin C helps the body to produce a substance called *collagen* that is responsible for binding the muscles and bones together. Vitamin C particularly boosts up the immune system and increases body resistance to heart diseases and various kinds of cancer.

From a chef's point of view, it is important to treat food in the most appropriate manner as the water soluble vitamins can easily be destroyed through the following:

- *Exposure* Water soluble vitamins can be lost if the foods are peeled, cut, and stored uncovered for long time
- *Heat* Too much of heat can also destroy these vitamins. It is therefore advisable to keep the cooking time as less as possible

- *Water* Since this vitamin is water soluble, it should not be stored in water or cooked in water for too long. For health reasons, it is better to poach such foods in oil as the vitamins will not be leeched out. Cook such foods by dry cooking methods such as roasting or grilling.

Fat-soluble vitamins Vitamins A, D, E, and K are soluble in fat and are absorbed by the body through fat. These vitamins are far more stable than their water-soluble counterparts as they do not get destroyed by factors such as heat, air, water, etc. Each of these vitamins is present in different sources.

Vitamin A It is commonly found in meat such as beef and chicken liver. Interestingly, plant sources do not contain vitamin A, but plants such as carrots and tomatoes contain compounds that help the body to produce its own vitamin A.

Vitamin D It is very important for bone formation in the body. Its deficiency can cause arched bones also known as rickets. Vitamin D is abundantly available in egg yolk, fish liver oils, and in some cereals and milk. It is also produced by the skin when exposed to sunlight. The cholesterol in the body helps in making vitamin D in presence of sunlight.

Vitamin E It is particularly helpful in cell protection, as it contains antioxidant properties that prevent the cells from the damage of reactive oxygen ions or free radicals that are formed as a by-product of fat metabolism. It is found in whole grains and nuts.

Vitamin K It is particularly responsible for the clotting of blood, and also produces proteins that are important for strong bones. Dark leafy green vegetables are rich source of vitamin K. This vitamin is also produced by the bacteria present in the intestine.

Minerals

Minerals are inorganic substances that are required by the body in very small quantities to carry out several functions such as regulating hormones, building strong bones, regulating blood pressure, etc. Minerals are again divided into macro and micro as discussed in case of nutrients. Minerals such as calcium, phosphorous, sodium, magnesium, and phosphorous are considered to be macro as they are required in large quantities. Many of these minerals are obtained from fruits, vegetables, and animal sources, yet some are supplied externally by elements such as common salt (sodium) and mineral supplements. Foods such as milk and dairy products and fruits such as apples are rich sources of calcium. The sodium intake of a healthy adult should not include more than 2,400 mg of salt on a daily basis.

Phytochemicals and Antioxidants

Phytochemicals are relatively new additions to nutritional science. Research has shown that these organic compounds present in various foods are directly responsible for fighting cancer. They are present in a range of fruits, especially berries, oranges, strawberries, vegetables, legumes, grains, and nuts. There are many types of phytochemicals that can be present in a single ingredient. For example, tomato may contain as many as 100 different types of phytochemicals.

Antioxidants are sub-category of phytochemicals. When a metabolic process happens in a body, not all oxygen is used up efficiently. Some free oxygen molecules move freely in the body, which can often damage some cells. Such oxygen molecules are known as free radicals. Antioxidants are the compounds that can combine with such free radicals and flush them out of the system. Antioxidants are present in abundance in green leafy vegetables and fruits. It is believed that foods rich in phytochemicals and antioxidants help the body fight cancer and delay the ageing process.

BALANCED DIET AND NUTRITIONAL ANALYSIS

Now that we have gathered basic information on the nutritional aspects of food, let us discuss various factors that need to be considered while cooking food for a 'balanced and healthy' diet. Eating healthy is not only a lifestyle, but an attitude. It is important that our body gets a balanced diet, which is a proportionately adequate composition of carbohydrates, fats, proteins, and various kinds of vitamins and minerals. The recommended adequate proportion of various macro and micro nutrients of a healthy menu are mentioned in Table 9.2.

There are, however, no particular value requirements for vitamins and minerals as they are required in very small quantities. It is also important to follow the food pyramid as shown in Fig. 9.3, which throws light on the recommended daily, weekly, and monthly consumption of various kinds of food products to keep us in good shape and health.

The broader base of the pyramid indicates that your diet should comprise bulk of these items and as the pyramid becomes narrower at the tip, the food indicated therein should be consumed accordingly.

This is a broad indication of a balanced meal but there are many kinds of nutritional softwares that can give you the exact count of calories and nutrients which an individual should consume. Many hospitals and food packaging industries use such software wherein the recipe is fed into the system and it in turn, calculates the various kinds of components. The recipes are also altered and fine-tuned to obtain the required nutritional components. One such sample of calculated nutritional analysis from a software called 'mastercook' is depicted in Exhibit 9.1. It is for a menu comprising coffee, main course, and a dessert that is mentioned at the top right-hand corner of the screen. The top left-hand corner mentions the total calories provided by the menu. Here we can see that the menu is balanced in terms of percentages from carbohydrates, proteins, and fats (refer Table 9.3). All the other nutrients, such as description of fats, cholesterol, and various vitamins and minerals, are listed in the middle part of the screen under the heading nutrition facts/per cent daily values per serving.

Table 9.2 Daily values required for a 200 kcal menu

Nutrients	Composition*
Carbohydrates	55–60%
Proteins	25–30%
Fats	20–30%
Sodium	1,500 mg
Fibre	12 g

*The values given herein are for a menu of calorific value 1,200 kcal

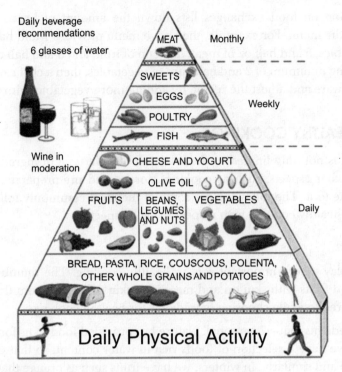

Daily beverage recommendations

6 glasses of water

Wine in moderation

Fig. 9.3 Food pyramid guide to healthy eating
Source: www.oldwayspt.org, accessed on 2 May 2011

Exhibit 9.1 Nutritional analysis of a menu

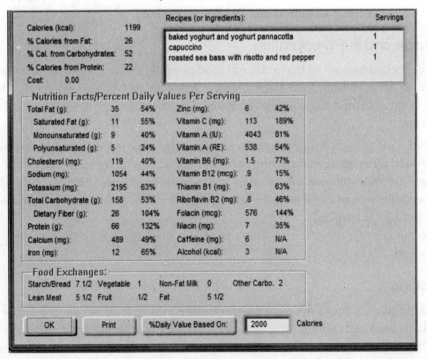

Calories (kcal):	1199
% Calories from Fat:	26
% Cal. from Carbohydrates:	52
% Calories from Protein:	22
Cost:	0.00

Recipes (or Ingredients): / Servings

Recipes (or Ingredients):	Servings
baked yoghurt and yoghurt pannacotta	1
capuccino	1
roasted sea bass with risotto and red pepper	1

Nutrition Facts/Percent Daily Values Per Serving

Total Fat (g):	35	54%	Zinc (mg):	6	42%
Saturated Fat (g):	11	55%	Vitamin C (mg):	113	189%
Monounsaturated (g):	9	40%	Vitamin A (IU):	4043	81%
Polyunsaturated (g):	5	24%	Vitamin A (RE):	538	54%
Cholesterol (mg):	119	40%	Vitamin B6 (mg):	1.5	77%
Sodium (mg):	1054	44%	Vitamin B12 (mcg):	.9	15%
Potassium (mg):	2195	63%	Thiamin B1 (mg):	.9	63%
Total Carbohydrate (g):	158	53%	Riboflavin B2 (mg):	.8	46%
Dietary Fiber (g):	26	104%	Folacin (mcg):	576	144%
Protein (g):	66	132%	Niacin (mg):	7	35%
Calcium (mg):	489	49%	Caffeine (mg):	6	N/A
Iron (mg):	12	65%	Alcohol (kcal):	3	N/A

Food Exchanges:

Starch/Bread	7 1/2	Vegetable	1	Non-Fat Milk	0	Other Carbo.	2
Lean Meat	5 1/2	Fruit	1/2	Fat	5 1/2		

| OK | Print | %Daily Value Based On: | 2000 | Calories |

The section on food exchanges lists down the amount of broad food categories provided by the menu. For example, the above menu provides 7 and half oz of starch, 1 cup of vegetables, 5 and half oz of meat, half cup of fruit, and 5 and half oz of fat. If a diet requires having minimum of 2 and half cups of vegetables, then a chef can know the same from this software and adjust the recipe by adding more vegetables into the dish.

PRINCIPLES OF HEALTHY COOKING

Healthy food is not only limited to the selection of right type of ingredients, but it also has various other aspects, such as cooking, storage and pre-preparation, utensils, etc., that contribute to it. The following are some of the most commonly followed principles pertaining to healthy cooking with respect to each aspect.

Ingredients

Ingredients play a very important role in healthy cooking. The thumb rule is to serve vegetables and fruits with skin on and meat with skin off. Apart from this, the following must be adhered to while choosing ingredients for healthy cooking.

- Select ingredients that are seasonal. Nature has provided food to us for each season. In summers, we have a selection of foods rich in water content, so that one does not get dehydrated and similarly, in winters, we have fruits such as orange that are rich source of vitamin C that help to combat ailments such as cough and cold.
- Use of fresh produce is advisable as compared to canned and tinned products as they contain preservatives and high sugar content.
- Always emphasize on organic ingredients that are free from pesticides and insecticides.
- Select lean meat and trim excess fats before cooking.

Storage and Pre-preparation

It is important to store all the processed food carefully and in proper storage temperatures, more so, while storing food for patients in hospitals and people on special diets. Let us look at some of the crucial points regarding the storage and processing of food for healthy cooking.

- Store food at right temperatures to conserve the nutrition value of the ingredients.
- Always serve meat without the skin and serve vegetables and fruits with skin on as they are more fibrous and contain more nutritional value. Some skins of fruits and vegetables are not edible and chefs need to make a choice to peel certain fruits and vegetables accordingly.
- Do not cut vegetables too small in size or else they will lose their nutritional value once cooked.

Cooking

Cooking plays a very important part in healthy foods. By now, we are aware of various kinds of cooking methods that are employed for preparing food in hotels and other catering establishments. While preparing healthy food, one must choose the most apt methods of cooking such as steaming, boiling, stewing, etc. The following points would be handy in this regard.

- Methods commonly applied for cooking healthy food are boiling, steaming, poaching, stewing, braising, roasting, grilling, baking, and sautéing. Avoid methods such as deep fat frying, as it increases the intake of fats and oil.
- Use fat commodities such as oil spray cans, are good substitutes, as they only coat the surface of the pans to give a browning texture to the food.
- Always choose unsaturated oils for cooking and change different sources of fats on a periodic basis.
- Cook food for as little time as possible to preserve its nutritional value.
- Use salt sparingly and instead try and use a wide range of seasonings to compensate the salt. It is also good to sprinkle salt when one finishes the dish instead of salting it while cooking. Though salt is present in most of the foods naturally, deficiency of this mineral is very rare in the human body. Excessive salt can aggravate hypertension in healthy individuals. Sodium is used in many forms in food such as:

  Sodium chloride—used as common salt

  Sodium benzoate—used as preservative in canned and tinned foods

  Monosodium glutamate—or MSG used as flavour enhancer in packed foods as well as commercially available Chinese food

  Sodium nitrate—used as preservative and colour enhancer in cured meat

  Sodium phosphate—used as an emulsifier and stabilizer in various products
- Incorporate contemporary sauces, such as fruit juices, salsas, and chutneys, to add interesting flavours to the dish.

Utensils

Selection of cooking utensils and equipment is also very important while preparing healthy food. One has to choose utensils that can give the same appearance to the food product without adding too much oil or fats. Some of these points are explained as follows.

Sautéing   While sautéing it is important to use non-stick or Teflon-coated pans which enable minimum application of oil.

Grilling   While grilling, use grills that can collect the juices that overflow from the meat and can be incorporated back into the sauces. Wire grills and charcoal grills are not suitable as the dripped moisture and juices from the meat are wasted.

Portion Size

Another aspect of eating healthy is to eat the right portion size or else the extra calories will get stored in the body in form of fats. Many diet consultants suggest eating small portion-sized meals more frequently. The United States Department of Agriculture (USDA) has recommended guidelines for portion sizes that are followed around the world. These are explained as follows.

- It is important to serve the right kind of portion size that has the optimum satiety value or else a person will keep feeling hungry even when he or she has been able to meet their dietary requirements.

- The right portion size would differ from food item to food item but a broad classification by USDA says that one should consume the portions shown in Table 9.3 on a daily basis. These are calculated on the basis of 2,000 kcal of diet.

Table 9.3 Portion sizes for various commodities

Commodity	Portion size (daily)
Whole grains	180 g
Vegetables	2 and half cups
Fruits	2 cups
Milk	3 cups
Meats and beans	150 g

Various health menus along with recipes are attached in the accompanying CD. The recipes are calculated on the basis of 1,200 kcal menu and comprise three courses, namely appetizer, main course, and a dessert. Nutritional analysis of each menu provided is also given and you will be able to see that though each dish by itself might not be able to meet the dietary guidelines as discussed in the chapter, but collectively as a menu, it meets all dietary requirements and thus, makes for a healthy menu. If you hand-picked an appetizer, a main course, and dessert from various menus and created a new menu, it might not be balanced in all respects and on contrary, one could cause serious misbalance in the nutrition as well. Therefore, it is important that help of nutritional software is taken to create a nutritional balance in the menu and then follow the recipes exactly to create them. One could use recipes from any region in the world and feed it in the software. The adjustments can then be made to the recipe to fine-tune it to meet the guidelines as mentioned in Table 9.2.

SUMMARY

This chapter is quite unique as it deals with the science of food, nutrition, and cooking to create a dish that is balanced in nature. The chapter disproves the theory 'lean cuisine is healthy cuisine', as it is understood that an adequate amount of fat is also required by the body to carry out vital functions. Nowadays, busy and sedentary lifestyles, have given rise to stressed lives and culture of unhealthy 'fast food' that is rich in carbohydrates and sugar. Such stressed and sedentary lifestyle with little or no exercise and odd eating habits have led to many health disorders across the world. It is very common to see young people suffering from food-related disorders and abnormalities such as obesity, diabetes and blood pressure, which were not as common in yesteryears when people used to eat healthy and also exercise a lot.

In this chapter, we constantly stressed upon a balanced menu, but before a menu is balanced, it is important to understand the various components that contribute to a balanced diet. We discussed two types of nutrients, micro (those required in less quantities such as vitamins and minerals) and macro (those required in large quantities by the body such as carbohydrates, proteins, and fats). We also discussed important terms such as essential and non-essential nutrients. Essential nutrients are so called because they cannot be produced by the body and need to be supplied through external food.

We discussed various components of food, such as carbohydrates, proteins, fats, vitamins, and minerals required by the body. Under each group, we studied about the various types of carbohydrates, proteins and most importantly, different types of fats such as MUFA and PUFA and their importance in a healthy diet. We also learnt about water-soluble and fat-soluble vitamins and understood the cooking principles that needed to be applied to them to preserve the nutritional value of food. We also came across the recent and most-talked about elements such as phytochemicals and antioxidants that help strengthen the immune system and increase resistance against various disorders including cancer.

We discussed the range of foods that are rich in such elements so that chefs can choose to use them while creating healthy menus for guests. We also discussed the food pyramid that can broadly guide a person to choose the kinds of food and the quantities that he/she should consume to remain fit and healthy.

In this chapter, we also focused on the role of various nutrition software that helps to calculate the amount of calories and nutrient content of a particular food item. Many dieticians in hospitals rely on such software to balance their menus. We also discussed the various principles involved in preparing healthy food ranging from selection of ingredients to cooking, and storage of food to service and portion sizes involved in healthy menus. The CD contains well-balanced menus with recipes and nutritional analysis of the same.

KEY TERMS

Amaranth   It is a green leafy vegetable.

Amino acids   These are the building blocks of proteins.

Charaka Samhita   It is an ancient text book on healthy eating written by sage Atreya Purnavarsu.

Cholesterol   It is a non-essential nutrient produced by the body and also supplied through animal fats.

Complete proteins   It is a term used for a food item containing all essential types of amino acids.

Essential nutrients   These are nutrients that cannot be produced or manufactured by the body.

Fibre   It is a type of carbohydrate that forms bulk of the diet.

Flax oil   It is oil obtained from seeds of the flax plant.

Glycaemia   It is the level of glucose in the blood stream.

Macro nutrients   These are nutrients that are required in large quantities by the body. For example, carbohydrates, proteins, and fats.

Micro nutrients   These are substances such as minerals, vitamins, phytochemicals, and antioxidants that are required in small quantities by the body.

MUFA   It is an acronym for monounsaturated fatty acid.

Non-essential nutrients   These are nutrients that can be produced by the body.

Non nutritive nutrients   These are nutrients that do not provide energy to the body. For example, vitamins and minerals.

Nutritive nutrients   These are nutrients that provide energy to the body. For example carbohydrates, proteins, and fats.

Omega 3   It is a type of fatty acid naturally found in oily fish.

PUFA   It is an acronym for polyunsaturated fatty acid.

Quinoa   These are protein-rich seeds of quinoa plant.

SPA   It is an acronym for *salus par aquam* which means healing/health through water.

Teflon coated   It is black coating of non-reactive organic compound teflon that provides non-stick ability to a utensil.

Trans fats   These are fats where the chemical structure gets altered by adding hydrogen or by heating a fat beyond smoke point.

CONCEPT REVIEW QUESTIONS

1. What do you understand by the word healthy cooking?
2. What do you mean by the term balance in the food?
3. Define nutrients and their types.
4. What do you understand by the term essential nutrients?
5. Define the term nutritive and non-nutritive nutrients.
6. What are carbohydrates and its types?
7. What is the difference between a monosaccharide and disaccharide?
8. Why do complex carbohydrates provide the feeling of satiety and fullness?
9. Define fibre. Name the various types of fibres and their function.
10. What are proteins made up of?
11. What do you understand by the term complete proteins?

12. Give at least three sources of plant-based proteins.
13. How much calories are provided by 1 g of carbohydrates, fats, and proteins, respectively?
14. Give at least five sources of complete proteins.
15. Why should one be careful about the type of fat in diet?
16. What is the difference between MUFA and PUFA oils?
17. What are trans fats and why are they unhealthy?
18. Give at least three sources of monounsaturated fatty acids and polyunsaturated fatty acids.
19. What are the effects of MUFA, PUFA, and saturated fats on the body?
20. Define vitamins and their types.
21. Name at least three types of water-soluble and fat-soluble vitamins.
22. Name three food sources that are rich in vitamin C.
23. What factors are responsible for destruction of water soluble vitamins?
24. Name at least three sources of vitamin D and vitamin E respectively.
25. Define phytochemicals and their role in a healthy menu.
26. What are antioxidants and how do they prevent ageing?
27. Give three food sources of phytochemicals and antioxidants.
28. What should be the approximate percentage of calories from carbohydrates, proteins, and fats in a balanced menu?
29. Describe a food pyramid with respect to a balanced diet.
30. Explain the principles involved in healthy cooking with regards to ingredients, storage, cooking, and serving.

PROJECT WORK

1. In groups of five, undertake a market survey of hotels and speciality restaurants that serve health food on their menu. Record your observations with regard to the choice of the menu, ingredients, equipment used in cooking, and portion-size and analyse the menu from health point of view. Share your learning with other groups.

2. From the menus provided in the CD, cook a menu and critique the same with regard to satiety value, presentation, textures, and flavours?

3. Using the knowledge from this chapter, prepare a menu with the guidelines mentioned in Table 9.2. You could take the help of nutrition software for the purpose.

CHAPTER 10

ORIENTAL CUISINES

Learning Objectives

After reading this chapter, you should be able to

- understand the basic concept of Oriental cuisine
- comprehend the different kinds of cuisines in China, Japan, and Thailand along with their variations
- identify various kinds of tools and equipment used for making food in China
- comprehend the use of uncommon ingredients in Japanese cooking
- examine the effects of demography on the cuisines of various countries in South-East Asia
- identify the ingredients of various countries and what makes them unique
- analyse the techniques used in the preparation of South-East Asian food
- identify various types of sushi and sashimi and what makes them unique
- identify a range of dim sums and their shapes
- appreciate the use of varied tools and equipment in Chinese, Japanese, and Thai cooking

INTRODUCTION

In the last few chapters, we discussed various international cuisines such as Western and European cuisines, as also the concept of Western plated and healthy food. Apart from these cuisines, food from the Orient or Eastern world, specially China, Japan, Thailand, Indonesia, Malaysia, Vietnam, and Philippines, is gaining international popularity and being featured on the menus of world-class hotels. In this chapter, we will discuss some popular cuisines from Asia, especially from China, Japan, and Thailand. These are categorized under Oriental, Asian, or Pan Asian cuisine in the industry. Although Chinese food is one of the most popular cuisines in the world, yet it is mostly perceived as takeaway food as there are many kiosks around the world that serve Chinese stir-fries with noodles or rice. Japanese cuisine is considered to be the food of the rich and famous and it is very common to see high-end restaurants flaunting sushi and sashimi bars serving the most exquisite dishes. Thai cuisine is also very popular for its stir-fries and curries. Thai curries are very different from Indian curries, which we will find out later in this chapter.

The Asian or Oriental cuisines are by far the most diverse cuisines in the world. Like Indian cuisine, Chinese, Japanese, Thai, Malaysian, Indonesian cuisines, etc. also have different styles of cooking and the ingredients used in cooking also differ from one country to another. Apart from the differences within a country, each province also has its own kind of cuisine. For instance, Chinese food in one province is very different from the other provinces and so is the case in other Asian countries because of the cultures and traditions of people inhabiting those regions. Broadly, Asian cuisine is studied under the following five heads.

East Asian cuisine

This cuisine mainly comprises cuisines of China, Japan, and Korea. Apart from Korean food, we will largely discuss Chinese and Japanese cuisines in this chapter, as they are among the most popular cuisines around the world today.

South-East Asian cuisine

This cuisine comprises cuisines of countries such as Thailand, Indonesia, Malaysia, Singapore, Brunei, The Philippines, Vietnam, Cambodia, and Laos. But for a few similarities, the food of each country is unique in its own way and also the regional cuisine of each country is diverse. In this chapter, we will discuss Thai food in detail as it is also one of the most popular cuisines served in hotels nowadays.

South Asian cuisine

The south Asian cuisine comprises cuisines of countries such as India, Sri Lanka, Burma, Bhutan, Tibet, and Pakistan. We will not discuss these in this chapter. Indian cuisine has been discussed in detail in the book, *Quantity Food Production Operations and Indian Cuisine.*

Central Asian cuisine

Central Asian cuisine refers to the cuisines of countries such as Afghanistan, Iran, Armenia, and Cyprus. Though this part of Asian cuisine is not very popular and famous around the world, these countries also have a rich culinary heritage and gastronomy.

Middle Eastern cuisine

Middle Eastern cuisine comprises cuisines from Saudi Arabia, Lebanon, Turkey, Jordan, etc. Some of these cuisines have been discussed under Mediterranean cuisines in Chapter 6.

When referring to Asian cuisines, it is usually the food of China, Japan, and Thailand that are among the most popular in hotels and restaurants worldwide, as they are easily accepted by most of people. Let us now discuss various kinds of popular Oriental cuisines.

CHINESE CUISINE

Chinese cuisine is one of the most diverse cuisines in the world, which is understandable given the large size of the country and its geographical location. In this country of more than one billion people, there are five major religions, eight dialects with Mandarin as the common language. From the gastronomic perspective, there are four main styles of cooking: Canton, Peking, Shanghai, and Szechwan, which correspond to the southern, northern, eastern, and western regions, respectively. As we will read more about these four regions, it will become evident that Cantonese is by far the most preferred cuisine because of flavoursome dishes and the combinations of sweet and sour taste in food.

The gastronomy of China is considered as one of the greatest in the world. The use of rice and wheat is extensive with rice being the staple ingredient and almost everything being cooked in a wok or a steamer. The sequence of courses is not followed in a Chinese meal as several dishes are laid on the table together; it is a family style of eating where the members help themselves. The dishes progress from light to heavy and back to light again at the end of the meal.

The use of chopsticks (Fig. 10.1) implies that everything is cut small or diced before it is cooked and the chefs use only a chopper called *cleaver* for most of their work. Duck and other foods, such as meat and vegetables, are given a glossy finish with sesame oil just before taking it out from wok. A lot of dishes are cooked by steaming method.

Peking features noodles rather than rice and other farinaceous (starchy) products such as steamed dumplings and pancake dishes. The dishes are more substantial (filling and balanced) and the cooking is more cosmopolitan than elsewhere in the country, more foods are deep-fried and generally there is more crispness of structure. Shanghai cooking is more robust with more use of flavours and oil, greater emphasis on garlic, ginger, and other spices and a more peppery result. Here too, the tradition of serving noodles is more popular than rice. The cookery of the western region of Szechwan, bordering India and Myanmar, is noted for its hot spices and includes the use of chillies in sharp contrast to other parts of the country.

Chinese food is popular all over the world, mainly due to extensive travel by the Chinese people. It is not uncommon to see 'a little China' in the USA, England, Australia, and even India. Chinese food is successful because of its flavours and the ease of eating. Though Chinese food all over the world has been associated with takeaway food, yet

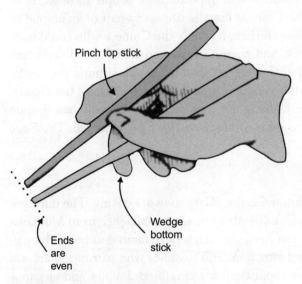

Pinch top stick

Ends are even

Wedge bottom stick

Fig. 10.1 Using chopsticks

Chinese cuisine can vary from simple to complex dishes served in high-end restaurants. The success of Chinese food can also be attributed to the use of fresh ingredients and balance of tastes or a combination of flavours, such as light and robust, in conformity with the country's overriding philosophy. The Chinese philosophy revolves around the yin and yang where yin (female principle) is the dark, cold, and inactive face of the world and thus, bland flavours and yang (male principle) is the strong flavour corresponding to the active, bright, and sunny side of life. The combination of chicken with ginger or shiitake mushroom with scallions are examples of yin and yang.

The Chinese are very particular about their ingredients, especially fish. They spend time in buying fresh fish and inspect each ingredient carefully before paying for it. They also believe that food has to appear fresh, taste good, and smell divine. Thus, it is common to see Chinese food being garnished and decorated beautifully.

Geographic Location

China is among the largest countries in Asia with a very diverse geography. The eastern half of the country is a region of fertile lowlands, foothills and mountains, deserts, steppes, and subtropical areas. Consequently, it is the most densely populated part of the country. The western half of China, which is in the interiors and is thinly populated, is a region of sunken basins, rolling plateaus, and towering mountain ranges. The north of China borders Mongolia, which has an arid climate and largely comprises deserts. The south-western part is humid and wet and is very prone to floods and that is the other reason as to why it is not highly populated. The two most famous rivers, namely Yellow River in the North and Yangtze River in central China cuts the country horizontally into three parts. The southern part is not as cold as northern China. Typhoons are common phenomena in southern China, whereas sandstorms are a common feature in the northern lands of China. Frequent earthquakes and other natural calamities have had a big influence on the cuisine in China. Due to shortage of food and opportunities, people have learnt to value food and not waste anything. The Chinese literally use every part of an animal or vegetable. For example, when processing chicken, it is only the Chinese who could have successfully utilized parts like feet, neck, and parson's nose and transformed them into the most delicious and gelatinous dishes that are relished by people around the world. There could be much confusion over the various regional Chinese cuisines; but clearly, there are four major regional styles of Chinese cooking which are broadly based upon the geographical location of the regions from where the styles have emerged. These are as follows

Northern region: Peking style

The cuisine of northern China is also known as the *Peking* style of cooking. The northern part of the country borders Mongolia. Considerable amount of influence from Mongolia is seen on this cuisine. Historically, the northern region has been famous as hub of human activity and saw the emergence of small kingdoms and royalties who patronized art and culture. Also, the cuisine became more sophisticated and refined. Luxury and elegance are the two words that aptly summarize the cuisine of this region.

The cold weather inhibits the growth of rice; but the Yellow River basin is a fertile basin for the cultivation of wheat, millet, barley which forms the staple food of northern cuisine. The tribes of northern China in the olden times were mainly nomadic and could hardly wait to rear crops. They walked around with herds of sheep and goats that formed a large part of their meal. Game meat, such as quails, duck, and goose, are also commonly consumed in this region. Aquatic food from the Yellow river such as crabs, prawns, and freshwater fish are also common in the *Peking* style cuisine. It is, however, strange to see that pork is not on the list of favourites in this cuisine. This could be because many of the invaders and travellers to this region from Mongolia were Muslims who do not consume pork and related products because of religious reasons.

The cold and harsh climate of the north not only affected the way the people ate and prepared food but also the preference for ingredients that provided warmth to the body. Thus, sesame oil can be commonly seen in the northern style of Chinese food. The food, which is rather oily, encompasses the use of scallions and garlic to absorb the oiliness of food. Due to the cold temperatures, tabletop cookery called Mongolian hotpot cookery, was introduced to keep food warm and hot. The *Peking* style underwent a lot of refinement under the reign of the Manchu dynasty (1644–1911). Unlike the Mongols, the Manchus had no cuisine of their own to boast about. Over the years, they refined the way the northern region cooked and popularized food from different regions of China. This is possibly the reason that today northern China does not have its own distinct cuisine, but has picked up the best from other regions.

Southern region: Cantonese style

The cuisine of this region is popularly known as *Cantonese* cuisine. This is by far the most popular style of Chinese cooking around the world. The two provinces, *Kwangsi* and *Kwangtung* that make up the Cantonese cuisine have a distinctive taste and flavour of cooking. It is one of the regions that have traditionally been very friendly to farmers. The mild winters and moderate monsoon rarely destroy the crops and the subtropical climate with its large coastline to South China Sea makes it the second-largest producer of rice after eastern China. Other commodities such as sugarcane, oranges, and other citrus fruits are found in abundance. Seafood, beef, and pork dominate the cuisine of this region, whereas lamb is rarely found on the menus. Due to the large sea coast, many kinds of live fish and shellfish catch form a large part of their livelihood.

Due to the coastal geographical location, Canton was a preferred place for travellers and traders who settled here from Portugal and Arab countries to do trade with China. Southern China flourished as a trade centre and was visited by many traders and people from around the world who demanded exotic food and also had the capacity to pay a price for the same. This demand for exotic and refined food led the chefs to create one of the most exotic and expensive cuisines of China. Exotic dishes such as shark fins soup and bird's nest soup, are some of the most popular and expensive dishes sold in very high-end Chinese restaurants. The fame of Cantonese food reached far and wide and this is the reason why the Manchus living in the north brought Cantonese chefs to their region to influence the food of *Peking*. *Kwangtung* suddenly became the favoured destination of the imperial household because of its delectable and exotic dishes.

The popular preparation 'little hearts' or dim sums is also the creation of Cantonese chefs. Cantonese food is all about less oil, and different flavours such as sweet and sour. In this style of cooking ingredients are more stir-fried and steamed so as to retain their flavour and nutritional value.

Cantonese food is famous all over the world because of the coastal location of Canton, where the people had access to sea and migrated to different parts of the world in search of fortunes and better prospects. Also, the Americans favoured the immigration of Chinese labourers to work on their railway network that was being built in the nineteenth century. Since these immigrants missed home food, some of them began cooking in Chinese style. In the absence of authentic ingredients, the cooks concocted a mix and match of a few available commodities and masked the textures with heavy sauces and flavours. This led to the creation of the famous chop suey which is very popular around the word, but rarely ever eaten in China. Other such dishes include *chowmein, manchurian*, and *chilli chicken,* which could take an original Chinese chef by surprise.

Eastern China

Eastern China has a large coastline, wherein the southern part borders South China Sea while the north borders Yellow Sea. The rest of eastern China borders the East China Sea. Yangtze River also passes through the east and this makes the life of the people more prosperous. They have access to sea as well as river. Provinces of eastern China such as Kiangsu *(Jiangsu),* Fukien *(Fujian),* Chekiang *(Zhejiang),* Anhwei *(Anhui)* and Kiangsi *(Jiangxi)* are considered to be the rice bowls of the country. The vast and varied landmass is capable of producing almost anything and everything. The climate is subtropical with warm and wet summers. Some areas of Shanghai can become severely cold and experience snowfall as well. The northern area of east China produces barley and wheat, whereas the southern part of east China is the largest producer of rice. The land is well irrigated with Yangtze River, thus fresh fruits and vegetables grow in abundance. The mountain ranges in the south of east China are warmer as compared to the north and thus the climate is most apt for tea plantations. Fukien *(Fujian)* is one of the best known regions for tea in China and Chinese tea is exported to many parts of Europe.

Traditionally, there was no dearth of ingredients to inspire cooks to create sumptuous dishes. Pork meat was the most popular, but in some towns, one can find exotic meat such as donkey and venison as well. Being a coastal belt, seafood is very popular, especially the special hairy crab of Shanghai. The lifestyles of major parts of eastern China were influenced by frequent travellers from Europe, and the USA who added a cosmopolitan touch to this region and Shanghai became the international hub for the rich and famous. The Kiangsu *(Jiangsu)* province is also proud of two other cities apart from Shanghai: Nanking *(Nanjing)* and Hangchow *(Zhengzhou).* Nanjing is famous for its ducks while Chekiang *(Zhejiang)* is famous for vinegar and Shaoxing *(Chongqing)* is known for its wine. Hangchow *(Zhengzhou)* was described by renowned traveller Marco Polo as one of the noblest cities in the world. It was also chosen by Mongols during their exile in the thirteenth century. The influence of imperial kingdom also led to some refined and specialized cuisines in this part of China.

Western China: Szechwan (Sichuan) style

The food of western China is starkly different from other regions and is popular as *Szechwan* cuisine. The use of spices and chillies dominates cooking in this region. The reason is very simple—Western China shares borders with Bhutan, Burma, and India and first century AD onwards, many Buddhists travelled from India to China and spread their religion throughout the country.

The western region comprises provinces such as Yunnan, Kweichow *(Guizhou),* Hunan, Hupei *(Hubei)* and Szechwan *(Sichuan).* Yangtze River flows through the entire region, rendering it fertile and conducive to the growth of many kinds of fruits and vegetables. The chilli peppers of Szechwan *(Sichuan)* are very popular and so are the milder version called Szechwan *(Sichuan)* peppercorns that are hotter than black pepper corns with a hint of star anise flavour. Other popular flavours commonly found in Szechwan *(Sichuan)* cuisine are that of black beans, hot and sour tastes, ginger and garlic.

In India, Szechwan *(Sichuan)* cuisine is preferred over other Chinese cuisines because of the presence of chillies and spices that is more acceptable here. The cuisine of Szechwan *(Sichuan)* is not coated or masked in sauces and that is the reason why it is common to see stir fried chicken paired with chillies, cashew nuts, and even walnuts with little or no sauce. Stir-frying in large woks is done to reduce the sauces so that they barely adhere to the meat or vegetables.

The food of Yunnan is well known for its glutinous rice and fermented bean curd.

The food of Yunnan province is also unique and quite different from in other parts of China. This region is mostly mountainous and the climate is also not very favourable to farming. Maintaining livestock is the main occupation and food is much influenced by its neighbours such as Laos, Vietnam, and Thailand. Centuries ago, Kublai Khan invaded Yunnan to colonize the area and hundreds and thousands of its Muslim cooks, influenced the cuisines of the province.

Commonly used Ingredients in Chinese Cuisine

Every cuisine in the world is unique because of its ingredients and the way they are processed and cooked. The growth of ingredients such as fruits and vegetables are governed by the quality of soil and the climatic conditions of that place. Chinese geography and cuisine are diverse and so are the ingredients. For instance, in the Szechwan *(Sichuan)* region alone, it is not uncommon to see more than 15 varieties of beans. Apart from fruits and vegetables, the Chinese are famous for eating various kinds of food such as preserved and salted fish skins, scorpions, lizards, and snakes. This is because of the harsh climates in certain parts of the country, where one has to rely upon some unusual food that is available throughout the year. Some of the commonly used ingredients in Chinese cuisine are described in Table 10.1.

Table 10.1 Commonly used ingredients in Chinese cuisine

Ingredients	Description	Photograph
Gailan	Also known as *kai-lan*, it is commonly referred to as Chinese broccoli. It is a leafy vegetable unlike the green broccoli heads. It is mainly stir-fried by itself or paired with other meat to make many dishes. *Gailan* is mainly seen in the Cantonese style of cooking.	
Napa cabbage	This cabbage is popularly known as *napa* cabbage or celery cabbage. It is commonly found near Beijing region. It is often stir-fried with ginger, garlic, and soy sauce or paired with mushrooms. The word *napa* comes from the Japanese word *napa,* which means leafy cabbage.	
Bok choy	Many a times referred to as Chinese cabbage, this small leafy vegetable with a bulbous base is commonly stir-fried or boiled and combined with other meat or eaten by itself. It is very popular in eastern China and is known by various names such as *pak choi, choy sum,* or *mei quin choi.*	
Tofu	Tofu is bean curd. It is made by coagulating soy milk and pressing the curds into soft white or creamy blocks. Tofu is used in almost all Oriental cuisines including Japan, Thailand, China, and even Malaysia and Vietnam. There are many varieties of tofu. It can be deep-fried, steamed or stir-fried with vegetables. It is a rich source of plant-based protein and is considered a highly esteemed commodity for health reasons.	
Noodles	Noodles are the most important staple food of Chinese cuisine. They can be made from wheat called *mein* or from rice or mung beans called *fen.* Wheat noodles are very popular in northern China, whereas in other regions *fen* noodles made from rice and *mung* beans are popular. There are various ways of making noodles. They can be rolled into sheet and cut like pasta, or can be extruded through machines. However, the most popular and skilful method is hand pulling the noodles. Some high-end restaurants popularize their cuisine by having a chef pull noodles in front of the guests.	
Soy sauce	This condiment is made by fermenting soybean along with water and salt. This commodity is used in all the Oriental cuisines. It is available in different flavours and colours ranging from brown to dark black. There are usually two types of soy sauce used in Chinese cuisines, namely light soy sauce and dark soy sauce. The light soy has more flavour, but dark soy sauce is used for adding colour to meat and sauces.	

(Contd)

Table 10.1 (Contd)

Ingredients	Description	Photograph
Salted black beans	These are made from soy beans which are salted and fermented until they become dark black. They are very popular in Cantonese cooking. Since they are flavoursome, they are paired with strong flavours such as garlic, pepper, and ginger.	
White fungus	Also known as white tree fungus or snow fungus, it is quite similar in appearance to cloud ear mushroom, the only difference is that it is white to creamy in colour. This is served dried and is commonly used in soups and with chicken and fish.	
Shiitake mushrooms	*Shiitake* mushroom is a delicacy and is used in almost all Oriental cuisines, especially China and Japan. *Shiitake* is a Japanese term, which literally means tree mushroom. This mushroom is cultivated on dead tree logs, hence the name. In China, these mushrooms are called *xiang gu,* which literally means fragrant mushroom. *Note:* It is important to cook this mushroom thoroughly; raw or undercooked *shiitake* can cause rashes all over the body after 48 hours of consumption, that last up to 10 days.	
Cloud ear fungus	Also known as black fungus, this fungus is so called because of its ear-like shape and rubber like appearance. This fungus grows on dead wood, has a dark brown colour, and is somewhat translucent. It is quite perishable and sold dried. When it dries up, it become black in colour. It is rehydrated in water and used in stir-fries and soups.	
Agar-agar	This product with gelatinous properties is obtained from a kind of red alga. It is a vegetarian substitute for gelatine, which is obtained from the bones of animals. Agar-agar is used in desserts in the entire South-East Asia. It is also known as China grass or Japanese *isinglass.* It is available in the form of flakes or powder.	
Conpoy	It is dried scallop which is commonly used in Chinese cuisine. The pungent smell of this dried seafood is particularly liked by the Chinese. *Conpoy* is made by first cooking the scallops and then drying them. It is one of the main components of the famous XO sauce.	
XO sauce	It is a spicy seafood sauce used in Cantonese cuisine. It is a fairly recent in origin and contains products such as dried scallops (*conpoy*), fish, and shrimps, as also chilli peppers, onions, garlic, and oil. The name XO comes from the French cognac which denotes luxury and prestige.	

(Contd)

Table 10.1 (Contd)

Ingredients	Description	Photograph
Five spice powder	As the name suggests, this powder is a mixture of five spices, namely cinnamon, cloves, star anise, *Sichuan* pepper, and fennel seeds. This balance of spices originates from the yin and yang theory. It is used for marination of Peking duck, Cantonese roasted duck, pork, and seafood as well.	
Shark's fin	The fin of shark fish is sold dried and is used for making shark's fin soup that is served at royal banquets and weddings. It is one of the exotic components in a Chinese cuisine and is used mainly for its texture.	
Bird's nest	This is a commodity that is made by a species of birds called swifts. The birds make the nest by using their saliva. Upon drying, they become unusual ingredients for use as bird's nest soup. This ingredient has been used in China for more than 400 years and is believed to be loaded with medicinal properties.	
Szechwan/ Sichuan peppercorn	This is also known as *Sichuan* pepper and is a commonly used spice in Szechwan cuisine and hence the name. It is obtained from the outer pod of tiny fruit of special species. In India, it is also called *tirphal*. It is also called *fagara*.	
Longan berries	Longan berries are obtained from the longan tree which grows in tropical climates around South-East Asia. The fleshy white fruit is quite similar to lichee in texture, but has a peculiar sweet and fruity flavour.	
Abalone	It is also known as sea ear or sea snail and is a kind of mollusc that is eaten raw or cooked. In China, it is commonly known as *bao yu* and is considered to be a luxury item on banquets.	
Frog legs	Frog legs are delicacies served in both French and Cantonese cuisines. A special type of frog called bull frog or pig frog is used for this purpose. When cooked, the frog legs almost taste like chicken.	
Sea cucumber	Sea cucumber is a marine animal with leathery skin that is served on new year and other special occasions. It is often used fresh and is also available canned. This seafood is believed to have high medicinal properties.	

(Contd)

Table 10.1 (*Contd*)

Ingredients	Description	Photograph
Century egg	Also known as the preserved egg or thousand year egg, it is a typical Chinese ingredient made from duck eggs. The eggs are wrapped in a mixture of clay, ash, lime, and rice or wheat bran and are preserved up to three months or 100 days. In this process, the yolk turns to a dark green colour and the shell becomes dark brown and transparent. They are commonly eaten on their own or paired with pickled ginger and eaten as starters.	
Ginkgo nuts	These nuts are obtained from gingko trees that grow between heights of 30–50 metres. The nuts obtained from these trees are used in *congee* (Table 10.2).	
Ginseng	The word *ginseng* is derived from the Chinese name meaning man root, because of the unique fork shape of the plant root resembling legs of a man. *Ginseng* root is used in Chinese cooking as well as for making herbal teas and medicine, as they are believed to improve potency in human beings.	
Chinkiang (*Zhejiang*) vinegar	This is the famous rice vinegar made from fermented rice and is used in many Asian countries such as Japan, China, and even Vietnam. It comes in clear and dark brown colours. This vinegar comes from Chinkiang (*Zhejiang*) province and is considered to be one of the finest black vinegars.	
Shaoxing	This is the traditional Chinese wine obtained from fermenting rice. It comes from Shaoxing (*Chongqing*) region of eastern China and hence, the name. It is drunk as a beverage and is often used in cooking. Many of the dishes called *drunken* utilize this wine to soak the meat in it.	
Sesame oil	This oil is derived from sesame seeds and is popularly used in almost all regions of China. It is particularly used in Cantonese cooking and is one of the main ingredients for flavouring food. Sesame oil is always used to enhance the glossiness of stir-fries and is added in the last minute just before the dish is finished on the range.	

(*Contd*)

Table 10.1 (Contd)

Ingredients	Description	Photograph
Hoisin sauce	*Hoisin* or *haixian* is the proprietary sauce used in Cantonese cuisine. The word is derived from the Cantonese word for seafood. This sauce is made from potato starch, rice starch, soy beans, vinegar, red chilli peppers, and garlic. Though the name stands for seafood, there is no fish product in this sauce. In China, this sauce is used as a dipping sauce.	
Oyster sauce	This sauce is commonly used in Chinese, Thai, and Vietnamese cuisines and is made from sugar, salt, and water that is thickened with cornstarch and flavoured with extract or essence from oysters. It is usually available as dark brown sauce and is used in stir frying. The vegetarian version of this sauce is made by using oyster mushrooms or *shiitake* mushrooms and may contain some taste enhancers as well.	
Monosodium glutamate	Also known as MSG or *ajinomoto* salt, it is obtained from fermentation of carbohydrates with nitrogen source. It is often used in Chinese cooking. There are few concerns over the usage of this salt, as it is believed to be a cancer causing agent. It is mainly used as a flavour enhancer in the food.	
Wonton skins	*Wonton* skins are pieces of flattened dough that are filled with various ingredients and are steamed or fried to make a dish called *wontons. Wonton* skins are made using flour, egg, water, and salt and are available in various colours.	
Potato starch	This is the starch extracted from potatoes. Though corn starch is commonly used as thickening agent in Chinese sauces for thickening, potato starch is commonly used in high-end restaurants as it is required in less quantity and does not interfere with the colour of the dish. It adds a clear colour to the sauces.	

Speciality Dishes

Since Chinese cuisine is so diverse in nature, hotels tend to specialize in food from one or two regions only. Hotel and restaurant cooking is majorly based on different types of sauces, such as sweet and sour sauce, *Szechwan* sauce, black bean sauce, and hot garlic sauce, that are prepared beforehand and kept as part of *mise en place* and when the order is placed, the main dish such as meat or vegetables are either deep-fried, steamed, or boiled and then combined with the sauces. As the sauces are kept ready, it is efficient and easy for chefs to cook a variety of dishes by combining them with different vegetables and seasonings. Some of the most internationally famous dishes from the Chinese kitchen are given in Table 10.2.

Table 10.2 Specialities from the Chinese kitchen (see also Plates 9 and 10)

Dish	Description	Photograph
Dim sums	Dim sum literally means little hearts in Cantonese. These are small stuffed dumplings that are mostly steamed, deep-or pan-fried and served in traditional bamboo baskets known as dim sum baskets. Usually, the dim sums are served off dim sum trolleys, where the bamboo baskets are piled on top of each other and are moved around in the restaurant offering various choices to the guests. The name of a dim sum is based on its shape or the type of flour used for making it. Some popular dim sums are as follows: *Hargao* These are dumplings made of rice flour and turn translucent upon cooking. The traditional shape of these dumplings is like a scallop shell.	*Hargao*
	Char siu bao These are steamed or baked bread dumplings with various kinds of fillings. The most common is sweetened Chinese barbecue pork. These are fluffy buns that resemble the white bread with regard to its texture.	*Shaomai*
	Shaomai These dumplings are made by stuffing *wonton* skins in such a way that the filling is exposed and is just wrapped with the skin. The exposed top can be garnished with crab roe or sliced mushrooms.	*Char siu bao*
	Lo mai gai This dim sum is usually made from sticky rice and other fillings and wrapped in a lotus leaf, before it is steamed. The subtle flavour of lotus leaf flavours the rice.	*Lo mai gai*
Hot and sour soup	This soup is a speciality from the Szechwan (*Sichuan*) region and Beijing. It can be made with vegetables or meats and is dark brown in colour. Dark mushrooms such as *shiitake* mushrooms, cloud ear fungus are a must. It is flavoured with hot chilli paste and soured by Chinkiang (*Zhejiang*) vinegar. The soup is traditionally served garnished with egg whites which coagulate and form thread-like strands in the soup.	

(Contd)

Table 10.2 (Contd)

Dish	Description	Photograph
Wonton soup	The Chinese like their food to be varied in texture and good flavours. This simple soup is made with clear chicken stock and *wontons* are boiled and added to the soup. The soup may contain vegetables and meat, but is usually served clear with natural flavours. This is a very popular Cantonese dish.	
Congee	This is a rice porridge served in many Asian countries and is popularly eaten for breakfast. However, the eating of *congee* is very dependent upon local culture and traditions. Many people like to have it as a meal in itself, while some pair it with meat and vegetables. *Congee* is often served with a choice of ingredients such as chopped coriander, fried onions, dried shrimps, soy sauce, ginger, chilli paste, etc., so that guests can flavour their congee according to choice.	
Spring roll	It is known as *chun juan* in Chinese. Shredded vegetables such as Chinese cabbage, carrots, and beans are stir-fried with salt and pepper and flavoured with sesame oil and soy sauce. These are then rolled into thin sheets and deep fried until crisp. Spring rolls can have many fillings apart from vegetables, but the ones with vegetables are more common. These are usually eaten during the spring festival in China and hence, the name.	
Kung pao	Also known as *gung po* or *gung bao*, it is a classical Szechwan (Sichuan) dish. It is usually made with chicken, but other meat such as seafood and lamb can also be used. The chicken is stir-fried with chilli peppers, Sichuan pepper, leeks, and peanuts and flavoured with Shaoxing (chongqing) wine. In some recipes, peanuts are substituted with cashewnuts.	
Peking duck	This dish is eaten for its crisp duck skin. It is quite unique and requires special skills in not only cooking but also while serving the guests. In this preparation, the duck is first blown with a pipe to loosen out the skin from the meat. It is then marinated with five spice powder and quickly blanched in hot water. Thereafter, the duck is allowed to dry for at least 6 hours, during which it is glazed with maltose syrup to impart the traditional red colour. It is then cooked in *Peking* duck oven until the skin is crisp and cooked. Serving this dish is also an art. It is usually carved in front of the guests. The skin is first served with sugar and garlic sauce. Thereafter, the meat is sliced meat and served along with thin rice pancakes, scallions, and *hoisin* sauce. The guests can roll the meat with scallions and *hoisin* in the pancakes and eat them. The remaining fat and bones may be made into a flavoursome broth and served at the end of the meal.	

(Contd)

Table 10.2 (Contd)

Dish	Description	Photograph
Drunken chicken	This is a term for dishes that involve the use of wine or alcohol in Chinese cooking. Traditionally, these dishes originate from eastern China where *shaoxing* wine is used. The meat is cooked and then soaked in the wine and aromatic vegetables from a few days to weeks to get the deep flavour of alcohol. The drunken dish is usually served cold as heating would evaporate all of the wine as also the flavour.	
Beggar's chicken	This dish is believed to have originated in Hangzhou region of eastern China. There are many stories regarding its origin. A popular lore suggests one day a beggar stole a chicken and hid it in mud near a river, on fear of being caught. On his return after few hours, he cooked it on spit roast. The mud had hardened around the chicken and sealed it like a clay pot. When the mud was cracked open, the feathers came off easily exposing the juicy chicken beneath. Even today, the dish is elaborate in preparation. The chicken is marinated with *shaoxing* wine, soy sauce, star anise, and cloves and left to sit for at least 5 hours. It is then stuffed with various kinds of meat like pork, seafood, or vegetables and wrapped in a lotus leaf. It is finally wrapped in potter's clay and baked in an oven for a few hours. When dish is done, the clay is cracked open and the chicken is cut and served with glutinous rice.	
Sweet and sour pork	This is a popular Cantonese dish famous all over the world. In this, marinated pork cubes are deep-fried until cooked and then stir-fried in a sweet and sour sauce consisting of pineapple, green peppers, onions, soy sauce, and ketchup, and thickened with cornstarch.	
Char siu	This is a popular Cantonese dish which literally means barbecued pork. The word *char* means pork and *siu* means to roast. Strips of marinated pork are skewered on thin skewers or forks and roasted on an open fire. The pork, usually cut from shoulder, is marinated in soy sauce, *hoisin* sauce, five spice powder, honey, and sherry and rice wine. Maltose is often used to give the traditional red coloured glaze on the skin.	
Mapo doufu	This is a popular dish from Szechwan (*Sichuan*) region. It is a combination of tofu and a spicy chilli and bean sauce. This dish is often combined with minced meat such as beef or pork. The characteristic flavours of this dish are its spicy bean paste.	
Dan dan noodles	Also known as *dan dan mian,* it is a spicy noodle dish from Szechwan (*Sichuan*) region. Spicy broth flavoured with chilli oil, Sichuan pepper, and minced pork is served over noodles.	

(Contd)

Table 10.2 (Contd)

Dish	Description	Photograph
Hai nan kai fann	It is a very popular dish of Hainan region and is popularly served as street food in Singapore, Malaysia, and even Thailand. It comprises a serving of poached chicken in stock on a bed of cucumber and lettuce accompanied with glutinous rice, chilli and garlic pastes. This dish is a perfect balanced meal and is often eaten during lunch.	
Mongolian hotpot	Imbibed from the Mongols, this Chinese dish is representative of northern cuisine. In this, a flavoursome simmering stock is placed at the centre of the table with accompanying meat and sauces arranged around it. The hotpot dishes, such as thinly sliced meat, dumplings, leafy vegetables, mushrooms, and seafood are served and guests dip these in the simmering stock and eat it with the accompanying sauces and rice. This dish is preferably eaten during winter as the food remains hot on the table.	
Shantung chicken	In this dish from Szechwan (*Sichuan*) region, chicken is marinated in soy sauce, Chinese rice wine, sugar, and salt and then deep fried until cooked. It is then tossed with garlic, soy sauce, *hoisin* sauce, vegetables, and chilli paste and served hot with rice or noodles.	
Cantonese-style steamed fish	It is one of the most internationally famous Cantonese dishes, perhaps due to its intense flavours and minimalistic approach to cooking. A whole fish is gutted, cleaned, and given a few slashes on the skin. It is then marinated with salt, scallions, sesame oil, soy sauce, and shredded ginger and allowed to steam for 10 minutes or until cooked. The fish is carefully lifted and put on the serving platter. It is then covered with fresh herbs such as cilantro, shredded scallions, and celery and the juices from the steamed fish. Oil is heated to a smoke point in wok and poured over the fish before serving.	
Hakka noodles	Hakka is a community in China which is believed to have originated in northern China and then migrated to Fukien (*Fujian*) and Kwangtung in eastern China. Hakka noodles are commonly dry stir-fried noodles with vegetables and meat and stir-fried with soy sauce and seasonings.	
Moon cake	As the name suggests, this dessert is popularly eaten during the mid-autumn festival in which lunar worshipping takes place. Typically made in round shapes with inscriptions on the top, moon cakes are made from eggs, flour and are filled with sweet lotus seed paste. They are often eaten with Chinese tea.	
Shaobing	Also known as *huoshao*, it is a baked layered bread filled with sweet bean paste and black sesame seed paste. There can be a variety of fillings in this sweet bread which is commonly consumed in northern China.	

(Contd)

Table 10.2 (Contd)

Dish	Description	Photograph
Date pancakes	Known as *tsao ni kwo ping* in Chinese, it is a very popular traditional dessert in China. In this, a batter is made from eggs and flour and made into pancakes in a wok. The pancakes are then stuffed with a mixture of date paste and shaped into a rectangle. The pancake are then fried until crisp and served with vanilla ice cream.	
Daarsaan	These are honey tossed fried flat noodles, garnished with sesame seeds, and served with vanilla ice cream. The noodles are made from dough of flour, eggs, and water and rolled to form sheets. These are then cut with knife and deep-fried until crisp. Honey and sugar is heated in a wok and when it is light golden in colour, the fried noodles are tossed and served hot with vanilla ice cream.	
Toffee banana	Often found in many Chinese restaurants, this dessert is made by dipping banana in flour and egg batter and deep frying it until crisp. The fried banana is then coated in sesame flavoured caramel sugar syrup and dipped into ice cold water to harden the sugar. This dessert is also served with vanilla ice cream.	

Tools and Equipment in Chinese Cooking

In order to understand the unique equipment used in Chinese cooking, it would be worthwhile to understand how food is prepared out of a single cooking range. In any hotel's Chinese kitchen, it is not uncommon to see one or more of cooking ranges as shown in Fig. 10.2. All the cooking—boiling, steaming, stir-frying, deep-frying—happens on these ranges. It is very important to be very organized as all the cooking can be

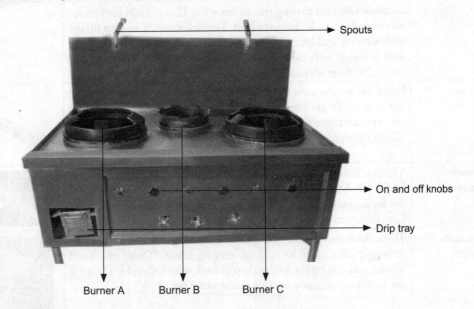

Fig. 10.2 A cooking range used in Chinese kitchen

conducted on a single cooking range without the cook moving places. The two burners, namely A and C (refer Fig. 10.2), can be used for cooking, whereas the back burner B contains stock. The water from the spouts is used for cooking and cleaning the woks as also the cooking range. The extra water drains down to the drip tray or is connected to the drain directly. These cooking ranges are also known as high-pressure ranges as their inlet pipe is connected to an air pressure gauge that induces an air-pressure to make the fire fierce which is desirable for quick stir-fried dishes.

Very basic cooking equipment, such as steamers, spoons, woks, spatulas, and strainers, are used for Chinese cooking. Large strainers allow the fried food to be strained while the wok is readied for cooking.

Chinese cooking is minimal and therefore, very fast. Only two or three cooks would be on the cooking ranges, implying that they have to dispense food for guests very quickly and efficiently. Therefore, they would have to conduct all styles of cooking on the same range. Let us discuss some of the common tools and equipment used in a Chinese kitchen in Table 10.3.

Table 10.3 Common tools and equipment in a Chinese kitchen

Equipment	Description	Photograph
Wok	The wok is a versatile utensil used in all oriental cuisines. It can be used for stir-frying, deep frying, and even cooking sauces and other items. A Chinese wok is a round, shallow, concave utensil made from light weight cast iron, which allows the flipping or tossing of food with ease. There are various sizes and shapes of wok. *Note:* The wok has to be seasoned well or it may be very irritating when the food sticks to the surface. Some Chinese chefs keep separate woks for tossing rice or noodles. There could be various ways in which woks are seasoned. The favourite of all is to fill the wok with oil and let it smoke. The oil is then drained off and the wok is wiped with clean cloth. The other way is to roast salt and scrub the same with an old cloth.	
Chinese broom	Since the wok is used for many purposes, it is important to clean the wok while cooking on the range. Hot water is poured onto the wok and scrubbed with a broom with wooden bristles. This allows cleaning of the wok, without damaging its seasoning.	
Chinese cleaver	This is a heavy chopper that is used for many tasks in the Chinese kitchen. It is used to flatten meats by beating the meats down with the flat surface. It is used for mincing, slicing, and even chopping. Cleavers come in different thickness and weights.	
Dim sum basket	These baskets, which are made from bamboo, are used for steaming dim sums as well as serving them. These are hand woven and can be stacked on top of each other, thereby allowing the steaming of many baskets at the same time.	

(Contd)

Table 10.3 (Contd)

Equipment	Description	Photograph
Earthenware cooking pot	Earthenware pots, also known as sand pots, are one of the most important cooking utensils in the Chinese kitchen. These are used for preparing various kinds of hotpots and stews from northern China. Sometimes, food is also served in the same dish as it retains hot for long time.	
Steamers	Though these days, electric or gas steamers are used in Chinese cooking, but in old times, the wok itself was used for steaming. Small steamers made from bamboo are still used in a few kitchens for steaming rice and other things.	
Peking duck oven	This oven can be of metal or even bricks or clay. A small fire is lit at the base with wood. Traditionally, wood from peach or pear tree is used for this purpose. When the fire burns out, the duck is hung till it cooks.	
Metal spatula	This spatula is used for stir-frying food in the wok. The curved shape allows it to easily scrape things from the bottom of the wok and the raised edges help hold the food while stir-frying.	
Chinese spoon	This spoon is used for cooking soups or even stir-fries in a wok. The spoon is used for lifting condiments as well as cooking. It is used in Chinese cooking for various purposes.	
Strainers	Chinese cooking happens on a single unit as explained earlier. Therefore, it is important that tools and equipment are at hand for easy operation. Since frying, stir-frying, boiling, etc. are done on the same range, it is important to strain foods quickly and easily. Large strainers are used for this purpose. The fried items are usually not fished out, but many a time an ingredient is deep fried and the entire contents are strained into another bowl with the help of these large strainers. This way, the fried item can be allowed to drain, while the wok is ready for cooking again.	

JAPANESE CUISINE

Japanese cuisine, as we see it today, has developed and evolved over 2,000 years. It shows strong influences from the cuisines of neighbouring countries such as China and Korea. Japanese cuisine became popular around the world, particularly the Western world, over the last 300–400 years and today it is one of the most famous cuisines in the world. Some of the best Michelin star chefs hail from Japan and have their own restaurants in the UK and the USA.

Most of the culinary habits can be traced to external influence. For instance, rice was introduced to the Japanese by the Koreans sometime in the third century BC. The techniques of growing rice were carried by migrating tribes from Korea who settled in Japan. Soon it became the staple food, rather staple ingredient of the entire country as later it began being used to make paper, fuel, building material, wine, etc. The other ingredients which became an integral part of the Japanese cuisine were soybeans, wheat, and soy sauce that were introduced from China. The oldest form of noodles *sakubei* produced by adding rice powder to flour was also introduced from China. Tea and chopsticks are more evidences of Chinese influence on Japanese food habits.

Japan, being an island nation, has one of the largest coastlines in the world. Thus, living on seafood is integral to Japanese cuisine. The Japanese always believe that the fish should be so fresh that it can be eaten raw. Even if it has been fished a few hours earlier, it must be cooked, steamed, or boiled. The habit of eating raw fish has been there since time immemorial, but combining raw fish with soy sauce was popularized around seventeenth century and this came to be known as sashimi.

Sushi, on the other hand, has been an accidental creation of the Japanese. In their quest for keeping the fish fresh in times prior to refrigeration, the Japanese perfected the art of preserving fish packed in cooked rice. The rice would ferment and the acid produced would help preserve the fish for later use. One day, someone tasted this rice and liked it. Thereafter, the Japanese mastered art of making rice with sugar and vinegar to arrive at the fermented taste and combined the same with raw fish to make the most popular sushi.

However, the people were quick to figure out that raw fish preserved in this manner could cause food poisoning, so they introduced an element called wasabi, which is a pungent horseradish with antiseptic properties that could kill any harmful bacteria in the stomach. The flavour was enhanced by pickled ginger called *gari*. To this date, every sushi is served with wasabi, soy sauce, and *gari*.

During the sixteenth century, the Japanese perfected the art of making sushi and started combining it along with sashimi and other products to create an array of displays. Many sushi bars opened during this time and chefs came up with more creative ideas to design different types and shapes of sushi. During this time, Japan was frequented by the Portuguese and Dutch, who too began to influence the food of Japan through their interactions. At that time, the Japanese were strictly vegetarian as both prevailing religions—Buddhism and the indigenous Shinto—disallowed animal slaughter for consumption. Also, there were no fried dishes and spices in their food. The Portuguese introduced the concept of frying which gave a rise to the Japanese speciality tempura, which we have read about in Chapter 3 on appetizers and garnishes.

Notwithstanding the aforementioned external influences, Japanese cuisine has managed to carve out its own niche with certain ingredients and dishes. The staple ingredients of Japanese food are rice and wheat. Japanese rice called *gohan* is eaten with soups called *okazu* and is accompanied with various pickles called *tsukemono*. A Japanese meal is much organized with a lot of emphasis on presentation, flavours, and textures. If any Japanese dish is served, then the accompaniments would all be prepared by different methods such as boiled, grilled, steamed, or raw. The food is flavoured commonly with *miso* and *dashi*. *Miso* is a soybean paste and *dashi* is a flavoursome stock prepared from seaweed and dried fish flakes of skipjack tuna called *katsuboshi* or from small bonito flakes called *hondashi*. Noodles are eaten commonly and mainly two types of noodles *udon* and *soba* are popular. *Udon* noodles are thick wheat noodles, while *soba* noodles are thin noodles made from buckwheat flour.

The volcanic and mountainous terrains have lush forests and heavy monsoons; due to more number of islands, there is a scarcity of land, so mainly the farms are used for hunting and gathering food. Thus, marine resource has become a significant part of the Japanese culinary traditions.

Geographical Location

Japan is a country of many islands located in the North Pacific Ocean, which directly contribute to the cuisine of the country in a broader aspect. It is composed of four major islands—*Hokkaido, Honshu, Shikoku,* and *Kyushu*— and thousands of smaller ones. Honshu, the largest island, is generally referred to as the mainland. The capital Tokyo is located on the Honshu Island. The country has some of the highest mountain ranges such as Mount Fuji which is an active volcano. As Japan is situated in active seismic zone, low tremors of earthquake and volcanic activity are felt in the country throughout the year.

The climates vary along the islands of Japan due to its geographical location. The northernmost islands have warm summers and long and cold winters with heavy snowfall. The mainland has mild winters with no snowfall, but hot and humid summers. The island of Kyushu, on the other hand, has subtropical climate.

Every region has its own unique identity and cooking style, though not as varied as seen in India or China as life revolves around seafood and vegetables that are available in all places. Cold climates though have led to the art of preserving and pickling vegetables, which are commonly served with Japanese dishes.

Ingredients used in Japanese Cuisine

The Japanese people have always been very open to cultures and relationship with foreign civilizations since the dawn of history. This openness about them gave rise to new ideas and helped Japan develop its own culture. The Buddhists came to Japan from China and influenced their culture significantly. It is mainly because of this Buddhist influence that the Japanese did not eat meat and other animals. It is quite rare to see non-vegetarian food except seafood on their menus even today. Japanese cuisine is very popular internationally and people around the world find that the food and unique ingredients from Japan are among the healthiest dishes and also have medicinal benefits. Some of the unique ingredients used in Japanese cooking are described in Table 10.4.

Table 10.4 Unique ingredients used in Japanese cooking

Ingredient	Description	Photograph
Japonica rice	Japonica rice or Japanese rice, or *gohan* as known in Japanese, is a short-grain variety of rice, which is characterized by its unique stickiness and texture. The variety of rice is known as *mochigome*. Rice is cultivated throughout Japan. The northernmost parts of Japan produce rice with hardier and starchier grains than the ones growing in the southern parts. In Honshu, the Japanese mainland, varieties such as *koshihikari, uonuma,* and *hinohikari* are grown.	
Soba noodles	*Soba* is a type of thin Japanese noodle made from buckwheat flour. The most famous Japanese *soba* noodles come from Nagano in Hokkaido. *Soba* noodles are usually served cold with dipping sauces or as salad.	
Sōmen noodles	*Sōmen* are very thin, white Japanese noodles made of wheat flour. The noodles are usually served cold and are less than 1.3 mm in diameter.	
Japanese *amberjack* or *yellowtail*	This fish is very popular in Japan. It is generally used for preparing sushi and sashimi. A 3 kg fish is called *hamachi*, and a 5 kg one is called *buri*.	
Nori	It is a seaweed used for making *maki* sushi. In English, it is also known as *laver*. It is cultivated in Ariake Bay, off the Kyushu Island.	
Wakame	*Wakame* is a sea vegetable or edible seaweed. It has a subtle sweet flavour and is most often served in soups and salads. It is native to cold temperate coastal areas of Japan. It is mostly procured in dried form and needs to be rehydrated in water before use in soups and salads.	
Daikon	*Daikon* which means a large root in Japanese, is also called white radish, Japanese radish, and Oriental radish. It is long and white in colour and is used in garnishes, salads, or even pickled and served with dishes.	

(Contd)

Table 10.4 (Contd)

Ingredient	Description	Photograph
Wasabi	Also known as Japanese horseradish, it is a pungent root which is used as a condiment while serving sushi and has an extremely strong flavour. It also has antibacterial properties which is why it is served with sushi and sashimi. Wasabi is used in many forms—it can be freshly grated and used; it is also available in dried powder and paste forms. The dry powder has to be rehydrated with water to achieve a dough-like consistency.	
Enokitake	These are long, thin white mushrooms used in east Asian cuisine. Although it is available fresh or canned, the fresh mushroom is preferred. They are traditionally used for soups, but can also be used for salads.	
Kobe beef	*Kobe* is a meat from a special breed of *wagyu* cattle called *tajima-ushi*. The meat is considered to be a delicacy because of its well-marbled texture that makes it one of the most expensive commodities in the world. Like the cheese varieties in Europe, *Kobe* beef also has been accorded a DOP kind of status. Kobe is the sixth largest city in Hyogo in Japan and it can be called *Kobe* beef only when the beef comes from this region and has been reared with the customary practices of this region.	
Sake	*Sake* is a rice wine from Japan. Though known as wine, the process of making *sake* is somewhat similar to that of making beer. *Sake* can be drunk warm or cold, and also find extensive use in Japanese cooking.	
Mirin	*Mirin* is a rice wine very similar to *sake*, but it contains higher percentage of sugar—from 40–50%. More sugar content would also mean lower alcohol. It is often drunk as sweet *sake*, but usually finds its use in culinary applications.	
Miso	*Miso* is an ingredient in Japanese cooking that has been used for centuries. It can be described as a seasoning which is made by fermenting rice, barley, or soybeans with addition of salt and fungus culture. The most commonly made *miso* is with soybeans, and the taste can range from salty to savoury to earthy depending upon the production. *Miso* is often used for pickling; it is boiled with *dashi* stock to make *miso shiro* soup that is a staple of Japanese people. *Miso* can also be used as a curing agent for eggs.	

(Contd)

Table 10.4 (Contd)

Ingredient	Description	Photograph
Shoyu	*Shoyu* is a Japanese soy sauce particularly used as seasoning in almost all dishes. The famous brand associated with Japanese soy sauce is Kikkoman Soy Sauce. All soy sauces are made by fermenting soybeans, but the Japanese also add wheat to their soy sauce which gives it a characteristic flavour.	
Tofu	Also known as *kinugoshi* tofu in Japanese, it is smooth and can be pureed if blended. It is a coagulated mass of soy milk and needs extreme care in handling. The cut tofu can be eaten raw, coated in flour and deep fried, or stir-fried in woks like Chinese. Tofu formed a large part of Japanese diet during the Buddhist regime as it was a unique source of plant-based protein.	
Kombu	*Kombu* or *konbu* are large seaweeds that belong to the species of brown algae known as *kelp*. Today, these are cultivated in the seas of Japan and extensively used for flavouring Japanese stock called *dashi*. *Kombu* is never eaten and is discarded after it has been boiled for 20 minutes in water.	
Hondashi	*Hondashi* is a seasoning powder used for making *dashi* stock. It is available as a proprietary product with flaked skip jack tuna and *monosodium glutamate*.	
Shichimi togarashi	Literally meaning seven flavour chilli pepper, it is a Japanese spice mixture comprising coarsely ground red chilli, *Sichuan* pepper, black and white sesame seed, ginger powder, dried orange peel, *nori*, and hemp seeds. It is used for flavouring soups and salads and is often used for making spicy versions of sushi.	
Su	*Su* is Japanese for vinegar. Japanese vinegar is sour and sweet and is mainly used for flavouring the rice for making sushi. The base of vinegar is rice but it also contains *monosodium glutamate*.	
Junsai	*Junsai* is a kind of rhizome like ginger that grows in lakes and ponds. *Junsai* plant produces deep maroon flowers. The most prized part of the plant is its sprout that is covered in transparent jelly and extensively used by chefs to make delicacies.	

(Contd)

Table 10.4 (Contd)

Ingredient	Description	Photograph
Matsutake	Also known as pine mushroom, it is extensively used in Japanese cuisine. It is particularly liked for its aromatic flavour. *Matsutake* mushrooms grow under the fallen leaves and are difficult to find. This explains the high price of these mushrooms.	
Gari shoga	*Gari* can be described as a *tsukemono* or pickled vegetable. Thin slices of young ginger are pickled in a solution of sugar and vinegar. This gives them the characteristic pink colour. *Gari* is usually eaten between sushi to cleanse the palate. It also has antiseptic properties like *wasabi*, which can counter the effect of any micro-organisms.	
Umeboshi	These are pickled Japanese plums that are extremely salty and sour. They are popularly eaten for breakfast and are served along with rice. Traditionally pickled and dyed red in colour using vegetable based dyes, these are often placed in the centre of rice to symbolize the national flag of Japan.	
Yuzu	*Yuzu* is a citrus fruit from east Asia. The fruit has an appearance of grapefruit, but is small like a lemon. Though largely eaten as fruit, its tart juices are used as seasoning in sauces and salads.	
Adzuki beans	These small oval and plum red beans are mostly used in desserts in Japanese cuisine. It is also used in Chinese and Korean cuisines. It is usually cooked with sugar and then pounded to a paste and used in many desserts.	

Styles of Cooking—Japan

Japanese cuisine is very unique in itself and there are various types of cooking methods employed to create some world famous dishes. Some of these styles of cooking discussed ahead are internationally popular with some fine dining restaurants specializing in these cooking styles.

Teppanyaki

Teppan means iron plate or griddle and *yaki* means to grill, hence *Teppanyaki* is a style of grilling or cooking food on hot plates. This style was introduced in Japan around 1945. The entire course of meal, starting from appetizers to dessert, is prepared live in front of the guests with lots of flair and showmanship. Though this kind of showbiz is not very popular among the native Japanese, the foreigners love it. This is why this style of cooking is more popular in the West than in Japan itself.

Fig. 10.3 Chef working at *teppan* table

Japanese food is considered to be bland by most people outside Japan. Since there were many people who visited Japan for business purpose, it became necessary to cater to such people. Hence, this style of cooking evolved in a bid to cater to such. The *teppanyaki* style of cooking also utilizes non-Japanese ingredients to prepare the dishes. Today, chefs have practised and perfected the art of show cooking in front of the guests. Eggs are flipped and broken in a bowl midway, prawns are grilled, and the prawn's tail is flipped into the chef's hat or pocket or sometimes into a guest's glass, which are few of the gimmicks performed at the *teppan* table. Figure 10.3 depicts a chef working at *teppan* table.

Teriyaki

Since Japanese food is considered to be bland by many Westerners, Japanese chefs have always tried to create new styles to suit to the Western palate. One such cooking style is called teriyaki, wherein meats are boiled or grilled in sweet soy marinade.

In many Japanese restaurants, this style of cooking is commonly used for appetizers, where chicken, fish, or any meat is skewered on to a bamboo stick along with leek or scallions and then grilled on a charcoal grill. The word teri is derived from Japanese word, which means shine or lustre. The meat while grilling is brushed several times with a mixture of soy sauce and *mirin*, which gives it its natural shine. This marinade is also used for marinating the meat before it is cooked. Figure 10.4 shows some dishes cooked in teriyaki style.

Sukiyaki

Influenced from the Chinese Mongolian hotpot, *sukiyaki* is popularly eaten in northern Japan during winters and at the new year party known as *bonenkai*. *Sukiyaki* consists of thin slices of meat usually prime quality Kobe beef and vegetables neatly arranged in a pot which contains a flavoursome stock seasoned with soy, *mirin*, and sugar (refer Fig. 10.5). The stock usually prepared with water as a base is known as *warishita*. The only

Salmon teriyaki   Chicken teriyaki

Fig. 10.4 Dishes made in teriyaki style

Fig. 10.5 Dish made in *Sukiyaki* style

difference from the Mongolian hotpot is that the cooked pieces of meat are dipped in raw egg, before they are eaten.

Sukiyaki is prepared in different ways across Japan. In some places, the meat is stewed in a mixture of soy, *mirin,* and sugar while in some other parts, it is seared first and then deglazed and flavoured with *mirin,* soy, and sugar.

Shabu Shabu

Shabu shabu is another Japanese variation of *sukiyaki* and is commonly eaten throughout the year. It is a tabletop cookery style, which means that the dish is literally cooked at the guests table. It can be said that this style of cooking relates more to the Mongolian hotpot than *sukiyaki.* Figure 10.6 depicts the *shabu shabu* style of cooking and presentation.

Fig. 10.6 *Shabu shabu* style of cooking and presentation

In this style, thinly sliced meat and vegetables are served separately, along with dipping sauces and rice. *Dashi* stock is used for dipping and cooking. The guests pick up the slices of meat and cook it in the simmering pot of *dashi* stock. It is customary to swish the meat back and forth with chopsticks several times before it gets cooked. The name of this style comes from the swishing of meat in stock, as *shabu shabu* literally translates to 'swish-swish' in Japanese. The cooked meat and vegetables are then poured over rice and eaten with dipping sauces. The most common dipping sauce used in *shabu shabu* is *ponzu* sauce and *goma* sauce.

Ponzu is a thin sauce of tart consistency and is flavoured with *yuzu* lemons. Traditionally, *ponzu* sauce is made by simmering *mirin* with rice vinegar, bonito flakes, and *kombu* and then strained off and seasoned with the juice of yuzu lemon.

Goma sauce is a sesame seed sauce that is made by flavouring *dashi* stock with sesame oil and roasted sesame seeds.

Speciality Dishes

Japanese cuisine is very unique and versatile. To the uninitiated it might seem like an overdose of sushi and sashimi, but Japanese cuisine is more than that. There are many styles of cooking in Japan some of which have gained popularity outside Japan. The northern Japanese food mostly comprises potatoes and various barbecued meat, food of western Japan is more delicately flavoured than that of east Japan. Green tea is often consumed as a national drink at the end of Japanese meal. It is a rich antioxidant.

Any discussion on Japanese cuisine would be incomplete without the understanding of sushi and sashimi, which are arguably the most popular Japanese dishes.

Sushi and sashimi

As discussed, sushi was an accidental creation discovered by the Japanese while preserving their fish in rice. Today, sushi bars specialize in various kinds of sushi using *nori* sheets, sushi rice, vegetables, and even raw fish. The popular demand all over the world has also led to the preparation of vegetable sushi even as American chefs have gone a step further to make a version of sushi called Californian rolls.

There are various shapes of sushi, which get their name from the way they are prepared and served. Some popular kinds of sushi and their shapes are described in Table 10.5.

Table 10.5   Kinds of sushi (see also Plate 10)

Sushi	Description	Photograph
Maki	This is a rolled sushi wherein the sushi rice is evenly spread onto a *nori* sheet and different types of fillings are placed in the centre and rolled with the help of sushi mat called *makisu*. The sushi is then cut into 6 to 8 pieces and served.	
Futomaki	This is same as *maki* roll, but usually thicker. Typically, a *futomaki* would be 1.5 inches in diameter that is made with two or more fillings. It is usually prepared with vegetables but meat and seafood are also used often.	
Hosomaki	This is also a kind of *maki* roll but thinner than it. The diameter of the *hosomaki* would be around 2 cm only. The fillings of *hosomaki* can sometimes change its name. For example, when only cucumber is rolled inside, it is known as *kappamaki* (*kappa* means cucumber in Japanese) or *tekka maki* when it is filled with tuna.	
Temaki	*Temaki* sushi is made by placing rice and fillings in crisp *nori* sheet and rolling it to form a cone. It is served on special stands where the cones can be placed and are consumed as soon as they are made or else they can get soggy.	
Uramaki	These are inside out rolls, which means that filling is rolled in *nori* sheet which is surrounded by sushi rice. *Uramaki* is more popular in Western countries and is often known by different names based on fillings. This kind of sushi is also known as Californian roll when filled with avocado, crab, cucumber, and fish roe called *tobiko*.	
Chirasi sushi	It literally means scattered sushi. A bowl is filled with sushi rice and topped with various toppings such as fish, condiments, and garnishes.	

(Contd)

Table 10.5 *(Contd)*

Sushi	Description	Photograph
Inari sushi	This sushi is a pouch of fried tofu skin that is stuffed with sushi rice. The tofu skins that are available proprietary can be cut into rectangles or into triangles.	
Nigiri sushi	These are hand-formed sushi, in which a rice ball is shaped into oblong rectangles between the palms of the hand and a slice of fish is placed on top, along with a small helping of wasabi. The sushi can sometimes be wrapped in a thin strip of *nori* sheet, especially when using cooked ingredients such as octopus, eel, or Japanese omelette called *tomago yaki*.	
Gunkan maki	It actually means battleship. A small dumpling of rice is wrapped with a strip of *nori* sheet and soft fillings are placed and topped with fish roe such as salmon caviar, *tobiko*, and herring roe.	
Oshi sushi	This is also known as box sushi, as the sushi rice is pressed in a special wooden mould called *oshibako*. The bottom of the box is lined with slices of fish and condiments and rice is placed on top and pressed in moulds to yield a perfect rectangular sushi, which can be cut into various sizes.	

Sashimi, on the other hand, is raw slice of ocean or sea fish that is served along with pickled ginger, soy sauce, and wasabi. River fish is generally not preferred as it is not considered to be clean and fit for raw consumption. It is an art to cut fish for sashimi. Usually tuna is the most preferred fish for sashimi and the most popular variety are *ahi* tuna or yellowfin tuna also known as *Albacore* tuna. *Maguro*, which is also known as bluefin tuna, is another preferred variety, though it is leaner than the *ahi* tuna.

Sushi tuna is further divided into sub-types based on their fat content. The fattier the tuna, it will have a buttery texture and will melt in mouth. Figure 10.7 depicts the various cuts on the tuna belly. The belly part of the tuna is used for making sashimi and can be divided into the following parts.

Akami   It is the cut from the lean side of belly and has the least fat content.

Toro   It is the fatty part of the tuna belly and is more expensive due to better taste. Toro is further subdivided into *chutoro* and *otoro*.

Chutoro   This is the cut from belly between *akami* and *otoro* and is not as fatty as *otoro*.

Otoro   This is the most prized cut of the tuna which is obtained from under the belly side. It has highest fat content and thus a texture which melts in the mouth.

Sushi and sashimi are presented on boats or in coloured decorative boxes called bento boxes as shown in Fig. 10.8.

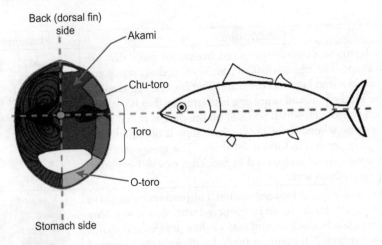

Fig. 10.7 The belly of the tuna

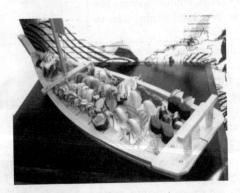

Fig, 10.8 Sushi boat and bento box

Apart from the various styles of sushi listed above, there are some very unique dishes in Japanese cuisine, some of which have been discussed in Table 10.6.

Table 10.6 Speciality dishes in Japanese cuisine (see also Plates 10 and 11)

Dish	Description	Photograph
Mochi	This is a rice cake that is usually prepared from glutinous rice called *mochi*. It is usually prepared on the occasion of the Japanese new year and during a ceremony called *mochitsuki*. This cake is made by soaking rice overnight and cooking it the next day. The cooked rice is then pounded until it becomes a smooth paste, which is then it is shaped into bars or spheres.	
Dango	These are dumplings made from *mochi* rice flour, which are steamed or boiled, then finished by broiling, and eaten with bean jam and a sprinkling of soybean sauce.	

(Contd)

Table 10.6 (Contd)

Dish	Description	Photograph
Tamagoyaki	This is a Japanese omelette prepared in special pans that are square in shape. The egg is whisked with *mirin* and soy sauce and then spread in a thin layer on the plate. The cooked egg is rolled like a pipe on the pan and more egg is poured in thin layer. The pre-formed rolled egg, which was still on the pan, is rolled again and this is done several times until a thick pipe is obtained. This is then slightly pressed to form a flat shape. The *tamagoyaki* thus, obtained is now sliced and served in breakfast or can be used as a topping on sushi as well.	
Tempura	One of the most popular Japanese dishes, tempura was brought to Japan by the Portuguese. It can be prepared with almost anything although vegetables, chicken, and seafood like prawns and squids are the most popular. Tempura is made by dipping the prepared vegetable or meat in a batter, which is prepared with flour, eggs, rice flour and deep frying it until very crisp, without getting too much colour on the food. Tempura can be served as appetizer or even eaten as main course.	
Black *miso* cod	This fish is not an authentic Japanese dish, but famous chefs have popularized it around the world. Black cod fish, also known as Chilean sea bass, is used for making this dish. A thick steak of black cod is marinated in the mixture of white *miso* paste, sake, sugar, and *mirin* and left for at least 3–4 days in fridge. It is then allowed to bake for 10–12 minutes or until a dark golden colour is achieved. The fish is then served with sautéed vegetables.	
Donburi	*Donburi* is the name given to any dish that is served in a bowl over a bed of cooked rice. There are many types of *donburis* such as *gyudon donburi*, in which the beef slices are stewed in *sake*, *mirin*, and soy sauce and *dashi* stock and served on a bed of rice in a bowl. Another popular *donburi* is *katsudon*, wherein *tonaktsu* or 'breaded pork' cutlet is served over the rice.	
Chazuke	This dish is usually made with leftover rice, which is mixed with green tea, and other ingredients such as tofu, salmon, and roe of cod fish.	
Tonkatsu	This dish was invented in the late nineteenth century and is a very popular in Japan. It is made by marinating a thick slice of pork, usually from the neck, in *sake*, soy, and *miso* paste and is breaded with breadcrumbs and deep-fried. It is usually served with steamed rice, *miso* soup, and shredded cabbage. It can also be served as a *donburi*, where it is known as *katsudon*.	
Gyoza	It is like Chinese dim sums with fillings of pork, cabbage, scallions, ginger, garlic, soy sauce, sesame oil, and sake. A thin sheet of dough, made with flour and water, is rolled in to desired shape and stuffed with various fillings. Thereafter, it is folded and shaped	

(Contd)

Table 10.6 (Contd)

Dish	Description	Photograph
	like a dim sum. It is then fried in a pot. When done, water is poured over the *gyozas* immediately and the pot is covered tightly to let them steam. These are served hot with soy sauce. In Malaysia, a similar dish is called pot stickers.	
Okayu	Also known as *kayu*, it is very similar to the Chinese rice *congee*. Rice is cooked like a porridge with addition of chicken, vegetables and can be served with assortment of toppings such as *tomagoyaki*, herbs, and *umeboshi*.	
Yakitori	Yakitori are grilled pieces of meat skewered onto bamboo sticks in the same way as *Thai satays*. Pieces of marinated meat are skewered onto bamboo sticks along with leeks or spring onions and then grilled until cooked. These are served traditionally with teriyaki sauce.	
Age bitashi	This is a very simple dish of assorted vegetables such as okra, pumpkin, and *shiitake* mushrooms that are deep-fried and then marinated in *dashi* stock. It can be served as a soup, but in Japan, it is often eaten as a main dish and is usually served chilled.	
Hiyayako	This is a very traditional dish served in many Japanese restaurants. In this preparation, the silken tofu is cut into a large rectangular piece and served with assorted toppings such as bonito flakes, grated ginger, and chopped chives. It is usually eaten as an appetizer in hotels and restaurants.	
Udon	*Udon* is a dish of thick Japanese noodles boiled in *dashi* stock and vegetables such as spinach and *shiitake* mushroom. The dish is presented attractively in a bowl and is eaten as a main course.	
Tsukemono	These are Japanese pickled vegetables which are made with a variety of ingredients such as cabbage, cucumber, pumpkin, and *umeboshi* plums. These are served as an accompaniment with rice or even served as snacks. *Tsukemono* is generally prepared by mixing salt in vegetables and pressing them with a heavy weight and allowed to pickle for a couple of days.	
Gomae	This is a popular Japanese sidedish, which literally means sesame dressing (*goma* means sesame). One could use almost any ingredient to make *gomae*. The dish is made by blanching spinach and then mixing with a dressing of sesame, *miso*, *sake*, and sugar.	
Chawanmushi	*Chawanmushi* is a savoury egg custard that is served traditionally in a tea cup. Variety of ingredients such as *shiitake*, roots of lily plants, and boiled shrimps are mixed with egg, soy sauce, *dashi*, *mirin*, and *ginkgo* nuts and are allowed to steam until cooked. It is usually served as an appetizer.	

Special Equipment in Japanese Kitchen

Japanese cuisine is a specialized cuisine of the orient. Unlike other oriental cuisines, cooking rarely happens in wok and over high-pressure burners. The Japanese believe in presenting their food with intricate garnishes and decorations. They particularly like to adorn their tables with food placed in symmetrical and decorative fashion. To make such an elaborate work easy, many unique tools and equipment are used in a Japanese kitchen. Some of the most common ones are described in Table 10.7.

Table 10.7 Special equipment and tools used for Japanese cooking

Equipment	Description	Photograph
Makisu	This is a mat made of bamboo strips that are woven together with a thread. *Makisu* is commonly used for rolling and making sushi called *maki* and hence the name. Apart from making sushi, these mats have many other uses such as shaping the Japanese omelette, and squeezing out moisture from foods.	
Hangiri	These are wooden bowls traditionally made from the wood of the Cypress tree. The porous quality of this wood makes it ideal equipment for cooling and mixing sushi rice in order to become fluffy and shiny. The wood absorbs the extra moisture from the rice and makes it ideal for sushi.	
Shamoji	*Shamoji* is a flat wooden rice serving or mixing spoon that is used along with *hangiri*. These spoons are made from bamboo or Cypress wood. Traditionally, the wooden *shamoji* is used for mixing sushi rice, as it does not slice the rice grains.	
Wasabi grater	Fresh wasabi root is grated in Japan and served with sushi and sashimi. The wasabi grater, made of dried shark skin, is traditionally used for this purpose. This grater has a coarse skin on one side and a fine skin on the other side to grate the wasabi into coarse or fine paste.	
Makiyakinabe	It is a square or rectangular cooking pan that is used for making Japanese style rolled omelettes called *tamagoyaki*. The pans are also known as *tamagoyakiki*, which means a griddle used for making *tamagoyaki*.	
Suribachi	This is a Japanese mortar and pestle used for crushing sesame seeds and other items in the kitchen. The *suribachi* is usually ceramic pottery bowl that is glazed on outside but inside the grinding area, it is a coarse unglazed pottery. The pestle however is made of wood and has a rounded end, which makes it ideal for grinding.	
Saibashi	*Saibashi* are Japanese kitchen chopsticks, which are slightly different from the regular chopsticks called *hashi*. They are usually used as a cooking tool and not used for eating. The length of these chopsticks can range from 30–60 cm. Many of these *saibashis* are joined together at the end with a twine, which makes it easy to hold and cook.	

(Contd)

Table 10.7 (Contd)

Equipment	Description	Photograph
Rice cooker	A rice cooker or rice steamer is a self-contained tabletop kitchen appliance for cooking rice.	
Santoku	*Santoku bōchō* or *bunka bōchō* as known in Japan is a multipurpose knife used for mincing, chopping, and slicing food in Japanese kitchens.	
Sachimi bocho	These flat and long knives are used for slicing thin slices of raw fish for sashimi and sushi. Due to the unique shape and cutting edge of this knife, it is an ideal tool for slicing fish. The knife is sharpened only from one side and this unique feature enables it to cut only by dragging fashion, which leaves a clean cut on the fish.	
Oshizushihako	An *oshizushihako* (which literally means pressed sushi box) is a box or mould used to make *oshizushi* or pressed sushi. The unique shape of this box allows placing the topping on the base of the box and filling with sushi rice and then pressing with a flat piece of wooden covers. The sushi is now removed and sliced to any size.	
Nori heater	This is a metal box with a heating element inside it in order to keep the *nori* sheets crisp. This heated box also allows light toasting of the *nori* sheet for a wonderful flavour. The *nori* in a sushi should be crisp.	

THAI CUISINE

Thai cuisine stands out from all the other Oriental cuisines of South-East Asia. Also, it is one of the widely accepted foods in the world today because of its immense flavours and taste. Traditionally, Thailand has been very open to foreign culture and thus is described as 'crossroads of Asia'. The use of herbs and ingredients, such as lemon grass, *kaffir* lime, and bird-eye chillies, makes it scented, spicy, and acceptable to almost all the palates in the world. There are three distinct features about this cuisine. First, unlike other East Asian countries, it does not use chopsticks for eating, rather the food is eaten with fork and spoon, wherein the fork is used for pushing the food onto the spoon through which the food is eaten. Second, Thai cuisine has lots of curries, which are very different from their Indian counterparts. Each curry has a unique paste and flavouring which is combined with coconut milk, herbs, and sauces and eaten with rice. Third, the main dish is always rice and all the dishes are served as accompaniment to it.

Thai food has been accepted all over the world, perhaps because of a unique harmony of cooking methods that are seen separately in other cuisines, as also their ability to create five different tastes—sweet, sour, pungent, spicy, and bitter—in one dish with each of them being in unison with the others. This cuisine uses methods of stir frying, stewing for curries, grilled and barbecued meat such as satay and grilled meat, and also steaming. Although the Thais use a lot of chillies in their food, yet there are dishes that do not contain any chillies. An ideal Thai meal aims at achieving a harmonious blend of the spicy, sweet, and sour tastes, and is meant to be satisfying to the eye, nose, and palate. Sometimes several of these flavours are subtly blended in a single dish, while sometimes any one flavour could predominate. In addition to rice, a typical meal might include a soup, a curry or two, a salad, a fried dish, and a steamed one. Buddhism being the most practised religion in the country; people do not use large chunks of meat in their food. Rather, meat is chopped or shredded and then cooked along with a variety of ingredients that include typical Thai herbs like *kaffir* lime, lemon grass, hot and sweet basil. The meat could be beef, duck, and pork, or fresh seafood such as clams, mussels, crab, and prawns.

There are also a considerable variety of sauces and condiments: *nam pla*, the essential salt substitute made from fermented fish; *nam prik*, which is *nam pla* combined with chopped chillies and other ingredients; crushed dried chillies as well as fresh ones for those who like their food really hot; pickled garlic; locally made chilli sauce; and fresh vegetables such as cucumbers, tomatoes, and spring onions. The most common dessert is one or more of the delectable fruits that are so abundant in Thailand, while on special occasions; more elaborate desserts may be served.

This extreme versatility and harmonious blend of different tastes have made the Thai cuisine a gourmet's delight around the world. Whatever be the food or wherever it is eaten, be it in a restaurant, on a city sidewalk, on an open verandah of a farmhouse, or in the middle of a rice field at harvest time—a Thai meal is nearly always a social affair. Today, in most urban areas, a table and chair are likely to be used for dining, though a floor covered with several soft reed mats still suffices in many rural homes. Western cutlery has come into general use with the exception of knives as nothing is large enough to need cutting in a proper Thai meal. A large spoon to scoop out individual portions of rice and a fork to help move the food on one's plate were needed and found their way to the Thai dining table. In the north and north-east, where steamed glutinous rice is preferred, it is convenient to use fingers to form small balls and dip them into more liquid dishes. Chopsticks may also be provided for Chinese-style noodles dishes and a ceramic Chinese spoon for soups and certain sweets.

A large container of rice is always the centrepiece. Around this are placed all the other dishes and condiments, with the possible exception of the sweet, if one is served. Guests are free to help themselves, in any way they want, mixing dishes at will and seasoning them with a wide variety of condiments to achieve the desired taste. The soup may thus be eaten at either the beginning or the end of a meal, and the salad likewise. The only constants are the rice, which accompanies almost everything, and the sweet, which is usually brought after the dishes have been removed.

Eating is regarded as a ritual in the country and people love to eat. They like the food to be in different forms like small snacks as in spring rolls along with some dips; flavoursome salads like *som tam*; tasty soups like *tom yam*; delicate or spicy curries like green curry or *massaman* curry; or dishes which are a meal in itself, which mainly includes different varieties of noodles cooked with a combination of meats, seafood, or vegetables, and certainly desserts. The use of coconut as well as palm sugar is significant in the desserts.

Each of these dishes has a typical characteristic and taste differently. Thai cuisine, however, does not have a variety of starch to be served. Rice is the only common staple, which is again mainly cooked by steaming and without any salt. This blandness is countered when it is consumed along with curries which are salty as well as spicy. The dressing which are used in the salads are also very simple, like salt or lemon juice, rather than being of complex character as in the cases of European dressings. They also have different dips which are made from a paste of chillies, garlic, and other ingredients such as dried shrimps, shrimp powder, and fish sauce. The dips are commonly called *prik*.

Due to its extreme versatility, Thai cuisine definitely stands apart from other cuisines. It has gained popularity outside Thailand very quickly and people from other countries are increasingly taking to it. Before we start discussing Thai cuisines, it would be worthwhile to make ourselves familiar with some common terms that we shall often come across during this discussion. Some common terms that we often come across on Thai menu cards and while cooking Thai food are listed Table 10.8.

Table 10.8 Common terms in Thai cuisine

Thai name	English name	Thai name	English name
Ahan	Food	*Koong*	Prawns
Ahan thalay	Seafood	*Kung mang*	Lobster
Bahmee	Egg noodles	*Magroot*	*Kaffir* lime
Bai	Leaf	*Man*	Potato
Het	Mushroom	*Manao*	Lime
Horapa	Basil	*Maprao*	Coconut
Kaeng	Curry	*Moo*	Pork
Kai	Chicken	*Nam*	Water
Kapi	Shrimp paste	*Nam prik*	Spicy dipping sauce
Kaeng phet	Red curry	*Nam pla*	Thai fish sauce
Kaeng wan	Green curry	*Nam pla siew*	Soy sauce
Kha	Galangal, Siamese ginger	*Neua*	Beef
Khai	Egg	*Phat*	Stir-fried
Khao	Rice	*Phad*	Deep-fried
Khao niao	Sticky rice	*Penang*	Peanut paste
Krachai	Lesser Siamese ginger	*Prik*	Chilli
Kratiem	Garlic	*Pla*	Fish

(Contd)

Table 10.8 *(Contd)*

Thai name	English name	Thai name	English name
Plaow	Steamed	*Tom yam*	Soup with chilli paste
Phak	Vegetables	*Wan*	Sweet
Poo	Crab	*Woon sen*	Glass noodles
Takrai	Lemon grass	*Yam*	Salad
Tom	Boiling	*Yang*	Grilled
Thod	Fried		

Now, with reference to Table 10.8 it will be fairly easy to understand some of the Thai dishes on a given menu. Let us try few examples:

1. *Yam woon sen* – Salad of glass noodles
2. *Tom kha het* – Boiling ginger mushroom (soup of galangal mushrooms)
3. *Kaeng kiew wan koong* – Green curry with prawns
4. *Manthod kratiem prik Thai* – Deep-fried potatoes stir-fried with garlic and Thai chillies

Geographical Location

Thailand is also known as pink elephant as its geographical map resembles the trunk of an elephant. The Kingdom of Thailand is located in the heart of South-East Asia which is surrounded by Laos on the north-east, Myanmar on the west, Cambodia to the south-east, and Malaysia on the south. The southern part of the country extends like a peninsula touching Malaysia, and is therefore known as Malay Peninsula. Since a large part of the country is covered with water, seafood and fresh vegetables are part of everyday food.

Being a tropical country, Thailand enjoys a very pleasant climate as well as abundance of food ingredients (both vegetarian and non-vegetarian), which are masterfully prepared with different herbs, dips, or curries to stimulate the taste buds of a gourmand. The Thai cuisine has evolved through the ages. Earlier, there were demarcations between royal food which was exclusively for the king and peasant's food, which was for the common man. As and when the Thais came in contact with the people of other parts of the world and their culture, these demarcations got blurred as they picked up pleasing ingredients and items from external cuisines to enrich their own. For example, the cooking methods of Thais earlier included steaming, stewing, baking, or grilling. They were introduced to stir frying by the Chinese. Later, as a result of Portuguese influence, they started using chillies in their dishes. The concept of curry is understood to have travelled to Thailand from India. With the increase of trade and commerce, the Thais incorporated the use of coconut in its different forms in their cuisine. As they got exposed to different foreign foods, they tried mixing and matching few ingredients in their food, which resulted in a much wider variation of Thai food ranging from spicy to mild, with an array of ingredients such as Thai chilli to *kaffir* lime or lemon grass to *galangal.*

Distinguished by its geographical location, Thai cuisine is divided into four major regions or cuisines, such as northern cuisines, north-eastern cuisine, central cuisine, and southern cuisine.

Central cuisine

The central part of Thailand has always been a region of historical importance. With the major Chao Phraya River flowing through it, the land is very fertile and conducive to the abundant growth of fresh fruits and vegetables. It is also the rice bowl of the country. Due to its unique topography and climate and its extensive network of canals and irrigation projects, rice abundantly grows here and thus, forms an important part of Thai cuisine. Bangkok, the capital of Thailand, is situated in central Thailand and is famous for its food.

Northern cuisine

The north had generally remained isolated from the rest of Thailand and it was only in 1921 that the first railway link between Bangkok and Chiang Mai in the north was established. This is a thickly forested region that engages in teak business through the neighbouring countries of Myanmar and Laos. Due to its isolation, the region's cuisines have been influenced immensely by the cuisines of Myanmar and Laos. The rice produced here is sticky and often rolled into balls and eaten with curries and more saucy dishes. The cuisine of the north is milder as compared to that of central Thailand. The traditional eating style *khantoke* is understood to have originated in northern Thailand. It entails eating on a low-lying table, usually made of oak wood, with people sitting around the table on the floor and eating the meal together as a family.

Cuisines of north-east

Of all the regions of Thailand, the north-east is the least frequented or known to foreign travellers. Thais call this region *Isaan*. It is also the poorest region of the country as the land here is unfertile and drought-prone, which has forced many people to migrate to other parts of the country in search of work. Since this part neighbours Laos, it is common to see the effect of Laos cuisine on north-eastern Thai food. The locals here like their food to be heavily seasoned with robust flavours. Glutinous rice is the staple food. Due to scarcity of cattle and other meat, fish and seafood are the primary sources of proteins. Two most important and popular dishes of this region are the raw papaya salad also known as *som tum isaan* and *laab,* which is a salad of minced meat.

Southern cuisine

The southern part of Thailand is also known as Malayan peninsula, as it juts out and borders Malaysia on its rugged limestone mountains. On the eastern side, the peninsula faces the Gulf of Thailand while the western side faces the Malaccan straits in the Indian Ocean. The long coastline naturally means that seafood forms a large part of their diet. Due to its proximity to Malaysia, a Muslim-majority country, the Muslim community here also thrives on beef. The cuisines of southern Thailand are as distinct as its serene beauty. Coconut plays a large role in local diet as it abundantly grows on the coastal belt. The famous Thai curry called *massaman* curry, which literally means Muslim curry, is made with coconut milk and spices such as white cardamom, coriander, and cumin. Many food items are influenced by Malaysia and Indonesia.

Apart from the regional cuisines, the cuisines of the royal courts have also gained international popularity and are often showcased in hotels and restaurants, and on special occasions. This food is commonly known as *Royal Cuisines of Thailand*. It not only focused on the art of blending flavours, but also on adorning the table with carved fruits and vegetables.

Commonly used Ingredients in Thai Cuisine

Taste of Thai food is easily distinguishable due to the presence of unique ingredients and aromatic herbs and vegetables. Some popular ingredients, such as *galangal* (a rhizome-like ginger), fish sauce, garlic, and basil, combine together to create a harmony of flavoursome food, the experience of which is truly unforgettable. Thai food was introduced in India about a decade ago and immediately found favour among people. Ever since, its popularity has grown to such an extent that one can find common Thai ingredients at a local grocery shop nowadays. Floating markets in Thailand are known to people from around the world. Lavish boats adorned with fresh produce of the day sell ingredients while they sail through backwaters of towns and cities. People often buy their ingredients from these floating markets. Some of the most unique ingredients in Thai cooking are described in Table 10.9.

Table 10.9 Ingredients used in Thai cuisine (see also Plate 11)

Ingredient	Description	Photograph
Lemon grass/ *takrai*	Called *takrai* in Thai, lemon grass grows well in moderate climate and has a lemony fragrance. Only the bulb-like structure at the base of the plant is used. It can be peeled and chopped or used in a paste along with other ingredients. Lemon grass is also commonly chopped with a *cleaver* and added to soups and stocks.	
Thai ginger/ *Galangal*	An underground stem like ginger, *galangal* or Thai ginger is also called *ka, kha,* or *laos,* as it is commonly used in Laos cuisine too. The rhizomes of this plant are larger than ginger. It is used in place of ginger but the taste is more pungent. *Galangal* is a very important ingredient in Thai curries. It is pounded with different ingredients such as chilli, peppers, shallots, and garlic, for making pastes. It can also be sliced or bruised and cooked in soups.	
Palm sugar	This sugar is prepared by taking the sap of palm trees and reducing it by boiling down. Different types of palms are used such as palmyra palm, coconut palm, and sugar palm. The texture of palm sugar is similar to that of Indian jaggery and it is used extensively in the cooking of southeast Asian cuisine.	

(Contd)

Table 10.9 (Contd)

Ingredient	Description	Photograph
Kaffir lime/ *Makrut*	It is called *makrut* in Thai. Leaves of the plant and, rarely, the rind of the fruit are used in Thai cooking. The leaves are used in many ways in cooking and they impart a strong lemon fragrance to the preparations. *Kaffir* lime is usually hand torn and added to the soups and curries, but it can also be sliced thinly or finely chopped and added to dishes.	
Mango ginger/*Krachai*	This ingredient is also commonly known as lesser ginger or lesser *galangal*. It has a rhizome-like appearance and it grows in the form of fingers in bunches. It is mildly flavoured as compared to the regular *galangal*.	
Tofu/*Tou hu*	Tofu or bean curd is prepared by soaking soybeans to extract milk. The soaked soybean is then ground into pulp in a stone grinder. The stone grinder is useful as it produces less heat which does not spoil the quality of the milk. The milk is then heated to separate the solids from it; when the skin formed on the milk is dried, it is sold as dried bean curd sticks. If the milk is heated further and a coagulant (calcium chloride or calcium sulphate), is added, it acts like rennet and curdles the milk which is then pressed to make bean curd or tofu.	
Fish sauce/ *Nam pla*	This is a condiment that is used for salting and flavouring food. It is impossible to imagine Thai food, without the distinctive taste of this condiment. *Nam pla* is usually golden brown in colour and is prepared from fermented fish and salt. Apart from being used in cooking, it is also at times served as a dipping sauce or table accompaniment.	
Curry paste	Curry pastes are the backbone or base of all Thai curries. There are many types of curry pastes and each one has a different proportion of ingredients as well as different types of ingredients. All the spice pastes have chillies as the major base and the colour of the curry would depend upon the type of chilli used therein. Green chilli is used for green curry paste, yellow Thai chillies for yellow paste, and red chillies for red curry pastes. Apart from herbs such as *galangal*, lemon grass, and *kafir* lime, curry pastes also contain spices such as cumin, coriander, and nutmeg. The various types of curry pastes used in Thai cuisine are: green, red, yellow, *massaman,* and *penang* curry paste.	

(Contd)

Table 10.9 (Contd)

Ingredient	Description	Photograph
Bird's eye chillies/*Prik kee noo*	These are very small chillies that are available in different colours such as red, yellow, and green. Thai bird's eye chillies are very spicy and should be used with care. Thai curry pastes often use a combination of bird's eye chillies and large chillies. *Note:* The seeds of bird's eye chillies can be removed prior to cooking. This helps in reducing the spice levels.	
Red and yellow chillies	These are large Thai chillies that are available in different colours such as red, yellow, and green. They are not as hot as the bird's eye chillies and can be used for various kinds of stir-fries and also for garnish.	
Green papaya/ *Malagao*	Commonly called *paw paw*, the green papaya is also known as raw papaya. It is usually peeled with a special peeler that has wavy edges, which yields long and thin shreds of papaya that is used for making raw papaya salad commonly known as *som tam*.	
Long beans	Also known as runner beans or *barbati* beans in Hindi, they are thin and long beans that can be used in various preparations such as stir-fries, salads, and even curries.	
Mountain sauce	This is a seasoning which is soy sauce based and contains certain aromatic substances that are used for seasoning curries and stir-fries. *Note:* Care has to be taken when using mountain sauce and fish sauce as both of them are salty. If they are added in more than required quantities, these can over-season the food.	
Pea aubergines/ *Makua puong*	These are small berries that belong to the aubergine family and hence the name. They are not used as vegetable, but are added to Thai curries and even stir-fries to add flavour and aroma to the food. They are often added whole and are allowed to boil in a curry.	

(Contd)

Table 10.9 (Contd)

Ingredient	Description	Photograph
Pandan leaves/*Bai toey hom*	These are a fragrant leaves of screw pine family and are used for flavouring rice, and are even used in desserts. *Pandan* leaves are also used for wrapping chicken, which is first steamed and then deep-fried to serve as an appetizer. Essence of pandan leaves is also used for flavouring ice creams and desserts.	
Mung bean noodles/*Woon sen* noodles	These noodles are also known as glass noodles because of their transparent appearance. These are made with mung bean starch and are available in dried form. These noodles are very thin and should be allowed to soak in warm water until they soften. They are popularly used for making salads.	
Flat rice noodles/*Goew tiew*	These flat noodles are made from rice and are commonly used to prepare a dish called *phad Thai*. These noodles are available in dried form and must be rehydrated in water for at least 4 hours or for a shorter time in warm water. These noodles are never blanched in water as this would make them mushy.	
Fresh egg noodles/ *Bahmee* noodles	These are wheat noodles with eggs and are used for making stir-fried noodles that are commonly known as *bahmee*. This preparation is very different from Chinese stir-fry noodles as the cuts of vegetables are larger and the vegetables are often blanched and then stir-fried along with the noodles.	
Shrimp paste/ *Kapi*	Many types of dried shrimp pastes are available and used in southern Thailand. These can range from pink to dark grey colour. The pink variety is mild and used for making curries, whereas the darker one is used for making sauces. The shrimp paste needs to be toasted on fire before it can be used so as to enhance the flavours.	
Thai chilli paste	This is a proprietary chilli paste made from Thai red chillies, onion, and garlic and is often used for seasoning as well as in soups and stir-fries. It is not very spicy and is mainly used for flavouring.	
Thai cardamom/ *Loog gra waan*	Also known as Siamese cardamom in Europe, this is plump and white in colour and has an aromatic flavour that is very different from the Indian green and black cardamom. In Thai cooking, it is usually used in southern Thailand in curries and desserts.	
Holy basil/ *Krapao/Tulsi*	It is known as holy basil or hot basil, as it is commonly used in holy ceremonies and offerings in Thailand and even in India. It is commonly known as *tulsi* in Hindi and is a variety of basil with peppery flavour which is the reason it is called hot basil or *krapao* in Thai.	

(Contd)

Table 10.9 (Contd)

Ingredient	Description	Photograph
Sri racha sauce	This is a chilli sauce that is prepared from Thai chillies, vinegar, sugar, and salt. It is usually prepared and sold in bottles. Sri Racha is the most popular brand of this sauce and the term is also used generically for the sauce.	
Bean curd sheets	These are proprietary sheets of dried bean curd that resemble a sheet of wrinkled paper. They are extremely difficult to work with when dry. They need to be soaked in water for at least 10 minutes before they can be used. These are usually used as a wrap for snacks that can be deep-fried or steamed.	

Speciality Dishes

Thailand is a land of festivities and celebrations, which (as in India) are incomplete without special dishes and sweets. The Thais are not only fond of eating but love to decorate their food like the Japanese. The dishes are arranged symmetrically and many of them are presented with carved fruits and vegetables. Some restaurants specially employ people for exclusively carving fruits and vegetables.

It is the lightness of the dishes that have made Thai cuisine so popular around the world. Thai dishes use cuts of meat that are without fat and also many herbs and vegetables that have medicinal properties. The food is quickly stir-fried on high-pressure burners to retain nutrition and texture. The food is seldom cooked for long and is always served fresh.

Like in other parts of the world, there are dishes for everyone. People at home would eat a simple curry with rice, yet in hotels and restaurants or on special occasions, elaborate dishes are served along with accompaniments and sauces. Some of the most popular Thai dishes are described in Table 10.10.

Table 10.10 Popular dishes of Thai cuisine (see also Plates 11 and 12)

Dish	Description	Photograph
Satay	Satay are thin slices of meat marinated in curry paste, seasonings, and skewered onto bamboo sticks and char-grilled on satay grillers. It is believed that satay originated in Indonesia, but these are popular in all South-East Asian countries such as Singapore, Malaysia, Philippines, and Thailand. Thai satays are served with peanut sauce.	
Thod man khao phod	Commonly known as Thai corn patties, these are prepared by mixing creamed corn and chopped corn kernels with red curry paste, *Kaffir* lime, chopped lemon grass, cornflour, and fish sauce like a batter. These are then dropped in hot oil and fried until it can hold shape. They are taken out of oil, reshaped, and flattened to make a round shape and fried again until crisp. Thai corn patties are traditionally served with plum sauce.	

(Contd)

Table 10.10 (Contd)

Dish	Description	Photograph
Thod man pla	Also known as Thai fish cakes, this is a dish commonly eaten as starters. Fish is minced and then mixed vigorously with red curry paste, *kaffir* lime, and seasonings. It is then flattened into patties and deep-fried. It is usually served with plum sauce.	
Larb gai	This famous dish from Isaan (north-eastern region) is a salad of minced meat, usually pork or chicken, that is mixed with toasted and crushed rice and seasonings. In Thailand, food is not eaten course wise and everything comes to the table and eaten in family style. However, in hotels and restaurants, *larb gai* features on the starter menu.	
Som tam	It is one of the most famous dishes of Thailand and is made from raw papaya. It is also known as raw papaya salad or *som tam isaan*, as it originates from north-eastern Thailand. The green raw papaya is peeled to expose the white skin, which is then peeled off using a special zigzag peeler to make thin shreds of raw papaya. These shreds are now lightly crushed along with tomatoes, peanuts, palm sugar, coriander roots, bird's eye chillies, and fish sauce in wooden mortar and served as salad. *Note:* Raw papaya salad should not be eaten by pregnant women as it can cause abortion due to high content of the enzyme, *papain*.	
Yam woon sen chae	Also known as glass noodle salad, it is made by soaking *woon sen* noodles in warm water until they soften. A handful of noodles are placed on a chopping board and cut at intervals to facilitate eating. These are then warmed in a steamer for a minute as cold glass noodles do not give a good texture. The warm noodles are mixed with chopped vegetables, seasonings, and served warm.	
Tom yam	This is one of the most famous soups of Thailand. It is a spicy, hot and sour broth of aromatic vegetables such as lemon grass, *kafir* lime, galangal, Thai chilli paste. Few vegetables such as mushrooms and crushed shallots are also added. *Tom yam* gets its name from the meat or ingredients used in it. For example, *tom yam gai* would mean it has chicken, *tom yam koong* would mean it has prawns, and *tom yam phak* would mean that it is prepared with vegetables.	
Tom kha	This soup is a broth made by boiling chicken stock with aromatic vegetables such as lemon grass, *kafir* lime, *galangal*, mushrooms, bird eye chillies, and coconut milk. Just like *Tom yam*, it also gets its name from its main ingredient. If the main ingredient is mushroom, the soup is called *tom kha het*.	
Krathong thong	It literally means golden flowers that are made by dipping the moulds in a batter of rice flour, tapioca flour, and wheat flour with egg and coconut milk, and deep-fried until crisp tartlets are obtained. These are then filled with assorted fillings and served as snacks.	

(Contd)

Table 10.10 (Contd)

Dish	Description	Photograph
Kai takrai	*Kai* means chicken and *takrai* is lemon grass. This is a stir-fried dish of chicken flavoured with lemon grass, vegetables such as onions and peppers. It is stir-fried with seasonings such as mountain sauce, light soy and fish sauce.	
Krapao	*Krapao* usually means hot basil and when this word is used in menu, it always is pre-fixed with the name of the ingredient that it is cooked with it. The main ingredient is usually minced or finely chopped. A bunch full of hot basil is minced along with onions, black pepper, green spring onions, and bird's eye chillies and kept aside. This dish is made by stir frying the minced meat or vegetable with *krapao* mix and seasoned with light soy sauce, fish sauce, and oyster sauce.	
Patani	This is a dish made by slicing lamb into thin slices which are blanched in hot water to remove any strong flavour and impurities. The blanched lamb is then tossed with ginger, onions, and seasonings such as light soy sauce, fish sauce, and oyster sauce.	
Kaeng kiew wan	*Kaeng kiew wan* or green curry is one of the most popular curries of Thai cuisine. The process of making all the curries is similar. They are made in a pot and not in a wok. To make a curry, first the main ingredients such as meat or vegetables are sautéed in small quantity of oil, along with the desired curry paste and small amount of stock. It is then allowed to stew for 5–7 minutes; then the first extract or thin coconut milk is added and cooked for another 3–4 minutes. Thereafter, aromatic vegetables such as *kaffir* lime, *galangal,* and pea aubergines are added along with a thick extract of coconut milk and cooked until the curry becomes thick. Curries are served with steamed rice. All curries are served garnished with fresh basil and sliced bird's eye chillies.	
Paneng	This curry is a spicy red curry that is traditionally prepared with sliced beef. The only difference between this curry and other curries is that it uses less coconut milk and thus, is spicier than all of them.	
Massaman	This curry is also prepared in the same way as green curry with an addition of potatoes and spices such as white cardamom and crushed peanuts.	
Kaeng phet	This is red curry and is the second spiciest of all curries. The procedure of making this curry is same as green curry with an addition of mountain sauce as seasoning.	

(Contd)

Table 10.10 (Contd)

Dish	Description	Photograph
Bahmee	These are stir-fried egg wheat noodles that are usually stir-fried with meats and vegetables, along with seasonings such as light soy sauce, fish sauce, and mountain seasoning. Though the style of stir frying is similar to Chinese noodles, in this case the vegetables are pre-cooked and are cut into chunks and not sliced or shredded as in case of Chinese cooking.	
Phad Thai	This is a dish made from flat rice noodles that are stir-fried and tossed in a sweet and sour sauce with other ingredients such as tamarind, tomato ketchup, chilli paste, peanuts, bean sprouts, and fresh coriander. The dish is eaten on its own and is served as main course.	
Kai hor bai toey	This dish is made by marinating chicken morsels in sesame oil, light soy sauce, and seasonings and then wrapping them in *pandan* leaves and securing the same with a knot. Thereafter, they are steamed so that the chicken gets cooked and then deep-fried until crisp.	
Sangkaya	This is a pudding made from coconut milk that is infused with pandan leaves and then thickened with cornstarch and eggs, and sweetened with palm sugar. It is served chilled, garnished with condensed milk.	
Tab tim krob	This is a popular dessert of Thailand. Water chestnuts are cut into small pieces and dipped for sometime in pomegranate syrup until they acquire a deep red colour. They are then strained and coated generously with tapioca flour. At this stage, they resemble pomegranate seeds. Thereafter, they are boiled in water until they float to the surface. They are then mixed with sweetened coconut milk and served with crushed ice. Sometimes other canned fruits like jackfruits are also added.	
Khanom krok	These are rice pancakes prepared in a special mould. The batter is made by combining rice flour, palm sugar, coconut milk, and freshly shredded coconut. The batter is poured into a hot and greased mould to make these sweets that are served as tea time snacks.	

Tools and Equipment used in Thai Cuisine

Most of the South-East Asian countries utilize high-pressure burners and woks for cooking as most of the cooking is done by stir frying, steaming, and boiling. The same holds true for Thai cooking. Apart from stir frying, Thai cuisine boasts of various kinds of curries that are prepared in pots and pans. Most Chinese equipment, such as wok, spatulas, cooking spoons, and strainers, are common to all Asian cuisines. However, some equipment unique to Thai cooking are listed and discussed in Table 10.11.

Table 10.11 Tools and equipment unique to Thai cooking

Equipment	Description	Photograph
Kude maprow or coconut grater	Known as *kude maprow* in Thailand, the coconut grater is available in various designs. The common ones are in shape of a rabbit, where a person can sit on the rabbit's back and grate the coconut for its milk and oil.	
Krok and *saak* or mortar and pestle	*Krok* and *saak* is the traditional mortar and pestle used for grinding curry pastes that form the base of Thai curries. It is traditionally made of stone or wood. It can be of two types: deep and flat. The deep ones are used for pounding, while the flat ones are used for grinding. The deep wooden mortar and pestle is still used in hotels to make the famous raw papaya salad.	
Bamboo basket	It is one of the frequently used equipment in Thai kitchen. A basket made from bamboo is used for lowering foods in boiling water or even into woks for deep frying or steaming rice. In modern hotel kitchens, metal strainers are used for this purpose, but in households, use of these baskets is still prevalent.	
Krathong thong maker	This equipment is made of brass and is like shells attached to along handle. It is dipped in batter and then lowered into oil to make crisp shells called *krathong* that are filled with various fillings and served as snacks.	
Satay griller	This is a charcoal grill used for grilling satay. Though traditionally charcoal grills are still commonly used, modern versions running on gas or electricity are also available in the market.	
Papaya peeler	This is a peeler with zigzag teeth. The unique design of this peeler allows it to shred papaya into thin and long shreds that are used for preparing the raw papaya salad.	
Tom yam steam boat	This equipment is used for serving Thai hotpot dishes and is also commonly used for serving soups such as *tom yam kai*, *tom yam phak*, and *tom yam koong*. The soup is poured into a bowl which has a vent in which glowing charcoals are added, so that it can keep the soup hot for a long time.	
Khanom krok pan	This is a cast iron utensil used for making Thai cakes called *khanom krok*. The dish is placed on fire and the batter is added into the indentations and covered with a lid.	

Over the last few chapters, we discussed a very broad range of cuisines from around the world. However, there are many more countries, each of which has its own regional cooking styles and influences that have not been discussed in this book. The reason is that many of those cuisines are not popularly served on the menus of international hotels; but sometimes we come across those cuisines at international food festivals. We also learnt that the focus of food preparation in Asian countries is by and large on the use of fresh and prime quality ingredients, and the art of presenting food with decorations and garnishes.

In the next chapter, we will discuss the art of making cakes and pastries and their importance in the menu.

SUMMARY

In the last few chapters, we discussed food around the Western and European cuisine and in this chapter, discussed the foods of East Asian countries, especially China, Japan, and Thailand. Though there are many other countries, such as Malaysia, Indonesia, Vietnam, Laos, Cambodia, Korea, and Philippines, in the Orient, yet a large part of these cuisines are influenced from the three main cuisines discussed in this chapter.

Chinese cuisine has always been very popular in India and the world due to the extensive travel of the Chinese, who migrated to various parts of the world in search of better fortune and prospects. Asians have always tried to use locally available ingredients to cook food which makes these cuisines more acceptable to people around the world.

Chinese food is more diverse than Indian food. Harsh environmental conditions, such as floods and droughts, taught the Chinese people to respect every grain of food. Thus, it is common to see the Chinese utilizing almost each and every part of any commodity available to them. For instance, in a chicken, every part except feathers is made into delicacies that are not only popular locally but also around the world.

It was also important to discuss Japanese cuisine, as this cuisine too has become popular in the world. It is quite common to find most of the modern hotels featuring Japanese dishes and opening up of speciality Japanese restaurants, and all-day dining restaurants having a section of sushi and sashimi dishes in India.

Thai food, on the other hand, has acquired immense popularity in hotels and restaurants around the world over the last decade. It is considered to be one of the healthiest cuisines in the world because of low consumption of oil in cooking and the use of fresh herbs and vegetables which have immense medicinal values.

In this chapter, we discussed Oriental cuisines with regard to their flavour profile and the evolution they have undergone over the years. We discussed the geographical location of these countries and understood its impact on the development of their respective cuisines. Every cuisine has a set of its local flavours, which are affected by a range of commodities available in that region. We discussed the local and commonly used ingredients in each of these cuisines. Apart from the ingredients, even tools and equipment play an important role in cooking; we discussed the same lucidly in tables along with photographs. Each cuisine's special and popular dishes have been discussed as well. The recipes of these dishes are described in the CD.

KEY TERMS

Bird's nest It is the nest of a bird species, which is built by the spit of the bird and is a delicacy in China. It is used in making soups.

Black beans These are salted and cured soybeans that turn black over a period of time.

Buri It is a Japanese term for *yellowtail* tuna weighing around 5 kg.

Chilli chicken It is a popular Chinese dish in India, prepared by deep-frying the chicken and stir-frying it with dry red chillies, dark soy sauce and chilli sauce.

Chop suey It is an American Chinese preparation of fried noodles with meat in a sauce.

Chowmein These are stir-fried noodles with chilli sauce and soy.

Cloud ear fungus Also known as black fungus, it is a type of mushroom used in Oriental cuisines.

Congee It is Chinese rice porridge often eaten for breakfast.

Crab roe These are eggs of crab or other fish that resemble caviar. These are available in different colours.

Dim sum These are small bite-sized savoury dumplings of wheat flour or starch, usually stuffed and steamed.

Dipping sauce It is a term for any sauce that can be served as an accompaniment to finger food or snacks. The food can be dipped into it and eaten.

Eel It is a type of fish that resembles a long snake.

Family style This is a style of service in which the food items are served together and the guests can share and help themselves informally without following courses.

Farinaceous It is a term used for classical course in the French menu that comprises starchy dishes such as rice, pasta, and noodles.

Hamachi It is a Japanese term for *yellowtail* tuna weighing around 3 kg.

Hemp seeds These are seeds of the hemp plant that are used in food, medicine, and even textile industry.

High-pressure burner These are cooking ranges designed for Asian cooking, wherein air is forced through an outlet to increase the pressure of gas flame which makes it ideal for stir frying.

Hotpot It is a style of cooking wherein the hot stock is placed on heat source and the food is dipped and cooked on the table.

Isaan This is local Thai reference for people from the north-eastern part of Thailand.

Khantoke It is a style of eating in Thailand, where food is served and eaten at low tables, while sitting on the floor.

Kiosks These are small shops that sell food.

Manchurian It is a term for crisp-fried dumplings of meat or vegetables stewed in soy-flavoured sauce, which is more popular outside China.

Marbling It is the interwoven texture of fat and muscle in an animal tissue.

Oriental cuisines It is a term used for cuisines from the Orient or the Eastern world.

Pan Asian cuisines It is a term used for cuisines from Asian countries. In the hospitality industry, the term is used interchangeably with Oriental cuisines.

Parson's nose It is the rear end of the chicken which is an excretory organ.

Quail It is a small bird, often classified as game.

Rennet It is an enzyme found in the stomach of calves, used as a coagulant for preparing cheese.

Sand pots These are earthenware pots used for stewing dishes in China.

Scallions These are the green portion of spring onions.

Scallops It is a type of mollusc obtained from large fan-type shells.

Shark fin These are dried fins of shark, popularly used in soups.

Sichuan pepper It is a kind of peppercorn used in Szechwan (*Sichuan*) cuisine. It is also known as *tirphal* in Hindi and *fagara* in English.

Stir-fry It is a method of cooking wherein the food is tossed in a wok on high flame.

Tempura It is a deep-fried dish from Japan, which is known for its light colour and crispness.

Tonkatsu It is crumb-fried pork cutlet from Japan.

Venison It is the meat of deer.

Wagyu It is a Chinese breed of cattle that has high content of marbling in meat.

Wonton It is a savoury filled thin sheets of dough that resemble *tortellini* pasta. *Wontons* are boiled in soups or deep-fried as snacks in Chinese cuisine.

CONCEPT REVIEW QUESTIONS

1. What countries contribute to Oriental cuisine or Pan Asian cuisine?
2. What are the major differences among Chinese, Japanese, and Thai cuisines?
3. Describe the geographical location of China and the role it plays on Chinese cuisine.
4. Describe the cuisine of the four regions of China.
5. What are the popular food commodities that come from the northern region of China?
6. What regions are included in eastern and western China? What famous commodities come from this region?
7. How is the food of eastern China different from that of southern China?
8. Which regional Chinese cuisine is most popular in the world? Give reasons for the same.
9. What is the philosophy of yin and yang applied to Chinese cooking?
10. What are dim sums and which region of China do they originally come from?
11. Describe the Mongolian hotpot cookery.
12. Name two most exotic dishes from the Canton region of China.
13. What are Chekiang (Zhejiang) vinegar and Shaoxing (Chongqing) wine and which part of China do they come from?
14. Differentiate between a Chinese cabbage and a napa cabbage.
15. Name few types of noodles used in Chinese cooking.
16. How does the soy sauce differ in China, Japan, and Thailand?
17. Describe three types of mushrooms commonly used in Chinese cooking.
18. Why is it important to cook shiitake mushrooms?
19. What is the five spice powder and what are its components?
20. What is the difference between abalone and sea cucumber?
21. Name and describe at least three types of dim sum.
22. What is the process of making a Peking duck?
23. Describe any three desserts from China.
24. Describe the cuisine of Japan with regard to its geographical layout.
25. 'Japan is only famous for its sushi and sashimi.' Critique the statement.
26. Describe the origin of sushi and its types and varieties.
27. What is a sashimi? How is it graded?
28. How is Japanese rice different from Chinese rice?
29. Describe at least three dishes made with Japanese rice.
30. Describe at least three Japanese noodles.
31. What is the difference between hamachi fish and buri fish?
32. Describe at least three seaweeds used in Japanese cuisine.
33. What accompaniments are served with sushi and sashimi and what are their roles?
34. What is kobe beef? What is unique about it?
35. Differentiate between sake and mirin.
36. How is silken tofu different from regular tofu?
37. Differentiate between togarashi and hondashi.
38. Name at least three mushroom varieties used in Japanese cuisine.
39. Describe the teppanyaki style of Japanese cooking.
40. What is the difference and similarities between the sukiyaki and shabu shabu style of cooking?
41. What is tomagoyaki and how is it made?
42. Describe a donburi and name at least two common ones.
43. Describe at least five unique instruments used in Japanese cuisine.
44. Evaluate the uniqueness of Thai cuisine with regard to Chinese and Japanese cuisines.
45. How are Thai curries different from Indian curries?
46. What are the regional cuisines of Thailand? How are they different from each other?
47. What are the differences among ginger, Thai ginger, and krachai?
48. Name at least five sauces used in Thai cuisine.
49. How many types of curry pastes are used in Thai cuisine? What are the differences among them?
50. Name at least three types of noodles used in Thai cuisine.
51. Describe a tom yam soup.
52. What is a som tam? How is it made?
53. Describe at least three Thai desserts.
54. What is the importance of mortar and pestle in Thai cuisine?

PROJECT WORK

1. In groups of five, do a market survey of hotels and speciality restaurants that specialize in Japanese food. Record your observations with regard to the choice of the menu, ingredients, equipment used in cooking and serving. Share your observations with the other groups.

2. In groups of five, prepare at least two popular dishes from China, Japan, and Thailand and make them ready for tasting and evaluation. Record your observations and share with other groups.

3. Do a market survey of fruits and vegetable markets that sell Oriental herbs and spices and list the various kinds of ingredients. Now classify these ingredients according to their country of origin and find out their uses.

4. In groups, visit a Chinese restaurant that serves a range of dim sums. Write down the names and make a note of various shapes of the same. Prepare a presentation of the same and share with the other groups.

5. In groups of four, do a cuisine research for the other Asian cuisines such as Malaysian, Philippines, Laos, Vietnam, Cambodia, and Indonesia and list the similarities with Chinese and Japanese cooking. Share your learning with the other groups.

PART III

ADVANCED PASTRY AND CONFECTIONERY

CHAPTER 11

CAKES AND PASTRIES

Learning Objectives

After reading this chapter, you should be able to
- understand the basic concept of cakes and pastries
- appreciate the components of a cake and their importance
- analyse the techniques used in making cakes and pastries
- claim an insight into various types of cakes and pastries and their classification
- know the various kinds of icings used on a cake
- distinguish between various kinds of sponges used in the production of cakes and pastries
- comprehend the step-by-step approach to layer and decorate cakes and pastries
- value the portioning and serving of cakes

INTRODUCTION

When we talk about bakery and confectionery, cakes and pastries are the first things that come to our mind. The spongy cakes packed with whipped cream and delicious flavours are synonymous to pastries; but in the real sense, a pastry is much more than just sponge and filling. In confectionery parlance, a pastry can be referred to as a paste or even dough made with various kinds of ingredients such as flour, sugar, butter, and eggs. In this chapter, we shall discuss the various kinds of cakes and pastries and their evolution over a period of time. Most of the cakes and pastries that are patented, were made in old hotels and pastry shops, and are known as classical cakes. Nowadays, with more and more experimenting chefs around, it is very common to see a fusion of flavours from around the world like a French cream cake flavoured with lemon grass from Thailand. This category of cakes is known as contemporary cakes. When a small piece of cake is individually garnished and served, it can be sold as a pastry. The pastries can be layered separately to form various shapes such as circles, rectangles, and squares. With different kinds of moulds available in the market, one can also make three dimensional shapes such as pyramids, and cones. When cakes are prepared as bite sized, they are often referred to as *petits fours glacés*, which is a generic title that covers all small bite size pastries and cakes that are 'iced'. *Petits fours glacés* are served with coffee after a meal, particularly for special functions, buffets, etc. A cake in commercial terminology refers to a cake made from flour, sugar, fat, and eggs. It may also contain milk, baking powder, fruit, nuts, etc. A cake is usually heavier than a sponge. However, 'cakes' have a broader interpretation that includes *gateau* (French) and *torte* (German). These are made of layers of sponge, *Genoese* sponge, meringues, creams, and pastries. A cake generally takes its name from its main filling and the flavour, such as lemon cream *gateaux*, pineapple *gateaux*, fresh strawberry *gateaux*, etc. The foundation of a good cake begins with its base. Thus, every effort and care needs to be taken in preparing a good base as decorating poor quality bases in an attempt to make them look better could prove counterproductive. The purpose of decorating a cake is to make it more appealing to the eye and to the palate. The decoration of a cake is very satisfying task as it enables one to express oneself in a creative manner.

Preparing a cake is a skill that requires a lot of precision when it comes to intricate details such as measurement and the quality of ingredients being used. The base of a cake can be either a sponge or thin layers of flaky pastry, or other ingredients such as crushed biscuits. Sponge cakes are so called because their texture resembles a sponge with well-distributed holes that are formed when the air trapped in the batter while folding gets released as the cake bakes. The gluten (a protein) in the flour helps the cake to retain its shape while the air escapes leaving the holes behind.

Many sponges can be served on their own but most of them are used as bases for classical cakes and other desserts. In this chapter, first we shall discuss various types of classical cakes and pastries and then discuss the modern trends.

CLASSICAL CAKES AND PASTRIES

Before we go on to learn different types of classical cakes and pastries, it is important to understand the basic composition of any cake.

Basic Composition

A classical cake has the following parts: base, cake, filling, topping, garnish, moistening agent. Figure 11.1 depicts the various layers of a basic cake or pastry.

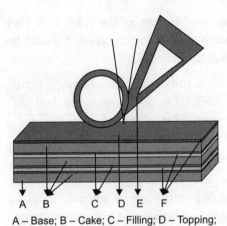

A – Base; B – Cake; C – Filling; D – Topping;
E – Garnish; F – Moistening agent

Fig. 11.1 Cross-section of a cake/pastry

CHEF'S TIP
All cakes of a light nature need a weaker soft flour (one with low gluten) to obtain a more crumbly result. If this type of flour is not available, an all-purpose flour can be used with the addition of some cornflour to make it softer.

CHEF'S TIP
Dried fruits should be washed and well drained. The purpose of doing this is not only for hygienic reasons but to increase the moisture content in the dried fruits, giving the cake a moist quality. Another way of achieving this is to macerate the dried fruits in spirits or liqueurs.

Base This is the base of the cake or pastry. It is not necessary for every cake to have a base, but most have one. A base serves many purposes such as the following

- It adds a texture to the cake. For example, a Black Forest cake, which is a soft cake layered with whipped cream and sponge, has a base of sweet paste biscuit that offers a crunch to the soft textured cake to create an interesting mouth feel.
- The base helps to lift the soft cakes and pastries from the plate for consumption; if the cake is too soft it will fall apart.
- The base prevents the spongy cake to soak up any odd flavours if refrigerated on a tray.

Cake This is the body of the cake. Various types of sponges can be used for this purpose. The most basic of all is *Genoese* sponge that is made by whisking eggs and sugar until light and fluffy. Flour is folded in along with melted fat and baked until cooked. A mixture of cocoa powder and flour can also be used to make chocolate sponge, which would be used for making a chocolate flavoured cake. Sometimes other kinds of bases can also be used instead of sponge or with a combination of sponge to layer a cake.

Filling This is the main flavouring of the cake from which it gets its name. For example, a chocolate truffle cake would have the filling of truffle inside. The base of the cake is layered with various kinds of flavoured creams and fillings to prepare the cake or pastry. The fillings can vary from jams and creams to jellied fruit juices. Sometimes baked custard is also used for filling a contemporary cake.

Topping The topping is the glaze of the cake, which is given for various reasons such as the following.

- It gives an attractive appearance to the cake
- It forms a cover on the cake and prevents it from drying out.
- It adds flavour and texture to the cake.

There can be various kinds of toppings used for the cake. Some cakes are covered only with dusted icing sugar, whereas some are covered with caramelized sugar. Various kinds of fillings used in cakes and pastries have been covered earlier in Chapter 20 of *Food Production Operations*.

Garnish This is one of the most important parts of a cake or a pastry that are used to decorate the cake for visual appeal, hence the term. Garnishes can range from fresh fruits to chocolate and sugar garnishes that would complement the flavour and texture of the cake. It is very important to choose the right kind of garnish to finish a cake. For instance, it would be odd to garnish a dry fruit cake with chocolate garnish or vice versa.

Moistening agent The moistening agent in a cake is usually a flavoured sugar syrup, that adds flavour as well as moistness to the cake. Each layer of sponge is brushed with liberal amounts of sugar syrup. This is done for the following reasons.

> **CHEF'S TIP**
> Always spread sugar syrup with a wide painting brush. This helps to spread the syrup equally on the sponge. Do not put too much of syrup on the base of the sponge as it will make the cake too soft and it will be difficult to lift the cake.

- To add sweetness to the cake
- To add flavour to the cake
- Some of the syrups flavoured with liqueurs are traditional for classical cakes, for example, a black forest cake is moistened with kirsch flavoured liqueur.
- Syrups are added to wet the sponge, which allows the fillings to stick to the sponge and it does not let the sponge give out its crumbs, while spreading the cream with a palette knife.

Kinds of Bases and Sponges

Before we start discussing different types of cakes and pastries, it is important to have an understanding of the various kinds of bases and sponges that are used for making a classical cake. Table 11.1 presents some popular kinds of sponges and bases that are used for making cakes.

Table 11.1 Types of bases used for making cakes and pastries (see also Plate 12)

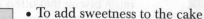

Base	Description	Photograph
Sponge	Sponge cakes are usually made with eggs, flour, and sugar and the texture of the baked product is light and airy. As it resembles the texture of a sponge, it is called so. A sponge cake can be of various types and the method of preparation differs for each one. Though the basic recipe for all sponge cakes includes eggs, flour, and sugar, and sometimes fat, it is the method of folding, that gives a different texture to each sponge. Sponge with addition of melted fat is known as *Genoese* sponge. It is the most commonly used sponge for cakes and pastries. A chocolate sponge can be made by substituting 25 per cent of flour with cocoa powder.	
Swiss roll	This is a very light and airy sponge made by whipping yolks and egg whites separately with sugar and then folding them together, along with flour and powdered nut flour such as almond and hazelnut. Swiss roll sponge can be made according to the cake or pastry that it would be required for. A lemon Swiss roll would be made using a sponge that is flavoured with lemon zest and is of a light lemon colour.	

(Contd)

Table 11.1 (Contd)

Base	Description	Photograph
Baumkuchen Other names: *Kue lapis* (Indonesia), Asian tree trunk cake, Indonesian layer cake	This cake is known as the king of cakes. Though its origins are in Germany, this cake is commonly made in Indonesia where it is known as *Kue lapis.* In India, it is known as *bebinca.* Traditionally, this cake is made on rollers that work on the principle of spit roasting. A large wooden roller revolves in front of a heat source such as gas jets or heated elements. The batter is prepared by creaming butter and sugar. A mixture of flour, cornflour, and almond powder is added to the creamed butter and sugar and yolks and whites of the egg that are separately whisked and are folded into the batter. This batter is poured over the wooden roller to coat it. It is allowed to brown on all sides and only when the first layer has browned, another layer of batter is poured and let to brown in a similar way, until the batter has been used up and the cake is fairly large. Experienced chefs can prepare this cake with up to 25 rings. Each brown coating on top of the cake makes one visible ring as more batter is poured over it. With the advent of technology, this cake can also be made in a pan under salamander. Though this cake will not have a traditional ring shape, it will have a flat cake like structure. This cake can also sometimes be sliced thin and put around any other cake or pastry for decoration or garnish.	*Baumkuchen* Process of making *baumkuchen*
Pound cake	This cake is also known as English cake or Madeira sponge or tea cake. It is known as pound cake because it contains a pound (454 g) of butter, flour, sugar, and eggs. This cake is made by creaming butter with sugar until light and fluffy. Eggs are added one by one taking care that the mixture does not curdle. Lastly, the flour is folded in with hands. Sometimes a small amount of baking powder is added for aeration. This cake can be flavoured with various kinds of ingredients such as citrus fruit zest and juices. They can also be flavoured with artificial flavours and colours. Candied fruits can also be mixed along with a batter to prepare dry fruit cakes. This cake is usually served sliced for afternoon tea and high tea.	
Meringue	Meringues are prepared by whipping egg whites with sugar and a pinch of salt. Heavy or light meringue can be achieved by addition of more or less sugar. Meringues can be divided into three categories. These are as follows: *French meringue* It is also known as cold meringue. To make this egg whites are whipped until frothy and sugar is added in small amounts, while whipping continuously. This meringue is supposed to be used instantly as it can separate if it is left outside for a longer period of time. *Swiss meringue* This is a hot meringue. To make this egg whites are whipped on a warm water bath until frothy, sugar is added in smaller amounts, and the mixture is whisked over the hot water bath until creamy and stands in peaks.	Cake covered with Swiss meringue sticks

(Contd)

Table 11.1 (Contd)

Base	Description	Photograph
Meringue	*Italian meringue* This is the most stable meringue of all. In this method, the egg whites are whipped with small amount of sugar until frothy and then hot melted sugar boiled to 118°C is added while continuously whisking the mixture until a thick meringue is obtained. Meringues can be used in variety of ways. They can be used as a base for cakes and pastries and even used for garnishes and decorations.	
Japonaise	This is a very crunchy base often used for high-end cakes and pastries. To make *Japonaise*, add two-third of almond powder or hazelnut powder to 1 part of meringue and mix well. It can be piped on to a baking mat with a round nozzle to form a circle starting from the centre and piping all the way towards the ends or it can be spread with a palette knife to form a circular base. *Japonaise* are commonly used as a base for small pastries and *petit four*, as it gives a rich taste and feel to the finished product.	
Macaroon	Macaroon is a crunchy paste made by combining nut flour, egg whites, and sugar. The nut flour can be of almonds, walnuts, desiccated coconut, etc. These can also be baked individually and served as cookies or spread into thin bases and baked for use as base for cakes and pastries.	
Sweet paste	Sweet paste is made by combining creamed butter and sugar with flour and eggs in such a way that the flour does not get over-mixed. Sweet paste is a versatile paste that sets into dough after being refrigerated for 30 minutes to 1 hour. It can be rolled into circles and baked until golden brown. This baked sweet paste base is traditionally used as a base for Black Forest cake (Table 11.2). Sweet paste can also be used for making cookies and bases for tarts, flans, and pies.	
Choux paste	*Choux* paste or pastry is a boiled pastry made by boiling butter and water together and then adding flour to it. It is cooked together for one minute and then removed from the fire. Eggs are incorporated one by one, stirring all the time until the paste is thick. This paste finds numerous uses in both bakery as well as Western kitchen to prepare sweets as well as savouries. *Choux* pastry can be piped to make various shapes, which can be decorated and filled for various kinds of pastries.	
Biscuit base	Dark chocolate cookies or English Marie biscuits are commonly used to make this crunchy base that is often used as a base for baked and chilled cheese cakes. The biscuits are crushed to a coarse powder and then kneaded with cold softened butter. It needs to be refrigerated for at least 30 minutes, before it can be rolled to desired thickness and then baked in the oven for 20 minutes until golden brown. The biscuit base needs to cool down before being used as a base.	

(Contd)

Table 11.1 (Contd)

Base	Description	Photograph
Dacquoise	*Dacquoise* is a French biscuit that was originally made in Dax, in south-western part of France. It is made by combining French meringue with powdered hazelnut and almond flour. It is then piped in circles and baked until crisp. It can be used only as a base or the entire cake can be made using this sponge.	
Joconde	This is a decorative sponge and is mostly used for lining the sides of the cakes. It is a modern invention that is made in two stages. Stage one involves making a *deco* paste by combining egg whites, flour, sugar, and butter in equal parts. It can be coloured to give designer effects. It is spread on a silicon baking mat as it sticks to other surfaces. Freeze the *deco* paste and then spread the special sponge mix onto the design in a layer and bake at high temperatures. The resulting sponge gets the design from *deco* paste printed on the sponge. The sponge is made by whipping up egg yolks with sugar. Mixture of flour and almond powder is folded in along with whipped meringue. Lastly, melted butter is folded in and the batter is spread over the baking mat with designs made with *deco* paste.	
Puff pastry	Puff paste or flaky pastry is often used as a base for making cakes and pastries. The famous *Napoleon gateaux* are made by layering baked puff pastry (*mille feuille*) sheets with whipped pastry cream. The puff pastry is also used as a base for many other classical cakes.	
Eggless sponge	This is very famous in India because of religious implications. The sponge is made by creaming butter and condensed milk until light and fluffy. Flour, baking powder, and soda water is folded carefully into the mixture and the sponge is baked until cooked.	

Kinds of Classical Cakes

Now that we have learnt about the various kinds of bases that can be layered with different kinds of creams and fillings to make some of the most popular cakes and pastries around the world. Some popular classical cakes and pastries are discussed in Table 11.2. It should be understood that each cake can also be served as a pastry. Though pastries can be referred to as smaller or individual cakes, there are certain pastries that are prepared only as a pastry and rarely as a cake. A few classical pastries are discussed separately in Table 11.3. Those are served as they are and not made into cakes.

Kinds of Classical Pastries

The word pastry is derived from the word paste. Various kinds of pastes are used in the pastry kitchen either to make bases for cakes, as discussed in Table 11.2, or for creating indigenous desserts called pastries. There is a thin line of difference between a cake and a pastry. All cakes when presented in a miniature form can be classified as pastries. However, there are certain pastries that are only prepared and served as pastries and not as cakes. Various kinds of classical pastries are described in Table 11.3.

Table 11.2 Classical cakes and pastries (see also Plates 12 and 13)

Cake/Pastry	Base and sponge	Filling	Garnish	Photograph
Sacher torte This is a chocolate cake, patented by Chef Franz Sacher, who was the head pastry chef to Prince Metternich. He invented it for the Congress of Vienna in 1832. The cake was an instant hit and has been famous ever after.	The *Sacher* is made from a dark chocolate sponge. In this cake, butter is melted along with the chocolate and whipped egg yolks are folded into the mixture. Flour sifted along with cornflour and cocoa powder is then folded in. Lastly, whipped meringue is folded in the batter. The sponge is baked, cooled, and sliced into two.	The *Sacher* sponge is moistened with sugar syrup and then the two halves are sandwiched with apricot jam. The jam is also spread on sides as well as top and smoothened out to give an even finish.	The cake is usually finished with melted chocolate truffle. Since this is a patented cake, it is customary to write the *Sacher* on top of the cake.	
Dobos torte This cake was created in Budapest by a Hungarian chef, Joseph Dobos. It became so famous that people from other countries wanted to import the cake. Chef Dobos thought of a novel idea to spread a thin layer of caramel on top of the cake to preserve and package it. Since then, the caramel coating on this cake has become synonymous to *Dobos torte.*	It is a white sponge that is prepared by creaming butter and sugar till fluffy. Whipped egg yolks and lemon zest is added and folded in. After this, meringue is folded along with flour, almond powder and the sponge is baked until cooked.	The cake is sliced into as many as five layers. Each layer is moistened with vanilla flavoured sugar syrup and layered with caramel flavoured butter cream. Two parts of white butter is whipped along with one part of icing sugar to prepare butter cream.	Sugar is heated over a moderate heat until it turns to a caramel. This is then spread onto a thin slice of sponge. This facilitates the cutting of the caramel. When the caramel sets, divide into equal pieces with a hot knife and arrange it on top of the cake like a fan.	

(Contd)

Table 11.2 (Contd)

Cake/Pastry	Base and sponge	Filling	Garnish	Photograph
Malakoff torte It is a popular *torte* that originated in France during the Crimean war between France and Russia. The *torte* is named after Malakoff hill, where it was created.	The base is a combination of sponge fingers—made by baking a special sponge in the shape of fingers. In this case egg yolks and whites are whipped along with sugar separately and then combined together with sifted cornflour and flour. This is piped on to the baking trays in finger shapes and then dusted with icing sugar before baking in the oven. The cake is moistened with rum-flavoured sugar syrup.	The cake is filled with rum-flavoured whipped cream. Layer of sponge fingers are arranged on the base and moistened with rum flavoured sugar syrup. More sponge fingers are arranged on the cream and topped with rum flavoured cream.	The cake is decorated by arranging sponge fingers on the sides of the cake. A swirl of whipped cream is piped on the edges of the cake and garnished with more sponge fingers.	
Linzer torte It is very famous tart that has its origins in the Linz city of Austria. *Linzer* is basically a tart which is eaten as a cake or as a dessert. It is one of the oldest tarts.	A shortcrust pastry is prepared by creaming butter and sugar with eggs and combining it lightly with flour and hazelnut powder. It is flavoured with lemon zest and left to chill for 30 minutes or until set. This forms the base of the cake. The dough is rolled to 5 mm thickness and lined on a tart or a pie mould.	The lined pie shell is filled with red currant jam or raspberry jam.	The dough is rolled and cut into strips. The strips are arranged in a criss-cross fashion on top of the torte and the cake is brushed with egg whites and baked at 180°C for 20 minutes. The cake should be chilled before cutting and is garnished with almond flakes.	

(Contd)

Table 11.2 (Contd)

Cake/Pastry	Base and sponge	Filling	Garnish	Photograph
Battenberg This cake is believed to have been created in 1884 in honour of the marriage of the granddaughter of Queen Victoria to the Prince of Battenberg. The traditional chequered yellow and pink colour is synonymous to this cake. This cake is from Great Britain.	This cake is made with pink and yellow coloured *Genoese* sponges that are cut into bars of square shape. These squares are joined to each other with the help of apricot jam and covered with marzipan.	The cake is not filled but the sponge bars are joined with apricot jam.	The cake has no particular garnish but is covered with marzipan and served exposing the chequered sponge.	
Black Forest gateaux This cake, which is very popular, comes from the Swabia region of Germany, which is famous for the Black Forest. The appearance of the cake represents the forests of this region. In Germany, this cake is known as *Schwarzwälder Kirschtorte*.	The cake usually has a base of baked sweet paste biscuit and apricot jam is spread in a thin layer over the biscuit and a slice of chocolate *Genoese* is put on top. Sugar syrup flavoured with *Kirsch* liqueur is used to moisten the sponge.	The cake is layered with fresh whipped cream, chopped dark chocolate chips and *morello* cherries. Some recipes also use sour cherries, which should be cooked with sugar and corn starch.	The cake is covered with whipped cream from all the sides and top. Dark chocolate flakes are put on top with swirls of whipped cream that are decorated with cherries. The sides can be left plain or can be decorated with chocolate flakes.	
Napoleon gateaux It is a classical French cake made with baked puff pastry also known as *mille feuille* that literally translates to thousand layers. It is believed that the cake was developed during the nineteenth century.	The base for the cake is made by rolling the puff pastry into thin sheets and baked until crisp and golden brown. This cake is not layered with sponge and hence it is not moistened with any syrup.	The sheets of baked puff pastry are layered with whipped pastry cream that is flavoured with orange flavoured liqueur.	Traditionally, the top of the cake is brushed with hot apricot jam after which warm fondant is poured on the top. Chocolate is piped in straight lines on the fondant. Further, a toothpick is used to create a feather design.	

(Contd)

Table 11.2 (Contd)

Cake/Pastry	Base and sponge	Filling	Garnish	Photograph
Gateaux St Honore This is a traditional French *gateau* that is named after the patron saint of pastry cooks.	This cake utilizes a base of puff pastry on which *choux* pastry is piped all around the rim and the gateau is baked blind.	The dessert is filled with two different types of fillings: 1. *Chiboust cream:* One part of pastry cream is mixed with one part of Italian meringue 2. *Diplomat cream:* One part of pastry cream is mixed with one part of melted chocolate and little gelatine. These are piped alternately in the empty space of *gateaux.*	The cake is decorated and garnished with small profitroles that are filled with orange flavoured pastry cream and dipped in caramel. The cake can also be garnished with cut fresh fruits and spun sugar.	
Praline gateaux This is a French gateau. Praline is made by heating nuts and sugar until caramelized. The mixture is then poured on to a marble slab and left to cool. It is then crushed coarsely and stored until further use.	This cake utilizes vanilla-flavoured Genoese sponge that is cut into three slices. Vanilla-flavoured sugar syrup is used to moisten the sponge.	The cake is layered with praline flavoured butter cream and some crushed praline is also sprinkled between the layers and it is covered on all sides with praline butter cream.	The sides of the cake are decorated with roasted almond flakes and the top is covered with crushed praline.	
Charlotte russe This cake was made by French Chef Marie-Antoine Carême who named it in honour of his Russian employer.	This cake is lined with sponge fingers and the base for this cake is also sponge fingers that are soaked in rum flavoured sugar syrup. This cake is usually made in a half sphere shaped mould known as *bombe.*	The lined cake is filled with a mixture of fruits and custard that is prepared by cooking milk and sugar with egg yolks and then cooled down. This is then mixed with whipped cream and gelatine.	The cake is usually garnished with fresh fruits and powdered icing sugar.	

(Contd)

Table 11.2 *(Contd)*

Cake/Pastry	Base and sponge	Filling	Garnish	Photograph
Opera gateaux This cake is a classical French *gateau* that was first made in the early 1900s. It is also known as *gateaux Clichy* after the name of the chef who is credited with having created it. Another Parisian pastry chef reintroduced the cake as *Gateaux Opera* after the Paris Grand Opera and it is believed to have been served at a French American reception held at the Opera house in 1930.	The opera sponge is a kind of *Japonaise* that is made by using almond powder. This cake consists of at least 5 slices of sponge that is moistened with sugar syrup that is flavoured with strong coffee, rum, and *kahlua*.	The sponge is layered alternately with coffee flavoured butter cream and *ganache*. The top of the cake is covered with butter cream.	The cake is glazed with melted *ganache* or chocolate glaze and decorated with gold leaf. It is also customary to write the word 'opera' on top of the cake.	
Devil's food cake It is a moist, rich chocolate cake which was made in America in the early 1900s. There is no historical reference to the name, but it is believed that since this cake is very rich and moist with chocolate, it is considered 'sinful', hence devil's food cake.	This cake is made by using dark cocoa powder, along with eggs, sugar, and acidic medium such as sour cream. The acid helps to draw out rich dark red colour from the cocoa, thus giving the cake its characteristic dark colour. The cake is moistened with sugar syrup.	The cake is filled with dark chocolate truffle and covered on all sides with chocolate truffle.	The cake is garnished with chocolate garnishes and dusted with cocoa powder.	
Mud cake It is also referred to as Mississippi mud slice and is believed to have originated in America in the late 1970s. The baked cake crumbs are said to look like the sand along the banks of the Mississippi river, hence the name.	This is a dark chocolate sponge that is quite similar to brownie, but in this case, the eggs are whipped and the cake has the texture of a *Genoese* cake. It is cut into two and moistened with rum flavoured sugar syrup.	The cake is usually layered with dark chocolate fudge. The sides of the cake are also finished with fudge.	The cake is garnished with dusted cocoa powder and chocolate garnishes.	

(Contd)

Table 11.2 (Contd)

Cake/Pastry	Base and sponge	Filling	Garnish	Photograph
Walnut brownie The walnut brownie originated in America in early 1900. It is a flat dark chocolate cake somewhat between a cookie and a cake. It is often eaten with tea and can be paired with vanilla ice cream and hot chocolate sauce also.	Brownie is a special sponge that is made for various kinds of desserts. The mixing technique here is very important as it decides the texture of the brownie. Chocolate is melted along with butter and kept aside to cool. Eggs and sugar are mixed together, but not whipped as whipping would result in a crumble texture and the brownie would not get the desired fudgy texture. To the mixture of eggs and sugar, the butter-chocolate mixture is added and flour is folded along with walnut powder and crushed walnuts.	This cake is served as it is and is not filled or layered. The rich fudgy texture of the cake acts as a moistening agent for this cake.	This cake can be served warm, dusted with icing sugar. It can sometimes be covered with chocolate fudge also.	
Baked cheese cake It is a unique American cake made with cream cheese. There is an interesting lore connected with the cream cheese that goes into the creation of this delicacy. While trying to create the famous *Neufchâtel* cheese from France, the Americans accidentally stumbled upon the recipe for unripened cheese which they called cream cheese. In 1912, a method was developed to pasteurize cream cheese, and thus the Philadelphia cream cheese was born.	Unlike other cakes, the baked cheese cake is not layered. In this case the cake ring is lined with a biscuit base and baked blind. The cheese is creamed along with sugar, eggs, and cream. The prepared batter is then put into the mould and baked in a water bath.	This cake does not have any filling.	The cake is served dusted with castor sugar. Sometimes it is spread with castor sugar and caramelized under radiated heat.	

(Contd)

Table 11.2 (Contd)

Cake/Pastry	Base and sponge	Filling	Garnish	Photograph
Chilled cheese cake This popular French cake has a smooth creamy texture that comes from a creamy cheese. Unlike the baked cheese cake, this cake is set in a mould with the help of gelatine.	The chilled cheese cake traditionally has a base of Genoese sponge, but one can also use other bases such as *Japonaise, Dacquoise,* or even meringue. The sponge used in the base is moistened with sugar syrup. This cake is prepared in a ring shaped mould which is lined with sponge. The cheese mixture is spread on the sponge and another layer of sponge is placed over it and moistened with sugar syrup. The remaining cheese cake mixture is filled and smoothened on the top and the cake is chilled.	The cake is usually filled with a cream cheese mixture that is made by using a variety of cream cheese such as Philadelphia, *mascarpone,* or even yoghurt cheese. Egg yolks are whipped with sugar and folded with cream cheese. The cake can be flavoured with any flavourings such as zest and juice of any citrus fruits, berries, chocolate, etc. Gelatine is added to the mixture and this mixture is poured into moulds and set.	The cheese cake can be garnished in a variety of ways. Traditionally, it is covered with a fruit gel and garnished with fruits.	
Croquembouche This is a very popular French cake. The name comes from a French word *croque en bouche* which means crunch in the mouth. This cake is traditionally used as an artistic showpiece that is served on various occasions such as weddings, naming ceremonies, and baptism ceremonies.	The cake has a base of thick sweet paste biscuit on top of which, small profiteroles made from *choux* pastry are arranged to form a cone shape.	The profiteroles can be filled with various fillings such as orange flavoured pastry cream, chocolate cream, etc. The filled profiteroles are dipped into caramel and stuck to the base and then built on each other to form a cone.	The cake is garnished with spun sugar, roses made with marzipan, and garnishes made with sugar.	

(Contd)

Table 11.2 *(Contd)*

Cake/Pastry	Base and sponge	Filling	Garnish	Photograph
Alhambra gateaux This cake was made in honour of the Spanish city Alhambra, which is famous for its lush green gardens and flowers. The chocolate glazed cake is garnished with marzipan rose flowers and green pistachios to resemble the gardens of Alhambra.	The base is a *Genoese* sponge flavoured with hazelnut powder. The sponge is sliced into two and moistened with rum and coffee flavoured sugar syrup.	The cake is layered with chocolate *ganache* and the sides are also covered in *ganache*. It is then chilled and finished with a thin layer of chocolate glaze.	The base of the cake is covered with chopped green pistachios in such a way that it covers at least 1 cm from the base. The top is decorated with white roses made from marzipan and the word *Alhambra* is piped on top.	
Yule log Yule logs are logs of wood that are used to burn in the hearths to keep the house warm during winters in Europe, which is Christmas time there. The French prepared the cake in the shape of logs. As the cakes become popular, they came to be known as yule log cake or *Buche de Noel*.	This cake is made by preparing *Genoese* sponge in sheets. The sponge can be flavoured with coffee, chocolate, or any other desired flavour. The sponge is moistened with vanilla flavoured sugar syrup.	Traditionally, the cake is filled with flavoured butter cream. It is then rolled and wrapped in paper and refrigerated until chilled.	The cake is covered with butter cream and groves are made on top to resemble a bark of log of wood. Green coloured butter cream is piped to resemble the ivy vine and meringue mushrooms are placed on the log to give it a natural look.	
Christmas cake Christmas cakes originated in Scotland, where these were made with candied fruits and whisky. It was also known as whisky Dundee. It is decorated with royal icing to resemble snow and Christmas decorations are placed on top.	It is a dark and moist cake which is enriched with candied fruit and nuts, macerated in alcohol. Eggs, flour, sugar, and butter are combined with molasses and soaked fruits to make this dark and rich moist cake. Fruit soaking for these cakes a couple of months before Christmas is a popular custom in the West. It is celebrated with great enthusiasm and fervour as a mark	The cake is not layered but served as whole.	The Christmas cake can be decorated in many ways. The traditional style is to cover the cake with royal icing or frosting and decorate it with X'mas decorations such as holy leaves, Santa Claus' face, and stars.	

(Contd)

Table 11.2 (Contd)

Cake/Pastry	Base and sponge	Filling	Garnish	Photograph
Gateaux Pithivier This cake is a kind of pie that is prepared with puff pastry. As the name suggests, it originated in the Pithivier region in France.	of ushering in the Christmas season also called yule tide. The cake is made by pinning out the puff pastry to a round circle of 7 mm thickness. Another circle slightly larger than the base is also cut out as it will be placed on top of the cake after being filled.	The cake is traditionally filled with an almond cream mixture that is also known as *crème frangipane.* It is made by creaming butter, sugar, and eggs, along with almond powder and rum.	The sides of the cake are brushed with egg yolks and another disc is placed on top of the mixture. The top of the cake is brushed with egg yolks and then with the tip of the knife, grooves are made on to the top by starting from the tip of the *gateau* and working at a slant through to the base. The cake is baked and served dusted with icing sugar.	
Pavlova This cake was made in Austria in honour of a Russian ballet dancer, Anna Pavlova, when she visited Austria for one of her performances in the 1920s.	The base of the *Pavlova* is made by baking Italian meringue in such a way that the exteriors are crisp and the interior is soft and chewy. It can be spread on to a baking sheet in circles or in shape of a *quenelle.* It can also be piped in smaller circles one on top of another to create an encasing, which can be filled with cream and fruits or served as individual pastries called *vacherins.*	The cake is not layered.	The *Pavlovas* are topped with *crème chantilly* and decorated with an assortment of fruits such as berries, tropical fruits such as kiwi, passion fruit, etc.	
Cardinal Schnitten This cake is also known as Vatican cake in English although it has its origins in Austria. This Viennese speciality is made with different textures of sponge and meringue.	The base of this cake is unique. *Genoese* sponge and meringue are piped on to a baking sheet in alternate layers and baked together. The sheets are then moistened with coffee flavoured rum syrup.	The cake is made by layering these sheets with a coffee flavoured butter cream.	The cake is served plain dusted with icing sugar. The pattern of sponge and meringue is exposed so as to enhance the appearance of the cake.	

Table 11.3 Classical pastries

Pastry	Description	Uses	Photograph
Choux pastry Also known as the boiled paste, it is one of the most common pastes used in pastry kitchen.	Water is boiled along with butter and flour is added and cooked until it leaves the sides of the pan. The dough kind of consistency is then made into a paste by incorporating eggs one at a time.	*Choux* paste can be used for bases of many cakes and also for creating individual pastries such as the following.	Eclairs
		Eclairs It is piped in tube shape (usually 4 inches long) and after baking, it is filled with flavoured cream or custard and glazed with melted chocolate or fondant.	
		Paris Brest This is a ring-shaped *choux* paste baked and piped with whipped cream and decorated with fresh fruits and berries. It is decorated with sifted icing sugar.	Paris Brest
		Profitroles These are round balls of *choux* paste baked and filled with flavoured creams and glazed with chocolate, caramelized sugar, sifted icing sugar, fondant, etc.	Profitroles
		Swans *Choux* paste is piped in shape of tear drop and baked to get swans. The top is cut and then split in half length wise to make the wings of swans. The neck is piped in a thin curved-shape and baked separately. The swans can be filled with *Crème Chantilly* and assembled to resemble a swan.	Swan

(contd)

Table 11.3 (Contd)

Pastry	Description	Uses	Photograph
Puff pastry It is also called flaky pastry.	A puff pastry consists of a laminated structure made of alternate layers of dough and fat. This is achieved by rolling out the paste and giving it sufficient turns until there are hundreds to thousands of layers of dough and fat. When this pastry is baked, the expanding air and water vapour 'puff' the separate layers apart from each other, resulting in a delightful, crisp, light, flaky pastry.	It has many uses in pastry kitchen like being used as a base for cakes such as *Napoleon, Pithivier gateaux St Honore,* etc. (Table 11.2). Some pastry products made by using puff paste are the following. *Eccless* These are sweet snacks often eaten during afternoon tea. Roll the puff to a 4-inch circle with 6 mm thickness. Place the filling of raisins, brown sugar, mixed spice, and little softened butter. Bring all the sides of circle together and form a ball. Now roll the ball into a 3-inch circle, wash with egg white, and dip in castor sugar and give two to three small slits on top and bake at 180°C till golden brown. *Banbury cakes* These are same as eccles as mentioned above. The only difference is that these are rolled into boat shapes or oval shapes and baked in the same way. *Jalousies* These are thin broad strips of puff paste, filled with cooked fruit, and covered with another strip of puff and baked. These are glazed with melted apricot jam and served as dessert.	Eccless Banbury cakes Jalousies

(contd)

Table 11.3 (Contd)

Pastry	Description	Uses	Photograph
Sweet pastry/*Pâté sucre*	It is a dough made by creaming butter and sugar and eggs and lightly folding in the flour. The flour is not overworked in the dough because this paste needs to be crisp and should have a bite when eaten. The paste is refrigerated until it is firm to handle and roll.	Sweet paste can be used for many products in pastry kitchen. It can be used for making cookies and biscuits and can also be used as the base for many cakes as discussed in Table 11.2 In pastries, this paste is used for making tart shells that can be filled with numerous fillings such as whipped cream with fresh fruits, and lemon curd.	
Short paste/*Pâté brisée*	This pastry is known as short crust pastry and is very flaky and crumbly. It is made by rolling chilled fat, along with flour and mixing with eggs and chilled water to make a paste that is then refrigerated until further use.	It is commonly used in making savoury items, but it can be used as a base for some cakes and tortes which need to be sugar free.	
Breakfast pastries	These are sweet baked goods that are often served in the breakfast buffet so the name breakfast pastries. These can be made from laminated dough such as croissant dough, puff dough, or cake batters such as tea cake.	Various kinds of products are made and served in breakfast and these are referred to as breakfast pastries. Some of these are as follows. *Croissant* Croissants are usually baked plain, but sometimes they could be stuffed with grated chocolate to make chocolate croissants. They can be glazed with melted chocolate after baking or simple dusted with icing sugar. *Danish pastries* These can be made in various shapes. It is often garnished with fruit and glazed with apricot jam. Some Danish pastries are also decorated with melted fondant stripes.	 Croissant Danish pastries

(contd)

Table 11.3 (Contd)

Pastry	Description	Uses	Photograph
Breakfast pastries		*Muffins* These are also known as cup cakes as they are made in small tart moulds. After baking, they pop out of the mould. These are made from the tea cake batter and can be flavoured with various flavourings.

Muffins |
| | | *Palmiers* It is often used as a breakfast pastry and is known as French hearts because of the heart shape. It is also called by other names such as pig's ears or *papillon*. The puff pastry is rolled with castor sugar into a rectangle and it is given folds inwards from both the ends to meet in the centre. It is finally folded just like a book fold and sliced 1 cm thick. The open ends twisted to resemble a 'T' shape and it is baked to form a heart shape. |

Folding puff for palmiers

Baked palmiers |
| | | *Doughnuts* These are fried sweet dough popular in many western countries. It is made from yeast-leavened soft dough that is rolled to 1 cm thickness and cut with a round cutter. A small hole is cut out in the centre of the doughnut as a custom. It is then left to proved (rise) and then deep fried until cooked. It is often served dredged in cinnamon-flavoured castor sugar. |

Doughnuts |

MODERN TRENDS IN CAKE AND PASTRY MAKING

With changing times the look and feel of cakes has undergone a tremendous change. So have the commodities and tools available for preparation of cakes and pastries. The cakes and pastries of yesteryears were very creamy and bulky compared to modern day cakes, where the emphasis is more on style and health. Contemporary cakes and pastries are sleek and stylish, thanks to tools and equipment that has enabled innovations in presentation. Also, as people get more health conscious, creamy layers making way for custards and fruits. Some of the modern trends in cake and pastry preparation are discussed in the succeeding sections.

Health Aspects

The pastries of earlier times were layered with butter cream and fresh cream. With people getting more health conscious over the years, butter cream has been replaced with healthier options such as custard creams, berries, and cheese. The heavy icings and frosting, and sweet icings have been replaced with more fresh fruits and glazes. Many manufacturers have started producing organic products such as organic sugar, flour, eggs, and even organic chocolates for some health-conscious people. Many pastry shops sell their products, labelled with nutritional analysis of the products, so that the customer can choose according to their requirement.

Even for cheese cakes, curd cheese is obtained by draining curd overnight in cheese cloth. The resulting cheese is less in fat content than the proprietary cream cheeses. Similarly, the use of low-fat butter and margarine is in vogue for the production of pastries and cakes. Butter and other fats are saturated and oil is preferred over fats. Many chefs have altered recipes to make cakes and pastries with oil. Carrot cakes and banana cakes are often made with oil and baked like a tea cake.

Service Styles

The service styles of cakes and pastries have evolved immensely during the last decade. Earlier, the display of cakes and pastries were laden with lots of artistic showpieces made of sugar and chocolates. The desserts, cakes, and pastries were presented as whole dishes. These were usually kept sliced or even whole, giving the guest the option of slicing out a portion according to his/her desire. The dessert buffet thus, looked cluttered and every product looked the same. The modern trend is to make small individual desserts of different shapes and sizes. This gives the buffet a 'full' look and even gives the guest a bigger choice. Figure 11.2 provides a glimpse of how the presentation of cakes and pastries has changed over the years.

Tools and Equipment

The modernization of tools and equipment has not only increased productivity but also given a new dimension to cakes and pastries. Until a few decades ago, one could only see cakes in basic shapes such as rounds, ovals, and squares, but now the availability of moulds in three-dimensional structures such as pyramids, cubes, spheres, etc. has given a whole new look to cakes and pastries.

Yesteryears   Contemporary

Fig. 11.2 Trends in presentation of cakes and pastries

Fig. 11.3 Pastries prepared in *flexipan* moulds (see also Plate 13)

Over the last few years, silicone rubber is being used to create flexible moulds called *flexipans* that can be baked at temperatures as high as 350°C. There are numerous designs and sizes available and one can be very creative in giving various shapes to cakes and pastries. Figure 11.3 depicts some pastries made in these moulds.

Apart from *flexipan* moulds, many other types of equipment and tools are used in modern pastry kitchens to decorate cakes and pastries. Table 11.4 provides an overview of some modern equipment that have become integral to pastry kitchens nowadays. The basic tools were described in Chapter 20 of *Food Production Operations*.

Product

Various kinds of pre-mixes and ready-made products have also changed the pastry products in the modern times. In olden days, everything had to be processed from scratch and it was often too time consuming. With the advances in food industry, almost any kind of product is now readily available and in any season. A range of canned fruits and berries, processed nuts, dehydrated fresh fruits, etc. are available in the market. Many pre-mixes, such as eggless cake mixes and mousses, are available that can be reconstituted with liquids to create a fine product.

> **CHEF'S TIP**
> If the sponge or any base gets stuck to the parchment paper, then turn the sponge upside down and brush the paper with water. Leave it for 1 minute and then peel off the paper.

Table 11.4 Modern equipment for making cakes and pastries

Equipment	Description	Photograph
Cake moulds (metal)	Various kinds of non-reactive and non-corrosive metals, such as stainless steel and aluminium, are used for making various kinds of cake moulds and rings. The advantage of a cake ring is that it can be used for baking sponges as well as cheese cakes and mousses that utilize gelatine as a setting agent. The use of the ring also does not require the lining of the moulds on all sides with parchment paper. These days, it is easy to fabricate the moulds by giving the design to the manufacturer. Modern kitchens use shapes such as teardrop, hexagonal, pyramid, triangle, and other geometrical shapes to enhance the appearance of cakes and pastries.	
Silicone moulds	Many companies around the world are manufacturing moulds in silicone that can withstand high temperatures. Other benefits of using silicone moulds include the following. • These do not require greasing and the product does not get stuck to the base. • These come in various designs and shapes and give a very modern look to the products. • These can also be used for preparing garnishes such as caramel and chocolates.	
Silpats	These are flat silicone mats used as a base on baking trays. Many products in pastry kitchen, such as *Japonaise* sponge, *joconde*, and Opera sponge, get stuck on parchment paper, which is very difficult to remove. *Silpats* are useful in these cases as things do not stick to them. Modern kitchens use Silpats to bake all their products.	

(Contd)

Table 11.4 (*Contd*)

Equipment	Description	Photograph
Silicone paper	This is a special kind of paper that is similar to the *silpat*. It is often found stuck to the back of stickers. The purpose of silicone sheets is to bake products that otherwise would get stuck on a parchment paper. It is less expensive than *silpat*, but unlike *silpat*, silicone paper cannot be reused.	
Spray gun	It is a simple apparatus that contains a jet spray attached to a compressor. Various kinds of spray guns are used in pastry and cake decorations. Atomiser sprays are available for spraying colours or even chocolates for an even coating and finish on cakes and pastries. Many high-end chocolate pastries and cakes are sprayed with a chocolate mixture to give a modern matt kind of finish to the product.	
Butane torch	It is a small torch burner attached to a butane canister. It comes in very handy to spot caramelize products. This tool has various uses. It can be used to extract chilled cakes out of metallic moulds by heating the sides of the mould with the torch burner. It can also be used for caramelizing sugar on many desserts such as *crème brûlée*, fruit gratins, and tarts.	
Modelling tools	Also known as marzipan tools, they are used mostly for making decorations from marzipan. They come in a set of various shapes and each tool has a specific purpose. The tools are used for making flowers, figures, figurines, etc.	
Sugar working apparatus	Sugar work is a highly skilled art, where the sugar is cooked, then stretched and pulled many times to get the natural shine. The sugar apparatus is used for making decorations from sugar. It consists of a heating surface with an infrared lamp that keeps the sugar at a particular temperature so that it does not harden. This apparatus also comes along with a sugar blow pump that is used for pumping air into a sugar ball to create fruits and other structures. Though this art form is very old, but modern equipment and tools have made the task a lot easier than yesteryears.	
Stencils and cut-outs or decorating stencil grills	Different kinds of stencils and cut outs are used for creating various kinds of decorations and garnishes for cakes and pastries. The stencils can be used in various ways. For instance, it can be placed on top of a cake or pastry and sprayed with colours or chocolate to imprint the design onto the pastry. It can also be used for making garnishes such as *touilles* that can be used for decoration.	

(*Contd*)

Table 11.4 (Contd)

Equipment	Description	Photograph
Stencils and cut-outs or decorating stencil grills	Various kinds of plastic or stainless steel sheets are available with various design cut-outs such as polka dots, stars, and Christmas bells. These can be used for making decorative *joconde* sponges and also imprinting any design onto a cake or a pastry. These are also known as decorating stencil grills.	
Relief mats	These are thick sheets of silicone rubber with three dimensional designs engravings. Relief mats are available in rounds or rectangle sheets and can be used for various purposes. The basic purpose is to make the decorative sides and top of a cake or pastry. The sponge cake mixture can be baked in these sheets. As a result, the sponge would get a three-dimensional imprint. The sponge can then be cut and used as desired. Apart from sponge batters, even melted chocolate can be poured on these mats for the designs.	
Acetate sheets	These are thick plastic sheets that are used for making various chocolate garnishes for cakes and pastries. Modern cakes can be decorated in numerous ways with the use of two or more tools. For example, one can place a stencil on an acetate sheet and spread a thin layer of chocolate *ganache* on the stencil. Then, carefully remove the stencil and the desired pattern would be created on the acetate sheet. Now place the ring mould on top of the acetate sheet and pour the cheese cake mixture over the design. Now put a layer of sponge and moisten it with syrup. Add more cheese cake mixture and finish the tip with sponge. After the cake is frozen for hour, it can be inverted and the acetate sheet peeled off. The design from the acetate sheet gets printed on top of the cake.	
Cold plates	These are electric cold plates that have a surface temperature of less than –5°C or sometimes even less. Some of this equipment comes in handy while preparing chocolate garnishes for cakes and pastries. Melted chocolate can be poured on to the cold plate and smoothened with a palette knife. It can then be scraped immediately to wrap around cakes and pastries.	

(Contd)

Table 11.4 (Contd)

Equipment	Description	Photograph
Foamers	These are quite unique equipment powered by nitrogen canisters that get plugged into a jar. The jar can be filled with any viscous liquid item such as fresh cream, fruit purees, chocolate creams, etc. and upon shaking vigorously, the liquid inside gets foamy and whipped up. It can then be piped on to cakes to garnish.	
Transfer sheets	These are plastic sheets with computerized patterns printed on them. The prints are made with cocoa butter and once the melted chocolate is spread on these sheets the designs get transferred on to the chocolate sheet that can be used for garnishing cakes and pastries. One can also custom-design these sheets by printing logos and designs of clients as they give a personal touch to the products.	
Textured sheets	These are flexible hard plastic sheets with various kinds of textures on it. The range of textures can be that of leather finish to bubbles. These sheets are also used for chocolate garnishes on cakes and pastries.	
Combs	Various kinds of combs are used for creating designs on the sides or top of the cake. They are available in various materials such as metal, plastic, or high grade silicon rubber. These combs are used for preparing various garnishes for cakes and pastries.	

(Contd)

Table 11.4 *(Contd)*

Equipment	Description	Photograph
Wood engraving tools	These are special kind of silicone rubber equipment that have semi-circular grooves engraved on it. The equipment is used for preparing designs on chocolate or on *joconde* sponge. Moving this equipment to and fro while dragging it creates a pattern of shaved wooden grains.	
Printing apparatus	This is a fairly new equipment added to the confectionery world. It uses a normal inkjet printer to print computerized images on a special edible paper made from rice. Edible food-coloured cartridges are used for this purpose. Any design can be printed on these sheets and placed on top of cakes or pastries.	

TYPES OF CAKES AND THEIR CLASSIFICATION

There are many kinds of cakes, which is why these cakes are classified on certain parameters. We studied about classical cakes in Table 11.2 and discussed contemporary trends later. A common way of classifying cakes is based on the occasions that they are made for. For example, wedding cakes, high-tea cakes, birthday cakes, speciality cakes for festive occasions such as Twelfth Night, Christmas, etc. Let us discuss some of these cakes.

Birthday Cakes and Ornamental Cakes

Cakes are synonymous to birthdays. It is customary for people to celebrate their birthdays by cutting cakes with their names piped on them. Various kinds of flavours and kinds of cake can be made on this occasion. Sometimes cakes are made based on a theme of the event, or on popular cartoons, toys, etc. (for children). Such cakes, known as ornamental cakes, can be made in various shapes matching the theme of the event. Some ornamental cakes can be in shapes of dolls, cars, or any object in a three dimensional design. The flavours of these cakes generally depend on the choice of the person celebrating the birthday.

CHEF'S TIP
To prevent cakes from over-colouring on the top during the baking process, place them under a greaseproof paper and reduce the top heat.

High-tea Cakes

High-tea is a western concept which is often confused with afternoon tea. A high-tea was usually an early dinner for children, so that they could eat and go to bed, while the parents could go out for dining and celebrating. A high-tea comprises many kinds of cakes, pastries, and savoury items such as sandwiches and quiches. Most of the cakes served in high-tea are dry cakes. Some of the commonly prepared high-tea cakes are described in Table 11.5.

Table 11.5　Various kinds of high-tea cakes (see also Plate 14)

High-tea cake	Description	Photograph
Victorian sponge	Victoria sponge is named after Queen Victoria, who popularized this cake in her afternoon teas. Unlike basic sponge, this sponge is made by creaming method and is usually sandwiched with jam and whipped cream. The top is not iced and can be dusted with icing sugar.	
Madeira cake	This is slightly different from Victorian sponge. In this cake, butter and sugar are creamed with egg yolks and the egg whites are stiffly beaten and folded in along with flour. The resulting cake has a good volume and a very spongy texture. It can be served plain as a tea cake or some candied and dry fruits can be added to the same.	
Dundee cake	This is a rich fruit cake from Scotland that is traditionally garnished with almonds on top. The cake is made by the creaming method as done for pound cake. Spices, such as cinnamon, are used along with candied fruits such as raisins, sultanas, black currants, orange and lemon peels, and candied cherries.	
Banana bread	Banana bread is also commonly served as a breakfast pastry or even in high-tea. Soft and pulpy bananas that have become black over a period of time are used for preparation of this cake. Banana is pureed along with vegetable oil and then mixed with whipped eggs, sugar, and flour and baked in loaf tins. The cake is then sliced and served.	
Carrot cake	Carrot cake is a very famous cake from Switzerland. It is made by grating carrots and combining with eggs, sugar, butter, flour, and sometimes almond powder. The cake is usually covered with marzipan and each slice is decorated with carrots made from marzipan.	
Fruit loaf	Various kinds of fruits are used for making dry cakes for hi-tea. Apples, mangoes, pineapple, etc. are some fruits that can be combined in a pureed form or in small chunks to make moist and soft cakes that are served at high-tea.	

(Contd)

Table 11.5 (Contd)

High-tea cake	Description	Photograph
Marble cake	This is same as English pound cake but the batter divided in two parts. One part is mixed with cocoa powder and the other is flavoured with vanilla. Both the batters are put in a baking tin and randomly stirred with a small rod to intermingle the designs. The resulting baked cake is marbled in texture.	

Wedding Cakes

As the name suggests, these cakes are made on weddings. It is customary to have these cakes in three or more tiers, each of which represents the strong base for the new relationship, the wonderful present, and the bright future of the bride and groom. Since these cakes have to be decorated in lavish designs, which take time to prepare, these are made from products that have a longer shelf life. The layering and coating of the cake is known as icing. Nowadays, these cakes can be made from various bases and flavours; but in olden times, dark rich plum cakes were used for making wedding cakes. This is very common till date and most of the wedding cakes are still made the old way with intricate decoration and icing. The size of the wedding cake depends upon the gathering—if the number of people attending a wedding function is very small, then the middle and the top partiers are dummy tiers and only the base is edible.

Conventionally, a wedding cake sponge is made by combining butter, brown sugar, eggs, flour, along with molasses, treacle, honey, and candied fruits soaked in dark rum. The moist dark cake is rich in flavours and can last for a few weeks without getting spoilt.

CHEF'S TIP
To check for 'doneness' in small cakes and sponges, press lightly on the surface. The impression made should spring back immediately. For heavy fruit cakes, insert a clean skewer. On withdrawal, the skewer should not have any moist mixture clinging to it.

Parts of a wedding cake

Traditionally, the wedding cake has the following components.

Stand Various kinds of stands and bases are used for presenting wedding cakes. Some of these stands are straight, whereas some are curved or spiral depending upon the style. These are available in metal as well as other materials like plastic. On a three-tiered cake where the cake would be kept on top of each other, the bases are separated with decorative pillars. These can be made with edible sugar pastes or can be procured ready-made from the market. Figure 11.4 illustrates some stands used for wedding cakes.

Icing Covering of the cake and its decoration is called the icing of the cake. The icing of wedding cakes is a time-consuming process as utmost care has to be taken to have

Fig. 11.4 Various kinds of wedding cake stands

a smooth finish on top of the cake. The following steps are carried out while icing a traditional wedding cake.

Level the cake   The cake has to be first trimmed from all the sides and the top to have clean edges, also known as shoulder of the cake. If there are any cracks or holes in the cake, the trimmings should be kneaded together with the tip of fingers and filled in, so that the cake has a uniform and flat top, sides, and base. It is important to turn the cake upside down and use the base of the cake as the top, as it would be flat and smooth.

Prepare the coating   This is usually done by boiling apricot jam and covering the cake with the same. The boiled apricot jam fills up any small holes and crevices in the cake and also helps the next layer of icing to stick on it. It also adds sweetness and moisture to the cake and seals it, thus increasing its shelf life. Apart from jam, other icings such as butter cream or royal icing are also used for the same purpose.

Prepare the base   Before the final icing is put on the cake, it is important to prepare the base for it. This is done by neatly covering the entire cake with rolled out marzipan. Care should be taken while covering the entire cake with marzipan. There should not be any creases on the sides and if there are any, they should be smoothened out with the help of a palette knife or a rolling pin. Marzipan or the almond paste adds flavour and richness to the cake, helps preserve the cake and prevents it from drying out, and also ensures that the final layer of icing on top has a smooth finish.

Put icing   There are various kinds of icings that can be used for decorating wedding cakes. The traditional ones are rolled fondants and royal icing (refer Table 11.7). These days ready-made sugar pastes in bright white colour are commonly used to cover wedding cakes. Royal icing is used for piping lace and filigree designs on the cake and other decorations such as sugar paste flowers, bells, and figurines are also used to decorate the cake.

Decorate   Various kinds of decoration are used to present wedding cakes. It is common to see gold- and silver-frilled satin, plastic figurines of a couple, bunch of fresh flowers, bells, etc. being commonly used for enhancing the appearance of the cake. It is also an art to portion the cake, while serving the guests (discussed later in the chapter).

Table 11.6 Cakes made on festive occasions

Cakes	Description	Photograph
Twelfth Night cake	This is a very popular cake in Europe and is known by various names such as King's cake or *tortell*. It is usually consumed on the Twelfth Night after Christmas and marks the end of the festive season. In France, this cake is made with puff pastry with a filling of almond cream. A bean is hidden in the cake and the person who finds the bean in his portion gets to wear a small paper crown and has his chance of ruling the feast until midnight.	
Christmas cake	Discussed earlier in Table 11.2	
Moon cake	Moon cakes are usually round or rectangular pieces of cakes or pastries that are specially made on the occasion of mid autumn festival called *Zhongqiu* in China. It is celebrated to worship the moon, thus moon cakes are served on this day. These are made in a specially designed mould with Chinese engravings so that the Chinese inscriptions or designs get imprinted on the top. The cake may be covered with a sweet crust. It contains sweet lotus seed paste and sometimes yolks from salted duck eggs.	
Pumpkin cake	These cakes are made by combining pureed pumpkin with eggs, butter, sugar, and flour. These are a speciality served on Halloween. There are various kinds of silicone moulds that come in the shape of a pumpkin. Once the cake is sandwiched and iced, it looks like a real pumpkin.	

Festive Cakes

This is a category of speciality cakes that are made on festive occasions, like hot cross buns are made on Easter. Table 11.6 describes some cakes made on festive occasions.

APPROACH TO CAKE DECORATION AND SERVING

Decorating a cake is an art, which, apart from skills, needs a creative mind to be able to craft and prepare cakes and pastries for various occasions and guests' needs. Some cakes require a large degree of planning and craftsmanship. Ornamental cakes can range from a simple face of a character to a palace of fairies with forts and people. Some cakes can be in a shape of a free-standing shoe on top of a cake box, or a three-dimensional cake in the shape of a musical instrument such as piano and guitar. Slowly and steadily, one can master this art. In this section, we shall discuss the basic principles of decorating a cake and a few significant points to be kept in mind while decorating a cake.

For an easy understanding, let us divide the procedure into the following simple steps.

1. Preparing the sponge base
2. Slicing the cake
3. Layering the cake
4. Coating
5. Decorating and garnishing

Preparing the Sponge Base

There are three methods of making sponge cakes—warm, cold, and commercial methods, each of which produces a sponge with different textures. The methods are described below.

Warm

In this method, eggs and sugar are warmed together to approximately 32°C, whisking over a bain-marie until it becomes thick like the consistency of thick cream (ribbon stage). When this stage is reached, continue to whisk the mixture away from the heat until it cools to approximately 24°C. The flour is carefully folded in along with the melted butter, if any is used. This method allows the sponge to be of good volume as warm eggs whip better in volume than cold eggs and also cooking the mixture removes any smell of raw eggs. Genoese sponges are commonly made in this way.

CHEF'S TIP

When using eggs in a cake preparation, you should warm the eggs either by placing the eggs in hot water or by warming them along with the weighed sugar with a gentle heat over a bain marie. The reason for doing this is to produce strong whisked foam that has the stability to withstand the additional mixing of other ingredients. If the foam loses its incorporated air, the result will be a heavier cake.

Warming the eggs will also prevent the curdling of mixtures when fat, sugars, and eggs are creamed together. Eggs can be separated and the whites whisked separately to increase the lightness of the cake.

Cold

In this method, the eggs are separated into yolks and whites. Whisk the yolks with half of the sugar. Whisk the whites with the remaining sugar. Blend the two together before carefully folding in the flour. Add the melted butter at the final stage if you are using it. Sponge made by this method is very airy and light. It is usually made for Swiss rolls or making sponge fingers for cakes and pastries.

Commercial

The eggs, sugar, water, emulsifier, and flour are all combined together in a machine bowl and whisked for approximately five minutes. The melted butter is folded into this emulsified mixture and the cake sponge is baked in moulds or sheets. This kind of sponge is very stable because of the presence of emulsifier.

Slicing the Cake

Slicing the cake is both an art and a skill. A saw-edged knife is used for slicing a delicate sponge. The cake should be kept on a flat surface and the knife should be placed at the point where we want to slice the cake. The kind of cake will decide whether the sponge has to be divided into half or three or more layers. Usually a cake is split equally into three layers. Start cutting the cake from the base in such a manner that the knife is flat on the cake base and ensure that you slice the cake in a sawing motion.

Layering the Cake

This is one of the most crucial steps in icing and decorating a cake. Layering refers to sandwiching the slices of cakes with various kinds of icings as discussed in Table 11.6. The choice of icing would depend upon the kind of cake that is being prepared. The thumb rule is to use light and airy icing with light sponge cakes and heavy icings such as royal icing on heavy ones such as fruit or Christmas cakes. Before layering cakes, it is important to select the slice of sponge. The top layer of the cake and the bottom layer should be the best slices as the base will make it easier to lift the cake and the top layer would give the final finish to it.

The application of sugar syrup comes next. The syrup can be flavoured with essences, liqueurs, etc. It is important to spread enough syrup with a brush so that each and every part of the sponge is coated.

Once the sugar syrup is applied on the base, put the icing in the centre and spread it with a palette knife. Care should be taken while doing so. It is important to spread the mixture in a uniform manner. The thickness of the icing should be even. Similarly, all the other layers are sandwiched one on top of each other. The next step is to refrigerate the cake so that the icing becomes firm and it is easier to handle the cake. The cake is now put on the cake turntable also known as *Lazy Suzanne*. First cover the top of the cake, smoothing the cream with the palette knife. Once the top is covered, cover the sides a little at a time by turning the cake, the final smoothing can be best achieved with the help of a rectangular plastic scraper.

When layering cakes with butter creams and whipped creams, it is advisable to coat the cake at least twice between refrigerating them. The final smooth layering would give a final finish to the cake, when it will be glazed or coated.

Coating

This is the last coating on top of the cake. There can be various kinds of toppings and coatings spread on top of the cake. Chocolate cakes are usually coated with melted truffle or chocolate glaze. The cake is now kept on the wire grid which is kept on a tray and the glaze is poured in the centre of the cake. It is allowed to spread with the help of palette knife and the wire grid is tapped couple of times to allow the extra coating to fall down on a tray beneath the wire grid.

Chilled cheese cakes are glazed while they are still in the ring and the ring is lifted after the coating has set.

Icings are also known as frostings and these are always sweet in taste. Icings are done for various reasons. The most important of these are as follows.

- They add sweet taste to the cakes and pastries
- They improve the appearance of the product
- They help in preserving cakes, as it covers all the sides and top of the cake, thus preventing the cakes from drying out
- They add moistness and flavour to the cake and pastries

We have discussed various types of creams and fillings used in cakes and pastries in the book *Food Production Operations*. It is important for you to be aware of the basics before we go further to discuss various types of icings. The various kinds of icings that can be done for decorating cakes are discussed in Table 11.7.

Table 11.7 Various types of icings

Icing	Description
Butter cream	This is a light and fluffy mixture of unsalted butter and icing sugar. The butter is creamed along with the sugar until air is incorporated thereby making the icing light, creamy, and fluffy. There are various kinds of butter creams and there could be slight variations to enhance the textures and flavour. These are commonly used for decorating and filling many types of cakes and pastries. Few of the common variations of butter cream are:
	Italian butter cream In this type of butter cream, half of the butter cream is folded along with Italian meringue (refer Table 11.1). The butter is creamed with less amount of sugar as Italian meringue would already be high on sugar content.
	French butter cream This is made by whipping egg yolks, along with boiling sugar syrup until the mixture is thick and creamy. It is then folded along with creamed and fluffy butter.
	Pastry butter cream In this kind of butter cream, one part of butter cream is mixed with whipped pastry cream. This kind of butter cream can sometimes be very soft and hence it can be bound with small amounts of melted gelatine.
	Fondant butter cream This butter cream is made by creaming butter until it is light and fluffy, then fondant is added to the butter and whipped again until it is smooth and creamy.
	Flavoured butter creams These kinds of butter creams are flavoured with various kinds of flavourings and colours to make ornamental cakes and various other types of cakes and pastries. Some of the most common flavourings used in butter creams are vanilla pods, melted chocolate, coffee, nut pastes such as hazelnut, chestnuts, and almond paste, liqueurs such as rum, and *Grand Marnier*.
	Even natural and artificial flavours can be used for flavouring butter creams.
Fondant	Fondant is a sugar-based icing that is mostly used on festive and wedding cakes. This icing requires lot of skill and art to be prepared in the kitchen; therefore, it is normally purchased readymade from the market. The consistency of this icing is such that it can be rolled and then used for covering cakes or pastries. The consistency can be regulated by warming the icing over the double boiler to make it viscous. It can then be used for dipping petit four, pastries such as eclairs and also as a topping for Napoleon and Danish pastries. After setting in this manner, it becomes smooth, shiny, and non-sticky.

(Contd)

Table 11.7 (contd)

Icing	Description
Fondant	Fondant is prepared by heating sugar and water until it reaches 105°C. Then liquid glucose or acids, such as cream of tartar, are added and the syrup is cooked until it reaches 118°C. It is then spread on a wet marble table and allowed to cool down until it reaches 45°C. The sugar is then folded and kneaded until soft dough is obtained. This dough can be rolled and used for covering cakes.
Chocolate icing	Various kinds of chocolate icings are used to cover and decorate cakes and pastries. The two major ones are truffle and *ganache* (refer the book *Food Production Operations*). Some other kinds of chocolate icings used on cakes and pastries are:
	Chocolate glaze It is made by cooking cocoa powder, water, fondant, and liquid glucose until the mixture is thick and shiny. Add soaked gelatine leaves and let the mixture cool down to 35 °C. It can then be used to cover top of the cakes. Gelatine allows the glaze to set on the cake with a shiny appearance.
	Chocolate fudge Chocolate truffle is whipped until it becomes fluffy and has a matt finish. Softened butter is incorporated into the mixture to create fudge icing. The fudge icings are spread with palette knife and lifted up to form peaks on top of the cakes.
Foam-type icings	These icings are made by whipping egg whites along with boiled sugar syrup. These are often referred to as boiled icings. An Italian meringue is an example of a foam-type icing. The disadvantage of these icing is that it is not a very stable form of icing and should be used on cakes and pastries which would be consumed immediately. To stabilize this icing, another variation of this icing is made and it is known as marshmallow icing. The Italian meringue is whipped along with melted gelatine and used immediately. The gelatine however stabilizes the icing.
Royal icing	Royal icing is prepared by beating egg whites and icing sugar until a thick paste is obtained. The icing should only be beaten with a flat paddle and never whipped. The amount of icing sugar used will guide the consistency of the icing.
	Royal icing has a unique property of setting to a brittle consistency and this is used by chefs to the best of its ability. Royal icing is used for decorating wedding cakes and piping icing to make lace structures. It is also used as a glue to stick decorations to the cake. Thus royal icing finds many uses in the pastry kitchen. Since this icing is very sweet in nature, it is mostly used for decoration only.
Glazed icings	Glazed icings can further be of the following types.
	Hot and cold gel Proprietary cold and hot gels are also available in modern times and they are neutral in flavour. These cold gels can be mixed with flavourings and colours and can be spread on top of the cakes and pastries. The hot gels are required to be heated along with a little quantity of water and flavourings and then spread over chilled cakes or pastries.
	Care should be taken while spreading the hot gel, as it can melt the top layer of the cake thereby creating an unwanted effect.
	Jams and preserves Apricot jam is the most commonly used jam in the pastry for various kinds of decorations of cakes and pastries. Danish pastries are iced with boiled apricot jam. Boiling and applying the jam allows it to spread in a thin consistency and it sets like a gel after cooling down.
	Hot sugar glaze This icing is like a mock fondant. It is the quickest icing to make, as icing sugar is combined with very little water and heated over moderate heat until it becomes opaque and has a flowing consistency. This can be used to glaze and decorate cakes and pastries.

Decorating and Garnishing

When decorating a cake, the aim should be to keep simple designs evenly piped and neatly executed. Compatible creams, soft icings such as *crème Chantilly*, and chocolate should be used on lighter varieties of cakes or a sponge base cake. When coating the cake with *crème Chantilly*, butter cream, etc., it is important that the cake is iced two times. For the first time, the icing should be spread, smoothened out, and allowed to rest in the freezer for a couple of hours, before the next layer can be spread. This ensures a smooth finish on the cake, which is desirable.

If you are decorating a cake with piped designs and patterns, planning is essential. Piping these designs and patterns may require practice, prior to decorating.

There is a variety of garnishes that can be used for decorating and garnishing cakes and pastries. Chocolate is the most commonly used garnish because it can be transformed into various shapes and patterns that enhance the appeal of the cake. Table 11.8 illustrates some of the commonly used garnishes on cakes and pastries.

Table 11.8 Various types of garnishes used on cakes and pastries (see also Plate 14)

Garnish	Description	Photograph
Sugar	*Sugar art* Sugar is used in various forms to decorate cakes. Sugar work is a skill in itself that is dedicated to making garnishes, such as spirals, flowers, pulled sugar structures, etc., which are used on festive and wedding cakes. *Spun sugar* It is the thread of sugar which can be achieved by passing the threads of caramelized sugar from the fork or special wire whisk or on a sheet of baking paper or foil. Dip the fork in sugar and then move it back and forth to create thin strands of sugar. This can also be achieved by making these strands on two pieces of metal rods that are protruding out from the edge of the working table. Make sure to oil the metal rods for easy removal of the spun sugar. The sugar must be spun just before serving as it quickly dissolves, particularly when the weather is humid. *Caramelized sugar* The sugar is caramelized and poured on to *silmats* to form sheets that resemble glass. These can then be broken into pieces and used to decorate the cake. Thin lines and figures can also be made by pouring the sugar on to silmats and then after drying, it can be used as a garnish. *Sugared flowers* Each flower is coated with egg white, placed on a sheet of paper thickly coated with castor sugar. Sprinkle more sugar over the top. If any part is not coated, gently dab on more sugar egg white and sprinkle with a little more sugar. Then place on a rack in an airy place to dry. Then we can use then to decorate cakes, desserts, and home made chocolates.	Sugar work Spun sugar Spun sugar dome Spun sugar tool Sugared flowers

(Contd)

Table 11.8 (Contd)

Garnish	Description	Photograph
Touille and *snap*	*Touille* is a paste made by using flour, butter sugar, and eggs. The paste is spread in very thin sheets on *silmats* and baked until golden brown. It can be given various shapes while it is hot, as it sets to a brittle texture, when cold. *Snap* on the other hand is high in sugar and butter content and upon baking, it has small and large holes that look very attractive. It also sets to very brittle when cold.	
Chocolate	It is the most versatile of all ingredients and many decorations and garnishes can be made with chocolates. We would read about chocolates and garnishes in Chapter 12.	
Cookies and sponges	Various cookie doughs, such as sweet paste or shortbread, are used for decorations of cakes and pastries. These doughs can be rolled out and cut into various shapes and sizes and baked. Even decorative sponges such as *joconde* sponge and *baumkuchen* can be sliced and used for decorating cakes.	
Fruits	Various kinds of fruits, such as berries and other exotic fruits, are used for decorating cakes and pastries. The choice of the fruit garnish depends on the type of cake. For example, a Black Forest cake is decorated with cherries as it the prime ingredient in the cake, pineapple cake is decorated with wedges of pineapple and in contemporary style of decorations, it is common to see dried slices of fruits called chips being used as a garnish.	
Icings and creams	Many a time, cake is decorated with icings and cream as well. Whipped cream can be piped from various kinds of nozzles to achieve decorative results such as basket weaves and rosettes. Icings can be used for piping figures of animals, and even flowers on top of a cake.	

(Contd)

Table 11.8 (Contd)

Garnish	Description	Photograph
Icings and creams	Royal icing can be used for creating figures by keeping a plastic sheet on top of any figure and tracing the outline of the same by piping the icing over it. The gaps can be filled with coloured royal icing. It is allowed to set and when the icing has dried off, the figure can be peeled off from the sheet and used with the face side up for garnishing. Similarly, lace and filigree designs are piped with royal icing and chocolates. These can then be used on cakes to give it a very classical and festive look. Piped meringue sticks, broken pieces of meringue sheets, etc. are other commonly used garnishes that add both a contemporary look and texture to a cake.	

WRITING AND PIPING ON CAKES

The writing and piping on cakes are skills that need to be mastered. Even mixing of the colours and deciding which colour would go well with a particular mood is important for the chef decorating the cake. To decide on colours, let us first talk about the colour wheel represented in Fig. 11.5.

Colours Yellow, blue, and red are primary colours. These are so called because all the other colours can be made by combining any of these colours.

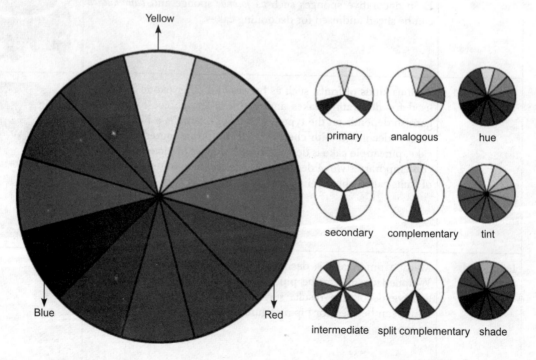

Fig. 11.5 Colour wheel (see also Plate 15)

Secondary colours These colours are formed by mixing any two primary colours. For example red and yellow combine to make orange, red and blue combine to make purple and blue and yellow combine to form green colour.

Tertiary colours These are colours made by the combination of secondary colours. These colours are rarely used in cake decoration. The only exception is when one has to make coffee or chocolate colour. Coffee colour can be made by combining green and orange in equal proportion and the chocolate colour can be achieved by mixing green and mauve in equal proportions.

Intermediate colours These are the colours that are seen between the primary and the secondary colours.

Analogue colours The range of colours between two primary colours are called analogue colours.

Complementary colours These colours are seen right opposite each other on the colour wheel. There are a total of six complementary colours on a colour wheel. For example blue and orange are complementary colours. This is important to know, as the choice of colours will make your decoration look pleasing to the eye.

Split complementary colours These are colours that appear on the left and the right of a complementary colour On the colour wheel.

Tint colours Any colour which is mixed with white is said to be tinted or pastel shade. The range of tinted colours combines very well on a cake for high end functions.

Shade colours Shades are the colours obtained when a colour is mixed with a small quantity of black or brown.

Monochrome colours The tints and shades of one colour would be referred to as monochrome colours.

Triad colours Any three colours on the colour wheel that are equidistant from each other are known as triads. For example, orange, green, and mauve form a triad.

Neutral colours Apart from the colours listed above, there are neutral colours. Black, white, gray, silver, and gold are called neutral colours. Black and white are also known as achromatic colours which means that they have no colour.

Let us now understand why it is important for a budding pastry chef to be aware of the colour wheel. Some colours are categorized into moods such as warm and cool. The seven colours on the colour wheel having red in them in different proportions are referred to as warm colours while the other colours are categorized as cool colours.

While decorating a wedding cake, the base of the cake is white or light pastel tints and the contrasting colours are given in deeper tones by arriving at a balance of cool and warm colours. If the base is darker, then the lighter colours and tints should be used to bring out the contrast on the cake and pastries.

Some of the colours are said to have an affinity with the seasons as well. It may be because during those times the flowers that bloom create that mood and we associate those colours with that season. Some of the seasons and the colours associated with them are as follows.

Spring   Yellow, green, lilac

Autumn   Yellow, gold, brown

Summers   Pink, dark green

Winters   White, blue, red

Some colours are believed to regulate and stimulate our moods. Table 11.9 gives us an idea of various colours and the moods associated with them.

Table 11.9   Colours and the moods they represent

Colour	Moods
Red	exciting, stimulating, daring, dynamic, bold, and sexy
Blue	comfort, loyalty, security, stability, serenity, and peace
Yellow	caution, bright, cheerful, energetic, mellow, hope, and happiness
Green	money, health, food, nature, fresh, healing, soothing, and prestige
Brown	nature, aged, eccentric, earth, substance, durability, and security
Orange	warm, excitement, friendly, vital, inviting, energetic, and playful
Pink	soft, healthy, childlike, energy, and feminine
Purple	royal, religion, elegant, sensuality, spirituality, and creativity
Black	dramatic, serious, strong, mysterious, elegant, and powerful
Grey	business, cold, and distinctive
White	clean, pure, and simple

Source: www.j6designs.com, accessed on 10 August 2011

Piping Exercises

Before starting to pipe, it is important to know how to make a good piping bag. Let us see how a good piping bag is made. Figure 11.6 shows the various steps involved in making a piping bag. The following are the steps for the procedure.

(a) Select a square piece of butter paper or greaseproof paper. Any other paper will absorb the moisture from the icing and break while piping. Fold the piece of square to obtain a triangle.

CHEF'S TIP
Always smoothen the icing with a palette knife on a flat surface to dissolve any small particles that can get stuck in the fine opening of a piping bag.

(b) Hold the paper in your hand so that the tip of the triangle is facing towards you. Mentally draw a line from the tip of the triangle to the base.

(c) Place your left thumb on the point where the line from the tip meets the base, holding the paper from the right end, roll it to the point where the thumb is to form a cone

(d) Roll it now to join the left end of the paper to get a cone

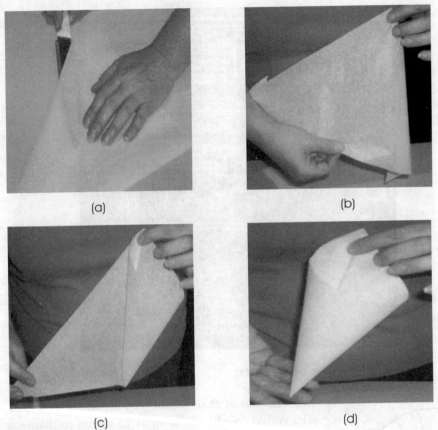

(a)

(b)

(c)

(d)

Fig. 11.6 Steps for making a piping bag

The piping bag may now be sealed with a tape to secure the shape. Use a pair of scissors to snap off the tip. The size of the hole you cut will determine the font of the piping.

Once the bag is made, a beginner can attempt to start the piping exercises. There is nothing highly technical about piping; it just needs a lot of practice as one has to have a stable hand and the movement of wrist has to be practised. The amount of pressure applied on the bag also needs to be practised, as this will result in even thickness of the piping. Some designs can be practised on a plastic sheet as shown in Fig. 11.7. One can keep practising until the right pattern is obtained.

CAKE SERVING

It is an art to cut and serve a cake. Each cake is cut into equal portions and it largely depends on the size and shape of the cake. It is fairly easy to divide a rectangular or a square piece of cake, but the challenge comes when one has to portion out a large three tier wedding cake for 400 people.

Usually, the portion size is around 80 g per person, but it also depends mainly on the size of the cake and the gathering or function. With that calculation, one can safely

Fig. 11.7 Exercises for piping

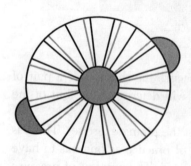

Fig. 11.8 Cake dividing tool

say that one kilo of cake would feed around 8 to 10 people. A 1 kg cake would roughly be around 10 inches in diameter and so the cake can be equally divided into 8 or 10 portions. When the diameter of the cake increases, one has to cut 16–20 wedges out of the cake and the trick is to cut each wedge into equal sizes. There are plastic or metal cake dividers available in the market, which once placed on top of the cake, can leave imprints and one can safely cut each slice of equal size. Refer Fig. 11.8 that depicts a cake dividing tool.

In case this tool is not available, we would normally cut the cakes in the following manners as shown in Figs 11.9, 11.10, and 11.11.

Portioning an 8-inch Cake

The 8-inch cake is simple to divide into eight pieces (see Fig. 11.9). Cut the cake into four quarters by cutting it in the shape of a plus sign. Thereafter, divide each quarter into half, which will yield 8 pieces of equal dimensions. It is now easy to divide the cake further into 16 pieces.

To divide an 8-inch cake into 10 pieces, follow the pattern shown in Fig. 11.10. Divide the cake into half (line AB). Then divide it along line CD. The rest of the cake can now be cut as for eight pieces shown along the dotted lines in the figure to yield 8 pieces. Thus the total pieces of the cake are 10. One can also cut 20 pieces like this.

To divide the cake into 12 pieces, refer Fig. 11.11. Divide the cake into half as shown along line AB; then divide into half along lines CD. Thereafter, divide the cake as shown along dotted lines E and F. The remaining quarter can now be split into half and this would yield 12 pieces or 24 pieces.

Portioning a Large 3-tier Wedding Cake

In order to cut a large 3-tier wedding cake or any other cake whose diameter is more than 12 inches, follow the pattern as shown in Fig. 11.12.

To cut a large cake, first cut all around the cake in a circular manner so that you have equal sized rings. A smaller round piece of 8 inches can be left as it is in the centre and portioned out in the same manner as shown in Figs 11.9 to 11.11. The rings thus, cut off can be then sliced into individual portions as shown in Fig. 11.12.

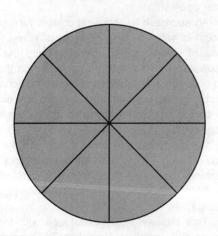

Fig. 11.9 Portioning an 8-inch cake into 8 pieces

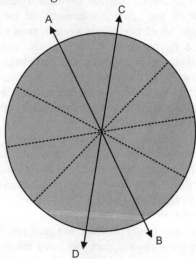

Fig. 11.10 Portioning an 8-inch cake cut into 10 pieces

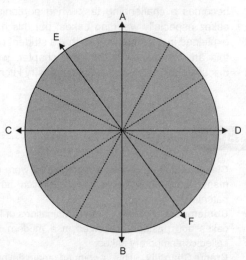

Fig. 11.11 Portioning an 8-inch cake into 12 pieces

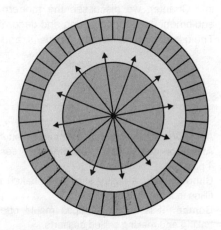

Fig. 11.12 Portioning large cakes

SUMMARY

In this chapter, we discussed cakes and pastries in detail. Both pastries and cakes are used as desserts, but pastries in a professional pastry kitchen are also referred to many other dough and pastes such as *choux* pastry, puff pastry, and so on. We discussed these pastries also as they play an important role in the preparation of cakes and pastries. Both 'cakes' and 'pastries' are always linked together as miniature cakes can be presented as pastries and even smaller pieces can be served as petit four that are often served along with the coffee at the end of the meal.

We discussed classical cakes and pastries and understood the basic components of cakes. We discussed about the various kinds of bases that can be used for preparing them. We also understood the importance of choosing the right kind of cake or sponge and the right kind of filling to provide textures in the cake. We then discussed the other components such as moistening agents, garnishes, and decorations.

This chapter also explained some famous classical cakes with a brief idea of the kind of sponge, moistening agent, decoration, and filling used in their preparation. It also dwelt a little on the history of those cakes as also their origins.

This chapter also discussed the modern trends in cake and pastry making and decoration. It explained the various factors that have influenced the making and presenting of cakes and pastries in a different way and style. While various basic tools and equipment used in the pastry kitchen were discussed in the first book *Food Production Operations,* in this Chapter, we discussed the modern tools and equipment used for preparing and decorating cakes. The use of silicone moulds, *flexipans*, and relief mats provide two-dimensional designs on top of the cakes and pastries.

We also discussed various kinds of cakes such as ornamental cakes, tea cakes, festive cakes, and wedding cakes. Varieties of icings along with their uses and application techniques were also taken up in this chapter. In the later part of this chapter we discussed the approach to cake decoration and serving. We discussed the layering of cakes from scratch and discussed the importance of each step in detail. Various kinds of garnishes were also discussed in a tabular form along with illustrations for better understanding.

An approach to choosing colours for icings was discussed with the help of a colour wheel. Various kinds of colour combinations as also the moods associated with colours are explained so that chefs can choose the combinations to suit the occasion for which they are preparing a cake. We also discussed the choice of colours to match the moods and the seasons.

We discussed the art of piping and the importance of being able to write with a piping bag. Certain exercises have been provided in the chapter with which the students can practice their piping and writing skills.

This chapter finally concluded with the art of serving and portioning the cakes. The representation of cakes through figures teaches the art of dividing the cake into various pieces. Cake portioning becomes a challenging task when portioning large cakes especially wedding cakes; but this has been explained in a simple way so that a student can learn this art with ease. In the next chapter, we would discuss chocolates and its use in pastry kitchen.

KEY TERMS

Aeration It is incorporating air into a mixture.

Afternoon tea This is tea or coffee served around 4 p.m.

Blind baked A pastry shell often baked without any filling in it is called blind baked.

Bombe It is a dome-shaped mould often used for baking and making chilled desserts.

Candied fruits These are dried fruits and their peels that are candied and sold packed.

Classical cakes These are cakes that were prepared many years ago, the recipes of which have been patented.

Contemporary cakes New combinations of flavoured cakes and pastries presented in a modern style are called contemporary cakes.

Crème Chantilly This is whipped cream flavoured with vanilla pods.

Deco paste It is a mixture prepared by mixing equal

quantities of flour, butter sugar, and egg whites. It is used for making designs on a *joconde*.

Desiccated coconut It is finely shredded and dried coconut used for making cookies, etc. in bakery and confectionery.

Feather icing This is piping of the lines on a liquid base and creating a design with the help of a toothpick to create a design that resembles feathers.

Filigree It is netted designs piped on wedding and other ornamental cakes.

Flexipans These are silicone moulds that are available in various shapes and sizes.

Frangipane It is a mixture prepared by creaming butter, sugar, almond powder, and eggs with small amounts of flour.

Frosting These are thick icings that stay in peaks.

Ganache This is two parts of cream melted with one part of chocolate and whipped together after it is cold, to achieve a thick whipped cream consistency.

Grand Marnier This is an orange-flavoured liquor from France.

Hazelnut It is a kind of nut used in Western cuisine.

High-tea Tea, coffee served with sandwiches and cakes at around 6 p.m.

Kahlua It is coffee-flavoured liquor, often used in cakes and pastries.

Kirsch Kirsch is German for cherries; cherry flavoured.

Lazy Suzanne It is another name for cake turntable.

Marie biscuits It is proprietary brand of English biscuits.

Marzipan It is proprietary almond paste that is used for modelling or covering cakes.

Mascarpone It is cream cheese from Italy, often used for making desserts.

Morello cherries These are a kind of cherries traditionally used in Black Forest cake.

Nougatine These are almonds caramelized along with sugar and allowed to cool on an oiled marble slab. It is then crushed to small pieces for use.

Nut flour It is obtained from powdered nuts such as almond, hazelnut, and peanut.

Organic It is a style of farming in which only natural fertilizers are used. No artificial pesticide or fertilizer is used in cultivation.

Ornamental cakes These are cakes made in various shapes representing a theme of a birthday party or any occasion.

Palette knife It is a flat spatula, often used for icing or spreading toppings on the cakes.

Pastry cream This is custard powder cooked along with sugar, eggs and cornflour, and milk. Once it is cooled, it is whipped and mixed with equal parts of whipped cream.

Petit four glace It is a small individual glazed baked product served along with coffee after the meal.

Philadelphia cheese It is cream cheese from Philadelphia region in the USA, popularly used for making baked cheese cakes.

Praline It is paste of *nougatine*.

Profiteroles These are choux pastry piped in rounds and baked in oven.

Proof It is a process wherein yeast-leavened goods are allowed to rise in size due to yeast action.

Quenelle A soft mixture shaped into oval shape by moving it between two spoons.

Relief mats These are thick sheets of thick silicone rubber, engraved with designs and used for making decorating sponges.

Salamander It is an equipment used in the hot kitchen, which emits radiated heat.

Short It is a texture of the baked product, where it snaps into two when folded.

Sour cherries A variety of cherry that is sour in taste. It is usually cooked with small amounts of starch and served packed.

Spit roasting It is a method of cooking where the food is cooked in front of an open flame.

Sponge fingers A kind of cookie made with sponge method. It is piped in shape of fingers and dusted with icing sugar prior to baking in the oven.

Truffle A common ingredient in the pastry kitchen, truffle is made with equal amount of cream and chocolate cooked together and then chilled to obtain a dark paste used for filling or covering cakes and pastries.

Vacherins These are shells made with meringue and baked. These can be filled with various kinds of fillings and decorated with fruits and berries.

CONCEPT REVIEW QUESTIONS

1. How would you differentiate between a cake and a pastry?
2. How would you differentiate between a classical cake and a contemporary cake?
3. How are petit fours different from pastries?
4. What is the difference between a *gateau* and a *torte*?

5. How does sieving help in increasing the volume of a cake?
6. Describe the various components of a cake.
7. What is the importance of a base in a cake?
8. Why is a cake moistened while layering?
9. Explain a sponge and describe at least three types of sponges used for making cakes and pastries.
10. What is *baumkuchen*? What are the other names by which it is known?
11. Why are pound cakes called so?
12. Describe the different types of meringue and their uses.
13. How is a *Japonaise* different from a *Dacquoise*?
14. Describe a *joconde* and its various uses.
15. Describe a *Sacher torte* and explain how it is made.
16. Why is *Dobos torte* covered with sugar?
17. What is the history behind the *Malakoff torte*?
18. Name one Austrian tart that utilizes jam as a filling.
19. Describe *Alhambra* cake and its uniqueness.
20. What is *Scwarzwalder kirsch torte*?
21. What two kinds of fillings are used in making *Gateau St Honore*?
22. How is devil's food cake different from a mud cake?
23. Differentiate between a chilled cheese cake and a baked cheese cake.
24. Why are yule logs so popular during Christmas?
25. How are breakfast pastries different from cakes and pastries?
26. How are the cakes and pastries of modern day different from the ones made in the old times?
27. How has the service style of cakes and pastries changed on a dessert buffet over the years?
28. Briefly describe the new kinds of tools and equipment used in making and decorating cakes and pastries in modern times.
29. What are silicone moulds? What are their advantages over metallic moulds?
30. What is the difference between a textured sheet and a transfer sheet?
31. How are cakes classified?
32. What is an ornamental cake?
33. Briefly describe at least five types of high-tea cakes and pastries.
34. What is special about wedding cakes and what are the steps involved in decorating them?
35. What is a Twelfth Night cake? What is its importance?
36. Explain different types of icings used on cakes and pastries.
37. What is the difference between royal icing and fondant icing?
38. How is truffle different from chocolate fudge?
39. What are the few methods of making sponge cakes?
40. Briefly describe few garnishes that are used for decorating cakes and pastries.
41. Describe a colour wheel. What is its importance in decorating cakes?
42. How do colours impact on the occasion of a cake?
43. What are the principles behind portioning out cakes?
44. How would you portion out a large wedding cake?

PROJECT WORK

1. In groups of five, do a market survey of various pastry shops and make a list of the kinds of cakes and pastries they are serving. Record your observations with regard to the choice of the menu, ingredients, equipment used in cooking and serving and share with the other groups.
2. From the recipe provided in the CD, make the basic *Genoese* sponge and layer the cake with various kinds of fillings and icings. Sample the cakes and record your observations.
3. In groups of five, prepare one wedding cake each and decorate it with various types of garnishes. Critique the cakes and record your feedback and share with the team
4. In groups of five, research at least three cakes from countries such as France, Germany, Spain, America, Austria, India, and China. Share the information with the rest of the team and discuss the components of each cake.

CHAPTER 12

CHOCOLATES

Learning Objectives

After reading this chapter, you should be able to

- understand the basic origin of chocolates
- appreciate the methods involved in production of chocolate from cocoa beans
- acquire in-depth knowledge about various kinds of chocolates and the properties that make them so unique
- work with chocolate by melting it for various applications
- appreciate the need for tempering chocolate and various methods to do the same
- analyse the various uses of chocolates and their techniques
- get a basic knowledge of making artistic showpieces of chocolate
- appreciate the use of the right kinds of tools and equipment for creating chocolate products
- select and store a chocolate according to its properties

INTRODUCTION

The very word 'chocolate' brings a twinkle in the eyes of people of all age groups—from a small child to an aged person. They find this ingredient, used in various food products, rich, smooth, creamy, and delicious.

For chefs working in the pastry kitchen, chocolate is the most sought-after ingredient that is widely used for various reasons. The first and the foremost is the sublime taste of chocolate. Chefs believe one can never go wrong in a dessert that has chocolate as an ingredient. The second reason is the variety of ways in which it can be used in the confectionery world. One can create beverages, cakes, pastries, hot and cold desserts, chocolate confections, and also showpieces of chocolate. It is commonly used for garnishing and decoration, as chefs conjure up showpieces that are commonly displayed in restaurants, buffets, and pastry shops.

In this chapter, we will first discuss the origin and history of chocolates, so that we can understand how this unique product became popular across the world. There are various kinds of chocolates available in the market. A layperson would classify a chocolate on the basis of brands, such as Cadbury, Amul, Nestlé, Lindt, and Toblerone, but a professional pastry chef sees it much differently. This chapter will introduce you to the various types and kinds of chocolates and the uses that it is put to. We will also talk about the various ways in which chocolate is used in the pastry kitchen and how one can create garnishes and showpieces for decorative purposes.

HISTORY OF CHOCOLATE

Chocolate is made from cocoa beans or the seeds of the cocoa tree. The origin of chocolate can be traced to Mexico, where the cocoa tree was revered and worshipped by the natives. *Theobroma cacao,* as the Aztecs called it, meant food for the gods. The Mayans and the Aztecs made a drink from cocoa beans and flavoured it with vanilla and spices. They called this beverage *Xocolatl,* which meant a bitter drink in their language. The cocoa beans were considered to be so valuable that they were bartered for other commodities such as cloth, jute, silk, and even jewels. Although there are many tales on how chocolate was first made, it is the Spanish who are credited with popularizing this versatile product and launching it in Europe and the rest of the world. The Spanish invaded Mexico in the sixteenth century. By that time, the Aztecs had set up a powerful empire, but the Spanish were successful in capturing Mexico and Don Cortes was appointed as the first governor general of Mexico. On his return to Spain in 1528, he brought with him a full load of cocoa beans, which became instantly popular among the rich and famous in Spain. The Spanish started flavouring chocolate with vanilla and sugar instead of spices and chillies used by the Aztecs. This became one of the most sought after food items and the Spanish are believed to have kept the procedure of making chocolates a secret for almost 100 years. Throughout centuries this versatile product has remained the most sought after food item worldwide. However, it was not the taste of the chocolate, but the monetary value of the cocoa beans that excited the Spanish for their trade and business. The Spanish used cocoa beans, which were the much preferred mode of payment in those times for buying slaves from Mexico. The cocoa beans came to be commonly known as the 'gold of the new world'. It was only in the later parts of the fifteenth century that people got to known the medicinal benefits of chocolate. A substance present in cocoa beans, known as *theobromine,* is considered to be good for the heart and that is the reason why chocolates were commonly made into heart shapes. It, thus, became the symbol of love and affection.

The Industrial Revolution of the eighteenth and nineteenth centuries changed the way chocolate was consumed as this bitter drink was transformed into the chocolate as we know of it. The Spanish started flavouring chocolate with vanilla and sugar instead of spices and chillies used by the Aztecs. This became one of the most sought after food items and the Spanish are believed to have kept the procedure of making chocolates a secret for almost 100 years. Throughout centuries this versatile product has remained the most sought after food item worldwide.

Cocoa beans, sugar, and vanilla are the three essential ingredients that have survived the tradition of chocolate making. Even though machines are used nowadays for making chocolate, the techniques used by the Spanish to make their first sweet chocolate remain much the same today.

Cocoa trees thrive in the equatorial forests along the Equator, which has a warm and humid climate. Direct sunlight and wind are enemies of this plant, which is why it is always grown under the shade of other tall trees. Africa is the largest grower of the cocoa trees in the world. Other places where it is also grown are the Amazon forests, areas around Honduras in Mexico and Venezuela, and few parts of Asia. Cocoa from the plantations of Africa around the regions of Ivory Coast and Ghana are more popular among chocolate lovers.

CHOCOLATE PRODUCTION

The transformation of these unique beans into chocolate is a lengthy process. It involves the following steps.

Step 1: Harvesting

Harvesting of beans is undertaken twice a year—from October to March and from May to August. The trees produce pink and white flowers throughout the year but only a few of them bear the cocoa pod. The pods on the trees look like a green, oval-shaped melon, which changes its colour from green to maroon, into orange to yellow (refer Fig. 12.1) which indicates that the beans are ready for harvesting. The pods are harvested very carefully so that the branches do not get damaged.

Step 2: Ripening and Fermentation

After the pods are harvested, they are left to further ripen for a few days [Fig. 12.2(a)]. This process of ripening also helps to loosen out the exterior skin from the pulp in which

(a)   (b)   (c)

Fig. 12.1 Stages of ripening of cocoa pods on the tree

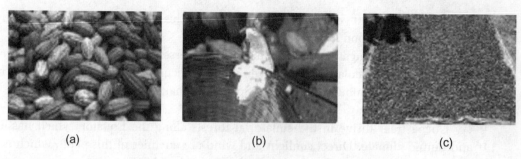

(a) (b) (c)

Fig. 12.2 Extracting cocoa beans from pods

the beans are embedded. The pods are split open with a sharp blow in a swift manner so that the seeds are not damaged [Fig. 12.2(b)]. The shell opens up exposing the concealed seeds that are creamy yellow in colour. These beans are sticky and pulpous at this stage and are collected in large containers or pits and left to ferment for a period of at least five to six days covered with banana leaves. These undergo biochemical changes during which the bitterness subsides and flavour develops. The yellow creamy beans transform into light brown coloured beans, now called cocoa seeds [Fig. 12.2(c)].

Step 3: Drying in Sun

After the seeds are obtained, they are further dried in the sun for a period of six days. At this point, they are frequently turned around so that they retain only a fraction of the moisture. It is essential to dry the seeds to arrest the fermentation or else the beans will get overfermented and lose their flavour. Drying also ensures that the seeds can be stored for longer duration. The cocoa seeds after drying are known as raw cocoa.

The first three steps are performed in villages or at sites where the pods are harvested. Thereafter, the raw cocoa has to be transported to factories where the humble seeds get transformed into chocolate—the most loved product on the planet.

Step 4: Selection and Blending

At the chocolate factory, the cocoa seeds are inspected as per the quality standards laid down by each factory. Only the best seeds are selected for producing chocolates. After careful selection of the right seeds, they are cleaned of any stones, wooden barks, and any other impurities. Thereafter, they are subjected to blending to produce chocolates. The process of blending cocoa seeds is very similar to the blending of tea or coffee. Blending is done very carefully to help create the exact desirable flavour for a particular kind of chocolate.

Step 5: Roasting and Crushing the Beans

Once blended, the seeds are roasted under red hot grills or in large rotating vats, anywhere between 30 minutes to 2 hours. This is done very carefully and for a brief time. The roasting of the seeds helps in many ways: it helps reduce moisture content to enable easier crushing of seeds; it aids the removal of the shell around the seed kernels; it also helps the seeds to acquire a dark brown colour that is desired to produce a dark coloured chocolate with the necessary aroma. The roasted seeds are then cooled and passed on to a crushing machine, where the machine splits up the seeds and separates the exterior shell from the remaining cocoa bits called cocoa nibs that are ready to be processed further (refer Fig. 12.3).

Fig. 12.3 Separating the nibs from the cocoa seeds

Step 6: Grinding

The nibs are then transferred to grinding mills, where they pass through a series of grinders starting from the ones that grind them coarse to the ones that grind them into super fine texture [refer Fig. 12.4(a)]. The grinding process not only grinds the cocoa nibs into a smooth paste, but it also generates pressure and heat due to the friction which slowly melts the cocoa butter present in the mass resulting in a thick liquid mass, known as cocoa liquor or chocolate liquor. This smooth shiny mass contains cocoa mass and cocoa butter that can be used for making chocolate and its by products. The mass obtained after grinding is primarily made up of two components: cocoa powder and cocoa butter. To separate these, the cocoa liquor is passed through hydraulic machines, where a certain amount of pressure is applied to extract the cocoa powder in the form of dry cakes and cocoa butter in the melted form (refer Fig. 12.4(b)]. The dry cakes can be crushed to obtain cocoa powder that finds its application in production of various products in the pastry kitchen. The cocoa butter, on the other hand, is used for making chocolates or sold in that form for various uses in the pastry kitchen.

(a) Grinding of cocoa beans

(b) Separating cocoa powder and butter

Fig. 12.4 The grinding process

Step 7: Conching

The art of making good quality chocolate entails the mixing of a variety of ingredients into the chocolate mass or liquor to obtain the chocolate of desired flavour and texture. Milk is added to make milk chocolates; sugar is used for regulating the sweetness and extra amount of cocoa powder is added to regulate the desired bitterness, while soy lecithin is added to help stabilize the chocolate, so that it helps the chocolate to flow easily when melted. All this is added to the chocolate mass during the stage known as conching. This is used for development of flavours in a chocolate. The cocoa liquor is fed in large machines, which has powerful stirring mechanism that almost performs a kneading motion and paddles or rolls the chocolate mass. The movement of chocolate mass results in many physical and chemical

Fig. 12.5 Conching

reactions that are much desirable for a good quality chocolate. The fats from cocoa butter and milk solids, if added, get mixed homogenously into the cocoa mass. The volatile acids also evaporate, thereby impacting the flavour of the chocolate. During conching, since there is small amount of continuous heat generated, it helps to caramelise the sugar and milk solids, thereby adding to the flavour of chocolate. The process of conching can last few hours up to a few days depending on the type of chocolate. During conching, chocolate obtains a smooth and velvety texture (refer Fig. 12.5). At the end of the conching process, cocoa butter and soy lecithin are added to the chocolate liquor. Soy lecithin helps in the emulsification of the chocolate, whereas cocoa butter helps to regulate the viscosity of the melted chocolate. Some confectionery products require thick chocolate, whereas some other preparations require liquid chocolate. Many companies custom make chocolates for such usages by regulating the amount of cocoa butter in the chocolate.

Step 8: Tempering

In this step, the conched chocolate is carefully brought to low temperatures stirring constantly all the time. The process of tempering is discussed in detail later in the chapter. It is only after tempering that the chocolate can be moulded into various shapes and blocks. Melted and tempered chocolate is shaped into drops, often called *callets*, small chips, or in sheets or blocks and then passed through cooling tunnels before it being packed for sale in the market or distribution to hotels and other commercial users.

TYPES OF CHOCOLATE

Chocolate is classified on various parameters. The most common one is on the basis of its colour, taste, and texture. The other popular classification is from the place that it originates from. Two kinds of chocolates are commonly used in the pastry kitchen: *couverture* and compound, both of which are available in dark, milk, and white colour. Each of these has different applications and uses in the professional pastry kitchen. The use of different types of chocolate would call for a particular process to be used for a particular product which is why it is important for students to understand these types of chocolates and their applications. It is also important to be familiar with certain terminologies, so that they can read the labels of the chocolates and comprehend the quality of the chocolate and its uses for a particular product.

Various types of chocolates, their respective uses along with the corresponding available brands are described in Table 12.1.

Table 12.1 Types of chocolates

Chocolate	Description and uses	Brands
Couverture	*Couverture* is the French term for covering chocolate. It is a high-quality chocolate preferred by pastry chefs across the world for making chocolate confections. *Couverture* chocolate is a high-class product, smooth, and refined. It is manufactured from cocoa mass, sugar, and cocoa butter. To produce a milk *couverture*, full-cream milk solids are added to cocoa butter and sugar during the conching stage. The cocoa butter gives the impression of cooling the mouth as it melts because the melting point is just below body temperature. A chocolate should have minimum 32 per cent of cocoa butter and at least 22 per cent of cocoa solids or mass, to be labelled as *couverture. Couverture* is available in milk, dark, and white colour and can be used for dipping, moulding, coating, and making garnishes. It is always necessary to temper the *covertures* before being used.	SCHARFFEN BERGER CHOCOLATE MAKER USA DAGOBA ORGANIC CHOCOLATE USA Guittard CHOCOLATE COMPANY USA PIERRE MARCOLINI Belgium VALRHONA France GODIVA Belgium CALLEBAUT Belgium Lindt OF SWITZERLAND Switzerland

(contd)

Table 12.1 *(Contd)*

Chocolate	Description and uses	Brands
Compound chocolate	This is less expensive than *couverture* as it is a combination of various other ingredients apart from cocoa liquor. Other ingredients include hard tropical vegetable fats and oils such as palm kernel oil. Compound chocolate does not require tempering as it contains very little or no cocoa butter at all. It is used for enrobing chocolates and preparing garnishes as some people prefer it because of its easy to use approach. Unlike *couvertures*, compound chocolates can just be melted and used for the same uses as the *couverture* would be used after tempering.	Switzerland Switzerland Malaysia Belgium CALLEBAUT MORDE India
White chocolate	This is not a real chocolate as it does not contain any cocoa liquor or mass. It contains ingredients such as cocoa butter, sugar, milk solids, emulsifiers, vanilla, and other flavourings. Since it does not contain any of the cocoa mass, hence the colour is off-white. In some countries, it is not called chocolate as it does not contain any cocoa liquor. White chocolates can be sold as compound or *couverture*, which have a higher content of cocoa butter. These are used to prepare coloured chocolates as one can add oil soluble colours dissolved in cocoa fat to the white chocolate to give various shades of colours for decorations and showpieces. These are also used for making desserts such as mousses, soufflés, and cakes.	Côte d'Or — Belgium HVIT DRONNING — Norway Prestige of Belgium — Belgium Divine — Ghana, Africa GODIVA — USA

(contd)

Table 12.1 (Contd)

Chocolate	Description and uses	Brands
Milk chocolate	This is a shade of chocolate that can be obtained by combining dark chocolate with white chocolate. Milk chocolate is a sweet chocolate that contains around 10–12 per cent cocoa solids that include cocoa mass and cocoa butter. It should not be confused with milk *couverture*. It is mostly used to flavour chocolate cookies and dough.	USA UK Brazil
Semi-sweet chocolate	This is a classic dark chocolate that is often referred to as cooking or baking chocolate. It frequently finds its use in making cookies and brownies. It has a slightly bitter taste as it contains 40–65 per cent cocoa solids.	Switzerland USA Grenada
Bittersweet chocolate	This is dark chocolate that has very little amount of sugar added to the cocoa mass in the conching process. Cocoa solids can range between 60–80 per cent depending upon the brand. Bitter sweet chocolate is used for preparing various desserts and also in *couverture* for enrobing and coating.	Switzerland Columbia UK

(contd)

Table 12.1 (Contd)

Chocolate	Description and uses	Brands
Unsweetened chocolate	It is a pure bitter chocolate that has an intense flavour of cocoa as there is no sugar added to the cocoa mass. It is preferred by die hard chocolate lovers. This can be used for preparing desserts and baking but since it does not contain any sugar, so many people find it unsuitable for eating raw. Bitter chocolate usually contains around 100 per cent cocoa solids, out of which 40–50 per cent is cocoa butter.	Switzerland USA Italy
Single-origin chocolates	As we read earlier, cocoa beans are blended to create the right blend for a particular brand. This is done because the beans from different countries and regions have different characteristics. For example, the African cocoa has a strong body and aroma whereas cocoa from the central parts of America and Asia have distinguished flavours of flowers and herbs. Single-origin chocolates are made from cocoa beans of same variety, soil, climatic conditions, and region. Like wines, the crop of cocoa differs from year to year; this would mean that the aroma and flavour of the single-origin chocolate could vary from one year to another. Single-origin chocolates are more expensive and are used for making chocolates, desserts, enrobing, and coating.	Venezuela Sao Tome, Africa Madagascar Manjari (France)

(contd)

Table 12.1 (Contd)

Chocolate	Description and uses	Brands
Organic chocolates	An organic cocoa bean is extracted from a plant that has never been sprayed with any pesticide or chemical. Such a plant grows in its natural habitat. The procedure for harvesting and production are same as other chocolates. Even the flavourings like milk solids, sugars, etc. that are added are organic in nature. The by products such as cocoa butter and cocoa powder obtained from these are also sold as organic products. It is the need of the hour and more and more people are demanding products that are organic.	SCHARFFEN BERGER CHOCOLATE MAKER USA Lake Champlain CHOCOLATES USA
Kosher chocolates	Several chocolate companies have started producing chocolate that conform to Jewish food laws known as kosher. Apart from the Jewish community, there are millions of people who eat kosher food products and many brands have specially created chocolates for such a diverse market.	CALLEBAUT INSPIRED BY YOUR CRAFTSMANSHIP Belgium
Sugar-free chocolates	This range of chocolates should not be confused with bitter chocolate that is made without any sugar. The range of sugar-free chocolates uses sugar in other forms such as *maltitol*. This chocolate is a favourite amongst people in various age groups and hence companies have started producing sugar free chocolates for people who have specific dietary requirements.	VALRHONA France CALLEBAUT INSPIRED BY YOUR CRAFTSMANSHIP Belgium

MELTING CHOCOLATE

Chocolate contains cocoa liquor and cocoa butter. It is because of the cocoa butter present in chocolate that one needs to be very careful while melting it. Cocoa butter is composed of crystals, the knowledge of which is very important for any budding pastry chef as it would help in the tempering and working of chocolate. When a chocolate is melted, the crystals present in the cocoa butter also melt, making the chocolate liquid and runny. This usually happens at a temperature of ±25°C. At round ±36°C all the crystals usually melt away. But in order to make sure that all the crystals have melted, it is advisable to melt the chocolate to 40°C but not more than that. When melting chocolate, there are two most commonly followed methods: melting over a double boiler and melting in a microwave oven. There are also machines that are used to melt chocolates, which ensure that the temperature does not go beyond 40°C.

While melting chocolate, one must keep the following points in mind:

1. Ensure that the chocolate never comes in direct contact with the heat source. Always melt the chocolate on a double boiler. Though one could use a microwave oven for

the same, it is advisable to use the double boiler. One cannot control the heat in a microwave and there are chances that chocolate can get burnt.

2. While melting the chocolate on the double boiler, ensure that the bowl which holds the chocolate is bigger than the pot containing water. This will ensure that the steam rising from the pot does not come in contact with the chocolate. Moisture is an enemy of the chocolate and even a small drop of water will result in thickening of the chocolate.

3. Make certain that the pot containing the chocolate does not directly touch the hot water in the pot below. This will result in spot heating of the chocolate and impact the final product.

4. Break the chocolate into small pieces for even melting and stir from time to time to ensure that the chocolate has melted evenly.

5. While melting in microwave, do not cook the chocolate; instead melt it by spurt method. Heat the chocolate only for 20 seconds. Stir and again melt for 20 seconds. Repeat this process until the chocolate has completely melted. Though this method is not very conducive for melting chocolates, but chefs use it to save on time. It is difficult to regulate the temperature of the chocolate in a microwave oven and sometimes the chocolate can get scorched as a result of overheating.

> **CHEF'S TIP**
> To melt chocolate, chop it into small pieces and place in a double-jacketed container or bain-marie with water not exceeding 49°C and chocolate temperature not exceeding 40°C.

Now that we have learnt to melt the chocolate, we move on to the most important aspect of a chocolate known as tempering or pre-crystallization.

TEMPERING OF CHOCOLATE AND ITS APPLICATION

The untempered chocolate will not have the desired sheen and the all important snap that is required for relishing a chocolate. If a melted chocolate is moulded and allowed to set, it will become hard, and acquire a greyish matte finish colour that is often referred to as bloom. Blooming is a common problem in the world of chocolates. There can be two kinds of blooms: fat bloom and sugar bloom. Fat bloom occurs when the chocolate is heated so much that the butter separates out from the mixture and then when the chocolate sets, it shows streaks that are discoloured and hazy. Sugar bloom occurs when the chocolate is allowed to cool too quickly or rapidly. The condensation on top of the chocolate dissolves the sugar present in the chocolate and when the moisture evaporates, it recrystallizes the sugar on the surface, thereby giving a hazy and dull appearance to the finished chocolate product. So, a fat bloom is related to temperature and sugar bloom is related to moisture.

Tempering is the answer to avoid blooms in chocolates. Because *couverture* contains cocoa butter, it needs to be 'tempered' prior to using. This process is necessary because cocoa butter, which is a component of the chocolate, has six types of fat crystals with different melting points. The longer a fat crystal takes to melt, the longer it will take to set and vice versa. If the *couverture* is not tempered, the cocoa butter would set slowly and when melted, they would separate and rise to the surface, giving the finished product a grey, patchy appearance. Tempering is a process where the *couverture* chocolate is melted to specific temperatures and then cooled to enable the cocoa butter fat crystals to bind together. As this process requires considerable skill, time, and effort, most establishments do not bother with it, preferring to use compound chocolate that only requires melting to be ready for use.

Out of the six types of crystals in cocoa butter, only one is a stable crystal. The art is to achieve the temperature of the chocolate to a degree that can form maximum of these stable crystals which in turn would help the chocolate to set into hard texture with the right shine and snap. The temperatures in tempering process are very important.

Tempering can thus, also be defined as the process in which the chocolate is melted to 40°C and then cooled to 27°C and then the temperature is slowly brought back to working temperature. These temperatures vary in dark, milk, and white chocolates due to their composition and are as follows.

Dark chocolate	± 31 to 32°C
Milk chocolate	± 30 to 31°C
White chocolate	± 28 to 29°C

CHEF'S TIP

Do not let the chocolate become contaminated by moisture, as it will have a harmful effect on the chocolate by changing its consistency and gloss. Excess heat will make the chocolate separate, lose its gloss, and become granular in texture.

There are several ways of tempering or pre crystallizing the chocolate and all these methods give the same results. The choice of method solely depends upon the user. However, one has to be careful as there is a very thin line of difference between tempering and pre-crystallization. If a small amount of chocolate on the tip of the knife does not set within 3–4 minutes, it means that the tempered chocolate has few crystals formed and if there is no sheen in the chocolate, it means that there are far too many crystals in the tempered chocolate. The various methods of tempering are described in Table 12.2.

Table 12.2 Methods of tempering chocolate

Method	Description
Table-top method or tabling method	In this method of tempering, smooth surfaces such as granite or marble are used to cool the chocolate as they retain a cooler temperature for a longer period of time. It involves three steps: First, the chocolate is melted to 40°C until smooth. Then, two-third of the chocolate is poured on the marble slab and scraped and moved constantly with a spatula. One would notice that the chocolate starts to thicken, which means that stable crystals are forming. The temperature of chocolate at this stage would be roughly 27°C.
	The third step is to mix this chocolate with the remaining one-third chocolate at 40°C. The chocolate is then brought to the working temperature.
	Time, temperature, and mixing of the chocolate are three major factors that would influence the end product. If we just leave the melted chocolate to cool down, it would be tempered, but moving the chocolate regularly while cooling will help in bringing the right kind of stable crystals together. Also, while mixing chocolate, never use a wire whisk, as that would incorporate air bubbles in the chocolate, which when moulding would burst and leave a hole in the figures.

(contd)

Table 12.2 *(Contd)*

Method	Description
Grafting method/ seeding method/ injection method	In this method, 75 per cent of the chocolate is melted to 40°C and brought down to 2°C more than the working temperature. For example, if the working temperature for dark chocolate is 32°C, then it is cooled to 34°C. Twenty-five per cent of the grated chocolate is added to the mixture and stirred until the temperature comes down to the working temperature. In this method, the stable crystals from the hard chocolate block are utilized to coagulate or stabilize the remaining crystals in the melted chocolate.
Microwave method	Though not a preferred method by professional chefs, it comes in handy while tempering small quantities of chocolate instantly. In this method, the chocolate is heated in the microwave in spurts. After every 15–20 seconds, mix the chocolate and heat again to a stage where small amount of chocolate is still hard and unmelted. Take it off from the microwave and keep stirring until the chocolate has completely melted. The unmelted chocolate pieces that contain stable crystals get mixed with the chocolate and this brings about pre-crystallization in the chocolate.
Machine method	Tempering machines with different capacities are available in the market. A machine automatically melts the chocolate and stirs it constantly so that it melts evenly. The temperature settings in the machine cool the chocolate to the set temperature and heat it again to the working temperature which varies for different kinds of *couvertures*.

COOLING CHOCOLATE

The two most important aspects of a chocolate are melting and tempering. Another significant process for the chocolate to have the right intensity of shine and snap is its cooling. When the chocolate cools down, it shrinks during the process. This property of chocolate enables the demoulding of chocolate figures. If the chocolate cools down too slowly then it will have a greyish tinge called bloom, as discussed earlier, and it will also be difficult to demould it from the mould. If the chocolate is allowed to cool too rapidly, then it will not only lose its shine but it might also result in condensation of moisture on top, which again discolours the chocolate.

CHEF'S TIP
To check if the chocolate is tempered, dip the point of a knife in the chocolate. If the chocolate sets with a shine within 3 to 4 minutes, then it has tempered successfully.

Temperatures play a very important role in the products made by using chocolates. It is advisable to work in a room that has a temperature of around 20°C and the place where the chocolate is left to cool should be around 10°C. Cooling in freezers or fridges at low temperatures might result in bloom.

USES OF CHOCOLATE

Chocolate can be used in many ways—they can be piped in different designs directly onto sweets, cakes, and petit fours; piped into silicon or greaseproof paper to make decorative chocolate filigree. Some chocolates may need to be thickened for piping purposes. Spirits, liquors, and glycerine are recommended for such uses. The chocolate is melted and a few drops are added at a time until it reaches the desired viscosity. Thinly spread chocolate can be cut into a variety of shapes and used for decorative purposes.

Chocolate can also be used to cover a cake. For that, a chocolate needs to be mixed with dairy cream that has been brought to boil and allowed to set to form paste. This product is called truffle. A cheaper variety can be made by using a mixture of cream and milk, or by using milk alone. The consistency of truffle may be adjusted by decreasing or increasing the proportion of chocolate. Truffle can also be used for piping purposes or can be mixed with whipped cream and used as a filling or for cakes, pastries, or variety of desserts. The various uses of chocolates are discussed below.

Moulding

Moulding is a technique wherein the chocolate is poured into various kinds of moulds to give it a particular shape and size. Many chocolate show pieces such as Easter eggs, Christmas figures, etc. are commonly made by pouring chocolate into a mould and

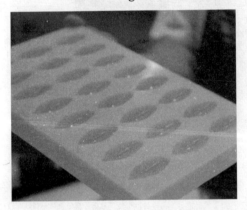

allowing it to set. The chocolate is then taken out from the shell and decorated and packed for sale. Moulded chocolates are also commonly made in pastry kitchens and sold in pastry shops or sent to hotel guests as amenities.

Some basic steps that should be followed for moulding a chocolate are explained as follows.

Step 1

Select a clean mould of any desired shape (Fig. 12.6) that you want to use and polish it well. Polishing of the mould is done with a lint free cotton cloth. Polishing helps to remove any moisture in the mould and the shiny surface would help in easy removal of the chocolate besides providing the necessary shine to it.

Fig. 12.6 A chocolate mould

Step 2

Pour the melted and tempered *couverture* into the mould and tap it to expel any air bubbles as showed in Fig. 12.7. The tapping should be done with a wooden material to avoid any damage to the moulds. Let the chocolate rest in the mould for at least 30 seconds to form a coating. If you want the coating to be thicker, allow the chocolate to stand for longer duration. In certain moulds that have complex corners and curves, it is a good idea to first brush the tempered *couverture* into the mould to avoid any bubbles or holes in the final product.

Fig. 12.7 Pouring the chocolate in the mould

Step 3

Invert the mould and tap it to remove the excess chocolate from the mould (Fig. 12.8). Now keep the mould inverted on a wire rack so that all the extra chocolate drips from the mould. This allows even coating of the mould with chocolate. In case of three dimensional figures, both the front and the back part of the moulds are held together with the help of clips and the chocolate is poured in the mould. The larger the figure to be moulded, the thicker should be the coating and vice versa. One can also give more than single coating, but each time it is important to remove the excess chocolate from the mould.

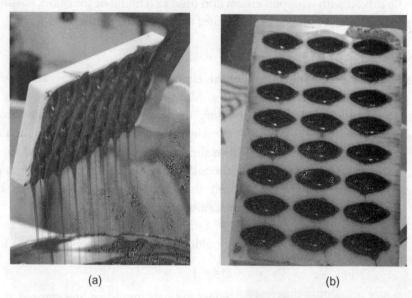

(a)   (b)

Fig. 12.8 Invert the mould and allow the excess chocolate to drip

Step 4

While making moulded chocolates, often known as pralines, one needs to pour flavoured fillings such as *ganache*, truffle, fondants, etc. in such a manner that little space of at least 2–3 mm is left on top. The filling is allowed to set for a couple of minutes (Fig. 12.9).

Step 5

When the filling is set, spread more tempered *couverture* on the mould to form a covering. Use a scraper and scrape the chocolate from all the sides and top so that each side of the shape is clearly visible as shown in Fig. 12.10.

Fig. 12.9 Allow the filling to set for few minutes

Fig. 12.10 Scrapping chocolate from the sides of the mould

Step 6

The moulded chocolate is allowed to set in a refrigerator at 10°C for 20 minutes. Thereafter, the chocolate is ready to be demoulded. When it has left the sides of the mould, which can be seen clearly as most of the moulds are of polycarbonate material, twist the mould slightly and tap it to remove the moulded chocolates. If the *couverture* is tempered well and the temperatures are followed, the chocolate would have a shine and would easily come out of the mould as seen Fig. 12.11.

While moulding figures such as Santa Claus, Easter bunny, or Easter egg, the moulds are slightly different in that those

Fig. 12.11 Demoulded chocolates

are three dimensional and can be pulled apart. The process of moulding the chocolate, however, remains the same, the only difference is that these moulds are not filled with any fillings as these would become heavy and break. The two moulds are filled individually and then joined together. The two sides are joined together with the help of chocolate. Another way is to keep the chocolate on a hot surface for a couple of seconds, so that the chocolate melts, and this helps in sticking the sides together. Another way of making these shapes is to clamp both parts of the moulds together with clips and then fill the mould with chocolate, rest for a couple of minutes, so that the chocolate sets in the plastic mould. The mould is then inverted to let the extra chocolate flow out to obtain the hollow figure mould. If the chocolate is not allowed to flow out, then the resulting figure would be solid and very heavy and cannot be eaten.

Faults in moulding chocolates

Moulding, as we have seen, is a task that involves a lot of skill and precision. A small oversight can mar flawless moulding. Some common faults while moulding chocolates along with the causes and ways to avoid them are highlighted in Table 12.3.

Table 12.3 Common faults in moulded chocolate

Faults	Causes	Prevention
Chocolate gets stuck in the mould	• The moulds were not clean.	Clean the moulds with lint free cotton.
	• Chocolate is not tempered properly.	Temper the chocolate as explained.
	• Cooling temperature is too low.	Ensure that cooling temperature is not below 10°C.
	• The layer in the mould is too thin.	See the thickness of the product. If required, coat the mould more than one time.
The chocolate lacks sheen	• The moulds were not clean.	Clean the moulds well.
	• Chocolate is not tempered properly.	Temper the chocolate as described.
	• Moulds have been cooled too slowly.	Cool the moulds in refrigerator at a temperature of 10°C.
	• *Couverture* has been over tempered.	Start the process again.
The moulded structure is cracked	• The coating in the mould is too thin.	Coat the moulds with optimum thickness.
	• The mould was cooled too quickly in low temperatures.	Cool the moulds at 10°C in refrigerator.
Chocolate pieces have finger marks on it	• The moulded chocolate has been touched with warm fingers.	Handle the moulded figure only with gloves to avoid any finger marks.

Coating

Coating is another important use of chocolates. Cakes and pastries are coated with melted chocolate truffle, so that the entire sides and top are coated with chocolate. Refer Chapter 11 on decorating cakes to know more about coatings of chocolates on cakes and pastries.

Various kinds of hand rolled truffles are also coated with tempered *couvertures* to create an array of chocolates that can be used in the same way as moulded chocolate. The following steps are followed to create hand rolled truffles:

Step 1 Make a *ganache* (refer the recipes on moulded chocolate in the CD).

Step 2 Pipe *ganache* into drops on to a tray lined with plastic and put in the freezer for at least 30 minutes, so that the *ganache* hardens.

Step 3 Remove the *ganache* from the freezer and shape into round balls, between the palms of hand. Freeze again for 30 minutes or until hard.

Step 4 Coat the balls with tempered *couverture* and roll it in various ingredients to create different textures and designs on the hand rolled truffle. The truffles can be coated in icing sugar, cocoa powder, chocolate flakes, chocolate vermicelli, crushed nuts, etc. The hand rolled truffle can also be kept plain or drizzled with contrasting coloured chocolate. Sometimes various textures are given to the hand rolled truffles by rolling them on a wire mesh or a rough surface.

Enrobing

Enrobing is a process where the prepared chocolate filling is firm enough to be cut into various shapes and then dipped into tempered chocolate to create fancy chocolate creations. This process is applied to create an array of enrobed chocolates that are sold in high end pastry shops and outlets. The procedure is similar to coating. The steps in making enrobed chocolates are as follows.

Step 1 Prepare *ganache* and spread it into a sheet of 7–10 mm thickness. This is achieved by using square moulds to give a neat finish and also there would be no wastage, when the *ganache* has to be cut into equal small squares.

Step 2 Refrigerate the *ganache* in the fridge for 20 minutes or until the *ganache* sets. Take it out from the refrigerator and spread a very thin layer of melted chocolate on both the sides. After one side is covered and the chocolate is set, invert the sheet and coat another side.

Step 3 Remove the chocolate from the mould and trim off the sides. Cut the prepared sheet into the desired shapes with the help of a sharp knife. In professional pastry kitchens, an equipment known as chocolate guitar (refer Table 12.5) is used for cutting the *ganache*.

Step 4 Dip the cut pieces of coated *ganache* into tempered *couverture* and let the excess chocolate drip off. Place the enrobed chocolate on a cocoa transfer sheet or textured plastic sheets (refer Table 12.5) to print designs on the surface of the enrobed chocolates.

Casting

This method is usually used for making chocolate figures and showpieces (discussed later in the chapter). Melted chocolate is poured into a prepared shape and removed when the chocolate is set hard. Various kinds of moulds or cake rings can be used for this purpose. One can also use flexible metal ribbons to shape them into desired shapes to create a mould. Using plasticine or clay is also very common to make space for casting of chocolate. One can also pour the chocolate into a ring and then cut out the desired shape when the chocolate is set until soft.

Garnishes

Chocolate is the most versatile pastry ingredient that is used for preparing garnishes, which add a whole new dimension to pastry products. Because of the unique properties of chocolate, it is the most preferred garnish with pastry chefs around the world. White chocolate can be coloured into interesting shades and used for garnishes and creating chocolate show pieces. Since water is the biggest enemy of a chocolate, one cannot use liquid colours to colour chocolate. Powder colours are first dissolved in small amounts of cocoa butter and then added to the melted chocolate. There are also edible metallic colours available that can be brushed over the chocolate to give it a metallic finish. These colours can be applied in their dry form or they can be mixed with cocoa powder and brushed on to the prepared chocolate garnish. Table 12.4 shows a few garnishes and the procedure of preparing them.

Table 12.4 Chocolate garnishes (see also Plate 15)

Garnishes	Description	Photograph
Cigars	The cigars are made by using tempered or untempered chocolate. Spread chocolate thinly on a marble slab and wait for a minute or until the finish of the chocolate looks cloudy. Put a metal scraper at an angle of 45° under the chocolate layer and scrape the chocolate. This will curl the chocolate couple of times to yield cigars. If the chocolate sets too hard, it will not curl easily. In that case, rub the chocolate in the palm a couple of times to soften it. One can prepare various types of cigars by alternating the colours of the chocolate. This effect is achieved by spreading a dark chocolate and then running a comb scraper to create grooves. When the chocolate sets, pour white chocolate and spread on top. The resulting cigars would be striped. The second photograph here shows a three-tier cake with black and white chocolate cigars.	
Feuillant (pronounced as *fyu-ee-awn*)	This garnish looks very pretty and classy on cakes, pastries, and plated desserts. For this type of garnish, only untempered *couverture* is used. A clean metal sheet is warmed at a temperature of 160°C for 4–5 minutes. The sheet should not be too hot, but should be little hotter than warm. Spread the melted chocolate on the warm sheet. Warm sheets help in spreading the chocolate to a thin layer. The sheet is then refrigerated for a couple of minutes or until the chocolate sets. Keep the tray at room temperature until the chocolate is soft yet firm. Scrape the chocolate, while holding the other end of the scraper with thumb and forefinger to curl the chocolate in such a way that it pleats or ruffles itself. Set the *feuillant* in the fridge and use as per choice.	
Chocolate leaves	Natural leaves, such as those of mint and rose, are used for preparing chocolate leaves for garnishes. One can use any type of leaf that has visible veins on the back surface. The leaves are cleaned and wiped dry and the melted and tempered *couverture* is applied with the help of a brush. It is sometimes necessary to give at least two coatings of chocolate to create this garnish. Set the leaves in refrigerator for a couple of minutes and peel off the leaf with the tip of knife. The sharp veins would get printed on the leaves, giving them a natural look. One can always give a more natural look to the leaves by brushing green coloured tempered *couverture* on the leaves to give natural shadings and then coat the leaves with dark or milk *couverture*.	

(Contd)

Table 12.4 (Contd)

Garnishes	Description	Photograph
Chocolate flowers	Metallic moulds as shown here are available to make flowers and leaves. This set has around 14–15 different shapes and it should be kept in the freezer for at least 30–60 minutes before we can use them. The moulds are dipped into the tempered chocolate and within few seconds, they can be removed from the moulds. These flowers and leaves can be used for decorating cakes and pastries.	
Chocolate cut-outs	Acetate sheets are commonly used for this purpose. Spread the chocolate in a thin layer with the help of a plate knife. Let the chocolate stand for a few minutes until the surface gives a cloudy appearance. The chocolate should be set, but not hard. At this point, one can use the tip of the knife to cut the desired shapes and sizes. One can be creative and cut any geometric shapes. The sheet should now be allowed to stand in cool place until hard. This will help the chocolate to peel off easily with a shine. There are many ways which one can use to make more attractive garnish by giving decorative effects onto the acetate sheet. These are as follows. 1. Splash few streaks of contrasting chocolate on the acetate sheet and when the same is set, apply dark chocolate over and make cut outs. The streaks of the chocolate can also be piped on to the sheet in straight lines or criss-cross fashion to create a more refined effect. 2. One can pipe small dots of contrasting chocolate, for example white and spread dark chocolate to make polka dotted cut outs. 3. Spread the white chocolate on a sheet and drag it with a comb scraper to make grooves. Let it set and apply dark chocolate over in a thin layer. Cut the desired shapes. 4. One can spread the chocolate over a textured plastic sheet (refer Table 12.5) to create a chocolate cut out with various textures. The bubble plastic used for packaging can also be used for making textured sheets with holes as shown in the photograph. 5. One can achieve a marbled effect by combining two or three colours of chocolate and then spreading it over acetate sheets. 6. To create a shaved wood effect, spread dark chocolate in a thin layer on an acetate sheet and drag the wood engraving tool (refer Table 12.5) over the chocolate by moving it to and fro to create a wooden effect. When set spread white chocolate and the resulting finish would resemble a sheet of shaved wood These are just few ideas; creativity is the key to preparing these garnishes.	

(Contd)

Table 12.4 (Contd)

Garnishes	Description	Photograph
Flames	Put the dark chocolate in large drops at 2-inch distance on an acetate sheet. Cover with another acetate sheet and drag the drop with a thumb to form thin shapes that resemble flames. Set until hard and then peel off and use as desired.	
Pipes	Chocolate pipes are commonly used in chocolate show pieces. There are two ways of making pipes. One is to spread the chocolate on an acetate sheet and roll the sheet to form a pipe. The other way is to make a pipe with an acetate sheet and then fill with melted tempered *couverture* and proceed as discussed in the section on moulding chocolate. The height of pipe will be determined by the width of the acetate sheet. You can also pipe the chocolate on the sheet to create a net design and then roll up the sheet to form a pipe.	
Nets	Tempered *couverture* is filled into a piping cone and piped on to an acetate sheet in a criss-cross fashion to create net like structure. After the chocolate is set, it can be peeled off and used as a garnish.	
Sides and collars	Take two acetate strips to make a longer strip. One can make various kinds of decorative strips as described in the cut out. The strips can then be used to cover sides of the cake. The acetate is peeled off when the chocolate is set. The strips can also be cut out into squares and then arranged around the cake overlapping each other.	
Twists and curls	The amazing property of a chocolate whereby it can be shaped before it sets hard is creatively used by chefs to make various kinds of garnishes. Chocolate can be twisted and curled by using acetate sheets. One can make the following designs using this method. 1. Spread a thin layer of chocolate and comb it with a comb scraper. Allow the chocolate to rest for a couple of seconds and then roll from one corner in such a way that the strips curl like a spring. Tape the end to hold the sheet in place and keep in a cool place for at least 10 minutes. Peel off the acetate sheet to yield curled strips. 2. Spread a thin layer of chocolate and allow it to set until it sets but is still soft. Cut shapes such as small and long triangles, etc. and roll the sheet as above. The resulting garnish would be curled triangle.	 Process of preparing spiral chocolate garnish

(Contd)

Table 12.4 *(Contd)*

Garnishes	Description	Photograph
Bows	Bows are again made by using acetate sheets. The acetate sheets are cut into desired length and width and tempered *couverture* is spread in a thin layer. Take the ends and join together to form a teardrop shape. Clip the ends or secure with tape. When the chocolate sets, peel of the sheet and stick the chocolate pieces with the help of melted chocolate.	
Chocolate baskets	Baskets are simple to make. Use any size mould—a cup, mixing bowl, or fluted mould. Make sure it is clean. Line the mould with a plastic wrap or tin foil (avoid creases). You may brush the mould with melted butter, which will help the foil stay against the sides of the mould. Paint a number of layers of chocolate in the mould and make sure the top edge is straight and clean. Let the chocolate set, remove it from the mould, and take off the foil or plastic. Trace out the handle on paper (make sure that the tracing fits the exact measurement of the basket). Pipe the handle over the tracing with tempered *couverture*. You may pipe the handle with thick chocolate to strengthen it. When the chocolate is set, attach the handle to the basket. You can fill the basket with dipped fruit, chocolates, or petit four.	
Chocolate boxes	Pour melted chocolate on to a greaseproof paper, spreading it in an even layer. Lift the paper with a palette knife to remove creases and air bubbles. When set, cut into 4-5 cm squares. Assemble the boxes with a little melted chocolate. They may be filled with *parfait*, mousse, fresh or dipped fruit. The chocolate boxes can also be used to fill up truffles and moulded pralines and used as room amenities or even sold in pastry shops.	
Chocolate cones	Chocolate cones are made by using acetate sheets. Make a cone of desired size and secure with a tape. Fill the cone with tempered chocolate and pour out the excess chocolate as done in case of moulding. Peel the paper off when the chocolate is hard. The cones can be used in chocolate show pieces or simply filled with mousses, berries, or custards and served as a dessert.	

Chocolate Structures and Showpieces

Many pastry chefs display their art by creating artistic showpieces that can be used to enhance the visual appeal of the buffets. Creating artistic showpieces requires creativity and a lot of practice. Different textures and shapes of chocolate are used for creating a chocolate structure or showpiece. The showpieces mostly work towards a theme. They must always have a thick base that would support the entire structure. Symmetry is very important as the showpiece should be pleasing to the eye. Contemporary structures use geometrical designs and abstract art to create showpieces. Let us understand how the simple chocolate structure shown in Fig. 12.13 was created.

Fig. 12.13 Chocolate structure

A This is the base of the chocolate. It has to be thick and sturdy as the rest of the structure has to balance on it. To prepare this structure, we can use the method of casting as explained earlier. We can make various kinds of shapes and sizes, but the overall look of the structure has to be kept in mind as it should not look too bulky.

B This is a moulded chocolate made in a spherical mould. The spheres in this figure are prepared by the moulding method and are joined together. The ball is then sprayed with a golden colour mixed with cocoa butter.

C The figure of the small cat is created in a polycarbonate mould by moulding method. Milk chocolate is used in this case to give a subtle colour contrast to the structure.

D This is a chocolate pipe made by using the acetate sheet as explained in Table 12.4. This pipe helps give a height to the structure and is used as a platform for placing the central focal point which is the chocolate bow.

E This curled chocolate lace is prepared by using acetate sheet as explained in Table 12.4 in the techniques about twists and curls. This spaghetti of curled chocolates is used for giving an abstract look to the entire structure.

F This structure of a candle is made out by using the cut-out method as explained in Table 12.4. This cut-out has been done on a thick chocolate slab to make it sturdy. The flame is painted with golden metallic colour to add a more realistic touch to the chocolate candle. This structure could also have been made in a pipe shape, but then it would take away the look and feel of the pipe used as the focal structure. It is important to provide contrasting shapes and colours to make attractive showpieces.

G This is the focal point in this showpiece and is made by making chocolate bows using acetate sheet as explained in Table 12.4. In one section in the bow, a curled chocolate piece adds a realistic look to the bow. The bow has been prepared by spreading chocolate onto a cocoa printed transfer sheet to give that golden pattern.

Some important points about chocolate showpieces that should be borne in mind are as follows.

- The showpiece should reflect a work of art and should be of a considerable size to fit the surroundings and the area of display.
- Even if the structure is an abstract art, it must have a pleasing symmetry.
- Various kinds of shapes should be used to give a creative décor to the showpiece.
- Various colours and shades of chocolates should be used to give an artistic effect to the chocolate showpiece.
- The showpiece should have a focal point, which should be highlighted in the art work.

This is a very basic piece of art work. However, students can gradually master the art of chocolate work by practising basic shapes and then assembling the structure keeping in mind the basic guidelines mentioned here.

Piping Chocolate

Chocolate is mostly used in a flowing state. It becomes difficult to pipe when the chocolate is in a melted state as the piped structure becomes flat. The chocolate needs to be hardened for this particular use. Usually, glycerine or water is added in very minimal amounts to harden chocolate for piping designs and writing. Normally 250 g of melted *couverture* is mixed with six to seven drops of glycerine or water and mixed until smooth. If the mixture is too runny, add one or two more drops of glycerine or water. Once the chocolate is poured in the piping bag, cut the tip off, and write or make designs. Nozzles are not used, as the chocolate would set in the nozzle. The thickened type of piping chocolate enables you to create and pipe designs. These patterns add a nice finishing touch to baskets, boxes, and centre pieces.

Plastic Chocolate

Plastic chocolate also known as modelling chocolate is made by combining melted chocolate with liquid glucose or thick corn syrup. Both the mixtures are kneaded until it resembles dough. The modelling chocolate needs to be rested for a minimum of 6 hours, after which it can be rolled and used as desired. This kind of chocolate is mainly used for creating models and showpieces. If you are making a figure of Santa Claus for Christmas, one can make the clothes of the figure with modelling chocolate. The uses are unlimited and it solely depends upon the creativity of the chef.

TOOLS AND EQUIPMENT

There are various kinds of tools and equipment that are specifically used for making various kinds of chocolate products such as garnishes, moulded chocolates, and showpieces as well. Nowadays, there are many tools and equipment that are specially designed to accomplish chocolate work. Some of the tools and equipment used in the production of chocolate and its products are described in Table 12.5.

Table 12.5 Tools and equipment for doing chocolate work

Equipment	Description	Photograph
Palette knife	Various kinds of palette knives are used for spreading chocolate for making various products. Small angular palette knives that are bent at an angle are frequently used for spreading chocolate.	
Chocolate tempering machine	These are commercially available machines that work on temperature control. The machine automatically melts the *couverture* to 40°C and then cools it down to 28°C until all the good crystals are formed. The machine then brings the temperature to the working temperature, which is different for each kind of	

(Contd)

Table 12.5 (Contd)

Equipment	Description	Photograph
	couverture. This machine can be programmed, according to the specific requirement of the chocolate. The paddle in the chocolate tempering machine, keeps stirring the chocolate constantly ensuring that each particle of chocolate has evenly melted.	
Dipping forks	These are mainly used for coating truffles or for preparing enrobed chocolates. The specially designed forks help the excess chocolate to drip back into the bowl, leaving the right amount to coat the enrobed chocolates and truffles. These are available as a set of 6–12 pieces.	
Moulds	These are polycarbonate plastic moulds available in various shapes and designs, commonly used for making moulded chocolates. There are many kinds of moulds available in the market. Some moulds, such as eggs and spheres, are moulded and stuck together, whereas some moulds of figures, when joined together have an opening from where excess chocolate can be poured out as described earlier in the chapter.	
Chocolate scraper	This is a thin stainless steel sheet of metal with a handle attached for grip. They are available in various shapes such as rectangles and triangles and has multiple uses. It can be used for spreading chocolate, scraping moulds, and even making cigars and *fueillant*.	
Chocolate comb	These are metal or plastic sheets with pointed or flat grooves at equal or symmetrical distances depending upon the type of comb. These combs are used for creating designs on the chocolate sheets.	
Wood engraving tool	These are special kind of silicone rubber equipment with semi circular grooves. These are used for preparing designs that resemble a shaved slice of wood. Moving this equipment to and fro while dragging it creates a pattern of shaved wooden grains. The procedure of making a chocolate garnish using this equipment is mentioned in Table 12.4.	

(Contd)

Table 12.5 (Contd)

Equipment	Description	Photograph
Chocolate shaving machine	This machine is used in places where there is a large requirement of chocolate flakes. In this machine, a block of chocolate is secured in a place that moves to and fro over a sharp blade to scrape the chocolate very thinly to make chocolate flakes. These flakes should be hardened in the fridge and should be handled very carefully as chocolate flakes will melt even from the heat of the palm if handled for too long.	
Chocolate thermometer	A chocolate thermometer is available in various shapes and materials. The grading on this thermometer corresponds to the various degrees required by a particular kind of chocolate. It also has markings which display the correct working temperature of chocolate. They are also available in digital mode.	
Acetate sheets	These are thick plastic sheets that are used for making various chocolate garnishes as explained in Table 12.4. These sheets are also sometimes known as overhead projector sheets (OHP) as they are used for making presentations on overhead projectors.	
Transfer sheets	These are plastic sheets with printed computerized patterns. The prints are made with cocoa butter. Once the melted chocolate is spread on these sheets, the designs get transferred onto the chocolate sheet that can be used for garnishing cakes and pastries. One can also get these sheets printed with customised designs such as logos of organizations to give a personal touch to the products.	
Textured sheets	These are flexible hard plastic sheets with various kinds of textures on it. The range of textures can be that of leather finish to bubbles. These sheets are used for chocolate garnishes that would be used on cakes and pastries. The use of these sheets is explained in the section on enrobed chocolate.	
Expandable trellis cutter	These are small steel discs with sharp edges mounted on metal bars that can be stretched and closed to arrange the distance between the rollers. This equipment is used for cutting dough and marking the lines for cutting rectangular blocks of pastries. This equipment is useful in making chocolate strips of equal sizes that can be used on the collars of cakes or to make chocolate boxes.	

(Contd)

Table 12.5 (Contd)

Equipment	Description	Photograph
Nitrogen spray guns	These are canisters in which liquid nitrogen is packed under pressure. This tool is very handy while making chocolate showpieces. Certain thin structures need to be stuck with melted chocolate instantly as holding them with hands would warm them and melt. Thus, liquid nitrogen is sprayed on to the melted chocolate so that it hardens the chocolate in a few seconds.	
Chocolate spray gun	This is like an atomiser attached to a compressor. The jar holds melted chocolate mixed with melted cocoa butter and is sprayed onto chocolate figures to give a matte kind of finish.	
Confectionery funnel	This piece of equipment is commonly used in confectionery to fill liquid *ganache* into moulded chocolates while making pralines and truffles. The lever located on the top of this tool, helps to regulate the amount of filling into the mould for evenness and consistency.	
Chocolate guitar	This equipment is used for cutting a square piece of set *ganache* into equal and neat pieces. As this equipment uses stainless steel chords of a guitar, hence the name.	

STORAGE OF CHOCOLATE

Since chocolate is prepared in factories with precision and care, it is important that it is stored properly in order to maintain its quality. Store chocolate well wrapped in a cool well-ventilated area and not in the refrigerator. Wipe off any moisture that occurs as moisture is one of the biggest enemies of the chocolate. The ideal temperature for storage of chocolate is between 12°C and 20°C with humidity less than 70 per cent. At high temperatures chocolate becomes soft and loses most of its sheen. The working temperature of the area should also be a temperature of 18–20°C. That is the reason most hotels have a separate room known as chocolate room, where the temperature is maintained between 18–20°C. When you have melted chocolate and some of it is left over, that chocolate should be stored in a plastic wrap at room temperature only. Ready-made chocolate products should be stored refrigerated in a separate refrigerator as chocolate has the ability to absorb strong flavours from other foods. Specially designed refrigerators are used to display chocolate products, which do not let the chocolate product sweat, as accumulation of moisture would result in a poor finish on top of the chocolate.

Working with chocolate is an art and can be mastered along the way. It requires a great deal of passion and hard work to achieve the desired results. It is important to be aware of the basic techniques in handling and preparing chocolates and over a period of time, one can graduate to the next level and so on.

In the next chapter, we will discuss various kinds of ice creams and frozen desserts that are served in pastry kitchens.

SUMMARY

In this chapter, we discussed chocolates in detail. It is one of the main ingredients used in the pastry kitchen. Chefs use this unique product creatively for preparing cakes, pastries, desserts, chocolate confections, garnishes, and even showpieces. However, chocolate is a tricky ingredient to work with hence, the knowledge of various kinds of chocolates and how to handle them is one of the most important aspects of chocolate production. In this chapter, we discussed the origin of chocolates from ancient civilizations.

We discussed the various stages in production of chocolate. The growing and harvesting of beans to prepare cocoa seeds is done manually by local farmers who then transport the beans to the factory, where the cocoa beans are used for making chocolates. While learning about the production processes, we also understood the importance of cocoa butter and cocoa mass and how cocoa powder is separated from the mass with the help of hydraulic presses. We discussed one of the most crucial steps in the production of chocolate known as conching, in which the chocolate is mixed and constantly stirred to give it the necessary shine and desired texture.

We also discussed various kinds of chocolates such as *couvertures*, semi-sweet chocolate, bitter chocolate, single-origin chocolate, and organic chocolate. Each kind of chocolate was explained, along with a brand, so that students can remember various brands to be able to select the right kind of chocolate for the right kind of job. This section also differentiated normal chocolate from *couverture* or covering chocolate, which is the most commonly used commodity in the pastry kitchen.

We learnt about various kinds of techniques involved in the processing and handling of a chocolate while making chocolate confections. Even melting of a chocolate is an art and we have discussed this aspect in great detail, along with various methods of tempering a chocolate for production of chocolate garnishes and confections. Cooling of a chocolate is also an art, otherwise it would result in greyish discolouration on top of the chocolate referred to as bloom. We also discussed various kinds of faults and their prevention for better understanding. We discussed various uses of garnishes, along with examples and techniques. We also discussed various techniques of chocolate work such as moulding, casting, enrobing, in steps, so that a student can understand the importance of each technique and its step to be able to make the right choice of methods when doing chocolate work on their own.

In this chapter, we also explained the basic principles of creating chocolate showpieces and how chocolate can be transformed to other products by piping or modelling chocolate that have their own specific use. Finally, we stressed on the importance of storing chocolate and various kinds of tools and equipments that are used for making these chocolate confections and artistic showpieces.

KEY TERMS

Aztecs   This was an ancient civilization that existed in Mexico.

Bloom   It is a whitish or greyish patch on the surface of a chocolate that can be caused due to heat or moisture.

Callets   These are small drop-shaped pieces of chocolate available commercially.

Chocolate vermicelli   It is a ready-made product used for decorating the pastry and chocolate confections.

Cocoa liquor   Also known as cocoa mass, It is obtained after the nibs are ground to a smooth paste.

Cocoa nibs   These are small pieces obtained after roasting, crushing, and removal of the skin of cocoa beans.

Cocoa pod   It is the large fruit of the cocoa tree which contains cocoa beans that yield the edible cocoa mass.

Compound chocolate   It is a chocolate that contains stabilizers and hard oils. It is used mainly for making chocolate decorations and garnishes, because it is easy to use.

Conching   It is a process in chocolate production wherein the cocoa mass is mixed for long durations of time to get the necessary flavour, shine, and texture.

Couverture   It is the French word for covering chocolate. It is a chocolate with minimum 32 per cent of cocoa fat.

Dipping forks   These are a set of forks used for dipping and enrobing chocolates and fruits.

Enrobing   The process of coating the cut pieces of chocolate confections with tempered *couverture* is called enrobing.

Fat bloom   This is a common fault in chocolate production, which occurs due uneven melting of fat crystals in the chocolate.

Maltilol   It is a kind of sugar substitute used in production of sugar-free chocolates.

Moulding   A technique in which chocolate figures and shapes are prepared by putting tempered chocolate into a mould and removing it after it has set.

Mousse   It is a creamy dessert made by combining flavours with whipped cream.

Parfait   It is a kind of frozen dessert.

Polycarbonate   This is a kind of plastic material used for making moulds for chocolate structures and figures.

Pralines   These are small moulded chocolate confections with various kinds of fillings.

Pre-crystallization   See tempering.

Raw cocoa   It is the term used for cocoa seeds after those have been dried in the sun.

Soya lecithin   It is a protein obtained from soya beans that is used for stabilizing and emulsification of chocolate products.

Spurt method   It is a method of melting chocolate by putting it in the microwave at intervals of 20 seconds.

Sugar bloom   Sugar bloom occurs when the chocolate is allowed to cool too rapidly. Sugar particles dissolve in the vapours and re-crystallize on the surface of the chocolate giving it a patchy and hazy look.

Tempering   It is the process of heating and cooling the chocolate *couverture* as per the required temperature to obtain a stabilized product, which has the required sheen and snaps off when broken in half.

Theobroma cacao   This is the botanical name of the cocoa bean tree.

Xocolatl   It was a bitter beverage made by the Aztecs.

CONCEPT REVIEW QUESTIONS

1. How did the word chocolate come into existence?
2. Why did Aztecs worship the cocoa tree?
3. How did chocolate become popular in other parts of the world?
4. Why is chocolate considered good for heart?
5. Describe the harvesting of cocoa bean and its processing before its transportation to the chocolate factory.
6. Why are cocoa beans blended before production of chocolates?
7. What is the importance of roasting the beans in the production of chocolates?
8. What are nibs and how are they obtained?
9. What do you understand by the word chocolate liquor?
10. How is cocoa powder obtained?
11. Describe the process of conching. How is it important in chocolate production?
12. Describe the process and importance of tempering a chocolate.
13. List and describe at least 3 methods of tempering a chocolate.
14. What is a *couverture*? How many types of these are available?
15. Name at least five brands of chocolate *couvertures*.
16. How is compound chocolate different from a *couverture*?
17. Why is white chocolate not considered to be real chocolate?
18. What is the difference between bitter chocolate and sugar-free chocolate?
19. What product is used for preparing sugar-free chocolates?
20. Name at least three single-origin chocolates and the countries they originate from.
21. What are organic chocolates? List any two brands of organic chocolates.
22. What precautions would you keep in mind while melting a chocolate?
23. Define bloom in the context of chocolate production. What are the different types of blooms?
24. What are the key features to be kept in mind while cooling chocolates?
25. List the working temperatures of various types of *couvertures*.
26. Describe various steps involved in preparing moulded chocolates.

27. What could be the various reasons of chocolate getting stuck to the mould?
28. What could be the necessary reasons of lack of sheen on the moulded chocolate?
29. Describe the process of enrobing.
30. Describe at least five types of garnishes that can be made by using chocolates.
31. What are the few ways in which you can create attractive chocolate cut-outs?
32. What are the key points to be kept in mind while preparing artistic chocolate showpieces?
33. What is a piping chocolate and how do you make it?
34. Define a plastic chocolate and its uses.
35. What is the use of dipping forks?
36. Describe the wood engraving tool. How is it used?

PROJECT WORK

1. In groups of five, undertake a market survey of pastry shops in your city and make a note of various kinds of products made from chocolates. Make note of these and make a report on the various ways in which chocolates were used in such products. Share your findings with other groups.
2. In groups of four to five, create a showpiece by using variety of shapes and colours of chocolate. Plan the showpiece keeping a theme in mind and display your showpieces. Critically examine each others' work.
3. In groups of four to five, collect various labels or chocolate samples and make a chart of these. Find out the origin of these chocolates and the purpose that they are most suited for. Present your findings in the class.

CHAPTER 13

DESSERTS

Learning Objectives

After reading this chapter, you should be able to

- understand the various kinds of hot and cold desserts
- make different types of desserts of various categories
- utilize sauces and garnishes for various kinds of pre-plated desserts
- analyse the presentation of dessert for buffet as well as à la carte
- prepare a cyclic dessert menu with balanced products

INTRODUCTION

One of the last courses of the French classical menu called 'dessert' goes by the principle of the age-old saying 'all is well that ends well'. This course of meal leaves a long-lasting impression on the guest's mind and satisfies his/her sweet tooth, thus completing the dining experience. Dessert is usually a sweet food served as the final course of a meal. The use of the term dessert was first recorded in 1600 and it is derived from a French word *desservir,* which means 'to clear the table'. This etymology is reflected in current table service, where it is customary to remove everything that is not being used (salt/pepper shakers, bread baskets, sometimes even flowers) from the table before serving dessert.

Just as restaurant menus have undergone great changes in recent years, the bakery and pastry kitchen too has undergone many changes from what it once was. This is especially true of presentation, which must meet very high expectations these days. Taste is also important, of course. A good cook must be able to achieve economy in preparation, while maintaining high standards in all aspects of the dessert.

In the last few chapters, we have discussed various kinds of desserts such as cakes, pastries, ice creams, and frozen desserts. In this chapter, we will discuss a range of desserts and understand their classification. Interestingly, desserts are served hot as well as cold and we will discuss various kinds of desserts that fall under both the categories.

Desserts feature as a display on buffet or are listed on an à la carte menu. The presentation of a dessert changes with the style of service. Modern buffet arrangements have an assortment of desserts presented pre-portioned or whole on display. It would be worthwhile to understand how the desserts on buffet have evolved over a period of time. The range of pre-plated desserts has various components such as garnish, sauces, and the dessert itself. We will discuss sauces and coulis in Chapter 15 and read about garnishes in Chapter 11 on cakes and pastries. In this chapter, we will understand how to combine these to create an array of pre-plated desserts.

HOT AND COLD DESSERTS

> **CHEF'S TIP**
> Some butter-based desserts might be very hard and chewy if served cold, while some cream-based desserts can never be served hot as the cream would split and melt.

Many desserts can be served only hot while some can only be served cold; but there are a range of desserts that can be served either hot or cold. The decision to serve a dessert at a particular temperature is guided by many factors such as guest preference, climate, texture, and flavour of the dessert. Thus, depending on the temperature at which these are served, desserts may be hot or cold (see Fig. 13.1).

Hot Desserts

Hot desserts are the ones that are served warm or hot in buffets or à la carte. The various types of hot desserts, such as puddings, soufflés, tarts, and pies (see Fig. 13.1), are further classified into different types based on the ingredients used for making them. These are discussed in the succeeding paragraphs.

Puddings

In Western cooking, pudding may also refer to savoury items such as Yorkshire pudding, black pudding, and savoury pudding. But in the pastry kitchen, a pudding is a dessert that

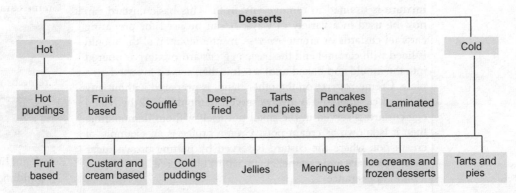

Fig. 13.1 Classification of desserts

is made with milk and sugar and contains starch as a thickening agent. In certain cases, the thickening can also come from eggs. Crème caramel is an example of such a pudding. Puddings can be served hot or cold based on their composition. Table 13.1 discusses some popular puddings along with their features.

Table 13.1 Various kinds of hot puddings

Puddings	Description	Photograph
Milk puddings	Milk puddings are made from rice, semolina, tapioca, or sago, or any starch-based cereal. These are simple to cook. All of them are cooked in sweetened milk. Flavourings, such as vanilla, orange or lemon peel, are optional. Puddings are simmered gently until cooked. Remove any peel, vanilla beans, etc. and serve immediately. If the French method is followed, egg yolks can be added at the right temperature to prevent curdling. Cooking of these puddings helps the starch to gelatinize, thereby, adding the smooth and thick consistency to the pudding. Butter may also be added on top and browned under a salamander. They are often served with a fruit or *anglaise* sauce. Both baking and boiling methods are used to prepare such puddings. While cooking milk-based puddings on hot stove, they need to be constantly stirred, so that they do not burn or stick to the bottom. Cooking on a double boiler is a safer method of making such puddings. Some puddings, such as French rice puddings, are baked. Rice is boiled in sugar and milk and enriched with egg yolks. Whipped egg whites are folded in and the pudding is baked before serving.	
Baked egg custards	Varieties of baked egg custards are made either in oven or on hot water bath such as bain-marie. The use of bain-marie keeps the temperature in control and does not let the custard split due to overheating. Eggs are the most important commodity in such puddings as both the yolks and white of an egg coagulate when heated, thereby setting the baked egg custard. The overheating of these puddings results in curdling of protein, which is also known as 'weeping of protein' or *syneresis*. Basic egg custard is prepared by heating 100 per cent of milk, with 20 per cent of sugar and 50 per cent eggs. Hot milk and sugar are mixed with eggs and the mixture is strained to remove any froth. This basic custard can now be used in a variety of ways. It can be used for preparing caramel custards or crème *renverse*. In crème caramel the mould is lined with caramel and the basic egg custard mixture is poured into the mould and baked until set. It is then served inverted on a plate. Crème *renverse*, on the other hand, is prepared without any lining of caramel and is always served demoulded. If the baked egg custard is served in the small pot itself without demoulding, then it is known as cream pots. Crème brûlée is an example of cream pot, where the custard is served by putting brown sugar over the surface and caramelizing it with a blowtorch, until it gives a burnt appearance.	Baked egg custard Crème caramel Crème brûlée Bread and butter pudding

(Contd)

Table 13.1 (Contd)

Puddings	Description	Photograph
Baked egg custards	Basic egg custard mixture is also used to moisten bread and butter pudding before baking. To make bread and butter pudding, mix left over breakfast rolls and bread with butter and brown in the oven. Arrange in a baking dish and pour the custard mix over it and bake until the custard is set and the pudding is brown. Cabinet pudding is made in the same manner as bread and butter pudding, but with addition of candied fruits such as glazed cherries, angelica, raisins, and sultanas. If the fruits are macerated in kirsch liquor for few hours, then the pudding is known as diplomat pudding.	
Sponge puddings	An array of desserts, very popular with the British is sponge puddings, which can be baked or steamed. These are usually made with flour, eggs, sugar, and butter and aeration in the product is done by mechanical aeration and leaveners such as baking powder, ammonium bicarbonate, baking soda, etc. Mechanical aeration is provided by creaming butter with sugar. In addition to the above mentioned ingredients, one can also use flavourings and milk or cream to provide richness to the end product. Puddings such as Christmas plum pudding or suet puddings are examples of steamed sponge puddings. These puddings are comparatively dry to eat and hence when serving as dessert, they need to be accompanied with sauce. Desserts such as pineapple upside down, Eve's pudding, etc. are examples of baked sponge puddings. To make eve's pudding, line a buttered mould with apples flavoured with lemon zest, rind, and apricot jam. Top up with sponge mixture and bake until cooked. Served un-moulded with vanilla sauce. For pineapple upside down, the mould is lined with sliced pineapple and when cooked, it is un-moulded and served glazed with hot apricot jam. *Summer pudding* It is kind of sponge pudding from Great Britain. The only difference is that the sponge is the old stale bread is soaked in summer berries, such as blueberries, red currants, and raspberries, and layered in a mould. It is served un-moulded with whipped cream. *Charlotte pudding* Another type of sponge pudding is *Charlotte* pudding. Appropriate moulds are lined with a short paste, brioche dough, puff paste, or thin slices of stale bread, brushed with melted butter for colour development during baking. The centre is then filled with a mixture of poached, sweetened fruit, such as apples or apricots, and baked in the oven. Casing should be crisp and brown.	 Christmas pudding Pineapple upside down pudding Summer pudding *Charlotte pudding*

Hot soufflés

These types of puddings originated in France and are very popular there. Earlier, the soufflés were savoury based such as fish soufflé, and cheese soufflé; but with the creativity of chefs, sweet soufflés became a rage. The basic components of soufflé remain the same, only sugar and flavourings replace the salt and meat products. Soufflé is traditionally starch based. In case of savouries, white sauce or béchamel is used as a base, but in pastry, this is replaced with pastry cream or any other milk based pudding. Whipped yolks, flavourings, and whipped egg whites are folded in and baked until the soufflé rises. The soufflé needs to be served immediately as it can collapse and this would be unacceptable as it loses its characteristics of being called a soufflé. Classically, any soufflé would have the following three components.

Base The base would be a starch base. It could be a pastry cream, milk-based pudding, or even sweetened white sauce. This starchy thick base is also known as *panada*. Once the base has cooled down, whisked egg yolks are mixed with the starchy bases to form a smooth and a creamy base. The base can be prepared well in advance and can be stored until further use.

Flavouring A whole range of flavours can be used for dessert soufflés. Chocolate, vanilla, lemon, and cheese are the most commonly used flavourings in soufflés, but chefs can use their creativity to flavour soufflés. While using citrus fruits, one can use the juice in the base and use zest and rind as the flavouring. Similarly, if flavouring the soufflé with chocolate, the base can be made by heating milk, sugar, and cocoa powder to make a chocolate flavoured pastry cream, which can then be enriched with chopped chocolate and nuts as well.

Eggs Egg white is the most essential ingredient that helps the soufflé to rise in a mould, giving it the traditional name. Yolks are added for enriching soufflé as they have little role in aeration. The egg whites and sugar are whipped to a meringue and then folded in the base and flavourings and baked immediately.

The following are some critical factors to be kept in mind while preparing hot soufflés.

1. Prepare the base or *panada*. Grease sugar-lined moulds. Set oven to correct temperature.
2. Stiffly beaten egg whites are the basis for a successful soufflé. Expansion of air in the egg whites will let the soufflé rise above the rim of the dish as it bakes. This is why it is important that moulds are properly greased.
3. First lighten the *panada* with a quarter of egg white. This will make it much easier to fold in the remaining whites, as beaten egg whites are not sufficiently stable to withstand extensive mixing.
4. Do not let the mixture stand or it will collapse.
5. Bake at 200°C. Draughts or disturbances during baking will cause the delicate structure to collapse.
6. The French tend to favour soufflés with a slightly underdone, creamy centre but well-done soufflés are more stable, and are generally preferred for this reason.
7. Dust soufflés with icing sugar, glazed (caramelized under the salamander), or dusted with cocoa powder, if it is a chocolate soufflé.
8. Serve soufflés immediately.

CHEF'S TIP
Always butter the soufflé mould very well and coat with castor sugar. This prevents the soufflé from sticking to the base.

Table 13.2 Types of deep-fried desserts

Dessert	Description	Photograph
Beignets	Also known as fritters, these are batter-fried fruits. Fruits such as apples, peaches, pears, and figs, are commonly used for this purpose. Apples can be peeled, cored, sliced, and coated with sugar and cinnamon powder. It is then coated with sweet batter and deep-fried. Most of the fritters are served dredged with powdered sugar. Some fruits, such as peach halves, prunes, and dates, can be stuffed with rice pudding, marzipan, nuts, etc. and coated with batter and crumbed like *à l'anglaise* and then deep-fried. *Beignets* are accompanied with vanilla sauce or ice cream.	
Choux fritters	*Choux* pastry is also served deep-fried. In France, *choux* pastry is shaped into oval shapes and deep-fried until crisp. It is also known as *choux* soufflé. In Mexico, a popular dessert called *churros* is made by piping 3–4 inch long ropes of *choux* pastry into hot oil. Once fried, they are coated with cinnamon flavoured sugar and served hot.	
Helado frito	Deep-fried ice creams are very popular in Mexico, where a chilled ice cream scoop is covered with batter and crumbed before frying. We will discuss it in detail in the next chapter on frozen desserts.	
Oriental desserts	Many oriental desserts commonly feature on the dessert menu of specialty restaurants. Two of them are: *Toffee fruits* Fruits, such as apple and banana, are batter-fried and coated with sesame flavoured caramelized sugar. This dessert is very popular in many high-end Chinese restaurants in India. *Daarsaan* These are deep-fried flat noodles, tossed in honey flavoured caramelized sugar. Most of these desserts are served with vanilla ice cream.	Toffee banana *Daarsaan*

Deep-fried desserts

Deep-fried desserts are another category of desserts that are popular all over the world. As the name suggests, these desserts are served deep-fried. Since these desserts would have sugar added to them, it is careful to control the temperatures, as they will get browned too quickly because of caramelization of sugar. A few of the commonly made deep-fried desserts around the world are described in Table 13.2.

Tarts and pies

This category of desserts can be served hot or cold depending on the type of product. Fruit tarts are served cold, whereas apple pies are served hot. Tarts, flans, and pies have been discussed in Chapter 21 of the book *Food Production Operations*. All tarts and pies have the following components.

Base   The base of these desserts can be made with various kinds of pastes such as sweet paste, shortcrust paste, and puff pastry. These pastes have been discussed in detail in the book *Food Production Operations*. Special moulds called tart moulds have raised edges and these are lined with the desired dough or pastry and baked with filling inside or the base can be docked and baked without any filling. This is also known as blind baking.

Filling   Various kinds of fillings can be used for making hot pies. These fillings could be custard based, starch based, or even purée based. The idea is to allow the filling to set after being baked, so that the tarts and pies can be cut into various portion sizes. Various kinds of fillings and the desserts are discussed in Table 13.3.

Topping   Every tart or pie is garnished with various kinds of products ranging from plain dusted icing sugar to various kinds of glazes. These are also known as toppings and they are added to impart a decorative look and texture to the prepared tart or pie. Following are the commonly used toppings.

Table 13.3   Fillings for pies and tarts

Filling	Description
Starch based	Pastry cream and milk puddings enriched with eggs are commonly used as fillings in tarts and pies. The eggs help the mixture to set like a jelly, which does not flow out when cut. One can add fillings of fruit, berries, jams, etc. on top of the pastry cream and bake the dessert.
Custard based	Egg custard comprising milk, eggs, and sugar can be used as a filling for tarts and pies. Cherry *clafouti* is one such classical dessert in which cherries are arranged in a tart shell and custard is poured over and baked until set. One can also bake plain egg custard in a tart shell like cream pots.
Purée based	Various vegetable or fruit purees can be combined with eggs and sugar and used as a filling for baked tarts and pies. Pumpkin pies are very commonly made by this method. Various desserts such as fruit cobblers, *Linzer tortes*, *clafoutis* are made by lining the tart mould with sweet paste and putting the base of pastry cream. Fruit purees are poured on top of pastry cream and baked topped with crumbled flour and butter also known as *streusel*. Raspberry purée cooked with sugar is a classical filling for *Linzer torte*.
Nut pastes	Many other fillings such as almond paste also known as *crème frangipane* are commonly used as filling for baked tarts and pies. Fruits such as pears, nectarines, and peaches pair up very well with almond paste to make delicious desserts. Almond cream is made by creaming butter and sugar to which almond powder, flour, and eggs are added to make a creamy mixture that resembles a thick batter.
Sugar	Mixtures cooked with sugar, liquid glucose, nuts, and butter make sticky fudge like filling, which is also commonly used in baked tarts and pies. Famous *engadine* walnut tart is made by combining honey, sugar, butter, and walnuts and cooked until sticky and caramelized. This is then added to the baked tart shell and baked at high temperature in the oven for a couple of minutes. *Macaroon* tarts are made by cooking sugar and egg whites with flavourings and adding them into the tart shell.
Cake batters	Various kinds of cake batters, such as brownie, and *Genoese* sponge, can also be poured into a tart shell and baked. New York baked cheesecake can be made in a tart shell to create large cheese cake pies or even small individual desserts.

Jams   Apricot jam is boiled and brushed over tarts to give them a glaze.

Streusel   Also known as crumble, it is made by rubbing butter, flour, and powdered sugar to obtain a chunky mixture that is spread generously over the tarts before baking. It gives a rustic look to tarts and pies and also adds flavour.

Icing sugar   It is dusted with a sieve on top of tarts and pies to make them look more appealing.

Meringues   Many tarts and pies are decorated with meringue and gratinated under salamander or caramelized with blow torch. Lemon meringue pie is a classical dessert made by pouring lemon custard in a baked tart shell and covering with meringue and baking in the oven until the meringue is crisp and coloured. Alternatively, the dessert can be gratinated under a salamander.

Crêpes and pancakes

Crêpes and pancakes are synonyms. In English, they are called pancakes and in French, it is crêpes. However, in hotels, a crêpe refers to a product prepared by pouring batter into a pan and pouring out the excess to create a thin crêpe, whereas pancakes are poured thick on a griddle and cooked on both the sides. But in this chapter we would discuss these as one product.

Pancakes are a popular sweet, convenient and simple to make. A batter is made from milk, flour, eggs, butter, or oil and appropriate seasoning, salt, sugar, lemon, and orange zest depending on use. Pancakes or crêpes are thin, flat cakes that are served rolled or folded around a filling, or infused with a warm sauce or syrup. Maple syrup is a popular choice for American pancakes that are commonly served during breakfast.

The crêpe mixture should be free of lumps, have a consistency of cream, and run freely from the spoon. The batter may have to be adjusted with milk. Crêpes should be neatly arranged on plates with the appropriate filling. Keep in mind that the colour combination and the flavour of the sauces used have to complement the dish. Decorate with a piece of fruit, e.g. strawberry, melon, pineapple, and mint. Certain classical crêpes, such as *crêpe Suzette*, are cooked in orange-flavoured caramelized sugar syrup and are prepared in front of the guests.

The pancakes are usually served hot and can be garnished and topped with sauces and nuts or gratinated under a salamander.

Laminated pastries

Laminated pastries such as puff pastry and *phyllo* pastry are commonly used to prepare varieties of hot desserts. You can read about the laminated pastries in detail in Chapter 22 of *Food Production Operations*. These pastries are used to prepare both hot and cold desserts. Puff pastry can be used to line tarts to make crispy tarts and fruit pies. Some of the commonly made hot desserts using laminated pastries are described in Table 13.4.

Table 13.4 Hot desserts with laminated pastries

Hot desserts	Description	Photograph
Eccles	This is a sweet snacks made from puff pastry and is usually served during afternoon tea. Roll the puff to 4-inch circle and 6 mm thick. Place the filling of raisins, brown sugar, mixed spice, and little softened butter. Bring all the sides of circle together and form a ball. Now roll the ball into a 3-inch circle, wash with egg white, and dip in castor sugar and give two to three small slits on top and bake at 180°C till golden brown. It is served hot dusted with icing sugar.	
Turnovers	The puff is rolled into discs or squares and filled with sweet fillings of fruits mixed with almond cream or pastry cream and turned over or folded over. These are then glazed with egg yolk and baked.	
Lebanese baklava	This dessert can be served hot as well as cold. It is commonly made from thin pastry sheets called *phyllo* or *filo*. It is made by layering a sheet of filo and brushing it with melted butter in a pan. Thereafter, placing another sheet on top and repeating the process, until at least six sheets are layered. Then sprinkle with crushed nuts and sugar and repeat the process until the baklava is 2 inches thick. Brush the top with melted butter. Traditionally, they are cut into diamond shapes, prior to baking, as the crisp pastry will be difficult to cut after baking. Bake till golden brown and while it is hot, pour in rose flavoured sugar syrup. The cuts help to let the syrup percolate down. Serve the pastry warm or cold.	
Strudel	This is a famous dessert from Austria. It is made by stretching the dough very thin and then brushing the surface with melted butter. Filling, usually of fruits, such as apple, and pineapple, are mixed with nuts, raisins, spices, and sponge crumbs and rolled to form a pipe, which is then baked at 180°C. It is served hot with vanilla sauce.	
Tarte tatin	This is a classical French dessert made by using apples and puff pastry. Apples are sliced and arranged over a cast iron pan that is lined with butter and sugar. The pan is heated over stove until golden and caramelized. The pan is covered with thick round piece of puff pastry and baked in the oven until cooked. *Tarte tatin* is served upside down revealing the caramelized sliced apples.	

Fruit-based hot desserts

Many fruits are also served as hot desserts. They can be served as they are or combined with other ingredients to make fruit pies and tarts as discussed in Table 13.2. Certain fruits, such as Japanese melon, peaches, and pineapple, are grilled on hot plates and served with ice creams. Grilled fruit *brochettes* are also very commonly served in France, along with sauces. Let us read about various kinds of fruit-based desserts served hot in Table 13.5.

Table 13.5 Fruit-based desserts

Dessert	Description
Baked	A variety of fruits can be baked as they are or can be used in fillings for pies, tarts, strudels, etc. Some fruits like apples and pears are wrapped in puff pastry and baked until cooked. Figs wrapped in filo and baked are a classical dessert served in Greece.
Compote	It is a sweet made from fruit peeled and poached, whole or halved, quartered or diced, and served with syrup. *Compotes* can be served as a sauce or topping or it can be served as a dessert with whipped cream. Some blind baked tart shells are also served filled with fruit compotes.
Flambéed fruit	Flambé are popular and impressive, if cooked in front of customers with expertise and flair. The fruits are cooked in sauce and then alcohol (such as brandy, vodka, and liqueurs) is poured on top and flamed. The flames rise out of the pan and continue until all the alcohol has evaporated. These dishes can also be quite adequately prepared in the kitchen, keeping the following in mind. • A successful flambé is not judged by the height of the flame • Alcohol will evaporate or is burnt away • When the sauce is reduced, the taste of strong flavoured liqueurs will intensify and may overpower the delicate taste of the dish.

Cold Desserts

Cold desserts can be prepared by a variety of methods. We have discussed some of these desserts in previous chapters on cakes and pastries, chocolates, ice creams and frozen desserts. We will look at a range of cold desserts, from very simple to more complex types in this section.

Today many of the classical cold sweets are back in vogue, albeit with new flavour combinations and presentation, and presentation techniques. Many of the classical creations were over-decorated, a style which has gone out of fashion. We will discuss about the modern plating and presentations of desserts later in this chapter. In the succeeding paragraphs we will discuss various kinds of cold desserts.

Cold puddings

Cold puddings are the same as hot puddings, the only difference is that these are served cold. All the hot puddings mentioned in Table 13.1 can be served cold. However, all cold puddings cannot be served hot. One such dessert is blancmange, which is made by heating milk and sugar, thickened with cornflour. These are chilled and served demoulded with jam sauce. Custard like lemon custard are made by cooking lemon juice, egg yolks, sugar, and butter over low heat until a thick custard is formed. This is used for making lemon meringue pies. Some cold puddings are described in Table 13.6.

Table 13.6 Various kinds of cold puddings

Cold puddings	Description	Photograph
Blancmange	*Blancmange* has an almond-flavoured milk base. It is set with agar-agar, gelatine, or starch (such as cornflour). *Blancmanges* can be flavoured with lemon, vanilla, coffee, chocolate, pistachio nuts, hazelnuts. Whipped cream can be added to achieve a creamy texture. They are served demoulded with sweet sauce such as berry coulis or jam sauce.	
Flummery	*Flummeries* are puddings usually thickened with cornflour, semolina, jelly or sago. They are based on fruit juices or milk. Examples are chocolate, semolina, or blackberry *flummery*. They are set, chilled, and moulded. They can be served in the pot or served demoulded with sauce.	
Rice *conde*	These rice desserts are cooked with milk and enriched with egg yolks. When they are cooled, whipped cream is added. They can be made using gelatine and a variety of flavours, such as vanilla or orange zest. If gelatine is added, they should be set in moulds immediately. *Note:* Any *conde* on a menu indicates a rice-based dessert. For instance, peach *conde* would refer to rice, moulded and covered with a poached peach half, and masked with Melba sauce.	
Fruit custard	Milk is cooked with sugar and thickened with custard powder until thick. Diced fruits and nuts are mixed and served chilled garnished with jellies.	

Fruit-based cold desserts

Fruits are a favourite amongst people especially for those who are health conscious. Fruits can be prepared in various ways. They can be cut into fancy shapes and served arranged as a fruit platter. Beautiful patterns can be created by using colourful fruits on plates. Sauces or purée may be used and often make this as an interesting dessert.

Some of the commonly made fruit-based desserts are described in Table 13.7.

Custard and cream-based desserts

Custards are generally mixture of milk, sugar, and eggs over a double boiler or hot water bath, so that the eggs thicken the mixture. This mixture is the basic custard and is also known as Bavarian cream or *crème anglaise* (discussed in Chapter 15). A classical example of baked custard is undoubtedly crème caramel. There are others that are served in their containers. They may be flavoured and perfumed in many ways: vanilla, coffee, and caramel, orange or lemon peel. Other names for this sweet are *pot de crème* and Peruvian cream.

CHEF'S TIP
For best results, leave the peeling and slicing of the fruit until the last possible moment. Once cut, some fruits, such as apple, pears, peaches, and bananas, discolour quickly. To prevent this happening, they must be immersed in lemon juice and water or in syrup.

Table 13.7 Fruit-based cold desserts

Desserts	Description	Photograph
Fruit platter	Sliced fruits in various shapes and cuts can be arranged on a platter to create interesting patterns. The important factors to consider when preparing a fruit platter are as follows: *The precision of the layout* Neatly arranged fruit looks attractive and appetising. Handle fruit as less as possible and use a sharp knife to cut them. *Colour combinations* Use a variety of colours such as red (watermelon, strawberries, etc.) and green (kiwi, honeydew melon, etc.) *Items are used in proportion* Make sure to cut the fruit in symmetrical size, so that an even design is created. Glass plates and white plates give fruits a better appeal. Do not use bright coloured plates, as they will interfere with the natural colours of the fruit.	
Fruit salad	Unlike western salads, a fruit salad is a mix of cut fresh fruits macerated with sugar syrup and flavours. It can be served with a scoop of ice cream or freshly whipped cream. Preparing fruit for dessert, particularly ripe and fresh fruit, is governed by the availability of ingredients and taste. To keep the flavour of each fruit distinct, use only 5 to 6 varieties. If possible, leave the peeling and slicing until the last moment to keep the colour of the fruit bright. Fresh or poached fruit may be used, mainly diced, moistened with syrup or juices, sometimes with spirits or liqueurs added. Fruit salad should have a fresh and appetising appearance. The fruit should be cut at the correct size to be identifiable. Approximately 125 g are served per portion.	
Compotes or poached fruits	Peeled, whole, half, quartered, or diced fruit is poached in sugar syrup or sometimes in wine, with the addition of spices such as cinnamon and cloves. These can be served as an accompaniment such as peach Melba and sometimes as a dessert accompanied by sauces and ice creams. Most fruits can be poached without addition of sugar; but some fruits such as apples, plums, and rhubarb, need sugar to develop their full flavour. Individual fruits may be prepared in a variety of ways: cherries in red wines, pears poached in coffee, *strawberries Romanoff* marinated in Curaçao, etc.	

Thickening of a baked egg custard depends on the coagulation of the egg protein. The ratio of eggs to milk controls the firmness of the custard.

When preparing the mixture, always strain your custard for impurities. This will also enhance its quality and smoothness. Using heated milk helps to blend the mixture, and to dissolve the sugar more quickly. Skim off any foam from the surface, because it will result in a porous texture, and spoil the appearance of the dessert.

Cook the custard in a moderate oven. Using a water bath will slow the heat penetration. The water acts as an insulator, giving even heat distribution and cooking. In other words, the outside of the custard will not overcook before the inside is set. The coagulation temperature will be reached gradually.

When turned out, the caramel custard should have a nice golden brown caramel sauce in the right proportion, with no air bubbles or signs of overcooking. As options, you can flavour the caramel mixture with melted chocolate, roasted nuts, coffee, or liqueurs. Making caramel is an art. If you are attempting to make it for the first time, adhere to the following guidelines.

- In a heavy-bottom copper pan, put the required amount of sugar and water over medium heat and cook until the mixture is a light amber colour.
- All sugar has to be dissolved and one should never stir the caramel with a metal spoon, or it could crystallize. Caramel and its density must be tailored to the requirements of the dessert.

A few of the common desserts using creams and custards are discussed in Table 13.8.

Table 13.8 Cream-based desserts

Cream-based desserts	Description	Photograph
Bavarois	*Bavarois* is a dessert-based on sauce *anglaise*. It is moulded, stabilized with gelatine, and enriched with cream and flavours. Various shapes can be created depending on the moulds used. They can be prepared for buffets or prepared in individual moulds. Bavarian desserts can have several flavours made from the same basic mixture. Some factors need to be kept in mind while preparing Bavarian desserts: • Avoid overheating as the eggs may curdle. • Soak gelatine in cold water to make it swell so that it dissolves when heated. In case of using leaf gelatine, soak in cold water, and then melt over low heat or add to hot custard mixture. • Strain the custard and allow to cool before adding the whipped cream. • Whip the cream until it forms a soft peak. • The mixture may be cooled over ice to speed up the process of setting.	

(Contd)

Table 13.8 (Contd)

Cream-based desserts	Description	Photograph
Bavarois	*Bavarois* may be layered, using a variety of colours and flavours, e.g., chocolate, vanilla, strawberry. Allow each layer to set before adding the next. Alternatively, pipe raspberry Bavarian cream into the centre of vanilla cream, which must still be soft. Or half fill a glass with Bavarian orange cream and pour on a chocolate sauce and serve. Again, varieties are only limited by your imagination.	
Mousse	Mousse is a cream-based dessert that can be made in variety of ways. Mousses range from the delicate, smooth sweet containing sweetened, flavoured whipped cream, to the more heavy egg yolk, gelatine, and cream based mixture to the very light and airy mixtures lightened with beaten egg whites. They must be chilled and served cold. A mousse is made by combining either fruit purée and syrup, or fruit purée and Italian meringue. It is stabilized with gelatine and enriched with fresh whipped cream. Keep in mind the fruit pulp should not be too sloppy. For stronger flavour, use a fresh fruit purée. Mousses can be made by cooking egg yolks and sugar to form a thick *sabayon* to which whipped cream is folded. Bavarian cream listed above can also be classified as a mousse.	
Charlotte	This type of cold sweet is usually a *bavarois* encased with Swiss roll slices or finger biscuits, ice wafers, or *Genoese* sponge. *Charlotte* moulds can be fluted or plain. They are lined with slices of Swiss roll placed as closely as possible otherwise there would be gaps created and when the mixture is poured, it will leak from the holes. If you are using finger biscuits, neatly line the base and sides of your charlotte mould, fill the centre, and leave to set. Trim off the finger biscuits in line with the mould. If setting individual portions in a serving dish or glass, you can reduce the gelatine content, but you must then allow at least 4 hours setting time. Quicker setting needs more gelatine, which then produces a rubbery consistency. Gelatine acts as a stabilizer, encasing the air you have beaten into the cream, making the dessert light and airy. Cover with plastic wrap, if you need to prevent undesirable flavours from affecting the taste. To demould any cream-based dessert, attempt only when the dessert has set and is firm to the touch. Loosen it in the mould. Another method is to immerse the mould briefly into tepid water. Do not overdo it, or the dessert may start to melt and ripple the surface.	

(Contd)

Table 13.8 (Contd)

Cream-based desserts	Description	Photograph
Soufflé	These are sweets based on a sauce *anglaise*, stabilized with gelatine, enriched with whipped cream, and lightened with beaten egg whites and flavourings such as spirits and liqueurs, and pastes of nuts. These are then set in special soufflé moulds, wrapped in greaseproof paper 2.5 cm higher than the mould. The paper is removed after chilling and the soufflé is decorated.	
Fools	A fairly stiff fruit purée is carefully mixed with whipped cream and allowed to set in the refrigerator. Because of the richness of this dessert, fruits which are highly acidic, such as raspberries, gooseberries, and rhubarb, are the most suitable. This old English dessert is often served with finger biscuits.	

Tarts, pies, and flans

As discussed in hot desserts, varieties of tarts, pies, and flans can be prepared and served hot or cold. Some flans are baked and served cold while some are served hot.

Some classical tarts, pies, and flans are discussed in Table 13.9.

Table 13.9 Tarts, pies, and flans served as dessert

Tarts, pies, and flans	Description	Photograph
Lemon tart	A lemon tart is made by lining the flan or tart mould with sweet paste and baking blind. It is then filled with lemon curd and served decorated with meringue or as plain. Key lime pie is a popular American dessert made with special lime called Key lime.	
Fruit tart	Fruits tart and flan can be made by using baked sweet paste tarts shells and lining them with melted chocolate. The base of the chocolate prevents the shell from getting soggy. Pipe whipped pastry cream into the prepared shell and decorate with freshly cut fruits. Glaze with a gel to protect the fruit from discolouring. These can be served as afternoon tea desserts or arranged and served on buffets.	
Bakewell tart	This dessert is prepared by lining the tart mould with sweet paste and filling the centre with raspberry jam and *crème Frangipane*. The leftover sweet paste is cut into strips and arranged in a lattice formation on top and baked until cooked. The tart is served cold garnished with water icing (refer Chapter 11 on cakes and pastries).	

(Contd)

Table 13.9 (Contd)

Tarts, pies, and flans	Description	Photograph
Cherry *clafouti*	Cherry *clafouti* is a classical dessert in which cherries are arranged in a tart shell and custard is poured over and baked until set. It is served cold and is a very popular dessert in England.	
Baked custard flan	This dessert is made by pouring basic egg custard into a prepared sweet paste flan and baked at 140°C until cooked. The tart is allowed to cool and is served with sauce.	
Chocolate tart	This dessert is made by lining the tart shell with cocoa flavoured sweet paste and is baked blind. A mixture is made by heating chocolate and liquid glucose and pouring into the baked shell. It is served cold.	

Jellies

Sweet jellies are made either with liqueur, a dessert wine, or fruit juice combined with sugar and gelatine. The liquid is usually heated with sugar until it dissolves. The mixture is then strained to remove any undissolved particles and softened gelatine is added to it and stirred until it dissolves completely. The jelly is set into moulds before the gelatine sets. Jelly moulds or dishes can be lined or attractively arranged in layers. If you mould your jelly, you will need more gelatine, so that the jelly can support its own weight once it is demoulded.

Jellies can be mixed with diced and chopped fruits and herbs to make attractive combinations. Jellies are rarely served as desserts these days, but they form an attractive garnish. A jelly can be set into a flat mould and can be cut with various cutters to make garnishes of different shapes.

Sponges and yeast-leavened desserts

We have discussed a range of desserts made with various kinds of sponges and bases in Chapter 11 on cakes and pastries. Those apart, various other desserts are made by combining sponge with other ingredients such as pastry cream, *ganache*, and nuts, to make some classical desserts. Yeast-leavened dough, such as brioche and *savarin*, dough are commonly used for preparing various kinds of desserts. Some of these desserts are decribed in Table 13.10.

Meringues

Meringue is a mixture of either, egg white and sugar or egg white and boiled sugar. The second type is known as Italian meringue. There are also convenience meringue mixtures in the market, usually dehydrated, which produce very satisfactory and reliable results.

Table 13.10 Sponge and yeast-leavened desserts

Sponge and yeast-leavened dessert	Description	Photograph
Fruit trifle	Fruit trifle is a very popular dessert from England. In this, a sponge is sandwiched with red coloured jam and then cut into cubes. The dessert is layered with pastry cream, diced fruits, nuts, sponge cubes, and whipped cream. Sponge sprinkled with sherry or other fortified wine, such as Madeira or Marsala, is used to add to the flavour and aroma. One can also add any sort of fruit, cut or pureed, or even omit it altogether and include extra jam or fruit jelly in its place. Fruit trifles are layered in glass bowls to make them look appealing and appetising. The top of trifle is traditionally iced with a feather icing of jam, cream, and pastry cream.	
Zuccotto	*Zuccotto* is a popular dessert from Italy that is made in a bombe mould and filled with chocolate sponge, ricotta cheese, *ganache*, nuts, and raisins and served covered with melted *ganache*.	
Tiramisu	This is a very famous Italian dessert that literally means 'pick me up'. It is made by layering a creamy mixture made by combining *mascarpone* cheese, egg yolks, sugar, and whipped egg whites or meringue, with coffee soaked sponge fingers also known as *Savoiardi*. It is a very common dessert served in most five-star hotels around the world.	
Baba au rhum	*Babas* and *savarin* are made from yeast dough and are proved and baked in a ring shaped mould known as *savarin* mould or a *dariole* mould. These are baked and then soaked in a sweet flavoured liquid usually, rum. These are then filled with fruit and garnished with whipped cream. To enhance the flavour they are glazed with hot jam glaze and served chilled.	

Meringues are prepared by whipping egg whites with a pinch of salt and sugar. Heavy or light meringue can be achieved by addition of more or less sugar. Meringues can be divided into three categories such as French meringue, Italian meringue, and Swiss meringue. Please refer Table 11.1 of Chapter 11 for detailed information on different types of meringue. Meringues can be used in variety of ways. They can be used as a base for cakes and pastries and even used for garnishes and decorations as in case of lemon meringue pie. Some commonly prepared desserts using meringue are described in Table 13.11.

Table 13.11 Meringue-based desserts

Dessert	Description	Photograph
Vacherin	Traditionally, these are meringue disks which are baked at 50°C for few hours or until dried. These are then sandwiched together with ice cream, and sides are finished with whipped cream like a cake. *Vacherins* can also be made by piping meringue from a round tube one on top of another to resemble a shell. The shells are then baked dried and then filled with whipped cream or pastry cream and decorated with fruits, berries, whipped cream, ice cream, etc.	
Pavlova	Another of the meringue favourites, it is made by combining meringue with cornflour, vinegar, and vanilla essence. It is shaped into *quenelles* for plated desserts or spooned over a baking sheet and made into round shape using the back of the spoon. The texture of the pavlova is uneven when baked. It is baked at low temperatures between 50–60°C for approximately 1.5 to 2 hours until crisp and dry. It is mainly served with sweetened whipped cream filling and fresh fruit. Coulis or tropical fruit salsas go well with pavlova.	
Marshmallows	Marshmallows are sweet confections that are usually served for children's parties or on festive occasions. They can also be used as a topping for ice creams and sundaes. Marshmallows are made by combining meringue with melted gelatine and cornflour and set in trays heavily dusted with cornflour until set. It is then cut with sharp knife and rolled in cornflour. Marshmallow can be flavoured with essence and colours.	

PRESENTATION OF DESSERTS

Chefs in today's world are artists in their own right; only instead of a canvas and palette they deal with plates, sauces, and cut food items laid out in an appealing manner to seduce customers into succumbing to their visual delights and exotic flavours. Even the most delectable dessert dish can be off-putting, if it is badly presented. The variety and combination of ingredients and styles are only limited by one's imagination. However, a sense of balance must be achieved when working with ingredients and the subtle blending of flavours. One needs to be aware of the changing trends in all aspects of dessert preparation and presentation to keep up with the modern and changing tastes of guests.

Classical Desserts and Modern Approach to Plated Desserts

In this section, we will discuss presenting desserts for both buffet and à la carte. We read about presenting cakes and pastries in Chapter 11 and learnt the modern trends in presenting them. Presentation of desserts generally follows the same rules, but with some more complexity especially à la carte or plated desserts. Desserts allow a larger area of freedom of expression, from the simplest product, such as a raspberry *fool* served in a champagne glass, to fresh strawberries placed in an almond *touille*. There are few limitations while working with shapes, colours, and textures but the combinations of these are infinite. The presentation of a dessert is of utmost importance as it is the last course on the menu and is designed to leave a lasting impact on the guest's mind.

Salient features of presenting desserts

As it is important to present food in such a way that it looks attractive and appealing to the guest, desserts also need to be presented in a manner that they create a lasting impression on the guest. Therefore, one has to keep in mind all aspects of presenting desserts. The following are some of the salient features that guide the presentations of desserts.

Visual appeal Chefs use a range of plates and garnish to decorate their desserts to impress their guests. For instance, a white coloured dessert will not create the same impact on a white plate, whereas a dark chocolate based dessert would stand out distinctively on a white background. Sometimes when options for coloured plates are limited, chefs often spray the plates with chocolate spray guns to provide contrasting colours to desserts. Sauces too are selected based on their colours and the flavours they would lend to the dessert. Since all desserts are not presented with sauces, it is important to select the right garnish for the dessert. The whole idea is to make the dessert look appealing, but care should be taken to keep it simple and not clutter the plate.

Balance and harmony It is very important to look at the balance of the dessert or any dish while presenting it. There should be a fine balance in terms of flavours, colours, textures and taste, which should complement each other rather than create confusion in the guest's mind. For example, sweet meringue *Pavlovas* are served with a tropical fruit salsa. The astringent flavour in the tropical fruits balances the too sweet taste of meringue. Soft-textured desserts, such as mousses and soufflés, are served with crunchy garnishes such as brandy snaps and *touilles*. We have discussed a range of garnishes in Chapter 11 on cakes and pastries in Table 11.8. It is important to keep the presentations simple. If the desserts are rich in cream, keep cream in the decoration to a minimum. The decoration or garnish should complement the texture of the dessert. The same principle applies to sauces—keep them simple and complementary.

Components of the dessert It is important to be careful in selecting the components of the desserts. The three basic components of dessert are:

- The dessert itself
- Sauce
- Garnish

Sometimes a dessert can be accompanied with ice cream, *sorbet*, or even a hot or cold liquid known as *shooter*. The total weight of the pre plated dessert should be in the range of 80–120 g. However, this also depends on the light texture of the dessert in which case the portion would be determined by the size of the dessert.

Easy to eat and serve This is where most of the chefs go wrong. A chef's job does not stop at presenting the dish; it is equally important that the presentation is such that it can be carried easily by the stewards to the guest's table and also easy for the guest to eat it. Some protruding garnishes such as caramel sticks, sugar coated spaghetti, etc. are sharp and can hurt the eye if not seen by the guest. Some chefs paint the plates with melted chocolate or berry sauce that gets dried and cannot be eaten by the guest.

Thus, plated desserts should be of the texture that they can be cut with spoon and fork as these are the standard cutlery served with desserts.

Easy to prepare   It is important for the presentation to be modern, elegant, yet simple to prepare by the staff. It is no good having complicated presentations that cannot be achieved by the staff in timely manner. The maximum time limit for presenting a dessert should be between 5 and 10 minutes.

Fresh and seasonal   The best approach to presenting desserts is to use fresh and seasonal items in presentation. Few fresh berries on the plate are any day better than frozen berry coulis that was prepared when berries were in season. Fresh fruits are the most preferred garnish for desserts as they are nutritious, colourful, and add texture to the dessert.

Classical and contemporary   It is important to be trendy and modern, but at the same time it is important to have a strong basic foundation. Time-tested classical desserts are always in vogue; only difference is that they are presented in more contemporary styles. It is important to have a blend of classical and contemporary desserts on the menu to suit to the varied taste of a guest. *Tiramisu*, chocolate mousse, etc. are classical desserts that are served in modern styles to make them more appealing.

Components and Presentation Techniques of Plated Desserts

To understand the components and presentation techniques of plated desserts, let us refer Table 13.12 wherein some classical desserts are presented in contemporary style. This section would complete your understanding of dessert presentation, the skills of which can be refined with practice and experience.

Table 13.12   Modern pre-plated desserts (see also Plate 16)

Pre-plated dessert	Description	Photograph
Dark chocolate mousse with caramel sauce	*Dessert* This is a chocolate mousse prepared in a ring mould and frozen. After demoulding, it is smoothened out and melted truffle is poured on top and iced like a cake. *Garnish* This dessert is garnished with pink coloured chocolate spiral (refer Table 12.4 in Chapter 12 on chocolates). To add to the texture, a candied and dried lotus root chip is placed on top with a sprig of mint for flavour and colour. To prepare candied fruit chip, brush the sliced fruit with egg whites and roll in castor sugar. It is then dried on top of an oven for couple of days. One can candy and dry a range of fruits in this manner. *Sauce* The butterscotch sauce (refer Table 15.6, Chapter 15) is poured into the designs created with softened truffle.	

(Contd)

Table 13.12 *(Contd)*

Pre-plated dessert	Description	Photograph
Gratinated summer berries with fresh strawberry ice cream	*Dessert* This dessert is gratinated summer berries. It is served along with a fresh strawberry ice cream. The berries are stewed with small amounts of sugar and then flavoured with liquor. In this particular dessert, the chef selects a large plate with small indentation where the berries were placed. Flavoured *sabayon* sauce (refer Table 15.6) was poured on top and gratinated under a salamander. This dessert is served warm. *Garnish* A fresh herb, in this case *bergamot* (refer Chapter 5) is served as a garnish. Seasonal herb compliments the seasonal berries. *Sauce* Sabayon sauce is used in this dessert, but unlike conventional style of serving sauce, here the sauce is poured over and gratinated. The purpose of the sauce in this case is to hold the dessert together.	
Peach Melba	*Dessert* This is an example of classical dessert peach Melba served in a modern presentation. Here the stewed peaches are layered on a plate to give a height and is served with a scoop of vanilla ice cream with the classical sauce. *Garnish* Brandy snap (refer Table 11.7) is used for adding a crackling texture to the smooth ice cream and stewed peach. Though it is not used classically in peach Melba, but in the modern adaptation, it is being used for another purpose. One can use a range of garnish to make the dessert look appealing. A sprig of fresh mint leaf is added for colour. *Sauce* The sauce used here is Melba sauce with a combination of juices obtained from stewed peaches. The juice from the peach adds sweetness and nutrition to the final dessert.	
Dark chocolate mousse	*Dessert* This dessert is a rich chocolate mousse presented in modern style. Glass plate is used here to add a fine dining touch. Melted chocolate is sprayed to create a base for presenting the dessert. *Garnish* Spiral of chocolate strip is used as a garnish (refer Table 12.4). In this dessert, the chocolate strip is given a design with a piping of white chocolate. *Sauce* Vanilla sauce is served here to add colour onto a dark background. Though this soft dessert did not require any sauce, but here the sauce has been added to break the monotony of chocolate colour.	

(Contd)

Table 13.12 (Contd)

Pre-plated dessert	Description	Photograph
Mille feuille of blueberry mousse with poached pears	*Dessert* This dessert is a combination of several desserts on a plate. Here the main dessert is nutty chocolate sheets sandwiched together with blueberry mousse. Pears poached in white wine and cinnamon is presented in a brandy snap cup and warm poached liquor is served as a *shooter*. *Garnish* A sprig of mint, brandy snap cup, and a stick of cinnamon are used as a garnish. *Sauce* There is no sauce served with this dessert, as the dessert is accompanied by a *shooter* which compensates for the sauce.	
Fresh peach *gelato*	*Dessert* This dessert is also served in a large plate with a small indentation. This dessert is a quenelle of fresh peach *gelato* served as a dessert. *Garnish* It is served with a brandy snap flavoured with peach skin dust and cracked peppercorns. *Sauce* This dessert does not require any sauce but few dots of berry coulis are served to break the monotony of the white background.	
Fruit trifle and chocolate tart with fruit salad	*Dessert* This is a classical combination of fruit trifle in a tall glass, fresh fruit salad, and chocolate tart served with sauces. The creamy textured trifle is balanced with a crunchy tart shell made of sweet paste. *Garnish* The dessert is garnished with chocolate flakes and spirals along with sprig of mint. A bunch of fresh red currants and dragon fruit also serves the purpose of garnish. *Sauce* The dessert is accompanied with caramel sauce and chocolate sauce. Caramel sauce complements the fruit salad whereas chocolate tart is accompanied with chocolate sauce. Trifle is eaten as it is, as it does not require any sauce.	
Banana chocolate *marquise*	*Dessert* This is again a modern presentation of a banana chocolate *marquise* served as a pre plated dessert. Chocolate *marquise* is a rich chocolate dessert made by combining melted chocolate, honey, and liquid glucose mixed with whipped cream. The dessert in the picture is presented with a quenelle of smoked honey ice cream on a bed of caramelized banana slices. *Garnish* The dessert here is garnished with a chocolate ring and thin chocolate spaghetti. Sliced bananas are spread in a circular fashion over a silpat, brushed with honey, and caramelized with a blow torch. These are then carefully lifted and placed on a plate. *Sauce* Caramel sauce is served with this dessert as it complements the caramelized bananas.	

Thus, we have seen that the modern style of presenting desserts involves various kinds of plates, sauces, and combinations of desserts and garnishes to make the dish look appealing and attractive. Classical favourites are preferred and presented in a modern style. Please refer Chapter 11 on cakes and pastries, where changing modern trends impacting the cakes and desserts have been described in detail.

Always remember to keep the desserts simple and elegant.

Nowadays garnishes are used more for decoration rather than being used in their traditional form. The kind of establishment style, pricing policy, and clientele will determine the time, money, and decoration you can devote to garnishes and plate presentation.

Tips for Presenting Pre-plated Desserts

As food fashions are constantly changing, it is important to be abreast of new tools and techniques that can be used for making desserts more appealing. The availability of a range of modern tools and equipment as discussed in the previous chapters has helped develop the skill of presentations into a veritable art in the hot kitchen as well as pastry sections. It is the view of most pastry chefs that a good presentation enhances the impact of a dessert. Modern desserts are designed to be a delight to the eye as well as to the palate. With skilled hands and some creative flair, you can achieve delicate and satisfying results, even with simple ingredients. Whatever dessert you plan to put on plate, always remember to do the following.

Keep the presentations simple   Simplicity is the key to success. Simple things are easy to understand, prepare, and serve to the guest. Complicated presentations would involve more handling, clash of flavours, and a messy concoction on a plate.

Use a particular dessert as the visual focus on the plate   Many a time the accompaniments or the garnish are bigger than the dessert itself. In such cases, the main dessert gets eclipsed and the rest of things on the plate dominate the actual dessert. Use garnishes, accompaniments, and sauces that complement the dish and do not take away the individuality of the main dessert itself.

Garnish with a combination of fresh ingredients   Always use what is fresh, seasonal, and crisp. Remember dessert is the last meal on the menu and it is important to leave a long lasting impression on the guest's mind.

Use natural products   Use natural colours and flavours. Essences and artificial colours are passé and do not go with the image of a high-end establishment. It is also important that all garnishes used on the plate must be edible. The desserts have always made use of ingredients like flours and starches, sugars and other sweeteners, dairy products, fats and oils, gelatin, flavourings, nuts, but these days, the desserts lay more stress on fresh fruits and fresh ingredients with minimal of garnishes. More emphasis is laid on the freshness in taste, a balanced appearance and small portions of each; so that the taste can be enjoyed to the last bite. Though, traditional marriage of flavours like apple-cinnamon, rum and raisins, molten chocolate-fruits are never going to fade away, they are now being used in new ways, i.e. apple based hot pastry with a cinnamon-flavoured cold custard, etc.

The desserts are also being served in a combination of flavours i.e. more than one small fresh fruit mousse on a single plate. This is also known as the *assiette* concept. This never leaves a repetitive taste in the mouth as different fruit flavours can be appreciated separately, each one being new to the taste buds. Not only flavours, but different textures, colours, temperatures, and consistencies are being used in unison on a single plate to give an assortment of textures to the taste buds.

More than the visual appeal, where elements might just be added without actually adding to the taste appreciation, desserts now go in for elements, which add to a taste experience, for it is the taste which is remembered. Also, freshly cut fruits or fresh fruit purées or coulis are being used to accompany desserts.

Thus, modern trends call for

- Smaller portions of the dessert, also presented in small individual platters (a feature for the buffets)
- Multiple elements with varying textures, colours, temperatures, etc. on a single plate
- Extra emphasis on freshness (freshly cut fruits and freshly made purees and coulis used instead of readymade crushes and synthetic products) and taste with minimum decoration
- Making desserts simpler with tastes that can be appreciated and not confusing the taste buds.

BUFFET DESSERTS

Buffet has always been a very interesting concept of serving as well as having food. A buffet provides an opportunity to the guests to experience different types of food with variety of texture, taste, and ingredients. Also, it provides an opportunity to the restaurants to serve a larger number of guests in a shorter period of time. The concept of buffet is very old. It dates back to ancient times when the communities were small and people used to dine together. It also helps the restaurants and food outlets to make more money, which results in controlling the food cost and increasing revenue.

A buffet includes different courses starting from the appetizers, salads, main courses, and desserts. Desserts form a very important part of the buffet. Also, it is that part of the buffet which is most elegantly presented. Since olden days, the dessert buffet has been seen as an opportunity for chefs to showcase their finesse in preparing and presenting desserts.

The concept of buffet has changed a lot over the years, mainly in terms of the presentation and techniques of preparing the desserts. Buffet desserts always have a variety of textures and flavours which are presented beautifully in a highlighted part of the buffet. A good and balanced buffet should be carefully planned as the selection of desserts play a large role in successful buffet presentations.

It is important to make a master chart according to the classification of desserts and prepare rotational menus for your buffets. It is necessary to make 10 rotational menus so that the repeat guests also get a different menu on different days. If you have only seven menus in rotation, then each day of the week will have a repetitive menu. For example, let us see in Table 13.13, the rotational menu classified under various subheadings.

Table 13.13 Buffet matrix for dessert buffet

Items	Monday	Tuesday	Wednesday	Thursday	Friday	Saturday	Sunday
Puddings	Cherry *clafoutis*	Cabinet pudding	Diplomat pudding	Ginger and wild honey pudding	Coconut and cinnamon pudding	English Bread and butter pudding	Queen's Pudding
Mousse cakes (individual portions)	Capucinno slice	Bailey's Irish mousse	Black Forest slice	Nougatine mousse cake	Apple mousse	*Charlotte* russe	Blueberry mousse
Eggless cheese cakes	Lemon-scented cheese cake	Mango Cheese cake	*Pandana* cheese cake	Vanilla Bean Cheese cake	Strawberry cheese cake	New York cheese cake	Chocobanana mousse cake
Tarts	Almond *frangipane* tart	Mix fruit dutch tart	*Tarte tatin*	Citron tart	Peach *frangipane* tart	Walnut *frangipane* tart	Tangerine pine nut tart
Chocolate cakes	Hazelnut truffle *torte*	Devils food cake	The Opera	Pistachio truffle torte	*Sacher*	*Dobos*	*Alhambra*
Cream cakes	Rose and fig cream cake	Oregon cherry cream cake	*Panna cotta* cream cake	Kiwi cream cake	Strawberry cream cake	Raspberry cream cake	Lamingtons
Eggless desserts in glass	Raspberry *fool*	Kir royal	Summer berry *compote*	Hazelnut cream	Pistachio and praline *fool*	Pineapple *panna cotta*	Butter scotch cream cake
Classical dessert	*Tiramisu*	Cream caramel	Cardinal *schnitten*	Fruit trifle	St Honore	*Napoleon gateaux*	Gateaux Pithivier
Low-calorie desserts	Fruit *compote*	Apple crumble pie	Grilled pineapple skewers	Almond *blancmange*	Baked yoghurt	Bitter chocolate tart	Crêpe with banana

Classifying deserts in this manner will help chefs to design better buffet menus and at a glance, one would be able to see the balance in colour, taste, texture, and flavour of the dessert. Creating categories helps chefs to plan the dessert menus in better and creative way. If you plan to give 12 desserts on the menu, then create 12 separate categories and list your menus accordingly for a period of ten days. Doing this in a tabular form is called creating a matrix. A matrix ensures that you are not repeating the flavours or the ingredient more than once on a given day.

On buffet, there have to be different types of desserts, such as soufflés, mousses, pastries, eggless, sugar free, cheese cake based, as well as quite a handful of regional desserts. Among all these desserts, there have to be one or two hot desserts. Also, recently there have been concepts of serving hot desserts prepared in front of the guest or in show kitchens wherever possible in restaurants or banquet functions. The desserts which are prepared in front of guests include desserts such as crêpes, sizzler brownies, and baked Alaska.

Earlier, all these desserts used to be presented in large portions and in large platters. Now the concepts have totally changed. The units are striving to put more attention to the guests individually. This concept is reflected in the presentation of the buffet. Now all the dishes, especially the desserts, are individually presented in small serving crockery, so that the guest can come and just pick the item he or she wants to have and proceed. This enables the guest to have a taste of all the ingredients which are used to make the particular dish as well as facilitates easy replenishments of the dishes from the kitchens.

This kind of service definitely requires proper planning and execution of the plans, but its cuts down on the time of service during the meal period and makes it efficient and faster.

There are many types of ingredients which are used to make mousses or soufflés, such as purees of fresh fruits or candied fruits, or *compotes* of berries, such as blueberry *compote*, raspberry *compote*, or sour cherry *compote*. Also, different packaged fruit purees are used in these preparations like mango purees, passion fruit purees, or rhubarb purees. Soft cheese, such as *mascarpone*, is also used in the making of various desserts such as *tiramisu*, which is very popular both as a buffet dessert as well as à la carte delicacy. The soufflés or mousses are now set in individual moulds which are filled in, set into freezers, demoulded and served. Fresh fruits are used in pastries, *gateaux*, as well as other desserts such as fruit custards, puddings, or tarts and pies. The use of classical pastries cannot be denied as *mille feuille*, *roulades*, as well as pies, tarts, and flans are provided in the buffet on a very regular basis. One of the most important ingredients which is most extensively used in any dessert buffet is the old and trustworthy chocolate. There are many desserts which are made with chocolate including chocolate mousses in different varieties. Both dark and white chocolates are used to give different effects and variations of tastes. Ice creams and frozen desserts are included on the buffet menu but are served from the kitchen itself as it becomes difficult to hold ice creams on the buffet for long periods of time.

SUMMARY

Dessert is an integral part of any meal and it is, thus, very important to focus on its presentation as well as taste. Since it is the last meal on the menu, it is important for chefs to create an everlasting impression on the guest's mind. This chapter covered various kinds of desserts in detail. In previous chapters, we read about cakes and pastries, chocolates, etc. In this chapter, the primary objective was to let the students have a thorough understanding about various kinds of desserts. Though the broader classification is hot and cold desserts, each of these categories have further classifications based on the ingredients used.

This chapter covered various hot and cold desserts with descriptions. The recipes for these desserts are provided in the accompanying CD and students can prepare the desserts after reading this chapter. The classification of dessert is explained with help of tables so that it is easy for students to see the difference at a glance. Each of these categories have been discussed in detail under various sub-headings.

Various kinds of fillings have been explained in Chapter 11 on cakes and pastries, however those not mentioned earlier in chapters were listed and explained here. It is also important to revisit the book *Food Production Operations* as it lists various kinds of creams and fillings that are used as base for various desserts explained in this book.

In this chapter, we emphasized on presentations of the desserts, both in à la carte as well on the buffet. Factors important for presenting desserts were also listed and explained in detail so that students can understand why a dessert is presented in a particular way.

A range of pre-plated desserts has been listed with photographs in tabular form and each dessert was discussed with regard to presentation, balance in flavour, and colour combination. The students can understand different ways and techniques of presenting the desserts, which has been explained with garnish and sauces. This table also explains the classical desserts presented in a more modern style. Many tools and equipment, such as silicon moulds, were explained in Chapter 12 and the same tools are also used in preparing the modern desserts.

The modern approach to buffet dessert was also given in detail. Earlier, the desserts on buffet were presented in large platters and bowls with a whole range of decorative items on the buffet. The modern style is to be minimalistic and yet classy. The desserts are presented in individual platters and the guests can choose what they want to have. When the desserts are presented whole, it tends to look messy after few guests have selected their portions. Individually presented dessert, thus, helps to keep the appeal of the buffet clean and fresh at all times.

In this chapter, we also discussed about creating a buffet matrix that would help the chefs to plan balanced cyclic menus for their buffets.

KEY TERMS

Agar-agar It is a seaweed that is used as a setting agent like gelatine.

Almond touille It is a garnish made from *touille* paste (refer Chapter 12)

Angelica These are candied stems of angelica plant used commonly in desserts.

Assiette It is French for a plate.

Bailey's Irish cream It is a kind of liqueur, often used in confectionery.

Blow torch It is an equipment attached to a butane cylinder or any gas source, which emits a sharp narrow flame often used for spot colouring of sugar as in case of crème brûlée.

Brioche It is yeast-leavened dough enriched with butter and eggs.

Convenience meringue It is powdered and dried egg white and sugar that can be reconstituted with water to make meringues.

Crème frangipane Also known as almond paste, it is made by creaming butter, sugar, eggs, and almond powder to a paste like consistency.

Crème renverse It is baked custard that is un-moulded and served.

Curaçao It is a kind of blue-coloured liqueur that has a flavour of orange.

Dariole mould This is another name for *savarin* or a ring-shaped mould.

Docked It is a term used to denote the pricking of lined tart or pie with a docker or a fork to prevent the pastry from shrinking.

Dragon fruit It is a fleshy fruit from South-East Asia, which has a purple skin that resembles a dragon. The white pulp is dotted with black spots.

Feather icing It is a kind of design created with help of a toothpick.

Finger biscuit Also known as sponge fingers or *Savoiardi*, it is a sponge batter that is piped like fingers and baked in oven until crisp.

Key lime It is a kind of lime usually found in America.

Kirsch liquor This is cherry-flavoured liquor.

Liquid glucose It is a kind of sweet sticky and viscous liquid obtained by treating corn syrup with acid.

Maple syrup It is sweet syrup obtained from maple trees often served as an accompaniment with pancakes and waffles.

Mascarpone cheese It is creamy cheese from Italy often used for desserts.

Nectarine It is a kind of stone fruit with smooth and shiny skin and resembles a peach.

Panada It is a thick starchy paste of milk or any liquid with starch cooked together.

Peruvian cream It is another name for baked custard served in the pot itself.

Phyllo pastry Also known as filo, it is a Greek preparation comprising thin sheets of flour dough. It is used in preparation of both sweet and savoury products.

Pineapple upside down This is a dessert made by lining a cake mould with pineapple slices dredged in sugar and filled up with a cake sponge mix and baked.

This dessert is served upside down to display the pineapple, hence the name.

Rhubarb It is a plant, the stems of which are used in desserts as they have a sweet and sour taste.

Ricotta cheese It is a type of soft cheese from Italy. It resembles fresh cottage cheese.

Salamander It is an equipment that radiates heat from above. It is commonly used for gratinating.

Shooter This is a liquid served as drink along with desserts in small quantities.

Strawberries Romanoff It is a classical dessert made by stewing strawberries with sugar and flavouring with Curaçao liqueur.

Swiss roll It is a dessert made by spreading a sponge sheet with filling and then tightly rolling the sheets to form a roulade. When sliced, the slices depict a pinwheel design.

Syneresis It is a term used to denote overcooking of proteins.

Tapioca Tapioca is a kind of tuber. Its starch is commonly used for culinary purposes.

Yorkshire pudding It is a savoury product made with a flour batter, baked and served with roast beef.

CONCEPT REVIEW QUESTIONS

1. How are desserts classified?
2. How would you further classify hot desserts and cold desserts?
3. What do you understand by the term pudding? Give a few examples.
4. Describe at least three different kinds of puddings made with different bases.
5. Differentiate among Peruvian cream, crème *renverse*, crème brûlée and *pot de crème*.
6. What is the difference between a cabinet pudding and queen's pudding?
7. What are sponge-based puddings? Give a few examples?
8. How are hot soufflés different from cold soufflés?
9. Explain the components of hot soufflé and the role played by each of these.
10. List at least five critical factors that should be kept in mind while making hot soufflés.
11. Describe at least three deep-fried desserts and their methods of preparation.
12. List and describe the components of flans, pies, or tarts.
13. Describe at least three different fillings that can be used for naked tarts.
14. Describe at least two desserts that use crêpe or pancakes as a base.
15. What are laminated pastries and how are they used for making hot desserts?
16. What do you understand by the word flambé and why is it done?
17. Differentiate between a *fool* and a *flummery*.
18. What are the factors that you would keep in mind while preparing fruit platters?
19. Describe custard-based desserts and their applications.
20. What care should be taken while preparing caramel?
21. How should gelatine be used in cold desserts?
22. What are *Charlottes* and what are the different ways of making the same?
23. Describe a bakewell tart.
24. Name few desserts that are made by using yeast-leavened products.
25. How are meringues used in preparation of desserts?
26. Differentiate between *vacherin* and *Pavlova*.
27. What are pre-plated desserts?
28. What are the components of a plated dessert? Describe them?
29. What factors guide the presentation of pre-plated desserts?
30. What is the importance of classical desserts? Give examples of how you can present at least three classical desserts in modern style.
31. What is different in the style of presenting buffet desserts as compared to a decade ago?
32. List a few trends that are followed in presenting à la carte and buffet desserts.
33. What is a buffet matrix? How does it help in making balanced menus?
34. How do equipment and tools help in presentation of desserts? Give examples.
35. Make a list of five buffet desserts that you would serve differently on a buffet.

PROJECT WORK

1. In groups of five, undertake a market survey of hotels and speciality restaurants and note the components of a dessert buffet? Observe how the desserts are balanced with regard to textures, temperatures, etc. Record your observations and share your findings with other groups.

2. Divide the class into groups and prepare a range of hot puddings using different bases as explained in Table 13.1. Compare the taste, textures, and flavours and observe what desserts can be served hot or cold. Share your learning with the other groups and record them.

3. Revisit Chapter 11 on cakes and pastries and in groups prepare a miniature version of cakes and pastries for presenting on à la carte. Decide on the accompanying sauces and use appropriate garnish to present the same. Critique dessert presentations of other groups and write down your observations.

4. In groups of three to four, prepare a rotational menu for 10 days with a total of 12 desserts in each. Devise your own category and place desserts under the same. Critique each others' menu with regard to balance in flavours, colours, textures, shapes, and taste.

CHAPTER 14

ICE CREAMS AND FROZEN DESSERTS

Learning Objectives

After reading this chapter, you should be able to

- know the range of frozen desserts
- understand the role of ingredients in the preparation of frozen desserts
- comprehend basic terms such as overrun, churning, and still freezing, which are used in the production of frozen desserts
- prepare a range of frozen desserts ranging from ice creams, sorbets, *gelatos*, *granitas*, *parfaits*, *bombe*, sundaes, and *coupes*
- differentiate among the textures of various frozen desserts and faults associated with them
- use various kinds of equipment in the preparation of frozen desserts

INTRODUCTION

Ice creams are favourite among people of all age groups. Be it summer or bone-chilling winter, frozen desserts never lose their popularity. In the pastry kitchen, a range of frozen desserts are prepared and served in à la carte and buffet operations all over the world. Ice creams do not need any introduction as they are easily available commercially. Many discerning customers demand a selection of home-made ice creams on the menu, which is why making ice creams and frozen desserts has become an important skill for pastry chefs. High-end hotels and restaurants prepare their ice creams in-house, which are termed as home-made ice creams.

In this chapter, we will discuss various kinds of ice creams and other frozen desserts such as sorbets and *parfaits*. Ice creams can be transformed into wonderful desserts by

Table 14.1 Types of frozen desserts

Churn-frozen	Still-frozen	Others	Classical frozen desserts
French ice cream	*Granita*	*Bombe*	Baked Alaska
American ice cream	*Kulfi*	Frozen mousse and soufflé	*Cassata*
Ice milk	*Parfait*	Iced *Charlotte* (*Charlotte glace*)	Fried ice cream
Frozen yoghurt		Iced *gateaux* (*torte glace*)	Sundaes and *coupes*
Gelato			
Basic ice creams			
Sorbet			

combining two or more flavours, or with sauces and other toppings to create various kinds of *coupes* and sundaes. In this chapter, we will also discuss some classical sundaes and *coupes* and learn about the various kinds of equipment used in the preparation of frozen desserts. Table 14.1 provides an overview of the various types of ice creams and frozen desserts.

There are various kinds of frozen desserts that are mainly classified on the basis of the method employed for preparing them. The two most commonly adopted methods for preparing frozen desserts are churn freeze and still freeze. In case of churn freeze, the mixture is allowed to freeze while it is being churning all the time. This method helps in producing a product that is smooth on the palate because of very small ice particles. Churning also incorporates air into the mixture, thereby making it light and foamy. Ice creams and sorbets are made by this method. Still-frozen desserts, on the other hand, are mixed and frozen without churning; they also need a smooth texture and soft mouth feel. Depending upon the kind of dessert, the mixture is churned prior to freezing or air is incorporated in many other ways such as adding whipped eggs, and cream. Let us now look at the two methods of preparation.

CHURN-FROZEN DESSERTS

As the name suggests, these desserts are churned constantly during the freezing cycle. The process of churning and freezing at the same time does not allow water crystals to form and the resulting desserts are smooth and creamy. There are many types of churn-frozen desserts, ice creams being among the most common ones. An ice cream can be defined as a smooth frozen mixture of milk, cream, sweeteners, and flavours with some amount of air incorporated in it as described above. There are many kinds of ice creams, each of which has a typical texture or mouth feel because of the kinds of ingredients used in its making. All the ingredients play a very important role in the production of ice creams and especially sorbets. Sugar is the most crucial of them all. The texture or the mouth feel of the churn-frozen desserts depends upon several factors such as the following.

- Type of the churn-frozen dessert
- Ingredients used in its preparation
- The process of making the mixture
- The equipment used in churning

Types of Churn-frozen Desserts

All churn-frozen desserts have one thing in common—the method of preparation, in which the mixture is churned while it is being frozen. The two most common churn-frozen desserts are ice creams and sorbets. The basic difference between the two is that an ice cream is smooth and creamy and has a dairy base, such as milk and cream, whereas a sorbet is made with liquids such as juices, paired with sugar. Some common types of churn-frozen desserts are described in Table 14.2.

Table 14.2   Common types of churn-frozen desserts

Churn-frozen desserts	Description
French ice cream	This type of ice cream is commonly enriched with egg yolks and butter. Full-cream milk is combined with dairy cream and sugar and is cooked with whipped egg yolks until a thick sauce is formed. Thereafter, flavours and stabilizers are added and the mixture is allowed to cool in the refrigerator for at least 24 hours before it can be churned. Refrigerating the mix overnight develops flavours and matures the ice cream mixture.
American ice cream	American ice cream is made in the same manner as French ice cream, but without the addition of eggs. Eggs have an ability to stabilize the mixture and make it creamier because of its emulsifying properties. Since American ice creams do not have eggs, it is necessary that some ice cream stabilizers (refer Table 14.6) are added to the mixture.
Ice milk	These are ice creams made with dairy products that have low butterfat content. These are very popular among people who are conscious of their calorie intake and have dietary restrictions. Eggs and butter are never added to these ice creams.
Frozen yoghurt	This ice cream can be made in French, American, or ice milk style. It contains yoghurt in addition to the milk and cream. The recipes are always adjusted for milk and cream when the yoghurt is added. The total proportions of the fat, liquid, and emulsifiers need to be constant for a standard product. Too much of fat, e.g., will precipitate out while churning and give the ice cream a curdled appearance. The preparation of frozen yoghurt can yield a better product when regular ice cream mixture is set with a culture of yoghurt and then churned as a normal ice cream. This method results in a smooth and a creamy product.
Gelato	*Gelato* (plural: *gelati*) is the Italian version of ice cream. It is generally made with very low fat content and are often made using only milk and no dairy cream. Some fruit-based *gelati* are made by combining fruit purée, sugar, stabilizers, and cream and churned until smooth. Though there is cream in fruit *gelati*, yet it is low in fat content as compared to conventional ice creams. Also, fruit purée content comprises a large percentage of the ingredients. Since most of the gelati are made without cream, fat, and other emulsifiers and stabilizers, the resulting product does not have too much of overrun. This gives the ice cream rich mouths feel, since it easily melts down in the mouth.
Sorbet	Sorbet is derived from the Persian word, *sherbet*. In English, the term 'water ice' is commonly used in place of sorbet. In Italian, these are called *sorbetto*. Sorbets are used as one of the courses in the French classical menu and usually are served in the middle of the meal before the main course is served. They are used as an interval in the gastronomic fare. It is because of this reason that sorbets are usually made using citrus fruits, such as lemon, orange, and berries, that aid in digestion as well as cleanse the mouth for other courses to follow.

Methods of Preparing Churn-frozen Desserts

By now we know that churn-frozen desserts are frozen as they are being churned. However, it is important to understand that the methods of making the mixture are unique in the case of different kinds of desserts. It is one of the factors that affect the final product. We shall discuss the methods of preparing each type of churn-frozen desserts separately in this section.

Preparing the ice cream mix

First of all let us discuss the method of preparing a basic ice cream mixture. There are two kinds of ice creams: eggless or the ones enriched with eggs. The method of preparing the mix will follow the same process in both cases. The steps for preparation of basic ice creams are as follows.

Step 1 Heat milk in a clean pan and bring to a boil. Meanwhile, whisk egg yolks and sugar in a bowl until creamy and thick.

Step 2 Add the whisked egg yolks to the milk and cook until the mixture thickens or coats the back of a spoon. Cool the mixture and add any flavours at this stage. If an eggless ice cream mix is being prepared, then add the desired stabilizers at this stage and cook the mix until it comes to a temperature of 80°C.

> **CHEF'S TIP**
> Maturing the mix in the refrigerator helps in bonding the proteins of milk, cream, and eggs with water molecules. This in turn helps in making smoother ice creams as the resulting mixture becomes homogenous, thereby not allowing the water molecules to form ice crystals.

Step 3 Remove the mixture from the fire and add cream and mix well. This will also help to bring the temperature down. Chill the ice cream mixture in the refrigerator overnight to mature the mix.

Step 4 Churn the mixture in a churning machine until smooth and creamy.

Step 5 Immediately transfer the mixture to a clean container and freeze in freezers at a temperature of –20°C.

Preparing sorbets

Sorbets in the modern times have also replaced ice creams, as they are made without any cream and fat and are thus, light and healthy. They are a combination of water, fruit juice, and sugar and are commonly known as water ice. Sugar plays an important role in sorbets and one has to be careful about the density of sugar in the syrup. Since this is the only ingredient that has to play an important part is deciding the texture of the final product, equipment such as saccharometer and baumanometer are used to measure the density of sugar. The production of sorbets become trickier as the density of sorbet mixture would change with the type of fruit being used in the mixture as concentration of sugar in each fruit or juice varies. For best freezing, the density of the sorbet mixture must be between 18°–20° Baume. If on measuring, one finds that sugar density is too high, the mixture can be diluted with water and vice versa. Many recipes also add 1–2 per cent of egg whites to the mixture before churning. The egg white helps in giving a smooth and airy texture to the sorbet. In many Italian sorbets, a part of sugar is whipped with egg whites to make an Italian meringue, which is then mixed along with water and flavours. The resulting sorbets are smooth and airy and many a time, a customer can get confused between a *gelato* and a *sorbetto*.

The following are some precautions that need to be taken while making sorbets.

- The density of the sugar should be measured as discussed above.
- Sorbets should be rapidly frozen while being churned. It is important to chill the mixture at low temperatures, so that it quickly freezes in the churner. Freezing sorbets at slow rate would result in crystal formation. Sometimes sweeteners such as corn syrup are used to prevent the formation of ice crystals.

To understand the methods of preparation of other churn-frozen desserts such as *gelatos*, frozen yoghurt, and ice milk (refer Table 13.1). As we read above, churn-frozen desserts like ice creams and sorbets are constantly churned while being frozen. If this is not done, the mixture would set into a block of ice. The churning incorporates air into the mixture, which is termed overrun. An overrun is measured in percentage. It signifies the percentage of air incorporated into the mixture. For example, if the mixture doubles in volume then the overrun is said to be 100 per cent and so on. Overrun is more desirable for ice creams as lower overruns would result in a dense and pasty ice cream. On the other hand, too much of overrun would make the ice cream very light and foamy and the end product would lack in flavour and mouths feel. Many home-made ice creams have an overrun between 20 and 30 per cent, whereas commercial ice creams could range between 20 and 100 per cent, depending upon the choice of customers.

Factors That Affect Overrun in Churn-frozen Desserts

There are four major factors that affect the overrun in churn-frozen desserts, namely freezing equipment, fat content in the mix, mixture, and amount of liquid in the freezer.

Type of freezing equipment

Modern freezing equipment works on the same principle as the age-old churning machines, which were also known as hand-cranked freezers. It consisted of a drum that was filled with ice, chilled water, and salt. A tub containing the ice cream mixture was placed in the drum containing the freezing mixture (ice and salt). The tub was placed in such a way that the ice covered the entire tub, thereby allowing the freezing of ice-cream mixture on the sides of the tub. To the tub was attached a scraper device called paddle or a dasher which was used to constantly stir the ice cream manually. This scraped the freezing mixture from the walls of the tub into the ice cream mixture. The churning was carried out till the mixture attained the desired smooth and creamy texture with air incorporated into it. Refer Table 14.7 for pictures.

Modern ice cream freezers operate on the same principle; the only difference being that the refrigeration is provided with electricity and not with ice and salt as the freezing agent. There are two kinds of freezers available in the market: vertical and horizontal freezers. Vertical freezers are similar to olden machines where the paddle moves in the tub vertically. This produces a lower overrun in the ice cream mixture as compared to the horizontal ice cream churners which incorporate more air into the ice cream mix and give a bigger overrun. These, however, are more suited for home-kitchens. On a commercial scale, which entails bulk production, there are many more kinds of freezers, also known as continuous ice cream freezers. These freezers produce almost 100 % overrun and sometimes more. As the name suggests, the mixture continuously runs from one end and is extruded as ice cream from the other end.

Fat content in the mix

The fat content in the mixture also influences the amount of air that can be incorporated in the ice cream mixture. The more the fat content, the lower the overrun, and vice versa. The fat content in the ice creams comes either from butter, cream, or even egg yolks that are added to the mixture.

Mixture

The overrun of the churn-frozen desserts also depends upon the texture and consistency of the ice cream mixture. The consistency of the mixture depends upon solids such as fruits, chocolates, nuts, etc. present in the mixture. The more the solids, lower the overrun, and vice versa.

Amount of ice-cream mixture in the freezer

The amount of ice cream mixture put in the freezing tub is another factor that affects the overrun of the frozen dessert. If more mixture is added to the churning machine, then very little space will be left for the air to get incorporated in the mix. That would yields heavy and dense ice creams. Ideally, the ice cream freezers should be half filled with the ice-cream mixture to get a good overrun. An overrun between 20 and30 per cent is considered optimum; thus one must ensure that no more than two thirds of the freezing tub is filled when the churning process begins.

STILL-FROZEN DESSERTS

As the name suggests, this range of frozen desserts is not churned or stirred but allowed to freeze as it is. Some examples of still-frozen desserts are *granitas*, *kulfi*, *parfait*, etc., which have their own unique tastes and texture. These are frozen without any further mixing or agitation. The resulting mixture is not airy or fluffy as it does not have any overrun. Nonetheless, it is important that the still-frozen desserts too have a smooth mouth feel and texture. Therefore, a range of ingredients and methods are involved in making different types of still-frozen desserts. In some cases, the mixture is whipped and air is incorporated prior to chilling the desserts while in other cases ingredients such as whipped creams and meringues, are used to give volume and smooth mouth feel. The still-frozen technique without incorporation of air is sometimes used for a product to give it a unique texture.

Types of Still-frozen Desserts

Just like churn-frozen desserts, still-frozen desserts too are of various types depending on the process involved and the ingredients that are used for preparing the same. Some common still-frozen desserts are described in Table 14.3.

Table 14.3 Types of still-frozen desserts

Still-frozen dessert	Description
Granitas	*Granitas* or *granita* is an Italian frozen dessert that is similar to sorbet with regard to ingredients. *Granitas*, however, have low concentration of sugar. This is so because large ice crystal formation is the desired texture for this dessert. *Granitas* can also be called shaved ice in English. This is made by combining fruit juices and sugar and allowing it to still-freeze in a large flat container such as gastronome trays. When the mixture is frozen, the *granita* is shaved off and served with additional syrups or as they are. It often replaces sorbet in a course.
Kulfi	*Kulfi* is among the most common still-frozen desserts in India. In this, the milk is reduced to thick sauce-like consistency which is known as *rabri*. The *rabri* is then flavoured with sugar, chopped nuts, saffron, and other flavourings as required and poured into small conical moulds made of clay or metal. The traditional way to quickly freeze this dessert was to put in a clay pot with ice water and salt and shake the pot to and fro to allow the mixture to freeze. Nowadays, the moulds are kept in freezers and served along with cornstarch vermicelli known as *falooda*, which is commonly flavoured with rose syrup.
Parfait	*Parfait* in French means perfect and that is kind of true for this still-frozen dessert. It has a creamy texture that is not a result of churning. A *parfait* in the USA would mean scoops of ice cream with different flavourings and toppings in a tall glass, but in France, where the dessert originated, it is a mixture of creamed egg yolks combined with whipped cream and flavourings frozen in tall moulds, which are un-moulded at the time of service. The *parfait* can be flavoured with a range of ingredients but flavours such as coffee, vanilla, chocolate, liqueurs such as kirsch and orange are most commonly used for flavouring them.

Methods of Preparing Still-frozen Desserts

The methods of preparing still-frozen desserts differ from one type to another. Since these desserts are not churned, their texture is decided by the ingredients and the way these are prepared and frozen. Let us discuss the preparation of these still-frozen desserts.

Preparing granitas

Granitas are fairly easy to make as they are made by combining liquid such as fruit juice with sugar syrup. The mixture is prepared in the same manner as for sorbets, the only difference is that it is not churned like a sorbet and is allowed to freeze in a shallow utensil and then shaved. The shavings of the frozen dessert are shaped into a scoop and served as *granitas*.

Preparing parfaits

The basic ingredients used for making *parfait* are sugar, eggs, and cream. There are more than one methods of preparing the basic *parfait* mix. Let us discuss the most commonly followed method in hotels in simple steps.

Step 1 Bring sugar and water to a boil and then cook the syrup to a temperature of 118°C. Remove from fire and dip bottom of the pan in cold water to arrest the cooking.

Step 2 Whisk egg yolks until creamy and further whisk it by adding hot syrup into the egg yolks. The whipping process should be carried out until the egg yolks become thick and creamy and double in volume.

Step 3 Add any flavouring at this stage and incorporate well. Fold in whipped cream.

Step 4 Put the prepared mixture in a long mould and freeze until required.

Preparing kulfis

Kulfi is a famous Indian dessert that is quite popular across the world. The texture of *kulfi* is very important and depends on the degree to which the milk and sugar are cooked. *Kulfis* are available in many flavours and shapes. Some people set it in a clay pot, while the most traditional way is to freeze it in aluminium conical moulds that are put into a pot with ice and salt and shaken periodically to freeze the *kulfi*.

The stepwise preparation of *kulfi* is as follows.

Step 1 Bring milk to a boil; reduce the heat and cook it stirring continuously until it is reduced to one-third its original volume. At this stage it is known as *rabri*.

Step 2 Remove from the flame and add sugar and condensed milk. One can add flavourings and other ingredients at this stage and cool the mixture over ice.

Step 3 Pour the *kulfi* into desired moulds and freeze until required.

OTHER TYPES OF FROZEN DESSERTS

There is another category of desserts that neither falls in the category of still-frozen nor churn-frozen desserts. These desserts are also referred to as miscellaneous frozen desserts. Some of them are made in their own unique style, whereas most of them are a combination of churn-frozen and still-frozen desserts, e.g., *bombe*. It is one dessert that can be made with various combinations of ice creams, sorbets, and *parfaits* layered together in a mould with or without cake sponge. Sometimes mousses are prepared and frozen, though one can say that those are kinds of *parfaits* which can be categorized into still-frozen desserts, but sometimes a mousse might not be prepared with eggs as all *parfaits* are. Some of these desserts are also classical and still feature on the menus of many hotels. Common desserts in this category are described below.

Bombe

Bombe is a dessert made with a combination of churned-frozen desserts such as ice creams or sorbets and *parfaits*. That is the reason why at times, the *parfait* mixture is also known as *bombe* as it is used for making this classical dessert in a spherical-shaped dome mould. Depending upon the chef's creativity, *bombes* can be made in many flavours and combinations. The inner surface of the mould is lined with an ice cream or sorbet and the cavity is filled with parfait mixture and frozen again. The *bombe* is then un-moulded and decorated with syrups, nuts, whipped cream, and fresh fruits. Figure 14.1 provides a pictorial representation of a *bombe*. Some classical *bombes* with their coverings and fillings are given in Table 14.4.

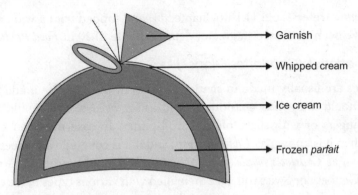

Fig. 14.1 Representation of a *bombe*

Table 14.4 Classical *bombes*

Classical bombe	Covering ice cream/sorbet	Parfait filling
Africaine	Dark chocolate ice cream	Vanilla and apricot
Aida	Strawberry ice cream	Kirsch liqueur
Alhambra	Vanilla bean	Fresh strawberry
Bresilienne	Pineapple sorbet	Vanilla, Caribbean rum, and chopped pineapple
Cardinale	Fresh raspberry sorbet	Vanilla bean and crushed praline
Ceylon	Coffee ice cream	Dark rum
Copella	Coffee ice cream	Praline
Diplomat	Vanilla bean	Maraschino liqueur and candied fruits
Florentine	Raspberry sorbet	Crushed praline
Formosa	Vanilla bean	Strawberry with chopped strawberries
Zamora	Coffee ice cream	Curaçao liqueur

Frozen mousses and soufflés

Mousses and soufflés are classical French desserts that are served chilled or used as a filling for various cakes and pastries. A whole range of desserts can be prepared by still-freezing mousses and soufflés to impart a different texture altogether to the final product. The concept is similar to that of a *parfait* as mousses are also made with various bases, such as *sabayon* and *crème anglaise*, and are folded along with whipped creams and flavours. There are no different ingredients for soufflés, but it is only the look of the dessert that gives an impression as if it has risen out of a mould. This effect can be given in a variety of ways. The most common one is to line a serving mould with a plastic sheet which is higher than that of the rim of the mould. The mousse or *parfait* mixture is still-frozen in these prepared moulds. Once the dessert is frozen, it is served by peeling off the plastic, which gives the impression of a soufflé. Frozen mousses and soufflés may be lined and layered with various kinds of sponges and bases such as meringues, biscuit bases such as *Dacquoise* and *Japonaise* (refer Table 11.1 in Chapter 11) and topped with a wide range of garnishes. They have been discussed in greater detail in Table 21.10 in *Food Production Operations*.

Iced Charlottes (Charlottes Glaces)

Charlottes are usually made in shapes of cakes or they can be made in spherical dome shaped mould known as charlotte mould as for *bombes*. The mould can be lined with sponge fingers or with slices of Swiss roll pastry. In case the outer covering is sponge fingers, then it is known as *Charlotte russe,* and if it is covered with slices of Swiss roll, then it is known as *Charlotte royale* (Fig. 14.2). *Charlotte* moulds are lined with sponge fingers, strips of Genoese or Swiss roll, and then filled with various types of ice cream and covered with a piece of sponge, to ensure stability when turning out. Keep frozen until required and serve with fruit pulp or sauce. There are as many varieties available as ice cream combinations are possible. The *Charlotte* generally takes its name from the ice cream content in the dessert. For example, vanilla *Charlotte* is a mould lined with *Genoese* strips, filled with vanilla ice. Figure 14.2 depicts a cross-section of *Charlotte royale*.

Iced gateaux (tortes glaces)

This frozen dessert is inspired from various cakes and gateaux. The concept is the same as discussed in the chapter on cakes. The cake sponge is moistened with flavoured syrups and layered with ice cream or choice of ice creams. The top of the cake is iced with whipped cream or as per the chef's choice. To prepare an ice cream cake, a cake ring of the required size is set onto greaseproof paper, lined with a layer of sponge, and filled with 3 cm thick layers of ice cream (same or different flavours) and finally covered with a layer of sponge. Fruit or nuts can be added to the ice creams and the sponge may be splashed with liqueurs. When frozen, remove the cake ring and finish gateau with whipped cream, decorate with nuts, almonds, chocolate, fruits, and cut into slices or wedge shaped portions for serving. Figure 14.3 shows a cross-section of an ice cream cake.

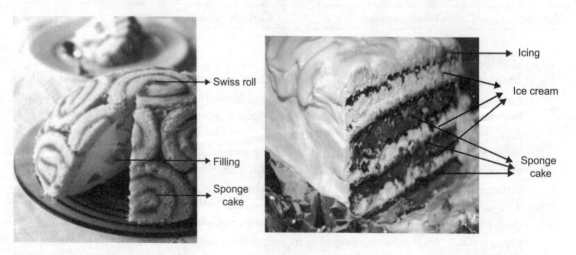

Fig. 14.2   *Charlotte royale*

Fig. 14.3   Cross-section of an ice cream cake

CLASSICAL FROZEN DESSERTS

A range of desserts are also made by combining ice creams and sorbets with various toppings and garnishes. Though the combination of these largely depends upon the creativity of the chef, yet there are some classical combinations that are still very popular around the world and hence passed on from one generation to another. Some of the classical frozen desserts have been discussed in this section.

Baked Alaska

It is also known as *soufflé omelette surpris* because of the baked look of whipped egg whites on the outside and frozen ice cream inside. Baked Alaska is also commonly known as *Norwegian omelette* and is made by lining a mould with *Genoese* sponge. Layers of ice creams, depending upon the choice, are put on the sponge and the base is also sealed with a layer of sponge. The dessert is frozen again until set. The baked Alaska is then unmoulded and covered with Italian meringue from all sides. It is then baked at a very high temperature for a very short duration. Refer Fig. 14.4 that shows a cross-section of Baked Alaska. Nowadays, a blow torch is used to colour the meringue. This equipment is attached to a small butane cylinder. It emits a jet of flame that is commonly used for gratinating in pastry kitchen. The baked Alaska can be garnished with cut fresh fruits.

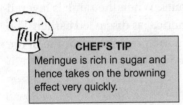

CHEF'S TIP
Meringue is rich in sugar and hence takes on the browning effect very quickly.

Cassata

Cassata is almost like *bombe* but the filling is not of *parfait*. This dessert popularly comes from Italy and is made by layering three different kinds of ice creams and sorbets lined with a layer of *Genoese* sponge. Some cassatas are also made by layering the moulds with ice creams and filling with a mixture of Italian meringue, whipped cream, and candied nuts. One such classical *cassata* is *Cassata Napoletana*. Figure 14.5 depicts a cross-section of a *cassata*.

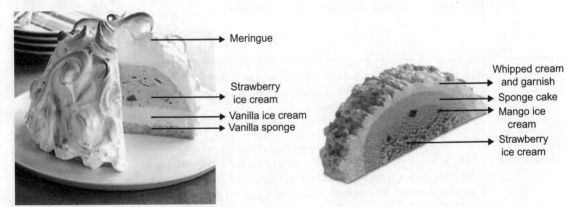

Fig. 14.4 Cross-section of baked Alaska

Fig. 14.5 Cross-section of a *cassata*

Fried Ice Cream

This dessert hails from Mexico where it is commonly known as *helado frito*. It is also commonly seen in China. A scoop of ice cream is wrapped in a covering such as pancake or sponge and allowed to freeze again until it is hard. The covered ice cream is then dipped into a sweetened batter of flour sugar and milk and usually covered with varieties of coatings ranging from crushed nuts to corn flakes. The ice cream is frozen again until set. Before being served it is dipped in hot oil and removed within a couple of seconds. This helps to brown the coatings giving a fried look to the ice cream. The surface of the ice cream is hot while the core is frozen and cold. The preparation comes as a surprise to customers when they see fried ice cream listed on the menu.

Sundaes and Coupes

Assorted ice creams and sorbets are combined in small metal cups known as *coupes* and hence the name. Sundaes are combined in shallow dishes allowing the coupes to be decorated liberally with fresh whipped cream, fruits, and nuts. When the same is layered in long glasses, they are commonly known as *parfaits* in America, as discussed earlier. The name of the coupe comes from the major flavouring used in the preparation. Some of the classical combinations for coupes and sundaes are described in Table 14.5.

Table 14.5 Classical *coupes* and sundaes (see also Plate 16)

Name	Description	Photograph
Arlesienne	This is prepared by putting diced candied fruits soaked in kirsch liqueur in a cup and a scoop of vanilla bean ice cream over it. The ice cream is topped with half of poached pear and apricot sauce.	
Black Forest	This is chocolate ice cream garnished with dark cherries soaked in cherry brandy. It is topped with freshly whipped cream and decorated with large shavings of dark chocolate.	
Jacques	This is prepared with a scoop each of lemon sorbet and strawberry ice cream in a shallow dish. The mixture is topped with cut fresh fruits marinated in cherry liqueur.	
Marie Louise	This is made in a long glass by arranging fresh raspberries in the glass with a scoop of vanilla bean ice cream over them. The topping consists of raspberry sauce and whipped cream.	

(Contd)

Table 14.5 (Contd)

Name	Description	Photograph
Peach Melba	In a coupe, put a scoop of vanilla bean ice cream and top with half of poached peach. Spoon over the Melba sauce and garnish with slivered almonds. Melba sauce is made by stewing fresh raspberries with sugar and making a purée of the same. The purée is combined with stewed red currants.	
Pears belle helene	It is prepared in a *coupe* with a scoop of vanilla bean ice cream and topping with half of poached pear. Spoon over chocolate sauce and garnish with slivered almonds.	
Banana split	This sundae is prepared in a boat shaped shallow dish. A banana is split lengthwise and arranged on either sides of the dish. Thereafter three kinds of ice creams are arranged as shown in the picture and topped with syrups, nuts, and freshly whipped cream.	

COMMODITIES USED IN MAKING FROZEN DESSERTS

There are various kinds of ingredients that are used in the preparation of frozen desserts. Every ingredient has a role and contributes to making the dessert unique in texture as also taste. Thus, it is very important to understand the role of ingredients in the making of desserts. Sugar, for example, plays a significant part in churn-frozen desserts. If it is less, then there will be large water crystals in the resulting dessert and if the sugar is too much, then the dessert will not freeze well. Apart from sugar, several other ingredients such as starches, eggs, and even stabilizers play a major role, which needs to be understood well so as to be able to make them as per standards. Table 14.6 highlights the role of various ingredients in a frozen dessert.

Table 14.6 Role of ingredients in frozen desserts

Ingredient	Role played
Sugar	Sugar is the most crucial of all ingredients in frozen desserts as the ratio of sugar to the overall mix determines the texture and the consistency of the preparation. Too much of sugar in the mix will prevent freezing and the mixture will not become firm whereas low concentration of sugar will result in a product that is not very smooth and has large ice crystals. Sugar is responsible for smoothness of the frozen dessert. Usually 18 to 20 per cent of the weight of the mixture should be sugar, but this can change with the addition of other ingredients in the mixture that also would contain certain amount of sugar. In case of sorbets, the amount of sugar is even more crucial as there is no cream or milk. In those cases, it is important to determine the density of the sugar in the mixture, which is measured with the help of a *saccharometer*. Density of sugar syrup is measured in *Brix* or *Baume*.

(Contd)

Table 14.6 (Contd)

Ingredient	Role played
Eggs	Eggs are used in various forms in frozen desserts. Egg yolks are commonly used in ice creams, whereas egg whites are used in the preparation of sorbets and some other frozen desserts. Eggs whites are sometimes whipped with sugar to form meringues that give a smooth texture to sorbets. Eggs also help in emulsifying the mixture, thereby producing smooth textures in ice creams. Egg whites in sorbets trap water molecules by forming a thin film around them thereby preventing the crystals from being formed in the mixture.
Milk and other dairy products	Usually milk of high fat content is used in making ice creams and desserts, unless the ice creams are specific to certain dietary requirements. Other kinds of dairy products such as skimmed milk, buttermilk, and yoghurts are also used to produce frozen desserts. Each of these dairy products yields a product with a characteristic texture and flavour. Cream of rather high fat content is used in frozen desserts and should never be boiled along with milk. Boiling the cream would result in melting of fat which will surface out during the cooling process and would precipitate out when churned in the freezer. The proportion of cream to milk is usually 25 to 30 per cent.
Starch	Many kinds of starch are sometimes used for adding base and texture to frozen desserts. The most commonly used starch is custard powder but it can vary with the type of ice cream. In some cases, rice powder is also used to thicken the mixture. Starch works on the same principle that it binds all the water molecules together to form a homogeneous mass which produces a smooth textured ice cream. One has to be careful in adding starch to the mixture as too much of starch will make the ice cream bulky and heavy.
Stabilizers	Stabilizers play a pivotal role, especially in the making of ice creams on a commercial scale. Though products such as fat, eggs, etc. act as natural stabilizers, there are a range of chemicals that are used as stabilizers in the commercial production of frozen desserts. The main function of stabilizers is that they hold the dessert molecules together and do not let it melt away easily. The ice cream thus retains its shape and texture for longer duration as compared to those without any. Many natural ingredients such as *xanthin*, *guar* gum, and gelatine, are used as stabilizers in ice cream production.
Emulsifiers	As the name suggests, an emulsifier is an agent that helps the mix to come together and impart homogeneity to the product by preventing the formation of ice crystals during the freezing process. Apart from the range of natural stabilizers, such as eggs and starch, chemical emulsifiers are used in combinations with stabilizers to obtain a smooth and airy product. Home-churned ice creams lack volume, but the taste and mouths feel is rich and flavoursome. That is the reason many fine dining establishments serve a range of home-churned ice creams and frozen desserts. However, there are many people who find home-made ice creams not up to the mark because of their comparison with commercially made ice creams that use stabilizers and emulsifiers to create foamy and airy product.
Butter	Unsalted fresh dairy butter is sometimes used in French ice creams. The fat in ice creams is responsible for giving the smoothness and rich mouths feel. One has to be careful in adding fat to recipes because even cream has an amount of fat that surfaces as butter fat from the churning process. Too much of fat in an ice cream would congeal up together during the churning process to form tiny lumps, which would make the ice cream granular and spoil the texture. On the other hand, the right amount of fat in ice cream prevents water molecules to come together, thereby resulting in a smooth texture.

(Contd)

Table 14.6 (Contd)

Ingredient	Role played
Flavours	Many kinds of flavours can be added to the basic ice cream mixture (refer steps involved in preparing basic ice cream). Flavours in frozen desserts should be added in adequate large quantities, otherwise, one would feel very little taste because when frozen desserts are consumed they numb the taste buds on the tongue. On the contrary, too much of flavour would spoil the taste of the frozen dessert. Scrapings of vanilla pods, melted chocolate, chocolate chips, cookie dough, caramel drops, fudges, fruits, and purees are most commonly used flavourings added to frozen desserts. Creativity and style of menu is the key to flavouring a frozen dessert. Many a speciality restaurant have taken a step further and made a combination of ice creams such as bacon ice cream, smoked salmon and ice cream.

EQUIPMENT USED IN THE PRODUCTION OF FROZEN DESSERTS

Apart from the ice cream churning machine, there are many more tools and equipment that are used in the production of frozen desserts. As desserts are highly prone to bacterial contamination, it is of utmost importance that health and hygienic standards are maintained while preparing ice creams. It is also extremely necessary that each equipment is properly washed and sanitized before use. Various kinds of equipment used in preparing frozen desserts are described in Table 14.7.

Table 14.7 Equipment used in preparing frozen desserts

Equipment	Description	Photograph
Hand-crank ice cream machines	These are hand-operated ice cream churners which have a tub that can fit inside another tub. The space around the inner tub is filled with ice, salt, and chilled water. As ice lowers the freezing point of the water, it is helpful in freezing the contents inside the inner tub. A scraper is attached to a handle which is moved by hand to continuously scrape the mixture while churning.	
Vertical freezing machines	These can be hand-operated or machine operated. The inner tub is designed to be in a vertical position. Vertical churning incorporates lesser air into the mixture.	
Horizontal freezing machines	These can be hand operated or machine operated. The ice-cream tub is designed to be in a horizontal position. Horizontal churning incorporates more air into the mixture, thereby making ice creams light and airy.	

(Contd)

Table 14.7 (Contd)

Equipment	Description	Photograph
Continuous freezing machines	These are commercially used machines for preparing ice creams and sorbets for volume catering. In this machine, an ice cream mixture is poured on one end and ice cream is extracted from the other end.	
Bombe mould	These are semi-spherical moulds made of metal, silicone, or plastic. They are available in various sizes and used for making *bombe* and other frozen desserts.	
Saccharo-meter	It is an equipment used for measuring the density of sugar syrup. It looks like a thermometer, with a weight at one end, which helps the saccharometer to float vertically in the syrup. The saccharometer is vertically placed inside the sugar syrup. Due to buoyant force, it floats at a point where the reading determines density of the syrup.	
Vermicelli press	This equipment is used in Indian cuisine for making *falooda* that is usually served along with *kulfi*. It is a cylindrical instrument that has dyes of various perforations. The mixture of cooked corn flour and water is put inside and pressed to extract the *falooda*.	
Ice cream containers	These are metal containers usually made of aluminium as stainless steel is not a good conductor of heat and does not retain cold temperatures for long when compared to aluminium. These containers are used for freezing ice cream and storing those in freezers. Modern ice cream containers are double-walled which is filled with silicon liquid. The silicon liquid freezes at low temperatures and keeps the temperature constant even if the container is kept on buffet for at least 30 minutes. The container can be charged again by freezing it up to 12 hours.	
Ice cream scooper	Scoops are used for serving and removing ice creams from the storage containers. The ice cream is scraped from the container using a scoop to yield a ball or an oval shape depending upon shape and size of the scoop.	

STORAGE AND SERVICE OF FROZEN DESSERTS

Storage and service of frozen desserts is of prime importance. Water freezes at 0°C. Thus, freezing temperatures start from –1°C. But ice creams and other frozen desserts must be stored at much lower temperatures to get the right texture and consistency. Once a frozen dessert is prepared, it should be rapidly frozen to avoid melting otherwise ice crystals would be formed in frozen desserts. Ice creams and sorbets are stored at a temperature between –18°C and –20°C. However, before serving it is important to move the ice cream to a temperature of –10°C to –11°C. This temperature will ensure that the ice cream and sorbets are soft to serve.

CHEF'S TIP
Never refreeze a melted or soft ice cream, as it can form large crystals. Instead, use this ice cream to prepare cold milk-shakes and smoothies.

One must always use an ice cream scoop to serve an ice cream or a sorbet. A scoop is used for scraping the ice cream until the mixture rolls to a ball in the scoop. For large banquet operations, ice creams can be scooped in advance, put on a base such as a small piece of sponge to secure the ice cream in its place. The batch can then be frozen and removed just before service. Sorbets also can be pre-portioned in chilled glasses and stored in the freezer.

SUMMARY

To a common man any frozen creamy dessert is an ice cream, but pastry chefs know it little differently. In this chapter, we read about the concept of frozen desserts and their various kinds, such as ice creams, sorbets, *granitas*, and *bombe*. We discussed a range of frozen desserts that are classified on the basis of their method of production such as churn-frozen and still-frozen. Ice creams, sorbets, and water ice are made by churn-freezing, i.e., the mixture is constantly churned while being frozen. This method does not allow the formation of ice crystals and results in a smooth and creamy product. Other frozen desserts such as *parfaits*, *granitas*, *bombes*, frozen mousses, and soufflés are prepared by the method of still freezing. Though these products also require some amount of air to be incorporated into the mix, the mixture is whipped before freezing or ingredients such as whipped eggs and cream are folded in the mixture before freezing. We discussed some of the important aspects of churn-frozen desserts such as overrun and the factors that affect the overrun in an ice cream.

We discussed the various kinds of ice creams such as French ice cream, American ice cream, *gelato*, ice milk, and frozen yoghurt. We also discussed the various steps involved in the production of ice creams and factors that need to be kept in mind while preparing them.

Ingredients play a very important role in production of frozen dessert. Sugar and fat are the most crucial of these all. In this chapter, we discussed the role played by each ingredient in the preparation of frozen desserts and some useful tips regarding the use of these ingredients.

A whole range of still-frozen desserts, such as *parfaits* and *bombes* were discussed in detail. The concept of American and French *parfait* and the difference between the two were also briefly explained. Step-by-step production of *parfait* was also discussed.

Various kinds of classical bombes are illustrated in tabular form for easy understanding. This chapter also discussed various kinds of other classical frozen desserts such as baked Alaska, *Cassata*, *kulfi*, fried ice cream, and various classical sundaes and coupes. Lastly, equipment and instruments used in the production of frozen desserts are also discussed along with illustrations.

In the next chapter, we will discuss various kinds of sauces that can be served along with desserts as à la carte or in buffets.

KEY TERMS

American ice cream It is an ice cream made without the addition of eggs.

Baked Alaska Also known as Norwegian omelette or soufflé omelette surprise, it is a frozen dessert made by covering assorted ice cream in sponge and then covering with meringue prior to baking.

Baume See Brix.

Bombe It is a kind of multi-layered still-frozen dessert set in a dome-shaped mould.

Brix It is a unit of measuring density of sugar. It is measured in percentage.

Buttermilk It is the liquid obtained after butter is churned out or separated from cream.

Candied fruit It is a term used for commercially available dried fruits candied in sugar.

Caribbean rum It is a white-coloured rum from Caribbean islands.

Cassata Napoletana It is a classical *cassata* from Italy.

Continuous freezers These are ice cream freezers put to commercial use.

Crème anglaise As learnt earlier, it is made by cooking milk, sugar, and egg yolks in a bain-marie until the sauce coats the back of the spoon.

Curaçao It is a blue-coloured orange-flavoured liqueur from France.

Emulsifiers These are natural and chemical ingredients used to help frozen desserts attain a smooth and a creamy texture and retain homogeneity.

Falooda This is noodle-shaped vermicelli made with a paste of cornflour and water cooked until transparent. The paste is passed through a press to obtain strands of desired thickness. It is a common accompaniment with *kulfi* in India.

French ice cream It is ice cream made with egg yolks.

Gelato It is an Italian ice cream made with little or no cream at all.

Guar gum It is gum obtained from the endosperm of *guar* beans, used as a stabilizer.

Helado frito It is a fried ice cream from Mexico.

Horizontal freezer It is an ice cream freezer in which the tube moves horizontally while being frozen.

Hydrometer A *hydrometer* is an instrument used to measure the specific gravity (or relative density) of liquids, i.e., the ratio of the density of the liquid to the density of water.

Ice milk It is a term used for ice creams made with low fat content.

Kirsch It is liqueur obtained from cherries.

Maraschino It is a type of red cherry.

Maturing It is a term in ice-cream making that involves allowing the ice cream mixture to rest in a freezer for at least 24 hours, so that the proteins mix homogeneously with liquid ingredients.

Meringue It is a type of dessert in which egg whites are whipped along with sugar until a thick creamy product is obtained.

Norwegian omelette See baked Alaska.

Overrun It is a term used to denote the amount of air incorporated into the frozen desserts while churning.

Parfait It is a still-frozen dessert made by whipping eggs and combining with whipped cream and various flavours.

Praline It is caramelized sugar and almonds, crushed into a coarse texture.

Rabri It is an Indian dessert obtained by reducing milk until it becomes thick and coats the back of a spoon.

Red currants These are small red berries with a sweet and sour taste.

Sabayon It is a sauce based on a foamy mixture of egg yolks whipped with small amounts of sugar and liquid over a bain-marie.

Saccharometer It is a tool used to measure the density of the sugar in a liquid.

Sherbet Water and flavourings sweetened with sugar is called sherbet.

Sorbet Served as a course in French classical menu, it is churned water and sugar with flavourings. It is also known as *sorbetto* in Italian.

Soufflé omelette surprise See baked Alaska.

Stabilizers These are natural and chemical ingredients that prevent the ice creams to melt away rapidly.

Vertical freezer This is an ice cream freezer in which the tube moves vertically while being frozen.

Water ice See sorbet

Xanthan gum It is a kind of polysaccharide made by fermenting glucose or sucrose with bacteria.

CONCEPT REVIEW QUESTIONS

1. What do you understand by the term frozen dessert?
2. Why are home-made ice creams popular with only certain customers?
3. What are the two most common methods involved in production of frozen desserts? Explain.
4. What do you understand by the term overrun? How does it impact upon the texture of the ice cream?
5. What are the advantages and disadvantages of large or less overrun in an ice cream?
6. List the factors that affect the overrun in a frozen dessert.
7. What is the principle behind the churn-freeze method?
8. List three kinds of ice cream churners commonly used in the manufacture of ice creams.
9. How would you differentiate between American, French, and Italian ice creams?
10. Why is it important to keep the mix in the refrigerator to mature and how does this help?
11. Differentiate between ice milk and frozen yoghurt.
12. What is the difference between *gelato* and sorbet?
13. What factors would you keep in mind while preparing the basic ice cream mixture?
14. Explain the role of sugar in frozen desserts. Why is it so crucial, especially in case of sorbets?
15. Explain the use of saccharometer while preparing frozen desserts.
16. What is the role of eggs in frozen desserts?
17. How do emulsifiers and stabilizers help in ice cream production?
18. What is the role of fat in a frozen dessert? What care should be taken when adding fat to an ice cream mixture?
19. What precautions should be kept in mind while making sorbets?
20. Differentiate between sorbet and *granita*.
21. What is the difference between *parfait* and *kulfi*?
22. Describe the step-by-step procedure of making a *parfait*.
23. Name and describe at least five classical *bombe* and their components.
24. Describe a baked Alaska.
25. Differentiate between *cassata* and *bombe*.
26. What is a fried ice cream? How is it made?
27. Describe peach Melba and *pears belle helene*.
28. Describe at least five classical sundaes or coupes.

PROJECT WORK

1. In groups of five, conduct a market survey of hotels and speciality restaurants and make a list of various kinds of frozen desserts they serve. Further, make a note of commercially available and home-churned ice creams and share with rest of the group.
2. In groups of three or four, make at least two sundaes or coupes with sauces, garnish, and accompaniments. Present the dishes to other groups and get your product evaluated and critiqued. Make standard recipes of the same and distribute to everybody.
3. In groups of three or four, use the information from the book and prepare health ice creams with dietary requirements. Present to the other groups and get your product evaluated and critiqued. Make standard recipes of the same and distribute to everybody.
4. Take a field trip to an ice cream factory in your area and make a report on the processing of the various kinds of ice creams and other frozen desserts.

CHAPTER 15

SAUCES AND COULIS

Learning Objectives

After reading this chapter, you should be able to

- understand the various kinds of sauces used in pastry kitchen
- make different types of sauces with various bases
- utilize sauces for various kinds of uses
- analyse the use of sauces with different products
- make various types of classical and contemporary sauces
- learn the *dum* techniques of creating dishes
- obtain an insight into storage and service of various types of sauces

INTRODUCTION

In the last few chapters, we discussed various kinds of cakes, pastries, chocolates, and ice creams. In all of these chapters, we read about the various ways in which sauces are used in the pastry and confectionery department. Unlike hot kitchens, sauces in pastry have many other uses apart from being served as a component that adds flavour, nutrition, colour, texture, etc. to the main dish or being served as an accompaniment to various desserts. We would discuss these uses in detail in this chapter.

Many pastry cooks believe that a good sauce is the main feature of good cooking. Like Western sauces, pastry sauces also require a lot of skill. A pastry chef would clearly understand the importance of a sauce in dessert and the role that it plays when it is paired with dessert. Sauces are basic but versatile commodities in the pastry kitchen and the professional pastry chef realizes the importance of making good sauces. There is no doubt that sauce making requires skill. Over the years, culinary techniques have been developed to produce good quality sauces.

In this chapter, we will discuss a variety of hot and cold sauces, including a liquid fruit purée, often known as coulis. We will also learn about the various components of sauces, their uses, as well as the use of correct thickening agents and how to store and reconstitute sauces correctly.

COMPONENTS OF SAUCES

A sauce is a liquid seasoning, usually thickened, that is generally prepared separately from the food with which it is to be served. The function of a sauce in a dessert is to add flavour and colour that complement, support, or contrast the main ingredients of the dish. The components of a sauce, however, remain the same, whether we are talking about the savoury sauces served with meat in Western cuisine or preparing the sauces for desserts.

Figure 15.1 shows the various components of a sauce. Let us understand each of these components and the impact that they have on the overall product.

Liquid

Liquid component in a dessert sauce can range from plain water to milk and even liqeuers. Unlike Western hot kitchen sauces, where juices from the roasted piece of meat can form a flavoursome base of the sauce, in pastry kitchen, the chef has to rely on the addition of external liquid to prepare a sauce.

Some of the commonly used liquids and their effects on the final product are described in Table 15.1.

Fig. 15.1 Components of sauces

Table 15.1 Liquid components of a sauce

Liquid	Description and effects
Water	Water is commonly used in preparing pastry sauces. Since water is neutral in flavour, it is important to flavour the sauce with other flavourings. The use of water results in clear sauces. Water can be used in a variety of ways to prepare sauces. For example, water and sugar are combined and heated to yield a clear caramel sauce. Sometimes water and sugar are heated to make thick syrups that can be flavoured with herbs and chopped fruits to make chunky fruit sauces.
Fruit juices	Juices and pulps from fruits are most commonly used in pastry kitchen to make sauces. The selection of fruit for a sauce would depend upon the particular dessert that is being made. Juices from citrus fruits, such as lemon and orange, are commonly combined with chocolate-based desserts. Pulps from fruits, such as passion fruit and mango, are combined with thick sugar syrup to make sauces that can be served as toppings for various ice creams, sundaes, and other desserts.

(Contd)

Table 15.1 (Contd)

Liquid	Description and effects
Milk	Dairy products, such as milk and cream, are synonymous to the pastry kitchen as their use is very varied and unique. Milk can be used for making cakes, breads, sauces, and many more dishes. Milk is combined with sugar and thickened with eggs, starch, etc. to yield an assortment of sauces.
Cream	The art of skilfully blending cream with other ingredients yields some of the most popular sauces that are used along with desserts and put to other uses in the pastry kitchen. Cream can be boiled along with chocolate to yield *ganache* and truffle that are used as sauces as well. Whipped cream is also adjusted to the desirable consistencies and used as a sauce.
Spirits and alcohol	Spirits and alcohols such as rum, whisky, brandy and a range of liquors are used for preparing sauces. Wines are also commonly used for making sauces. They are boiled off to get rid of the alcohol content, after which these are thickened with eggs or other thickening agents (discussed in Table 14.2).

Thickening Agents

Thickening gives body (consistency) to a sauce. If the sauce is not thick, it will run on the plate and will be difficult for the guest to relish it with the dessert. When referring to thickness in a dessert sauce, it is the consistency that can coat the back of a spoon. Too thick consistency would spoil the texture of the sauce. Depending on the nature and flavour of the source, and final use of the sauce, thickening agents also vary greatly. Table 15.2 provides an insight into some commonly used thickening agents in pastry sauces.

Table 15.2 Thickening agents for sauces

Thickening agents	Description and effects
Starches	Various kinds of starches, such as custard powder, corn starch, flour, tapioca, potato starch, cocoa powder, are used for thickening sauces. Pastry cream is made by boiling milk and sugar with eggs and flour. Pastry cream can be thinned down with milk and sugar syrup to make custard-based sauces. It is important to cook the starch-based sauces for a longer duration to get rid of the starchy flavours.
Eggs	Whole eggs or yolks are the most commonly used ingredient to thicken sauces. Since eggs give a wonderful colour and texture, these are widely preferred over other ingredients. Eggs yolks whisked with sugar and spirits over a bain-marie (water bath) result in very flavoursome sauces that are used with many popular desserts. Care should be taken to cook such sauces on slow heat, such as bain-marie, and gentle agitation to prevent overcooking.
Chocolates	Chocolates are also commonly used for providing thickness to the sauce. Care has to be taken as consistency of chocolate-based sauce fluctuates with temperature. If after chilling, the sauce is too thick, it can be thinned down with either more cream or sugar syrup. Thinning down with cream will give a muddy finish, whereas thinning down with sugar syrup will yield a dark and shiny sauce.

(Contd)

Table 15.2 (*Contd*)

Thickening agents	Description and effects
Gelatine	Gelatine is sometimes used to give necessary thickness to thin sauces. For example, a fruit juice would be thickened with gelatine and then rested in a cool place until set. The set gel is then blended and strained through a sieve to obtain a thick sauce. It can also be used for controlling consistency for cold *sabayon* and thin sauces to regulate the texture of the sauce.
Cream	Cream can be reduced for thickening. It can also be whipped to the required consistency and then flavoured to yield a sauce. Whipped cream can also be added to liquids to yield sauces. The degree of whipping for cream will impact the final consistency of a sauce.
Sugar and its products	Sugar heated until it melts is also used as a thickening agent in sauces. The consistency of the sugar syrup depends upon the temperature of the syrup. Sugar syrup can be used as a base for many fruits sauces. Many other forms of sugar such as treacle, corn syrup, honey, and molasses are also used for adding thickness to sauces because of their viscous nature.
Air	Air increases viscosity of purées. Purées agitated in mixer at high speed incorporate many small air bubbles that give thickness to the sauce.
Fruits and vegetables	Fruits and vegetables, usually puréed, are commonly used for thickening the sauces. The consistency of the sauce can be adjusted by adding the required amount of purée and then adjusted to a coating consistency. Various fruits and vegetables, such as berries, mango, apricots, pumpkin, and sweet potato, are commonly used for thickening sauces.

Table 15.3 Seasoning used in sauces

Seasoning	Description and effects
Salt	Salt is the material most widely used for seasoning of food; but its application in preparation of sweets is limited. It is used to bring out the natural flavours in food.
Acids	Acids in the form of citric juices such as orange and lemon juice are commonly used for seasoning and flavours.
Sugar	Sugar in many forms is used for adding seasoning to dessert sauces. Honey, corn syrups, treacle, and molasses are also used for both flavouring and seasoning the sauce.

Seasoning

Seasoning in desserts is the addition of sugar and sometimes salt to bring out the tastes and to heighten the flavours in a sauce. Table 15.3 describes some of the common seasonings used in pastry sauces.

Flavouring

Flavour is described as the total sensory impression formed when food is eaten. It is a combination of the sensations of taste, smell, and texture. Many of the sweet sauces are based on specific flavouring agents, e.g., vanilla, fruit pastes, nuts, spirits, etc. Skilful blending of flavouring agents with the basic sauce is the key to successful sauce making. The result is an almost endless range of sauces that have individual and characteristic

Table 15.4 Flavourings used in sauces

Flavourings	Description and effects
Extracts	Extracts are derived from natural flavouring material. The flavour is extracted by macerating the natural source, e.g. vanilla in ethyl alcohol. These extracts are the best flavouring materials, but also the most expensive.
Herbs and spices	The most frequently used spices are cinnamon, nutmeg, cloves, and green cardamom. Refer Chapter 5 for various kinds of spices that are used for flavouring sweet sauces.
Essential oils	Essential oils contain the principal flavour of all fruits, nuts, and flowers. Lemon and orange oils are most useful in patisserie work, as they withstand high temperatures without deterioration.
Essences	Many flavours can now be made artificially. Used with discretion, these essences are very useful when the natural substitute is not available.
Blended flavours	Blended flavours are compounded from both natural and artificial sources. Such essences have the true bouquet of natural flavour, reinforced with strength of the artificial essence.
Fruit pastes and concentrates	Fruit pastes and concentrates are products that impart true flavour of the fruit. The fruit pastes and concentrates are sold packaged and can be procured from the market at any time of the year. Chefs also tend to make fruit purées and concentrates in hotels when the fruit is in season. These can then be frozen and stored for off-seasons, when the fresh fruit will not be available. Fruit pastes can be combined with liquids to adjust consistency for the sauce.
Spirits and liqueurs	Spirits and liqueurs are expensive; therefore, these should be used with discretion. Since these are very volatile substances that can evaporate when heated, their use should be confined to creams, icings, sauces, etc. Some of these are available as concentrates and are ideal for cooking purposes.

flavours. If you have a natural alternative, it is best to avoid artificial flavours, which can be overpowering and synthetic at times.

Condiments, herbs, spices, and flavouring are used to modify, blend, or strengthen natural flavours. The use of these substances may make the difference between a highly palatable and visually appealing dish and a drab, tasteless dish. Some flavouring commonly used in pastry sauces are described in Table 15.4.

TYPES OF SAUCES

Sauces used in pastry, do not have any classifications such as Western sauces, but broadly, the sauces are classified on the basis of the major ingredient used to prepare these. Certain sauces are made by stewing soft fruit especially berries. These are then puréed and served strained or unstrained. These are commonly referred to as coulis. Few examples of such coulis are strawberry coulis or raspberry coulis. Most sauces can be served hot or cold depending upon their use. Various types of sauces used in pastry kitchen are described in Table 15.5.

Table 15.5 Types of sauces used in pastry kitchen

Classification	Description
Fruit based	Fruits can be used in various ways to make sauces. Some of the most elegant sauces are simple and made from simple ingredients. As we read above, fruits can be stewed and puréed to yield coulis or can be stewed in water or juice and then thickened with starch to prepare sauces.
Custard based	This is one of the most commonly made sauces in pastry kitchen. It is commonly known as *crème anglaise* or vanilla custard. It is prepared by bringing sugar and milk to boil and then thickened with creamed egg yolks and stirred until the custard coats the back of the spoon. This is basic custard and then can be flavoured with various flavourings to prepare a range of sauces. Brandy sauce, served traditionally with Christmas plum pudding, is made in a similar manner. Another kind of custard sauce is made by reconstituting pastry cream with milk or cream to arrive at the desired consistency.
Chocolate based	Chocolate sauce is frequently used as a topping for various ice creams and served along with desserts and puddings. Chocolate-based sauces can be made in various ways such as the following. • Boiling cream and chocolate yields truffle that can be thinned down with milk, cream, or sugar syrup to obtain chocolate sauce. The colour of chocolate sauce can be regulated by adding milk and cream in required proportions. • Another kind of chocolate sauce is obtained by adding chopped chocolate to the *crème anglaise* while the mixture is still hot. • Chocolate sauce can also be made by combining water, sugar, cocoa powder, and butter and cooked like a pastry cream. The consistency of the sauce can be adjusted using sugar syrup or cream. • Another method of making chocolate sauce is boiling water and liquid glucose and then adding chopped chocolate to obtain a smooth sauce.
Cream based	Reduced cream with flavourings is widely used in confectionery. Cream can also be added to caramelized sugar to make butterscotch sauce or it can be reduced with sugar to make caramel fudge sauce.

CLASSICAL AND CONTEMPORARY SAUCES

A whole range of classical and contemporary sauces are used in the pastry kitchen for various purposes, as discussed earlier. Some of the most classical and contemporary sauces used in the pastry kitchen are discussed in Table 15.6.

Table 15.6 Classical and contemporary desserts sauces

Sauce	Description
Crème anglaise/ Vanilla custard/ Vanilla sauce/ Bavarian cream	*Crème anglaise* is warm egg custard sauce that apart from being served on its own is used as the basis for other sweets such as cold *soufflés*, Bavarian creams, and ice creams. This sauce contains no starch. Egg yolks, sugar, and warm milk with the addition of a few drops of vanilla essence are mixed together, and over gentle heat on a water bath, stirred with a wooden spoon until it thickens and coats the back of the spoon. This sauce has to be strained and kept warm in a warm water bath. It is not recommended for reheating.

(Contd)

Table 15.6 (Contd)

Sauce	Description
Crème anglaise/ Vanilla custard/ Vanilla sauce/ Bavarian cream	Sauce *anglaise* base must be held in a warm place at about 37°C. This is critical because if the temperature is too hot, the sauce will separate (split). Egg yolk-based sauces, such as sauce *anglaise*, need slow heat (water bath) and gentle agitation to prevent overcooking.
Chocolate sauce	Chocolate sauce can be made in a variety of ways as discussed in Table 14.5. Chocolate sauces must always be reheated before adjusting consistency as the consistency varies with temperature. Chocolate sauce is served along with ice creams and hot chocolate brownies and fudge as well.
Melba sauce	This is one of the most classical sauces and utilized commonly as a topping for *coupe* known as peach Melba. Melba sauce is a coulis that is made by stewing fresh or frozen raspberries with sugar and water and then passed through a wire mesh strainer to obtain a smooth sauce. It can be seasoned with few drops of lemon juice. Melba sauce is usually served cold.
Caramel sauce	Caramel sauce is a basic sauce that forms the base for many other caramelized sauces such as fudge and butterscotch. Basic caramel sauce is made by heating a mixture of sugar, water, and liquid glucose until the sugar starts to caramelize and attain a dark golden colour. The pan is removed from the heat and the bottom is immersed in cold water to arrest the cooking. This sauce will set hard after setting, so water is added to the mixture and brought to boil again, so that the crystals that were formed after adding water get dissolved and the sauce is syrupy and flowy.
Butterscotch sauce	Butterscotch sauce is made in the same way as caramel sauce described above. The only difference is that softened butter is incorporated into the caramel sauce after it has cooled down to 30°C. Sometimes cream is also added to give a rich and creamy texture.
Crêpe Suzette sauce	This sauce is classically served with French pancakes also known as crêpes and hence the name. It is one of the most classical desserts that are prepared in front of the guest on a *guéridon* trolley. To make this sauce, orange juice, lemon juice, and zest are combined and heated in a pan until warm. It is then left to macerate for few minutes. Sugar is allowed to caramelize in another pan over low heat until golden colour. The pan is removed from heat and chilled butter cubes are added and cooked again until the butter is dissolved in the sauce. The warm juice of citrus fruits is now added. Traditionally, this sauce is flambéed with brandy. Flambéing is a technique used in kitchen, where alcohol is poured over a dish and then lighted with fire, so that the alcohol burns off. This creates an unusual visual impact in the restaurant and also helps to burn the excessive alcohol away.
Strawberry coulis	Cut strawberries into quarters and cook with sugar and water. When the strawberries are soft, remove from heat and blend until smooth or pass through a wire mesh. The choice of blending or passing through the wire mesh will determine the texture and consistency of the coulis.
Apricot jam sauce	Commonly made in France, this jam sauce can be made with any jam. The jam is combined with sugar and allowed to boil. The consistency of the sauce is adjusted with corn flour slurry.

(Contd)

Table 15.6   (Contd)

Sauce	Description
Sabayon sauce	This sauce is very unique, as it has to be served immediately and cannot be stored for long. The *sabayon* based sauce is made by combining egg yolks, sugar, and the desired flavour in the form of alcohol. The alcohol base also helps in providing liquid to the mixture, which is now whisked over a water bath, so that it becomes thick and frothy. If alcohol is being omitted, then few teaspoons of water should be added to the egg yolks.
Brandy sauce	Brandy sauce is a classical accompaniment to plum puddings served on Christmas day. This sauce is made by adding brandy (usually cognac) to *crème anglaise* sauce.
Tropical fruit salsa	This is a contemporary sauce made in a variety of ways. The acidic flavour of tropical fruits makes it an ideal accompaniment for meringue based desserts as it helps to cut down on the excess sweetness. Fruits, such as kiwi, pineapple, and strawberry, are cut into small dices and combined with thick sugar syrup or thickened fruit juices to make this chunky fruit salsa.

VARIOUS USES OF SAUCES

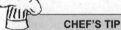

CHEF'S TIP
Do not allow the sauce to re-boil as it will curdle. There is the danger of overheating and toughening of proteins.

Unlike Western kitchen, sauces made in the pastry kitchen have many more uses other than being served along with a dessert. In the previous chapter on ice creams and frozen desserts, we read about certain sauces that are served along with ice creams as a topping and in the chapter on cakes and pastries, we read how certain chocolate based sauces are also used as icing. So, sauces in pastry kitchens have unique and varied uses. Some of the uses are as follows

Sauces as Accompaniments

When the sauce is used as an accompaniment to a dessert, it serves the same purpose as sauces in western kitchen. The sauces are primarily served to enhance flavour of the dish, to add moistness, colour contrast, nutrition, and flavour to the main dish. Sometimes a sauce is used to enhance presentation of the dessert on a plate. Selection of sauces for this purpose is very important as the accompanying sauces should not overpower the main dessert, but should complement them.

Sauces as Toppings and Fillings

Sauces are commonly used as toppings on ice creams, coupes, and sundaes. They can also be mixed with gelatine and used as a topping or icing for cakes and pastries. Sauces can also be used for filling tarts, pies, and even moulded chocolates and truffles. Sauces should be reconstituted to desired consistency for each use.

Sauces as a Base for Desserts

This is one of the most versatile uses of sauces in pastry kitchen. *Crème anglaise* is the most commonly used sauce base to create many desserts apart from being served as a sauce by itself (refer Table 15.6). Sauces are combined along with whipped creams to create desserts such as mousse, soufflés, and fools. Sauces can be heated and thickened with starch and made into desserts such as fruit cobbler which we will discuss in the next chapter. *Crème anglaise* is also known as Bavarian cream and it is combined with whipped cream, gelatine, and flavours to create desserts called *bavarois*.

CHOOSING AN ACOMPANYING SAUCE

Choosing the right kind of sauce for the right product is very important and this depends upon various factors such as sweetness of dessert, texture, mouth feel, and even the style of service of the dessert.

Sweetness of Dessert

The amount of sugar in the dessert also determines the kind of sauce that would be served with it. Meringue-based desserts which are very high on sweet content are served with tarty sauces such as citrus sauces and tropical fruit salsas or coulis (Table 15.6). The acid in the sauce would cut down on the sweetness in the dessert and provide a contrasting taste and flavour. *Crêpe Suzette* is a classical dessert that is served with caramelized sugar-based sauce. Since the crêpes have little or no sugar, the sweet sauce complements the crêpes.

Texture of the Dessert

The texture of the dessert is also a guiding factor towards selection of the sauce. A creamy dessert would be served with a chunky sauce or sauce that has crushed nuts or any substance that can break the creamy texture of the dessert. Desserts with crumbly textures would rather be served with smooth sauces. For example, plum pudding is classically paired with brandy sauce.

Service of the Sauce

The style of service and presentation of sauces at the time of service also determines the kind of sauce or consistency of the sauce. There are many factors that must be kept in mind while deciding on what kind of sauce should be served with what dish. The following guidelines will help you to effectively use sauces to enhance the presentation of the dish.

- In silver service, the sauce is always served separately. This allows the customer to decide how much sauce will be served. Too thick sauces would be difficult to serve and too thin would flow on the plate. Medium thick sauces that coat the back of the spoon are the best option in this case.
- For pre-plated desserts, consider whether the sauce will be best:
  - on the dessert
  - under the dessert
  - or partially coating the dessert as in case of ice cream toppings

  The placement of the sauce would determine the consistency of the sauce
- Should the sauce be spooned, ladled, poured, or piped? Sometimes sauces are served decorated on the plate in which case the sauce needs to be piped in designs. All these factors would determine the kind of sauce and the consistency of the same.

- To strain or not? Should you strain a sauce to remove, say raspberry pips or chips of chocolate? This is often simply a matter of taste and style. Think about the effect that you want to create.

Colour Combinations

The colour of sauces will vary, but it must be appropriate to the sauce being made. Try to avoid artificial colours, though they may be useful on occasion and festive preparations. Using contrasting colour of sauces would also determine the choice of the sauce to be served. Sometimes dark and white coloured sauces, such as chocolate sauce and *crème anglaise*, are placed on the plate and given a marbled effect to create designs and enhance the presentation.

STORAGE AND SERVICE OF SAUCES

The storage and service of a sauce would depend upon its temperature. If the sauce is to be served cold or hot, this would determine the consistency and style of service of the sauce. Ideally hot sauce should be made immediately before serving. However, very few establishments can afford the time and expense this entails, and many will prepare sauces beforehand. But there are disadvantages in keeping a hot sauce in a bain-marie. These disadvantages could be as follows.

- The consistency of the sauce may change. Chocolate sauce may become too thin if it becomes very hot.
- The colour and structure of the sauce may change.
- If cream has been added, fat separation may occur.
- If the sauce has cream added to acid, curdling may happen.

The temperature for holding and serving hot sauces should be around 80°C. The temperature for a cold sauce would depend on its application. Warm sauces that are thickened with eggs, such as custard, vanilla sauce, and sabayon, should not exceed 50°C or else there are chances that it may curdle.

When serving sauces, the general guideline is to serve approximately 50 ml of sauce per person. However, the amount of sauce to be served will be guided by the nature of dish and type of establishment. Sauces used as a base on a plate may be considerably less than if served separately in silver service.

Storage of sauces is one of the most crucial aspects of pastry kitchen. Since the pastry sauces are rich in high protein foods like milk, cream, and eggs, they are more susceptible to bacterial contamination. If a cooked sauce is to be stored for any period of time it is used, it must be cooled as quickly as possible, then covered and refrigerated. The best method of cooling a sauce is to place it on a rack to allow air to circulate around. It should be stirred frequently to ensure an even rate of cooling.

Because of evaporation from the surface, a skin will form rapidly on a sauce, if it is left to stand. This can be prevented if the sauce is covered with a plastic wrap or a tight-fitting lid.

Sauces may be stored at temperatures of 1°C to 4°C. Depending on the ingredients used, they may not hold for any length of time. It is a good practice to make fresh supplies as often as required, if sweetened fruit purées are used as a sauce, there is danger of fermentation and rapid bacteria growth. To extend the keeping time, coulis and purées can be cooked before storage.

It is important that all sauces are labelled and date tagged in order to follow first-in first-out (FIFO) procedure.

SUMMARY

Sauces are one of the most important aspects of a pastry kitchen. The most delectable dessert would not look as appealing if served without a sauce. Imagine a scoop of ice cream without any topping and imagine one with sauce and garnish.

Sauces of pastry kitchen are very different from the ones used in the Western kitchen. Unlike Western or hot kitchen where the sauces are made from the liquid in which the food has been cooked, in pastry kitchen, a range of liquids are used to transform them into many different kinds of sauces. However, the components of a sauce are similar to that of Western kitchen. Every sauce has to have a liquid or a base which has flavourings, thickening, and seasoning. Though the seasoning of the pastry sauces does not necessarily require the use of salt and pepper, but addition of a pinch of salt does enhance the flavours of certain sauces. In this chapter, we discussed various components in detail and discussed a range of ingredients used as components in sauces.

We discussed various types of sauces, such as fruit based, custard based, chocolate based, and cream based, in detail along with examples. Unlike Western kitchen there are no mother sauces in pastry kitchen, yet many variations can be made from one type of sauce. For example, chocolate sauce can be made from crème anglaise as a base or it can also be made by starch-based method or by boiling water with liquid glucose and adding chocolate to it.

We also discussed the uses of sauces in pastry kitchen. Apart from being served along with the main dessert, these sauces can be used as a base for various desserts and pudding, ranging from soufflés, mousses, to even ice cream mixtures. Some sauces are served as toppings on ice creams while some are piped on a plate or spooned over desserts. We talked about various factors that determine the choice of sauce that would accompany the dessert. These factors are sweetness of dessert, texture, and style of service. We also discussed various kinds of classical and contemporary sauces served with desserts and what makes them unique and special. Sauces such as Melba sauce and crêpe Suzette sauce are among the oldest used sauces in confectionery. We also discussed the factors to be kept in mind while storing and serving sauces. The storage of sauce is of utmost importance as the ingredients used in pastry kitchen are very prone to bacterial contamination. Thus, they must be stored under refrigeration and wherever possible, they should be made fresh and served fresh.

KEY TERMS

Bavarois　This is a dessert made by combining crème anglaise with gelatine and whipped cream.

Brownies　It is a rich chocolate dessert often served hot with chocolate sauce.

Cognac　It is a kind of brandy from France.

Corn syrup　It is chemically refined syrup obtained from corn kernels.

Coulis　It is sauce obtained by stewing and puréeing fruits.

Crêpe Suzette　These are flat pancakes cooked in citrus-flavoured caramel sauce.

Flambé It is adding alcohol to a dish and flaming it with fire to burn it off.

Fruit cobbler It is a hot dessert made by baking cooked fruit sauce.

Guéridon trolley It is a mobile trolley used in restaurant, often used for cooking live in front of the guest.

Liquid glucose It is sticky syrup obtained by treating corn syrup with acid. Liquid glucose prevents the crystallization of sugar.

Macerate Soaking a food (generally a fruit) in a liquid, such as alcohol, and fruit juice, for long period of time so that the flavour of the liquid is infused in it is called maceration.

Molasses It is the dark residual syrup obtained from refining sugar.

Passion fruit It is a kind of fruit, which contains pulp that is acidic in nature.

Plum pudding It is a steamed dessert prepared during Christmas.

Potato starch Also known as fecule, it is the starch obtained from potatoes.

Silver service It is a style of serving food, where the food is served from platter to plate.

Tapioca It is a kind of vegetable tuber rich in starch.

Treacle It is a syrup obtained as a by-product of refining sugar.

CONCEPT REVIEW QUESTIONS

1. How are sauces used in pastry kitchen different from the ones used in Western kitchen?
2. What is a coulis?
3. Describe the components of a sauce.
4. Describe at least four types of liquids that can be used for making sauces.
5. What thickening agents are used in preparing sauces for the pastry?
6. What care should be taken while using eggs in thickening the sauces?
7. List few methods of making chocolate sauce.
8. What are the differences among extracts, oils, and essence used in flavouring of sauces?
9. How are sauces classified?
10. Differentiate between cream-based and custard-based sauces.
11. Apart from being served along with desserts, what are the other ways in which sauces can be used?
12. Define a Bavarian cream.
13. What factors are considered while choosing the sauce as an accompaniment?
14. How does the service of sauce impact the kind of sauce to be served?
15. Define a *Melba* sauce and its use.
16. What is the difference among caramel sauce, butterscotch sauce, and *crêpe Suzette* sauce?
17. What is a *sabayon* and how is it made?
18. What kind of sauce would you serve with extra sweet desserts? Why?
19. Why is storage of sauces of utmost importance in pastry kitchen?
20. List four disadvantages of keeping hot sauces in bain-marie or hot water bath.

PROJECT WORK

1. In groups of five, prepare chocolate sauce by the listed methods and compare the results.
2. Undertake a market survey of restaurants and hotels serving desserts with various sauces and toppings. Analyse the importance of any one sauce and discuss how that particular sauce is most apt for the dessert with which it is served. Also suggest a few other sauces that can be served along with that dessert.
3. From the recipes given in the CD, prepare various kinds of sauces and pair those with desserts. Justify your selection and share the records with the rest of the group.
4. In groups of three, prepare at least three types of sauces by using a liquid, flavouring, seasoning, and thickening agent. Taste and record your observations. Make standard recipes after making adjustments and share it with the rest of the groups.

CHAPTER 16

COOKIES AND BISCUITS

Learning Objectives

After reading this chapter, you should be able to
- understand the basic difference between a cookie and a biscuit
- claim an insight into the different methods used in the preparation of cookies
- analyse the type of cookies and how their baking techniques impact upon the texture of the final product
- prepare various kinds of classical cookies and biscuits
- Evaluate a cookie and be able to rectify any fault in a cookie

INTRODUCTION

Though the terms 'cookie' and 'biscuit' are used interchangeably and generally substituted for each other, yet there are theories and opinions that tend to differentiate between the two items. A cookie is commonly known so in the USA, while in the UK it is known as a biscuit. Though both are accorded the same significance and served as snacks nowadays, it is quite probable that these were different at one point in time. For instance, the Dutch made small tidbits from leftover cake batters and called them *koekje*, which meant little cake. They mastered the art of making soft as well as crisp *koekjes*. The word 'cookie' is understood to have derived from *koekje* in North America. Biscuit, on the other hand, is understood to have come from the Latin word *panis biscotus*, which meant bread cooked twice. Leftover bread or cakes were baked until crisp and eaten as biscuits. Even the popular *bioscotti* from Italy is prepared in the same manner till date. The dough is shaped into a *roulade* and baked. It is then sliced thinly and baked again until crisp. Even in France, biscuit means to cook twice. Many sponge bases, such as *Dacquoise*, almond sponge, and hazelnut sponge, are referred to as biscuits.

For simplifying the classification, a cookie is a product that is soft centred, usually made in the style of preparing cake batter and is traditionally sweet. A biscuit, on the other hand, is crisp and hard like a cheese cracker, which can be savoury. With globalization, more awareness, and cross-cultural intermingling, chefs became more creative and cookies and biscuits evolved as separate recipes with the use of creaming butter, sugar, and other ingredients. Earlier, these products were limited to leftover baked products only. With the development of different kinds of flours, sugar, and chemical and leavening agents, the production of biscuits and cookies got commercialized and hit the market as separate entities. Like cakes, cookies began to be prepared on festive occasions, especially Christmas. Nowadays, there are a whole range of cookies that are manufactured and distributed on other popular festivals, such as Diwali, as well.

In this chapter, we will discuss various types of cookies and their methods of preparation. We will also discuss the importance of cookies in five-star hotels and establishments as amenities and some more cookies that are specially prepared on festive occasions. This chapter will complete our understanding of the bakery and pastry section.

PREPARATION OF SIMPLE COOKIES

In olden times, a biscuit was a hard, unsweetened, and dry product that was made from leftover dough and bread in a cooling baker's oven. It had a long shelf life and could easily be carried in boxes or paper bags and was ideally preferred by the poor, who could not afford expensive cakes and breads. By the seventh century AD, the Egyptians and Persians had learnt the art of flavouring breads with spices such as ginger and cardamom, and sweeteners such as honey and candied fruits. This style of preparation gave rise to the popular gingerbread cookies, which are traditionally prepared on Christmas even today.

Nowadays the typical distinction between cookies or biscuits does not hold; these can be sweet or savoury depending upon the choice of the guest. There are various ways of making cookies and biscuits. Some of the common methods of preparing cookies are highlighted in Table 16.1.

Table 16.1 Methods of making cookies

Method	Description	Examples
Straight method	It is one of the simplest methods in which all the scaled ingredients are put in a bowl and mixed together until uniform dough or batter is obtained. This method is apt for cookies that have no or very less moisture in the dough. However, a disadvantage of this method is that it is difficult to regulate the over-mixing of ingredients, which can result in chewy cookies and biscuits.	Sweet paste cookies, short-bread cookies, raisin spice bars, gingerbread cookies, macaroons, *biscottis*

(Contd)

Table 16.1 (Contd)

Method	Description	Examples
Creaming method	One of the most common methods for preparing cookies and biscuits, in this method the butter and sugar is creamed until fluffy. Liquid ingredients, such as eggs, milk, and cream, are added all at once and then flour is folded into the mixture. The consistency of the dough or batter can be regulated by regulating the moisture content in the mix. One can make a range of cookies with this method.	Piped butter cookies, *Anzac* cookies, chocolate chip cookies, oats and raisin cookies.
Sponge method	This method of making cookies is similar to that of cakes. Eggs and sugar are whipped together until light and fluffy and dry ingredients are folded in to prepare batters. Various biscuits and cookies are made by this method.	*Savoiardi, amaretti* cookies, anise cookies, chocolate brownie cookies.

TYPES OF COOKIES

Cookies are classified on the basis of their method of production and baking technique. Some cookies are piped whereas some are shaped in hands and then baked. The consistency of a piped cookie is softer than the one rolled in hands. The texture of the cookie too largely depends upon the recipe and the style of baking. Some cookies are baked at high temperatures for a short duration to achieve a soft centre and texture, while some are baked at low temperatures for long duration to make crisp cookies. Cookies are made with various ingredients, such as flours (refined, whole wheat, rye), and custard powder; fats such as butter, peanut butter, oil, and margarine; sweeteners such as sugar, honey, brown sugar, and molasses; spices such as ginger powder, cloves, cinnamon, cardamom, caraway, and anise; candied fruits; dried nuts; and chocolates. Moisture in cookies is very rarely given with water. The thinning of batter is done with the help of eggs or butters. Various types of cookies along with their examples are described in the following paragraphs.

Drop Cookies

This type of cookie is made from soft dough. The cookie dough or batter is dropped with a spoon or even a piping bag. Dropping through a piping bag would give better control over shape and size which is the most important aspect of baking cookies. When the cookie dough contains ingredients such as chocolate chips, candied fruits and nuts, it is advisable to use a spoon as these ingredients can get stuck in the nozzle of the piping bag. Some large cookies, such as American choco chip cookies, also use ice cream scoops to drop the cookie dough onto a baking mat for baking. Space out the cookies appropriately to allow them to spread. Some common examples of drop cookies are described in Table 16.2.

Table 16.2 Examples of drop cookies (see also Plate 16)

Cookie	Description	Photograph
Oatmeal raisin cookie	This is a healthy cookie as it uses oats and raisins in the recipe. The raisins should be soaked in water overnight for softening. It is made by creaming. Butter and brown sugar are creamed together using a flat paddle. Eggs are added one by one until incorporated. Then, dried ingredients such as flour, rolled oats, baking soda, and baking powder are combined together with soaked and drained raisins. If the mixture is not of dropping consistency, add milk or egg whites to adjust the consistency. The cookie is then dropped on the baking mat with a spoon and baked until crisp.	
Chocolate chip cookie	This is a popular cookie that can be made by dropping method or the dough can be refrigerated and rolled in hands before baking. This cookie is also made by creaming method, wherein butter and sugar is creamed together until well blended. Do not overmix. Add eggs and cream again. Mix all the dry ingredients such as flour, chocolate chips, chopped walnuts, baking powder together and fold it into the butter and sugar mixture. Drop on baking sheets and bake until still soft as the cookie tends to become crisp when it cools down.	
Macaroon	This cookie can be flavoured with chocolate and nuts. Coconut and chocolate macaroons are among the most popular flavours in these cookies. These are made by cooking egg whites, sugar, and desiccated coconut or chocolate until warm. Small quantity of flour is added to the mixture and the mixture is dropped onto a greased tray with the help of a round nozzle. These cookies are baked at 180 °C for not more than 15 minutes. These cookies tend to be soft, when baked, but they get crisp after cooling. If over-baked, they become hard and chewy.	
Crunchy drop	This cookie is made by creaming method. Butter and sugar are creamed until fluffy. Eggs are added one by one until fully incorporated. Dry ingredients such as flour, baking soda, and baking powder are alternately folded in, along with milk and mixed together. Chopped walnuts, dates, glazed cherries, and chopped raisins are added into the mixture, which is dropped onto cornflakes and coated with them. It is then baked on a baking sheet. The cookies spread and the cornflakes give a crackled effect to the cookies.	
Florentine	These are one of the classical cookies that are finished with a zigzag design of melted chocolate on top. For the mixture, butter and sugar, honey and double cream are cooked to a strong boil at 115°C. Thereafter, it is removed from the heat source and other ingredients such as flour, and candied fruits (orange, black currants, cherries, and sliced almond flakes) are added. The batter is then dropped onto a baking sheet while it is hot or else it will become very stiff when cooled.	

(Contd)

Table 16.2 *(Contd)*

Cookie	Description	Photograph
Florentine	After the cookies are baked, they are pulled back together to a round shape with the help of a round cookie cutter and allowed to cool down. Melted chocolate is spread on the flat side of the cookie and given a zigzag design with the help of a comb.	
Amaretti	It is a famous Italian cookie made by combining sugar, egg whites, almond powder, and corn flour until a thick paste is obtained. The paste is then dropped onto a greased and floured baking tray and baked at 200°C for 6–7 minutes or until light golden brown colour. These cookies are traditionally packed in special plastic sheets inscribed with the name *amaretti*.	
Rock cake	This is known as rock cake because of its appearance. This cookie originated in Great Britain. To make these cookies, butter and sugar are creamed together until they are fluffy. Eggs are added one by one and dry ingredients such as flour, baking powder, baking soda, milk, dried and candied fruits, and spices such as cinnamon, nutmeg, and cloves are added and the cookie is dropped onto the greased surface and pressed down with the fork. The top is dusted with sugar and cinnamon mixture and the cookie is baked until golden brown.	
Anzac biscuits	These biscuits are very popular in Australia and New Zealand. They are made by creaming butter and brown sugar. Sweeteners, such as honey and golden syrup, are boiled and added to the mixture along with desiccated coconut, soda bicarbonate, rolled oats, and flour. The cookie is then dropped onto a baking sheet and rolled in oats before baking.	

Piped Cookies

As the name suggests, these cookies are piped through a piping bag or piping tube onto a baking tray. The dough for this cookie has to be of right consistency. If the dough is too thick, then it will be difficult to pipe through a bag and if it is too soft, then it will spread too much while baking. Designs can be given by choosing the kind of nozzle. The top of the cookie can be garnished with nuts, candied fruit, etc. before baking. One can pipe stars, rosettes, or straight ridged lines through various kinds of nozzles. Some common piped cookies are described in Table 16.3.

Table 16.3 Examples of piped cookies

Cookie	Description	Photograph
Anisette	Also known as anise cookie, this is a famous cookie from Switzerland. It is made by whipping eggs or egg whites with sugar until thick and creamy. Aniseed and flour is folded in and the mixture is piped onto a baking sheet using a plain nozzle. The mixture is then dusted with castor sugar and allowed to dry for an hour. These are then baked at 180°C for around 5 minutes or else the cookie will become hard and chewy.	

(Contd)

Table 16.3 *(Contd)*

Cookie	Description	Photograph
Butter cookie	This cookie originated from Holland, which is one of the producers of best quality dairy products. Butter cookie is the most commonly prepared cookie in hotels. It can be piped in various shapes and sizes by choosing the appropriate nozzles. They can also be garnished with various items, such as almond halves, glazed fruit, jam, seeds such as caraway, fennel, and carom (*ajwain*), before baking. The dough is made by creaming method. Butter and sugar are creamed together until fluffy. Eggs are added one by one and creamed. Flour and flavourings are mixed lightly with hand and the cookie is piped through a nozzle into shapes such as rosettes, swirls, and long sticks. If the mixture is too stiff to force through the piping bag, then one can add egg whites to the batter to make it soft.	
Langues de chat	Also known as cat's tongue, they are often confused with lady-finger biscuit (see *Savoiardi*). Cats tongue is prepared by creaming butter and icing sugar until fluffy. Egg whites are incorporated in the mixture and creamed well. Flour is folded in to prepare a thick batter. It is then piped through a round nozzle with an opening of 6–8 mm on a silicon mat. It is piped around 5–6 cm long. When it is baked, the mixture spreads to yield a cookie that is thin, flat, and crisp. The shape resembles the tongue of a cat and hence the name. This cookie can be used as decoration on the sides of cakes and can also be used as a garnish for ice cream sundaes and *coupes*.	
Savoiardi	It is also known as ladyfinger biscuit because of its shape, colour, delicate structure and taste. This cookie is made by sponge method. Egg yolks and whites are stiffly beaten, along with castor sugar until creamy and fluffy. Dry ingredients such as flour and corn flour are sifted together and folded in carefully. The mixture is piped through a round nozzle of 10–12 mm diameter and 5–6 cm long. Icing sugar is dredged over each biscuit before baking. This helps to form a crisp layer on top of the biscuit, which prevents it from becoming soggy. It is baked at 200°C until creamy white colour. *Savoiardis* are used in making the famous Italian dessert *tiramisu* or for decorating cakes, or as a garnish for ice creams and sundaes.	
Spritz	This cookie is also made by creaming method. Marzipan and small quantity of eggs in the recipe are creamed until a smooth paste is obtained. Softened butter is added to the mixture and creamed again with addition of the rest of the eggs. Flour is folded in and the cookie is piped into a baking sheet through a star shaped nozzle into flowery pattern. The cookie can be garnished with candied fruit or nut before baking.	

Hand-rolled Cookies

These types of cookies are usually made with stiff dough such as sweet paste dough, short-crust dough, and salt dough. If the cookie dough is soft, then put it in the refrigerator to obtain stiffness. Hand-rolled cookies are shaped into rounds between the palms and then put on the baking sheet. These can be pressed further with help of a fork to add a design as in case of *melting moments* cookies. Table 16.4 highlights some common hand-rolled cookies.

Table 16.4 Types of hand-rolled cookies

Cookie	Description	Photograph
Snicker doodles	These are thin flat cookies that originated in Germany. They are made by creaming method. Butter and sugar are creamed together along with eggs. Dry ingredients such as flour, baking powder, and cream of tartar are folded in the mixture. It is allowed to rest in the refrigerator for an hour. Small balls of dough are pinched and rolled between the hands. They are then rolled into sugar and cinnamon mixture and baked at 180°C. The crackled texture of this cookie is much desired.	
Parkins	These biscuits are quite popular in Great Britain and are also known as Victorian Parkin biscuits. Flour and spices such as cinnamon and ginger are sifted together and mixed along with oatmeal. Treacle or golden syrup is warmed, along with sugar and butter and added to the dry ingredients. Baking soda is dissolved in milk and added to the mixture and blended together to obtain a soft dough. They are then pinched and rolled between the palms and placed on the baking tray. These are then flattened and washed with eggs. A split almond is placed in the centre and the biscuits are baked at 180°C until crisp.	
Sweet paste cookies	Sweet paste is one of the most common pastes that are used for making various types of cookies. The basic dough can be flavoured and coloured as per choice of flavours and moulded into various shapes and baked. Sweet paste can be rolled between palms and flattened before baking. The top surface can be brushed with egg whites and rolled in various toppings, such as granulated sugar, brown sugar, and desiccated coconut, and baked until golden brown.	
Melting moments	Soft and crumbly, melting moments are popular cookies. These are made by combining flour and custard powder with butter and sugar. It is made by creaming method, wherein the fat is creamed along with sugar until fluffy. Dry ingredients such as flour, custard powder, and baking powder are folded in and the dough is rested in the refrigerator for at least one hour. The dough is pinched and rolled between the palms and flattened with the help of a fork. It is baked until light brown in colour. *Note:* These cookies need to be stored carefully as they are very crumbly.	
Crescents	These cookies are named after their moon shape. Crescents can be shaped from sweet paste or any other soft dough. The dough is rolled into a small ball and then rolled on a floured surface to form a log that is tapered from both the sides. It is then arranged like a crescent or semi-circle and baked.	

(Contd)

Table 16.4 (*Contd*)

Cookie	Description	Photograph
Pretzel fondant	This cookie is made by combining flour, sugar, butter, and eggs together to form soft dough. Small balls are pinched away from the dough and rolled in the shape of a rope and given the classical pretzel shape. The top surface is brushed with egg and dredged with nib sugar and baked until golden brown. After the cookies are baked, fondant can be drizzled over to give it the sweet taste and appearance.	
Ginger snap	This cookie can also be made by piped method or the dough can be chilled in a refrigerator and then shaped and baked. Classically, ginger snaps are made by creaming butter, molasses, and sugar until a thick paste is obtained. Baking soda is mixed in water or milk and added to the mixture. Lastly, the flour is folded in. The dough can now be piped or left in the refrigerator to cool. The cookie is rolled between hands and then put on a baking tray. Flatten the cookies before baking at 180°C until golden brown.	
Nan khatai	This is a very famous cookie made in India. It is made by creaming equal quantities of vegetable shortening with powdered sugar. Flour is added along with small amount of curd and green cardamom seeds. The flour is very lightly added to the creamed mixture to avoid overmixing. The dough is then shaped between hands and baked until light creamy in colour. This cookie is very soft and crumbly and should be handled carefully.	

Cutter-cut Cookies

These cookies are made by rolling the dough to a desired thickness and then cutting it with cutters of required shape. These cookies are much more symmetric and look neat as they are cut with cutters. The choice of rolling or shaping with hands is purely the chef's choice as it affects the final texture and the look of the cookie. Some cookies containing raisins and candied fruits cannot be cut with cutters as it becomes difficult to cut the cookie if the raisin comes in the way. In such cases, the dough is moulded in hands and baked. Some common cutter-cut cookies are described in Table 16.5.

Table 16.5 Some examples of cutter-cut cookies (see also Plate 16)

Cookie	Description	Photograph
Bannocks	These famous cookies are from Scotland. To make these cookies, dry ingredients such as oats, flour, baking powder, and soda bicarbonate are combined in a large mixing bowl. Water and sugar are warmed until 50°C and mixed along with softened butter and dry ingredients to form soft dough. The dough is rested in refrigerator and then pinned out at least 5 mm thick. Dock and cut into round circles with a cookie cutter. Bake at 200°C for 10 minutes or until golden brown.	

(*Contd*)

Table 16.5 (Contd)

Cookie	Description	Photograph
Shortbread	Also from Scotland, this cookie is very soft and crumbly. Traditionally, it is made without any eggs. Butter and sugar are creamed and mixed very lightly with flour and corn flour. Since this dough is tough to roll out, it is pressed onto special moulds and then baked. But in modern applications, egg is added to the mixture to form soft dough. It is then rolled out and cut with a rectangle cutter and baked.	
Bull's eye	This cookie is made by using sweet paste, which is rolled to 4mm thickness and cut with a round cutter. Place half of the cut cookies on the baking tray and the other half in refrigerator for 30 minutes. When chilled, cut out the centre with a smaller cutter to form a ring. Bake at 180°C till golden brown. Now place the ring over the flat cookie base and fill the centre with boiled raspberry jam.	
Bolero	This cookie is made by rubbing flour and butter together to resemble breadcrumbs. Then other ingredients such as almond powder, sugar, and eggs are mixed lightly to form dough. The dough should be refrigerated for at least 15 minutes before rolling out to 4 mm thickness. It is cut with a round cutter, washed with egg, sprinkled with nib sugar, and baked until golden brown.	
Derby cookie	This cookie is made by rubbing flour and butter together to resemble fine powder. Then a well is made in the centre and sugar and eggs are poured in the well and mixed along with the flour and black currants to obtain a smooth paste. Care should be taken not to overmix the paste. Refrigerate until firm and roll to 4 mm thickness. Cut with fluted cutter and place on a baking tray. Egg wash the top and sprinkle with castor sugar before baking.	
Nice biscuit	This biscuit comes from France and usually comes packaged with an inscription of the word 'nice'. To make the biscuits, sift the dry ingredients such as flour, corn flour, fine desiccated coconut, and soda bicarbonate together. Dissolve ammonium carbonate into milk and keep aside. Cream the icing sugar and butter and fold in the dry ingredients, golden syrup, and milk and combine to form smooth dough. Pin out the dough and cut into rectangular shape using a fluted cutter. Place on the baking tray, wash with egg and sprinkle surface with granulated sugar and bake at 200°C.	
Shrewsbury biscuit	This is a famous biscuit from Great Britain. To prepare this cookie, rub flour and butter together to form a texture of bread crumbs. Make a well in the centre and combine eggs, sugar, and cinnamon in the well working with fingers from inside out to incorporate the dry ingredients to form a smooth paste. Refrigerate the paste until it is ready to be rolled out. Roll out the dough to 4 mm thickness and cut with a 2-inch plain cutter and bake the cookies at 200°C until creamy white in colour.	

Bar Cookies

These types of cookies are shaped in bars or long ropes or pipes and then baked till half done. Then the cookies are sliced to the required thickness while the dough is still warm and placed again on the baking sheets and baked until crisp. This type of baking is also known as baking twice or *biscotti* in Italian. Sometimes, the *biscotti* is frozen and then sliced on a meat slicer to obtain very thin pieces that are baked till crisp and served with coffee or as garnish with ice creams and sundaes. Some common bar cookies are described in Table 16.6.

Sheet Cookies

Many chefs confuse these cookies with the bar cookies described earlier. There are various methods of preparing this type of cookie. In some cases, the dough is baked in sheets and cut later, while in some cases, they are lined on a tray and the topping is spread onto the base before being baked. Most of the popular sheet cookies are made by this method. Some popular sheet cookies are described in Table 16.7.

Table 16.6   Common bar cookies

Cookie	Description	Photograph
Raisin spice bars	This is not a perfectly shaped cookie as the dough is very soft to handle. It is made by combining butter, sugar, eggs, molasses, flour, spices such as cinnamon, cloves, and ginger, baking soda, and soaked and drained raisins. The dough is sticky when made. It should be left in a refrigerator to chill and then shaped into long bars and baked for 10 minutes at 180°C. Remove and cut into 8 mm thick bars and bake again at 180°C for another 7–8 minutes or golden brown.	
Biscotti	This is a broad term used for biscuits baked twice in the earlier times. There can be varieties of flavours and combinations in a *biscotti*, which is popular throughout Europe and North America. In making *biscotti*, the sponge method is followed. Eggs, sugar, and a pinch of salt are mixed over double boiler until all the sugar has dissolved. The mixture is then whipped until it becomes creamy and light. Thereafter, vanilla, lemon, and orange zest, are folded in along with flour, baking powder and almonds. The mixture is thick and sticky and not flowy as for a sponge. It is then shaped into logs and brushed with eggs. Bake at 160°C for 30 minutes or until golden brown. Remove and let it cool slightly. Slice diagonally to required thickness and length and bake again at 130–140°C until toasted or dry. Store in airtight boxes to retain the crispness.	

Table 16.7 Types of sheet cookies

Cookie	Description	Photograph
Bee sting	It is a very popular cookie from Germany made from yeast leaved dough known as *kuchen* dough. The dough is smooth and is made from flour, sugar, eggs, butter, and milk. It is sheeted to 4 mm thickness and spread on a baking sheet. The bee sting mixture is prepared by cooking butter, sugar, honey, heavy cream, almond flakes, and chopped almonds. The mixture is allowed to cook until it leaves the sides of the pan. It is then poured on top of the prepared *kuchen* dough. It is then allowed to proof for 30 minutes and baked at 180°C for 30 minutes. When it is cool enough, it is cut into squares and served. The bee sting cookies can also be sandwiched along with vanilla flavoured cream.	
Almond bars	This cookie is made by sheeting out the sweet paste to 4 mm thickness and spreading it on a baking sheet. Dock the sweet paste and bake blind. Now combine cream, sugar, honey, and almond slices in a heavy bottom pan and cook until the mixture starts to leave the side of the pan. Spread the mixture on to the prepared sweet paste base and bake for another 10 minutes at 180°C. As soon as the cookie is cool, cut into rectangular shapes.	
Brownie	Brownie batter is a unique one. It can be baked into a cake or dropped onto a baking sheet to prepare brownie cookies. (Refer Chapter 11 on the basic batter for brownies). One method of preparing a brownie cookie is to spread the batter on a baking sheet and bake until fudgy. Cut into bars when cooled down.	
Honey bee	The procedure for making honey bee cookies is the same as for almond bars. The only difference is that these have candied fruits and black currants in addition to the almond slices.	
Toscani	This cookie comes from the Tuscany region in Italy and hence the name. To prepare this cookie, base and topping are separately prepared as in case of all bar cookies. The unique base of this cookie is made by creaming marzipan and butter together. Eggs are slowly incorporated along with flour and the mix is spread onto a baking sheet and baked till half done. The topping is prepared by boiling butter, sugar, liquid glucose, flaked almonds, and water for around 2–3 minutes. The mixture is now spread onto half baked base and then baked at 180°C until cooked. The cookie should be cut into small squares while it is warm or else the sugar mixture will set hard. When it cools completely, dip the cookie into melted chocolate and serve.	
Nut squares	This cookie is made by creaming method as in case of pound cake. The batter of pound cakes is spread onto a thin sheet on a baking tray and is sprinkled with a generous topping of chopped pecan nuts, walnuts, and almond slices, and cinnamon powder. It is then baked at 180°C. It is cut into squares and served and hence the name.	

Frozen and Cut Cookies

As the name suggests, this cookie is shaped into logs or square bars and sliced when frozen. Such methods are adopted for various reasons such as the dough is too soft to handle or to give it shape, or to save on time of sheeting the dough when it is chilled, as this facilitates cutting with a cutter. The most common way of preparing such cookies is by using sweet paste. One can mix various nuts and flavourings into the sweet paste and roll it into logs or squares and then freeze them. They are then sliced to 7 mm thickness and arranged on baking sheets. Slicing the cookie in this manner, results in evenly sliced nuts which gives it a good appearance. Some commonly prepared cookies with this method are described in Table 16.8.

Table 16.8 Examples of frozen and cut cookies (see also Plate 16)

Cookie	Description	Photograph
Sable	This popular cookie from Switzerland is prepared by creaming butter, icing sugar, and vegetable shortening until creamy. Flour and egg whites are folded in until a thick paste is obtained. The paste is chilled in a fridge until it can be rolled into logs. After shaping logs of 1-inch diameter, they are frozen for at least an hour or until they are ready to be sliced. The logs are then brushed with egg whites and rolled in castor sugar before being cut into 5 mm thickness. The cookies are baked until golden brown at 200°C.	
Pinwheel	This cookie is also made with sweet paste. One part of the sweet paste is mixed with cocoa powder to make chocolate sweet paste. To prepare pinwheel cookies, roll out the white sweet paste to 3 mm thickness and brush with egg whites. Sheet the chocolate sweet paste to 3 mm thickness and place on top. Roll the sheet to form a log of 1-inch diameter. Freeze for an hour and then slice to 4 mm thickness and bake at 180°C until cooked.	
Chequered	This cookie is made by using sweet paste. One part of the sweet paste is mixed with cocoa powder to make chocolate sweet paste. To prepare chequered cookies, roll out the white sweet paste to 1 cm thickness and brush with egg whites. Sheet the chocolate sweet paste to 1 cm thickness and place on top. Refrigerate for an hour until firm. Now cut into half and sandwich again with help of an egg white to yield a sheet of 4 layers alternating with dark and white sweet paste. Refrigerate again and then slice into 1 cm thickness and lay flat on a tray. Brush with egg white and place another sheet on top in such a way that the white covers the dark to create a chequered pattern. Repeat the process until there are four sheets. Roll another sweet paste sheet of 1mm thickness and brush with egg white. Place the prepared square log onto the sheet and roll so that it is encased in the sheet from all sides. Freeze for an hour and then slice to 4mm thickness and bake at 180°C until cooked.	

(Contd)

Table 16.8 (Contd)

Cookie	Description	Photograph
Cressini	A popular cookie from Italy, *cressini* is prepared by freezing the dough. To prepare this cookie, combine flour, icing sugar, butter, and egg yolks to form pliable dough. It is then rolled to logs and then flattened from all sides to make a square log. Freeze for an hour and cut into 5 mm thick slices and bake at 180°C. When baked, this cookie is often decorated with spots of coloured fondant.	
Friggies	This cookie prepared by creaming method. Vegetable shortening and butter are creamed together along with sugar and mixed with peanut butter. Eggs are incorporated one by one until the mixture is smooth and creamy. Dry ingredients, such as flour, baking soda, pinch of salt, and lemon zest are mixed and the dough, is rolled into logs and frozen for an hour or until firm. They are sliced into 4 mm thick slices and docked with a fork three times in a straight line to create a pattern of 12 dots. The slices are baked at 180°C until golden brown.	
English tea cookie	This cookie is popularly eaten during tea time and hence the name. To prepare the dough for this cookie, combine flour along with salt and mix together. Butter and granulated sugar are creamed until creamy. Add egg yolks, lemon juice, and zest and cream again. Add shredded coconut and flour mixture to form soft dough. Chill the dough in refrigerator if it is too soft to handle. Roll into logs and freeze again in refrigerator. Cut into 3 mm thick slices and bake for 15 minutes at 180°C. This cookie is sometimes dipped half in melted chocolate as well.	

Stencil Cookies

As the name suggests, these cookies are made by spreading in thin sheets on a baking tray. Since these cookies are made using very soft batters that spread very thin on the sheet and can lose shape, they are spread on to a sheet with the help of stencil (Fig. 16.1). Such stencils can also be handmade by cutting desired shapes, such as square, round, star, and flower, on a cardboard. Most of these types of cookies are used as a garnish or as an accompaniment with ice creams and sundaes. These cookies are also rich in butter content that helps in the spread.

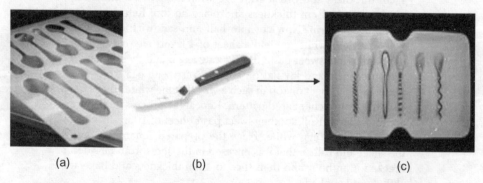

(a)　　　　　　　　　(b)　　　　　　　　　(c)

Fig. 16.1 Making stencil cookies (a) stencil of spoon (b) offset spatula to spread easily (c) baked cookies

Preparation

To prepare stencil cookies, use a *silpat* or silicone paper. Place the stencil on a baking sheet and spread the cookie batter with the help of offset spatula. Lift the stencil and prepare another cookie and keep repeating the process until the sheet is full. The cookie can be topped with various toppings, such as sliced almonds, and sesame seeds, as per the recipe before baking.

Some of these cookies can also be shaped into curls and curves as they are soft when taken out from the oven and usually set into brittle texture upon cooling. This property of the cookie makes it a wonderful garnish. Some common stencil cookies are described in Table 16.9.

Table 16.9 Stencil cookies

Cookie	Description	Photograph
Walnut Duchess	This is a famous cookie from Germany. In this case, the egg whites and sugar are whipped to a meringue, and chopped walnuts and sifted corn flour is added to the mix. Melted hot butter is folded in last and the cookie is spread in an oval shape on a stencil and baked at 180°C until baked. Two cookies are sandwiched together with nougat paste and the top is covered with melted covertures and garnished with a half walnut.	
Almond rolls	This cookie is made by mixing almond powder, flour, and icing sugar along with egg whites until a smooth paste is obtained. The cookie batter can be flavoured with lemon zest. It is then spread through a round stencil and baked until golden brown. The cookie is rolled around a thin rolling pin to form a cylindrical shape.	
Sesame *touille* cookies	This cookie is made by mixing flour, sugar, and nutmeg, along with beaten egg whites. Then sesame seeds are added to the paste and mixed well till a smooth batter is obtained. It is then spread onto a sheet using a triangle shape stencil and sprinkled with more sesame seeds before baking. The cookie can be given any shape when it is just taken out from oven.	
Ginger snap	This cookie (also discussed in Table 16.4) is made by cooking honey, sugar, and butter until it comes to a boil. Flour and ginger powder are added and cooked for around one minute. The cookie is now spread thinly on a baking sheet and baked. The resulting cookie is full of holes and makes an attractive garnish. One can prepare ginger snaps in various shapes.	
Biarritz cookie	This cookie is almost similar to the almond cookie and made by grinding sugar and almond together until a fine powder is obtained. The powder is mixed with egg whites and creamed further until a smooth paste is obtained. The paste is now spread on a baking sheet with the help of a stencil and baked. The cookie is cooled until it becomes crisp. Spread the bottom of the cookie with melted chocolate.	

(Contd)

Table 16.9 (Contd)

Cookie	Description	Photograph
Richelieu	This is a very famous cookie from France made by whisking egg whites with sugar until a thick meringue is obtained. Ground almond powder and flour is mixed with the meringue. The mixture is then spread onto a baking sheet using an oval-shaped stencil. When baked and cooled, two cookies are sandwiched together using a praline flavoured *ganache* and then dipped in milk couverture. This cookie can also be classified as a sandwich cookie.	

Sandwich Cookies

As the name suggests, these cookies are baked separately and then sandwiched together with a choice of fillings. The fillings could be butter cream, chocolate *ganache*, nut pastes, or even jam. Some of the cookies discussed in this section have classical fillings as described, but chefs can be creative and decide on their own fillings. Though one can prepare sandwich cookies by using any type of cookie and filling, some of the classical sandwich cookies are described in Table 16.10.

Table 16.10 Sandwich cookies

Cookie	Description	Photograph
Duchess cookie	This cookie from France is prepared by whisking egg whites with sugar until a stiff meringue is obtained. Ground hazelnut powder is folded in the mixture and the batter is piped from small rods onto a baking sheet and then baked. When the cookies have cooled down, they are sandwiched with praline-flavoured hazelnut *ganache*.	
Pischinger	It is a popular Swiss cookie made from sweet paste. Sweet paste is rolled to 3 mm thickness and then cut with a round cutter and baked until golden brown. When cool enough, the cookies are sandwiched with chocolate praline nougat. The cookie is then dipped in tempered chocolate and garnished with a piece of roasted hazelnut in centre.	
Taragona	This cookie from France is made by creaming butter and sugar until fluffy. Egg yolks are then added and the mixture is creamed until pale in colour. Sifted flour, cocoa powder, hazelnut powder is folded into the mixture, along with a small amount of milk until a smooth paste is obtained. The paste is rested in a refrigerator until it is ready to be rolled out. Once rolled thinly, the cookies are cut with a round cutter and baked until cooked. Thereafter, they are sandwiched with vanilla *couverture*.	
Zurich nuts	This famous cookie from Switzerland is made by creaming butter and sugar and then combining with eggs until the mixture is smooth but not fluffy. Flour and ground almond powder are added to the mixture and mixed until a smooth texture is obtained. *Note:* Do not overmix, as the cookies will lose their short properties.	

(Contd)

Table 16.10 (Contd)

Cookie	Description	Photograph
Zurich nuts	Pipe the cookie mixture with a star shaped nozzle into a long pipe and bake to a golden brown. When cold, sandwich the cookies with nougat paste and dip the tops in a melted *couverture.*	
Chocolate kisses	This French cookie has a strong Italian influence. Italian meringue is prepared and melted chocolate couverture is carefully folded in. The mixture is then piped into small round bulbs through a plain round tube and baked at a temperature of 160°C for 30 minutes. The cookies are sandwiched together with vanilla flavoured chocolate *ganache.*	

Festive Cookies

Western festivals or celebrations are incomplete without cookies. These are popular tidbits that have found their way into all cuisines cutting across cultures. Festivals are special occasions that provide an opportunity for traditional cooks and chefs to showcase their culinary skills. Thus, we have a wide variety of cookies being made for Christmas, Easter, Halloween, etc. Some of the classical cookies that are prepared on various festive occasions are described in Table 16.11.

Table 16.11 Cookies for festive occasions (see also Plate 16)

Cookie	Description	Photograph
Basler Läckerli	This Swiss cookie is typically prepared on Christmas. Honey and sugar is warmed and dry ingredients such as flour, cinnamon, baking powder, chopped candied fruits, nibbed almonds, and lemon zest are mixed together to form a dough. The dough should be soft to handle and be rested in a refrigerator until it is firm to roll out. It is rolled out to 4 mm thickness and baked at 210°C until golden. While hot, the cookie is brushed with a hot sugar glaze. The sugar glaze is applied with a stiff brush and worked forward and backward until the glaze gives a grainy appearance. The cookie is cut into rectangles and served.	
Pizzelle	This popular Italian cookie is made for celebrating the festival of snakes also known as 'feast day of San Domenico'. According to folklore, a small village called Colcullo in Abruzo region of Italy was once swarmed with snakes forcing the people to leave. After the snakes were chased out, the people celebrated their return with wafer-thin cookies called *pizzelle,* which meant round and flat. This cookie is made in special pans that resemble waffle pans and are cooked on stove tops. Eggs and sugar are whipped together and melted butter is added to the mix. Sifted flour and baking powder are then folded in to make a batter of dropping consistency. The mixture is placed in a mould (like flat pan) that closes like a waffle batter machine. The cookie is cooked on the stove top, until crisp.	

(Contd)

Table 16.11 (Contd)

Cookie	Description	Photograph
Spekulaas	This popular cookie from Holland is prepared by creaming method. Butter and sugar are creamed together until just smooth and not fluffy. Eggs, spices such as cardamom, cloves, and cinnamon powder are mixed along with flour and lemon zest to form dough. This cookie is usually made in moulded style. The dough is pressed onto special wooden *spekulaas* moulds and then demoulded and placed on baking sheets. Designs are embossed on it with special instruments.	
Ginger bread	This cookie is popularly made during Christmas by warming honey, sugar, and butter and mixing with rye flour, gingerbread spice, eggs, and molasses. The dough is left to mature for at least 12 hours before it can be rolled out and cut into different shapes. The cookie is glazed with hot sugar syrup. There are many recipes of preparing gingerbread. Its dough can be used for making cookies as also for making tiles that can be used for preparing gingerbread houses and other Christmas figurines.	
Cinnamon stars	This cookie is a German recipe popularly made during Christmas. Ingredients such as ground almond powder, egg whites, marzipan, granulated sugar, cinnamon, and flour are mixed together to form a firm dough and rolled out to at least 6mm thickness. Stiffly prepared meringue is spread in a thin layer on top of the rolled dough and cut with a special cutter known as cinnamon star cutter. The cutter is designed like a tong and helps in releasing the cookie after being cut. The cookie is briefly baked in the oven (180°C for around 6–7 minutes only) or until the meringue turns beige in colour.	
Brunsli	It is a popular cookie from Germany made usually on Christmas. The dough is made by combining almond powder, icing sugar, melted dark chocolate, egg whites, cinnamon powder, and orange essence. It is rolled out by dredging with castor sugar to 6mm thickness and cut with clover shape cutters and baked for 6–7 minutes only.	
Pertikus	This popular cookie from Switzerland is also usually made on Christmas. The dough is made by creaming butter and sugar until soft and then mixing it with flour, egg whites, cinnamon, nutmeg and hazelnut powder. It is soft dough. The cookies are piped into horseshoe shape with the help of a star-shaped nozzle and baked until golden brown.	

USES OF COOKIES

Cookies and biscuits have many uses in the pastry kitchen. They can be used as a base for cakes and pastries or served as an accompaniment with tea and coffee. Cookies are also commonly served as amenities in the guestroom. (Amenities are add-on facilities given to the guests as part of the package.) These could range from shampoo and soaps

Fig. 16.2 Presentations of cookies as amenities

to arrangement of fruits and canapés in a room. These facilities are not directly charged to the guests but are built in the guest's package. Cookies are the most preferred choice as an amenity, as these do not require any refrigeration and can stay for a few days in the room. Care should be taken to serve cookies that do not get too soggy over a period of time. Cookies are arranged on various kinds of platters and placed as room amenity. Figure 16.2 illustrates some cookie presentations that are served as an amenity.

In large hotels, the room-service section is usually responsible for placing the amenities in the guestroom. The front office tips the room service section on the rooms that would be occupied and need to be readied. The latter then coordinates with the pastry kitchen and gets the cookies picked up and placed in the room.

Apart from being placed as an amenity in the guestroom, cookies can also be sold in the hotel's pastry shop. These are usually sold by weight, but some large-size cookies are also sold per piece.

COMMON FAULTS IN COOKIE PREPARATION

The cookies discussed in this chapter are classical cookies that have unique texture and mouth feel. Some cookies are designed to be crisp, yet some taste good only when they are crumbly. Some cookies require spread, whereas some cookies need to be baked only for a few minutes. Any deviation from the standard product is termed as fault. Chefs can use the knowledge of faults to give a particular texture to the cookie or even correct a texture of a particular cookie. Some of the common faults that crop up in the preparation of cookies are discussed in Table 16.12.

Table 16.12 Common faults in making cookies

Faults	Causes
Cookies stick to pans	• It is important to grease the baking sheets and one has to be careful while doing so as excessive greasing will aid in spreading of the cookie. • Certain cookies need to be taken off the baking sheet while they are hot. If they are left on the pan to cool for a long time, they could stick. On the other hand, soft cookies should be allowed to cool down before they can be lifted off. • Too much sugar in the recipe also leads to cookies sticking to the pans. • Improper mixing of the cookie dough or batter could also result in sticking of cookies.

(Contd)

Table 16.12 (*Contd*)

Faults	Causes
Too crumbly	• Too much sugar in the recipe can make the cookie crumbly • Improper mixing of the cookie dough or batter could also result in crumbly cookies. • Too much of fat or shortening in the cookie dough can also make it crumbly. If you observe *nan khatai* cookie, you would understand what makes it crumbly. • Too much leavening and eggs could also result in crumbly cookies.
Cookie is very brittle and hard	• Too much flour in the dough could result in tough cookie. • Less quantity of fat in dough could result in hard cookie. • Dough mixed for too long will result in tough cookie as the gluten in the flour would develop hence, the cookie will lose its shortening properties. • There is less liquid. • Low baking temperature also aids in hard cookies.
Cookie does not get proper colour	• Baking temperature is too low. • Sugar is not enough in the recipe.
Cookie spreads too fast	• Low baking temperature aids in spread of cookies • Overgreased baking sheets leads to cookie spreading. • There is not enough flour in the dough or batter. • Too much creaming of the dough also leads to spread of cookies. • Too much liquid in the recipe also leads to spreading of the cookies
Cookie does not spread	• Baking temperature is high • There is too much flour in the dough or batter. • Less sugar in the recipe also prevents the cookie from spreading. • Insufficient greasing of pans does not allow the cookies to spread

The information in Table 16.12 is very important for the budding pastry chefs, as they can alter the textures of cookies by taking care of the faults. If chefs want a particular property in the product (cookie), they can use this knowledge to tailor their product accordingly.

SUMMARY

This chapter concludes our section on pastry. Here, we discussed the origin of cookies and biscuits and how they have transformed over the years. The earlier cookies were dry and were made from leftover batters or dough of breads. The main purpose of these goodies was to serve as an accompaniment with tea and coffee. Today, cookies are specially made for occasions using various instruments and techniques. Some of the cookies are individually decorated by using various icings and toppings such as fondants, chocolates, or sugar glazes.

In this chapter, we discussed various methods of preparing cookies such as straight method, creaming method, and sponge method. Apart from this, we also discussed various types of cookies such as drop cookies, where the moisture in the dough is regulated in such a manner that the batter forms a dropping consistency. The liquid ingredients used in cookie batter are usually eggs, and on rare occasions, milk is used. Piped cookies along with description and examples are explained in brief. The recipes of these cookies can be found in the CD. Many other cookies, such as hand-rolled cookies, rolled and cutter-cut cookies, bar cookies, sheet cookies, frozen and cut cookies, stencil cookies, sandwich cookies, and festive cookies, were also discussed, along with description and illustrations, so that the students can easily identify these products.

Chefs can be creative with preparation of cookies, as long as they are aware of the basic methods of preparation of cookies and also the knowledge of giving the required texture and mouth feel. Common faults that occur while making cookies are discussed along with tips on how the chefs can identify and rectify them.

KEY TERMS

Baking blind   It is a term used for denoting baking of a pastry shell without any filling.

Candied fruit   These are peels of fruits, such as orange, lemon, and ginger, steeped in sugar syrup and then allowed to mature until they are dry and crunchy.

Dacquoise   It is a type of sponge made from eggs, sugar, flour, and almond powder.

Dock   Dock means to prick the rolled or sheeted dough with a docker or fork to create small holes which prevents the dough from rising.

Fondant   It is an icing that is prepared by cooking sugar and liquid glucose with water to the soft ball stage and kneaded on an oiled marble slab until a smooth dough is obtained

Gingerbread spice   This is a mixture of ground spices, such as cloves, dry ginger, cinnamon, nutmeg, and cardamom, used for flavouring gingerbread dough and other Christmas specialities.

Glazed cherries   These are candied red cherries often used as garnish on cookies before baking.

Gluten   It is the protein present in flour that determines its strength.

Golden syrup   This is sweetened corn syrup marketed under various brand names.

Koekje   This is Dutch for little cake. It is believed that the term cookie originated from this word.

Kuchen dough   This is yeast-leavened dough from Germany used in preparation of bee sting cookies.

Ladyfinger biscuit   This is another name for Italian *savoiardi* biscuit.

Nougat paste   It is a paste obtained by grinding caramelized sugar and almonds. It is also known as nougat praline.

Offset spatula   This is a kind of flat palette knife that is bent at an angle.

Panis bicotus   It is Latin for bread cooked twice. The word is considered to be the origin of the term biscuit.

Pretzel   It is a German bread that has a criss-cross pattern that resembles the Nazi symbol.

Rye flour   It is a kind of flour made from rye seeds.

Tiramisu   It is an Italian creamy dessert made by using *mascarpone* cheese.

Treacle   It is a dark sweetened liquid obtained from sugar refining process.

CONCEPT REVIEW QUESTIONS

1. How did the word cookie originate?
2. What is the difference between a cookie and a biscuit?
3. How have cookies and biscuits evolved over the last few decades?
4. Describe the straight method of preparing cookies.
5. Describe creaming method of making cookies with some examples.
6. What is sponge method? What does it do to the cookie?
7. What points must be kept in mind while baking cookies?
8. Explain the principle of making drop cookies and give three examples.
9. Describe the florentine cookie and *Anzac* cookie.
10. Explain at least three types of piped classical cookies.
11. What is the difference between *langues de chat* and *Savoiardi*?
12. Explain the concept of hand-rolled cookies and examples of any three cookies made by this method.
13. What are cutter-cut cookies and what precaution should one follow while preparing such cookies?

14. Explain the difference between *Shrewsbury* biscuit and shortbread cookie.
15. Differentiate between a bar cookie and sheet cookie.
16. Explain the procedure of making a *biscotti*.
17. Describe *sable* cookie and explain the method for preparing it.
18. Explain the procedure of making chequered cookies.
19. What are stencil cookies? What is their importance?
20. Explain the concept of sandwich cookies.
21. What do you understand by the term festive cookies? Explain at least five kinds of festive cookies?

22. What is the role of cookies in hotels and restaurants?
23. What could be the possible causes if the cookie sticks to the baking sheet?
24. If the cookie is too crumbly, then what could be the possible reasons for the same?
25. How can you prevent the cookies from becoming brittle and hard?
26. If you do not want your cookie to get too much colour then what should you do?
27. If the cookie does not spread on the baking sheet, what could be the possible causes?
28. If you want your cookie to spread more, what could you do without altering the recipe?

PROJECT WORK

1. In groups of five, conduct a market survey of various pastry shops in the city and make a list of cookies and biscuits sold there. Using the knowledge given in the chapter, classify the cookies on its type and method of preparation. Discuss how you could alter the product to make it more appealing.
2. Divide yourself in groups of three. Select one common recipe amongst yourselves and apply all the faults listed in Table 16.12. Share your observation with the group and see how each fault affects the texture of the cookie.
3. In groups of five, prepare at least three festive cookies and present it to the other groups for tasting and evaluation.

Part IV

FOOD PRODUCTION MANAGEMENT

- *Production Management*
- *Research and Product Development*

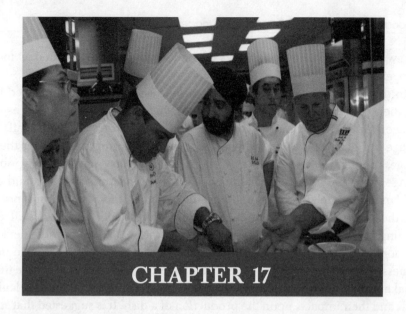

CHAPTER 17

PRODUCTION MANAGEMENT

Learning Objectives

After reading this chapter, you should be able to
- comprehend the difference between organizing a kitchen and kitchen organization
- organize a kitchen with regard to resources and manpower
- allocate people to various job roles and differentiate between a job description and job responsibility
- plan the duty rosters and annual leave planners for the staff
- appreciate the role of production planning in the kitchen
- forecast and budget for portions, equipment, and manpower
- compute cost of a menu with regard to portion costs and sales price
- convert a recipe from *x* number of portion to *y* number with constant or variable portion size
- prepare Gantt charts and comprehend their role in scheduling production
- exercise control over quality and quantity of production
- comprehend yield management and its importance
- calculate food cost percentage, waste percentage, price of the menu, and selling price of the menu by using particular formulas

INTRODUCTION

In the previous chapters, we learnt about different aspects of cooking and types of cuisines that are produced in hotels and restaurants. Whether it is a hotel or a stand-alone restaurant, apart from producing and selling food and services, a profit has to be made to sustain the business. Wherever production occurs, it automatically calls in for exercising control so that the profits are maximized and waste is eliminated or at best, minimized. This exercise of controlling production, organizing it, evaluating the need for new equipment, and better ways of production is simply termed as food production management.

In this chapter, we will discuss the various aspects that are managed by chefs other than their core competency, cooking. A chef needs to be a good cook as well as a great manager. Apart from being great cooks and role models for their staff, chefs need to manage the daily operations which start from purchasing to selecting the right quality, storage, production, and also waste management. Every stage of their job role includes managerial functions such as planning, organizing, staffing, directing, and controlling.

Planning in the kitchen is of utmost importance. If the operation is not well planned, then there would be guest complaints, loss of revenue, and also staff de-motivation. Planning in the kitchen calls for day-to-day planning, planning for the next day, and for a few months in advance. Apart from the managerial functions, chefs also need to act like businesspersons, understanding the bottom line and cost factors to enable the organization to make profits. So, it is important that chefs understand the financial calculations such as yields and their impacts upon the production of a dish. It is suggested that students refresh their knowledge by reading Chapters 2 and 3 of the book *Food Production Operations*. They should have a sound knowledge of various types of kitchens and staffing levels before reading this chapter.

KITCHEN ORGANIZATION

Organizing is a managerial function that involves bringing together the physical, financial, and human resources to achieve the goals of a large organization. To organize a kitchen in simple language would mean providing the kitchen with cooks, necessary tools and equipment to do the job, and raw materials required for the preparation of the menu.

Once this is clear in our minds, the first obvious step of organizing would be to list the activities that would be performed in the kitchen on a daily basis. These activities will differ from one food business to another because most of these activities will be based upon the type of catering establishment, the menu, and the skill set of the staff. Let us discuss a normal kitchen of a five-star establishment. As a head of the department, if you were to list the kind of work or activities that will be carried out in the kitchen, it would be as follows.

- Procuring, receiving, storing, and issuing raw materials
- Preparing of vegetables, meat, fish, etc. with regard to the menu and meal service
- Cooking and dispensing soups, salads, hot food, etc.
- Cooking and dispensing breads, desserts, chocolates, cookies, etc.
- Cooking specialized regional cuisines
- Cooking food for banquets, restaurant, etc.
- Dispensing food to guests
- Performing ancillary work such as cleaning and maintenance of equipment and area
- Preparing of food for staff

Apart from these activities, there could be many more tasks that may be carried out in a kitchen such as laying and clearing of buffets, dispensing amenities, creating buffet sculptures and showpieces.

The next step is to group or classify these activities into subgroups so that tasks can be performed efficiently. This is why we come across various departments in the kitchen, such as the larder kitchen, hot kitchen, bakery, room service, and satellite kitchens. The larder kitchen has been discussed in detail in Chapter 1 of this book while all the other kitchens have been discussed in Chapter 3 of *Food Production Operations.*

Every successful business has a defined set of people at various levels responsible for a set of objectives that they have to achieve. Once the departments are finalized, the next step is manpower planning or deciding on the number of people that would be required to do the job. This is generally done with the help of the human resource department (HRD) and decision-making in this regard is based on several factors such as the prior education and experience of the person and his/her skill level. Furthermore, duties are assigned to various people, following which responsibilities, authority, and power of delegation determine the level of each staffer in the organizational hierarchy. The first professional organizational structure in the kitchen was introduced by renowned nineteenth century chef Auguste Escoffier, who termed it as brigade system. It the most followed system in the modern hotels and restaurants till date. The organizational structure is also known as hierarchy and depends on factors such as volume and type of business. We have discussed the different hierarchical structures and responsibilities of staff in Chapter 2 of *Food Production Operations.*

Once the above is established, it is important that the standards are laid out and specified. The standards are clearly spelt out not only because we want consistent product, but it also acts as a guideline to know where we are now (current status) and where would we like to position our business (desired status). That is the reason why most successful businesses keep upgrading their standards. Standards also keep a check on quality and act as a tool for managers and staff to control costs and other related functions of cooking. Chapter 4 of the book *Quantity Food Production Operations and Indian Cuisine* provides a deeper insight into the recruitment process and manpower planning in a kitchen.

ALLOCATION OF WORK—JOB DESCRIPTION, DUTY ROSTERS

Allocation of work is one of the most important aspects of kitchen organization. It depends upon several factors such as skill levels of staff, type of business, and kind of operation. We have discussed the job descriptions of people at various levels of hierarchy in Chapter 3 in *Food Production Operations.* Management of people is broadly termed as personnel management and it becomes the responsibility of all the people who have a set of people directly reporting to them. It could be a manager or even a cook who has a few apprentices reporting to him/her. To control the set of people, it is important that the job description of each staffer is properly outlined. It is against these job descriptions that the managers set up key performance objectives and benchmarks to measure or appraise staff performance from time to time. Personnel management deals with the management of people at work and their interpersonal relationships. The main job role of the head chef in the kitchen is to create an atmosphere in which the people put in their best efforts and work towards achieving the common goal of the organization. The chef needs to be viewed as a role model, where he/she is always fair and just to their subordinates and rewards or praises in public but criticizes behind closed doors at all times.

The job descriptions at every level must be completely spelt out in black and white and handed over to the employee at the time of joining. By doing this, one can eliminate ambiguity about a job and each person knows exactly what to do and how he/she can advance to the next level of hierarchy. In other words, job descriptions can also act as a motivational tool for people working at any level.

Let us see the job description, responsibilities, and other duties of the executive chef and *chef de partie* to understand this in detail.

Executive Chef's Job Description

The task or job profile of an executive chef of a five-star facility generally includes the following points.

- To direct and guide the food production team in providing a consistent quality of food as per international standards, in order to achieve maximum level of customer satisfaction in an atmosphere of high employee morale.
- To organize and direct a team that delivers top quality food products, with a prompt, accurate, and personalized service, to achieve optimum level of customer satisfaction and profitability.

Key responsibilities

The main responsibilities of an executive chef include the following.

- To ensure prompt, efficient, and accurate service to all customers so as to achieve high level of guest satisfaction
- To set up kitchen and ensure maintenance according to international standards
- To monitor and control quantities, costs, and quality of supplies for the kitchen
- To prepare capital and operational budget for the year.
- To ensure that the employees adhere to hotel policies and standards.
- To conduct daily briefings to communicate necessary information. Controls pilferage and spoilage in order to cut down operational cost.
- To ensure cost effectiveness of resources (material and staff) and exercise control to achieve optimum profitability.
- To ensure that all staff in the department are fully trained through constant on-the-job training.
- To ensure attendance during behavioural and vocational training programmes, and personally conduct key training for employees in the department.
- To define organization of work within the department including assignments, time schedules, and vacations of staff.
- To ensure the quality of food preparation, as per organizational standards
- To ensure availability of stocks and raw ingredients by proper planning and coordination.
- To establish yields and methods of effective processing to reduce waste and maximize profits.
- To be responsible for the hygiene and cleanliness of kitchen areas, equipment, and staff.

- To analyses and monitor costs (material, energy, and staff) to ensure high profitability on a regular basis.
- To ensure that storage of raw material is according to international standards.
- To remain updated with market knowledge and trends.
- To ensure practice of hygiene and safety precautions as well as compliance with hotel and company policies by the kitchen staff through training.
- To decides on hiring, promotion, disciplinary action, and performance related pay for subordinates.
- To develop friendly relationship with customers.
- To actively collect customer feedback and initiate remedial action whenever required.

Key performance measures

Once the job descriptions are set, some key performance measures have to be clearly spelt out so that the person's performance can be evaluated. Some of the key performance measures for an executive chef would be as follows.

Food cost   The food cost needs to be maintained at the level decided by the organization. The healthy average food cost can be in the range of 20–25 per cent.

Department productivity   This is measured by profit and loss statements at the end of the year and how the department has functioned with regard to the budgets.

Attendance and punctuality   Too many unplanned leaves and absenteeism directly reflect upon the performance of an executive or a manager.

Going beyond the call of duty to satisfy customer needs   This can be measured through guest comment cards and feedback from internal customers.

Multi-functional   The executive chef needs to be multi-skilled and should be able to coach and mentor people in every aspect of kitchen.

Eye for detail   This can be measured by weekly rounds and inspection of the department.

Duty Rosters

There are many operational challenges in the kitchen; one of them is preparing the roster and allocation of staff to maximize the output in such a way that no personnel is overworked or stressed. Every manager or supervisor is responsible for preparing a list of staff that is allocated on duty, keeping in mind that they get an off-day as per the company policy. This list or document is called duty roster. The frequency of preparation of a duty roster could be weekly, fortnightly, or even monthly as decided by the in charge or human resource (HR) policies. Preparing duty rosters is an art and the person preparing it must give a lot of thought to the process before making one. The hospitality industry is very demanding when it comes to customer satisfaction. This would mean putting up a smile even in case of emergency at home or a child's birthday celebration at home if one's shift reliever does not turn up and the staffer ends up doing a double duty.

Planning Sheet for Duty Rosters

NAME	7:00 a.m.	8:00 a.m.	9:00 a.m.	10:00 a.m.	11:00 a.m.	12:00 noon	1:00 p.m.	2:00 p.m.	3:00 p.m.	4:00 p.m.	5:00 p.m.	6:00 p.m.	7:00 p.m.	8:00 p.m.	9:00 p.m.	10:00 p.m.	11:00 p.m.
Amman																	
Siraj																	
Madhav																	
Amrita																	
Sonant																	
Chong																	

Fig. 17.1 Planning sheet for duty rosters

Figure 17.1 depicts a sample planner of a duty roster that will enable you to see how many people are needed at a particular time of the day. There will be some point of time when you would need more staff on duty, while sometimes when the operation is not busy just one person might be needed on a shift. Nowadays, there are several software, which one can use effectively to prepare duty rosters. Managers can make one in Excel format on computers like the one shown Fig. 17.1.

Sourcing staff is another big challenge in the service industry today and one has to do with bare minimum resources. One has to effectively use the available staff for maximizing the output. In the planning sheet discussed above, one can easily plan the shifts depending upon the lean and busy times. In Fig. 17.1, we can see that six staffers are allocated to effectively cover an operation that runs breakfast, lunch, and dinner service. It is quite evident from this roster that this operation is busier during breakfast and dinner and does minimal à la carte business for lunch and has a buffet style of service for lunch which can be managed by two people.

Once this sheet is established, it will be easy to allocate the staff on weekly or monthly duty roster. Some shift timings are more important than others, so it is important that another staff is allocated to cover such shifts when the other person is rostered off on that day. In such a way, everyone gets a weekly off and everyone covers each other when they are off.

Figure 17.2 shows the format of a duty roster wherein the staff can know their weekly schedules and offs. In the duty roster (refer Fig. 17.2), everyone gets a weekly off. No staff is allocated for weekly off on Saturday as it is probably the busiest day of the week. Also when a person is rostered off, another person covers his/her shift, so that the operation remains unaffected.

Duty Roster							
M: 7 a.m.–4 p.m./BS: 11–3 p.m.; 7–11 p.m./M–BS: 7–10 a.m.; 3–7 p.m./EVE: 3–11 p.m.							
Name	Monday	Tuesday	Wednesday	Thursday	Friday	Saturday	Sunday
Amman	**OFF**	M	M	M	M	M	M
Siraj	M	**OFF**	BS	BS	BS	BS	BS
Madhav	M–BS	BS	**OFF**	M–BS	M–BS	M–BS	M–BS
Amrita	M–BS	M–BS	M–BS	**OFF**	EVE	M–BS	M–BS
Sonant	EVE	EVE	EVE	EVE	**OFF**	EVE	EVE
Chong	EVE	EVE	EVE	EVE	EVE	EVE	**OFF**

Fig. 17.2 Weekly roster

There is yet another duty roster planned for annual leaves, which is called leave planner. It allows the departments to plan out long leaves for the staff without affecting regular operations. The annual leave planning can be done in various ways. Usually, the staffers are advised to plan their leave in the lean months. This can change from the type of business to the location of business. Let us look at the annual leave planner format in Fig. 17.3 to understand this aspect.

> **CHEF'S TIP**
> Planning a roster can sometimes get complicated as employees want leave because of their religious festivals, ceremonies, and social obligations. Therefore, good planning would be to have a staff with various religious backgrounds, so that the staff members can cover up for each other during festive occasions.

If one plans the leave planner in this manner, it will be easy to give equal amount of leave to the staff members depending upon the business exigencies. It may be noticed that some staff has been given leaves at a stretch of 30 days while others have been given scattered leave such as 15 days at one time, and the rest on other dates. In many organizations, staffers are allowed to carry forward their annual leaves up to 75 days only, beyond which any extra leave would automatically lapse. However, as a rule, accumulation of leave should only be allowed if there are business exigencies. Sometimes large accumulated leaves of staff poorly reflect upon the planning of the manager or the department head.

PRODUCTION PLANNING AND SCHEDULING

In the last two years in your professional studies and training, you have already learnt the basic principles of cookery and practically prepared various items in the food production sessions. It is expected that you must have spent adequate time in upgrading your knowledge about foods and beverages. It is up to you to make the best use of the available resources, which is one of the basic principles of management. You would have also been encouraged to ask questions, to plan, and to organize your time and facilities.

If you are prepared properly, the daily operations in a professional kitchen are well within your scope; they can quite easily be managed through careful planning and organization. This can only be achieved however, if you prepare in advance—it is absolutely pointless turning up on the final day and start planning for the production. Some items might require a pre-preparation that would involve soaking, fermenting, etc. which cannot be achieved if it was not planned earlier. It is thus important that for any kind of operation, the production is clearly planned out in advance, if you wish to achieve the level of success that is within your capabilities.

It is important that as a cook or even as a chef, you encourage your staff to use common sense at all times. Even if you are not an experienced cook, it is not hard to observe that something either feels or looks wrong. If in doubt, always seek answers to the doubts rather than going ahead blindly to make inevitable errors, which can so easily be avoided.

Before beginning production of the menu, it is important to make a menu specification sheet as shown in Fig. 17.4. This sheet acts as a tool for both production and service to plan out the operation. The sheet should be made for every menu, as it immediately tells us everything about a menu, such as the time taken for pick up of food, balance in the menu, and portion size. It helps us to organize resources such as crockery and other equipment required for the preparation.

Leave Planner

Name	January	February	March	April	May	June	July	August	September	October	November	December
Amman				1–15						1–15		
Siraj						1–30						
Madhav					1–15		1–15					
Amrita			1–30									
Sonant					15–30						15–30	
Chong							15–30				1–15	

Fig. 17.3 Leave planner

Menu	Key ingredient	Key flavourings	Method of cooking	Crockery	Portion size	P/UP time
Appetizers						
Roast vegetable organic salad	Pepper, artichoke, asparagus mixed leaves	Herb vinaigrette	Roasting	8-inch plate	80 g	5 mins
Smoked chicken Caesar salad	Chicken iceberg	Caesar dressing	Smoked	Pasta bowl	80 g	5 mins
Soups						
Minestrone	Beans, zucchini, potatoes, tomatoes, cauliflower, broccoli	Tomato and basil	Simmering, cartouche	Soup cup	120 ml	5 mins
Lamb *harira*	Lamb, beans, carrots, chickpea	Cumin	Simmering, sautéing	Soup cup	120 ml	5 mins
Main Course						
Penne with mushroom	*Penne*, assorted mushrooms	Parmesan cheese	Boiling, sautéing	Pasta bowl with under liner	140 g	10 mins
Eggplant *Parmigiano*	Eggplant, tomatoes, olives, parmesan cheese	Parmesan, tomato, basil	Baking, grilling	12-inch plate	140 g	10 mins
Penne with chicken and mushroom	*Penne*, assorted mushrooms, chicken	Parmesan cheese	Boiling, sautéing	Pasta bowl with under liner	140 g	10 mins
Grilled *bhetki*	*Bhetki*, zucchini, carrots, olives, tomatoes, baby potato	Olives, tomatoes, dill	Grilling, sautéing	12-inch plate	140 g	10 mins
Dessert						
Tiramisu	*Mascarpone*, eggs, coffee liqueur, sponge	Coffee and *mascarpone*	Steaming	Champagne saucer	70 g	5 mins
Fresh fruit platter	Grapes, papaya, pineapple, kiwi, apples, and pears			10-inch square plate	80 g	5 mins

Fig. 17.4 Menu specification sheet

Scheduling a production is not only about cooking of food, but it also involves planning for cooking equipment, resources, and even extra staff, if required. It is always a good idea to prepare a versatile chart called *Gantt chart* for this purpose. Gantt charts are plotting the allocated tasks against time. Such a chart provides the executive chef with a detailed structure of the event that you are planning to conduct. A sample of Gantt chart is provided in Fig. 17.5.

This chart is a sample Gantt chart, which is prepared for a menu of a starter, main course, and a dessert. The Gantt charts can be made for a single dish, or a menu, or even an event. Such formats allow plotting the tasks to be done on time scales, so that it can be used as an effective tool for planning a production.

PRODUCTION QUALITY AND QUANTITY CONTROL

After planning, organizing, and other managerial functions, it is important to monitor or evaluate the procedures and processes that are laid down in an organization. It is important to monitor the quality and quantities produced, as overproduction can not only lead to loss of revenue, but will also aid in fatigue of staff as well as faster wear and tear of machinery. Monitoring quality not only keeps the business in a healthy state , but act as a motivating tool not only for the staff and guests but also for the stakeholders.

Monitoring quality or controlling quality can be described as a continuous inspection which has to be undertaken throughout production and service. It is a process that takes place at the beginning as well at the end of the process. The check on quantity and quality must be done by the staffers themselves in the first place. If such a thing is only restricted to the chef or manager, it might result in a defective dish, which will result in loss of revenue as it cannot be served to the guests.

Generally, quality and quantity are measured at the following four most important points during the production.

At the receiving bay   The first check on quality and quantity is done at the time of ordering and receiving raw materials or ingredients. The food items must be weighed and received as per the quantity ordered. Quality as specified to the vendor at the time of signing a contract must be adhered to and under no circumstances one must receive a sub-standard quality of ingredients. Always remember that high quality ingredients produce high quality products and vice versa. In many contracts, there is a clause that if the supplier cannot supply the desired quality, then the hotel has the right to purchase the desired quality from the open market and in turn debit the cost to the supplier. This clause ensures that the supplier would deliver the items as mentioned in purchase specifications. Another aspect of quality management is to periodically review the procedures and specifications. It is also important to have proper methods of storage and control, so that the quality of ingredients received does not deteriorate due to improper storage and issuing procedures.

At the production bay   The chef has to ensure that the food is being prepared as per the planned production and by following standard recipes. Any deviation from the recipe

	11:00	11:30	12:00	12:30	01:00	LUNCH BREAK	02:00	02:30	03:00	03:30	04:00	05:00
Check the availability of ingredients, clean, and set up work table.												
Prepare sundried tomatoes for pesto and bake them on low heat												
Prepare ingredients for amuse bouche and let it hang till juice is extracted												
Prepare ravioli mixture												
Knead ravioli dough												
Sheet out ravioli and portion												
Prepare garnish for amuse bouche and appetizer												
Area clean and mise en place check												
Weigh ingredients for lemon curd, prepare lemon curd												
Ingredient and mise en place check												
Close for the day												

Fig. 17.5 Sample Gantt chart

will result in inconsistent quality as well as cost. Thus, chefs have to be very conscious at every stage of production and the most important of all of these is during the basic processing of meats and vegetables. Poor knife skills will not only give you a less yield for final product but will also impact upon the overall quality of food. Butchery is one such area where the chefs have to focus on knife skills and constantly monitor the yields to control the quality and quantity. We shall discuss more about yield management later in the chapter. They have to constantly improve the ways in which staff can work efficiently and deliver a consistent product. During the production process, each individual must be in sync with the goals and objectives of the department and chefs have to ensure that the staffers are provided with the right tools and equipment to produce quality with desired yield. Periodic inventories of food stores and refrigerators also act as a tool for checking quality and quantity of food and the kitchen team must understand the implications of over production and poor storage.

At the service bay   Quality does not stop at production, it is a continuous process. It is important to monitor the quality and quantity at the time of food service. Thus, the chef must taste and personally check every dish before it goes to the guests. At the time of presentation, the food must be presented as per the laid out standards such as portion size, presentation, accompaniments, etc. Right kinds of equipment such as measuring spoons and ladles should be used for effective portion control. If the portion size is too small, then the guest will feel that there is no value for money and on the contrary, if the portion size is too big, it will result in loss of revenue. Chefs must also periodically check the left overs in the guest's plate. This indicates if the guest enjoyed the food, if the portion was too big or small, and if there is anything on the plate that has not been eaten by the guests. This helps the chef to evaluate the quality assurance tests such as portion evaluation, yields, as well as recipe checks to ensure that the staff is following the standards.

At the garbage bay   This is one of the most neglected areas by the food service and production personnel and yet one of the most important when it comes to evaluating the production and wastage. Once in a while, chefs should check garbage disposal to monitor the wastage during production. This will give you an idea of what is being processed and how much is being wasted. Many hotels have a garbage sorting table, where the garbage is sorted to ensure the proper segregation of garbage into bio-degradable and recyclable products and also to ensure that no pilferage takes place.

FORECASTING AND BUDGETING

While planning a production, quantities to be made are done on the basis of approximation only depending upon the type of the day or any scheduled event. This judgment, which is a well-calculated guess, called *forecasting*. Whenever possible we shall not refuse a customer's request, it may therefore, be necessary to respond quickly to replenish stocks which have decreased beyond expectations. Certain dishes or products, however, cannot be replaced instantly. In that case, we will have to refuse if demand exceeds supply. But we should never refuse a request simply on the ground that the demand surpassed our forecasts. Forecasting can be done for various kinds of functions such as budgets, number of dishes to be prepared for a particular meal or event, staffing, etc.

We shall understand forecasting better with an example of a menu which is to be prepared for 32 covers (Exhibit 17.1) for an important event.

Forecast Production Numbers

The first step would be to establish forecasted production numbers. This forecasting would depend upon number of factors such as the following.

Type of clientele If the clientele is mostly vegetarian, then one would have to plan for more vegetarian salad.

Popularity of the dish If some dishes are speciality or popular, then they would sell more.

Past records Historical records give an indication as to how much of each dish would be sold.

Type of style of service The number of portions will differ from self service, à la carte service, fixed menu, etc.

Exhibit 17.1 A sample menu

MENU ONE

Roast vegetable and garden greens
Served tossed with herb vinaigrette
OR
Smoked Chicken Caesar salad
Crisp iceberg lettuce tossed with Caesar dressing and smoked chicken

Lamb Harira
Classical lamb and lentil broth from Morocco flavoured with cumin
OR
Minestrone
Traditional Italian soup with mixed vegetables and pasta, served with fresh bread drizzled with olive oil and garlic

Penne with Mushroom
Penne tossed with fresh mushrooms and cream sauce
OR
Penne with Chicken and mushroom
Penne tossed with fresh mushrooms, chicken and cream sauce
OR
Grilled Bhetki
Grilled Kokata *bhetki* served with sautéed vegetables
OR
Eggplant Parmigiano
Baked egg plant and tomatoes flavoured with basil and parmesan cheese

Tiramisu
An Italian dessert made with creamy mascarpone cheese and coffee liqueur
OR
Fresh Fruit Platter
Served with crème Chantilly

Table 17.1   Forecasted number of portions

Dish name	Production numbers
Roast vegetable salad	10
Chicken Caesar	30
Minestrone soup	25
Lamb *harira*	15
Eggplant *Parmigiano*	5
Penne with mushroom	10
Penne with chicken and mushroom	15
Grilled *bhetki*	10
Tiramisu	30
Fresh fruit platter	10

Since this is à la carte menu and the guests would choose their dish and keeping the above factors, a forecasted number of portions are done as shown in Table 17.1.

This menu is designed to accommodate approximately 32 covers. Actual bookings must be checked for each occasion. In spite of forecasting, there can be various factors that affect the actual sales of a dish. Thus, to avoid any last minute running around, an extra 10 per cent is produced which will allow for any problems, accidents, and choice. Flexibility in production is necessary, as it is difficult to be very accurate with the precise quantity included in some dishes.

Forecast portion numbers are indicated beside each dish in Table 17.6. These numbers are meant for general guidance and are not absolute. Production experience and sales history records would provide a closer guide for forecasting but can never be exact.

Computing the Cost of Menu

Computing the costing of menu is yet another aspect of business which must be carried out in consultation with food and beverage controls and with the involvement of the general manager. The end result of any business is to generate profit for the organization, and it can be achieved by controlling costs and wastage. The costing of a dish is done by first preparing the standard recipe. Standard recipe lists down the ingredients, its yield, prices, as well as methods of preparation. Once the standard recipe is done, the cost of the recipe is established by adding the net price of all the ingredients. Then the price of the dish is fixed to arrive at a standard food cost, which is generally guided by the standards of the company. There are two types of costs: actual food cost and potential food cost.

The food cost established on the basis of standard recipe is termed as potential food cost. It is measured as a percentage and is calculated by the following formula:

$$\text{Potential food cost percentage} = \frac{\text{Cost of the standrad recipe}}{\text{Sale price of the recipe}}$$

The food cost established on the basis of actual ingredients procured in the kitchen divided by total sales is called actual food cost. It is also measured in terms of percentage and is calculated by the following formula:

$$\text{Actual food cost percentage} = \frac{\text{Cost of the ingredients}}{\text{Total food sales}} \times 100$$

It is important that the standard recipe is followed to avoid any inconsistencies while computing the cost. It is also important to update the recipes on a periodic basis as the cost of ingredients as well as the yield of the product changes from time to time. Once the individual cost of each dish on the menu is done, it will be easy to establish the cost of the whole menu with regard to the forecasted number of portions. It becomes challenging, when one has to compute the cost for a fixed menu in which few choices are available to the guest. Let us look at Table 17.2 for the same.

Table 17.2 Total cost of the menu

Dish name	Production no.	Dish cost (₹)	Total cost (₹)
Roast vegetable salad	10	21	210
Chicken Caesar	30	30	900
Minestrone soup	25	8.5	212.5
Lamb harira	15	12	180
Eggplant Parmigiano	5	50	250
Penne with mushroom	10	28	280
Penne with chicken and mushroom	15	35	525
Grilled bhetki	10	70	700
Tiramisu	30	40	1200
Fresh fruit platter with ice cream	10	15	150
		Total	**4607.50**

With reference to Table 17.6, we can now calculate the following:

$$\text{Cost of menu} = \frac{\text{Total cost}}{\text{Actual number of covers}}$$

$$= \frac{4607.50}{32}$$

$$= ₹143.98 \text{ per cover.}$$

Note: Remember that we have to marginally overproduce to allow for customer choice. The excess costs are incurred because of overproduction.

If this is an à la carte menu, where the dishes are individually priced, then there is no concern; but in this case, which is a fixed menu with built in choices, three types of costs can emerge: maximum cost, minimum cost and average cost.

Maximum cost

If a customer chooses all of the most expensive items from the menu, then it would be the maximum cost of the menu. For example, chicken salad, lamb *harira*, grilled *bhetki*, and *tiramisu* = ₹152.00

Minimum cost

If a customer chooses all of the cheapest items from the menu, then it would be the minimum cost. For example, roasted vegetable salad, *minestrone, penne* with mushroom, and fresh fruit platter = ₹72.50

Average cost

If a customer chooses a selection of items from the menu that are a combination of maximum and minimum costs, then this would give us an average cost of the menu

For instance, Chicken Caesar, *minestrone, penne* with chicken, *tiramisu* = ₹113.50

In most cases, a vegetarian menu and meat menu are priced separately, but in case where the guests would choose from the common menu, then the costing would be done on the cost which will be the highest amongst all.

From the above menu, if the cost of the highest menu is ₹152.00 and if the company wants to maintain the food cost at 25 per cent, then they would sell this menu for ₹608.00 plus taxes.

While fixing a selling price for à la carte items, one cannot apply this rule of 25 per cent food cost to each and every dish, as this will result in some dishes being sold at very high prices and would become non-moving on the menu. In such cases, some dishes like soups and salads are sold at much higher margin, thereby maintaining a food cost of 5–10 per cent; whereas some high cost items can be sold at a food cost of 50 per cent. It is important that the overall food cost at the end of the day or at the end of the month is in sync with the standards set by the organization. The chefs must hold a regular briefing of the service staff to up sell dishes that are high profit and low cost margin.

YIELD MANAGEMENT

Yield management is a broad term used for revenue generating aspects of business. It is also known as revenue management and can be defined as the process of understanding customer behaviour, and anticipating their needs in order to strategize the pricing and maximize profits or revenue. This process is specifically used for very perishable products such as airlines, hotel rooms, and to some extent food in a restaurant. For instance, if a seat is not sold, then we would lose the revenue for that day and hence it is termed as perishable. A special branch or a department called revenue management has been very popular in hotels and other service industry selling perishable products. In other words, yield management can be described as a process wherein the product is sold to the right customer at the right price, and at the right time. The concept of *happy hours* in many restaurants and pubs is a good example of revenue management.

The chef's role in yield management is limited to an extent as this is mostly done by the revenue management department.

In this chapter, we will talk about yield management from the perspective of food only. The chef's role is to control waste percentage or obtain a net portion or yield of a commodity after processing. The yield in a kitchen is very important, especially expensive commodities such as imported vegetables, seafood, meats, etc. If the staff is untrained, then the final quantity obtained will be less and this will impact the profitability. Let us understand the impact of yields on the cost of a dish with the following example.

If a recipe calls for 1 kg of diced potato, then while placing an order for that recipe, we will have to order for more than 1 kg of potato because to obtain dices, we will have to peel and trim the potatoes to get dices. There are few questions that will come to our minds:

1. How much should we order?
2. What will happen to the remaining trimmings and peels?
3. What will be the final yield?

Let us answer these questions one by one to understand the calculation of yields in a kitchen. To understand how much we should order, first we need to understand a term called the *conversion factor*. The conversion factor is a numerical value, which will be used for converting a recipe from 10 portions to the desired number of portions.

For instance, if a recipe yields 10 portions of sautéed potatoes and the portion size of the potato is 180g. We will use the following formula:

$$\text{Recipe conversion factor} = \frac{\text{Desired yield}}{\text{Given yield}}$$

$$= \frac{\text{DY}}{\text{GY}}$$

This means if the given yield as per the recipe is 10 portions and we need to convert it to 23 portions, then as per the formula:

$$\text{Recipe conversion factor} = \frac{\text{DY}}{\text{GY}} = \frac{23}{10} = 2.$$

Therefore, the conversion factor is 2.3 in this case; hence, we would multiply each ingredient with this numerical value to obtain a yield for 23 portions.

There might still be another case in which the yield of a new recipe has to be created with a change in portion size. The above example was a fairly direct calculation; let's suppose that the 10 portions of potatoes with 180 g as a portion has to be converted to 23 portions of potatoes with 75 g as one portion of potato. The formula would still be same, but we will use both the yields together as shown below:

$$\text{Conversion factor} = \frac{\text{DY}}{\text{GY}}$$

The desired yield in this case is 23 portions of 75 g and the given yield is 10 portions of 180 g, so

$$\text{Conversion factor (CF)} = \frac{23}{10} \frac{0.75}{.180}$$

$$\text{CF} = .958$$
$$\text{CF} = .96 \text{ (rounded off)}$$

Hence, if we multiply 1800 g of potatoes with .96, we get

$$1800 \text{ g} \times .96 = 1728 \text{ g}.$$

This is the quantity of potatoes required for for 23 portions in which the new portion size is 75 g.

So the restaurant chef will order the required quantity of potatoes from the commissary kitchen.

But to obtain a yield of 1728 g of ready potatoes, the commissary chef has to order more quantity in order to get the desired yield. The yield tests are conducted on periodic basis. To calculate the yield for a potato dices, take 1kg of potatoes and peel them. The peeled potatoes are now weighed and the weight is recorded. Let us assume that 80g was the weight of the peel. If the peel is not used anywhere and will go into the garbage, then this amount will be treated as waste percentage. So let us look at the formula for waste percentage:

$$\text{Waste percentage} = \frac{\text{Waste}}{\text{Original weight}} \times 100$$

From the example above, the waste percentage of potato is

$$\text{Waste percentage} = \frac{80}{1000} \times 100 = 8\%$$

This means that 8% of the potato is not used anywhere and will be discarded. It also means that 92% of the potato is edible and can be used in other preparations. This formula extends into another formula that would give us the yield percentage that will be represented by:

$$\text{Yield percentage} = \frac{\text{Weight obtained or the edible portion}}{\text{Original weight}} \times 100$$

From the same example as described above, if the total weight obtained after peeling and washing is 920, then the yield percentage would be calculated as follows:

$$\text{Yield percentage} = \frac{920}{1000} \times 100 = 92\%$$

One can use any one of these factors while calculating recipes. This example is fairly easy to calculate because of small waste percentages; but in case of spinach and other greens such as amaranth leaves, mustard greens, etc., after cleaning and boiling, the yield percentage would be only 27%. This means that from 1 kg of spinach as purchased from market, only 270g of boiled spinach is obtained. This large figure becomes crucial in costing recipes. If a recipe calls for 1 kg of boiled spinach, then it is important for chefs to know that they will have to order at least a little more than 4 kg of raw spinach. Sometimes guess work might not work and will jeopardize the production planning. So here we will use yet another formula to calculate how much of spinach we should buy. For this, we first need to establish the required yield which is obtained by the following formula:

Yield required = Number of portions × portion size

So, if we know that we need 10 portions of spinach, where one portion is 75 g, then:

$$\text{Yield required} = 10 \times 75 = 750 \text{ g.}$$

This quantity would be ordered if one can get pre-blanched and cooked spinach from the vendor; but if one has to process it in-house, then we will have to order more in order to get the desired portion size. This is known as raw weight and can be calculated as follows:

$$\text{Raw weight required} = \frac{\text{Cleaned weight or Cooked weight}}{\text{Percentage of yield}}$$

So, if we know that the cooked weight required is 750 g and the yield percentage is 27%, we can easily calculate the required raw quantity as follows:

$$\text{Raw weight required} = \frac{750 \text{ g}}{27\%} = \frac{750}{.27} = 2777 \text{ g}$$

Thus, we can now easily order 2.7 kg or 3 kg of spinach to be able to make 10 portions of 75g each.

Now, it will become easy to calculate the food cost. It is easy for chefs to feed in the required formulas in excel sheet, which would automatically calculate the accurate figures. Before we start to understand how a food cost percentage is calculated, let us understand one more aspect of the same, which is called *portion cost*. A portion cost can be calculated by the following formula:

$$\text{Portion cost} = \frac{\text{Cost of all ingredients in a recipe}}{\text{Number of portions (recipe yield)}}$$

So, if the cost of ingredients used in preparing 10 portions of sautéed spinach is ₹160, then it will be easy to calculate the portion cost by applying the above formula:

$$\text{Portion cost} = \frac{₹160}{10} = ₹16 \text{ per portion}$$

Once the above formulae are available, it is easy to calculate the food cost percentage by using the following formula:

$$\text{Food cost \%} = \frac{\text{Portion cost}}{\text{Menu price}} \times 100$$

The price at which the dish should be sold is governed by the food cost factor. Assuming that the sautéed spinach is being sold at ₹200, let us calculate the food cost percentage of one portion of sautéed spinach by using this formula:

$$\text{Food cost \%} = \frac{₹16}{₹200} \times 100 = (.08) \times 100 = 8\%$$

Food service establishments have their own benchmarks for a food cost. Normally a food cost of 25% means that good quality of food is being maintained. But it is important to understand that every dish cannot be sold at 25 per cent food cost. In a range of dishes on the menu, some dishes will be sold at lower food cost as in case of sautéed spinach above, while some dishes would also be sold at 50 per cent food cost. But it is important that at the end of the day or at the end of the month, the benchmarked food cost is maintained.

We can also decide the price of a dish if we know how much food cost would be incurred in a particular dish. To do this, we will use the same formula as food cost % but use it in a different way as follows:

$$\text{Menu price} = \frac{\text{Portion cost}}{\text{Food cost percentage}}$$

Thus, if we wanted to achieve a food cost % of 25% while selling spinach, then we should have sold it at:

$$\text{Menu Price} = \frac{₹16}{25\%} = \frac{16}{25} \times 100 = ₹64$$

In a five star establishment, we can afford to sell this dish at a higher mark up by achieving low food cost percentage and similarly some high cost items will not sell if we sold them at 25% food cost. For example, if an imported steak with accompaniments on a plate would cost ₹1200, then to make a food cost of 25% we will have to sell this dish at:

$$\frac{₹1200}{25\%} = \frac{1200}{25} \times 100 = ₹4800$$

There will be very few buyers at this price and the dish will become *non-moving* in the menu.

The selling price is thus, decided to ensure that whatever is on the menu sells and adds a profit to the organization. Staff should be trained on such aspects and trained to sell dishes that have a higher profit margin. Every staff member must be educated on the costs and yields to be aware of the costs of production. This will not only make them accountable but will also motivate them in achieving the objectives of the organization.

SUMMARY

A chef has to be a great cook and at the same time be an effective manager, who can conduct all the functions of food production management. In this chapter, we discussed various responsibilities, which make chefs successful in the catering business.

Any professional set-up needs to have a structure of people and monetary and other resources to achieve the larger goals of the organization. This managerial function of setting up a place is described as organization skill. In this chapter, we discussed a step-by-step approach towards organizing a kitchen. Listing various jobs that would be performed in the kitchen would help the managers to establish many factors such as staffing levels, types of menus, and storage and preparation space.

We also discussed how tasks are allocated according to job descriptions and how to prepare duty rosters so that desired output can be achieved without overworking any staff member. This most crucial aspect of staff rosters was discussed in detail with examples and formats that can be used for the same. Thereafter, we discussed the finer aspects of production planning with an example of a menu. These aspects included menu specification sheets and Gantt charts that enable the chef to plan out and allocate time for the most crucial jobs in order of their importance.

We also discussed production quality and how the quantity can be controlled to maximize the profits.

It is always wiser and mandatory to cut wastage and not costs.

Monitoring quality and quantity is a function that is a continuous process and it starts right from the receiving bay until the disposal of garbage. It is also important for the chefs to be able to forecast the production levels in order to prepare the right quantity without over or under producing. In this chapter, we discussed forecasting with an example of a menu and explained how one can calculate the portions to be produced and how the cost of the menu can be computed. We also discussed various important formulas to calculate important values like potential and actual food cost percentages, menu cost, which eventually decides the selling price and profit margin. Lastly, we talked about various kinds of yields and waste percentages and how a student would be able to calculate the same. We also discussed the conversion factor that would enable students to calculate the recipes with complex calculations.

In the next chapter, we will read about another important aspect of a chef's job, i.e., product and research development and how a chef has to keep himself or herself updated with the latest technology and products in the world.

KEY TERMS

Actual food cost   It is cost of ingredients divided by the total sales for a period.

Amaranth leaves   It is a leafy vegetable with a peppery taste.

Brigade system   It is the formal hierarchy structure in a kitchen that is headed by the executive chef.

Capital budget   The money allocated for buying large machinery and equipment is called capital budget.

Conversion factor   It is a numerical value which can be used for converting recipes to higher or lower portion size.

Duty roster   This is the allocation of staff to various jobs on daily basis.

Forecasting   Based on previous data; it is a calculated guess of the future business or production.

Gantt chart   This is a chart where the things to be done are plotted against timings and deadlines.

Happy hours   A term used for promotional time when the food and drinks in a food outlet are sold at discounted price.

Inventory   The physical check of commodities or equipment at any given location is defined as inventory.

Key performance objectives   These are targets set for the staff against which their performance is measured.

Kitchen organization   It is a formal structure of hierarchy in the kitchen department, with reporting and responsibilities defined for every level.

Manpower planning   The task of assigning duties and responsibilities to staff and planning the required number of people for the job is called manpower planning.

Open market purchase   It is a term used for purchasing raw materials from market directly and not from a contracted supplier.

Operational budget   It is a term for money allocated for running the day-to-day operations of any entity.

Organizing   This is a management function for providing the staff with equipment and resources to perform their task.

Potential food cost   It is the cost of ingredients in a recipe divided by the sale price of the recipe.

Profit and loss statement   It is a statement of account that lists the expenses and earnings of an organization on a single sheet.

Purchase specification   This is a mutually agreed standard of quality of ingredients between a hotel and its suppliers on a contractual basis.

Standards   These are benchmark objectives that guide the operation of any business.

Waste percentage   This is calculated by dividing waste obtained by original weight multiplied by 100.

Yield management   It is the process of selling the right product to the right customer at the right price.

CONCEPT REVIEW QUESTIONS

1. What do you understand by the word kitchen organization?
2. What managerial functions have to be performed by the chef in the kitchen?
3. How is manpower planning done? What factors need to be kept in mind while doing so?
4. Define a brigade system.
5. What are duty rosters and how does one plan them?
6. What is the difference between a job description and a job responsibility?
7. Describe personnel management.
8. What do you understand by the term 'key performance measures'? List at least three key performance measures for an executive chef.
9. What are the challenges that come in the way of planning a duty roster?
10. How does a planning sheet help in making duty rosters?
11. How is annual leave planner different from duty roster?
12. What do you understand by the term 'production planning'?
13. What is a menu specification sheet and how does it help?
14. Describe a Gantt chart and its uses.
15. How does one control quality and quantity of production in a kitchen?
16. Describe four major areas where one can effectively control the quantity as well as the quality during the operations.
17. Describe forecasting. How is it relevant to kitchen operations?
18. What is the difference between potential food cost and actual food cost?
19. How does one compute the cost of a menu? Why is it important?
20. Differentiate among maximum cost, minimum cost, and average cost of a fixed menu.
21. Describe the term 'yield management'. How is it applicable in the kitchens?
22. What is a conversion factor in the context of food planning? What is its importance?
23. Differentiate between waste percentage and yield percentage.
24. How would you calculate the portion cost of a dish?
25. How would you decide the price of the dish with regard to food cost percentage?

PROJECT WORK

1. In groups of five, plan a small restaurant and decide upon the activities that will be conducted in the business. Now organize the kitchen with regards to equipment and organizational structure. Present your data to the other groups and be open to any questions and answers.
2. In groups of five, plan for an event and allocate staff on various shifts to optimize the production levels. Keep factors such as holidays, and exigencies, in mind while planning the same.
3. In groups of five, plan a Gantt chart for an event. Follow the Gantt chart on the day of the event and analyse what went right and what could have been improved upon.
4. In groups of five, conduct yield tests on various commodities and record your observations with regard to waste percentage and yield percentages.

CHAPTER 18

RESEARCH AND PRODUCT DEVELOPMENT

Learning Objectives

After reading this chapter, you should be able to
- understand the basic concept of product and research development
- appreciate the process of testing new equipment in a food establishment
- develop and create new recipes with regard to specific market segments
- differentiate between developing recipes for hotel kitchen and food industries
- participate in food trials and understand the process
- claim an insight into objective and organoleptic evaluations of food and understand how and why they are done

INTRODUCTION

The food and beverage (F&B) industry has changed and evolved over the years and will constantly change for the better in future. A whole new range of products, genetically modified fruits and vegetables, and new tools and equipment have taken food preparations and presentations to new heights. All this is expected to improve further with advancements in technology as well as in agriculture. Enhanced travel and tourism have further created a demand for all kinds of food from various parts of the world. Also, its procurement is no longer an issue thanks to liberal import and export regulations.

A decade ago, preparing Italian pasta or pizza at home was limited to only those households that had members who frequently travelled abroad and had savoured such products before. However, with the increase in demand, many food product companies have come up with ready-to-eat pastas, pizza breads, etc., which are increasingly become popular in the urban Indian households.

Furthermore, there has been a sea change in the lifestyles of societies across the world, especially after the addition of women to the workforce in vast numbers. With both life-partners working, packaged food has become very popular in the market. Today, apart from Indian dishes, such as *dal makhani, paneer masala,* and *biryani,* it is not uncommon to see packaged food from other countries sharing shelf space in grocery stores. Often, all that one has to do is just mix the ingredients with water and boil to create a dish. Companies are trying to come up with newer and better products and more variety to attract customers leading to new product development.

In this chapter, we will discuss product development in the kitchen including testing new equipment and upgrading the same with the change in menus. We will also discuss the art of developing creative recipes and how these should be introduced in the hotel and restaurant menus.

Chefs constantly need to upgrade the skills of the staff as well, so training and development of self and staff are also very important. A chef's role is also crucial when new staff is to be hired; one has to conduct tests to gauge the skill levels of aspirers seeking to chart a career in the kitchen department of leading hotels. Therefore, it becomes important to understand how to conduct food trials and how to evaluate the taste and flavour of food.

TESTING NEW EQUIPMENT

Apart from regular maintenance of kitchen equipment, it is tested at the time of installation. Whenever a new equipment is used for the first time, it must run for at least 4–6 hours before judging its performance. The testing of each equipment would depend on various factors such as

- Type of equipment
- Reason for testing the equipment
- To check if the planned facilities are working
- To check the operating instruction of the equipment

Type of Equipment

Various types of kitchen equipment, big and small, are introduced in the kitchen throughout the operations. This is done either to replace old equipment which is incurring high maintenance costs or to introduce new ones to improve the quality and speed of operations. One has to plan for procuring new equipment, which is generally undertaken once a year at the time of capital budgeting. An executive chef, along with the chief engineer and the general manager, has to provide reasons and justifications for purchase of equipment. The chief engineer is also involved in planning the facilities.

Each equipment, such as electrical loads, drainage systems, and water inlets, has its own significance. These must be planned in the existing kitchen, which might not have a provision in the first place. The new equipment thus installed is tested for its optimum performance. The engineer needs to check if the facilities provided in the equipment are in working condition and that there is no leakage. The equipment is run for at least 4 hours while in case of new refrigerators, they are run for at least 24 hours to test their defrosting cycles, temperature stabilities, etc.

The Reason for Testing the Equipment

There are various reasons for subjecting any equipment to tests, the foremost being to ensure that it operates efficiently as per its design specifications and provides the desired output. If not, then minor adjustments need to be made to make it run efficiently. It is very important that qualified technicians from the company that has supplied the equipment are called in for installation. There have been instances where hobs with inbuilt ovens have been ordered for a new kitchen and it was found upon arrival or installation that the equipment did not work at all. Later, the engineers found that the burners were designed to run only on piped natural gas (PNG) and not on the conventional LPG cylinders. This problem could have been avoided in the first place by carefully planning the equipment in consultation with engineers, so that they could study the facilities much in advance even before placing an order.

If the equipment is imported, alterations would have to be undertaken by concerned professionals to make it LPG-compliant. However, such changes must strictly be done in accordance with the manufacturing company's approval or else the warranty for the machine may become invalid.

To Check if the Planned Facilities are Working

Another reason for testing the equipment is to check if the facilities planned are working well and efficiently. Many a time, it has been found that the inlet or outlet pipe is too short to be connected to the municipal water line, or the electrical plug top does not conform to the country's standards. In all such cases, minor adjustments need to be made to the facilities or to the equipment itself. Further, such items must be tested for at least 4 to 6 hours to check that they are compatible with the facilities such as electrical loads provided, provided drainage, water inlets and outlets.

To Check Operating Instructions of Equipment

The equipment is also tested to check and verify the operating instructions of the machinery. This time is utilized to train end-users, such as chefs and cooks, in the kitchen, so that the equipment is used appropriately and not mishandled. In this context, let us take the example of a machine called retarder proofer in bakery. This equipment allows a baker to make breads and put in the machine for baking at a later stage. One can electronically set the timers on the machine from 24 to 48 hours. During the time set, the bread undergoes a freezing cycle, and then automatically goes on to thawing mode and then for leavening (as per the marked time). So, to test this machine, it is important that the machine is loaded with bread dough and checked for its operation for one complete cycle of at least 24 hours. Similarly, other equipment installed would have their own specific operating instructions, which need to be studied from the operating manuals that are supplied with the equipment.

DEVELOPING NEW RECIPES

Eating habits of people have changed around the world. Students can have an idea of the extent of this change by simply picking up cookery books of the last 20 years and see how food has developed from the braised *coq au vin* to deconstructed chicken recipes. To be on the top of business or, at least be seen as modern and updated, one must constantly develop new products, new processes, and new ways of doing things.

Developing new recipes is a common feature in almost all entities in food business, especially among branded food chains such as McDonald's and Kentucky Fried Chicken (KFC). These food chains need to constantly evolve their products to suit the market segment they are catering to. For example, McDonald's standards and processes would be same around the world, but in India, they do not serve beef burgers due to sensitive religious constraints. Instead, products suitable to the Indian palate are developed by a team of recipe developers who work as a separate team and may consist of chefs, food technologists, scientists, etc. and each one of them has a distinct job role. In hotels, chefs are essentially responsible for developing new recipes that are profitable and creative and can easily be made and dispensed by the kitchen staff. Recipe development comprises various stages, which differs on the basis of the organization. Thus, recipe development in hotels and restaurants is different from that in food chain segment. Let us refer Fig. 18.1 to understand the stages or levels in recipe development in hotels and restaurants.

According to the pyramid in Fig. 18.1, level 1 depicts the basic level of a cook where he/she is honing the basic cooking skills and scrupulously following recipes as specified to them. Level 2 is the comprehension stage when the cook begins to understand how a particular dish has to be done. He/She might still need to refer back to the recipes for clearing doubts. Level 3 is a stage of analysis; understanding the role of various ingredients in cooking, the way it will adapt to a cooking principle and what texture changes would it undergo. Level 4 can be described as the level where the cook can develop new recipes and products that can create an impact on the market segment. There is no particular time limit of each level as it solely depends on the kitchen professional as to how committed and passionate one is to advance his/her career in food production operations. Chefs create new recipes by different methods; the most common method is the trial and error method, where based on culinary knowledge and skills, a chef combines flavours and textures to create a new product that is first offered to eminent guests for food tasting. The feedback is collated and the recipe is further refined and then launched into the new menus. Many factors are built into the new recipe when it is ready to be listed on the new menu. The factors include production planning, forecasting the number of portions to be sold, and also creating a menu specification sheet. All these factors have been discussed in Chapter 17.

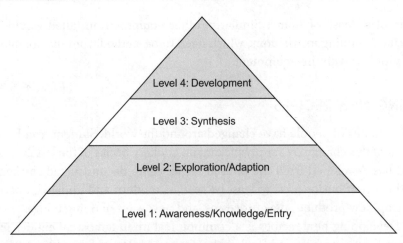

Fig. 18.1 Steps in recipe development

Developing recipes for a food chain is a bit more complicated than in a hotel or a restaurant. Developing recipe for a food chain, which is to be launched in various outlets across the globe, may at times take 6–8 months before the process is complete. It is like a project development plan, where a team of people work towards achieving a goal. Figure 18.2 provides an insight into the process involved in recipe development in a global food chain.

Figure 18.2 clearly explains the methodology that will be undertaken to develop a product or a recipe for a food chain. For this, the first step is to evaluate the objective of the organization as to what it wants to develop, and whether it is a product for long term or short term. The next step is to develop an action plan, may be in the form of Gantt charts, to be able to plan the things in a sequential manner. This step would include the making of the product as it would be done in a basic kitchen. Thereafter, the team of developers will figure out how this product can be made in bulk and deconstructed and reconstructed at the food premise. In a fast-food operation, the staff does not have much time at hand to cook the particular product from scratch as that would create inconsistencies besides leading to a huge business loss. Thus, products have to be prepared in such a way that it allows only reheating, frying, and dispensing from the counter. In order to achieve this, the product is tested for the temperatures and time that it would be cooked for at the premise, to make it look as original and close to the one that was crafted originally in the kitchen in the first step.

During the various steps, the judgement of physical factors such as environment, communication, and marketing, have to be kept in mind for the success of the launched product. Have you ever wondered how fast-food chains launch new products in the market and how much work and planning goes behind the same to achieve the desired results? All the activities shown inside the circle are guided by external factors such as time, resources such as people, equipment, raw materials, and even the budgets.

The recipe is thus created in a monitored environment by food technologists and scientists to see how it should be stored and dispensed to avoid microbial growth and contaminations. The biggest challenge is to obtain a product, which despite having undergone immense processes, is flavoursome, moist, and as fresh as it was when initially, at the time of delivery.

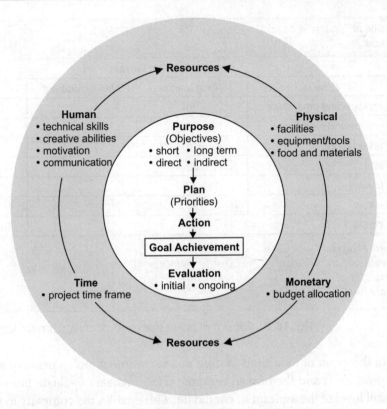

Fig. 18.2 Project plan for recipe development
Source: Hullah, E. 1984, *Cardinal's Handbook of Recipe Development, Canada*

FOOD TRIALS

Evaluating food by a panel for critiquing is termed as food trial. Food trials can be of two types, namely

- Trial while opening a new establishment, or introduction of new dishes or menu to existing establishment, and
- Trial as a recruitment tool for hiring new staff for a food production operation.

In the first case, food trials are done for two primary reasons: first to train the staff to be able to produce the food for the guest as per the standard recipe and presentations, and second, to moderate recipes and create new standard recipes before the launch of the hotel to the guests.

Many food service establishments invite esteemed guests to come to their restaurant and avail complimentary F&B services and evaluate the standards of food and beverage service. Sometimes, planning looks well on paper, but the proof of the pudding is in the pudding itself. Hence, it is important that the planned event is simulated or practised several times and the recipes refined with the advice of the guests as well as the staff who are preparing the same.

Name of Candidate:
Menu:

Trade Test Format			
Criteria	Total Marks	Marks Obtained	Remarks
Workflow and organization	20		
Hygiene and cleanliness	10		
Presentation	10		
Taste	20		
Flavours	20		
Texture	20		
Feedback			Total Average %

Time Allotted:
Time taken by candidate: _____ Hours _____ Minutes
Chef's Panel:
Signature: _____

Fig. 18.3 Format of trade test used as a recruitment tool

In the event of food trials as used as a recruitment tool, a panel of judges that usually comprise chefs and the human resource (HR) manager evaluate the food so as to judge the skill level of the aspirant or candidate. This enables the company to hire the right kind of person for the right job and is viewed as a fair practice by all. A popular format called 'trade test format' (shown in Fig. 18.3) is generally used for the purpose.

The format can differ from one organization to another. In this format, a candidate is provided with ingredients and resources and is allowed to prepare a menu for evaluation. Post presentation, the food is tasted and judged on various parameters such as work flow and hygiene, taste, flavour, textures, and presentation of the food.

This evaluation is done by at least three persons and the average scores decide the selection of the person. The role of the HR person is to evaluate the candidate on the basis of right attitude, while chefs on the panel check for knowledge and skills. These three components: knowledge, skills, and right attitude of the candidates make them the most suitable one.

Let us now understand how the food is tasted and judged on various parameters.

EVALUATING A RECIPE

A standard recipe is made for a product before it is finally introduced in the food production operations. The standard recipe should be clear to read and understand as it has to be used as a control tool by the organization to calculate the cost and the price of the food, which will eventually also decide the price of the dish and the profitability of the organization. The following are some common features of the standard recipe that must be considered, while making it.

Clarity

The recipe should be clear, concise, accurate, readable, and easy to comprehend. A recipe should specify the type and kind of ingredients. For instance, if a recipe calls for 200 g of boiled spinach, then it must mention the same as 200 g of boiled spinach and not 200 g of spinach, as upon boiling, 200 g of spinach will become 25 g or even less due to cooking loss (refer Chapter 17). Furthermore, it is important that the recipe is made for at least 10 portions to enable easy measurements for small weights such as spices and seasonings. It also facilitates the calculations if the recipe needs to be scaled up or down. It is also important to list the ingredients in the sequence that they would be used in cooking. This is done so that one can plan the making of the dish in one's own mind and then write down the ingredients as per the steps or methods. This method usually eradicates the chances of missing ingredients in a recipe.

Instructions

The method in a recipe is as important as the ingredient itself and the processing of an ingredient must be mentioned in each step. The recipe must also tell the cook how it would be served with appropriate accompaniment or garnish. The amounts mentioned in the recipe should also follow a consistent pattern. If plotting it on Excel format in computers, it is advisable that the measures are mentioned in weight and volume and not in numbers or pieces as the formula will calculate things accordingly. The instructions in the recipe should be foolproof and free from human errors. For example, if the recipe calls for a kilogram of whipping cream, then it must be specified whether we want 1 kg of cream that can be whipped or we want 1 kg of pre-whipped cream.

It is important that the product is audited periodically as per the standard recipe. This is done to ensure that the recipes are up-to-date and there is no deviation from the set standards. One must establish the yield or the output of the recipe, as sometimes the quality of ingredients and the tools used by the staff vary, and this could cause irregularities in the yield. Auditing a recipe also answers few questions such as the following.

1. Does it produce a quality product as determined by a score card? If not, why?
2. Is the product nutritious?
3. Is it economical in time, energy, and material?
4. Does it eliminate, as far as possible, the factor of human error?
5. Is the recipe suited to (i) clientele, (ii) available equipment, (iii) workers, (iv) type of service?
6. Is the per capita cost of the product in line with the selling price?

A sample of score card that can be used for evaluating the recipe is depicted in Fig. 18.4.

Sample Score Card for Evaluation of Each Dish

Name _____

Menu in serial order   1. _____   2. _____   3. _____

Menu	Appearance	Consistency (Thick/thin)	Texture Tenderness, Juiciness	Flavour Aroma, Taste	Total

Comments:

Scores –	Very Good	5
	Good	4
	Fair	3
	V. Poor–Poor	0–2

Fig. 18.4   Sample score card for evaluation of each dish

ORGANOLEPTIC AND SENSORY EVALUATION

Quality is the ultimate criterion of desirability of any food product. It can be evaluated by the following two methods.

- Sensory/subjective/organoleptic method
- Objective methods

Organoleptic Method

It is a combination of the different senses—sight, smell, taste, touch, and sound. The organoleptic senses are very perceptive in nature as everybody has their own perception of appearance, flavour, and mouth feel. This reaction is highly conditioned by a variety of psychological and social factors and the results of this tasting are different from one person to another. Therefore, it is important that a tasting panel of at least three to four persons are formed for an average scoring. Let us now discuss each organoleptic factors separately.

Sight

The appearance of the food to our eyes is most crucial, as it is an age-old saying that one eats with the eyes first. It is this feature of our senses that judges the features of the food such as freshness, colour appeall, dull, glossy, or juicy, etc. and can fairly indicate the texture of the food. Our mind is attuned to a particular colour and taste for a particular food that we have been eating for a while now. For example, we as Indians will not complain of a sweet fritter like apple fritters, but in our mind pakora can never be served or eaten sweet. An Indian will dislike pakoras if they were served sweet, but at the same time we have no issues with French apple fritters. Another aspect where the eyes judge the food is colour. A brown-coloured food would mean it is crusty and crunchy and a black surface would indicate burnt and over-flavoured food. The other attributes of the colour indicate the ripeness of fruits and vegetables, the strength of tea or coffee, and the sight of cooked spices in a curry.

Smell

The smell of the food is defined as flavour in cooking and the smell in a food can be of the following three major types.

1. Odour
2. Taste
3. Aroma

Odour   Odour contributes immensely to the pleasure of eating. Volatile molecules stimulate olfactory organs and they invigorate our perceptions of food being either sweet, bitter, astringent, spicy, sour, or acidic. All these perceptions are associated with taste. There are various food items which cannot be tasted, when they are raw. It is the flavours that can indicate to us whether the milk has gotten sour or the raw meat has turned acidic and is spoilt.

Taste   Taste is registered on the taste buds in the tongue. The taste buds register the sensation of the food being sweet, salty, acidic, bitter, spicy, or pungent. There is another taste known as the sixth taste, which is an undefined taste and hence, does not fall into any category. It is often known as kinaesthetic taste or *umami*, as known in Japanese. This taste actually cannot be described as it is a mix of many tastes that coat the tongue but one can feel the sensation on the palate for a long time. Chefs are researching continuously and trying to find the foods that are naturally rich in *umami* flavours.

Aroma   Aroma is the smell of the food mixed with the taste buds. Flavour alone can be obtained by smelling, but for judging the aroma of the dish, it is mandatory that the food is smelt and tasted at the same time. Many a times the spices are categorized into being flavoursome and aromatic. In such cases, the natural scent of the spices is associated with aroma. For example, green cardamom, cloves, etc. can be eaten without being cooked, whereas flavouring spices, such as red chilli powder and turmeric, can never be eaten raw.

Touch and sound

This feature of food can be defined in many ways such as texture, mouth feel, and even temperature of the food. We all expect tea, coffee, or soup to be hot and if cold, we will not like to eat or drink the same. However, it is iced tea, cold coffee, or cold soup, we will expect it to be chilled. Many adjectives, such as crunchy, soft, brittle, and smooth, describe the texture of the food. The texture of the food in a prepared dish is as much desirable as it is an indication that the correct method of cooking has been applied to the dish. If roast chicken does not have a crispy skin or samosas are soft, it will immediately indicate that the cooking methods applied are not correct.

Texture can also be described as a consistency. This is so in case of liquids and semi-liquid foods such as gravies, sauces, and soups. There is a fixed image of a dish in our minds as we have been eating it since ages. A chef expects the broth to be thin and pureed soup to be of certain consistency. If the soup is too watery or too thick, it again is an indication that the cook is not familiar with the textures in the food.

The crispy bite of fresh sliced onion rings or the crackling sound of poppadom would satisfy the sound element of the food. One can thus see that the balance of organoleptic tasting completes the feeling of satisfaction. If even one element in the meal is missing, the overall experience does not seem to be right in the first place. All such factors, though psychological, contribute to the acceptability of foods when there is pleasant association.

The tasting of the food is not only limited to the food trials and trade tests, but also extends intensively into other F&B industries. Today tea, coffee, and wine experts are being hired for tasting. Tasters are people whose sensitivity and consistency have been established by scientific training and repeated tests. Such people are called connoisseurs. The connoisseurs are responsible for selecting the right blends in tea, coffee, and other beverages, such as wines and liquors, and it is important that the ideal panel members have the following attributes.

- Are of good health
- Can distinguish appreciable difference between taste and smell
- Experienced in the field
- Are not prejudiced
- Willing to spend time
- Interested in sensory analysis
- Have the ability to derive proper conclusion
- Available for periodic tests

Organoleptic Tests

In large food industries, organoleptic tests are grouped into various categories such as the following.

Discrimination tests

These types of tests are performed to differentiate products from one another. There are three major types of discrimination tests.

Paired comparison test Several pairs of coded samples are given, which are different from each other. The testing is done to arrive at some criteria. For example, if a supplier gives us four to five samples of Basmati rice, we will do the testing by boiling all of them to arrive at the right texture and consistency. We will then decide which one suits our operation better with respect to quality and price.

Duo-trio test In this testing, the panel is presented with three samples, of which one is an original product, the second is similar to the original, and the third is the sample product to be tested. The job of the testing panel, in this case is to assess which of the two products resembles the original product the most.

Triangle tests This method of testing employs three samples, two of which are identical while the third is different. The testing panels have to pick up the odd with the degree of difference. Figure 18.5 shows how a typical triangle test card looks like.

Hedonic test

Also known as consumer tests, hedonic tests are based on pleasant/unpleasant experiences of consumers, or in short an honest expression of a consumer's personal feeling or liking.

Triangle Test Card

Name _____   Date _____

Product _____

Two of the three samples are identical. You are required to determine the odd sample _____

Set no.	Code no. of samples	Code no. of odd samples	Comment on odd samples
I	_____	_____	_____
II	_____	_____	_____
III	_____	_____	_____
IV	_____	_____	_____

_____
Signature

Fig. 18.5 Triangle test card

Hedonic Rating Test

Name _____   Date _____

Product _____

	Code	Code	Code		Code	Code	Code
Like extremely	___	___	___	Dislike slightly	___	___	___
Like very much	___	___	___	Dislike moderately	___	___	___
Like moderately	___	___	___	Dislike very much	___	___	___
Like slightly	___	___	___	Dislike extremely	___	___	___
Neither like nor dislike	___	___	___	Reasons			

_____
Signature

Fig. 18.6 A sample hedonic score card

These tests are generally carried out on more than 50 end-users. Hedonic testing gives an idea to a producer about the general likes of the end-user. It is also limited to a particular market segment. These tests can be conducted for a single product or for comparing two or three products, wherein an evaluator has to judge which of the given samples is more acceptable and appealing to him/her. In such cases, it is important that just a blind test is conducted or the samples are not labelled. If a sample is known, then there is a danger of the evaluators' perceptions and prejudices creeping in and rendering the whole exercise futile. Figure 18.6 shows the format of a hedonic rating test card.

Numerical scoring test

This testing is done by a trained panellist who follows the sensory characteristic corresponding to the agreed quality descriptions and scores. Such a testing is followed when a standard product is known and the evaluators judge the end product and give a numerical value as to how close it is to the standard product. Figure 18.7 shows a numerical scoring test card.

Numerical Scoring Test

Name _____   Date _____

Product _____

Please rate samples according to the following:

Score	Quality Description
90	Excellent
80	Good
70	Fair
60	Poor

Sample   Score   Comment

_____
Signature

Fig. 18.7 A numerical score card

Thus we see that there are numerous types of testing as described above and all of which form a part of sensory testing or organoleptic testing. Many food industries follow organoleptic testing methodologies, but they have their own advantages and disadvantages as well. As we can see from the above mentioned tests, the results can be variable in nature as the sensory tests are very subjective and driven by a particular segment.

Objective Evaluation

Apart from sensory evaluations discussed earlier, many food processing industries and, sometimes hotels and restaurants, resort to the objective method of evaluation. In these tests, the quality of food is measured along various parameters such as moisture, freshness, specific gravity, viscosity, and microbial contaminations. Such tests are conducted with sophisticated equipment and gadgets and are more reliable than the sensory evaluations, which differ from person to person. Nonetheless, objective testing has its own pros and cons. Table 18.1 highlights the advantages and disadvantages of the same.

With this chapter, we conclude the third volume of food productions. The first volume titled *Food Production Operations* taught you the basics of food production techniques and processes with regard to ingredients, storage, cooking principles, and basics of Western, pastry, and Indian cooking skills. The second volume was targeted towards volume

Table 18.1 Advantages and disadvantages of objective testing

Advantages	Disadvantages
Results are accurate and very minute difference can be noticed.	Time consuming as each process takes time.
Less subjected to errors when compared to sensory methods.	Sophisticated equipment are required and at times these may not be available.
It provides permanent record, e.g., Ph value, composition of fat, protein, etc.	Sound technical knowledge is required to conduct such tests.

cooking, purchasing, indenting, and regional cuisines of India. This book covers the advance level of culinary applications with regard to international cuisine and pastry applications.

Kitchen is one of the places where learning never stops. This book builds the base to start your career as a well-grounded kitchen professional, and with dedication, passion, and hard work, you will eventually climb the ladder to success.

SUMMARY

This chapter dealt with yet another dimension of scopes and responsibilities of an executive chef as a manager in the kitchen. Research and product development is a continuous process and food organizations constantly strive to improve their products by launching new menus, introducing new equipment and technologies to upgrade their products. All this is done because the tastes and demands of customers are evolving worldwide. Today, a global traveller expects to find the food of his/her own country in any place that he/she goes to.

In this chapter, we discussed various responsibilities of chefs such as upgrading and testing new equipment, creating and developing new products and recipes, as also the art of evaluating recipes and conducting food trials.

Food trials are of various types. These can be done when a new menu is launched, or even used as a recruitment tool. When we talk about food trials or food tasting as it is commonly known, we have to understand different types of sensory evaluation techniques that should be used for evaluating the food. Thus, we discussed the organoleptic tests of food and also by the professional food tasters in the food industries.

The process of food tasting in the food products companies are very sophisticated and require lots of data collection and storage of records for future reference. We also explained the same with formats and score cards for the better understanding of the students.

This chapter brings us to the end of this book. It is important to put this knowledge to practice and attain the right attitude and skills to be able to enhance your career in this industry.

KEY TERMS

Apple fritter   It is an apple slice coated with sweet batter and deep-fried.

Aroma   It is a term used for flavour of the food associated with nose and tongue.

Astringent   It is a taste associated with sensation of dryness or puckering on the tongue.

Capital budgeting   It is a budgeting exercise wherein large equipment and machinery is budgeted for the coming or current year.

Connoisseur   It is the term for experts who evaluate and taste food products.

Coq au vin   This is a classical French dish of chicken braised in red wine.

Defrosting   This is a process in freezers, which does not allow ice crystals to form in the machine.

Food trial   It is perfecting the cooking of a dish as per a standard recipe.

Genetically modified   It is a process of modifying the genes in a plant to obtain products of desired quality.

Kentucky Fried Chicken (KFC)   Kentucky Fried Chicken is an international food chain.

Kinaesthetic taste   It is the sixth taste.

Operating instructions   It is the set of instructions on how to use and install an equipment. The instructions are provided in the manual accompanying the equipment at the time of its sale.

Organoleptic tests   Tests carried out on food using senses such as sight, smell, touch, sound, and taste.

Pakora   These are savoury Indian fritters made with gram-flour batter.

Specific gravity It is the ratio of the density of a substance to the density of water.

Tasting panel This is a group of expert professionals who are trained to taste and evaluate food.

Umami It is Japanese for the kinaesthetic taste or the sixth taste.

Viscosity It is the thickness of a liquid.

CONCEPT REVIEW QUESTIONS

1. What do you understand by the term product development?
2. Why is research and development so important in food business?
3. What factors have lead to new product development?
4. What is testing of new equipment? Why is it done?
5. Mention the four factors that would guide the testing of new equipment.
6. How and why are recipes developed?
7. Describe the levels in the pyramid of recipe development.
8. How is recipe development accomplished in various types of food establishments?
9. Describe a food trial? Why is it done?
10. How would you use food trial as a tool for recruitment?
11. Why is it important to evaluate a recipe?
12. Describe the features of a good standard recipe.
13. What factors are evaluated in a recipe?
14. Describe organoleptic or sensory food evaluations.
15. What is a discrimination test and why is it done?
16. Differentiate between a paired comparison test and duo-trio test.
17. Describe the triangle test and its importance.
18. What are hedonic tests? Why are they performed?
19. What is objective testing? How is it different form sensory evaluation?
20. List the advantages and disadvantages of objective testing.

PROJECT WORK

1. In groups of five, select a recipe and modify it to suit a particular segment such as children, college students, adults, or old people. Record your observations as to what changes would you make in a recipe and give the reasons.
2. In groups of five, decide the new equipment that would suit your establishment and with the support of an engineer, establish the facilities required for the same. Now list the processes that you would follow to install the equipment and share your findings with the other groups.
3. In groups of five, prepare a recipe and get it evaluated by the other groups with a trade test card. Justify your evaluations and record the feedback.
4. In groups of five, select few products such as different types of mayonnaise, ketchups, and mustards, and carry out sensory tests such as pairing tests, duo-trio tests, triangle test, and hedonic tests and fill up the formats for the same. Discuss your findings with the other groups in the class.

INDEX

Related Titles by the Same Author

Food Production Operations [9780198061816]

Food Production Operations, aimed at first year students, introduces the various facets of the professional kitchen—ranging from the layout of the kitchen departments to menu planning to production of Indian, Western, and pastry food items.

The companion DVD contains 55 videos (such as preparation of cakes, pastries, breads, and sauces) showcasing various food production procedures and techniques to operate complex kitchen equipment and also includes 365 Excel-based recipes with built-in macros that allow users to calculate the right amount of ingredients required for preparing the dishes that have been divided into Indian, Western, and pastry.

WINNER OF BEST PROFESSIONAL BOOK FROM INDIA, GOURMAND AWARDS 2011

Quantity Food Production Operations and Indian Cuisine [9780198068495]

Quantity Food Production Operations and Indian Cuisine, targeted at second year students, familiarizes the reader with fundamentals of volume cooking and catering. Various regional Indian cuisines (such as Hyderabadi, Awadhi, Bengali) and ancient techniques of Indian cooking, such as *dum* and *tandoor,* have been discussed, along with traditional home style cooking.

The book has 32 colour plates and is accompanied by a CD with 337 macro-enabled recipes that allow users to determine the cost of raw materials used.

Related Hospitality Titles

- 9780198061090 *Hotel Housekeeping,* 2/e
- 9780198065272 *Food and Beverage Service*
- 9780195699197 *Hotel Front Office*
- 9780198064633 *Hotel Facility Planning*
- 9780198062912 *Hotel Engineering*
- 9780195694468 *Hotel Finance*
- 9780195689112 *Food Science and Nutrition*
- 9780198072362 *Tourism Principles and Practices*
- 9780198060017 *Tourism Operations and Management*
- 9780198066309 *Tourism Marketing*

Visit us at www.oup.co.in and www.oupinheonline.com